The Sporting

Trainers
Review

NH SEASON 1995-96

Compiled by
John Bigley and Colin Havercroft

Published 1996 by The Sporting Life
One Canada Square, Canary Wharf, London E14 5AP

© 1996 The Sporting Life

ISBN 0 901091 86 3

Editorial and Production by Martin Pickering Bloodstock Services
Cover designed by P.W. Reprosharp Ltd, London EC1
Cover printed by Graphic Techniques, Milton Keynes, Bucks
Text printed by The Bath Press, Bath and London

Cover pictures
Collage of Leading Trainers:
Top row: David Elsworth, Gordon Richards, Paul Nicholls, David Nicholson.
Middle row: Josh Gifford, Martin Pipe.
Bottom row: Nick Gaselee, Henrietta Knight, Jonjo O'Neill, Capt. Tim Forster.

(Photographs: Ray Wright)

CONTENTS

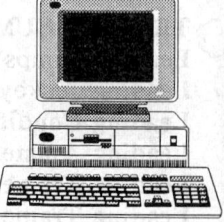

TRAINER SECTION

M J AHERN (Lambourn, Berks)

	Races Run	1st	2nd	3rd	Unpl	Per cent	£1 Level Stake
Hurdles	23	1	2	0	20	4.3	- 20.37
Chases	5	0	1	1	3	-	- 5.00
Totals	28	1	3	1	23	3.6	- 25.37

G Bradley	1-4	- 1.37	Bangor	1-1	+ 1.63

No of horses racing for the stable	8	Total winning prize-money	£2,710

J AKEHURST (Upper Lambourn, Berks)

	Races Run	1st	2nd	3rd	Unpl	Per cent	£1 Level Stake
Hurdles	11	2	1	0	8	18.2	- 0.17
Chases	0	0	0	0	0	-	0.00
Totals	11	2	1	0	8	18.2	- 0.17

J A McCarthy	2-2	+ 8.83

Stratford	1-1	+ 8.00	Plumpton	1-2	- 0.17

No of horses racing for the stable	4	Total winning prize-money	£5,045

R AKEHURST (Epsom, Surrey)

	Races Run	1st	2nd	3rd	Unpl	Per cent	£1 Level Stake
Hurdles	48	11	11	2	24	22.9	- 18.68
Chases	0	0	0	0	0	-	0.00
Totals	48	11	11	2	24	22.9	- 18.68

BY MONTH

	W-R	Per cent	£1 Level Stake		W-R	Per cent	£1 Level Stake
June	0-1	-	1.00	December	0-7	-	- 7.00
July	0-1	-	- 1.00	January	3-11	27.3	- 3.12
August	0-0	-	0.00	February	1-3	33.3	+ 2.00
September	1-1	100.0	+ 1.38	March	2-8	25.0	- 4.38
October	1-7	14.3	- 4.50	April	1-2	50.0	- 0.47
November	2-7	28.6	- 0.59	May	0-0	-	0.00

DISTANCE

	W-R	Per cent	£1 Level Stake		W-R	Per cent	£1 Level Stake
Hurdles				Chases			
2m-2m 3f	10-40	25.0	- 12.21	2m-2m 3f	0-0	-	0.00
2m 4f-2m 7f	1-7	14.3	- 5.47	2m 4f-2m 7f	0-0	-	0.00
3m +	0-1	-	- 1.00	3m +	0-0	-	0.00

TYPE OF RACE

	W-R	Per cent	£1 Level Stake		W-R	Per cent	£1 Level Stake
Novice hurdles	8-36	22.2	- 15.59	Selling	0-0	-	0.00
H'cap hurdles	3-12	25.0	- 3.09	Amateur	0-0	-	0.00
Novice chases	0-0	-	0.00	Hunter chases	0-0	-	0.00
H'cap chases	0-0	-	0.00	N H Flat	0-0	-	0.00

COURSE GRADE · FIRST TIME OUT

	W-R	Per cent	£1 Level Stake		W-R	Per cent	£1 Level Stake
Group 1	5-30	16.7	- 17.18	Hurdles	4-17	23.5	- 5.71
Group 2	3-6	50.0	+ 0.37	Chases	0-0	-	0.00
Group 3	3-11	27.3	- 0.87				
Group 4	0-1	-	- 1.00	Totals	4-17	23.5	- 5.71

JOCKEYS RIDING

	W-R	Per cent	£1 Level Stake		W-R	Per cent	£1 Level Stake
S Ryan	8-28	28.6	- 7.09	G Bradley	1-2	50.0	+ 2.50
N Williamson	1-1	100.0	+ 1.38	R Dunwoody	1-6	16.7	- 4.47

D Bridgwater	0-6	A Maguire	0-1	C Llewellyn	0-1
M A Fitzgerald	0-2	A P McCoy	0-1		

COURSE RECORD

	Total W-R	Nov Hdles	H'cap Hdles	Nov Chses	H'cap Chses	Hunter Chses	N H Flat	£1 Level Stake
Windsor	2-4	2-4	0-0	0-0	0-0	0-0	0-0	+ 3.63
Lingfield	2-4	2-4	0-0	0-0	0-0	0-0	0-0	+ 0.37
Ascot	2-9	1-7	1-2	0-0	0-0	0-0	0-0	- 4.97
Fontwell	1-2	1-2	0-0	0-0	0-0	0-0	0-0	0.00
Folkestone	1-2	1-2	0-0	0-0	0-0	0-0	0-0	+ 0.50
Aintree	1-2	0-0	1-2	0-0	0-0	0-0	0-0	+ 2.50
Cheltenham	1-5	1-4	0-1	0-0	0-0	0-0	0-0	- 2.62
Sandown	1-10	0-4	1-6	0-0	0-0	0-0	0-0	- 8.09

Kempton	0-3	Worcester	0-2	Taunton	0-1
Plumpton	0-2	Newbury	0-1	Wincanton	0-1

WINNING HORSES

	Races Run	1st	2nd	3rd	Unpl	Win £
Darter	6	3	2	0	1	11,135
Bimsey	3	1	0	1	1	10,236
Miroswaki	6	2	3	0	1	6,507
Admiral's Well	4	1	0	0	3	4,947
Silver Groom	5	1	1	0	3	4,947
Bolivar	5	2	1	0	2	4,896
Wishing	4	1	1	0	2	2,358

WINNING OWNERS

	Races Won	Value £		Races Won	Value £
A D Spence	5	18,440	The Silver Darling Partnership	1	4,947
Aidan Ryan	1	10,236	Bel Leisure Limited	2	4,896
Mrs A Naughton	2	6,507			

No of horses racing for the stable	17		Total winning prize-money	£45,026

Favourites	9-17	52.9%	+ 2.82	Average SP of winner		1.7/1
Longest win seq	1	Longest losing seq	8	Return on stakes invested		-38.9%

1994/95 Form	8-58	13.8%	- 17.21	1992/93 Form	13-104	12.5%	- 36.79
1993/94 Form	17-69	24.6%	- 6.60	1991/92 Form	18-137	13.1%	- 52.62

H ALEXANDER (Lanchester, Co Durham)

	Races Run	1st	2nd	3rd	Unpl	Per cent	£1 Level Stake
Hurdles	40	3	4	2	31	7.5	- 15.50
Chases	16	0	0	2	14	-	- 16.00
Totals	56	3	4	4	45	5.4	- 31.50

R McGrath	2-15	- 1.50	M Dwyer	1-3	+ 8.00
Carlisle	1-4	+ 7.00	Sedgefield	1-13	- 5.50
Perth	1-4	+ 2.00			

No of horses racing for the stable	9		Total winning prize-money	£7,399

G N ALFORD (Southampton, Hants)

	Races Run	1st	2nd	3rd	Unpl	Per cent	£1 Level Stake
Hurdles	8	1	0	1	6	12.5	+ 13.00
Chases	0	0	0	0	0	-	0.00
Totals	8	1	0	1	6	12.5	+ 13.00

R Greene	1-6	+ 15.00	Hereford	1-1	+ 20.00

No of horses racing for the stable	1		Total winning prize-money	£2,515

R ALLAN (Cornhill-on-Tweed, Northumberland)

	Races Run	1st	2nd	3rd	Unpl	Per cent	£1 Level Stake
Hurdles	38	6	3	5	24	15.8	+ 1.00
Chases	10	2	1	4	3	20.0	+ 0.33
Totals	48	8	4	9	27	16.7	+ 1.33

BY MONTH

	W-R	Per cent	£1 Level Stake		W-R	Per cent	£1 Level Stake
June	0-2	-	- 2.00	December	1-5	20.0	- 2.75
July	0-0	-	0.00	January	0-7	-	- 7.00
August	0-0	-	0.00	February	0-2	-	- 2.00
September	0-0	-	0.00	March	1-5	20.0	+ 1.00
October	2-4	50.0	+ 6.50	April	0-7	-	- 7.00
November	0-9	-	- 9.00	May	4-7	57.1	+ 23.58

DISTANCE

Hurdles	W-R	Per cent	£1 Level Stake	Chases	W-R	Per cent	£1 Level Stake
2m-2m 3f	6-32	18.8	+ 7.00	2m-2m 3f	2-7	28.6	+ 3.33
2m 4f-2m 7f	0-5	-	- 5.00	2m 4f-2m 7f	0-3	-	- 3.00
3m +	0-1	-	- 1.00	3m +	0-0	-	0.00

TYPE OF RACE

	W-R	Per cent	£1 Level Stake		W-R	Per cent	£1 Level Stake
Novice hurdles	1-13	7.7	- 11.75	Selling	0-7	-	- 7.00
H'cap hurdles	3-9	33.3	+ 22.50	Amateur	0-1	-	- 1.00
Novice chases	2-5	40.0	+ 5.33	Hunter chases	0-0	-	0.00
H'cap chases	0-5	-	- 5.00	N H Flat	2-8	25.0	- 1.75

COURSE GRADE

FIRST TIME OUT

	W-R	Per cent	£1 Level Stake		W-R	Per cent	£1 Level Stake
Group 1	1-5	20.0	- 0.50	Hurdles	3-14	21.4	+ 0.50
Group 2	0-0	-	0.00	Chases	0-0	-	0.00
Group 3	0-4	-	- 4.00				
Group 4	7-39	17.9	+ 5.83	Totals	3-14	21.4	+ 0.50

JOCKEYS RIDING

	W-R	Per cent	£1 Level Stake		W-R	Per cent	£1 Level Stake
S Melrose	4-25	16.0	+ 8.25	B Storey	2-11	18.2	- 5.25
L Wyer	2-7	28.6	+ 3.33				

B Harding	0-1	J Callaghan	0-1	N Bentley	0-1
G Bradley	0-1	Mr A Robson	0-1		

COURSE RECORD

	Total W-R	Nov Hdles	H'cap Hdles	Nov Chses	H'cap Chses	Hunter Chses	N H Flat	£1 Level Stake
Kelso	3-13	0-8	1-2	2-2	0-1	0-0	0-0	+ 3.33
Perth	2-5	1-3	0-0	0-0	0-1	0-0	1-1	+ 0.25
Newcastle	1-3	0-0	1-3	0-0	0-0	0-0	0-0	+ 1.50
Sedgefield	1-6	0-0	1-2	0-2	0-2	0-0	0-0	+ 15.00
Musselburgh	1-7	0-2	0-2	0-0	0-0	0-0	1-3	- 4.75

Carlisle	0-4	Hexham	0-4
Catterick	0-4	Ayr	0-2

WINNING HORSES

	Races Run	1st	2nd	3rd	Unpl	Win £
Briar's Delight	12	3	1	5	3	10,955
Adamatic	6	2	1	2	1	4,351
Astraleon	2	1	0	1	0	3,188
Triennium	9	1	2	1	5	2,734
Bit O Magic	1	1	0	0	0	1,966

WINNING OWNERS

	Races Won	Value £		Races Won	Value £
A Clark	3	10,955	J Stephenson	1	3,188
Geoff Adam	3	6,317	M C Boyd	1	2,734

No of horses racing for the stable	14	Total winning prize-money	£23,194

Favourites	2-7	28.6%	- 3.50	Average SP of winner	5.2/1
Longest win seq	2	Longest losing seq	15	Return on stakes invested	2.8%

1994/95 Form	5-50	10.0%	- 19.00	1992/93 Form	6-83	7.2%	- 54.47
1993/94 Form	7-83	8.4%	- 51.29	1991/92 Form	10-52	19.2%	- 27.41

C N ALLEN (Newmarket, Suffolk)

	Races Run	1st	2nd	3rd	Unpl	Per cent	£1 Level Stake
Hurdles	16	1	0	0	15	6.3	+ 5.00
Chases	0	0	0	0	0	-	0.00
Totals	16	1	0	0	15	6.3	+ 5.00

J Ryan	1-1	+ 20.00	Leicester	1-1	+ 20.00

No of horses racing for the stable	7	Total winning prize-money	£2,267

R H ALNER (Droop, Dorset)

	Races Run	1st	2nd	3rd	Unpl	Per cent	£1 Level Stake
Hurdles	76	4	5	7	60	5.3	- 59.07
Chases	122	21	21	17	63	17.2	- 7.64
Totals	198	25	26	24	123	12.6	- 66.71

BY MONTH

	W-R	Per cent	£1 Level Stake		W-R	Per cent	£1 Level Stake
June	0-2	-	- 2.00	December	1-13	7.7	- 10.75
July	0-1	-	- 1.00	January	1-28	3.6	- 7.00
August	2-7	28.6	- 2.64	February	3-18	16.7	- 0.50
September	0-5	-	- 5.00	March	1-36	2.8	- 33.00
October	3-15	20.0	- 3.37	April	3-31	9.7	- 10.00
November	9-28	32.1	+ 12.55	May	2-14	14.3	- 4.00

DISTANCE

	W-R	Per cent	£1 Level Stake		W-R	Per cent	£1 Level Stake
Hurdles				Chases			
2m-2m 3f	0-36	-	- 36.00	2m-2m 3f	7-31	22.6	+ 26.74
2m 4f-2m 7f	3-26	11.5	- 15.57	2m 4f-2m 7f	6-33	18.2	- 10.13
3m +	1-14	7.1	- 7.50	3m +	8-58	13.8	- 24.25

TYPE OF RACE

	W-R	Per cent	£1 Level Stake		W-R	Per cent	£1 Level Stake
Novice hurdles	3-47	6.4	- 36.57	Selling	0-0	-	0.00
H'cap hurdles	1-22	4.5	- 15.50	Amateur	2-8	25.0	+ 0.91
Novice chases	9-44	20.5	+ 0.96	Hunter chases	1-2	50.0	+ 2.50
H'cap chases	9-70	12.9	- 14.01	N H Flat	0-5	-	- 5.00

COURSE GRADE / FIRST TIME OUT

	W-R	Per cent	£1 Level Stake		W-R	Per cent	£1 Level Stake
Group 1	8-53	15.1	+ 16.63	Hurdles	2-26	7.7	- 17.70
Group 2	3-29	10.3	- 20.75	Chases	5-19	26.3	+ 31.21
Group 3	10-81	12.3	- 44.72				
Group 4	4-35	11.4	- 17.87	Totals	7-45	15.6	+ 13.51

JOCKEYS RIDING

	W-R	Per cent	£1 Level Stake		W-R	Per cent	£1 Level Stake
Mr P Henley	11-80	13.8	- 28.96	Miss D Harding	1-2	50.0	+ 2.50
Mr R Nuttall	4-10	40.0	- 1.46	J R Kavanagh	1-5	20.0	- 2.00
S McNeill	3-13	23.1	+ 16.50	A P McCoy	1-5	20.0	+ 16.00
R Dunwoody	2-5	40.0	+ 5.00	P Carey	1-11	9.1	- 8.62
D Bridgwater	1-1	100.0	+ 0.33				

R Johnson	0-10	Mr C Bonner	0-2	Mr A Wood	0-1
W McFarland	0-9	Mr J Culloty	0-2	Mr J Jukes	0-1
A Maguire	0-7	B Fenton	0-1	Mr M Armytage	0-1
C Maude	0-7	C Llewellyn	0-1	Philip Hughes	0-1
Miss S Barraclough	0-7	G E Tormey	0-1	S Burrough	0-1
A Thornton	0-4	G McCourt	0-1	Sophie Mitchell	0-1
D Gallagher	0-3	J Titley	0-1	T Dascombe	0-1
B Powell	0-2	M A Fitzgerald	0-1		

COURSE RECORD

	Total W-R	Nov Hdles	H'cap Hdles	Nov Chses	H'cap Chses	Hunter Chses	N H Flat	£1 Level Stake
Folkestone	3-5	0-1	0-0	0-1	3-3	0-0	0-0	+ 10.38
Kempton	3-8	0-0	0-0	1-4	1-3	1-1	0-0	+ 24.50
Fontwell	3-10	0-1	0-1	2-2	1-6	0-0	0-0	- 1.75
Exeter	3-23	0-6	0-3	1-5	2-8	0-0	0-1	- 12.37
Warwick	2-6	0-0	0-2	2-3	0-1	0-0	0-0	+ 4.00
Newbury	2-13	1-4	0-1	1-1	0-6	0-0	0-1	- 9.87
Ascot	2-13	0-4	0-2	0-1	2-6	0-0	0-0	+ 15.00
Towcester	1-3	0-0	1-1	0-0	0-2	0-0	0-0	+ 3.50
Huntingdon	1-4	0-0	0-0	0-2	1-2	0-0	0-0	- 2.64
Uttoxeter	1-7	0-1	0-2	0-2	1-2	0-0	0-0	- 5.09
Windsor	1-8	1-2	0-0	0-4	0-2	0-0	0-0	- 5.37
Plumpton	1-11	0-1	0-0	1-4	0-6	0-0	0-0	- 8.00
Cheltenham	1-11	1-2	0-4	0-1	0-3	0-1	0-0	- 5.00
Wincanton	1-28	0-14	0-2	1-5	0-6	0-0	0-1	- 26.00

Chepstow	0-10	Hereford		0-3	Haydock		0-1
Newton Abbot	0-6	Taunton		0-3	Market Rasen		0-1
Sandown	0-6	Bangor		0-2	Southwell		0-1
Nottingham	0-5	Lingfield		0-2	Stratford		0-1
Worcester	0-5	Aintree		0-1	Wetherby		0-1

WINNING HORSES

	Races Run	1st	2nd	3rd	Unpl	Win £
Harwell Lad	8	4	1	2	1	14,344
Vicosa	9	3	3	0	3	10,764
Beaurepaire	8	2	3	1	2	10,382
Hops And Pops	9	2	0	0	7	10,287
Uncle Eli	1	1	0	0	0	8,325
Super Tactics	8	2	2	3	1	8,277
Court Rapier	7	2	0	1	4	6,318
Columcille	7	2	3	0	2	6,108
Master Ryon	8	1	1	0	6	4,472
Bishops Hall	4	1	1	0	2	4,276
Rex To The Rescue	5	1	0	0	4	3,501
Malwood Castle	5	1	1	0	3	3,134
Winspit	5	1	0	2	2	2,906
Secret Bid	3	1	0	0	2	1,996
Cool Dawn	2	1	1	0	0	1,632

WINNING OWNERS

	Races Won	Value £		Races Won	Value £
H V Perry	4	14,595	H H Richards	1	4,472
H Wellstead	4	14,344	T J Carroll	1	4,276
Diamond Racing Ltd	3	10,764	P F Gough	1	3,501
Pell-Mell Partners	2	10,382	Mrs U Wainwright	1	3,134
The Happy Band	2	10,287	Mrs J E Purdie	1	2,906
James Burley	1	8,325	The Droop Partners	1	1,996
R Alner	2	6,108	Hon D Harding	1	1,632

No of horses racing for the stable			46		Total winning prize-money		£96,722

Favourites	11-32	34.4%	- 7.71	Average SP of winner	4.3/1
Longest win seq	3	Longest losing seq	32	Return on stakes invested	-33.7%

1994/95 Form	27-145	18.6%	- 39.77	1992/93 Form	3-23	13.0%	- 13.09
1993/94 Form	26-162	16.0%	- 50.23	1991/92 Form	4-24	16.7%	+ 7.25

E J ALSTON (Longton, Lancs)

	Races Run	1st	2nd	3rd	Unpl	Per cent	£1 Level Stake
Hurdles	34	3	2	3	26	8.8	- 12.50
Chases	0	0	0	0	0	-	0.00
Totals	34	3	2	3	26	8.8	- 12.50

R Garrity	1-2	+ 3.00	L Wyer	1-6	- 0.50
A Procter	1-3	+ 8.00			

Carlisle	1-2	+ 3.50	Ayr	1-5	0.00
Uttoxeter	1-5	+ 6.00			

No of horses racing for the stable	9	Total winning prize-money	£6,509

MRS E M ANDREWS (Luton, Beds)

	Races Run	1st	2nd	3rd	Unpl	Per cent	£1 Level Stake
Hurdles	0	0	0	0	0	-	0.00
Chases	2	1	0	0	1	50.0	+ 0.88
Totals	2	1	0	0	1	50.0	+ 0.88

Mr S R Andrews	1-2	+ 0.88	Plumpton	1-1	+ 1.88

No of horses racing for the stable	1	Total winning prize-money	£1,506

D W P ARBUTHNOT (Compton, Berks)

	Races Run	1st	2nd	3rd	Unpl	Per cent	£1 Level Stake
Hurdles	19	3	1	0	15	15.8	- 4.00
Chases	0	0	0	0	0	-	0.00
Totals	19	3	1	0	15	15.8	- 4.00

A P McCoy	1-1	+ 2.25	S McNeill	1-9	- 5.25
I Lawrence	1-2	+ 6.00			

Uttoxeter	1-1	+ 2.75	Warwick	1-5	- 1.75
Plumpton	1-2	+ 6.00			

No of horses racing for the stable	3	Total winning prize-money	£8,415

MRS S M AUSTIN (Burythorpe, North Yorks)

	Races Run	1st	2nd	3rd	Unpl	Per cent	£1 Level Stake
Hurdles	37	2	5	5	25	5.4	- 25.00
Chases	1	0	0	0	1	-	- 1.00
Totals	38	2	5	5	26	5.3	- 26.00

D Wilkinson	2-19	- 7.00				
Southwell	1-3	+ 1.00		Sedgefield	1-10	- 2.00

No of horses racing for the stable   10   Total winning prize-money   £4,409

N M BABBAGE (Cleeve Hill, Glos)

	Races Run	1st	2nd	3rd	Unpl	Per cent	£1 Level Stake
Hurdles	37	3	5	3	26	8.1	+ 11.00
Chases	20	2	1	4	13	10.0	+ 16.00
Totals	57	5	6	7	39	8.8	+ 27.00

A P McCoy	1-2	+ 8.00	Martin Smith	1-5	+ 21.00
M A Fitzgerald	1-2	+ 24.00	G Hogan	1-7	+ 2.00
S McNeill	1-3	+ 10.00			
Towcester	1-2	+ 24.00	Kempton	1-3	+ 23.00
Leicester	1-2	+ 7.00	Wincanton	1-4	+ 9.00
Taunton	1-3	+ 7.00			

No of horses racing for the stable   18   Total winning prize-money   £13,210

A BAILEY (Little Budworth, Cheshire)

	Races Run	1st	2nd	3rd	Unpl	Per cent	£1 Level Stake
Hurdles	18	1	3	2	12	5.6	- 11.50
Chases	2	0	0	1	1	-	- 2.00
Totals	20	1	3	3	13	5.0	- 13.50

T Kent	1-10	- 3.50	Sedgefield	1-1	+ 5.50

No of horses racing for the stable   9   Total winning prize-money   £1,996

K C BAILEY (Upper Lambourn, Berks)

	Races Run	1st	2nd	3rd	Unpl	Per cent	£1 Level Stake
Hurdles	199	25	21	25	128	12.6	- 79.82
Chases	231	43	36	35	117	18.6	- 51.35
Totals	430	68	57	60	245	15.8	-131.17

BY MONTH

	W-R	Per cent	£1 Level Stake		W-R	Per cent	£1 Level Stake
June	1-1	100.0	+ 1.63	December	3-44	6.8	- 30.75
July	0-8	-	- 8.00	January	4-40	10.0	+ 0.50
August	2-8	25.0	- 4.29	February	5-31	16.1	- 1.34
September	6-19	31.6	+ 5.70	March	10-62	16.1	- 21.58
October	10-43	23.3	- 12.21	April	5-61	8.2	- 43.16
November	13-66	19.7	- 5.09	May	9-47	19.1	- 12.58

DISTANCE

	W-R	Per cent	£1 Level Stake		W-R	Per cent	£1 Level Stake
Hurdles				Chases			
2m-2m 3f	16-106	15.1	- 48.70	2m-2m 3f	10-49	20.4	- 18.60
2m 4f-2m 7f	5-58	8.6	- 23.50	2m 4f-2m 7f	16-88	18.2	- 27.00
3m +	4-35	11.4	- 7.62	3m +	17-94	18.1	- 5.75

TYPE OF RACE

	W-R	Per cent	£1 Level Stake		W-R	Per cent	£1 Level Stake
Novice hurdles	15-125	12.0	- 58.29	Selling	0-1	-	- 1.00
H'cap hurdles	5-45	11.1	- 14.27	Amateur	2-9	22.2	+ 2.00
Novice chases	19-93	20.4	- 21.11	Hunter chases	0-4	-	- 4.00
H'cap chases	22-127	17.3	- 30.24	N H Flat	5-26	19.2	- 4.26

COURSE GRADE / FIRST TIME OUT

	W-R	Per cent	£1 Level Stake		W-R	Per cent	£1 Level Stake
Group 1	7-104	6.7	- 68.51	Hurdles	8-60	13.3	- 17.84
Group 2	8-48	16.7	- 10.88	Chases	11-41	26.8	+ 0.58
Group 3	34-165	20.6	- 8.09				
Group 4	19-113	16.8	- 43.69	Totals	19-101	18.8	- 17.26

JOCKEYS RIDING

	W-R	Per cent	£1 Level Stake		W-R	Per cent	£1 Level Stake
T J Murphy	17-103	16.5	- 34.50	S McNeill	4-23	17.4	- 6.70
R Dunwoody	14-65	21.5	- 16.04	W McFarland	2-8	25.0	- 3.42
N Williamson	10-33	30.3	+ 0.50	J Magee	2-19	10.5	- 14.15
A Thornton	7-77	9.1	- 31.92	Mr C Bonner	1-3	33.3	+ 2.00
J Osborne	5-33	15.2	- 3.57	J A McCarthy	1-6	16.7	- 3.37
G Bradley	4-14	28.6	+ 20.00	Mr M Armytage	1-13	7.7	- 7.00

J Railton	0-9	R Johnson	0-2	M Dwyer	0-1
C Llewellyn	0-6	A Maguire	0-1	Mr A Parker	0-1
G Hogan	0-3	B Fenton	0-1	Mr D Alers-Hankey	0-1
M A Fitzgerald	0-3	C F Swan	0-1	P Carberry	0-1
A P McCoy	0-2	D Bridgwater	0-1		

COURSE RECORD

	Total W-R	Nov Hdles	H'cap Hdles	Nov Chses	H'cap Chses	Hunter Chses	N H Flat	£1 Level Stake
Uttoxeter	7-33	2-13	1-4	3-6	1-10	0-0	0-0	- 12.01
Nottingham	6-14	0-2	2-2	3-6	1-3	0-0	0-1	+ 30.60
Ludlow	6-19	2-6	0-3	3-4	1-4	0-1	0-1	+ 5.69
Worcester	5-23	0-5	0-2	2-6	3-8	0-0	0-2	+ 2.88
Market Rasen	4-12	0-3	0-1	1-2	2-4	0-0	1-2	+ 1.82
Hereford	4-14	1-5	0-3	0-2	2-2	0-0	1-2	+ 3.63
Newton Abbot	4-16	3-7	0-1	0-1	0-4	0-1	1-2	+ 8.13
Towcester	4-16	1-5	0-2	1-1	2-8	0-0	0-0	- 3.87
Wincanton	3-11	0-3	0-0	0-1	3-7	0-0	0-0	+ 5.80
Windsor	3-11	1-3	0-2	1-4	1-2	0-0	0-0	+ 2.30
Fontwell	3-14	1-6	0-1	0-1	1-5	0-0	1-1	- 2.92
Stratford	3-18	0-5	0-2	1-3	2-8	0-0	0-0	- 9.73
Kempton	2-14	1-3	0-2	1-4	0-4	0-0	0-1	- 1.09
Huntingdon	2-16	0-3	0-1	1-4	1-5	0-0	0-3	- 7.25
Cheltenham	2-17	0-3	0-0	1-6	1-8	0-0	0-0	- 11.65
Ascot	2-18	0-7	1-2	0-1	1-7	0-0	0-1	- 2.50
Sedgefield	1-1	1-1	0-0	0-0	0-0	0-0	0-0	+ 1.20
Cartmel	1-2	1-1	0-0	0-1	0-0	0-0	0-0	- 0.20
Southwell	1-6	0-0	0-0	0-4	1-2	0-0	0-0	+ 0.50
Ayr	1-7	0-2	1-3	0-0	0-1	0-0	0-1	- 5.27
Lingfield	1-7	0-4	0-0	0-2	0-0	0-0	1-1	- 5.09
Perth	1-9	0-3	0-1	1-3	0-0	0-1	0-1	- 7.27
Warwick	1-10	0-4	0-0	0-3	1-3	0-0	0-0	- 5.50
Exeter	1-18	1-4	0-3	0-3	0-4	0-1	0-3	- 15.37

Bangor	0-12	Doncaster	0-7	Musselburgh	0-3
Sandown	0-12	Fakenham	0-7	Newcastle	0-2
Newbury	0-11	Aintree	0-6	Plumpton	0-2
Haydock	0-10	Taunton	0-6	Catterick	0-1
Leicester	0-9	Folkestone	0-5		
Chepstow	0-7	Wetherby	0-4		

WINNING HORSES

	Races Run	1st	2nd	3rd	Unpl	Win £
Alderbrook	3	2	1	0	0	26,396
Betty's Boy	4	2	1	0	1	17,058
Bertone	9	4	2	2	1	16,640
Docs Dilemma	5	2	1	1	1	12,838
Wise Approach	12	3	2	1	6	12,698
Persian Tactics	8	4	2	1	1	12,641
Over The Stream	6	3	0	1	2	10,264
The Bud Club	9	3	1	2	3	9,684

Bailey K C

Lake of Loughrea	11	3	2	2	4	9,474
Seekin Cash	5	1	1	1	2	8,598
Far Senior	5	2	0	1	2	8,314
Fellow Countryman	5	2	1	0	2	7,842
Full of Fire	6	2	2	0	2	7,585
Price's Hill	8	2	2	0	4	7,335
Andre Laval	2	2	0	0	0	6,841
Dominie	9	2	0	2	5	5,509
Waterford Castle	7	2	2	0	3	5,386
Pampered Guest	4	1	0	1	2	5,136
King Girseach	4	2	0	0	2	4,927
Act of Parliament	5	1	0	1	3	4,824
Shellhouse	4	2	0	1	1	4,641
Mr Jamboree	8	1	2	1	4	4,560
Stac-Pollaidh	9	2	2	0	5	4,330
Strong Medicine	7	1	1	2	3	4,221
Persian View	6	2	0	1	3	4,010
Sharp Performer	6	1	1	0	4	3,834
Glemot	7	1	3	2	1	3,720
Drumcullen	8	1	2	0	5	3,182
Lobster Cottage	4	1	0	0	3	3,106
Injectabuck	2	1	0	1	0	2,775
Cyrus The Great	8	1	4	2	1	2,668
Hoh Music	4	1	0	1	2	2,458
Sprung Rhythm	4	1	2	1	0	2,320
Porphyrios	9	1	1	2	5	2,142
Quiet Amusement	3	1	1	0	1	1,889
Granham Pride	2	1	0	0	1	1,605
Badger's Lane	1	1	0	0	0	1,413
Gaye Fame	2	1	0	0	1	1,354
Celtic Park	2	1	1	0	0	1,301
Lucia Forte	1	1	0	0	0	1,301

WINNING OWNERS

	Races Won	Value £		Races Won	Value £
Mrs Harry J Duffey	12	40,758	Blakeley Painters Ltd	2	4,927
E Pick	2	26,396	Raymond J Roberts	2	4,641
Scott Hardy Partnership	2	12,838	Mrs D Lousada	1	4,560
Mrs S Gee	3	12,698	I F W Buchan	2	4,330
Richard Shaw	1	11,274	Mrs S C Ellen	1	3,834
J D Gordon	3	10,264	Dennis Yardy	1	3,720
J Perriss	2	9,960	Martyn Booth	1	3,182
The Blue Chip Group	3	9,684	R L T Burges	1	3,106
W J Ives	3	9,587	K C Bailey	1	3,054
Mrs David Thompson	1	8,598	I M S Racing	2	2,959
A D Wardall	2	7,842	P J Vogt	1	2,668
J Michael Gillow	2	7,585	D F Allport	1	2,458
G D W Swire	2	7,335	Ian Bullerwell	1	2,142
Dr D B A Silk	2	6,996	Mrs Angela Fayers	1	1,889
Mrs Christopher Wright	2	6,841	Sir Gordon Brunton	1	1,413
T Benfield and W Brown	1	5,784	Mrs Lucia Farmer	1	1,301
A J Heyes	2	5,509	Urs E Schwarzenbach	1	1,301
Sybil Lady Joseph	2	5,386			

No of horses racing for the stable	102	Total winning prize-money	£256,820

| Favourites | 33-105 | 31.4% | - 21.63 | Average SP of winner | | 3.4/1 |
| Longest win seq | 3 | Longest losing seq | 26 | Return on stakes invested | | -30.5% |

| 1994/95 Form | 72-316 | 22.8% | + 12.44 | 1992/93 Form | 57-302 | 18.9% | - 60.00 |
| 1993/94 Form | 87-376 | 23.1% | - 35.43 | 1991/92 Form | 38-250 | 15.2% | - 20.91 |

R J BAKER (Stoodleigh, Devon)

	Races Run	1st	2nd	3rd	Unpl	Per cent	£1 Level Stake
Hurdles	84	1	4	8	71	1.2	- 78.50
Chases	4	0	0	1	3	-	- 4.00
Totals	88	1	4	9	74	1.1	- 82.50

D Bridgwater	1-1	+ 4.50	Taunton	1-18	- 12.50

No of horses racing for the stable	27	Total winning prize-money	£4,720

G B BALDING (Fyfield, Hants)

	Races Run	1st	2nd	3rd	Unpl	Per cent	£1 Level Stake
Hurdles	186	21	23	15	127	11.3	- 61.73
Chases	121	24	15	17	65	19.8	+ 21.40
Totals	307	45	38	32	192	14.7	- 40.33

BY MONTH

	W-R	Per cent	£1 Level Stake		W-R	Per cent	£1 Level Stake
June	4-8	50.0	+ 33.00	December	2-27	7.4	- 18.00
July	7-16	43.8	+ 20.18	January	1-36	2.8	- 26.00
August	1-7	14.3	- 4.62	February	2-22	9.1	- 4.50
September	4-16	25.0	+ 1.71	March	3-50	6.0	- 36.37
October	6-31	19.4	- 9.82	April	8-33	24.2	+ 20.66
November	5-41	12.2	- 0.50	May	2-20	10.0	- 16.07

DISTANCE

Hurdles	W-R	Per cent	£1 Level Stake	Chases	W-R	Per cent	£1 Level Stake
2m-2m 3f	17-112	15.2	- 15.23	2m-2m 3f	8-28	28.6	+ 8.71
2m 4f-2m 7f	4-64	6.3	- 36.50	2m 4f-2m 7f	11-54	20.4	+ 15.69
3m +	0-10	-	- 10.00	3m +	5-39	12.8	- 3.00

Balding G B

TYPE OF RACE

	W–R	Per cent	£1 Level Stake		W–R	Per cent	£1 Level Stake
Novice hurdles	10-98	10.2	- 43.11	Selling	1-6	16.7	+ 0.50
H'cap hurdles	8-67	11.9	- 16.62	Amateur	0-8	-	- 8.00
Novice chases	4-30	13.3	- 4.87	Hunter chases	0-2	-	- 2.00
H'cap chases	20-82	24.4	+ 35.27	N H Flat	2-14	14.3	- 1.50

COURSE GRADE FIRST TIME OUT

	W–R	Per cent	£1 Level Stake		W–R	Per cent	£1 Level Stake
Group 1	7-75	9.3	- 26.50	Hurdles	5-47	10.6	- 12.50
Group 2	7-42	16.7	- 7.24	Chases	4-15	26.7	+ 17.08
Group 3	22-113	19.5	+ 31.76				
Group 4	9-77	11.7	- 38.35	Totals	9-62	14.5	+ 4.58

JOCKEYS RIDING

	W–R	Per cent	£1 Level Stake		W–R	Per cent	£1 Level Stake
A P McCoy	33-138	23.9	+ 30.19	B Fenton	2-37	5.4	- 17.00
B M Clifford	9-68	13.2	+ 5.48	Mr A Balding	1-15	6.7	- 10.00

R Arnold	0-13	Mr T McCarthy	0-2	Mr E James	0-1
A Tory	0-7	D J Murphy	0-1	P Holley	0-1
R Greene	0-6	D Salter	0-1	R Dunwoody	0-1
J Frost	0-4	G Bradley	0-1	Ross Berry	0-1
J Railton	0-4	J A McCarthy	0-1	S Fox	0-1
L Wyer	0-2	Mr E Babington	0-1	S McNeill	0-1

COURSE RECORD

	Total W–R	Nov Hdles	H'cap Hdles	Nov Chses	H'cap Chses	Hunter Chses	N H Flat	£1 Level Stake
Worcester	12-31	3-6	2-6	0-2	5-12	0-0	2-5	+ 48.96
Fontwell	4-19	1-6	1-6	0-2	2-4	0-0	0-1	- 1.97
Stratford	3-16	2-3	0-4	0-2	1-7	0-0	0-0	- 0.50
Exeter	3-25	1-9	1-7	0-2	1-6	0-0	0-1	- 3.71
Market Rasen	2-5	1-2	0-1	0-0	1-2	0-0	0-0	+ 5.80
Huntingdon	2-5	1-3	0-0	0-0	1-2	0-0	0-0	+ 6.00
Ludlow	2-6	0-2	0-0	1-2	1-2	0-0	0-0	- 0.12
Sandown	2-12	0-4	1-1	0-2	1-3	0-1	0-1	+ 2.50
Wincanton	2-16	0-6	0-2	0-0	2-8	0-0	0-0	+ 7.00
Ascot	2-16	0-11	1-3	1-1	0-1	0-0	0-0	- 0.50
Cheltenham	2-20	0-5	1-7	0-1	1-7	0-0	0-0	- 12.50
Carlisle	1-1	0-0	0-0	0-0	1-1	0-0	0-0	+ 1.50
Leicester	1-4	0-1	0-0	0-1	1-2	0-0	0-0	+ 0.50
Lingfield	1-6	0-1	0-2	1-2	0-0	0-0	0-1	+ 7.00
Newton Abbot	1-7	0-2	0-1	0-0	1-4	0-0	0-0	- 5.27
Hereford	1-7	0-0	0-4	0-0	1-2	0-0	0-1	- 4.90
Bangor	1-8	1-1	0-4	0-0	0-2	0-0	0-1	- 5.62
Chepstow	1-10	0-4	0-4	1-1	0-1	0-0	0-0	- 7.00
Taunton	1-14	0-5	1-1	0-4	0-3	0-1	0-0	- 9.50
Newbury	1-22	0-10	1-8	0-1	0-3	0-0	0-0	- 11.00

Towcester	0-16	Nottingham	0-3	Doncaster	0-1
Warwick	0-16	Kempton	0-2	Newcastle	0-1
Windsor	0-8	Plumpton	0-2		
Folkestone	0-7	Aintree	0-1		

WINNING HORSES

	Races Run	1st	2nd	3rd	Unpl	Win £
Southampton	16	4	2	4	6	26,231
Conti D'Estruval	11	5	0	1	5	23,768
Polden Pride	15	6	1	3	5	20,633
Tug of Peace	9	2	2	0	5	19,493
Blair Castle	12	5	2	3	2	12,123
Goldenswift	8	3	1	1	3	9,335
Romany Creek	7	2	2	2	1	8,056
Fools Errand	9	2	2	2	3	7,456
Vicar of Bray	7	2	1	1	3	6,791
The Caumrue	8	2	1	0	5	6,090
Jimmy's Cross	9	3	3	1	2	5,767
Phar From Funny	6	1	0	1	4	5,084
Ask The Governor	9	1	1	0	7	4,590
Jewel Thief	8	2	4	0	2	4,176
Doonloughan	9	1	1	3	4	4,159
General Salute	4	1	0	0	3	3,267
Pampillo	5	1	3	1	0	2,898
Platini	3	1	2	0	0	2,472
Barbary Falcon	1	1	0	0	0	1,235

WINNING OWNERS

	Races Won	Value £		Races Won	Value £
Highflyers	10	40,826	The Cleric Partnership	2	6,791
Bernard Keay	5	23,768	The On The Run Partnership	2	6,090
D F Lockyer	6	20,633	Mrs E A Haycock	1	5,084
P Richardson	2	19,493	Mrs D Claessen-Brierton	1	4,590
Mrs S Watts	3	9,335	Derek Strauss	1	4,159
Mrs G B Balding	4	8,762	Leslie Garratt Racing	2	4,079
Duke Of Atholl	2	8,056	Lord Chetwode	1	3,267
Mrs David Russell	2	7,456	R P Shepherd	1	1,235

No of horses racing for the stable		66	Total winning prize-money		£173,624
Favourites	14-46	30.4% - 11.67	Average SP of winner		4.9/1
Longest win seq	3	Longest losing seq 40	Return on stakes invested		-13.1%
1994/95 Form	41-289	14.2% - 19.35	1992/93 Form	38-290 13.1%	-105.16
1993/94 Form	17-264	6.4% - 88.99	1991/92 Form	53-368 14.4%	- 7.25

I A BALDING (Kingsclere, Hants)

	Races Run	1st	2nd	3rd	Unpl	Per cent	£1 Level Stake
Hurdles	38	9	1	5	23	23.7	- 3.65
Chases	8	4	3	1	0	50.0	+ 2.23
Totals	46	13	4	6	23	28.3	- 1.42

BY MONTH

	W-R	Per cent	£1 Level Stake		W-R	Per cent	£1 Level Stake
June	0-0	-	0.00	December	3-8	37.5	- 1.00
July	0-0	-	0.00	January	0-2	-	- 2.00
August	0-0	-	0.00	February	0-7	-	- 7.00
September	0-1	-	- 1.00	March	2-10	20.0	+ 0.53
October	1-6	16.7	- 3.75	April	2-3	66.7	+ 7.00
November	1-4	25.0	+ 1.50	May	4-5	80.0	+ 4.30

DISTANCE

	W-R	Per cent	£1 Level Stake		W-R	Per cent	£1 Level Stake
Hurdles				Chases			
2m-2m 3f	6-27	22.2	- 1.93	2m-2m 3f	1-2	50.0	+ 1.00
2m 4f-2m 7f	3-10	30.0	- 0.72	2m 4f-2m 7f	2-4	50.0	+ 0.23
3m +	0-1	-	- 1.00	3m +	1-2	50.0	+ 1.00

TYPE OF RACE

	W-R	Per cent	£1 Level Stake		W-R	Per cent	£1 Level Stake
Novice hurdles	6-23	26.1	- 2.72	Selling	0-0	-	0.00
H'cap hurdles	3-13	23.1	+ 1.07	Amateur	0-0	-	0.00
Novice chases	0-1	-	- 1.00	Hunter chases	3-5	60.0	+ 2.73
H'cap chases	1-2	50.0	+ 0.50	N H Flat	0-2	-	- 2.00

COURSE GRADE

	W-R	Per cent	£1 Level Stake
Group 1	3-17	17.6	- 5.97
Group 2	1-4	25.0	- 0.75
Group 3	4-15	26.7	+ 4.23
Group 4	5-10	50.0	+ 1.07

FIRST TIME OUT

	W-R	Per cent	£1 Level Stake
Hurdles	1-9	11.1	- 6.75
Chases	0-1	-	- 1.00
Totals	1-10	10.0	- 7.75

JOCKEYS RIDING

	W-R	Per cent	£1 Level Stake		W-R	Per cent	£1 Level Stake
Mr A Balding	4-9	44.4	+ 1.98	J Osborne	4-11	36.4	+ 4.00
G Bradley	4-10	40.0	+ 3.10	J Titley	1-1	100.0	+ 4.50

B Fenton	0-5	B Powell	0-1	J Railton	0-1
R Dunwoody	0-4	D Byrne	0-1		
A P McCoy	0-2	G McCourt	0-1		

COURSE RECORD

	Total W-R	Nov Hdles	H'cap Hdles	Nov Chses	H'cap Chses	Hunter Chses	N H Flat	£1 Level Stake
Musselburgh	2-2	1-1	0-0	0-0	1-1	0-0	0-0	+ 1.75
Exeter	2-5	1-3	1-2	0-0	0-0	0-0	0-0	- 1.18
Market Rasen	1-1	0-0	0-0	0-0	0-0	1-1	0-0	+ 0.73
Lingfield	1-1	1-1	0-0	0-0	0-0	0-0	0-0	+ 2.25
Stratford	1-2	0-0	0-0	0-0	0-1	1-1	0-0	+ 1.00
Cheltenham	1-2	0-1	0-0	0-0	0-0	1-1	0-0	+ 1.00
Doncaster	1-2	1-1	0-0	0-0	0-0	0-0	0-1	- 0.47
Ludlow	1-3	0-2	1-1	0-0	0-0	0-0	0-0	+ 0.50
Wincanton	1-3	0-1	1-1	0-0	0-0	0-1	0-0	+ 6.00
Windsor	1-5	1-4	0-1	0-0	0-0	0-0	0-0	+ 0.50
Ascot	1-7	1-4	0-1	0-1	0-0	0-1	0-0	- 0.50

Chepstow	0-3	Aintree		0-1	Uttoxeter	0-1
Kempton	0-3	Newbury		0-1		
Warwick	0-3	Sandown		0-1		

WINNING HORSES

	Races Run	1st	2nd	3rd	Unpl	Win £
Blaze Away	6	3	0	1	2	8,775
Moat Garden	4	3	0	0	1	8,440
King's Treasure	6	3	2	1	0	6,397
Shaarid	5	2	1	1	1	5,664
Kilcoran Bay	10	2	0	2	6	5,176

WINNING OWNERS

	Races Won	Value £		Races Won	Value £
Paul Mellon	3	8,775	Peter Oldfield	2	5,664
Queen Elizabeth	3	8,440	Nigel Harris	2	5,176
Tunnel Vision	3	6,397			

No of horses racing for the stable   10   Total winning prize-money   £34,452

Favourites	8-11	72.7%	+ 6.58	Average SP of winner			2.4/1
Longest win seq	6	Longest losing seq	9	Return on stakes invested			-3.1%

1994/95 Form	10-33	30.3%	+ 0.35	1992/93 Form	6-46	13.0%	- 30.37
1993/94 Form	12-42	28.6%	- 7.29	1991/92 Form	12-36	33.3%	+ 0.73

J E BANKS (Newmarket, Suffolk)

	Races Run	1st	2nd	3rd	Unpl	Per cent	£1 Level Stake
Hurdles	15	1	3	3	8	6.7	- 9.00
Chases	0	0	0	0	0	-	0.00
Totals	15	1	3	3	8	6.7	- 9.00

J R Kavanagh	1-4	+ 2.00	Doncaster	1-2	+ 4.00

No of horses racing for the stable   6   Total winning prize-money   £2,268

M C BANKS (Waresley, Cambs)

	Races Run	1st	2nd	3rd	Unpl	Per cent	£1 Level Stake
Hurdles	18	3	3	3	9	16.7	+ 26.50
Chases	3	0	0	1	2	-	- 3.00
Totals	21	3	3	4	11	14.3	+ 23.50

D Skyrme	3-20	+ 24.50			
Windsor	1-2	+ 32.00	Towcester	1-3	+ 0.50
Fakenham	1-2	+ 5.00			

No of horses racing for the stable   3   Total winning prize-money   £7,805

R BARBER (Seaborough, Dorset)

	Races Run	1st	2nd	3rd	Unpl	Per cent	£1 Level Stake
Hurdles	0	0	0	0	0	-	0.00
Chases	13	1	1	3	8	7.7	- 11.33
Totals	13	1	1	3	8	7.7	- 11.33

Mr Tim Mitchell	1-6	- 4.33	Windsor	1-1	+ 0.67

No of horses racing for the stable   6   Total winning prize-money   £1,123

MRS ALTHEA BARCLAY (Oddington, Glos)

	Races Run	1st	2nd	3rd	Unpl	Per cent	£1 Level Stake
Hurdles	7	0	0	0	7	-	- 7.00
Chases	3	1	0	0	2	33.3	+ 7.00
Totals	10	1	0	0	9	10.0	0.00

S Joynes	1-2	+ 8.00	Uttoxeter	1-2	+ 8.00

No of horses racing for the stable   3   Total winning prize-money   £2,533

W L BARKER (Scorton, North Yorks)

	Races Run	1st	2nd	3rd	Unpl	Per cent	£1 Level Stake
Hurdles	16	3	0	1	12	18.8	- 3.75
Chases	18	0	5	2	11	-	- 18.00
Totals	34	3	5	3	23	8.8	- 21.75

G Harker	2-15	- 7.25		R Supple		1-14	- 9.50
Market Rasen	2-7	+ 1.25		Kelso		1-4	0.00

No of horses racing for the stable   6   Total winning prize-money   £6,410

SIR JOHN BARLOW (Malpas, Cheshire)

	Races Run	1st	2nd	3rd	Unpl	Per cent	£1 Level Stake
Hurdles	0	0	0	0	0	-	0.00
Chases	1	1	0	0	0	100.0	+ 1.50
Totals	1	1	0	0	0	100.0	+ 1.50

Mr D Barlow	1-1	+ 1.50		Carlisle		1-1	+ 1.50

No of horses racing for the stable   1   Total winning prize-money   £1,155

M A BARNES (Little Salkeld, Cumbria)

	Races Run	1st	2nd	3rd	Unpl	Per cent	£1 Level Stake
Hurdles	48	2	3	2	41	4.2	- 1.00
Chases	48	2	8	9	29	4.2	- 28.50
Totals	96	4	11	11	70	4.2	- 29.50

P Waggott	3-68	- 10.00		A Dobbin		1-5	+ 3.50
Bangor	1-1	+ 7.50		Perth		1-10	+ 3.00
Carlisle	1-6	+ 28.00		Sedgefield		1-15	- 4.00

No of horses racing for the stable   22   Total winning prize-money   £13,790

G BARNETT (Stoke-on-Trent, Staffs)

	Races Run	1st	2nd	3rd	Unpl	Per cent	£1 Level Stake
Hurdles	3	1	0	0	2	33.3	+ 18.00
Chases	10	1	3	0	6	10.0	+ 57.00
Totals	13	2	3	0	8	15.4	+ 75.00

D Walsh	1-3	+ 64.00	R Farrant	1-5	+ 16.00
Worcester	1-1	+ 66.00	Uttoxeter	1-2	+ 19.00

No of horses racing for the stable   3   Total winning prize-money   £5,307

M F BARRACLOUGH (Claverdon, Warwicks)

	Races Run	1st	2nd	3rd	Unpl	Per cent	£1 Level Stake
Hurdles	45	2	2	2	39	4.4	- 21.00
Chases	6	0	0	1	5	-	- 6.00
Totals	51	2	2	3	44	3.9	- 27.00

Ann Stokell	2-20	+ 4.00			
Huntingdon	1-2	+ 5.00	Market Rasen	1-7	+ 10.00

No of horses racing for the stable   10   Total winning prize-money   £4,448

T D BARRON (Maunby, North Yorks)

	Races Run	1st	2nd	3rd	Unpl	Per cent	£1 Level Stake
Hurdles	12	1	4	1	6	8.3	- 5.00
Chases	0	0	0	0	0	-	0.00
Totals	12	1	4	1	6	8.3	- 5.00

J Callaghan	1-2	+ 5.00	Hexham	1-2	+ 5.00

No of horses racing for the stable   2   Total winning prize-money   £2,061

A BARROW (Over Stowey, Somerset)

	Races Run	1st	2nd	3rd	Unpl	Per cent	£1 Level Stake
Hurdles	42	1	2	5	34	2.4	- 16.00
Chases	22	0	4	1	17	-	- 22.00
Totals	64	1	6	6	51	1.6	- 38.00

Sophie Mitchell	1-6	+ 20.00	Stratford	1-6	+ 20.00

No of horses racing for the stable   14   Total winning prize-money   £2,598

C R BARWELL (Stoodleigh, Devon)

	Races Run	1st	2nd	3rd	Unpl	Per cent	£1 Level Stake
Hurdles	33	2	4	6	21	6.1	+ 21.25
Chases	18	1	2	4	11	5.6	- 11.50
Totals	51	3	6	10	32	5.9	+ 9.75

B Fenton	1-2	+ 49.00		A P McCoy		1-7	- 3.75
D Bridgwater	1-3	+ 3.50					
Stratford	1-5	- 1.75		Worcester		1-7	+ 44.00
Taunton	1-6	+ 0.50					

No of horses racing for the stable   14   Total winning prize-money   £7,355

P BEAUMONT (Brandsby, North Yorks)

	Races Run	1st	2nd	3rd	Unpl	Per cent	£1 Level Stake
Hurdles	74	12	5	9	48	16.2	+ 9.50
Chases	34	9	5	4	16	26.5	+ 7.03
Totals	108	21	10	13	64	19.4	+ 16.53

BY MONTH

	W-R	Per cent	£1 Level Stake		W-R	Per cent	£1 Level Stake
June	1-2	50.0	+ 19.00	December	1-3	33.3	+ 3.00
July	1-3	33.3	+ 2.00	January	2-18	11.1	- 9.43
August	0-0	-	0.00	February	1-7	14.3	- 1.00
September	0-1	-	- 1.00	March	0-4	-	- 4.00
October	2-6	33.3	+ 4.75	April	3-21	14.3	- 3.00
November	4-23	17.4	- 3.03	May	6-20	30.0	+ 9.24

DISTANCE

	W-R	Per cent	£1 Level Stake		W-R	Per cent	£1 Level Stake
Hurdles				Chases			
2m-2m 3f	4-25	16.0	- 10.50	2m-2m 3f	0-10	-	- 10.00
2m 4f-2m 7f	3-29	10.3	- 5.00	2m 4f-2m 7f	0-2	-	- 2.00
3m +	5-20	25.0	+ 25.00	3m +	9-22	40.9	+ 19.03

TYPE OF RACE

	W-R	Per cent	£1 Level Stake		W-R	Per cent	£1 Level Stake
Novice hurdles	2-23	8.7	+ 4.00	Selling	1-8	12.5	- 2.00
H'cap hurdles	4-27	14.8	+ 3.00	Amateur	1-5	20.0	+ 1.00
Novice chases	6-16	37.5	+ 10.81	Hunter chases	0-0	-	0.00
H'cap chases	3-18	16.7	- 3.78	N H Flat	4-11	36.4	+ 3.50

COURSE GRADE					FIRST TIME OUT			
	W-R	Per cent	£1 Level Stake			W-R	Per cent	£1 Level Stake
Group 1	1-13	7.7	- 10.00	Hurdles		3-23	13.0	+ 8.75
Group 2	3-15	20.0	- 7.51	Chases		1-9	11.1	- 6.00
Group 3	4-29	13.8	- 12.25					
Group 4	13-51	25.5	+ 46.29	Totals		4-32	12.5	+ 2.75

JOCKEYS RIDING

	W-R	Per cent	£1 Level Stake			W-R	Per cent	£1 Level Stake
R Supple	9-60	15.0	+ 7.98	E Callaghan		1-2	50.0	+ 3.00
B D Grattan	6-24	25.0	+ 8.50	F Leahy		1-2	50.0	+ 1.00
A Dobbin	2-2	100.0	+ 6.83	M Dwyer		1-6	16.7	- 4.78
Mr R Ford	1-1	100.0	+ 5.00					

Mrs A Farrell	0-6	C Maude	0-1	J Callaghan	0-1
B Harding	0-1	D Bridgwater	0-1	Martin Brennan	0-1

COURSE RECORD

	Total W-R	Nov Hdles	H'cap Hdles	Nov Chses	H'cap Chses	Hunter Chses	N H Flat	£1 Level Stake
Perth	3-8	1-4	1-2	1-1	0-0	0-0	0-1	+ 29.50
Market Rasen	3-9	0-1	0-2	0-1	1-2	0-0	2-3	+ 5.00
Sedgefield	3-9	1-3	1-4	1-2	0-0	0-0	0-0	+ 5.57
Hexham	3-12	0-3	1-3	1-1	1-4	0-0	0-1	+ 14.00
Wetherby	3-15	0-7	0-5	2-2	0-0	0-0	1-1	- 7.51
Uttoxeter	1-2	0-0	0-0	0-0	0-0	0-0	1-2	+ 0.75
Cartmel	1-3	1-2	0-1	0-0	0-0	0-0	0-0	+ 3.00
Bangor	1-5	0-0	1-3	0-0	0-1	0-0	0-1	+ 2.00
Kelso	1-5	0-2	0-1	0-1	1-1	0-0	0-0	- 3.78
Southwell	1-6	0-0	1-4	0-2	0-0	0-0	0-0	- 1.00
Ayr	1-6	0-2	0-1	1-2	0-1	0-0	0-0	- 3.00

Catterick	0-12	Newcastle	0-3	Nottingham	0-1
Leicester	0-4	Haydock	0-2	Sandown	0-1
Carlisle	0-3	Doncaster	0-1	Stratford	0-1

WINNING HORSES

	Races Run	1st	2nd	3rd	Unpl	Win £
Jodami	4	1	1	0	2	10,650
Temple Garth	8	2	0	1	5	7,386
Westwell Boy	5	2	1	1	1	6,815
Irish Gent	4	2	0	1	1	6,292
New Charges	4	2	1	1	0	4,481
Topothenorthracing	8	1	1	3	3	3,599
Beggars Banquet	5	2	1	0	2	3,433
Island Chief	2	1	0	0	1	3,116
Misti Hunter	1	1	0	0	0	2,999
King Pin	3	2	0	0	1	2,823

Niki Dee	1	1	0	0	0	2,708
Young Kenny	5	1	0	0	4	2,480
Grate Deel	8	1	0	1	6	2,408
Applauder	3	1	0	0	2	2,253
Scrabo View	3	1	0	0	2	2,103

WINNING OWNERS

	Races Won	Value £		Races Won	Value £
J N Yeadon	1	10,650	The Foulrice Twenty	1	3,599
Mrs Jos Wilson	2	7,386	E H Ruddock	2	3,433
D N Yeadon	2	6,815	J G Read	1	2,480
The Morley Stud	2	6,292	Mrs M Ashby	1	2,408
George Dilger	2	5,824	Mrs J M Plummer	1	2,253
J N Hinchliffe	3	5,822	Robin Mellish	1	2,103
Mrs M R Beaumont	2	4,481			

No of horses racing for the stable	33	Total winning prize-money	£63,546

Favourites	6-13	46.2%	- 0.72	Average SP of winner	4.9/1
Longest win seq	3	Longest losing seq	14	Return on stakes invested	15.3%

1994/95 Form	11-138	8.0%	- 60.75	1992/93 Form	19-106	17.9%	+ 31.51
1993/94 Form	18-153	11.8%	- 55.04	1991/92 Form	5-106	4.7%	- 74.82

S B BELL (Burton Fleming, North Humberside)

	Races Run	1st	2nd	3rd	Unpl	Per cent	£1 Level Stake
Hurdles	22	2	3	2	15	9.1	- 12.17
Chases	1	0	0	0	1	-	- 1.00
Totals	23	2	3	2	16	8.7	- 13.17

N Smith	2-17	- 7.17	

Southwell	1-3	+ 1.33	Market Rasen	1-6		- 0.50

No of horses racing for the stable	8	Total winning prize-money	£3,810

J A BENNETT (Sparsholt, Oxon)

	Races Run	1st	2nd	3rd	Unpl	Per cent	£1 Level Stake
Hurdles	40	4	5	4	27	10.0	- 5.00
Chases	0	0	0	0	0	-	0.00
Totals	40	4	5	4	27	10.0	- 5.00

L Harvey	2-20	+ 3.00	Sophie Mitchell	1-5	- 2.00
C Llewellyn	1-4	+ 5.00			

Market Rasen	1-1	+ 12.00	Newton Abbot	1-4	- 1.00
Newbury	1-1	+ 9.00	Hereford	1-6	+ 3.00

No of horses racing for the stable	12	Total winning prize-money	£11,097

W A BETHELL (Arnold, Humberside)

	Races Run	1st	2nd	3rd	Unpl	Per cent	£1 Level Stake
Hurdles	13	0	2	0	11	-	- 13.00
Chases	23	4	2	3	14	17.4	- 1.92
Totals	36	4	4	3	25	11.1	- 14.92

A S Smith	4-25	- 3.92

Windsor	1-1	+ 12.00	Newcastle	1-4	- 0.50
Folkestone	1-2	+ 0.38	Wetherby	1-6	- 3.80

No of horses racing for the stable	10	Total winning prize-money	£13,133

P J BEVAN (Kingstone, Staffs)

	Races Run	1st	2nd	3rd	Unpl	Per cent	£1 Level Stake
Hurdles	39	1	3	8	27	2.6	- 31.00
Chases	1	0	0	0	1	-	- 1.00
Totals	40	1	3	8	28	2.5	- 32.00

W Worthington	1-14	- 6.00	Market Rasen	1-5	+ 3.00

No of horses racing for the stable	10	Total winning prize-money	£1,933

T T BILL (Smisby, Derbys)

	Races Run	1st	2nd	3rd	Unpl	Per cent	£1 Level Stake
Hurdles	10	0	1	1	8	-	- 10.00
Chases	9	1	2	1	5	11.1	- 6.37
Totals	19	1	3	2	13	5.3	- 16.37

J Railton	1-11	- 8.37	Leicester	1-2	+ 0.63

No of horses racing for the stable   7   Total winning prize-money   £2,956

J N R BILLINGE (Cupar, Fife)

	Races Run	1st	2nd	3rd	Unpl	Per cent	£1 Level Stake
Hurdles	0	0	0	0	0	-	0.00
Chases	1	1	0	0	0	100.0	+ 4.00
Totals	1	1	0	0	0	100.0	+ 4.00

Mr J Billinge	1-1	+ 4.00	Perth	1-1	+ 4.00

No of horses racing for the stable   1   Total winning prize-money   £2,136

J J BIRKETT (High Seaton, Cumbria)

	Races Run	1st	2nd	3rd	Unpl	Per cent	£1 Level Stake
Hurdles	44	1	3	2	38	2.3	- 40.50
Chases	22	2	0	3	17	9.1	+ 9.00
Totals	66	3	3	5	55	4.5	- 31.50

L O'Hara	3-25	+ 9.50			
Carlisle	2-10	+ 21.00	Hexham	1-17	- 13.50

No of horses racing for the stable   15   Total winning prize-money   £7,621

K BISHOP (Spaxton, Somerset)

	Races Run	1st	2nd	3rd	Unpl	Per cent	£1 Level Stake
Hurdles	50	1	0	4	45	2.0	- 45.67
Chases	15	0	1	1	13	-	- 15.00
Totals	65	1	1	5	58	1.5	- 60.67

L Harvey	1-12	- 7.67	Ludlow	1-3	+ 1.33

No of horses racing for the stable   18   Total winning prize-money   £2,108

MRS C J BLACK (West Felton, Salop)

	Races Run	1st	2nd	3rd	Unpl	Per cent	£1 Level Stake
Hurdles	4	0	2	0	2	–	– 4.00
Chases	3	2	0	0	1	66.7	+ 38.00
Totals	7	2	2	0	3	28.6	+ 34.00

D McCain	2-7	+ 34.00				
Uttoxeter	1-1	+ 14.00		Bangor	1-3	+ 23.00

No of horses racing for the stable   2   Total winning prize-money   £17,198

A G BLACKMORE (Little Berkhamsted, Herts)

	Races Run	1st	2nd	3rd	Unpl	Per cent	£1 Level Stake
Hurdles	5	1	0	0	4	20.0	+ 8.00
Chases	3	0	0	0	3	–	– 3.00
Totals	8	1	0	0	7	12.5	+ 5.00

D Skyrme	1-2	+ 11.00		Towcester	1-2	+ 11.00

No of horses racing for the stable   3   Total winning prize-money   £1,947

MISS C BLAKEBOROUGH (Scorton, North Yorks)

	Races Run	1st	2nd	3rd	Unpl	Per cent	£1 Level Stake
Hurdles	0	0	0	0	0	–	0.00
Chases	1	1	0	0	0	100.0	+ 2.75
Totals	1	1	0	0	0	100.0	+ 2.75

Mr S Brisby	1-1	+ 2.75		Hexham	1-1	+ 2.75

No of horses racing for the stable   1   Total winning prize-money   £1,440

M J BOLTON (Shrewton, Wilts)

	Races Run	1st	2nd	3rd	Unpl	Per cent	£1 Level Stake
Hurdles	20	2	0	1	17	10.0	+ 14.00
Chases	5	1	0	0	4	20.0	+ 21.00
Totals	25	3	0	1	21	12.0	+ 35.00

C Maude	1-3	+ 10.00		P Hide	1-14	+ 12.00
L Aspell	1-6	+ 15.00				

Fontwell	3-6	+ 54.00

No of horses racing for the stable   6   Total winning prize-money   £7,851

J F BOTTOMLEY (Norton, North Yorks)

	Races Run	1st	2nd	3rd	Unpl	Per cent	£1 Level Stake
Hurdles	17	1	4	2	10	5.9	- 14.37
Chases	5	3	0	0	2	60.0	+ 9.75
Totals	22	4	4	2	12	18.2	- 4.62

D Byrne	3-14	+ 0.75		L Aspell	1-1	+ 1.63
Huntingdon	2-3	+ 3.38		Hexham	2-7	+ 4.00

No of horses racing for the stable   7   Total winning prize-money   £10,392

P BOWEN (Haverfordwest, Dyfed)

	Races Run	1st	2nd	3rd	Unpl	Per cent	£1 Level Stake
Hurdles	26	1	6	2	17	3.8	- 15.00
Chases	30	6	3	4	17	20.0	+ 18.12
Totals	56	7	9	6	34	12.5	+ 3.12

BY MONTH

	W-R	Per cent	£1 Level Stake		W-R	Per cent	£1 Level Stake
June	0-0	-	0.00	December	1-3	33.3	+ 2.50
July	0-0	-	0.00	January	1-6	16.7	+ 5.00
August	0-0	-	0.00	February	1-4	25.0	+ 9.00
September	0-4	-	- 4.00	March	1-7	14.3	- 2.50
October	2-7	28.6	+ 16.50	April	0-5	-	- 5.00
November	1-11	9.1	- 9.38	May	0-9	-	- 9.00

DISTANCE

Hurdles	W-R	Per cent	£1 Level Stake	Chases	W-R	Per cent	£1 Level Stake
2m-2m 3f	1-21	4.8	- 10.00	2m-2m 3f	0-1	-	- 1.00
2m 4f-2m 7f	0-3	-	- 3.00	2m 4f-2m 7f	0-7	-	- 7.00
3m +	0-2	-	- 2.00	3m +	6-22	27.3	+ 26.12

TYPE OF RACE

	W-R	Per cent	£1 Level Stake		W-R	Per cent	£1 Level Stake
Novice hurdles	0-3	-	- 3.00	Selling	1-6	16.7	+ 5.00
H'cap hurdles	0-15	-	- 15.00	Amateur	0-1	-	- 1.00
Novice chases	0-1	-	- 1.00	Hunter chases	0-0	-	0.00
H'cap chases	6-28	21.4	+ 20.12	N H Flat	0-2	-	- 2.00

COURSE GRADE

	W-R	Per cent	£1 Level Stake
Group 1	0-7	-	- 7.00
Group 2	0-1	-	- 1.00
Group 3	2-24	8.3	- 5.50
Group 4	5-24	20.8	+ 16.62

FIRST TIME OUT

	W-R	Per cent	£1 Level Stake
Hurdles	0-6	-	- 6.00
Chases	0-3	-	- 3.00
Totals	0-9	-	- 9.00

JOCKEYS RIDING

	W-R	Per cent	£1 Level Stake		W-R	Per cent	£1 Level Stake
R Johnson	4-28	14.3	+ 19.50	A Maguire	1-1	100.0	+ 0.62
D Walsh	2-9	22.2	+ 1.00				

J R Kavanagh	0-3	D Gallagher	0-1	O Burrows	0-1
A P McCoy	0-2	G E Tormey	0-1	R Dunwoody	0-1
D Bridgwater	0-2	J Osborne	0-1	R Farrant	0-1
Mr R Thornton	0-2	M Perrett	0-1		
B McGiff	0-1	Mr J Jukes	0-1		

COURSE RECORD

	Total W-R	Nov Hdles	H'cap Hdles	Nov Chses	H'cap Chses	Hunter Chses	N H Flat	£1 Level Stake
Sedgefield	5-8	0-0	1-2	0-0	4-6	0-0	0-0	+ 32.62
Plumpton	1-1	0-0	0-0	0-0	1-1	0-0	0-0	+ 12.00
Catterick	1-6	0-0	0-3	0-0	1-2	0-0	0-1	- 0.50

Hereford	0-8	Aintree	0-1	Hexham	0-1
Warwick	0-7	Ascot	0-1	Market Rasen	0-1
Cheltenham	0-3	Bangor	0-1	Newbury	0-1
Taunton	0-3	Carlisle	0-1	Stratford	0-1
Uttoxeter	0-3	Exeter	0-1	Towcester	0-1
Huntingdon	0-2	Fontwell	0-1	Wincanton	0-1
Worcester	0-2	Haydock	0-1		

WINNING HORSES

	Races Run	1st	2nd	3rd	Unpl	Win £
Iffeee	12	6	0	1	5	23,725
Stately Home	9	1	3	1	4	2,094

WINNING OWNERS

	Races Won	Value £		Races Won	Value £
T M Morris	6	23,725	P Bowen	1	2,094

No of horses racing for the stable		14	Total winning prize-money		£25,819

Favourites	2-5	40.0%	- 0.88	Average SP of winner	7.4/1
Longest win seq	2	Longest losing seq	20	Return on stakes invested	5.6%

1994/95 Form	5-14	35.7%	+ 14.34	1992/93 Form	3-9	33.3%	+ 1.38
1993/94 Form	0-5			1991/92 Form	0-10		

S R BOWRING (Edwinstowe, Notts)

	Races Run	1st	2nd	3rd	Unpl	Per cent	£1 Level Stake
Hurdles	6	2	1	0	3	33.3	+ 2.00
Chases	0	0	0	0	0	-	0.00
Totals	6	2	1	0	3	33.3	+ 2.00

A S Smith	1-1	+ 4.50	G Lee	1-2	+ 0.50
Catterick	1-1	+ 4.50	Doncaster	1-1	+ 1.50

No of horses racing for the stable	3	Total winning prize-money	£3,926

MRS S C BRADBURNE (Ladybank, Fife)

	Races Run	1st	2nd	3rd	Unpl	Per cent	£1 Level Stake
Hurdles	26	3	1	2	20	11.5	+ 17.00
Chases	60	8	10	10	32	13.3	+ 28.08
Totals	86	11	11	12	52	12.8	+ 45.08

BY MONTH

	W-R	Per cent	£1 Level Stake		W-R	Per cent	£1 Level Stake
June	0-5	-	- 5.00	December	3-6	50.0	+ 27.50
July	0-0	-	0.00	January	4-10	40.0	+ 39.33
August	2-7	28.6	+ 32.50	February	0-7	-	- 7.00
September	0-5	-	- 5.00	March	1-16	6.3	- 10.00
October	0-3	-	- 3.00	April	0-14	-	- 14.00
November	1-5	20.0	- 2.25	May	0-8	-	- 8.00

DISTANCE

Hurdles	W-R	Per cent	£1 Level Stake	Chases	W-R	Per cent	£1 Level Stake
2m-2m 3f	0-9	-	- 9.00	2m-2m 3f	3-27	11.1	+ 32.33
2m 4f-2m 7f	2-13	15.4	- 4.00	2m 4f-2m 7f	3-21	14.3	- 4.75
3m +	1-4	25.0	+ 30.00	3m +	2-12	16.7	+ 0.50

TYPE OF RACE

	W-R	Per cent	£1 Level Stake		W-R	Per cent	£1 Level Stake
Novice hurdles	0-11	-	- 11.00	Selling	0-3	-	- 3.00
H'cap hurdles	3-13	23.1	+ 30.00	Amateur	1-2	50.0	+ 3.50
Novice chases	1-14	7.1	+ 20.00	Hunter chases	1-5	20.0	+ 1.00
H'cap chases	5-38	13.2	+ 4.58	N H Flat	0-0	-	0.00

COURSE GRADE

	W-R	Per cent	£1 Level Stake
Group 1	0-19	-	- 19.00
Group 2	0-2	-	- 2.00
Group 3	0-0	-	0.00
Group 4	11-65	16.9	+ 66.08

FIRST TIME OUT

	W-R	Per cent	£1 Level Stake
Hurdles	0-5	-	- 5.00
Chases	1-11	9.1	- 5.50
Totals	1-16	6.3	- 10.50

JOCKEYS RIDING

	W-R	Per cent	£1 Level Stake		W-R	Per cent	£1 Level Stake
A Watt	4-32	12.5	+ 19.25	K Johnson	1-3	33.3	+ 31.00
T Reed	3-13	23.1	+ 0.33	Mr M Bradburne	1-10	10.0	- 4.00
Miss L Bradburne	1-2	50.0	+ 3.50	B Storey	1-13	7.7	+ 8.00

A Dobbin	0-4	L O'Hara	0-1	P Carberry		0-1
L Wyer	0-3	Miss P Robson	0-1			
P Niven	0-2	N Williamson	0-1			

COURSE RECORD

	Total W-R	Nov Hdles	H'cap Hdles	Nov Chses	H'cap Chses	Hunter Chses	N H Flat	£1 Level Stake
Musselburgh	5-16	0-3	3-6	0-2	2-5	0-0	0-0	+ 41.50
Kelso	2-9	0-2	0-1	0-1	1-3	1-2	0-0	+ 1.33
Perth	2-22	0-3	0-1	1-6	1-12	0-0	0-0	+ 17.50
Sedgefield	1-5	0-0	0-1	0-0	1-4	0-0	0-0	+ 16.00
Hexham	1-7	0-1	0-0	0-1	1-5	0-0	0-0	- 4.25

Ayr	0-15	Newcastle	0-2	Doncaster	0-1
Carlisle	0-3	Wetherby	0-2		
Cartmel	0-3	Aintree	0-1		

WINNING HORSES

	Races Run	1st	2nd	3rd	Unpl	Win £
Charming Gale	16	2	4	4	6	7,216
Sonsie Mo	9	2	0	0	7	6,118
Blue Charm	9	2	1	2	4	5,093
Musket Shot	2	1	0	1	0	3,743
Ayia Napa	3	1	0	0	2	3,022
Native Crown	3	1	0	0	2	2,898
Willie Sparkle	11	1	4	1	5	2,846
Off The Bru	8	1	1	2	4	2,038

WINNING OWNERS

	Races Won	Value £		Races Won	Value £
Timothy Hardie	3	8,964	Mrs M C Lindsay	2	5,093
Mrs John Etherton	2	7,216	Mrs S C Bradburne	1	3,022
J G Bradburne	2	5,781	Tom Carruthers	1	2,898

No of horses racing for the stable	16	Total winning prize-money	£32,974

Favourites	2-3	66.7%	+ 2.75	Average SP of winner	10.9/1
Longest win seq	3	Longest losing seq	37	Return on stakes invested	52.4%

1994/95 Form	5-117	4.3%	- 95.87	1992/93 Form	18-152	11.8%	- 59.77
1993/94 Form	12-171	7.0%	- 90.81	1991/92 Form	9-94	9.6%	- 15.00

J M BRADLEY (Sedbury, Gwent)

	Races Run	1st	2nd	3rd	Unpl	Per cent	£1 Level Stake
Hurdles	131	8	8	14	101	6.1	- 82.80
Chases	59	7	7	11	34	11.9	- 6.50
Totals	190	15	15	25	135	7.9	- 89.30

BY MONTH

	W-R	Per cent	£1 Level Stake		W-R	Per cent	£1 Level Stake
June	0-4	-	- 4.00	December	1-20	5.0	- 12.00
July	1-4	25.0	+ 2.00	January	1-21	4.8	- 17.50
August	2-6	33.3	+ 4.20	February	1-17	5.9	- 10.00
September	1-13	7.7	- 5.00	March	1-18	5.6	- 13.50
October	1-21	4.8	- 16.50	April	3-27	11.1	+ 7.00
November	2-23	8.7	- 14.00	May	1-16	6.3	- 10.00

DISTANCE

Hurdles	W-R	Per cent	£1 Level Stake	Chases	W-R	Per cent	£1 Level Stake
2m-2m 3f	5-108	4.6	- 74.80	2m-2m 3f	2-25	8.0	- 10.00
2m 4f-2m 7f	1-15	6.7	- 9.00	2m 4f-2m 7f	5-17	29.4	+ 20.50
3m +	2-8	25.0	+ 1.00	3m +	0-17	-	- 17.00

TYPE OF RACE

	W-R	Per cent	£1 Level Stake		W-R	Per cent	£1 Level Stake
Novice hurdles	1-33	3.0	- 29.50	Selling	4-45	8.9	- 18.00
H'cap hurdles	3-38	7.9	- 10.50	Amateur	1-8	12.5	- 5.80
Novice chases	1-13	7.7	- 5.00	Hunter chases	0-0	-	0.00
H'cap chases	5-38	13.2	- 5.50	N H Flat	0-15	-	- 15.00

COURSE GRADE

	W-R	Per cent	£1 Level Stake
Group 1	1-13	7.7	- 6.00
Group 2	1-19	5.3	- 7.00
Group 3	5-68	7.4	- 39.50
Group 4	8-90	8.9	- 36.80

FIRST TIME OUT

	W-R	Per cent	£1 Level Stake
Hurdles	2-29	6.9	- 22.30
Chases	1-9	11.1	- 1.00
Totals	3-38	7.9	- 23.30

JOCKEYS RIDING

	W-R	Per cent	£1 Level Stake		W-R	Per cent	£1 Level Stake
Guy Lewis	4-38	10.5	- 7.50	T J Murphy	1-3	33.3	+ 3.00
J Titley	2-4	50.0	+ 7.50	D Fortt	1-3	33.3	+ 4.00
R Farrant	2-34	5.9	- 21.50	B Fenton	1-4	25.0	+ 11.00
R Johnson	2-52	3.8	- 41.80	A P McCoy	1-5	20.0	- 1.50
S Fox	1-1	100.0	+ 3.50				

Mr M Daly	0-5	P McLoughlin	0-2	Miss E Jones	0-1
N Williamson	0-4	W J Ryan	0-2	Miss P Jones	0-1
B Harding	0-3	B M Clifford	0-1	Mr P Henley	0-1
M A Fitzgerald	0-3	G Crone	0-1	Muredach Kelly	0-1
Mr J Culloty	0-3	G Hogan	0-1	S Joynes	0-1
B Powell	0-2	G McCourt	0-1	S Wynne	0-1
Mr D Price	0-2	J R Kavanagh	0-1	T Dascombe	0-1
Mr J Rees	0-2	K P Gaule	0-1	W Greatrex	0-1
Mr M Rimell	0-2	M Hourigan	0-1	W Marston	0-1

COURSE RECORD

	Total W-R	Nov Hdles	H'cap Hdles	Nov Chses	H'cap Chses	Hunter Chses	N H Flat	£1 Level Stake
Bangor	4-12	0-4	2-4	0-0	2-4	0-0	0-0	+ 13.50
Taunton	2-14	0-5	2-7	0-0	0-2	0-0	0-0	+ 5.50
Worcester	2-18	0-2	1-4	0-2	1-7	0-0	0-3	- 5.50
Wincanton	1-5	1-4	0-0	0-1	0-0	0-0	0-0	- 1.50
Doncaster	1-5	0-2	0-1	0-0	1-2	0-0	0-0	+ 2.00
Southwell	1-6	0-2	0-0	0-2	1-2	0-0	0-0	0.00
Newton Abbot	1-7	0-2	0-1	0-1	1-2	0-0	0-1	+ 5.00
Uttoxeter	1-7	0-0	0-3	1-1	0-2	0-0	0-1	+ 1.00
Nottingham	1-10	0-3	1-4	0-0	0-1	0-0	0-2	- 5.50
Hereford	1-21	0-7	1-8	0-0	0-6	0-0	0-0	- 18.80

Ludlow	0-22	Newcastle	0-3	Folkestone	0-2
Chepstow	0-11	Stratford	0-3	Towcester	0-2
Exeter	0-11	Windsor	0-3	Fontwell	0-1
Market Rasen	0-7	Ascot	0-2	Huntingdon	0-1
Leicester	0-6	Cheltenham	0-2	Sandown	0-1
Warwick	0-6	Fakenham	0-2		

WINNING HORSES

	Races Run	1st	2nd	3rd	Unpl	Win £
Chris's Glen	16	3	1	4	8	7,691
Jason's Boy	12	2	2	3	5	6,341
Boxing Match	6	2	0	0	4	5,497
Seal King	3	1	1	0	1	4,531
Its Grand	12	2	2	4	4	4,340
Veryvel	8	1	2	1	4	3,756
Nuclear Express	2	1	0	1	0	3,386
Asterix	1	1	0	0	0	2,556
Zingibar	13	1	0	2	10	2,355
Borrismore Flash	5	1	0	0	4	2,126

WINNING OWNERS

	Races Won	Value £		Races Won	Value £
The Tote End Racing Club	3	7,691	David S Lewis	1	3,756
W E Jones	2	6,341	G B Perry	1	3,386
S J Merrick	2	5,497	Clifton Hunt	1	2,556
Robert J Williams	1	4,531	D Holpin	1	2,355
Avon & West Racing Club Ltd	2	4,340	Lee Bowles	1	2,126

No of horses racing for the stable	42		Total winning prize-money	£42,579

Favourites	5-16	31.3%	+ 4.70	Average SP of winner	5.7/1
Longest win seq	1	Longest losing seq	26	Return on stakes invested	-47.0%

1994/95 Form	14-131	10.7%	- 49.00	1992/93 Form	7-121	5.8%	- 83.68
1993/94 Form	9-150	6.0%	- 45.00	1991/92 Form	2-114	1.8%	- 82.00

PAUL BRADLEY (Forsbrook, Staffs)

	Races Run	1st	2nd	3rd	Unpl	Per cent	£1 Level Stake
Hurdles	33	2	5	3	23	6.1	- 25.79
Chases	23	3	4	3	13	13.0	- 12.83
Totals	56	5	9	6	36	8.9	- 38.62

Mr R Armson	2-2	+ 4.67	S Wynne	1-7	- 4.12
Sophie Mitchell	1-1	+ 3.33	A Thornton	1-20	- 16.50

Nottingham	1-1	+ 3.33	Southwell	1-5	- 1.50
Cartmel	1-2	+ 3.00	Uttoxeter	1-10	- 8.33
Bangor	1-3	- 0.12			

No of horses racing for the stable	7		Total winning prize-money	£14,742

M BRADSTOCK (Letcombe Bassett, Oxon)

	Races Run	1st	2nd	3rd	Unpl	Per cent	£1 Level Stake
Hurdles	27	3	1	1	22	11.1	+ 18.00
Chases	15	1	3	2	9	6.7	+ 11.00
Totals	42	4	4	3	31	9.5	+ 29.00

P Holley	2-22	+ 19.00	Katharine Hambidge	1-5	+ 8.00
Mr R Thornton	1-1	+ 16.00			
Newton Abbot	2-3	+ 40.00	Wincanton	1-2	+ 11.00
Ludlow	1-2	+ 13.00			

No of horses racing for the stable   13   Total winning prize-money   £9,324

MRS S A BRAMALL (Hutton Sessay, North Yorks)

	Races Run	1st	2nd	3rd	Unpl	Per cent	£1 Level Stake
Hurdles	46	4	7	3	32	8.7	- 17.42
Chases	50	5	6	8	31	10.0	- 14.50
Totals	96	9	13	11	63	9.4	- 31.92

BY MONTH

	W-R	Per cent	£1 Level Stake		W-R	Per cent	£1 Level Stake
June	0-0	-	0.00	December	1-7	14.3	+ 2.00
July	0-2	-	- 2.00	January	3-25	12.0	- 5.67
August	0-2	-	- 2.00	February	0-16	-	- 16.00
September	1-2	50.0	+ 7.00	March	2-19	10.5	- 4.50
October	1-8	12.5	+ 1.00	April	0-0	-	0.00
November	1-15	6.7	- 11.75	May	0-0	-	0.00

DISTANCE

Hurdles	W-R	Per cent	£1 Level Stake	Chases	W-R	Per cent	£1 Level Stake
2m-2m 3f	1-18	5.6	- 13.67	2m-2m 3f	1-4	25.0	+ 5.00
2m 4f-2m 7f	0-15	-	- 15.00	2m 4f-2m 7f	2-9	22.2	+ 3.00
3m +	3-13	23.1	+ 11.25	3m +	2-37	5.4	- 22.50

TYPE OF RACE

	W-R	Per cent	£1 Level Stake		W-R	Per cent	£1 Level Stake
Novice hurdles	0-14	-	- 14.00	Selling	0-0	-	0.00
H'cap hurdles	3-18	16.7	+ 6.25	Amateur	1-5	20.0	+ 4.00
Novice chases	4-21	19.0	+ 5.50	Hunter chases	0-0	-	0.00
H'cap chases	0-26	-	- 26.00	N H Flat	1-12	8.3	- 7.67

COURSE GRADE

	W-R	Per cent	£1 Level Stake
Group 1	1-31	3.2	- 19.00
Group 2	0-6	-	- 6.00
Group 3	2-19	10.5	- 7.00
Group 4	6-40	15.0	+ 0.08

FIRST TIME OUT

	W-R	Per cent	£1 Level Stake
Hurdles	2-11	18.2	+ 2.33
Chases	1-11	9.1	- 2.00
Totals	3-22	13.6	+ 0.33

JOCKEYS RIDING

	W-R	Per cent	£1 Level Stake		W-R	Per cent	£1 Level Stake
Mr K Whelan	6-47	12.8	- 8.25	J H Burke	3-39	7.7	- 13.67

A K Smith	0-5	A Dobbin	0-1	G Bradley	0-1
J Callaghan	0-2	F Leahy	0-1		

COURSE RECORD

	Total W-R	Nov Hdles	H'cap Hdles	Nov Chses	H'cap Chses	Hunter Chses	N H Flat	£1 Level Stake
Hexham	2-5	0-0	0-1	2-2	0-1	0-0	0-1	+ 13.00
Carlisle	2-9	0-2	2-2	0-3	0-1	0-0	0-1	+ 3.25
Huntingdon	1-2	0-0	0-0	0-0	1-2	0-0	0-0	+ 7.00
Leicester	1-3	0-1	0-0	1-1	0-1	0-0	0-0	0.00
Musselburgh	1-4	0-1	0-2	0-0	0-0	0-0	1-1	+ 0.33
Kelso	1-9	0-1	0-0	1-4	0-4	0-0	0-0	- 3.50
Newcastle	1-14	0-0	1-4	0-3	0-5	0-0	0-2	- 2.00

Sedgefield	0-9	Aintree	0-4	Bangor	0-1
Catterick	0-6	Ayr	0-3	Newbury	0-1
Haydock	0-6	Towcester	0-3	Uttoxeter	0-1
Market Rasen	0-6	Cheltenham	0-2	Worcester	0-1
Wetherby	0-6	Ascot	0-1		

WINNING HORSES

	Races Run	1st	2nd	3rd	Unpl	Win £
Beauchamp Grace	4	2	0	2	0	6,321
Adrien	9	2	0	1	6	4,440
Canaillou II	6	1	2	0	3	3,648
Spanish Fair	7	1	2	1	3	3,556
Monokratic	4	1	0	1	2	3,371
Able Player	10	1	3	1	5	2,253
Colonel George	3	1	1	0	1	1,551

WINNING OWNERS

	Races Won	Value £		Races Won	Value £
Mrs S A Bramall	4	12,130	Leading Star Racing	1	3,371
Miss K S Bramall	2	4,440	Mrs Sandra Scott Bell	1	1,551
M Stanners	1	3,648			

No of horses racing for the stable		23	Total winning prize-money		£25,140

Favourites	3-11	27.3%	-	0.42	Average SP of winner		6.1/1
Longest win seq	1	Longest losing seq	18		Return on stakes invested		-33.3%

1994/95 Form	9-85	10.6%	+ 7.38	1992/93 Form	16-120	13.3%	+ 64.41
1993/94 Form	21-136	15.4%	+ 8.65	1991/92 Form	0-90		

G C BRAVERY (Newmarket, Suffolk)

	Races Run	1st	2nd	3rd	Unpl	Per cent	£1 Level Stake
Hurdles	17	1	0	3	13	5.9	- 10.00
Chases	0	0	0	0	0	-	0.00
Totals	17	1	0	3	13	5.9	- 10.00

G Lee	1-2	+ 5.00	Southwell	1-1	+ 6.00

No of horses racing for the stable		4	Total winning prize-money		£1,235

O BRENNAN (Worksop, Notts)

	Races Run	1st	2nd	3rd	Unpl	Per cent	£1 Level Stake
Hurdles	97	6	11	5	75	6.2	- 58.75
Chases	34	6	5	2	21	17.6	- 15.90
Totals	131	12	16	7	96	9.2	- 74.65

BY MONTH

	W-R	Per cent	£1 Level Stake		W-R	Per cent	£1 Level Stake
June	0-4	-	- 4.00	December	2-16	12.5	- 4.90
July	0-3	-	- 3.00	January	0-14	-	- 14.00
August	0-6	-	- 6.00	February	0-8	-	- 8.00
September	0-1	-	- 1.00	March	3-23	13.0	- 6.00
October	0-1	-	- 1.00	April	3-22	13.6	- 15.00
November	0-7	-	- 7.00	May	4-26	15.4	- 4.75

DISTANCE

Hurdles	W-R	Per cent	£1 Level Stake	Chases	W-R	Per cent	£1 Level Stake
2m-2m 3f	3-60	5.0	- 37.00	2m-2m 3f	0-4	-	- 4.00
2m 4f-2m 7f	3-30	10.0	- 14.75	2m 4f-2m 7f	5-19	26.3	- 3.65
3m +	0-7	-	- 7.00	3m +	1-11	9.1	- 8.25

TYPE OF RACE

	W-R	Per cent	£1 Level Stake		W-R	Per cent	£1 Level Stake
Novice hurdles	2-32	6.3	- 15.00	Selling	3-11	27.3	+ 7.50
H'cap hurdles	1-37	2.7	- 34.25	Amateur	0-1	-	- 1.00
Novice chases	5-16	31.3	- 1.90	Hunter chases	0-0	-	0.00
H'cap chases	1-17	5.9	- 13.00	N H Flat	0-17	-	- 17.00

COURSE GRADE

	W-R	Per cent	£1 Level Stake
Group 1	1-5	20.0	+ 3.00
Group 2	0-0	-	0.00
Group 3	5-71	7.0	- 48.25
Group 4	6-55	10.9	- 29.40

FIRST TIME OUT

	W-R	Per cent	£1 Level Stake
Hurdles	0-33	-	- 33.00
Chases	1-8	12.5	- 5.90
Totals	1-41	2.4	- 38.90

JOCKEYS RIDING

	W-R	Per cent	£1 Level Stake		W-R	Per cent	£1 Level Stake
Martin Brennan	9-78	11.5	- 32.90	Mr M Brennan	3-30	10.0	- 18.75
W Walsh	0-8			S O'Donnell	0-4		Mr A Walton 0-1
Miss V Haigh	0-7			S Fox	0-3		

COURSE RECORD

	Total W-R	Nov Hdles	H'cap Hdles	Nov Chses	H'cap Chses	Hunter Chses	N H Flat	£1 Level Stake
Fakenham	4-9	0-0	2-6	1-2	1-1	0-0	0-0	+ 9.85
Huntingdon	3-14	1-5	1-4	1-2	0-1	0-0	0-2	+ 4.50
Market Rasen	2-26	0-6	0-7	2-5	0-4	0-0	0-4	- 21.75
Doncaster	1-5	1-2	0-1	0-0	0-0	0-0	0-2	+ 3.00
Southwell	1-6	0-1	0-1	1-1	0-3	0-0	0-0	- 3.25
Towcester	1-28	1-11	0-7	0-4	0-3	0-0	0-3	- 24.00

Uttoxeter	0-9	Bangor	0-4	Ludlow	0-1
Nottingham	0-7	Hexham	0-3	Sedgefield	0-1
Warwick	0-7	Carlisle	0-2	Stratford	0-1
Worcester	0-7	Cartmel	0-1		

WINNING HORSES

	Races Run	1st	2nd	3rd	Unpl	Win £
Speaker Weatherill	5	3	0	1	1	11,139
Artic Wings	7	2	3	0	2	6,790
Shers Delight	6	2	0	0	4	4,985
Boston Rover	7	1	1	0	5	4,322
Marsh's Law	9	1	1	0	7	2,766
Far Out	7	1	1	0	5	2,185
Barney's Gift	7	1	1	1	4	2,178
Pinecone Peter	8	1	1	0	6	2,128

WINNING OWNERS

	Races Won	Value £		Races Won	Value £
Lady Anne Bentinck	5	17,929	Mrs Violet J Hannigan	1	2,766
O Brennan	2	6,507	Richard J Marshall	1	2,178
Gary Hudson	2	4,985	Mrs B A Burgass	1	2,128

No of horses racing for the stable	41	Total winning prize-money £36,493

Favourites	7-19	36.8%	+ 1.35	Average SP of winner	3.7/1
Longest win seq	2	Longest losing seq	29	Return on stakes invested	-57.0%

1994/95 Form	28-165	17.0%	- 28.70	1992/93 Form	25-133	18.8%	+ 4.12
1993/94 Form	30-178	16.9%	- 0.73	1991/92 Form	13-188	6.9%	- 61.87

R BREWIS (Belford, Northumberland)

	Races Run	1st	2nd	3rd	Unpl	Per cent	£1 Level Stake
Hurdles	10	1	2	1	6	10.0	- 1.00
Chases	4	0	0	0	4	-	- 4.00
Totals	14	1	2	1	10	7.1	- 5.00

A S Smith	1-2	+ 7.00	Hexham	1-1	+ 8.00

No of horses racing for the stable	4	Total winning prize-money	£2,899

J J BRIDGER (Liphook, Hants)

	Races Run	1st	2nd	3rd	Unpl	Per cent	£1 Level Stake
Hurdles	28	1	0	2	25	3.6	- 23.00
Chases	5	0	1	0	4	-	- 5.00
Totals	33	1	1	2	29	3.0	- 28.00

A Maguire	1-1	+ 4.00	Huntingdon	1-2	+ 3.00

No of horses racing for the stable	10	Total winning prize-money	£1,800

K S BRIDGWATER (Lapworth, Warwicks)

	Races Run	1st	2nd	3rd	Unpl	Per cent	£1 Level Stake
Hurdles	44	1	2	3	38	2.3	- 37.50
Chases	9	0	1	2	6	-	- 9.00
Totals	53	1	3	5	44	1.9	- 46.50

D Leahy	1-11	- 4.50	Hereford	1-10	- 3.50

No of horses racing for the stable	17	Total winning prize-money	£2,234

W M BRISBOURNE (Great Ness, Salop)

	Races Run	1st	2nd	3rd	Unpl	Per cent	£1 Level Stake
Hurdles	9	1	3	0	5	11.1	- 4.50
Chases	0	0	0	0	0	-	0.00
Totals	9	1	3	0	5	11.1	- 4.50

R Massey	1-3	+ 1.50	Nottingham	1-2	+ 2.50

No of horses racing for the stable   4   Total winning prize-money   £1,807

M BRITTAIN (Warthill, North Yorks)

	Races Run	1st	2nd	3rd	Unpl	Per cent	£1 Level Stake
Hurdles	17	0	0	0	17	-	- 17.00
Chases	11	1	3	1	6	9.1	- 8.00
Totals	28	1	3	1	23	3.6	- 25.00

D Wilkinson	1-17	- 14.00	Southwell	1-4	- 1.00

No of horses racing for the stable   6   Total winning prize-money   £2,768

C D BROAD (Elton, Glos)

	Races Run	1st	2nd	3rd	Unpl	Per cent	£1 Level Stake
Hurdles	66	2	4	5	55	3.0	- 49.50
Chases	26	1	5	4	16	3.8	- 23.25
Totals	92	3	9	9	71	3.3	- 72.75

M Dwyer	1-1	+ 1.75	G Hogan	1-20	- 10.00
R Farrant	1-3	+ 3.50			
Ascot	1-1	+ 9.00	Bangor	1-6	- 3.25
Warwick	1-5	+ 1.50			

No of horses racing for the stable   23   Total winning prize-money   £14,126

C P E BROOKS (Lambourn, Berks)

	Races Run	1st	2nd	3rd	Unpl	Per cent	£1 Level Stake
Hurdles	97	10	7	13	67	10.3	- 36.75
Chases	88	19	8	16	45	21.6	+ 19.91
Totals	185	29	15	29	112	15.7	- 16.84

BY MONTH

	W-R	Per cent	£1 Level Stake		W-R	Per cent	£1 Level Stake
June	0-2	–	– 2.00	December	3-17	17.6	– 7.00
July	1-4	25.0	+ 2.00	January	1-24	4.2	– 16.50
August	1-2	50.0	+ 0.63	February	5-25	20.0	+ 25.00
September	0-0	–	0.00	March	6-36	16.7	– 7.37
October	2-10	20.0	– 2.42	April	3-28	10.7	– 18.10
November	7-28	25.0	+ 17.92	May	0-9	–	– 9.00

DISTANCE

Hurdles	W-R	Per cent	£1 Level Stake	Chases	W-R	Per cent	£1 Level Stake
2m-2m 3f	8-57	14.0	– 8.25	2m-2m 3f	3-15	20.0	– 7.94
2m 4f-2m 7f	2-35	5.7	– 23.50	2m 4f-2m 7f	6-22	27.3	– 0.11
3m +	0-5	–	– 5.00	3m +	10-51	19.6	+ 27.96

TYPE OF RACE

	W-R	Per cent	£1 Level Stake		W-R	Per cent	£1 Level Stake
Novice hurdles	6-60	10.0	– 29.50	Selling	0-1	–	– 1.00
H'cap hurdles	2-19	10.5	– 5.50	Amateur	2-7	28.6	+ 1.41
Novice chases	2-20	10.0	– 5.60	Hunter chases	0-3	–	– 3.00
H'cap chases	15-59	25.4	+ 26.10	N H Flat	2-16	12.5	+ 0.25

COURSE GRADE

	W-R	Per cent	£1 Level Stake
Group 1	13-78	16.7	+ 11.64
Group 2	2-25	8.0	– 16.87
Group 3	11-58	19.0	+ 3.65
Group 4	3-24	12.5	– 15.26

FIRST TIME OUT

	W-R	Per cent	£1 Level Stake
Hurdles	2-37	5.4	– 20.75
Chases	6-16	37.5	+ 19.04
Totals	8-53	15.1	– 1.71

JOCKEYS RIDING

	W-R	Per cent	£1 Level Stake		W-R	Per cent	£1 Level Stake
G Bradley	14-111	12.6	– 27.28	Blythe Miller	1-3	33.3	+ 0.75
D Gallagher	8-34	23.5	+ 14.63	S McNeill	1-3	33.3	+ 10.00
Mr E James	2-14	14.3	– 5.59	T J Murphy	1-4	25.0	– 0.75
Richard Guest	1-2	50.0	+ 4.00	M Berry	1-5	20.0	– 3.60

B Powell	0-1	J Lower	0-1	M Dwyer	0-1
Capt E Andrewes	0-1	J Osborne	0-1	Mr J Culloty	0-1
J Frost	0-1	J Titley	0-1	W Marston	0-1

COURSE RECORD

	Total W-R	Nov Hdles	H'cap Hdles	Nov Chses	H'cap Chses	Hunter Chses	N H Flat	£1 Level Stake
Folkestone	3-4	1-2	1-1	0-0	1-1	0-0	0-0	+ 12.00
Doncaster	3-9	0-2	0-0	1-1	1-3	0-0	1-3	+ 20.75
Newbury	3-14	0-4	0-3	0-1	3-6	0-0	0-0	+ 1.13
Haydock	2-6	1-2	0-0	0-0	1-3	0-0	0-1	+ 1.88

Windsor	2-8	0-4	0-0	0-0	2-4	0-0	0-0	+ 2.25
Worcester	2-12	2-3	0-0	0-1	0-4	0-0	0-4	- 1.50
Cheltenham	2-13	0-4	0-1	0-2	1-5	0-0	1-1	+ 11.25
Newcastle	1-1	0-0	1-1	0-0	0-0	0-0	0-0	+ 5.00
Bangor	1-3	0-0	0-1	0-0	1-2	0-0	0-0	+ 1.33
Uttoxeter	1-3	1-2	0-0	0-0	0-1	0-0	0-0	+ 1.00
Plumpton	1-4	0-1	0-0	1-2	0-1	0-0	0-0	- 2.60
Hereford	1-4	0-1	0-0	0-0	1-3	0-0	0-0	- 2.09
Aintree	1-4	0-0	0-0	0-2	1-2	0-0	0-0	- 1.12
Nottingham	1-4	0-0	0-1	0-0	1-2	0-0	0-1	+ 9.00
Newton Abbot	1-5	0-1	0-0	0-2	1-2	0-0	0-0	- 2.37
Towcester	1-5	0-2	0-0	0-0	1-3	0-0	0-0	- 2.50
Leicester	1-5	0-1	0-0	0-0	1-4	0-0	0-0	+ 1.50
Fontwell	1-6	1-4	0-1	0-0	0-1	0-0	0-0	- 0.50
Sandown	1-12	0-3	0-2	0-0	1-5	0-0	0-2	- 8.25

Chepstow	0-10	Exeter	0-4	Huntingdon		0-2
Ascot	0-9	Lingfield	0-4	Ludlow		0-2
Kempton	0-8	Warwick	0-3	Southwell		0-2
Stratford	0-8	Ayr	0-2	Taunton		0-2
Wincanton	0-5	Fakenham	0-2			

WINNING HORSES

	Races Run	1st	2nd	3rd	Unpl	Win £
Couldnt Be Better	6	2	0	1	3	59,347
Padre Mio	3	1	0	0	2	18,860
Go Universal	7	4	1	1	1	16,702
Suny Bay	3	2	0	0	1	12,087
Mr President	6	2	0	2	2	7,853
Lonesome Glory	2	1	0	0	1	6,852
Harvest View	6	2	0	1	3	5,095
Florida Sky	5	1	0	0	4	5,061
Mr Flanagan	7	1	1	1	4	3,709
Good Insight	5	1	0	1	3	3,664
Youbetterbelieveit	2	1	0	0	1	3,440
Dark Stranger	5	1	2	0	2	3,235
Universal Magic	5	1	1	0	3	3,147
Time Enough	11	1	1	3	6	3,070
Mr Primetime	10	1	1	2	6	2,889
Big Ben Dun	5	1	2	1	1	2,812
Man Mood	4	1	0	1	2	2,801
Strokesaver	3	1	0	2	0	2,180
Foxtrot Romeo	9	1	1	3	4	2,119
Country Star	2	1	0	0	1	1,951
Wilde Music	2	1	0	0	1	1,716
Good Stuff	2	1	0	0	1	1,354

WINNING OWNERS

	Races Won	Value £		Races Won	Value £
R A B Whittle	2	59,347	Mrs Richard Stanley	1	3,709
Uplands Bloodstock	6	24,754	The Lewis Partnership	1	3,070
Universal Conference & Incentive	5	19,849	Anglia Telecom Centres Plc	1	2,889
Lady Lloyd Webber	1	18,860	Steel Plate & Sections Ltd	1	2,801
Mrs B Mead	2	7,853	The Bow Lane Partnership	1	2,180
Terry Neill	2	6,899	Lady Cobham	1	2,119
Mrs Walter M Jeffords	1	6,852	H R H Prince Fahd Salman	1	1,951
Dr P P Brown	2	5,095	A L Brodin	1	1,716

No of horses racing for the stable	54	Total winning prize-money		£169,944
Favourites	7-29 24.1% - 11.80	Average SP of winner		4.8/1
Longest win seq 2 Longest losing seq 28		Return on stakes invested		-9.1%
1994/95 Form	31-163 19.0% - 42.23	1992/93 Form 16-100 16.0% - 12.24		
1993/94 Form	24-126 19.0% - 39.60	1991/92 Form 29-169 17.2% - 50.25		

S A BROOKSHAW (Uffington, Salop)

	Races Run	1st	2nd	3rd	Unpl	Per cent	£1 Level Stake
Hurdles	9	1	1	1	6	11.1	+ 2.00
Chases	34	5	9	2	18	14.7	- 17.84
Totals	43	6	10	3	24	14.0	- 15.84

Mr R Ford	3-11	+ 1.00	Miss S Beddoes	1-8	- 6.47
R Johnson	1-5	- 2.37	J Railton	1-11	0.00
Warwick	1-2	+ 2.50	Aintree	1-4	+ 0.50
Cartmel	1-2	+ 1.00	Bangor	1-8	- 6.47
Hereford	1-4	- 1.37	Uttoxeter	1-12	- 1.00

No of horses racing for the stable	16	Total winning prize-money	£25,197

R BROTHERTON (Elmley Castle, H'ford & Worcs)

	Races Run	1st	2nd	3rd	Unpl	Per cent	£1 Level Stake
Hurdles	75	2	2	6	65	2.7	- 42.00
Chases	5	0	0	0	5	-	- 5.00
Totals	80	2	2	6	70	2.5	- 47.00

J Osborne	1-4	+ 8.00	C Llewellyn	1-16	+ 5.00
Uttoxeter	1-7	+ 14.00	Taunton	1-9	+ 3.00

No of horses racing for the stable	16	Total winning prize-money	£4,679

D H BROWN (Roche Abbey, South Yorks)

	Races Run	1st	2nd	3rd	Unpl	Per cent	£1 Level Stake
Hurdles	4	1	1	1	1	25.0	+ 30.00
Chases	5	0	1	0	4	-	- 5.00
Totals	9	1	2	1	5	11.1	+ 25.00

L Wyer	1-4	+ 30.00	Worcester	1-1	+ 33.00

No of horses racing for the stable	1	Total winning prize-money	£2,145

MRS J BROWN (York, North Yorks)

	Races Run	1st	2nd	3rd	Unpl	Per cent	£1 Level Stake
Hurdles	28	0	1	1	26	-	- 28.00
Chases	19	2	2	2	13	10.5	- 5.50
Totals	47	2	3	3	39	4.3	- 33.50

Mr S Swiers	1-5	+ 1.50	E Callaghan	1-18	- 11.00
Catterick	1-4	+ 3.00	Newcastle	1-6	+ 0.50

No of horses racing for the stable	13	Total winning prize-money	£7,063

R L BROWN (Grosmont, Gwent)

	Races Run	1st	2nd	3rd	Unpl	Per cent	£1 Level Stake
Hurdles	11	1	0	1	9	9.1	+ 4.00
Chases	1	0	0	0	1	-	- 1.00
Totals	12	1	0	1	10	8.3	+ 3.00

P McLoughlin	1-6	+ 9.00	Ludlow	1-5	+ 10.00

No of horses racing for the stable	2	Total winning prize-money	£2,598

D W BROWNING (Broadoak, East Sussex)

	Races Run	1st	2nd	3rd	Unpl	Per cent	£1 Level Stake
Hurdles	11	1	0	1	9	9.1	+ 6.00
Chases	1	0	0	0	1	-	- 1.00
Totals	12	1	0	1	10	8.3	+ 5.00

B Fenton	1-3	+ 14.00	Plumpton	1-4	+ 13.00

No of horses racing for the stable	4	Total winning prize-money	£2,175

MRS D BUCKETT (Southampton, Hants)

	Races Run	1st	2nd	3rd	Unpl	Per cent	£1 Level Stake
Hurdles	0	0	0	0	0	–	0.00
Chases	4	1	1	0	2	25.0	+ 9.00
Totals	4	1	1	0	2	25.0	+ 9.00

Mr R Nuttall	1-2	+ 11.00	Folkestone	1-1	+ 12.00

No of horses racing for the stable   2   Total winning prize-money   £1,527

R H BUCKLER (Melplash, Dorset)

	Races Run	1st	2nd	3rd	Unpl	Per cent	£1 Level Stake
Hurdles	89	12	6	6	65	13.5	+110.40
Chases	83	4	9	11	59	4.8	- 44.00
Totals	172	16	15	17	124	9.3	+ 66.40

BY MONTH

	W-R	Per cent	£1 Level Stake		W-R	Per cent	£1 Level Stake
June	0-1	–	- 1.00	December	1-12	8.3	- 2.00
July	0-6	–	- 6.00	January	3-28	10.7	- 0.50
August	1-6	16.7	+ 3.00	February	3-25	12.0	+ 91.50
September	0-6	–	- 6.00	March	2-21	9.5	- 8.50
October	1-15	6.7	- 3.00	April	4-20	20.0	+ 29.50
November	1-17	5.9	- 15.60	May	0-15	–	- 15.00

DISTANCE

Hurdles	W-R	Per cent	£1 Level Stake	Chases	W-R	Per cent	£1 Level Stake
2m-2m 3f	2-33	6.1	- 23.00	2m-2m 3f	3-36	8.3	- 4.00
2m 4f-2m 7f	3-27	11.1	+ 11.00	2m 4f-2m 7f	0-23	–	- 23.00
3m +	7-29	24.1	+122.40	3m +	1-24	4.2	- 17.00

TYPE OF RACE

	W-R	Per cent	£1 Level Stake		W-R	Per cent	£1 Level Stake
Novice hurdles	3-33	9.1	- 1.60	Selling	0-9	–	- 9.00
H'cap hurdles	9-39	23.1	+129.00	Amateur	0-3	–	- 3.00
Novice chases	1-21	4.8	- 10.00	Hunter chases	0-0	–	0.00
H'cap chases	3-56	5.4	- 28.00	N H Flat	0-11	–	- 11.00

COURSE GRADE					FIRST TIME OUT			
	W-R	Per cent	£1 Level Stake			W-R	Per cent	£1 Level Stake
Group 1	2-28	7.1	+ 81.00	Hurdles		0-28	-	- 28.00
Group 2	6-47	12.8	+ 28.50	Chases		0-13	-	- 13.00
Group 3	3-46	6.5	- 18.00					
Group 4	5-51	9.8	- 25.10	Totals		0-41	-	- 41.00

JOCKEYS RIDING

	W-R	Per cent	£1 Level Stake			W-R	Per cent	£1 Level Stake
B Powell	10-111	9.0	- 15.60	Mr J Culloty		2-4	50.0	+ 8.50
G Supple	3-25	12.0	+ 4.50	A Tory		1-4	25.0	+ 97.00

Miss S Cobden	0-4	A Maguire	0-1	P Holley	0-1
Mr G Baines	0-3	C Llewellyn	0-1	R Farrant	0-1
Mr R Thornton	0-3	M A Fitzgerald	0-1	R Johnson	0-1
R Greene	0-3	M Dwyer	0-1	R Massey	0-1
Mr B Dixon	0-2	M Richards	0-1	S McNeill	0-1
Mr C Bonner	0-2	Mr J Jukes	0-1		

COURSE RECORD

	Total W-R	Nov Hdles	H'cap Hdles	Nov Chses	H'cap Chses	Hunter Chses	N H Flat	£1 Level Stake
Taunton	3-11	1-2	2-4	0-2	0-3	0-0	0-0	+ 4.90
Fontwell	3-13	2-4	1-4	0-0	0-5	0-0	0-0	+ 28.00
Kempton	2-6	0-1	2-3	0-1	0-0	0-0	0-1	+103.00
Newton Abbot	2-22	0-2	2-4	0-5	0-10	0-0	0-1	+ 1.50
Plumpton	1-5	0-1	0-1	0-0	1-3	0-0	0-0	+ 2.00
Stratford	1-9	0-2	0-0	0-0	1-7	0-0	0-0	0.00
Worcester	1-10	0-0	0-3	0-2	1-4	0-0	0-1	+ 2.00
Hereford	1-10	0-3	1-1	0-1	0-5	0-0	0-0	- 4.50
Chepstow	1-10	0-2	0-3	1-1	0-3	0-0	0-1	+ 1.00
Exeter	1-20	0-3	1-6	0-3	0-6	0-0	0-2	- 15.50

Ascot	0-8	Warwick	0-4	Ludlow	0-1
Towcester	0-8	Windsor	0-4	Market Rasen	0-1
Wincanton	0-7	Aintree	0-2	Sandown	0-1
Newbury	0-5	Folkestone	0-2	Southwell	0-1
Cheltenham	0-4	Haydock	0-2		
Nottingham	0-4	Lingfield	0-2		

WINNING HORSES

	Races Run	1st	2nd	3rd	Unpl	Win £
See Enough	7	1	0	0	6	12,103
Ground Nut	10	2	1	2	5	8,541
Kings Cherry	5	1	0	0	4	8,420
St Ville	8	2	0	1	5	6,859
Miss Diskin	8	2	2	0	4	6,353
Tour Leader	9	2	1	0	6	5,627

Angelo's Double	4	1	1	1	1	4,013
Nos Na Gaoithe	3	1	1	0	1	3,743
Golden Opal	9	1	0	1	7	3,449
Starlap	11	1	3	5	2	2,903
Flow	6	1	2	0	3	2,868
Ballyedward	5	1	0	0	4	2,595

WINNING OWNERS

	Races Won	Value £		Races Won	Value £
J A G Meaden	1	12,103	John Henwood	1	4,013
Mrs R L Haskins	2	8,541	R A Read	1	3,743
T J Swaffield	1	8,420	R H Buckler	1	3,449
Melplash Racing	2	6,859	Mrs D A La Trobe	1	2,903
Martyn Forrester	2	6,353	Mrs C J Dunn	1	2,868
Peter Jones	2	5,627	Nick Elliott	1	2,595

No of horses racing for the stable	42	Total winning prize-money	£67,474

Favourites	3-11	27.3%	- 0.60	Average SP of winner	13.9/1
Longest win seq	2	Longest losing seq 25		Return on stakes invested	38.6%

1994/95 Form	12-143	8.4%	- 67.74	1992/93 Form	12-77	15.6%	+ 87.63
1993/94 Form	12-111	10.8%	+ 57.33	1991/92 Form	2-62	3.2%	- 52.17

D BURCHELL (Briery Hill, Gwent)

	Races Run	1st	2nd	3rd	Unpl	Per cent	£1 Level Stake
Hurdles	96	7	11	9	69	7.3	- 54.75
Chases	21	2	6	3	10	9.5	- 5.50
Totals	117	9	17	12	79	7.7	- 60.25

BY MONTH

	W-R	Per cent	£1 Level Stake		W-R	Per cent	£1 Level Stake
June	1-5	20.0	- 1.75	December	0-2	-	- 2.00
July	0-4	-	- 4.00	January	0-6	-	- 6.00
August	1-6	16.7	- 0.50	February	0-9	-	- 9.00
September	0-11	-	- 11.00	March	2-12	16.7	- 3.00
October	0-13	-	- 13.00	April	2-14	14.3	+ 6.00
November	1-21	4.8	- 15.50	May	2-14	14.3	- 0.50

DISTANCE

Hurdles	W-R	Per cent	£1 Level Stake	Chases	W-R	Per cent	£1 Level Stake
2m-2m 3f	5-79	6.3	- 51.00	2m-2m 3f	1-14	7.1	- 8.50
2m 4f-2m 7f	2-14	14.3	- 0.75	2m 4f-2m 7f	1-6	16.7	+ 4.00
3m +	0-3	-	- 3.00	3m +	0-1	-	- 1.00

TYPE OF RACE

	W–R	Per cent	£1 Level Stake		W–R	Per cent	£1 Level Stake
Novice hurdles	1-26	3.8	- 16.00	Selling	5-34	14.7	- 10.75
H'cap hurdles	2-33	6.1	- 19.50	Amateur	0-0	-	0.00
Novice chases	0-3	-	- 3.00	Hunter chases	0-0	-	0.00
H'cap chases	1-17	5.9	- 7.00	N H Flat	0-4	-	- 4.00

COURSE GRADE

	W–R	Per cent	£1 Level Stake
Group 1	0-15	-	- 15.00
Group 2	2-17	11.8	- 1.50
Group 3	4-42	9.5	- 21.75
Group 4	3-43	7.0	- 22.00

FIRST TIME OUT

	W–R	Per cent	£1 Level Stake
Hurdles	1-26	3.8	- 20.50
Chases	0-6	-	- 6.00
Totals	1-32	3.1	- 26.50

JOCKEYS RIDING

	W–R	Per cent	£1 Level Stake		W–R	Per cent	£1 Level Stake
D J Burchell	6-87	6.9	- 49.00	T Eley	1-4	25.0	- 0.75
Guy Lewis	2-8	25.0	+ 7.50				
J Prior	0-8			A Procter	0-3		
Miss E Jones	0-6			S Wynne	0-1		

COURSE RECORD

	Total W–R	Nov Hdles	H'cap Hdles	Nov Chses	H'cap Chses	Hunter Chses	N H Flat	£1 Level Stake
Uttoxeter	2-5	1-2	1-2	0-0	0-1	0-0	0-0	+ 1.75
Plumpton	1-1	0-0	0-0	0-0	1-1	0-0	0-0	+ 4.50
Southwell	1-2	0-1	1-1	0-0	0-0	0-0	0-0	+ 3.50
Bangor	1-6	1-3	0-3	0-0	0-0	0-0	0-0	- 0.50
Ludlow	1-7	0-1	0-4	0-0	1-2	0-0	0-0	+ 3.00
Chepstow	1-7	1-2	0-2	0-0	0-3	0-0	0-0	+ 3.00
Stratford	1-8	0-4	1-2	0-0	0-2	0-0	0-0	0.00
Newton Abbot	1-9	1-4	0-4	0-0	0-0	0-0	0-1	- 3.50

Taunton	0-13	Perth	0-4	Windsor	0-2
Worcester	0-10	Wincanton	0-3	Aintree	0-1
Cheltenham	0-6	Folkestone	0-2	Cartmel	0-1
Exeter	0-5	Leicester	0-2	Kempton	0-1
Haydock	0-5	Market Rasen	0-2	Lingfield	0-1
Hereford	0-5	Sandown	0-2	Nottingham	0-1
Huntingdon	0-4	Warwick	0-2		

WINNING HORSES

	Races Run	1st	2nd	3rd	Unpl	Win £
Coast Along	7	2	1	0	4	4,412
Wadada	4	2	0	0	2	4,400
Castle Secret	6	1	1	1	3	3,730
Channel Pastime	8	1	3	2	2	3,525
Emrys	3	1	0	0	2	2,445
Bright Sapphire	2	1	1	0	0	1,970
Colette's Choice	1	1	0	0	0	1,963

WINNING OWNERS

	Races Won	Value £		Races Won	Value £
Mrs Ruth Burchell	3	8,130	David Bond	1	2,445
T G Brooks	2	4,412	D Roderick	1	1,970
Mrs Sandra Worthington	1	3,525	J A Cooper	1	1,963

No of horses racing for the stable	33	Total winning prize-money	£22,445

Favourites	2-7	28.6%	- 0.25	Average SP of winner		5.3/1
Longest win seq	1	Longest losing seq	39	Return on stakes invested		-51.5%

1994/95 Form	15-106	14.2%	- 10.05	1992/93 Form	12-101	11.9%	- 40.23
1993/94 Form	13-105	12.4%	- 40.61	1991/92 Form	18-126	14.3%	+ 2.43

K R BURKE (Ginge, Oxon)

	Races Run	1st	2nd	3rd	Unpl	Per cent	£1 Level Stake
Hurdles	73	7	13	10	43	9.6	- 24.00
Chases	20	1	3	4	12	5.0	- 12.00
Totals	93	8	16	14	55	8.6	- 36.00

BY MONTH

	W-R	Per cent	£1 Level Stake		W-R	Per cent	£1 Level Stake
June	1-3	33.3	+ 5.00	December	0-10	-	- 10.00
July	3-6	50.0	+ 13.50	January	0-12	-	- 12.00
August	0-2	-	- 2.00	February	0-5	-	- 5.00
September	0-6	-	- 6.00	March	0-6	-	- 6.00
October	0-6	-	- 6.00	April	1-5	20.0	+ 1.50
November	2-20	10.0	- 1.00	May	1-12	8.3	- 8.00

DISTANCE

Hurdles	W-R	Per cent	£1 Level Stake	Chases	W-R	Per cent	£1 Level Stake
2m-2m 3f	6-55	10.9	- 12.50	2m-2m 3f	1-10	10.0	- 2.00
2m 4f-2m 7f	1-12	8.3	- 5.50	2m 4f-2m 7f	0-8	-	- 8.00
3m +	0-6	-	- 6.00	3m +	0-2	-	- 2.00

TYPE OF RACE

	W-R	Per cent	£1 Level Stake		W-R	Per cent	£1 Level Stake
Novice hurdles	0-15	-	- 15.00	Selling	3-20	15.0	- 7.50
H'cap hurdles	4-35	11.4	+ 1.50	Amateur	0-0	-	0.00
Novice chases	0-5	-	- 5.00	Hunter chases	0-0	-	0.00
H'cap chases	1-14	7.1	- 6.00	N H Flat	0-4	-	- 4.00

<table>
<tr><td colspan="4" align="center">COURSE GRADE</td><td colspan="4" align="center">FIRST TIME OUT</td></tr>
<tr><td></td><td>W-R</td><td>Per cent</td><td>£1 Level Stake</td><td></td><td>W-R</td><td>Per cent</td><td>£1 Level Stake</td></tr>
<tr><td>Group 1</td><td>1-7</td><td>14.3</td><td>0.00</td><td>Hurdles</td><td>3-21</td><td>14.3</td><td>- 1.50</td></tr>
<tr><td>Group 2</td><td>2-10</td><td>20.0</td><td>+ 2.50</td><td>Chases</td><td>1-4</td><td>25.0</td><td>+ 4.00</td></tr>
<tr><td>Group 3</td><td>3-52</td><td>5.8</td><td>- 21.00</td><td></td><td></td><td></td><td></td></tr>
<tr><td>Group 4</td><td>2-24</td><td>8.3</td><td>- 17.50</td><td>Totals</td><td>4-25</td><td>16.0</td><td>+ 2.50</td></tr>
</table>

JOCKEYS RIDING

	W-R	Per cent	£1 Level Stake		W-R	Per cent	£1 Level Stake
A Larnach	3-47	6.4	- 21.50	A P McCoy	1-4	25.0	+ 4.00
G Lee	1-1	100.0	+ 10.00	R Dunwoody	1-5	20.0	- 1.00
B Fenton	1-2	50.0	+ 0.50	M A Fitzgerald	1-12	8.3	- 6.00

R Supple	0-11	D Bridgwater	0-1	R Johnson		0-1
J Titley	0-2	G Bradley	0-1	S Fox		0-1
Mr J Culloty	0-2	G Ryan	0-1			
C Carnaby	0-1	P Carberry	0-1			

COURSE RECORD

	Total W-R	Nov Hdles	H'cap Hdles	Nov Chses	H'cap Chses	Hunter Chses	N H Flat	£1 Level Stake
Newton Abbot	2-7	1-3	1-1	0-0	0-3	0-0	0-0	+ 5.50
Market Rasen	1-2	0-0	0-0	0-0	1-2	0-0	0-0	+ 6.00
Bangor	1-2	0-1	1-1	0-0	0-0	0-0	0-0	+ 0.50
Cartmel	1-2	1-2	0-0	0-0	0-0	0-0	0-0	+ 2.00
Cheltenham	1-2	0-0	1-2	0-0	0-0	0-0	0-0	+ 5.00
Uttoxeter	1-7	0-3	1-3	0-0	0-0	0-0	0-1	+ 5.00
Worcester	1-11	0-3	1-8	0-0	0-0	0-0	0-0	0.00

Stratford	0-7	Sedgefield	0-3	Kempton	0-1
Huntingdon	0-6	Ascot	0-2	Lingfield	0-1
Towcester	0-6	Fontwell	0-2	Ludlow	0-1
Windsor	0-6	Leicester	0-2	Newbury	0-1
Hereford	0-5	Southwell	0-2	Plumpton	0-1
Warwick	0-4	Aintree	0-1	Wincanton	0-1
Exeter	0-3	Catterick	0-1		
Nottingham	0-3	Folkestone	0-1		

Burke K R

WINNING HORSES

	Races Run	1st	2nd	3rd	Unpl	Win £
Windward Ariom	12	2	2	2	6	5,014
Sian Wyn	7	2	2	1	2	4,729
Windsor Park	4	1	0	1	2	4,172
Miss Nosey Oats	4	1	1	0	2	2,397
Northern Trial	10	1	1	4	4	2,029
Bodantree	1	1	0	0	0	1,989

WINNING OWNERS

	Races Won	Value £		Races Won	Value £
R S Brookhouse	2	6,161	P A Matthews	1	2,397
Andrew Shaw	2	5,014	Jonathan Weal	1	2,029
D G & D J Robinson	2	4,729			

No of horses racing for the stable	28	Total winning prize-money	£20,330

Favourites	1-8	12.5%	- 5.50	Average SP of winner	6.1/1
Longest win seq	1	Longest losing seq	45	Return on stakes invested	-38.7%

1994/95 Form	8-96	8.3%	- 55.12	1992/93 Form	10-80	12.5%	- 18.42
1993/94 Form	11-146	7.5%	- 71.50	1991/92 Form	4-113	3.5%	- 49.88

P BUTLER (East Chiltington, East Sussex)

	Races Run	1st	2nd	3rd	Unpl	Per cent	£1 Level Stake
Hurdles	18	0	0	2	16	-	- 18.00
Chases	27	3	1	4	19	11.1	- 16.50
Totals	45	3	1	6	35	6.7	- 34.50

T J Murphy	2-14	- 6.00	M A Fitzgerald	1-5	- 2.50

Windsor	1-2	+ 2.50	Lingfield	1-9	- 5.50
Fontwell	1-8	- 5.50			

No of horses racing for the stable	12	Total winning prize-money	£8,637

PIERS BUTLER (Wimborne, Dorset)

	Races Run	1st	2nd	3rd	Unpl	Per cent	£1 Level Stake
Hurdles	0	0	0	0	0	-	0.00
Chases	4	1	0	0	3	25.0	- 1.75
Totals	4	1	0	0	3	25.0	- 1.75

Mr N Mitchell	1-4	- 1.75	Fontwell	1-1	+ 1.25

No of horses racing for the stable	1	Total winning prize-money	£1,548

N A CALLAGHAN (Newmarket, Suffolk)

	Races Run	1st	2nd	3rd	Unpl	Per cent	£1 Level Stake
Hurdles	5	0	1	0	4	-	- 5.00
Chases	6	3	1	0	2	50.0	+ 0.47
Totals	11	3	2	0	6	27.3	- 4.53

J Titley	2-5	- 0.15	A P McCoy	1-1	+ 0.62
Nottingham	1-1	+ 0.62	Fakenham	1-2	+ 0.10
Market Rasen	1-1	+ 1.75			

No of horses racing for the stable   3   Total winning prize-money   £11,101

P CALVER (Ripon, North Yorks)

	Races Run	1st	2nd	3rd	Unpl	Per cent	£1 Level Stake
Hurdles	7	1	0	0	6	14.3	+ 0.50
Chases	14	1	5	3	5	7.1	- 9.50
Totals	21	2	5	3	11	9.5	- 9.00

L Wyer	2-15	- 3.00			
Kelso	1-2	+ 5.50	Worcester	1-3	+ 1.50

No of horses racing for the stable   5   Total winning prize-money   £7,778

M J CAMACHO (Norton, North Yorks)

	Races Run	1st	2nd	3rd	Unpl	Per cent	£1 Level Stake
Hurdles	15	3	3	1	8	20.0	+ 6.75
Chases	4	2	2	0	0	50.0	+ 2.70
Totals	19	5	5	1	8	26.3	+ 9.45

P Niven	2-3	+ 3.75	D Byrne	1-3	+ 14.00
E Callaghan	1-1	+ 2.50	M Dwyer	1-10	- 8.80
Kelso	2-2	+ 16.25	Doncaster	1-1	+ 0.20
Catterick	1-1	+ 2.50	Newcastle	1-4	+ 1.50

No of horses racing for the stable   6   Total winning prize-money   £22,068

B R CAMBIDGE (Bishop's Wood, Staffs)

	Races Run	1st	2nd	3rd	Unpl	Per cent	£1 Level Stake
Hurdles	25	1	2	2	20	4.0	- 4.00
Chases	4	0	0	0	4	-	- 4.00
Totals	29	1	2	2	24	3.4	- 8.00

T J Murphy	1-5	+ 16.00	Uttoxeter	1-6	+ 15.00

No of horses racing for the stable   7   Total winning prize-money   £1,928

S W CAMPION (West Barkwith, Lincs)

	Races Run	1st	2nd	3rd	Unpl	Per cent	£1 Level Stake
Hurdles	21	1	1	1	18	4.8	- 8.00
Chases	1	0	0	0	1	-	- 1.00
Totals	22	1	1	1	19	4.5	- 9.00

G E Tormey	1-2	+ 11.00	Fakenham	1-1	+ 12.00

No of horses racing for the stable   10   Total winning prize-money   £3,745

D E CANTILLON (Newmarket, Suffolk)

	Races Run	1st	2nd	3rd	Unpl	Per cent	£1 Level Stake
Hurdles	4	0	2	1	1	-	- 4.00
Chases	6	3	1	1	1	50.0	+ 5.00
Totals	10	3	3	2	2	30.0	+ 1.00

G Bradley	2-2	+ 4.00	L Wyer	1-2	+ 3.00
Huntingdon	2-2	+ 4.00	Wetherby	1-2	+ 3.00

No of horses racing for the stable   1   Total winning prize-money   £13,088

MISS C M CARDEN (Macclesfield, Cheshire)

	Races Run	1st	2nd	3rd	Unpl	Per cent	£1 Level Stake
Hurdles	0	0	0	0	0	-	0.00
Chases	5	1	0	1	3	20.0	+ 21.00
Totals	5	1	0	1	3	20.0	+ 21.00

Mr S Prior	1-5	+ 21.00	Uttoxeter	1-1	+ 25.00

No of horses racing for the stable   1   Total winning prize-money   £1,810

D N CAREY (Nantyglo, Gwent)

	Races Run	1st	2nd	3rd	Unpl	Per cent	£1 Level Stake
Hurdles	22	1	0	3	18	4.5	- 7.00
Chases	6	0	1	1	4	-	- 6.00
Totals	28	1	1	4	22	3.6	- 13.00

B Fenton	1-3	+ 12.00	Hereford	1-5	+ 10.00

No of horses racing for the stable   4   Total winning prize-money   £2,472

D J CARO (Malmesbury, Wilts)

	Races Run	1st	2nd	3rd	Unpl	Per cent	£1 Level Stake
Hurdles	12	0	1	1	10	-	- 12.00
Chases	5	1	1	0	3	20.0	- 3.20
Totals	17	1	2	1	13	5.9	- 15.20

Mr A J Phillips	1-4	- 2.20	Sandown	1-2	- 0.20

No of horses racing for the stable   6   Total winning prize-money   £1,646

MISS C J E CAROE (Chichester, West Sussex)

	Races Run	1st	2nd	3rd	Unpl	Per cent	£1 Level Stake
Hurdles	20	1	2	3	14	5.0	- 15.00
Chases	17	1	2	3	11	5.9	+ 9.00
Totals	37	2	4	6	25	5.4	- 6.00

D Leahy	1-7	+ 19.00	I Lawrence	1-21	- 16.00
Plumpton	1-8	- 3.00	Fontwell	1-9	+ 17.00

No of horses racing for the stable   8   Total winning prize-money   £4,601

J M CARR (Norton, North Yorks)

	Races Run	1st	2nd	3rd	Unpl	Per cent	£1 Level Stake
Hurdles	19	2	3	2	12	10.5	- 4.62
Chases	0	0	0	0	0	-	0.00
Totals	19	2	3	2	12	10.5	- 4.62

F Leahy	2-10	+ 4.38			
Wetherby	1-3	+ 9.00	Haydock	1-4	- 1.62

No of horses racing for the stable   5   Total winning prize-money   £5,848

A W CARROLL (Inkberrow, H'ford & Worcs)

	Races Run	1st	2nd	3rd	Unpl	Per cent	£1 Level Stake
Hurdles	66	1	5	3	57	1.5	- 53.00
Chases	4	0	1	1	2	-	- 4.00
Totals	70	1	6	4	59	1.4	- 57.00

B Powell	1-10	+ 3.00	Leicester	1-5	+ 8.00

No of horses racing for the stable   18   Total winning prize-money   £3,444

T CASEY (Beare Green, Surrey)

	Races Run	1st	2nd	3rd	Unpl	Per cent	£1 Level Stake
Hurdles	30	2	4	0	24	6.7	- 25.75
Chases	31	5	7	5	14	16.1	- 12.51
Totals	61	7	11	5	38	11.5	- 38.26

BY MONTH

	W-R	Per cent	£1 Level Stake		W-R	Per cent	£1 Level Stake
June	0-0	-	0.00	December	0-4	-	- 4.00
July	0-0	-	0.00	January	1-8	12.5	- 4.75
August	0-0	-	0.00	February	2-12	16.7	- 6.67
September	0-0	-	0.00	March	1-12	8.3	- 4.00
October	0-2	-	- 2.00	April	1-4	25.0	- 2.50
November	2-14	14.3	- 9.34	May	0-5	-	- 5.00

DISTANCE

Hurdles	W-R	Per cent	£1 Level Stake	Chases	W-R	Per cent	£1 Level Stake
2m-2m 3f	2-23	8.7	- 18.75	2m-2m 3f	0-6	-	- 6.00
2m 4f-2m 7f	0-7	-	- 7.00	2m 4f-2m 7f	1-7	14.3	- 5.09
3m +	0-0	-	0.00	3m +	4-18	22.2	- 1.42

TYPE OF RACE

	W-R	Per cent	£1 Level Stake		W-R	Per cent	£1 Level Stake
Novice hurdles	2-20	10.0	- 15.75	Selling	0-4	-	- 4.00
H'cap hurdles	0-4	-	- 4.00	Amateur	0-2	-	- 2.00
Novice chases	3-17	17.6	- 10.51	Hunter chases	0-0	-	0.00
H'cap chases	2-12	16.7	0.00	N H Flat	0-2	-	- 2.00

54

COURSE GRADE					FIRST TIME OUT			
	W-R	Per cent	£1 Level Stake			W-R	Per cent	£1 Level Stake
Group 1	4-28	14.3	- 12.76	Hurdles		1-9	11.1	- 6.25
Group 2	2-15	13.3	- 9.00	Chases		1-6	16.7	- 4.09
Group 3	1-14	7.1	- 12.50					
Group 4	0-4	-	- 4.00	Totals		2-15	13.3	- 10.34

JOCKEYS RIDING

	W-R	Per cent	£1 Level Stake			W-R	Per cent	£1 Level Stake
M A Fitzgerald	3-17	17.6	- 4.42	R Dunwoody		1-5	20.0	- 1.00
E Murphy	3-17	17.6	- 10.84					

S Laird	0-3	B Powell	0-1	Miss C Wates		0-1
A P McCoy	0-2	D Bridgwater	0-1	Mr P Henley		0-1
B Fenton	0-2	D Gallagher	0-1	Muredach Kelly		0-1
J Osborne	0-2	D O'Sullivan	0-1	W Marston		0-1
R Johnson	0-2	G Bradley	0-1			
A Thornton	0-1	J A McCarthy	0-1			

COURSE RECORD

	Total W-R	Nov Hdles	H'cap Hdles	Nov Chses	H'cap Chses	Hunter Chses	N H Flat	£1 Level Stake
Kempton	3-12	0-3	0-1	2-4	1-4	0-0	0-0	- 4.76
Fontwell	2-8	1-3	0-1	1-2	0-2	0-0	0-0	- 2.00
Aintree	1-1	0-0	0-0	0-0	1-1	0-0	0-0	+ 7.00
Plumpton	1-6	1-5	0-1	0-0	0-0	0-0	0-0	- 4.50

Lingfield	0-7	Newbury	0-4	Sandown	0-3
Cheltenham	0-5	Towcester	0-4	Huntingdon	0-2
Windsor	0-5	Ascot	0-3	Warwick	0-1

WINNING HORSES

	Races Run	1st	2nd	3rd	Unpl	Win £
Rough Quest	6	2	3	0	1	172,134
Silverfort Lad	9	2	1	1	5	8,081
Flight Lieutenant	8	2	3	0	3	5,897
Even Flow	1	1	0	0	0	3,738

WINNING OWNERS

	Races Won	Value £		Races Won	Value £
A T A Wates	5	183,953	Mrs Laura Pegg	2	5,897

No of horses racing for the stable	16	Total winning prize-money	£189,850

Favourites	6-14	42.9%	+ 5.49	Average SP of winner		2.2/1
Longest win seq	2	Longest losing seq	16	Return on stakes invested		-62.7%

1994/95 Form	7-46	15.2%	+ 12.67	1992/93 Form	3-61	4.9%	- 49.25
1993/94 Form	2-31	6.5%	- 21.12	1991/92 Form	10-101	9.9%	- 47.17

P CAUDWELL (Abingdon, Oxon)

	Races Run	1st	2nd	3rd	Unpl	Per cent	£1 Level Stake
Hurdles	0	0	0	0	0	-	0.00
Chases	2	1	1	0	0	50.0	+ 2.00
Totals	2	1	1	0	0	50.0	+ 2.00

Mr A Sansome	1-2	+ 2.00		Fakenham	1-1	+ 3.00

No of horses racing for the stable   1   Total winning prize-money   £2,441

MRS J CECIL (Newmarket, Suffolk)

	Races Run	1st	2nd	3rd	Unpl	Per cent	£1 Level Stake
Hurdles	30	3	2	4	21	10.0	- 15.90
Chases	0	0	0	0	0	-	0.00
Totals	30	3	2	4	21	10.0	- 15.90

T Kent   3-30   - 15.90

Doncaster	2-2	+ 10.00		Haydock	1-3	- 0.90

No of horses racing for the stable   9   Total winning prize-money   £10,125

S G CHADWICK (Aspatria, Cumbria)

	Races Run	1st	2nd	3rd	Unpl	Per cent	£1 Level Stake
Hurdles	3	0	0	0	3	-	- 3.00
Chases	9	1	0	1	7	11.1	+ 25.00
Totals	12	1	0	1	10	8.3	+ 22.00

D Bentley	1-4	+ 30.00		Hexham	1-4	+ 30.00

No of horses racing for the stable   3   Total winning prize-money   £2,837

N CHAMBERLAIN (West Auckland, Co Durham)

	Races Run	1st	2nd	3rd	Unpl	Per cent	£1 Level Stake
Hurdles	31	1	2	1	27	3.2	- 24.00
Chases	11	1	0	4	6	9.1	- 5.00
Totals	42	2	2	5	33	4.8	- 29.00

Miss C Metcalfe   2-19   - 6.00

Nottingham	1-1	+ 5.00		Kelso	1-3	+ 4.00

No of horses racing for the stable   13   Total winning prize-money   £3,924

..MINGS (Basingstoke, Hants)

	..ces Run	1st	2nd	3rd	Unpl	Per cent	£1 Level Stake
	0	0	0	0	0	–	0.00
	16	4	1	0	11	25.0	+ 0.25
Totals	16	4	1	0	11	25.0	+ 0.25

Mr C Vigors   4-10   + 6.25

Lingfield	1-1	+ 2.00	Worcester	1-1	+ 6.00
Chepstow	1-1	+ 2.75	Cheltenham	1-3	- 0.50

No of horses racing for the stable   6   Total winning prize-money   £6,982

R CHAMPION (Newmarket, Suffolk)

	Races Run	1st	2nd	3rd	Unpl	Per cent	£1 Level Stake
Hurdles	3	0	0	0	3	–	- 3.00
Chases	12	4	1	2	5	33.3	+ 12.13
Totals	15	4	1	2	8	26.7	+ 9.13

A Dobbin	2-2	+ 12.50	M A Fitzgerald	1-4	- 1.37
D Bridgwater	1-2	+ 5.00			

Sedgefield	1-1	+ 1.63	Aintree	1-1	+ 9.00
Huntingdon	1-1	+ 6.00	Catterick	1-1	+ 3.50

No of horses racing for the stable   4   Total winning prize-money   £16,601

NOEL T CHANCE (Lambourn, Berks)

	Races Run	1st	2nd	3rd	Unpl	Per cent	£1 Level Stake
Hurdles	45	10	10	4	21	22.2	+ 7.64
Chases	8	3	1	1	3	37.5	+ 1.45
Totals	53	13	11	5	24	24.5	+ 9.09

BY MONTH

	W-R	Per cent	£1 Level Stake		W-R	Per cent	£1 Level Stake
June	1-2	50.0	+ 9.00	December	1-2	50.0	+ 3.50
July	0-0	-	0.00	January	1-6	16.7	- 2.00
August	0-0	-	0.00	February	2-6	33.3	+ 1.25
September	1-5	20.0	+ 1.50	March	1-8	12.5	- 2.50
October	2-7	28.6	+ 1.36	April	0-1	-	- 1.00
November	4-13	30.8	+ 0.98	May	0-3	-	- 3.00

DISTANCE

Hurdles	W-R	Per cent	£1 Level Stake	Chases	W-R	Per cent	£1 Level Stake
2m-2m 3f	5-34	14.7	- 3.87	2m-2m 3f	0-1	-	- 1.00
2m 4f-2m 7f	4-8	50.0	+ 9.51	2m 4f-2m 7f	0-0	-	0.00
3m +	1-3	33.3	+ 2.00	3m +	3-7	42.9	+ 2.45

TYPE OF RACE

	W-R	Per cent	£1 Level Stake		W-R	Per cent	£1 Level Stake
Novice hurdles	7-24	29.2	+ 9.51	Selling	0-0	-	0.00
H'cap hurdles	1-11	9.1	0.00	Amateur	0-0	-	0.00
Novice chases	3-6	50.0	+ 3.45	Hunter chases	0-0	-	0.00
H'cap chases	0-2	-	- 2.00	N H Flat	2-10	20.0	- 1.87

COURSE GRADE

	W-R	Per cent	£1 Level Stake
Group 1	2-13	15.4	- 4.25
Group 2	2-6	33.3	- 0.64
Group 3	3-19	15.8	+ 5.50
Group 4	6-15	40.0	+ 8.48

FIRST TIME OUT

	W-R	Per cent	£1 Level Stake
Hurdles	4-14	28.6	+ 10.28
Chases	0-1	-	- 1.00
Totals	4-15	26.7	+ 9.28

JOCKEYS RIDING

	W-R	Per cent	£1 Level Stake		W-R	Per cent	£1 Level Stake
R Johnson	8-29	27.6	+ 10.74	M Dwyer	1-1	100.0	+ 1.20
D Finnegan	3-13	23.1	+ 1.65	R Dunwoody	1-2	50.0	+ 3.50
B Powell	0-2			M A Fitzgerald	0-2		T Comerford	0-1
D Leahy	0-2			Richard Davis	0-1			

COURSE RECORD

	Total W-R	Nov Hdles	H'cap Hdles	Nov Chses	H'cap Chses	Hunter Chses	N H Flat	£1 Level Stake
Towcester	2-2	2-2	0-0	0-0	0-0	0-0	0-0	+ 7.15
Ludlow	2-3	1-2	0-0	0-0	0-0	0-0	1-1	+ 5.13
Wetherby	2-3	1-2	0-0	1-1	0-0	0-0	0-0	+ 2.36
Sandown	1-1	0-0	0-0	0-0	0-0	0-0	1-1	+ 4.50
Market Rasen	1-2	0-0	1-1	0-0	0-1	0-0	0-0	+ 9.00
Plumpton	1-2	1-2	0-0	0-0	0-0	0-0	0-0	+ 5.00
Bangor	1-2	0-0	0-0	1-1	0-0	0-0	0-1	+ 0.20
Ascot	1-2	0-0	0-1	1-1	0-0	0-0	0-0	+ 1.25
Uttoxeter	1-3	1-1	0-2	0-0	0-0	0-0	0-0	+ 3.50
Taunton	1-4	1-3	0-1	0-0	0-0	0-0	0-0	0.00

Wincanton	0-4	Worcester	0-2	Leicester	0-1
Cheltenham	0-3	Ayr	0-1	Lingfield	0-1
Hereford	0-3	Doncaster	0-1	Newbury	0-1
Huntingdon	0-3	Fakenham	0-1	Nottingham	0-1
Kempton	0-3	Folkestone	0-1		
Fontwell	0-2	Haydock	0-1		

WINNING HORSES

	Races Run	1st	2nd	3rd	Unpl	Win £
Mr Mulligan	6	5	1	0	0	39,328
Monty Royale	2	1	0	0	1	8,988
Cailin Glas	4	2	0	0	2	4,916
Nupdown Boy	5	1	0	0	4	2,861
Royal Thimble	8	1	3	1	3	2,579
Mead Court	9	1	1	0	7	2,071
Marching Marquis	2	1	1	0	0	1,417
Gracefield	3	1	1	0	1	1,130

WINNING OWNERS

	Races Won	Value £		Races Won	Value £
M Worcester	12	60,711	Mrs M Chance	1	2,579

No of horses racing for the stable		15	Total winning prize-money	£63,290
Favourites	3-11	27.3% - 4.19	Average SP of winner	3.8/1
Longest win seq	3	Longest losing seq 9	Return on stakes invested	17.2%
1991/92 Form	0-1			

M R CHANNON (Upper Lambourn, Berks)

	Races Run	1st	2nd	3rd	Unpl	Per cent	£1 Level Stake
Hurdles	7	0	0	1	6	-	- 7.00
Chases	4	1	0	0	3	25.0	+ 0.50
Totals	11	1	0	1	9	9.1	- 6.50

A Thornton	1-7	- 2.50	Leicester	1-2	+ 2.50

No of horses racing for the stable	5	Total winning prize-money	£2,846

M C CHAPMAN (Market Rasen, Lincs)

	Races Run	1st	2nd	3rd	Unpl	Per cent	£1 Level Stake
Hurdles	62	2	5	11	44	3.2	- 41.00
Chases	48	5	4	9	30	10.4	+ 2.75
Totals	110	7	9	20	74	6.4	- 38.25

Chapman M C

BY MONTH

	W-R	Per cent	£1 Level Stake		W-R	Per cent	£1 Level Stake
June	0-5	-	- 5.00	December	0-9	-	- 9.00
July	0-4	-	- 4.00	January	1-12	8.3	+ 5.00
August	3-5	60.0	+ 29.25	February	0-10	-	- 10.00
September	0-5	-	- 5.00	March	0-6	-	- 6.00
October	0-12	-	- 12.00	April	0-16	-	- 16.00
November	2-12	16.7	+ 2.50	May	1-14	7.1	- 8.00

DISTANCE

	W-R	Per cent	£1 Level Stake		W-R	Per cent	£1 Level Stake
Hurdles				Chases			
2m-2m 3f	2-52	3.8	- 31.00	2m-2m 3f	3-26	11.5	+ 1.75
2m 4f-2m 7f	0-5	-	- 5.00	2m 4f-2m 7f	2-17	11.8	+ 6.00
3m +	0-5	-	- 5.00	3m +	0-5	-	- 5.00

TYPE OF RACE

	W-R	Per cent	£1 Level Stake		W-R	Per cent	£1 Level Stake
Novice hurdles	0-20	-	- 20.00	Selling	1-8	12.5	+ 2.00
H'cap hurdles	1-31	3.2	- 20.00	Amateur	0-4	-	- 4.00
Novice chases	0-12	-	- 12.00	Hunter chases	0-0	-	0.00
H'cap chases	5-33	15.2	+ 17.75	N H Flat	0-2	-	- 2.00

COURSE GRADE / FIRST TIME OUT

	W-R	Per cent	£1 Level Stake		W-R	Per cent	£1 Level Stake
Group 1	1-31	3.2	- 20.00	Hurdles	1-11	9.1	- 1.00
Group 2	0-0	-	0.00	Chases	0-5	-	- 5.00
Group 3	2-52	3.8	- 14.00				
Group 4	4-27	14.8	- 4.25	Totals	1-16	6.3	- 6.00

JOCKEYS RIDING

	W-R	Per cent	£1 Level Stake
W Worthington	7-93	7.5	- 21.25

Mr M Mackley	0-4	D Finnegan	0-1	M Keighley	0-1
E Callaghan	0-2	D Thomas	0-1	Miss P Robson	0-1
G Supple	0-2	E Husband	0-1	S Lyons	0-1
Mr J Culloty	0-2	G E Tormey	0-1		

COURSE RECORD

	Total W-R	Nov Hdles	H'cap Hdles	Nov Chses	H'cap Chses	Hunter Chses	N H Flat	£1 Level Stake
Cartmel	2-10	0-4	1-3	0-1	1-2	0-0	0-0	+ 3.25
Fakenham	1-4	0-0	0-1	0-0	1-3	0-0	0-0	+ 2.00
Nottingham	1-5	0-1	0-1	0-0	1-3	0-0	0-0	+ 12.00
Ludlow	1-12	0-2	0-3	0-1	1-5	0-0	0-1	- 8.50
Ascot	1-25	0-7	1-10	0-3	0-5	0-0	0-0	- 14.00
Market Rasen	1-32	0-6	0-7	0-5	1-13	0-0	0-1	- 11.00

Leicester	0-7	Doncaster	0-1	Sedgefield	0-1
Huntingdon	0-3	Haydock	0-1	Stratford	0-1
Worcester	0-2	Newbury	0-1	Uttoxeter	0-1
Catterick	0-1	Newcastle	0-1		
Cheltenham	0-1	Sandown	0-1		

WINNING HORSES

	Races Run	1st	2nd	3rd	Unpl	Win £
Rupples	24	3	3	5	13	11,966
Sprowston Boy	8	2	0	2	4	7,495
Non Vintage	12	1	2	3	6	6,692
Britannia Mills	15	1	1	4	9	2,324

WINNING OWNERS

	Races Won	Value £		Races Won	Value £
C Hague	2	9,243	Geoff Whiting	2	7,495
Alan Mann	2	9,016	Exors of the Late C Hague	1	2,723

No of horses racing for the stable	16	Total winning prize-money	£28,477
Favourites	0-2	Average SP of winner	9.3/1
Longest win seq	2 Longest losing seq 39	Return on stakes invested	-34.8%

| 1994/95 Form | 6-107 | 5.6% | - 34.25 | 1992/93 Form | 4-103 | 3.9% | - 74.50 |
| 1993/94 Form | 5-81 | 6.2% | - 49.00 | 1991/92 Form | 9-113 | 8.0% | - 43.12 |

D N CHAPPELL (Whitsbury, Hants)

	Races Run	1st	2nd	3rd	Unpl	Per cent	£1 Level Stake
Hurdles	11	1	2	0	8	9.1	- 9.00
Chases	6	0	0	0	6	-	- 6.00
Totals	17	1	2	0	14	5.9	- 15.00

| G Upton | 1-8 | - 6.00 | Worcester | 1-4 | - 2.00 |

No of horses racing for the stable 5 Total winning prize-money £1,557

G F H CHARLES-JONES (Letcombe Regis, Oxon)

	Races Run	1st	2nd	3rd	Unpl	Per cent	£1 Level Stake
Hurdles	15	1	0	0	14	6.7	+ 11.00
Chases	18	1	1	2	14	5.6	- 9.00
Totals	33	2	1	2	28	6.1	+ 2.00

| D Walsh | 1-4 | + 5.00 | W McFarland | 1-22 | + 4.00 |
| Plumpton | 1-3 | + 6.00 | Towcester | 1-3 | + 23.00 |

No of horses racing for the stable 8 Total winning prize-money £5,301

J I A CHARLTON (Stocksfield, Northumberland)

	Races Run	1st	2nd	3rd	Unpl	Per cent	£1 Level Stake
Hurdles	30	1	2	2	25	3.3	- 21.00
Chases	31	8	5	3	15	25.8	- 5.59
Totals	61	9	7	5	40	14.8	- 26.59

BY MONTH

	W-R	Per cent	£1 Level Stake		W-R	Per cent	£1 Level Stake
June	1-5	20.0	- 2.75	December	1-7	14.3	- 3.50
July	0-0	-	0.00	January	2-10	20.0	+ 1.25
August	0-0	-	0.00	February	1-8	12.5	- 4.00
September	0-0	-	0.00	March	1-7	14.3	- 4.00
October	0-1	-	- 1.00	April	0-10	-	- 10.00
November	2-7	28.6	- 1.09	May	1-6	16.7	- 1.50

DISTANCE

Hurdles	W-R	Per cent	£1 Level Stake	Chases	W-R	Per cent	£1 Level Stake
2m-2m 3f	0-16	-	- 16.00	2m-2m 3f	8-20	40.0	+ 5.41
2m 4f-2m 7f	0-8	-	- 8.00	2m 4f-2m 7f	0-6	-	- 6.00
3m +	1-6	16.7	+ 3.00	3m +	0-5	-	- 5.00

TYPE OF RACE

	W-R	Per cent	£1 Level Stake		W-R	Per cent	£1 Level Stake
Novice hurdles	1-20	5.0	- 11.00	Selling	0-1	-	- 1.00
H'cap hurdles	0-8	-	- 8.00	Amateur	0-0	-	0.00
Novice chases	4-13	30.8	- 0.25	Hunter chases	0-0	-	0.00
H'cap chases	4-18	22.2	- 5.34	N H Flat	0-1	-	- 1.00

COURSE GRADE

	W-R	Per cent	£1 Level Stake
Group 1	3-13	23.1	- 1.50
Group 2	0-2	-	- 2.00
Group 3	3-17	17.6	- 2.25
Group 4	3-29	10.3	- 20.84

FIRST TIME OUT

	W-R	Per cent	£1 Level Stake
Hurdles	0-13	-	- 13.00
Chases	2-4	50.0	+ 2.25
Totals	2-17	11.8	- 10.75

JOCKEYS RIDING

	W-R	Per cent	£1 Level Stake		W-R	Per cent	£1 Level Stake
B Storey	5-42	11.9	- 21.34	K Johnson	1-4	25.0	- 1.75
A P McCoy	3-5	60.0	+ 6.50				

B Harding	0-6	E Callaghan	0-1	Richard Guest	0-1
A K Smith	0-1	P Niven	0-1		

Charlton J I A

COURSE RECORD

	Total W-R	Nov Hdles	H'cap Hdles	Nov Chses	H'cap Chses	Hunter Chses	N H Flat	£1 Level Stake
Catterick	3-15	1-2	0-4	2-5	0-4	0-0	0-0	- 0.25
Carlisle	2-7	0-3	0-0	0-0	2-4	0-0	0-0	- 1.09
Sandown	1-1	0-0	0-0	1-1	0-0	0-0	0-0	+ 2.00
Ascot	1-2	0-0	0-0	1-1	0-1	0-0	0-0	+ 2.00
Aintree	1-2	0-0	0-0	0-1	1-1	0-0	0-0	+ 2.50
Perth	1-3	0-1	0-0	0-1	1-1	0-0	0-0	- 0.75

Hexham	0-8	Ayr	0-2	Market Rasen	0-1
Kelso	0-6	Doncaster	0-2	Stratford	0-1
Newcastle	0-4	Musselburgh	0-2		
Cartmel	0-3	Wetherby	0-2		

WINNING HORSES

	Races Run	1st	2nd	3rd	Unpl	Win £
Lord Dorcet	8	4	1	0	3	21,774
Strong Approach	8	3	2	1	2	12,177
Golden Isle	3	1	0	0	2	3,355
Radical Choice	3	1	0	1	1	3,036

WINNING OWNERS

	Races Won	Value £		Races Won	Value £
John Hogg	5	25,129	J I A Charlton	1	3,036
Mrs R C Carr	3	12,177			

No of horses racing for the stable	17	Total winning prize-money	£40,342

Favourites	5-11	45.5%	+ 3.41	Average SP of winner	2.8/1
Longest win seq	2	Longest losing seq	15	Return on stakes invested	-43.6%

1994/95 Form	10-104	9.6%	- 2.55	1992/93 Form	9-94	9.6%	- 25.62
1993/94 Form	4-100	4.0%	- 63.00	1991/92 Form	9-128	7.0%	- 67.08

P CHEESBROUGH (Leasingthorne, Co Durham)

	Races Run	1st	2nd	3rd	Unpl	Per cent	£1 Level Stake
Hurdles	50	2	4	8	36	4.0	- 43.75
Chases	51	2	5	12	32	3.9	- 45.00
Totals	101	4	9	20	68	4.0	- 88.75

P G Cahill	2-6	0.00	R Supple	1-70	- 67.25
R Johnson	1-1	+ 2.50			
Hexham	2-15	- 8.75	Ayr	1-5	- 2.25
Market Rasen	1-3	+ 0.25			

No of horses racing for the stable	16	Total winning prize-money	£13,822

DR D CHESNEY (Charminster, Dorset)

	Races Run	1st	2nd	3rd	Unpl	Per cent	£1 Level Stake
Hurdles	3	1	0	0	2	33.3	+ 0.25
Chases	0	0	0	0	0	-	0.00
Totals	3	1	0	0	2	33.3	+ 0.25

S Burrough	1-2	+ 1.25		Taunton		1-1	+ 2.25

No of horses racing for the stable   1   Total winning prize-money   £1,912

S CHRISTIAN (Kinnersley, H'ford & Worcs)

	Races Run	1st	2nd	3rd	Unpl	Per cent	£1 Level Stake
Hurdles	26	3	5	2	16	11.5	- 6.00
Chases	12	0	3	3	6	-	- 12.00
Totals	38	3	8	5	22	7.9	- 18.00

S McNeill	1-3	+ 6.00		D Gallagher		1-5	- 1.00
J Osborne	1-4	+ 3.00					
Hereford	2-3	+ 10.00		Ludlow		1-3	+ 4.00

No of horses racing for the stable   17   Total winning prize-money   £6,014

B G CLARK (Stevenage, Herts)

	Races Run	1st	2nd	3rd	Unpl	Per cent	£1 Level Stake
Hurdles	0	0	0	0	0	-	0.00
Chases	3	1	0	0	2	33.3	+ 5.00
Totals	3	1	0	0	2	33.3	+ 5.00

Mr R Gill	1-3	+ 5.00		Fakenham		1-1	+ 7.00

No of horses racing for the stable   1   Total winning prize-money   £2,524

P C CLARKE (Ashburnham, East Sussex)

	Races Run	1st	2nd	3rd	Unpl	Per cent	£1 Level Stake
Hurdles	14	2	1	0	11	14.3	+ 0.50
Chases	16	0	2	4	10	-	- 16.00
Totals	30	2	3	4	21	6.7	- 15.50

B Fenton	2-25	- 10.50			
Newton Abbot	1-1	+ 6.00	Stratford	1-2	+ 5.50

No of horses racing for the stable	6	Total winning prize-money	£5,161

W CLAY (Saverley Green, Staffs)

	Races Run	1st	2nd	3rd	Unpl	Per cent	£1 Level Stake
Hurdles	129	6	7	8	108	4.7	- 42.75
Chases	18	0	1	5	12	-	- 18.00
Totals	147	6	8	13	120	4.1	- 60.75

Guy Lewis	4-83	- 25.00	Diane Clay	1-26	0.00
A S Smith	1-6	- 3.75			

Uttoxeter	2-32	- 22.75	Southwell	1-15	- 2.00
Taunton	1-3	+ 31.00	Bangor	1-20	- 16.00
Worcester	1-11	+ 15.00			

No of horses racing for the stable	39	Total winning prize-money	£13,336

MRS S COBDEN (Martock, Somerset)

	Races Run	1st	2nd	3rd	Unpl	Per cent	£1 Level Stake
Hurdles	0	0	0	0	0	-	0.00
Chases	6	2	1	0	3	33.3	+ 3.00
Totals	6	2	1	0	3	33.3	+ 3.00

Mrs J Reed	2-6	+ 3.00			
Ascot	1-1	+ 2.50	Stratford	1-2	+ 3.50

No of horses racing for the stable	1	Total winning prize-money	£5,113

S N COLE (Rackenford, Devon)

	Races Run	1st	2nd	3rd	Unpl	Per cent	£1 Level Stake
Hurdles	8	1	0	0	7	12.5	- 1.00
Chases	2	0	0	0	2	-	- 2.00
Totals	10	1	0	0	9	10.0	- 3.00

A P McCoy	1-2	+ 5.00	Stratford	1-2	+ 5.00

No of horses racing for the stable   4   Total winning prize-money   £2,960

R COLLINS (Newton Aycliffe, Co Durham)

	Races Run	1st	2nd	3rd	Unpl	Per cent	£1 Level Stake
Hurdles	12	1	1	1	9	8.3	- 9.00
Chases	0	0	0	0	0	-	0.00
Totals	12	1	1	1	9	8.3	- 9.00

R Dunwoody	1-3	0.00	Sedgefield	1-2	+ 1.00

No of horses racing for the stable   3   Total winning prize-money   £2,460

M J COOMBE (Fleet, Dorset)

	Races Run	1st	2nd	3rd	Unpl	Per cent	£1 Level Stake
Hurdles	8	1	0	1	6	12.5	+ 1.10
Chases	5	1	0	0	4	20.0	+ 3.00
Totals	13	2	0	1	10	15.4	+ 4.10

Miss M Coombe	2-11	+ 6.10			
Fakenham	1-2	+ 6.00	Newton Abbot	1-3	+ 6.10

No of horses racing for the stable   3   Total winning prize-money   £5,975

R CRAGGS (Sedgefield, Co Cleveland)

	Races Run	1st	2nd	3rd	Unpl	Per cent	£1 Level Stake
Hurdles	23	3	3	0	17	13.0	+ 5.88
Chases	3	0	0	0	3	-	- 3.00
Totals	26	3	3	0	20	11.5	+ 2.88

A Dobbin	2-3	+ 14.88	B Fenton	1-1	+ 10.00
Southwell	1-1	+ 10.00	Carlisle	1-4	- 1.12
Wetherby	1-3	+ 12.00			

No of horses racing for the stable   6   Total winning prize-money   £7,379

J K CRESSWELL (Oakmoor, Staffs)

	Races Run	1st	2nd	3rd	Unpl	Per cent	£1 Level Stake
Hurdles	22	1	2	2	17	4.5	- 10.00
Chases	0	0	0	0	0	-	0.00
Totals	22	1	2	2	17	4.5	- 10.00

T Eley	1-3	+ 9.00		Stratford	1-4	+ 8.00

No of horses racing for the stable   7   Total winning prize-money   £2,318

K CUMINGS (South Molton, Devon)

	Races Run	1st	2nd	3rd	Unpl	Per cent	£1 Level Stake
Hurdles	0	0	0	0	0	-	0.00
Chases	5	1	0	1	3	20.0	- 2.50
Totals	5	1	0	1	3	20.0	- 2.50

Miss J Cumings	1-3	- 0.50		Leicester	1-3	- 0.50

No of horses racing for the stable   3   Total winning prize-money   £2,364

W S CUNNINGHAM (Hutton Rudby, North Yorks)

	Races Run	1st	2nd	3rd	Unpl	Per cent	£1 Level Stake
Hurdles	27	0	1	3	23	-	- 27.00
Chases	23	3	6	2	12	13.0	- 8.68
Totals	50	3	7	5	35	6.0	- 35.68

W Fry	2-13	- 0.25		R Johnson	1-4	- 2.43
Market Rasen	1-3	+ 6.00		Newcastle	1-9	- 7.43
Southwell	1-6	- 2.25				

No of horses racing for the stable   15   Total winning prize-money   £11,111

K O CUNNINGHAM-BROWN (Stockbridge, Hants)

	Races Run	1st	2nd	3rd	Unpl	Per cent	£1 Level Stake
Hurdles	29	1	2	3	23	3.4	- 24.67
Chases	9	0	2	2	5	-	- 9.00
Totals	38	1	4	5	28	2.6	- 33.67

D Walsh	1-7	- 2.67		Fontwell	1-6	- 1.67

No of horses racing for the stable   10   Total winning prize-money   £1,977

B J CURLEY (Stetchworth, Cambs)

	Races Run	1st	2nd	3rd	Unpl	Per cent	£1 Level Stake
Hurdles	7	2	0	1	4	28.6	+ 1.75
Chases	0	0	0	0	0	-	0.00
Totals	7	2	0	1	4	28.6	+ 1.75

E Murphy	2-4	+ 4.75			
Folkestone	1-1	+ 4.00	Lingfield	1-2	+ 1.75

No of horses racing for the stable   4   Total winning prize-money   £4,412

J W P CURTIS (Beeford, North Humberside)

	Races Run	1st	2nd	3rd	Unpl	Per cent	£1 Level Stake
Hurdles	18	1	0	2	15	5.6	- 3.00
Chases	38	1	7	6	24	2.6	- 33.00
Totals	56	2	7	8	39	3.6	- 36.00

L O'Hara	2-26	- 6.00	Sedgefield	2-11	+ 9.00

No of horses racing for the stable   10   Total winning prize-money   £6,471

R CURTIS (Lambourn, Berks)

	Races Run	1st	2nd	3rd	Unpl	Per cent	£1 Level Stake
Hurdles	40	5	3	3	29	12.5	+ 10.83
Chases	47	11	10	6	20	23.4	- 10.81
Totals	87	16	13	9	49	18.4	+ 0.02

BY MONTH

	W-R	Per cent	£1 Level Stake		W-R	Per cent	£1 Level Stake
June	1-2	50.0	+ 3.50	December	2-7	28.6	+ 7.75
July	0-0	-	0.00	January	0-8	-	- 8.00
August	1-5	20.0	- 1.00	February	0-9	-	- 9.00
September	0-5	-	- 5.00	March	2-12	16.7	+ 10.00
October	0-8	-	- 8.00	April	3-12	25.0	- 1.79
November	2-9	22.2	- 4.02	May	5-10	50.0	+ 15.58

DISTANCE

Hurdles	W-R	Per cent	£1 Level Stake	Chases	W-R	Per cent	£1 Level Stake
2m-2m 3f	0-16	-	- 16.00	2m-2m 3f	0-1	-	- 1.00
2m 4f-2m 7f	4-20	20.0	+ 25.33	2m 4f-2m 7f	4-15	26.7	- 3.89
3m +	1-4	25.0	+ 1.50	3m +	7-31	22.6	- 5.92

TYPE OF RACE

	W-R	Per cent	£1 Level Stake		W-R	Per cent	£1 Level Stake
Novice hurdles	1-17	5.9	- 11.50	Selling	1-3	33.3	+ 8.00
H'cap hurdles	2-13	15.4	+ 17.00	Amateur	1-2	50.0	+ 2.33
Novice chases	2-10	20.0	- 3.90	Hunter chases	0-0	-	0.00
H'cap chases	9-36	25.0	- 5.91	N H Flat	0-6	-	- 6.00

COURSE GRADE

	W-R	Per cent	£1 Level Stake
Group 1	1-17	5.9	- 14.90
Group 2	1-16	6.3	- 13.12
Group 3	6-34	17.6	- 11.07
Group 4	8-20	40.0	+ 39.11

FIRST TIME OUT

	W-R	Per cent	£1 Level Stake
Hurdles	0-12	-	- 12.00
Chases	0-7	-	- 7.00
Totals	0-19	-	- 19.00

JOCKEYS RIDING

	W-R	Per cent	£1 Level Stake		W-R	Per cent	£1 Level Stake
D Morris	7-54	13.0	- 30.51	S McNeill	1-1	100.0	+ 14.00
D Walsh	6-17	35.3	+ 16.20	G Crone	1-5	20.0	+ 6.00
Mr G Chanter	1-1	100.0	+ 3.33				

G E Tormey	0-2	M A Fitzgerald	0-1	Mr J Culloty	0-1
G Bradley	0-1	Major G F Wheeler	0-1	P Niven	0-1
J Titley	0-1	Mr G Shenkin	0-1		

COURSE RECORD

	Total W-R	Nov Hdles	H'cap Hdles	Nov Chses	H'cap Chses	Hunter Chses	N H Flat	£1 Level Stake
Ludlow	4-6	0-0	3-3	0-0	1-3	0-0	0-0	+ 42.00
Towcester	3-6	0-0	0-1	0-1	3-4	0-0	0-0	+ 3.01
Plumpton	3-13	0-3	0-1	1-1	2-8	0-0	0-0	- 3.65
Huntingdon	1-1	0-0	1-1	0-0	0-0	0-0	0-0	+ 3.33
Hereford	1-2	0-0	0-0	0-0	1-2	0-0	0-0	+ 0.10
Folkestone	1-4	0-1	0-1	0-0	1-2	0-0	0-0	- 0.25
Uttoxeter	1-5	1-3	0-1	0-0	0-1	0-0	0-0	+ 0.50
Sandown	1-6	0-1	0-0	1-2	0-2	0-0	0-1	- 3.90
Fontwell	1-10	0-2	0-2	0-2	1-3	0-0	0-1	- 7.12

Chepstow	0-5	Nottingham	0-2	Haydock	0-1
Kempton	0-4	Warwick	0-2	Leicester	0-1
Cheltenham	0-3	Wincanton	0-2	Newton Abbot	0-1
Ascot	0-2	Windsor	0-2	Stratford	0-1
Exeter	0-2	Bangor	0-1	Taunton	0-1
Fakenham	0-2	Doncaster	0-1	Worcester	0-1

WINNING HORSES

	Races Run	1st	2nd	3rd	Unpl	Win £
Oh So Handy	12	5	3	2	2	15,156
Equity Player	9	3	3	2	1	12,185
Hillwalk	11	2	2	0	7	8,425
Captain Coe	6	2	0	1	3	4,981
Funcheon Gale	7	1	1	1	4	3,173
Mirador	5	1	1	0	3	2,285
Express Travel	3	1	1	0	1	2,145
Kreef	7	1	0	0	6	1,958

WINNING OWNERS

	Races Won	Value £		Races Won	Value £
Mrs R A Smith	5	15,156	Mrs J Whitehead, J McGivern &		
The Mrs S Partnership	3	12,185	Two Kates	1	2,285
M L Shone	2	8,425	Michael J Low	1	2,145
Heart of the South Racing (2)	2	4,981	HJS Racing	1	1,958
Kings of the Road P'ship	1	3,173			

No of horses racing for the stable	20	Total winning prize-money	£50,308

Favourites	8-13	61.5%	+ 8.19	Average SP of winner	4.4/1
Longest win seq	2	Longest losing seq	27	Return on stakes invested	0.0%

1994/95 Form	3-66	4.5%	- 52.50	1992/93 Form	14-119	11.8%	- 57.42
1993/94 Form	7-97	7.2%	- 66.37	1991/92 Form	7-96	7.3%	- 36.04

T A K CUTHBERT (Little Corby, Cumbria)

	Races Run	1st	2nd	3rd	Unpl	Per cent	£1 Level Stake
Hurdles	21	0	2	2	17	-	- 21.00
Chases	12	1	0	4	7	8.3	- 9.00
Totals	33	1	2	6	24	3.0	- 30.00

P Niven	1-4	- 1.00	Market Rasen	1-4	- 1.00

No of horses racing for the stable	6	Total winning prize-money	£7,035

P T DALTON (Bretby, Derbys)

	Races Run	1st	2nd	3rd	Unpl	Per cent	£1 Level Stake
Hurdles	8	0	1	0	7	-	- 8.00
Chases	21	2	2	2	15	9.5	- 10.67
Totals	29	2	3	2	22	6.9	- 18.67

C Maude	2-5	+ 5.33		
Haydock	1-3	+ 1.33	Uttoxeter	1-8	- 2.00

No of horses racing for the stable   8   Total winning prize-money   £7,756

VICTOR DARTNALL (Barnstaple, Devon)

	Races Run	1st	2nd	3rd	Unpl	Per cent	£1 Level Stake
Hurdles	0	0	0	0	0	-	0.00
Chases	4	4	0	0	0	100.0	+ 9.80
Totals	4	4	0	0	0	100.0	+ 9.80

Mr Richard White	2-2	+ 8.00	Mr N Harris	2-2	+ 1.80
Exeter	1-1	+ 2.50	Fontwell	1-1	+ 1.00
Folkestone	1-1	+ 0.80	Wetherby	1-1	+ 5.50

No of horses racing for the stable   2   Total winning prize-money   £6,789

D J S FFRENCH DAVIS (Upper Lambourn, Berks)

	Races Run	1st	2nd	3rd	Unpl	Per cent	£1 Level Stake
Hurdles	26	1	1	2	22	3.8	- 20.00
Chases	5	0	0	2	3	-	- 5.00
Totals	31	1	1	4	25	3.2	- 25.00

S McNeill	1-6	0.00	Stratford	1-4	+ 2.00

No of horses racing for the stable   11   Total winning prize-money   £3,633

R DENCH (Whitstable, Kent)

	Races Run	1st	2nd	3rd	Unpl	Per cent	£1 Level Stake
Hurdles	0	0	0	0	0	-	0.00
Chases	2	1	0	0	1	50.0	+ 3.00
Totals	2	1	0	0	1	50.0	+ 3.00

Mr P Hickman	1-1	+ 4.00	Folkestone	1-1	+ 4.00

No of horses racing for the stable   1   Total winning prize-money   £1,839

MRS JILL DENNIS (Bude, Cornwall)

	Races Run	1st	2nd	3rd	Unpl	Per cent	£1 Level Stake
Hurdles	0	0	0	0	0	-	0.00
Chases	5	1	1	1	2	20.0	+ 0.50
Totals	5	1	1	1	2	20.0	+ 0.50

Mr T Dennis	1-2	+ 3.50	Wincanton	1-1	+ 4.50

No of horses racing for the stable   2   Total winning prize-money   £1,970

R DICKIN (Stratford-upon-Avon, Warwicks)

	Races Run	1st	2nd	3rd	Unpl	Per cent	£1 Level Stake
Hurdles	55	1	1	2	51	1.8	- 52.62
Chases	74	9	12	10	43	12.2	- 24.29
Totals	129	10	13	12	94	7.8	- 76.91

BY MONTH

	W-R	Per cent	£1 Level Stake		W-R	Per cent	£1 Level Stake
June	0-5	-	- 5.00	December	0-10	-	- 10.00
July	1-6	16.7	- 3.62	January	0-12	-	- 12.00
August	2-3	66.7	+ 1.21	February	0-12	-	- 12.00
September	1-10	10.0	- 5.50	March	1-22	4.5	- 16.50
October	2-9	22.2	- 0.50	April	1-14	7.1	- 3.00
November	1-11	9.1	- 1.00	May	1-15	6.7	- 9.00

DISTANCE

Hurdles	W-R	Per cent	£1 Level Stake	Chases	W-R	Per cent	£1 Level Stake
2m-2m 3f	1-43	2.3	- 40.62	2m-2m 3f	6-40	15.0	- 0.62
2m 4f-2m 7f	0-5	-	- 5.00	2m 4f-2m 7f	2-14	14.3	- 7.67
3m +	0-7	-	- 7.00	3m +	1-20	5.0	- 16.00

Dickin R

TYPE OF RACE

	W-R	Per cent	£1 Level Stake		W-R	Per cent	£1 Level Stake
Novice hurdles	0-20	-	- 20.00	Selling	0-4	-	- 4.00
H'cap hurdles	1-27	3.7	- 24.62	Amateur	1-3	33.3	+ 1.00
Novice chases	2-15	13.3	- 10.79	Hunter chases	0-0	-	0.00
H'cap chases	6-56	10.7	- 14.50	N H Flat	0-4	-	- 4.00

COURSE GRADE

	W-R	Per cent	£1 Level Stake
Group 1	1-26	3.8	- 22.00
Group 2	1-13	7.7	- 8.50
Group 3	3-50	6.0	- 30.62
Group 4	5-40	12.5	- 15.79

FIRST TIME OUT

	W-R	Per cent	£1 Level Stake
Hurdles	0-18	-	- 18.00
Chases	1-9	11.1	- 4.50
Totals	1-27	3.7	- 22.50

JOCKEYS RIDING

	W-R	Per cent	£1 Level Stake		W-R	Per cent	£1 Level Stake
Mr R Thornton	2-4	50.0	+ 5.50	D Leahy	1-3	33.3	+ 1.50
Mr J Culloty	2-12	16.7	+ 5.00	R Dunwoody	1-6	16.7	+ 4.00
D Meredith	2-45	4.4	- 38.12	B Powell	1-12	8.3	- 9.62
A P McCoy	1-3	33.3	- 1.17				

Philip Hughes	0-19	N Williamson	0-2	Miss S Duckett	0-1
R Bellamy	0-9	A Maguire	0-1	Mr M Brennan	0-1
D Byrne	0-6	A Thornton	0-1	P Niven	0-1
M A Fitzgerald	0-2	D Bridgwater	0-1		

COURSE RECORD

	Total W-R	Nov Hdles	H'cap Hdles	Nov Chses	H'cap Chses	Hunter Chses	N H Flat	£1 Level Stake
Market Rasen	2-7	0-0	0-2	0-0	2-5	0-0	0-0	+ 10.00
Bangor	2-7	0-0	1-1	1-2	0-4	0-0	0-0	- 2.79
Hereford	2-10	0-4	0-1	0-2	2-3	0-0	0-0	+ 5.50
Newton Abbot	1-4	0-1	0-0	0-0	1-3	0-0	0-0	+ 0.50
Fakenham	1-7	0-1	0-0	0-2	1-4	0-0	0-0	- 2.50
Cheltenham	1-8	0-1	0-2	0-2	1-3	0-0	0-0	- 4.00
Worcester	1-16	0-5	0-4	1-3	0-4	0-0	0-0	- 13.62

Newbury	0-9	Nottingham	0-4	Kempton	0-2
Towcester	0-8	Uttoxeter	0-4	Taunton	0-2
Stratford	0-6	Warwick	0-4	Haydock	0-1
Ludlow	0-5	Plumpton	0-3	Newcastle	0-1
Chepstow	0-4	Aintree	0-2	Sandown	0-1
Fontwell	0-4	Ascot	0-2	Southwell	0-1
Leicester	0-4	Huntingdon	0-2	Wetherby	0-1

WINNING HORSES

	Races Run	1st	2nd	3rd	Unpl	Win £
Bally Parson	10	2	0	1	7	7,829
Sagaman	8	2	2	2	2	6,356
Lodestone Lad	3	1	0	1	1	4,031
Dr Rocket	17	1	4	4	8	3,534
K C's Dancer	8	1	1	0	6	3,469
Hurryup	10	1	1	0	8	3,354
Ketford Bridge	1	1	0	0	0	2,583
Dubai Falcon	5	1	1	0	3	2,169

WINNING OWNERS

	Races Won	Value £		Races Won	Value £
G Hutsby	2	7,829	King of Clubs Ltd (Gloucester)	1	3,469
Michael Doocey	2	6,356	Allan Bennett	1	3,354
Mrs D L Weaver	1	4,031	Mrs T L Benge	1	2,583
The Rocketeers	1	3,534	H Burford	1	2,169

No of horses racing for the stable	27	Total winning prize-money		£33,325
Favourites	4-14 28.6% - 3.41	Average SP of winner		4.2/1
Longest win seq	2 Longest losing seq 44	Return on stakes invested		-59.6%
1994/95 Form	12-166 7.2% -115.18	1992/93 Form	15-123 12.2%	- 42.16
1993/94 Form	12-130 9.2% - 37.37	1991/92 Form	17-168 10.1%	- 14.42

J E DIXON (Thursby, Cumbria)

	Races Run	1st	2nd	3rd	Unpl	Per cent	£1 Level Stake
Hurdles	20	1	1	1	17	5.0	- 10.00
Chases	9	0	1	0	8	-	- 9.00
Totals	29	1	2	1	25	3.4	- 19.00

B Storey	1-18 - 8.00	Carlisle	1-6	+ 4.00
No of horses racing for the stable	6	Total winning prize-money		£1,744

J P DODDS (Chatton, Northumberland)

	Races Run	1st	2nd	3rd	Unpl	Per cent	£1 Level Stake
Hurdles	25	1	6	0	18	4.0	- 21.75
Chases	8	0	1	0	7	-	- 8.00
Totals	33	1	7	0	25	3.0	- 29.75

Richard Guest	1-19 - 15.75	Perth	1-5	- 1.75
No of horses racing for the stable	9	Total winning prize-money		£2,961

M DODS (Piercebridge, Co Durham)

	Races Run	1st	2nd	3rd	Unpl	Per cent	£1 Level Stake
Hurdles	17	1	1	1	14	5.9	- 13.00
Chases	6	0	0	0	6	-	- 6.00
Totals	23	1	1	1	20	4.3	- 19.00

B Storey	1-5	- 1.00	Kelso	1-2	+ 2.00

No of horses racing for the stable   5   Total winning prize-money   £2,697

T W DONNELLY (Swadlincote, Derbys)

	Races Run	1st	2nd	3rd	Unpl	Per cent	£1 Level Stake
Hurdles	27	3	3	3	18	11.1	- 13.17
Chases	0	0	0	0	0	-	0.00
Totals	27	3	3	3	18	11.1	- 13.17

Mr R Armson	2-10	- 0.50	T Eley	1-9	- 4.67
Carlisle	1-1	+ 4.50	Uttoxeter	1-7	- 2.67
Musselburgh	1-1	+ 3.00			

No of horses racing for the stable   6   Total winning prize-money   £7,407

S DOW (Epsom, Surrey)

	Races Run	1st	2nd	3rd	Unpl	Per cent	£1 Level Stake
Hurdles	48	3	1	5	39	6.3	- 26.50
Chases	6	1	1	1	3	16.7	- 3.50
Totals	54	4	2	6	42	7.4	- 30.00

R Dunwoody	2-8	+ 3.00	A Dicken	1-23	- 14.00
D Bridgwater	1-4	0.00			
Sandown	2-8	+ 3.00	Cheltenham	1-7	- 3.00
Towcester	1-3	+ 6.00			

No of horses racing for the stable   17   Total winning prize-money   £50,100

MISS J S DOYLE (Eastbury, Berks)

	Races Run	1st	2nd	3rd	Unpl	Per cent	£1 Level Stake
Hurdles	40	3	4	2	31	7.5	- 21.75
Chases	0	0	0	0	0	-	0.00
Totals	40	3	4	2	31	7.5	- 21.75

S Curran	2-35	- 25.75	S McNeill	1-3	+ 6.00
Huntingdon	1-1	+ 2.75	Newbury	1-5	+ 0.50
Stratford	1-5	+ 4.00			

No of horses racing for the stable   9   Total winning prize-money   £8,532

J M DUN (Heriot, Borders)

	Races Run	1st	2nd	3rd	Unpl	Per cent	£1 Level Stake
Hurdles	15	3	0	2	10	20.0	+ 36.50
Chases	0	0	0	0	0	-	0.00
Totals	15	3	0	2	10	20.0	+ 36.50

D Parker	2-11	+ 6.50	Mr M H Naughton	1-1	+ 33.00
Kelso	2-6	+ 11.50	Hexham	1-2	+ 32.00

No of horses racing for the stable   3   Total winning prize-money   £7,176

T D C DUN (Heriot, Borders)

	Races Run	1st	2nd	3rd	Unpl	Per cent	£1 Level Stake
Hurdles	0	0	0	0	0	-	0.00
Chases	13	1	0	1	11	7.7	- 4.00
Totals	13	1	0	1	11	7.7	- 4.00

T Reed	1-7	+ 2.00	Ayr	1-5	+ 4.00

No of horses racing for the stable   2   Total winning prize-money   £3,096

A J K DUNN (Allerford, Somerset)

	Races Run	1st	2nd	3rd	Unpl	Per cent	£1 Level Stake
Hurdles	14	1	1	3	9	7.1	- 11.90
Chases	5	0	0	0	5	-	- 5.00
Totals	19	1	1	3	14	5.3	- 16.90

Peter Hobbs	1-5	- 2.90	Exeter	1-2	+ 0.10

No of horses racing for the stable   7   Total winning prize-money   £2,716

MRS P N DUTFIELD (Axmouth, Devon)

	Races Run	1st	2nd	3rd	Unpl	Per cent	£1 Level Stake
Hurdles	24	1	0	2	21	4.2	- 19.50
Chases	11	0	1	2	8	-	- 11.00
Totals	35	1	1	4	29	2.9	- 30.50

P Holley	1-18	- 13.50	Exeter	1-5	- 0.50

No of horses racing for the stable   14   Total winning prize-money   £1,916

C DWYER (Newmarket, Suffolk)

	Races Run	1st	2nd	3rd	Unpl	Per cent	£1 Level Stake
Hurdles	2	1	0	0	1	50.0	+ 0.20
Chases	0	0	0	0	0	-	0.00
Totals	2	1	0	0	1	50.0	+ 0.20

V Smith	1-2	+ 0.20	Plumpton	1-1	+ 1.20

No of horses racing for the stable   2   Total winning prize-money   £2,122

T DYER (Invergowrie, Tayside)

	Races Run	1st	2nd	3rd	Unpl	Per cent	£1 Level Stake
Hurdles	123	7	12	10	94	5.7	- 87.04
Chases	16	0	2	2	12	-	- 16.00
Totals	139	7	14	12	106	5.0	-103.04

BY MONTH

	W-R	Per cent	£1 Level Stake		W-R	Per cent	£1 Level Stake
June	0-2	-	- 2.00	December	2-9	22.2	+ 6.25
July	0-3	-	- 3.00	January	1-18	5.6	- 15.37
August	2-4	50.0	+ 4.83	February	1-19	5.3	- 15.75
September	0-11	-	- 11.00	March	0-19	-	- 19.00
October	0-10	-	- 10.00	April	0-15	-	- 15.00
November	1-21	4.8	- 15.00	May	0-8	-	- 8.00

DISTANCE

	W-R	Per cent	£1 Level Stake		W-R	Per cent	£1 Level Stake
Hurdles				Chases			
2m-2m 3f	6-99	6.1	- 67.37	2m-2m 3f	0-12	-	- 12.00
2m 4f-2m 7f	0-18	-	- 18.00	2m 4f-2m 7f	0-4	-	- 4.00
3m +	1-6	16.7	- 1.67	3m +	0-0	-	0.00

TYPE OF RACE

	W-R	Per cent	£1 Level Stake		W-R	Per cent	£1 Level Stake
Novice hurdles	2-47	4.3	- 40.04	Selling	1-24	4.2	- 19.50
H'cap hurdles	4-48	8.3	- 23.50	Amateur	0-4	-	- 4.00
Novice chases	0-9	-	- 9.00	Hunter chases	0-0	-	0.00
H'cap chases	0-5	-	- 5.00	N H Flat	0-2	-	- 2.00

COURSE GRADE / FIRST TIME OUT

	W-R	Per cent	£1 Level Stake		W-R	Per cent	£1 Level Stake
Group 1	1-38	2.6	- 35.37	Hurdles	1-25	4.0	- 20.67
Group 2	0-3	-	- 3.00	Chases	0-1	-	- 1.00
Group 3	1-16	6.3	- 3.00				
Group 4	5-82	6.1	- 61.67	Totals	1-26	3.8	- 21.67

JOCKEYS RIDING

	W-R	Per cent	£1 Level Stake		W-R	Per cent	£1 Level Stake
L Wyer	2-12	16.7	- 3.75	Peter Hobbs	2-22	9.1	- 13.17
A Dobbin	2-21	9.5	- 15.12	J Callaghan	1-8	12.5	+ 5.00

	W-R		W-R		W-R
A Linton	0-31	P Niven	0-3	M Foster	0-1
B Harding	0-8	B Fenton	0-2	Mr R Hale	0-1
B Storey	0-8	D Parker	0-2	Mrs A Farrell	0-1
E Callaghan	0-4	Mr J McGurgan	0-2	R Dunwoody	0-1
F Leahy	0-4	P G Cahill	0-2		
R McGrath	0-4	Richard Guest	0-2		

COURSE RECORD

	Total W-R	Nov Hdles	H'cap Hdles	Nov Chses	H'cap Chses	Hunter Chses	N H Flat	£1 Level Stake
Hexham	2-10	0-2	2-7	0-0	0-1	0-0	0-0	- 1.75
Perth	2-27	1-14	1-9	0-3	0-0	0-0	0-1	- 18.17
Catterick	1-10	0-2	1-7	0-0	0-1	0-0	0-0	+ 3.00
Kelso	1-16	0-7	1-7	0-1	0-1	0-0	0-0	- 12.75
Ayr	1-22	1-12	0-9	0-0	0-1	0-0	0-0	- 19.37

Musselburgh	0-11	Bangor 0-4	Worcester 0-3
Carlisle	0-9	Cartmel 0-3	Cheltenham 0-2
Newcastle	0-8	Market Rasen 0-3	Sedgefield 0-2
Haydock	0-5	Wetherby 0-3	Aintree 0-1

WINNING HORSES

	Races Run	1st	2nd	3rd	Unpl	Win £
Rachael's Owen	11	3	2	1	5	6,485
Stash The Cash	15	2	6	0	7	5,050
Marco Magnifico	11	1	0	2	8	2,140
Tony's Feelings	8	1	0	1	6	2,138

WINNING OWNERS

	Races Won	Value £		Races Won	Value £
Mrs Linda Dyer	3	6,433	S Bruce	2	4,330
G Shiel	2	5,050			

No of horses racing for the stable	26	Total winning prize-money	£15,813

Favourites	2-8	25.0% - 2.50	Average SP of winner	4.1/1
Longest win seq	1	Longest losing seq 51	Return on stakes invested	-74.1%

1994/95 Form	6-65	9.2% - 24.25	1992/93 Form	6-64	9.4% - 37.00
1993/94 Form	4-59	6.8% - 41.04	1991/92 Form	0-1	

SIMON EARLE (Sturminster Newton, Dorset)

	Races Run	1st	2nd	3rd	Unpl	Per cent	£1 Level Stake
Hurdles	22	0	1	1	20	-	- 22.00
Chases	26	6	3	2	15	23.1	+ 1.66
Totals	48	6	4	3	35	12.5	- 20.34

B Powell	3-10 + 8.41	S Earle	1-1 + 1.75
C Maude	2-19 - 12.50		

Cheltenham	2-3 + 5.75	Sandown	1-3 - 1.09
Fontwell	1-1 + 10.00	Worcester	1-6 - 3.25
Plumpton	1-1 + 2.25		

No of horses racing for the stable	18	Total winning prize-money	£29,938

M H EASTERBY (Great Habton, North Yorks)

	Races Run	1st	2nd	3rd	Unpl	Per cent	£1 Level Stake
Hurdles	74	19	11	8	36	25.7	- 5.65
Chases	21	9	4	5	3	42.9	+ 6.46
Totals	95	28	15	13	39	29.5	+ 0.81

BY MONTH

	W-R	Per cent	£1 Level Stake		W-R	Per cent	£1 Level Stake
June	0-0	-	0.00	December	7-21	33.3	- 2.79
July	0-1	-	- 1.00	January	7-28	25.0	- 9.33
August	0-0	-	0.00	February	0-0	-	0.00
September	1-5	20.0	+ 4.00	March	0-0	-	0.00
October	6-15	40.0	+ 13.70	April	0-0	-	0.00
November	7-25	28.0	- 3.77	May	0-0	-	0.00

DISTANCE

Hurdles	W-R	Per cent	£1 Level Stake	Chases	W-R	Per cent	£1 Level Stake
2m-2m 3f	14-55	25.5	- 2.95	2m-2m 3f	2-5	40.0	- 0.27
2m 4f-2m 7f	4-14	28.6	+ 0.94	2m 4f-2m 7f	2-6	33.3	- 1.00
3m +	1-5	20.0	- 3.64	3m +	5-10	50.0	+ 7.73

TYPE OF RACE

	W-R	Per cent	£1 Level Stake		W-R	Per cent	£1 Level Stake
Novice hurdles	11-40	27.5	+ 4.75	Selling	0-0	-	0.00
H'cap hurdles	7-29	24.1	- 7.90	Amateur	0-0	-	0.00
Novice chases	3-9	33.3	- 1.77	Hunter chases	0-0	-	0.00
H'cap chases	6-12	50.0	+ 8.23	N H Flat	1-5	20.0	- 2.50

COURSE GRADE / FIRST TIME OUT

	W-R	Per cent	£1 Level Stake		W-R	Per cent	£1 Level Stake
Group 1	12-42	28.6	- 7.04	Hurdles	3-24	12.5	- 3.00
Group 2	10-26	38.5	+ 12.39	Chases	2-5	40.0	+ 0.50
Group 3	1-12	8.3	- 7.50				
Group 4	5-15	33.3	+ 2.96	Totals	5-29	17.2	- 2.50

JOCKEYS RIDING

	W-R	Per cent	£1 Level Stake		W-R	Per cent	£1 Level Stake
L Wyer	23-74	31.1	+ 0.93	R Garrity	5-11	45.5	+ 9.88

F Leahy	0-3	B Fenton	0-1	Richard Guest	0-1
A Dobbin	0-1	G Lee	0-1	W Marston	0-1
A S Smith	0-1	J Callaghan	0-1		

COURSE RECORD

	Total W-R	Nov Hdles	H'cap Hdles	Nov Chses	H'cap Chses	Hunter Chses	N H Flat	£1 Level Stake
Wetherby	10-25	6-15	0-4	2-2	2-4	0-0	0-0	+ 13.39
Haydock	5-14	1-6	2-2	0-1	2-3	0-0	0-2	+ 1.63
Carlisle	2-5	0-1	1-3	0-0	0-0	0-0	1-1	- 0.40
Doncaster	2-5	0-0	1-3	0-0	1-1	0-0	0-1	+ 0.10
Sedgefield	2-7	2-4	0-1	0-2	0-0	0-0	0-0	+ 5.00
Newcastle	2-12	1-6	1-4	0-1	0-1	0-0	0-0	- 6.50
Hexham	1-1	1-1	0-0	0-0	0-0	0-0	0-0	+ 0.36
Warwick	1-1	0-0	0-0	0-0	1-1	0-0	0-0	+ 3.50
Sandown	1-2	0-0	1-2	0-0	0-0	0-0	0-0	+ 2.50
Aintree	1-2	0-0	1-2	0-0	0-0	0-0	0-0	+ 0.50
Ascot	1-3	0-0	0-1	1-2	0-0	0-0	0-0	- 1.27

Market Rasen	0-6	Bangor	0-1	Kempton	0-1
Catterick	0-4	Chepstow	0-1	Nottingham	0-1
Cheltenham	0-3	Kelso	0-1		

WINNING HORSES

	Races Run	1st	2nd	3rd	Unpl	Win £
Scotton Banks	5	4	1	0	0	37,782
Simply Dashing	6	5	1	0	0	22,016
Thornton Gate	7	4	1	0	2	18,299
Cumbrian Challenge	7	3	1	3	0	14,798
Toogood To Be True	5	2	1	1	1	11,526
Shining Edge	4	1	0	1	2	7,908
Chopwell Curtains	7	3	1	1	2	7,067
Golden Hello	3	1	0	0	2	5,109
Durham Drapes	3	1	1	0	1	3,729
Dawn Mission	4	1	1	1	1	3,050
Dally Boy	4	1	2	1	0	2,728
Balhernoch	3	1	1	1	0	2,495
Rye Crossing	5	1	2	0	2	2,234

WINNING OWNERS

	Races Won	Value £		Races Won	Value £
I Bray	4	37,782	G Graham	1	7,908
Steve Hammond	5	22,016	G E Shouler	1	5,109
T H Bennett	5	21,027	Mrs Jennifer E Pallister	1	3,050
Cumbrian Industrials Ltd	3	14,798	I Bell	1	2,495
Jim McGrath	2	11,526	C H Stevens	1	2,234
Durham Drapes Ltd	4	10,796			

No of horses racing for the stable	29	Total winning prize-money	£138,741

Favourites	18-30	60.0%	+ 12.06	Average SP of winner	2.4/1
Longest win seq	3	Longest losing seq	9	Return on stakes invested	0.9%

1994/95 Form	17-154	11.0%	- 87.96	1992/93 Form	39-218	17.9%	- 18.18
1993/94 Form	31-138	22.5%	+ 20.63	1991/92 Form	42-203	20.7%	- 56.24

M W EASTERBY (Sheriff Hutton, North Yorks)

	Races Run	1st	2nd	3rd	Unpl	Per cent	£1 Level Stake
Hurdles	66	7	2	9	48	10.6	- 31.93
Chases	34	6	7	6	15	17.6	0.00
Totals	100	13	9	15	63	13.0	- 31.93

BY MONTH

	W-R	Per cent	£1 Level Stake		W-R	Per cent	£1 Level Stake
June	1-2	50.0	+ 4.50	December	0-11	-	- 11.00
July	0-2	-	- 2.00	January	3-17	17.6	+ 6.50
August	0-1	-	- 1.00	February	3-14	21.4	- 2.00
September	0-4	-	- 4.00	March	3-16	18.8	- 6.18
October	0-9	-	- 9.00	April	2-8	25.0	+ 1.25
November	0-11	-	- 11.00	May	1-5	20.0	+ 2.00

DISTANCE

Hurdles	W-R	Per cent	£1 Level Stake	Chases	W-R	Per cent	£1 Level Stake
2m-2m 3f	6-48	12.5	- 16.18	2m-2m 3f	3-13	23.1	+ 5.00
2m 4f-2m 7f	1-17	5.9	- 14.75	2m 4f-2m 7f	2-8	25.0	+ 3.50
3m +	0-1	-	- 1.00	3m +	1-13	7.7	- 8.50

TYPE OF RACE

	W-R	Per cent	£1 Level Stake		W-R	Per cent	£1 Level Stake
Novice hurdles	3-33	9.1	- 25.68	Selling	0-0	-	0.00
H'cap hurdles	3-26	11.5	- 3.00	Amateur	0-0	-	0.00
Novice chases	1-10	10.0	- 5.50	Hunter chases	0-1	-	- 1.00
H'cap chases	5-23	21.7	+ 6.50	N H Flat	1-7	14.3	- 3.25

COURSE GRADE / FIRST TIME OUT

	W-R	Per cent	£1 Level Stake		W-R	Per cent	£1 Level Stake
Group 1	5-31	16.1	- 2.75	Hurdles	1-25	4.0	- 18.50
Group 2	3-26	11.5	- 9.75	Chases	0-5	-	- 5.00
Group 3	2-25	8.0	- 14.00				
Group 4	3-18	16.7	- 5.43	Totals	1-30	3.3	- 23.50

JOCKEYS RIDING

	W-R	Per cent	£1 Level Stake		W-R	Per cent	£1 Level Stake
R Garrity	7-27	25.9	+ 17.00	B Harding	1-4	25.0	- 1.75
A Thornton	3-5	60.0	+ 4.82	R Dunwoody	1-5	20.0	+ 0.50
N Williamson	1-1	100.0	+ 5.50				

J Driscoll	0-15	P Niven	0-3	A S Smith	0-1
M Dwyer	0-6	W Marston	0-3	C F Swan	0-1
M A Fitzgerald	0-4	B Fenton	0-2	G Lee	0-1
E Callaghan	0-3	J Supple	0-2	G Ryan	0-1
E Husband	0-3	J Titley	0-2	J Callaghan	0-1
Mr J Culloty	0-3	L Wyer	0-2		
Mr S Swiers	0-3	O Pears	0-2		

COURSE RECORD

	Total W-R	Nov Hdles	H'cap Hdles	Nov Chses	H'cap Chses	Hunter Chses	N H Flat	£1 Level Stake
Newcastle	4-11	1-3	1-4	0-0	1-3	0-0	1-1	+ 11.75
Wetherby	3-26	1-8	0-10	0-1	2-5	0-1	0-1	- 9.75
Sedgefield	2-9	0-1	0-1	0-2	2-3	0-0	0-2	+ 2.00
Stratford	1-2	0-1	1-1	0-0	0-0	0-0	0-0	+ 4.50
Hexham	1-7	1-2	0-2	0-1	0-1	0-0	0-1	- 5.43
Market Rasen	1-10	0-1	0-1	1-5	0-2	0-0	0-1	- 5.50
Haydock	1-16	0-10	1-5	0-0	0-1	0-0	0-0	- 10.50

Catterick	0-5	Carlisle		0-1	Newbury	0-1
Leicester	0-4	Cheltenham		0-1	Nottingham	0-1
Doncaster	0-2	Huntingdon		0-1		
Uttoxeter	0-2	Kelso		0-1		

WINNING HORSES

	Races Run	1st	2nd	3rd	Unpl	Win £
Issyin	7	2	0	3	2	8,269
Tresidder	10	2	1	0	7	6,944
Purevalue	7	2	1	1	3	6,288
Circus Line	5	2	0	0	3	5,247
Silver Stick	8	1	2	2	3	4,811
Aljadeer	7	1	2	2	2	3,925
Admirals Seat	3	1	0	0	2	3,048
Auburn Boy	1	1	0	0	0	2,819
Southern Cross	3	1	0	1	1	1,637

WINNING OWNERS

	Races Won	Value £		Races Won	Value £
Mrs H Brown	2	8,269	Mrs P A H Hartley	2	5,247
S H J Brewer	2	6,944	Lord Manton	1	4,811
A D Simmons	2	6,288	Miss V Foster	1	3,925
G E Shouler	2	5,867	R O M Racing	1	1,637

No of horses racing for the stable		31	Total winning prize-money	£42,988

Favourites	4-14	28.6%	- 3.68	Average SP of winner		4.2/1
Longest win seq	2	Longest losing seq	46	Return on stakes invested		-31.9%

1994/95 Form	10-102	9.8%	- 60.31	1992/93 Form	11-113	9.7%	- 62.18
1993/94 Form	11-114	9.6%	- 68.33	1991/92 Form	22-108	20.4%	+ 7.50

T D EASTERBY (Great Habton, North Yorks)

	Races Run	1st	2nd	3rd	Unpl	Per cent	£1 Level Stake
Hurdles	74	11	13	5	45	14.9	- 18.02
Chases	10	3	1	0	6	30.0	+ 2.25
Totals	84	14	14	5	51	16.7	- 15.77

BY MONTH

	W-R	Per cent	£1 Level Stake		W-R	Per cent	£1 Level Stake
June	0-0	-	0.00	December	0-0	-	0.00
July	0-0	-	0.00	January	0-0	-	0.00
August	0-0	-	0.00	February	5-32	15.6	- 6.25
September	0-0	-	0.00	March	6-23	26.1	+ 9.38
October	0-0	-	0.00	April	3-19	15.8	- 8.90
November	0-0	-	0.00	May	0-10	-	- 10.00

DISTANCE

Hurdles	W-R	Per cent	£1 Level Stake	Chases	W-R	Per cent	£1 Level Stake
2m-2m 3f	9-58	15.5	- 12.02	2m-2m 3f	1-3	33.3	+ 0.75
2m 4f-2m 7f	2-15	13.3	- 5.00	2m 4f-2m 7f	0-0	-	0.00
3m +	0-1	-	- 1.00	3m +	2-7	28.6	+ 1.50

TYPE OF RACE

	W-R	Per cent	£1 Level Stake		W-R	Per cent	£1 Level Stake
Novice hurdles	5-26	19.2	- 5.15	Selling	0-1	-	- 1.00
H'cap hurdles	5-41	12.2	- 15.37	Amateur	0-0	-	0.00
Novice chases	1-3	33.3	+ 2.50	Hunter chases	0-0	-	0.00
H'cap chases	2-7	28.6	- 0.25	N H Flat	1-6	16.7	+ 3.50

COURSE GRADE

	W-R	Per cent	£1 Level Stake
Group 1	4-35	11.4	- 15.87
Group 2	4-13	30.8	+ 6.75
Group 3	2-14	14.3	- 1.50
Group 4	4-22	18.2	- 5.15

FIRST TIME OUT

	W-R	Per cent	£1 Level Stake
Hurdles	0-2	-	- 2.00
Chases	0-0	-	0.00
Totals	0-2	-	- 2.00

JOCKEYS RIDING

	W-R	Per cent	£1 Level Stake		W-R	Per cent	£1 Level Stake
L Wyer	12-58	20.7	+ 3.13	R Garrity	1-10	10.0	- 5.00
P Niven	1-1	100.0	+ 1.10				

B Harding	0-3	A P McCoy		0-1	P Carberry	0-1
J Callaghan	0-3	A S Smith		0-1	R Johnson	0-1
B Fenton	0-2	F Leahy		0-1		
A J Roche	0-1	M A Fitzgerald		0-1		

COURSE RECORD

	Total W-R	Nov Hdles	H'cap Hdles	Nov Chses	H'cap Chses	Hunter Chses	N H Flat	£1 Level Stake
Wetherby	4-13	0-5	2-6	0-0	2-2	0-0	0-0	+ 6.75
Ayr	3-8	1-3	2-4	0-0	0-1	0-0	0-0	+ 5.63
Sedgefield	2-9	1-5	1-4	0-0	0-0	0-0	0-0	+ 2.00
Warwick	1-1	1-1	0-0	0-0	0-0	0-0	0-0	+ 2.00
Hexham	1-4	1-2	0-2	0-0	0-0	0-0	0-0	- 0.25
Catterick	1-4	0-0	0-2	0-0	0-0	0-0	1-2	+ 5.50
Kelso	1-5	1-3	0-2	0-0	0-0	0-0	0-0	- 2.90
Aintree	1-5	0-1	0-2	1-2	0-0	0-0	0-0	+ 0.50

Newcastle	0-7	Perth	0-2	Newbury	0-1
Haydock	0-6	Ascot	0-1	Nottingham	0-1
Uttoxeter	0-6	Bangor	0-1	Sandown	0-1
Doncaster	0-4	Carlisle	0-1	Stratford	0-1
Cheltenham	0-2	Market Rasen	0-1		

WINNING HORSES

	Races Run	1st	2nd	3rd	Unpl	Win £
Scotton Banks	3	1	0	0	2	39,156
Simply Dashing	2	1	0	0	1	7,880
Toogood To Be True	4	1	1	0	2	6,783
Sharkashka	5	2	1	0	2	5,783
Shining Edge	8	2	2	3	1	5,764
Cumbrian Challenge	4	1	0	0	3	4,500
Generator	6	2	0	1	3	3,389
Current Speech	7	1	2	0	4	3,020
Balhernoch	4	1	0	0	3	2,775
Cumbrian Rhapsody	3	1	0	0	2	2,637
Bridle Path	6	1	0	0	5	2,408

WINNING OWNERS

	Races Won	Value £		Races Won	Value £
I Bray	1	39,156	G Graham	2	5,764
C H Stevens	3	8,803	Mrs M H Easterby	2	3,389
Steve Hammond	1	7,880	I Bell	1	2,775
Cumbrian Industrials Ltd	2	7,137	Fred Wilson	1	2,408
Jim McGrath	1	6,783			

No of horses racing for the stable		21	Total winning prize-money	£84,095

Favourites	5-15	33.3%	- 0.27	Average SP of winner	3.9/1
Longest win seq	2	Longest losing seq	23	Return on stakes invested	-18.8%

P ECCLES (Lambourn, Berks)

	Races Run	1st	2nd	3rd	Unpl	Per cent	£1 Level Stake
Hurdles	16	1	2	0	13	6.3	- 11.50
Chases	16	4	3	1	8	25.0	- 7.50
Totals	32	5	5	1	21	15.6	- 19.00

A Maguire	2-4	- 0.63		R Johnson	1-3	- 0.25
A P McCoy	2-5	+ 1.88				
Huntingdon	1-1	+ 1.38		Windsor	1-2	+ 2.50
Fontwell	1-2	+ 0.75		Ludlow	1-4	- 2.20
Carlisle	1-2	- 0.43				

No of horses racing for the stable	9	Total winning prize-money	£13,445

B J ECKLEY (Llansbyddid, Powys)

	Races Run	1st	2nd	3rd	Unpl	Per cent	£1 Level Stake
Hurdles	7	1	1	2	3	14.3	+ 19.00
Chases	5	0	1	2	2	-	- 5.00
Totals	12	1	2	4	5	8.3	+ 14.00

R Bellamy	1-2	+ 24.00	Uttoxeter	1-2	+ 24.00

No of horses racing for the stable	2	Total winning prize-money	£2,484

R J ECKLEY (Lyonshall, H'ford & Worcs)

	Races Run	1st	2nd	3rd	Unpl	Per cent	£1 Level Stake
Hurdles	27	2	1	0	24	7.4	- 1.00
Chases	0	0	0	0	0	-	0.00
Totals	27	2	1	0	24	7.4	- 1.00

D Gallagher	1-1	+ 4.00	D Walsh	1-4	+ 17.00
Chepstow	1-2	+ 19.00	Hereford	1-10	- 5.00

No of horses racing for the stable	5	Total winning prize-money	£5,020

D EDDY (Ingoe, Northumberland)

	Races Run	1st	2nd	3rd	Unpl	Per cent	£1 Level Stake
Hurdles	24	0	4	1	19	-	- 24.00
Chases	12	2	0	2	8	16.7	+ 4.00
Totals	36	2	4	3	27	5.6	- 20.00

N Williamson	1-1	+ 7.00	J Callaghan	1-8	0.00
Stratford	1-1	+ 7.00	Market Rasen	1-2	+ 6.00

No of horses racing for the stable   11   Total winning prize-money   £6,456

G F EDWARDS (Wheddon Cross, Somerset)

	Races Run	1st	2nd	3rd	Unpl	Per cent	£1 Level Stake
Hurdles	31	4	4	5	18	12.9	- 2.50
Chases	2	0	0	2	0	-	- 2.00
Totals	33	4	4	7	18	12.1	- 4.50

M A Fitzgerald	3-11	+ 9.50	A P McCoy	1-7	+ 1.00
Exeter	3-7	+ 12.50	Newton Abbot	1-9	0.00

No of horses racing for the stable   4   Total winning prize-money   £8,962

G L EDWARDS (Telford, Salop)

	Races Run	1st	2nd	3rd	Unpl	Per cent	£1 Level Stake
Hurdles	0	0	0	0	0	-	0.00
Chases	2	1	0	1	0	50.0	+ 3.00
Totals	2	1	0	1	0	50.0	+ 3.00

Mr A Crow	1-2	+ 3.00	Bangor	1-1	+ 4.00

No of horses racing for the stable   1   Total winning prize-money   £2,736

J A C EDWARDS (Sellack, H'ford & Worcs)

	Races Run	1st	2nd	3rd	Unpl	Per cent	£1 Level Stake
Hurdles	95	3	5	10	77	3.2	- 84.92
Chases	35	7	4	5	19	20.0	- 4.67
Totals	130	10	9	15	96	7.7	- 89.59

BY MONTH

	W-R	Per cent	£1 Level Stake		W-R	Per cent	£1 Level Stake
June	0-1	-	- 1.00	December	1-19	5.3	- 15.25
July	0-0	-	0.00	January	2-17	11.8	- 7.17
August	0-0	-	0.00	February	0-13	-	- 13.00
September	0-2	-	- 2.00	March	2-18	11.1	- 5.00
October	0-1	-	- 1.00	April	3-23	13.0	- 14.67
November	0-12	-	- 12.00	May	2-24	8.3	- 18.50

DISTANCE

	W-R	Per cent	£1 Level Stake		W-R	Per cent	£1 Level Stake
Hurdles				Chases			
2m-2m 3f	1-51	2.0	- 49.00	2m-2m 3f	3-5	60.0	+ 8.25
2m 4f-2m 7f	1-24	4.2	- 19.67	2m 4f-2m 7f	2-7	28.6	- 1.92
3m +	1-20	5.0	- 16.25	3m +	2-23	8.7	- 11.00

TYPE OF RACE

	W-R	Per cent	£1 Level Stake		W-R	Per cent	£1 Level Stake
Novice hurdles	1-47	2.1	- 42.67	Selling	0-1	-	- 1.00
H'cap hurdles	2-19	10.5	- 13.25	Amateur	0-5	-	- 5.00
Novice chases	4-24	16.7	- 9.92	Hunter chases	1-3	33.3	+ 4.50
H'cap chases	2-8	25.0	+ 0.75	N H Flat	0-23	-	- 23.00

COURSE GRADE / FIRST TIME OUT

	W-R	Per cent	£1 Level Stake		W-R	Per cent	£1 Level Stake
Group 1	1-29	3.4	- 24.50	Hurdles	0-24	-	- 24.00
Group 2	6-24	25.0	+ 3.08	Chases	1-6	16.7	+ 1.50
Group 3	1-34	2.9	- 32.17				
Group 4	2-43	4.7	- 36.00	Totals	1-30	3.3	- 22.50

JOCKEYS RIDING

	W-R	Per cent	£1 Level Stake		W-R	Per cent	£1 Level Stake
M A Fitzgerald	4-7	57.1	+ 10.33	Mr J Culloty	1-1	100.0	+ 2.25
A P McCoy	2-10	20.0	- 1.92	Mr B Potts	1-8	12.5	- 0.50
R Johnson	2-28	7.1	- 23.75				

D Bentley	0-19	T Jenks	0-3	Mr M Rimell	0-1
P Niven	0-9	B Harding	0-2	Mr R Bevis	0-1
Mr M Daly	0-8	A Maguire	0-1	Mr T Edwards	0-1
M Dwyer	0-7	A Thornton	0-1	P Carberry	0-1
R Dunwoody	0-7	D Gallagher	0-1	S Wynne	0-1
J Titley	0-6	D Parker	0-1		
J R Kavanagh	0-5	Mr C Vigors	0-1		

COURSE RECORD

	Total W-R	Nov Hdles	H'cap Hdles	Nov Chses	H'cap Chses	Hunter Chses	N H Flat	£1 Level Stake
Chepstow	3-7	0-1	1-3	1-1	1-2	0-0	0-0	+ 2.75
Fontwell	2-6	1-3	0-0	1-3	0-0	0-0	0-0	+ 3.83
Lingfield	1-1	0-0	0-0	0-0	0-0	1-1	0-0	+ 6.50
Southwell	1-2	0-0	1-1	0-1	0-0	0-0	0-0	+ 1.75
Exeter	1-5	0-2	0-0	0-0	1-1	0-0	0-2	- 1.75
Ayr	1-5	0-2	0-0	1-1	0-0	0-1	0-1	- 0.50
Uttoxeter	1-8	0-5	0-1	1-2	0-0	0-0	0-0	- 6.17

Haydock	0-9	Aintree	0-3	Ascot	0-1
Newton Abbot	0-8	Leicester	0-3	Cartmel	0-1
Perth	0-8	Towcester	0-3	Catterick	0-1
Ludlow	0-7	Windsor	0-3	Doncaster	0-1
Worcester	0-7	Hexham	0-2	Fakenham	0-1
Hereford	0-6	Huntingdon	0-2	Kelso	0-1
Cheltenham	0-5	Newbury	0-2	Newcastle	0-1
Bangor	0-4	Sandown	0-2	Plumpton	0-1
Nottingham	0-4	Taunton	0-2	Sedgefield	0-1
Warwick	0-4	Wetherby	0-2	Wincanton	0-1

WINNING HORSES

	Races Run	1st	2nd	3rd	Unpl	Win £
Merlin's Lad	6	3	0	1	2	10,828
Hag's Way	6	2	0	2	2	6,586
Fourth In Line	7	1	1	1	4	5,119
Cracking Idea	8	1	0	1	6	3,267
Jultara	7	1	2	1	3	2,678
Father O'Brien	10	1	0	3	6	2,469
Direct	3	1	0	0	2	1,035

WINNING OWNERS

	Races Won	Value £		Races Won	Value £
H Messer-Bennetts	3	10,828	Alan Parker	1	3,267
Mrs G Jenkinson	2	7,588	Roger Barby	1	2,678
Mrs Alurie O'Sullivan	2	6,586	J A C Edwards	1	1,035

No of horses racing for the stable		30	Total winning prize-money	£31,982

Favourites	5-10	50.0%	+ 3.08	Average SP of winner			3.0/1
Longest win seq	2	Longest losing seq	32	Return on stakes invested			-68.9%

1994/95 Form	16-97	16.5%	- 0.41	1992/93 Form	29-253	11.5%	- 140.21
1993/94 Form	18-88	20.5%	+ 34.13	1991/92 Form	39-260	15.0%	- 69.30

MISS S EDWARDS (Sutton, Surrey)

	Races Run	1st	2nd	3rd	Unpl	Per cent	£1 Level Stake
Hurdles	0	0	0	0	0	-	0.00
Chases	4	1	2	0	1	25.0	- 0.25
Totals	4	1	2	0	1	25.0	- 0.25

Mr T Hills	1-4	- 0.25		Towcester	1-2	+ 1.75	

No of horses racing for the stable   3   Total winning prize-money   £1,294

C R EGERTON (Chaddleworth, Berks)

	Races Run	1st	2nd	3rd	Unpl	Per cent	£1 Level Stake
Hurdles	74	11	17	8	38	14.9	- 31.19
Chases	35	2	8	5	20	5.7	- 24.50
Totals	109	13	25	13	58	11.9	- 55.69

BY MONTH

	W-R	Per cent	£1 Level Stake		W-R	Per cent	£1 Level Stake
June	0-2	-	- 2.00	December	0-6	-	- 6.00
July	0-0	-	0.00	January	3-16	18.8	+ 0.91
August	2-4	50.0	+ 0.69	February	2-13	15.4	- 4.33
September	2-6	33.3	+ 3.50	March	0-20	-	- 20.00
October	1-8	12.5	- 2.50	April	1-10	10.0	- 6.50
November	2-9	22.2	- 4.46	May	0-15	-	- 15.00

DISTANCE

Hurdles	W-R	Per cent	£1 Level Stake	Chases	W-R	Per cent	£1 Level Stake
2m-2m 3f	10-57	17.5	- 21.69	2m-2m 3f	1-5	20.0	- 1.50
2m 4f-2m 7f	1-12	8.3	- 4.50	2m 4f-2m 7f	0-6	-	- 6.00
3m +	0-5	-	- 5.00	3m +	1-24	4.2	- 17.00

TYPE OF RACE

	W-R	Per cent	£1 Level Stake		W-R	Per cent	£1 Level Stake
Novice hurdles	9-38	23.7	- 8.19	Selling	1-12	8.3	- 4.50
H'cap hurdles	1-12	8.3	- 6.50	Amateur	0-0	-	0.00
Novice chases	2-12	16.7	- 1.50	Hunter chases	0-8	-	- 8.00
H'cap chases	0-13	-	- 13.00	N H Flat	0-14	-	- 14.00

COURSE GRADE					FIRST TIME OUT			
	W-R	Per cent	£1 Level Stake			W-R	Per cent	£1 Level Stake
Group 1	4-29	13.8	- 17.13	Hurdles		4-26	15.4	- 7.46
Group 2	0-15	-	- 15.00	Chases		0-9	-	- 9.00
Group 3	4-32	12.5	- 9.25					
Group 4	5-33	15.2	- 14.31	Totals		4-35	11.4	- 16.46

JOCKEYS RIDING

	W-R	Per cent	£1 Level Stake			W-R	Per cent	£1 Level Stake
J Osborne	5-32	15.6	- 8.80	A Maguire		1-3	33.3	- 1.33
J A McCarthy	4-30	13.3	- 18.56	Sophie Mitchell		1-4	25.0	+ 3.50
N Williamson	2-4	50.0	+ 5.50					

G Bradley	0-5	Mr E James	0-2	Mr A Sansome	0-1
Mr P Henley	0-5	Mr J Culloty	0-2	Mr J P Durkan	0-1
D Gallagher	0-4	R Massey	0-2	T J Murphy	0-1
J Railton	0-4	A P McCoy	0-1	T Jenks	0-1
R Johnson	0-3	A S Smith	0-1		
C Llewellyn	0-2	C Maude	0-1		

COURSE RECORD

	Total W-R	Nov Hdles	H'cap Hdles	Nov Chses	H'cap Chses	Hunter Chses	N H Flat	£1 Level Stake
Haydock	2-4	2-4	0-0	0-0	0-0	0-0	0-0	- 0.42
Stratford	1-1	1-1	0-0	0-0	0-0	0-0	0-0	+ 5.50
Leicester	1-1	1-1	0-0	0-0	0-0	0-0	0-0	+ 6.50
Southwell	1-2	1-1	0-0	0-0	0-0	0-0	0-1	- 0.56
Bangor	1-3	1-1	0-1	0-0	0-0	0-1	0-0	0.00
Towcester	1-3	0-0	1-2	0-0	0-1	0-0	0-0	+ 4.50
Exeter	1-4	0-0	0-1	1-1	0-1	0-0	0-1	- 0.50
Plumpton	1-4	0-0	1-1	0-2	0-0	0-1	0-0	+ 1.50
Market Rasen	1-6	1-2	0-1	0-0	0-1	0-0	0-2	- 2.75
Taunton	1-7	1-5	0-0	0-1	0-1	0-0	0-0	- 3.75
Newbury	1-7	0-3	0-1	1-1	0-1	0-0	0-1	0.00
Cheltenham	1-9	1-4	0-2	0-1	0-1	0-1	0-0	- 7.71

Hereford	0-9	Fontwell	0-3	Nottingham	0-2
Newton Abbot	0-8	Huntingdon	0-3	Chepstow	0-1
Uttoxeter	0-7	Lingfield	0-3	Sedgefield	0-1
Ascot	0-4	Sandown	0-3	Worcester	0-1
Ludlow	0-4	Windsor	0-3		
Warwick	0-4	Kempton	0-2		

WINNING HORSES

	Races Run	1st	2nd	3rd	Unpl	Win £
Mysilv	6	3	2	0	1	24,274
River Lossie	5	2	1	1	1	9,632
Woodrising	6	2	2	0	2	5,280
Stay With Me	2	2	0	0	0	4,944
Hawker Hunter	4	1	0	0	3	3,566
Frontager	3	1	1	0	1	2,790
Cast The Line	7	1	1	0	5	2,158
Whitebonnet	11	1	4	2	4	2,052

WINNING OWNERS

	Races Won	Value £		Races Won	Value £
Elite Racing Club	3	24,274	Dr G Madan Mohan	1	3,566
Chris Brasher	2	9,632	Charles Egerton & Partners	1	2,790
The Blue Chip Group	3	7,332	D P Barrie	1	2,158
Mrs Sandra A Roe	2	4,944			

No of horses racing for the stable	35	Total winning prize-money		£54,696

Favourites	7-28	25.0%	- 11.94	Average SP of winner		3.1/1
Longest win seq	1	Longest losing seq	24	Return on stakes invested		-51.1%

1994/95 Form	15-80	18.8%	- 2.62	1992/93 Form	15-56	26.8%	+ 15.13
1993/94 Form	26-119	21.8%	- 0.54	1991/92 Form	4-29	13.8%	+ 10.75

B ELLISON (Lanchester, Co Durham)

	Races Run	1st	2nd	3rd	Unpl	Per cent	£1 Level Stake
Hurdles	52	3	7	4	38	5.8	- 16.50
Chases	27	7	6	1	13	25.9	+ 17.13
Totals	79	10	13	5	51	12.7	+ 0.63

BY MONTH

	W-R	Per cent	£1 Level Stake		W-R	Per cent	£1 Level Stake
June	0-1	-	- 1.00	December	0-6	-	- 6.00
July	0-0	-	0.00	January	0-12	-	- 12.00
August	0-0	-	0.00	February	2-9	22.2	+ 8.00
September	0-4	-	- 4.00	March	0-10	-	- 10.00
October	0-2	-	- 2.00	April	4-16	25.0	+ 9.00
November	0-6	-	- 6.00	May	4-13	30.8	+ 24.63

DISTANCE

	W-R	Per cent	£1 Level Stake		W-R	Per cent	£1 Level Stake
Hurdles				Chases			
2m-2m 3f	1-35	2.9	- 18.00	2m-2m 3f	0-4	-	- 4.00
2m 4f-2m 7f	1-16	6.3	- 9.50	2m 4f-2m 7f	3-6	50.0	+ 12.63
3m +	1-1	100.0	+ 11.00	3m +	4-17	23.5	+ 8.50

TYPE OF RACE

	W-R	Per cent	£1 Level Stake		W-R	Per cent	£1 Level Stake
Novice hurdles	0-19	-	- 19.00	Selling	1-17	5.9	0.00
H'cap hurdles	2-14	14.3	+ 4.50	Amateur	0-1	-	- 1.00
Novice chases	1-14	7.1	- 9.00	Hunter chases	0-0	-	0.00
H'cap chases	6-12	50.0	+ 27.13	N H Flat	0-2	-	- 2.00

COURSE GRADE

	W-R	Per cent	£1 Level Stake
Group 1	0-9	-	- 9.00
Group 2	0-3	-	- 3.00
Group 3	0-12	-	- 12.00
Group 4	10-55	18.2	+ 24.63

FIRST TIME OUT

	W-R	Per cent	£1 Level Stake
Hurdles	0-10	-	- 10.00
Chases	0-3	-	- 3.00
Totals	0-13	-	- 13.00

JOCKEYS RIDING

	W-R	Per cent	£1 Level Stake		W-R	Per cent	£1 Level Stake
P G Cahill	5-13	38.5	+ 25.50	F Leahy	1-1	100.0	+ 16.00
B Harding	2-37	5.4	- 20.00	Mr C Bonner	1-2	50.0	+ 2.50
A Dobbin	1-1	100.0	+ 1.63				

M Foster	0-5	A Maguire	0-1	N Horrocks	0-1
M A Fitzgerald	0-3	D Byrne	0-1	N Williamson	0-1
Miss V Haigh	0-3	L Wyer	0-1	P Carberry	0-1
D Bentley	0-2	Mr M H Naughton	0-1	S Haworth	0-1
Mr K Whelan	0-2	Mrs J Speight	0-1	Scott Taylor	0-1

COURSE RECORD

	Total W-R	Nov Hdles	H'cap Hdles	Nov Chses	H'cap Chses	Hunter Chses	N H Flat	£1 Level Stake
Perth	2-5	0-1	1-2	0-1	1-1	0-0	0-0	+ 10.50
Hexham	2-9	0-3	0-1	0-2	2-3	0-0	0-0	+ 9.00
Sedgefield	2-21	0-4	0-9	1-4	1-4	0-0	0-0	- 11.50
Cartmel	1-1	0-0	1-1	0-0	0-0	0-0	0-0	+ 16.00
Bangor	1-2	0-1	0-0	0-0	1-1	0-0	0-0	+ 0.63
Musselburgh	1-4	0-2	1-1	0-1	0-0	0-0	0-0	+ 8.00
Carlisle	1-8	0-1	0-4	0-1	1-1	0-0	0-1	- 3.00

Catterick	0-5	Wetherby	0-3	Market Rasen	0-1
Kelso	0-5	Cheltenham	0-2	Stratford	0-1
Newcastle	0-5	Doncaster	0-2		
Leicester	0-3	Nottingham	0-2		

WINNING HORSES

	Races Run	1st	2nd	3rd	Unpl	Win £
Go Silly	11	3	4	0	4	11,204
Potato Man	3	2	1	0	0	8,803
Majic Rain	3	2	0	0	1	5,310
Urban Dancing	10	1	4	0	5	4,338
Bhavnagar	6	1	1	0	4	2,979
Clover Girl	10	1	1	0	8	2,514

WINNING OWNERS

	Races Won	Value £		Races Won	Value £
Ferrograph Limited	3	11,204	Ronald McCulloch	1	4,338
Chris Foster	2	8,803	E J Berry	1	2,979
D V Tate	2	5,310	Kevin M L Brown	1	2,514

No of horses racing for the stable		15		Total winning prize-money			£35,148
Favourites	1-3	33.3%	- 0.37	Average SP of winner			7.0/1
Longest win seq	2	Longest losing seq	35	Return on stakes invested			0.8%
1994/95 Form	0-22			1992/93 Form	3-22	13.6%	+ 18.00
1993/94 Form	2-35	5.7%	- 19.50	1991/92 Form	3-34	8.8%	- 14.00

D R C ELSWORTH (Whitcombe, Dorset)

	Races Run	1st	2nd	3rd	Unpl	Per cent	£1 Level Stake
Hurdles	73	10	8	7	48	13.7	- 39.95
Chases	30	4	2	2	22	13.3	- 10.59
Totals	103	14	10	9	70	13.6	- 50.54

BY MONTH

	W-R	Per cent	£1 Level Stake		W-R	Per cent	£1 Level Stake
June	0-0	-	0.00	December	2-10	20.0	+ 1.25
July	0-0	-	0.00	January	0-14	-	- 14.00
August	0-1	-	- 1.00	February	1-14	7.1	- 12.27
September	2-2	100.0	+ 4.00	March	1-12	8.3	- 7.00
October	2-13	15.4	- 9.60	April	2-11	18.2	- 3.09
November	3-21	14.3	- 8.33	May	1-5	20.0	- 0.50

DISTANCE

Hurdles	W-R	Per cent	£1 Level Stake	Chases	W-R	Per cent	£1 Level Stake
2m-2m 3f	10-61	16.4	- 27.95	2m-2m 3f	4-12	33.3	+ 7.41
2m 4f-2m 7f	0-11	-	- 11.00	2m 4f-2m 7f	0-8	-	- 8.00
3m +	0-1	-	- 1.00	3m +	0-10	-	- 10.00

TYPE OF RACE

	W-R	Per cent	£1 Level Stake		W-R	Per cent	£1 Level Stake
Novice hurdles	6-35	17.1	- 13.30	Selling	1-2	50.0	+ 2.50
H'cap hurdles	1-31	3.2	- 27.75	Amateur	1-5	20.0	- 3.33
Novice chases	3-12	25.0	+ 2.91	Hunter chases	0-0	-	0.00
H'cap chases	0-14	-	- 14.00	N H Flat	2-4	50.0	+ 2.43

COURSE GRADE

	W-R	Per cent	£1 Level Stake
Group 1	5-62	8.1	- 49.53
Group 2	3-10	30.0	+ 2.17
Group 3	2-12	16.7	- 6.10
Group 4	4-19	21.1	+ 2.92

FIRST TIME OUT

	W-R	Per cent	£1 Level Stake
Hurdles	4-24	16.7	- 14.60
Chases	0-1	-	- 1.00
Totals	4-25	16.0	- 15.60

JOCKEYS RIDING

	W-R	Per cent	£1 Level Stake		W-R	Per cent	£1 Level Stake
P Holley	5-49	10.2	- 31.03	Mr P Henley	2-10	20.0	- 3.83
A Procter	3-22	13.6	- 3.75	P Hide	1-2	50.0	- 0.09
A McCabe	2-5	40.0	+ 1.43	R Dunwoody	1-5	20.0	- 3.27

A P McCoy	0-3	Mr E James	0-1	P Carberry	0-1
A Thornton	0-1	Mr R Nuttall	0-1	S McNeill	0-1
Mr C Vigors	0-1	Mr T McCarthy	0-1		

COURSE RECORD

	Total W-R	Nov Hdles	H'cap Hdles	Nov Chses	H'cap Chses	Hunter Chses	N H Flat	£1 Level Stake
Exeter	3-11	1-3	1-5	1-2	0-1	0-0	0-0	+ 1.92
Sandown	2-12	1-2	0-7	0-1	0-0	0-0	1-2	- 8.17
Worcester	1-1	0-0	0-0	0-0	0-0	0-0	1-1	+ 3.33
Chepstow	1-2	1-1	0-1	0-0	0-0	0-0	0-0	+ 4.00
Newton Abbot	1-3	1-2	0-0	0-0	0-1	0-0	0-0	- 1.33
Fontwell	1-3	0-0	0-1	0-1	1-1	0-0	0-0	+ 1.50
Taunton	1-6	1-4	0-0	0-0	0-2	0-0	0-0	+ 3.00
Wincanton	1-6	1-3	0-1	0-0	0-2	0-0	0-0	- 4.43
Kempton	1-8	1-3	0-2	0-0	0-3	0-0	0-0	- 6.27
Newbury	1-11	0-1	0-6	1-1	0-3	0-0	0-0	- 6.00
Ascot	1-17	0-10	0-3	1-3	0-1	0-0	0-0	- 15.09

Cheltenham	0-6	Lingfield	0-2	Huntingdon	0-1
Aintree	0-3	Stratford	0-2	Newcastle	0-1
Ayr	0-2	Windsor	0-2	Towcester	0-1
Haydock	0-2	Hereford	0-1		

WINNING HORSES

	Races Run	1st	2nd	3rd	Unpl	Win £
Atours	6	3	3	0	0	31,058
Nemuro	12	3	1	0	8	11,592
Absalom's Lady	8	1	2	1	4	7,259
Bookcase	6	1	1	2	2	3,682
Neat Feat	4	2	1	0	1	3,327
Tango's Delight	6	1	0	0	5	2,490
Tony's Fen	1	1	0	0	0	2,142
Trade Wind	3	1	0	0	2	2,113
Persian Saint	5	1	0	1	3	1,944

WINNING OWNERS

	Races Won	Value £		Races Won	Value £
Oh So Rosie Partnership	3	31,058	Food Brokers Ltd	2	3,327
Turf City Racing	3	11,592	Edwin Fry	1	2,490
Whitcombe Manor Racing Stables	2	9,203	The Executive	1	2,142
Adept (80) Ltd	1	3,682	Ray Richards	1	2,113

No of horses racing for the stable		25	Total winning prize-money	£65,607

Favourites	8-9	88.9%	+ 6.63	Average SP of winner	2.7/1
Longest win seq	3	Longest losing seq	18	Return on stakes invested	-49.1%

1994/95 Form	13-96	13.5%	- 33.58	1992/93 Form	18-115	15.7%	- 18.97
1993/94 Form	19-112	17.0%	- 5.44	1991/92 Form	20-143	14.0%	- 16.52

MISS A EMBIRICOS (Newmarket, Suffolk)

	Races Run	1st	2nd	3rd	Unpl	Per cent	£1 Level Stake
Hurdles	30	2	0	2	26	6.7	+ 12.00
Chases	48	4	8	4	32	8.3	- 20.00
Totals	78	6	8	6	58	7.7	- 8.00

J Ryan	4-59	+ 2.00	J R Kavanagh	1-11	- 5.50
Miss A Embiricos	1-2	+ 1.50			

Market Rasen	3-14	+ 33.50	Huntingdon	1-5	+ 3.00
Towcester	1-2	+ 1.50	Uttoxeter	1-11	0.00

No of horses racing for the stable	19	Total winning prize-money	£18,953

G P ENRIGHT (Lewes, East Sussex)

	Races Run	1st	2nd	3rd	Unpl	Per cent	£1 Level Stake
Hurdles	22	1	0	2	19	4.5	- 20.00
Chases	13	2	2	3	6	15.4	- 4.00
Totals	35	3	2	5	25	8.6	- 24.00

J R Kavanagh	2-26	- 19.50	A Maguire	1-2	+ 2.50
Nottingham	1-1	+ 3.50	Lingfield	1-4	+ 0.50
Fontwell	1-2	0.00			

No of horses racing for the stable	6	Total winning prize-money	£9,646

T J ETHERINGTON (Norton, North Yorks)

	Races Run	1st	2nd	3rd	Unpl	Per cent	£1 Level Stake
Hurdles	28	4	6	2	16	14.3	+ 12.50
Chases	2	0	0	1	1	-	- 2.00
Totals	30	4	6	3	17	13.3	+ 10.50

R Rourke	3-15	+ 19.00	A Thornton	1-6	+ 0.50
Wetherby	2-3	+ 23.00	Southwell	1-3	+ 3.50
Hereford	1-1	+ 7.00			

No of horses racing for the stable	7	Total winning prize-money	£10,847

P D EVANS (Leighton, Powys)

	Races Run	1st	2nd	3rd	Unpl	Per cent	£1 Level Stake
Hurdles	17	2	2	0	13	11.8	- 5.67
Chases	0	0	0	0	0	-	0.00
Totals	17	2	2	0	13	11.8	- 5.67

P Carberry	1-1	+ 9.00	A P McCoy	1-2	- 0.67
Ayr	1-1	+ 9.00	Windsor	1-1	+ 0.33

No of horses racing for the stable	10	Total winning prize-money	£4,703

J L EYRE (Sutton Bank, North Yorks)

	Races Run	1st	2nd	3rd	Unpl	Per cent	£1 Level Stake
Hurdles	48	10	7	7	24	20.8	- 15.52
Chases	1	0	0	0	1	-	- 1.00
Totals	49	10	7	7	25	20.4	- 16.52

BY MONTH

	W-R	Per cent	£1 Level Stake		W-R	Per cent	£1 Level Stake
June	0-3	-	- 3.00	December	1-5	20.0	- 1.00
July	0-2	-	- 2.00	January	0-4	-	- 4.00
August	1-1	100.0	+ 3.00	February	3-7	42.9	+ 2.25
September	1-3	33.3	+ 1.50	March	1-3	33.3	- 1.50
October	1-7	14.3	- 3.50	April	0-3	-	- 3.00
November	2-10	20.0	- 4.27	May	0-1	-	- 1.00

DISTANCE

Hurdles	W-R	Per cent	£1 Level Stake	Chases	W-R	Per cent	£1 Level Stake
2m-2m 3f	5-22	22.7	- 5.77	2m-2m 3f	0-1	-	- 1.00
2m 4f-2m 7f	4-21	19.0	- 6.25	2m 4f-2m 7f	0-0	-	0.00
3m +	1-5	20.0	- 3.50	3m +	0-0	-	0.00

TYPE OF RACE

	W-R	Per cent	£1 Level Stake		W-R	Per cent	£1 Level Stake
Novice hurdles	4-20	20.0	- 9.25	Selling	2-8	25.0	0.00
H'cap hurdles	0-8	-	- 8.00	Amateur	2-3	66.7	+ 4.50
Novice chases	0-0	-	0.00	Hunter chases	0-0	-	0.00
H'cap chases	0-1	-	- 1.00	N H Flat	2-9	22.2	- 2.77

COURSE GRADE

	W-R	Per cent	£1 Level Stake
Group 1	2-8	25.0	- 4.27
Group 2	1-3	33.3	+ 0.50
Group 3	1-16	6.3	- 12.00
Group 4	6-22	27.3	- 0.75

FIRST TIME OUT

	W-R	Per cent	£1 Level Stake
Hurdles	2-14	14.3	- 7.50
Chases	0-0	-	0.00
Totals	2-14	14.3	- 7.50

JOCKEYS RIDING

	W-R	Per cent	£1 Level Stake		W-R	Per cent	£1 Level Stake
O Pears	6-23	26.1	- 5.27	T Eley	1-4	25.0	0.00
Miss P Robson	2-2	100.0	+ 5.50	C Elliott	1-9	11.1	- 5.75

G Harker	0-3	B Storey	0-1	N Smith	0-1
A P McCoy	0-2	F Perratt	0-1	R Dunwoody	0-1
A Dobbin	0-1	Mr K Whelan	0-1		

COURSE RECORD

	Total W-R	Nov Hdles	H'cap Hdles	Nov Chses	H'cap Chses	Hunter Chses	N H Flat	£1 Level Stake
Musselburgh	2-6	2-4	0-1	0-0	0-0	0-0	0-1	+ 1.25
Carlisle	2-8	1-2	0-3	0-0	0-0	0-0	1-3	- 2.00
Cartmel	1-1	0-0	1-1	0-0	0-0	0-0	0-0	+ 3.00
Ayr	1-2	1-2	0-0	0-0	0-0	0-0	0-0	0.00
Haydock	1-2	0-1	0-0	0-0	0-0	0-0	1-1	- 0.27
Hexham	1-3	0-2	1-1	0-0	0-0	0-0	0-0	+ 1.00
Wetherby	1-3	1-1	0-2	0-0	0-0	0-0	0-0	+ 0.50
Catterick	1-5	0-3	1-1	0-0	0-1	0-0	0-0	- 1.00

Market Rasen	0-8	Bangor	0-1	Nottingham	0-1
Kelso	0-2	Cheltenham	0-1	Perth	0-1
Aintree	0-1	Leicester	0-1	Uttoxeter	0-1
Ascot	0-1	Newcastle	0-1		

WINNING HORSES

	Races Run	1st	2nd	3rd	Unpl	Win £
Old Habits	9	3	3	0	3	8,412
Yacht Club	9	2	1	2	4	3,889
Peep O Day	4	1	1	1	1	2,941
Celestial Choir	2	1	0	1	0	2,621
Prizefighter	2	1	0	0	1	2,175
Fenwick's Brother	3	1	0	1	1	1,256
Rachael's Dawn	8	1	1	2	4	1,159

WINNING OWNERS

	Races Won	Value £		Races Won	Value £
R W Thomson	3	8,412	Diamond Racing Ltd	1	2,175
Ernest Spencer	2	3,889	Martin Firth	1	1,256
John L Holdroyd	1	2,941	Mrs C A Ward	1	1,159
Mrs Carol Sykes	1	2,621			

No of horses racing for the stable	15	Total winning prize-money	£22,453

Favourites	6-12	50.0%	+ 5.23	Average SP of winner	2.2/1
Longest win seq	2	Longest losing seq	11	Return on stakes invested	-33.7%

1994/95 Form	7-72	9.7%	- 45.44	1992/93 Form	4-74	5.4%	- 26.45
1993/94 Form	4-77	5.2%	+ 15.00	1991/92 Form	2-34	5.9%	- 21.75

C W FAIRHURST (Middleham, North Yorks)

	Races Run	1st	2nd	3rd	Unpl	Per cent	£1 Level Stake
Hurdles	12	1	1	2	8	8.3	- 7.67
Chases	0	0	0	0	0	-	0.00
Totals	12	1	1	2	8	8.3	- 7.67

J Callaghan	1-8	- 3.67	Kelso	1-1	+ 3.33

No of horses racing for the stable   3   Total winning prize-money   £2,108

J FANSHAWE (Newmarket, Suffolk)

	Races Run	1st	2nd	3rd	Unpl	Per cent	£1 Level Stake
Hurdles	8	3	0	1	4	37.5	+ 31.01
Chases	0	0	0	0	0	-	0.00
Totals	8	3	0	1	4	37.5	+ 31.01

P Hide	2-3	+ 2.01	T J Murphy	1-1	+ 33.00
Huntingdon	2-2	+ 3.01	Newbury	1-1	+ 33.00

No of horses racing for the stable   4   Total winning prize-money   £8,638

MRS A L FARRELL (Brandsby, North Yorks)

	Races Run	1st	2nd	3rd	Unpl	Per cent	£1 Level Stake
Hurdles	0	0	0	0	0	-	0.00
Chases	1	1	0	0	0	100.0	+ 3.50
Totals	1	1	0	0	0	100.0	+ 3.50

Mr N Bannister	1-1	+ 3.50	Cartmel	1-1	+ 3.50

No of horses racing for the stable   1   Total winning prize-money   £2,008

PADDY FARRELL (Taunton, Somerset)

	Races Run	1st	2nd	3rd	Unpl	Per cent	£1 Level Stake
Hurdles	22	0	4	0	18	-	- 22.00
Chases	9	1	1	0	7	11.1	- 4.00
Totals	31	1	5	0	25	3.2	- 26.00

M Foster	1-7	- 2.00	Plumpton	1-2	+ 3.00

No of horses racing for the stable   9   Total winning prize-money   £2,611

P S FELGATE (Grimston, Leics)

	Races Run	1st	2nd	3rd	Unpl	Per cent	£1 Level Stake
Hurdles	3	1	0	0	2	33.3	- 0.50
Chases	0	0	0	0	0	-	0.00
Totals	3	1	0	0	2	33.3	- 0.50

A P McCoy	1-1	+ 1.50	Ludlow	1-1	+ 1.50

No of horses racing for the stable   2   Total winning prize-money   £2,108

MRS R FELL (Roborough, Devon)

	Races Run	1st	2nd	3rd	Unpl	Per cent	£1 Level Stake
Hurdles	0	0	0	0	0	-	0.00
Chases	2	1	0	0	1	50.0	+ 3.00
Totals	2	1	0	0	1	50.0	+ 3.00

Mr K Heard	1-2	+ 3.00	Newton Abbot	1-1	+ 4.00

No of horses racing for the stable   1   Total winning prize-money   £1,219

J FFITCH-HEYES (Lewes, East Sussex)

	Races Run	1st	2nd	3rd	Unpl	Per cent	£1 Level Stake
Hurdles	34	1	3	4	26	2.9	- 17.00
Chases	19	0	1	2	16	-	- 19.00
Totals	53	1	4	6	42	1.9	- 36.00

B Fenton	1-20	- 3.00	Newton Abbot	1-4	+ 13.00

No of horses racing for the stable   13   Total winning prize-money   £3,469

G FIERRO (Hednesford, Staffs)

	Races Run	1st	2nd	3rd	Unpl	Per cent	£1 Level Stake
Hurdles	20	1	0	1	18	5.0	- 7.00
Chases	4	0	0	0	4	-	- 4.00
Totals	24	1	0	1	22	4.2	- 11.00

B M Clifford	1-6	+ 7.00	Uttoxeter	1-5	+ 8.00

No of horses racing for the stable   10   Total winning prize-money   £2,316

R F FISHER (Bardsea, Cumbria)

	Races Run	1st	2nd	3rd	Unpl	Per cent	£1 Level Stake
Hurdles	24	4	2	1	17	16.7	+ 8.00
Chases	0	0	0	0	0	-	0.00
Totals	24	4	2	1	17	16.7	+ 8.00

J Callaghan	2-7	+ 14.00	F Leahy	1-6	0.00
P Niven	1-3	+ 2.00			
Catterick	1-1	+ 16.00	Southwell	1-2	+ 4.00
Carlisle	1-1	+ 3.00	Ayr	1-4	+ 1.00

No of horses racing for the stable	6	Total winning prize-money	£9,203

J G FITZGERALD (Norton, North Yorks)

	Races Run	1st	2nd	3rd	Unpl	Per cent	£1 Level Stake
Hurdles	87	13	10	10	54	14.9	+ 60.76
Chases	54	9	9	12	24	16.7	- 13.75
Totals	141	22	19	22	78	15.6	+ 47.01

BY MONTH

	W-R	Per cent	£1 Level Stake		W-R	Per cent	£1 Level Stake
June	0-3	-	- 3.00	December	2-12	16.7	- 3.75
July	0-1	-	- 1.00	January	3-26	11.5	+ 26.50
August	0-1	-	- 1.00	February	5-24	20.8	+ 48.00
September	0-1	-	- 1.00	March	5-36	13.9	- 15.90
October	0-1	-	- 1.00	April	4-17	23.5	- 1.59
November	2-9	22.2	+ 7.00	May	1-10	10.0	- 6.25

DISTANCE

Hurdles	W-R	Per cent	£1 Level Stake	Chases	W-R	Per cent	£1 Level Stake
2m-2m 3f	8-56	14.3	+ 30.26	2m-2m 3f	1-20	5.0	- 17.00
2m 4f-2m 7f	5-27	18.5	+ 34.50	2m 4f-2m 7f	2-15	13.3	- 8.00
3m +	0-4	-	- 4.00	3m +	6-19	31.6	+ 11.25

TYPE OF RACE

	W-R	Per cent	£1 Level Stake		W-R	Per cent	£1 Level Stake
Novice hurdles	3-38	7.9	+ 27.00	Selling	1-5	20.0	- 1.75
H'cap hurdles	3-25	12.0	+ 22.50	Amateur	0-0	-	0.00
Novice chases	0-2	-	- 2.00	Hunter chases	0-0	-	0.00
H'cap chases	9-52	17.3	- 11.75	N H Flat	6-19	31.6	+ 13.01

COURSE GRADE

	W-R	Per cent	£1 Level Stake
Group 1	12-61	19.7	+ 32.85
Group 2	1-15	6.7	+ 36.00
Group 3	6-36	16.7	- 1.25
Group 4	3-29	10.3	- 20.59

FIRST TIME OUT

	W-R	Per cent	£1 Level Stake
Hurdles	6-28	21.4	+ 85.00
Chases	1-11	9.1	- 2.00
Totals	7-39	17.9	+ 83.00

JOCKEYS RIDING

	W-R	Per cent	£1 Level Stake
M Dwyer	9-52	17.3	- 8.59
F Leahy	5-29	17.2	+ 74.75
E Callaghan	3-20	15.0	- 8.40
W J Dwan	2-19	10.5	- 7.50
R Dunwoody	1-1	100.0	+ 6.00
A P McCoy	1-2	50.0	+ 1.75
L Wyer	1-5	20.0	+ 2.00

P Niven	0-5	G E Tormey	0-1	Mr C Bonner	0-1
D Byrne	0-4	J Osborne	0-1	P Carberry	0-1

COURSE RECORD

	Total W-R	Nov Hdles	H'cap Hdles	Nov Chses	H'cap Chses	Hunter Chses	N H Flat	£1 Level Stake
Newcastle	4-16	0-4	1-6	0-0	3-5	0-0	0-1	+ 32.50
Haydock	3-13	0-3	0-1	0-0	1-6	0-0	2-3	+ 5.75
Perth	2-4	0-0	0-1	0-0	1-2	0-0	1-1	+ 1.16
Ayr	2-5	1-2	0-0	0-1	1-2	0-0	0-0	+ 6.00
Uttoxeter	2-8	1-5	0-2	0-0	1-1	0-0	0-0	+ 2.75
Market Rasen	2-11	0-3	0-1	0-0	1-4	0-0	1-3	+ 4.50
Sandown	1-3	0-0	1-2	0-0	0-1	0-0	0-0	+ 4.00
Leicester	1-3	0-0	0-1	0-0	1-2	0-0	0-0	0.00
Cheltenham	1-5	0-0	1-2	0-0	0-1	0-0	0-2	+ 1.50
Catterick	1-5	0-2	0-0	0-0	0-0	0-0	1-3	+ 0.50
Doncaster	1-7	0-1	0-1	0-0	0-2	0-0	1-3	- 4.90
Hexham	1-8	1-2	0-1	0-0	0-5	0-0	0-0	- 4.75
Wetherby	1-15	1-9	0-0	0-0	0-5	0-0	0-1	+ 36.00

Aintree	0-6	Nottingham	0-3	Warwick	0-2
Sedgefield	0-5	Stratford	0-3	Musselburgh	0-1
Carlisle	0-3	Towcester	0-3	Newbury	0-1
Kelso	0-3	Ascot	0-2	Worcester	0-1
Kempton	0-3	Southwell	0-2		

WINNING HORSES

	Races Run	1st	2nd	3rd	Unpl	Win £
Trainglot	3	3	0	0	0	68,120
High Padre	5	3	0	0	2	18,312
Astings	6	2	1	1	2	15,468
Rustic Air	7	2	1	1	3	6,886
Richardson	4	1	1	0	2	4,488
Agistment	3	2	0	0	1	4,187
Alzulu	3	2	1	0	0	2,967

FitzGerald J G

Newlands-General	8	1	2	3	2	2,879
Claverhouse	5	1	0	0	4	2,684
Our Robert	5	1	0	1	3	2,568
Thursday Night	6	1	2	0	3	2,444
Bold Pursuit	2	1	0	0	1	2,339
Ballad Minstrel	2	1	0	0	1	1,746
China King	2	1	0	1	0	1,182

WINNING OWNERS

	Races Won	Value £		Races Won	Value £
Marquesa De Moratalla	5	72,307	W Hancock	1	2,879
J S Murdoch	3	18,312	Mrs Peter Corbett	1	2,684
W A A Farrell	2	15,468	Tony Fawcett	1	2,568
Mrs B V Eve	3	8,068	R J Wragg	1	2,339
R Haggas	2	6,932	J G FitzGerald	1	1,746
D Buckle	2	2,967			

No of horses racing for the stable	39	Total winning prize-money		£136,270

Favourites	9-28	32.1%	- 0.99	Average SP of winner	7.5/1
Longest win seq	2	Longest losing seq	16	Return on stakes invested	33.3%

1994/95 Form	37-188	19.7%	+ 10.32	1992/93 Form	62-268	23.1%	- 2.99
1993/94 Form	23-190	12.1%	- 93.72	1991/92 Form	33-198	16.7%	- 19.55

A L FORBES (Stramshall, Staffs)

	Races Run	1st	2nd	3rd	Unpl	Per cent	£1 Level Stake
Hurdles	3	1	0	0	2	33.3	+ 3.00
Chases	2	0	0	0	2	-	- 2.00
Totals	5	1	0	0	4	20.0	+ 1.00

T Eley	1-5	+ 1.00	Worcester	1-2	+ 4.00

No of horses racing for the stable	2	Total winning prize-money		£3,397

CAPT T A FORSTER (Downton-on-the-Rock, H'ford & Worcs)

	Races Run	1st	2nd	3rd	Unpl	Per cent	£1 Level Stake
Hurdles	95	16	7	16	56	16.8	- 2.66
Chases	83	18	15	10	40	21.7	+ 4.02
Totals	178	34	22	26	96	19.1	+ 1.36

BY MONTH

	W-R	Per cent	£1 Level Stake		W-R	Per cent	£1 Level Stake
June	1-1	100.0	+ 4.00	December	3-14	21.4	- 4.52
July	1-2	50.0	+ 2.00	January	5-26	19.2	- 13.17
August	0-3	-	- 3.00	February	4-16	25.0	+ 7.83
September	1-2	50.0	+ 0.63	March	5-43	11.6	- 12.37
October	2-9	22.2	+ 0.80	April	3-22	13.6	+ 7.00
November	7-30	23.3	+ 2.16	May	2-10	20.0	+ 10.00

DISTANCE

Hurdles	W-R	Per cent	£1 Level Stake	Chases	W-R	Per cent	£1 Level Stake
2m-2m 3f	9-42	21.4	+ 5.34	2m-2m 3f	0-12	-	- 12.00
2m 4f-2m 7f	6-43	14.0	- 3.00	2m 4f-2m 7f	6-36	16.7	+ 1.13
3m +	1-10	10.0	- 5.00	3m +	12-35	34.3	+ 14.89

TYPE OF RACE

	W-R	Per cent	£1 Level Stake		W-R	Per cent	£1 Level Stake
Novice hurdles	9-51	17.6	- 14.04	Selling	0-0	-	0.00
H'cap hurdles	6-35	17.1	+ 5.38	Amateur	0-5	-	- 5.00
Novice chases	3-33	9.1	- 20.87	Hunter chases	0-0	-	0.00
H'cap chases	15-47	31.9	+ 27.89	N H Flat	1-7	14.3	+ 8.00

COURSE GRADE

	W-R	Per cent	£1 Level Stake
Group 1	6-19	31.6	+ 13.83
Group 2	2-18	11.1	- 2.25
Group 3	11-67	16.4	- 4.37
Group 4	15-74	20.3	- 5.85

FIRST TIME OUT

	W-R	Per cent	£1 Level Stake
Hurdles	5-36	13.9	- 3.34
Chases	3-18	16.7	- 2.50
Totals	8-54	14.8	- 5.84

JOCKEYS RIDING

	W-R	Per cent	£1 Level Stake		W-R	Per cent	£1 Level Stake
S Wynne	8-61	13.1	+ 8.50	M A Fitzgerald	1-2	50.0	+ 5.50
R Dunwoody	6-13	46.2	- 0.13	C Llewellyn	1-2	50.0	0.00
A Thornton	6-36	16.7	- 12.50	D Gallagher	1-2	50.0	+ 2.50
A P McCoy	5-17	29.4	- 0.64	B Fenton	1-4	25.0	+ 11.00
B Powell	2-3	66.7	+ 4.00	Mr P Henley	1-4	25.0	+ 7.00
B Harding	1-1	100.0	+ 1.63	A Maguire	1-5	20.0	+ 2.50

J R Kavanagh	0-6	L Harvey	0-2	J Titley	0-1
J Osborne	0-3	Mr J Culloty	0-2	Mr C Ward Thomas	0-1
R Farrant	0-3	Christopher Webb	0-1	Mr R Thornton	0-1
D Bridgwater	0-2	G Hogan	0-1	R Johnson	0-1
G McCourt	0-2	J Railton	0-1	W Marston	0-1

Forster Capt T A

COURSE RECORD

	Total W-R	Nov Hdles	H'cap Hdles	Nov Chses	H'cap Chses	Hunter Chses	N H Flat	£1 Level Stake
Ludlow	6-25	2-8	0-3	0-3	4-10	0-0	0-1	- 6.19
Cheltenham	3-7	0-1	1-1	0-2	2-3	0-0	0-0	+ 14.50
Towcester	3-20	1-5	0-4	0-5	2-5	0-0	0-1	- 8.75
Haydock	2-4	1-2	0-1	0-0	1-1	0-0	0-0	- 0.17
Stratford	2-7	1-4	1-3	0-0	0-0	0-0	0-0	+ 5.50
Leicester	2-9	0-0	0-1	0-5	2-3	0-0	0-0	+ 11.75
Hereford	2-12	0-2	1-2	0-2	0-4	0-0	1-2	+ 5.63
Chepstow	2-18	0-9	1-5	0-1	1-3	0-0	0-0	- 2.25
Market Rasen	1-1	1-1	0-0	0-0	0-0	0-0	0-0	+ 4.00
Carlisle	1-1	0-0	0-0	0-0	1-1	0-0	0-0	+ 0.83
Exeter	1-2	0-0	1-2	0-0	0-0	0-0	0-0	+ 3.00
Taunton	1-2	1-1	0-1	0-0	0-0	0-0	0-0	+ 9.00
Kempton	1-2	0-0	0-0	0-1	1-1	0-0	0-0	+ 5.50
Huntingdon	1-3	1-2	0-0	0-1	0-0	0-0	0-0	- 0.37
Windsor	1-3	1-2	0-0	0-0	0-1	0-0	0-0	+ 2.00
Uttoxeter	1-5	0-2	0-0	0-0	1-3	0-0	0-0	- 1.00
Wincanton	1-7	0-1	0-3	1-1	0-2	0-0	0-0	- 5.00
Bangor	1-9	0-1	0-1	1-3	0-4	0-0	0-0	- 6.37
Nottingham	1-9	0-1	1-4	0-4	0-0	0-0	0-0	- 5.75
Warwick	1-13	0-6	0-1	1-3	0-3	0-0	0-0	- 5.50

Worcester	0-10	Southwell		0-3	Ayr	0-1
Newbury	0-4	Ascot		0-1		

WINNING HORSES

	Races Run	1st	2nd	3rd	Unpl	Win £
Dublin Flyer	3	2	0	0	1	45,537
Maamur	5	3	1	0	1	43,288
Class of Ninetytwo	6	4	0	1	1	14,081
General Wolfe	5	2	2	0	1	11,694
Sun Surfer	7	2	0	2	3	9,123
Nicklup	6	2	0	1	3	7,301
Silver Standard	9	2	0	2	5	5,943
Ruby Vision	6	2	1	1	2	5,434
Teinein	6	2	1	1	2	5,257
Coonawara	1	1	0	0	0	4,902
Bungee Jumper	5	2	1	1	1	4,775
Three Philosophers	6	2	0	0	4	4,678
Three Saints	4	1	0	1	2	3,649
Eastern River	4	1	0	1	2	3,534
Poppea	6	1	1	1	3	3,363
Sail By The Stars	4	1	0	1	2	3,134
Rectory Garden	5	1	2	2	0	2,983
Valiant	2	1	0	0	1	2,213
Nothingtodowithme	1	1	0	0	0	2,150
Cool Virtue	1	1	0	0	0	1,070

WINNING OWNERS

	Races Won	Value £		Races Won	Value £
J B Sumner	4	50,312	G J G Roberts	2	5,434
Mrs A L Wood	3	43,288	Lady Cadogan	1	3,649
Lord Cadogan	7	24,365	Gamston Equine	1	3,534
Simon Sainsbury	5	19,282	T F F Nixon	1	3,134
The Winning Line	2	11,694	Mrs H Jones	1	2,213
Anne Duchess of Westminster	3	8,041	Miles Gosling	1	2,150
G W Lugg	2	5,943	Stephen Lambert	1	1,070

No of horses racing for the stable	54	Total winning prize-money	£184,109

Favourites	15-41	36.6%	- 3.64	Average SP of winner		4.3/1
Longest win seq	2	Longest losing seq	14	Return on stakes invested		0.8%

1994/95 Form	32-182	17.6%	- 24.89	1992/93 Form	29-217	13.4%	- 94.99
1993/94 Form	33-244	13.5%	- 58.98	1991/92 Form	44-273	16.1%	+ 26.28

J C FOX (Winterbourne Stoke, Wilts)

	Races Run	1st	2nd	3rd	Unpl	Per cent	£1 Level Stake
Hurdles	16	1	3	3	9	6.3	- 11.00
Chases	0	0	0	0	0	-	0.00
Totals	16	1	3	3	9	6.3	- 11.00

S Fox	1-13	- 8.00	Ascot	1-2	+ 3.00

No of horses racing for the stable	4	Total winning prize-money	£5,220

R G FROST (Buckfastleigh, Devon)

	Races Run	1st	2nd	3rd	Unpl	Per cent	£1 Level Stake
Hurdles	88	7	12	16	53	8.0	- 44.00
Chases	43	1	6	8	28	2.3	- 38.00
Totals	131	8	18	24	81	6.1	- 82.00

BY MONTH

	W-R	Per cent	£1 Level Stake		W-R	Per cent	£1 Level Stake
June	0-8	-	- 8.00	December	0-9	-	- 9.00
July	0-6	-	- 6.00	January	0-18	-	- 18.00
August	1-3	33.3	0.00	February	0-9	-	- 9.00
September	0-5	-	- 5.00	March	2-13	15.4	- 1.50
October	1-12	8.3	- 7.50	April	1-10	10.0	- 7.00
November	1-21	4.8	- 8.00	May	2-17	11.8	- 3.00

DISTANCE

Hurdles	W-R	Per cent	£1 Level Stake	Chases	W-R	Per cent	£1 Level Stake
2m-2m 3f	4-68	5.9	- 38.50	2m-2m 3f	1-21	4.8	- 16.00
2m 4f-2m 7f	3-18	16.7	- 3.50	2m 4f-2m 7f	0-17	-	- 17.00
3m +	0-2	-	- 2.00	3m +	0-5	-	- 5.00

TYPE OF RACE

	W-R	Per cent	£1 Level Stake		W-R	Per cent	£1 Level Stake
Novice hurdles	3-38	7.9	- 20.00	Selling	0-22	-	- 22.00
H'cap hurdles	4-21	19.0	+ 5.00	Amateur	0-0	-	0.00
Novice chases	0-16	-	- 16.00	Hunter chases	0-1	-	- 1.00
H'cap chases	1-24	4.2	- 19.00	N H Flat	0-9	-	- 9.00

COURSE GRADE

	W-R	Per cent	£1 Level Stake
Group 1	0-6	-	- 6.00
Group 2	5-58	8.6	- 27.50
Group 3	0-19	-	- 19.00
Group 4	3-48	6.3	- 29.50

FIRST TIME OUT

	W-R	Per cent	£1 Level Stake
Hurdles	3-29	10.3	- 8.50
Chases	0-7	-	- 7.00
Totals	3-36	8.3	- 15.50

JOCKEYS RIDING

	W-R	Per cent	£1 Level Stake
J Frost	8-125	6.4	- 76.00

R Darke	0-3	B Powell	0-1
B Moore	0-1	Mr M Frith	0-1

COURSE RECORD

	Total W-R	Nov Hdles	H'cap Hdles	Nov Chses	H'cap Chses	Hunter Chses	N H Flat	£1 Level Stake
Newton Abbot	5-45	2-19	3-6	0-7	0-9	0-1	0-3	- 14.50
Exeter	3-25	1-7	1-8	0-3	1-5	0-0	0-2	- 6.50

Fontwell	0-9	Worcester	0-5	Windsor	0-2
Hereford	0-9	Chepstow	0-4	Aintree	0-1
Taunton	0-9	Haydock	0-3	Kempton	0-1
Wincanton	0-7	Market Rasen	0-3	Sandown	0-1
Southwell	0-5	Uttoxeter	0-2		

WINNING HORSES

	Races Run	1st	2nd	3rd	Unpl	Win £
Hold Your Ranks	6	2	1	1	2	5,760
Holdimclose	6	2	0	2	2	4,596
Abavard	10	1	4	1	4	2,853
Mr Playfull	9	1	4	3	1	2,411
Mr Woodlark	2	1	0	0	1	2,397
Clear Idea	7	1	1	1	4	2,015

WINNING OWNERS

	Races Won	Value £		Races Won	Value £
Brian Seward	2	5,760	D G Henderson	1	2,853
P A Tylor	2	4,808	A E C Electric Fencing Ltd	1	2,015
Mrs C Loze	2	4,596			

No of horses racing for the stable	36	Total winning prize-money	£20,032

Favourites	4-8	50.0%	+ 10.00	Average SP of winner	5.1/1
Longest win seq	1	Longest losing seq	56	Return on stakes invested	-62.6%

1994/95 Form	8-167	4.8%	-128.50	1992/93 Form	12-199	6.0%	- 99.66
1993/94 Form	13-170	7.6%	- 88.83	1991/92 Form	14-170	8.2%	- 41.67

D R GANDOLFO (Wantage, Oxon)

	Races Run	1st	2nd	3rd	Unpl	Per cent	£1 Level Stake
Hurdles	129	15	17	14	83	11.6	- 47.13
Chases	40	9	6	4	21	22.5	- 7.98
Totals	169	24	23	18	104	14.2	- 55.11

BY MONTH

	W-R	Per cent	£1 Level Stake		W-R	Per cent	£1 Level Stake
June	0-0	-	0.00	December	1-20	5.0	- 12.00
July	1-3	33.3	- 0.12	January	2-28	7.1	- 18.00
August	1-1	100.0	+ 2.50	February	5-22	22.7	+ 10.79
September	1-5	20.0	- 2.25	March	7-27	25.9	- 6.60
October	1-8	12.5	- 3.00	April	3-19	15.8	- 1.00
November	2-25	8.0	- 14.43	May	0-11	-	- 11.00

DISTANCE

Hurdles	W-R	Per cent	£1 Level Stake	Chases	W-R	Per cent	£1 Level Stake
2m-2m 3f	10-96	10.4	- 38.63	2m-2m 3f	4-16	25.0	- 2.46
2m 4f-2m 7f	5-28	17.9	- 3.50	2m 4f-2m 7f	4-16	25.0	- 1.02
3m +	0-5	-	- 5.00	3m +	1-8	12.5	- 4.50

TYPE OF RACE

	W-R	Per cent	£1 Level Stake		W-R	Per cent	£1 Level Stake
Novice hurdles	6-57	10.5	- 32.76	Selling	0-8	-	- 8.00
H'cap hurdles	6-45	13.3	- 17.37	Amateur	0-1	-	- 1.00
Novice chases	6-19	31.6	+ 1.02	Hunter chases	0-0	-	0.00
H'cap chases	3-21	14.3	- 9.00	N H Flat	3-18	16.7	+ 12.00

COURSE GRADE

	W-R	Per cent	£1 Level Stake
Group 1	3-30	10.0	- 16.50
Group 2	2-29	6.9	- 25.76
Group 3	10-57	17.5	- 10.89
Group 4	9-53	17.0	- 1.96

FIRST TIME OUT

	W-R	Per cent	£1 Level Stake
Hurdles	4-36	11.1	- 10.93
Chases	0-8	-	- 8.00
Totals	4-44	9.1	- 18.93

JOCKEYS RIDING

	W-R	Per cent	£1 Level Stake		W-R	Per cent	£1 Level Stake
R Dunwoody	10-19	52.6	+ 5.39	Sophie Mitchell	2-21	9.5	- 10.50
M Dwyer	7-42	16.7	- 5.50	D Leahy	1-43	2.3	- 35.00
D Fortt	4-24	16.7	+ 10.50				

J Osborne	0-5	G Upton	0-2	P Niven	0-1
A Dowling	0-3	A P McCoy	0-1	R Farrant	0-1
A Maguire	0-3	D Bridgwater	0-1		
C Llewellyn	0-2	Miss P Jones	0-1		

COURSE RECORD

	Total W-R	Nov Hdles	H'cap Hdles	Nov Chses	H'cap Chses	Hunter Chses	N H Flat	£1 Level Stake
Towcester	4-14	1-8	1-2	1-1	0-1	0-0	1-2	+ 8.79
Uttoxeter	2-2	1-1	0-0	0-0	1-1	0-0	0-0	+ 6.75
Worcester	2-6	0-0	2-3	0-1	0-0	0-0	0-2	+ 0.25
Cheltenham	2-6	0-1	0-2	2-3	0-0	0-0	0-0	+ 4.00
Wincanton	2-6	0-2	1-2	1-2	0-0	0-0	0-0	+ 4.73
Newton Abbot	2-12	2-6	0-3	0-1	0-1	0-0	0-1	- 8.76
Ludlow	1-2	0-1	0-0	0-0	0-0	0-0	1-1	+ 6.00
Stratford	1-3	0-2	1-1	0-0	0-0	0-0	0-0	- 0.12
Bangor	1-4	1-2	0-1	0-0	0-1	0-0	0-0	+ 4.00
Fakenham	1-4	0-1	0-1	1-1	0-1	0-0	0-0	- 0.50
Kempton	1-4	0-1	0-0	1-1	0-0	0-0	0-2	- 0.50
Nottingham	1-5	0-1	0-2	0-0	0-1	0-0	1-1	+ 6.00
Taunton	1-6	0-3	0-2	0-0	1-1	0-0	0-0	+ 0.50
Windsor	1-7	1-4	0-1	0-0	0-2	0-0	0-0	- 5.50
Warwick	1-11	0-4	1-4	0-1	0-1	0-0	0-1	- 6.00
Exeter	1-17	0-7	0-7	0-1	1-2	0-0	0-0	- 14.75

Chepstow	0-12	Leicester	0-5	Fontwell	0-2
Newbury	0-7	Folkestone	0-4	Huntingdon	0-2
Hereford	0-6	Lingfield	0-3	Aintree	0-1
Ascot	0-5	Market Rasen	0-3	Doncaster	0-1
Haydock	0-5	Plumpton	0-3	Sandown	0-1

Gandolfo D R

WINNING HORSES

	Races Run	1st	2nd	3rd	Unpl	Win £
Gales Cavalier	5	2	2	0	1	27,441
Garrylough	7	3	1	1	2	18,176
Trying Again	7	4	1	0	2	14,997
Khalidi	3	2	0	1	0	7,701
Nadjati	9	2	0	2	5	6,143
Around The Gale	6	2	1	0	3	5,642
Selatan	7	2	1	0	4	5,405
Mouse Bird	6	1	3	1	1	2,948
General Tonic	5	1	2	0	2	2,661
River Leven	5	1	1	1	2	2,040
Deymiar	6	1	3	1	1	2,040
Come On Penny	7	1	1	1	4	1,319
Sprig Muslin	2	1	0	1	0	1,264
Royal Event	3	1	0	1	1	1,229

WINNING OWNERS

	Races Won	Value £		Races Won	Value £
T J Whitley	11	40,931	R E Brinkworth	1	2,040
Starlight Racing	5	35,507	A E Frost	1	1,319
W H Dore	4	14,997	D R Gandolfo	1	1,264
Osbert Pierce	1	2,948			

No of horses racing for the stable 45   Total winning prize-money £99,006

Favourites	11-29	37.9%	- 3.36	Average SP of winner		3.7/1
Longest win seq	3	Longest losing seq 31		Return on stakes invested		-32.6%
1994/95 Form	29-139	20.9%	+ 9.31	1992/93 Form	12-147 8.2%	- 63.37
1993/94 Form	16-115	13.9%	+ 0.75	1991/92 Form	14-135 10.4%	- 8.69

A B GARTON (Macclesfield, Cheshire)

	Races Run	1st	2nd	3rd	Unpl	Per cent	£1 Level Stake
Hurdles	0	0	0	0	0	-	0.00
Chases	3	1	0	1	1	33.3	+ 9.00
Totals	3	1	0	1	1	33.3	+ 9.00

Mr T Garton   1-3   + 9.00   Uttoxeter   1-1   + 11.00

No of horses racing for the stable 1   Total winning prize-money £1,843

N A GASELEE (Upper Lambourn, Berks)

	Races Run	1st	2nd	3rd	Unpl	Per cent	£1 Level Stake
Hurdles	51	5	4	2	40	9.8	- 1.37
Chases	75	9	10	12	44	12.0	- 25.00
Totals	126	14	14	14	84	11.1	- 26.37

BY MONTH

	W-R	Per cent	£1 Level Stake		W-R	Per cent	£1 Level Stake
June	1-4	25.0	- 0.50	December	1-12	8.3	- 7.50
July	0-1	-	- 1.00	January	3-15	20.0	+ 26.50
August	0-1	-	- 1.00	February	2-22	9.1	- 6.00
September	0-1	-	- 1.00	March	0-22	-	- 22.00
October	2-8	25.0	+ 1.00	April	3-15	20.0	+ 2.63
November	1-14	7.1	- 12.50	May	1-11	9.1	- 5.00

DISTANCE

	W-R	Per cent	£1 Level Stake		W-R	Per cent	£1 Level Stake
Hurdles				Chases			
2m-2m 3f	0-18	-	- 18.00	2m-2m 3f	2-16	12.5	- 10.00
2m 4f-2m 7f	4-17	23.5	+ 30.00	2m 4f-2m 7f	6-32	18.8	+ 6.00
3m +	1-16	6.3	- 13.37	3m +	1-27	3.7	- 21.00

TYPE OF RACE

	W-R	Per cent	£1 Level Stake		W-R	Per cent	£1 Level Stake
Novice hurdles	4-23	17.4	+ 16.63	Selling	0-0	-	0.00
H'cap hurdles	1-20	5.0	- 10.00	Amateur	1-1	100.0	+ 3.50
Novice chases	4-17	23.5	+ 4.00	Hunter chases	0-7	-	- 7.00
H'cap chases	4-50	8.0	- 25.50	N H Flat	0-8	-	- 8.00

COURSE GRADE

	W-R	Per cent	£1 Level Stake
Group 1	3-41	7.3	0.00
Group 2	0-18	-	- 18.00
Group 3	7-40	17.5	+ 2.50
Group 4	4-27	14.8	- 10.87

FIRST TIME OUT

	W-R	Per cent	£1 Level Stake
Hurdles	1-12	8.3	- 7.50
Chases	2-16	12.5	- 8.00
Totals	3-28	10.7	- 15.50

JOCKEYS RIDING

	W-R	Per cent	£1 Level Stake		W-R	Per cent	£1 Level Stake
C Llewellyn	6-48	12.5	+ 14.00	Mr M Rimell	1-3	33.3	+ 1.50
R Dunwoody	2-4	50.0	+ 5.50	B Powell	1-4	25.0	- 2.50
A Thornton	2-6	33.3	+ 9.00	P Niven	1-4	25.0	- 1.37
D Gallagher	1-2	50.0	+ 2.50				

F Cooper	0-10	J Titley	0-2	M Perrett	0-1
J R Kavanagh	0-8	D Finnegan	0-1	N Mann	0-1
A Tory	0-7	G Bradley	0-1	N Williamson	0-1
M A Fitzgerald	0-7	G Upton	0-1	P Hide	0-1
J Osborne	0-5	J Railton	0-1	Richard Davis	0-1
Mr R Hall	0-5	M Dwyer	0-1	T Dascombe	0-1

COURSE RECORD

	Total W-R	Nov Hdles	H'cap Hdles	Nov Chses	H'cap Chses	Hunter Chses	N H Flat	£1 Level Stake
Worcester	2-6	0-0	0-2	0-0	2-4	0-0	0-0	+ 7.50
Warwick	2-7	0-0	0-1	2-3	0-3	0-0	0-0	+ 3.50
Windsor	2-8	1-4	0-1	1-2	0-0	0-1	0-0	+ 4.50
Perth	1-1	1-1	0-0	0-0	0-0	0-0	0-0	+ 1.63
Bangor	1-2	0-0	0-0	1-1	0-1	0-0	0-0	+ 2.50
Ludlow	1-3	0-0	0-0	0-0	1-2	0-1	0-0	+ 1.50
Stratford	1-5	0-0	0-2	0-0	1-3	0-0	0-0	+ 1.00
Ascot	1-5	1-1	0-1	0-1	0-1	0-0	0-1	+ 21.00
Kempton	1-6	0-1	1-1	0-2	0-1	0-0	0-1	+ 4.00
Sandown	1-6	0-1	0-0	0-0	1-3	0-1	0-1	- 1.00
Towcester	1-9	1-3	0-1	0-1	0-3	0-0	0-1	- 4.50

Newbury	0-12	Newton Abbot	0-3	Fakenham	0-1
Chepstow	0-10	Nottingham	0-3	Folkestone	0-1
Exeter	0-8	Aintree	0-2	Huntingdon	0-1
Haydock	0-5	Hereford	0-2	Taunton	0-1
Wincanton	0-5	Leicester	0-2	Wetherby	0-1
Cheltenham	0-4	Uttoxeter	0-2		
Lingfield	0-4	Doncaster	0-1		

WINNING HORSES

	Races Run	1st	2nd	3rd	Unpl	Win £
Destiny Calls	6	3	1	2	0	21,537
Bavard Dieu	6	2	0	0	4	12,226
Act of Faith	5	2	0	1	2	8,463
Commercial Artist	3	1	0	0	2	7,276
Mr Entertainer	8	2	1	1	4	7,168
Castle Court	7	1	0	2	4	4,075
Bucket of Gold	3	1	0	0	2	3,050
Erckule	4	1	0	0	3	2,931
Mystic Isle	7	1	1	0	5	2,740

WINNING OWNERS

	Races Won	Value £		Races Won	Value £
Simon Harrap	3	21,537	M A Boddington	2	7,168
Saguaro Stables	2	12,226	Mrs T J McInnes Skinner	1	3,050
Mrs David Thompson	2	11,351	The Saxon Partnership	1	2,931
Mrs R W S Baker	2	8,463	Mrs P Furse	1	2,740

No of horses racing for the stable	29	Total winning prize-money £69,466

Favourites	4-11	36.4% + 2.63	Average SP of winner 6.1/1
Longest win seq	2	Longest losing seq 40	Return on stakes invested -20.9%

1994/95 Form	17-127	13.4% - 22.71	1992/93 Form 13-121 10.7% - 36.40
1993/94 Form	19-130	14.6% - 18.88	1991/92 Form 15-140 10.7% - 53.13

MISS K M GEORGE (Princes Risborough, Bucks)

	Races Run	1st	2nd	3rd	Unpl	Per cent	£1 Level Stake
Hurdles	10	3	1	0	6	30.0	+ 4.25
Chases	7	2	0	0	5	28.6	+ 23.00
Totals	17	5	1	0	11	29.4	+ 27.25

A Larnach	3-6	+ 15.25	J R Kavanagh	2-5 + 18.00
Plumpton	3-7	+ 7.25	Worcester	1-2 + 13.00
Ludlow	1-1	+ 14.00		

No of horses racing for the stable	6	Total winning prize-money £14,024

T R GEORGE (Slad, Glos)

	Races Run	1st	2nd	3rd	Unpl	Per cent	£1 Level Stake
Hurdles	50	3	6	6	35	6.0	- 21.50
Chases	25	1	3	3	18	4.0	+ 9.00
Totals	75	4	9	9	53	5.3	- 12.50

G Hogan	2-4	+ 9.50	R Johnson	1-11 + 23.00
R Dunwoody	1-2	+ 13.00		
Nottingham	1-2	+ 32.00	Uttoxeter	1-5 - 0.50
Newton Abbot	1-5	+ 10.00	Ludlow	1-6 + 3.00

No of horses racing for the stable	16	Total winning prize-money £13,764

D P GERAGHTY (Barckley, Northants)

	Races Run	1st	2nd	3rd	Unpl	Per cent	£1 Level Stake
Hurdles	22	1	4	4	13	4.5	+ 45.00
Chases	1	0	0	0	1	-	- 1.00
Totals	23	1	4	4	14	4.3	+ 44.00

V Slattery	1-3	+ 64.00	Windsor 1-5 + 62.00

No of horses racing for the stable	6	Total winning prize-money £2,875

MRS D S C GIBSON (Hexham, Northumberland)

	Races Run	1st	2nd	3rd	Unpl	Per cent	£1 Level Stake
Hurdles	0	0	0	0	0	-	0.00
Chases	5	2	0	0	3	40.0	+ 23.38
Totals	5	2	0	0	3	40.0	+ 23.38

Mrs V Jackson	2-5	+ 23.38			
Sedgefield	1-1	+ 1.38	Perth	1-2	+ 24.00

No of horses racing for the stable	1	Total winning prize-money	£4,811

J T GIFFORD (Findon, West Sussex)

	Races Run	1st	2nd	3rd	Unpl	Per cent	£1 Level Stake
Hurdles	138	19	13	13	93	13.8	- 30.54
Chases	129	21	10	13	85	16.3	- 10.75
Totals	267	40	23	26	178	15.0	- 41.29

BY MONTH

	W-R	Per cent	£1 Level Stake		W-R	Per cent	£1 Level Stake
June	0-0	-	0.00	December	7-34	20.6	+ 7.20
July	0-0	-	0.00	January	4-57	7.0	- 24.18
August	0-0	-	0.00	February	0-26	-	- 26.00
September	0-0	-	0.00	March	6-51	11.8	- 18.00
October	4-11	36.4	+ 17.38	April	7-33	21.2	+ 1.32
November	9-41	22.0	- 1.01	May	3-14	21.4	+ 2.00

DISTANCE

Hurdles	W-R	Per cent	£1 Level Stake	Chases	W-R	Per cent	£1 Level Stake
2m-2m 3f	11-95	11.6	- 19.17	2m-2m 3f	7-39	17.9	- 12.43
2m 4f-2m 7f	7-36	19.4	- 15.37	2m 4f-2m 7f	9-35	25.7	+ 16.27
3m +	1-7	14.3	+ 4.00	3m +	5-55	9.1	- 14.59

TYPE OF RACE

	W-R	Per cent	£1 Level Stake		W-R	Per cent	£1 Level Stake
Novice hurdles	9-78	11.5	- 29.37	Selling	0-0	-	0.00
H'cap hurdles	6-41	14.6	- 11.67	Amateur	1-7	14.3	+ 14.00
Novice chases	7-36	19.4	- 16.16	Hunter chases	0-0	-	0.00
H'cap chases	13-86	15.1	- 8.59	N H Flat	4-19	21.1	+ 10.50

Gifford J T

<table>
<tr><td colspan="4" align="center">**COURSE GRADE**</td><td colspan="4" align="center">**FIRST TIME OUT**</td></tr>
<tr><td></td><td>W-R</td><td>Per cent</td><td>£1 Level Stake</td><td></td><td>W-R</td><td>Per cent</td><td>£1 Level Stake</td></tr>
<tr><td>Group 1</td><td>15-115</td><td>13.0</td><td>- 26.52</td><td>Hurdles</td><td>11-51</td><td>21.6</td><td>+ 20.96</td></tr>
<tr><td>Group 2</td><td>8-62</td><td>12.9</td><td>- 19.17</td><td>Chases</td><td>5-27</td><td>18.5</td><td>+ 3.50</td></tr>
<tr><td>Group 3</td><td>11-57</td><td>19.3</td><td>+ 11.65</td><td></td><td></td><td></td><td></td></tr>
<tr><td>Group 4</td><td>6-33</td><td>18.2</td><td>- 7.25</td><td>Totals</td><td>16-78</td><td>20.5</td><td>+ 24.46</td></tr>
</table>

JOCKEYS RIDING

<table>
<tr><td></td><td>W-R</td><td>Per cent</td><td>£1 Level Stake</td><td></td><td>W-R</td><td>Per cent</td><td>£1 Level Stake</td></tr>
<tr><td>P Hide</td><td>24-161</td><td>14.9</td><td>- 50.54</td><td>D O'Sullivan</td><td>1-2</td><td>50.0</td><td>+ 3.00</td></tr>
<tr><td>L Aspell</td><td>9-48</td><td>18.8</td><td>+ 6.00</td><td>B Powell</td><td>1-6</td><td>16.7</td><td>- 3.00</td></tr>
<tr><td>A P McCoy</td><td>2-4</td><td>50.0</td><td>+ 10.75</td><td>S McNeill</td><td>1-10</td><td>10.0</td><td>- 4.50</td></tr>
<tr><td>G Bradley</td><td>1-1</td><td>100.0</td><td>+ 11.00</td><td>Mr P O'Keeffe</td><td>1-21</td><td>4.8</td><td>0.00</td></tr>
</table>

L Manceau	0-2	Miss A Embiricos	0-1	R Johnson	0-1
R Dunwoody	0-2	Mr C Bonner	0-1	R Massey	0-1
W Marston	0-2	Mr T McCarthy	0-1	W Greatrex	0-1
E Murphy	0-1	Peter Hobbs	0-1		

COURSE RECORD

	Total W-R	Nov Hdles	H'cap Hdles	Nov Chses	H'cap Chses	Hunter Chses	N H Flat	£1 Level Stake
Towcester	5-20	1-6	0-2	2-2	2-10	0-0	0-0	- 2.25
Fontwell	5-34	1-9	2-7	0-5	2-12	0-0	0-1	- 9.67
Huntingdon	3-10	2-4	0-1	0-1	1-3	0-0	0-1	+ 12.50
Folkestone	3-12	0-3	0-1	1-1	1-3	0-0	1-4	+ 15.70
Newbury	3-16	0-4	0-3	1-2	1-6	0-0	1-1	- 2.00
Cheltenham	3-20	1-6	0-3	0-2	1-7	0-0	1-2	+ 13.00
Sandown	3-29	0-10	1-5	1-4	1-8	0-0	0-2	- 10.50
Ascot	3-30	2-12	0-4	0-3	1-9	0-0	0-2	- 22.34
Warwick	2-13	0-2	0-3	0-1	2-7	0-0	0-0	- 2.50
Kempton	2-19	0-5	2-3	0-3	0-6	0-0	0-2	- 5.25
Chepstow	2-21	0-6	0-3	0-3	2-8	0-0	0-1	- 10.00
Ayr	1-1	0-0	0-0	1-1	0-0	0-0	0-0	+ 0.57
Newton Abbot	1-2	0-0	1-1	0-1	0-0	0-0	0-0	+ 5.50
Stratford	1-3	1-1	0-0	0-0	0-2	0-0	0-0	- 0.62
Wincanton	1-3	1-3	0-0	0-0	0-0	0-0	0-0	+ 1.00
Windsor	1-6	0-2	0-0	1-2	0-2	0-0	0-0	- 4.43
Exeter	1-8	0-0	0-3	0-1	0-3	0-0	1-1	0.00

Plumpton	0-4	Worcester	0-3	Fakenham	0-1
Lingfield	0-3	Uttoxeter	0-2	Hereford	0-1
Taunton	0-3	Wetherby	0-2	Leicester	0-1

WINNING HORSES

	Races Run	1st	2nd	3rd	Unpl	Win £
Mandys Mantino	4	4	0	0	0	16,256
Major Summit	4	3	0	1	0	15,684
Yorkshire Gale	5	2	0	0	3	14,971
No Pain No Gain	9	3	3	0	3	11,489
Armala	5	3	0	0	2	11,362
Denver Bay	5	2	1	0	2	10,819
Redeemyourself	2	2	0	0	0	10,666
Run Up The Flag	6	1	0	4	1	10,406
Wee Windy	4	2	1	0	1	7,033
Rainbow Castle	9	2	0	1	6	7,002
Buck Willow	4	1	0	1	2	4,965
Around The Horn	4	1	0	0	3	4,500
Mr Felix	5	1	0	2	2	4,401
My Wizard	3	1	0	0	2	3,998
Marius	9	1	2	1	5	3,822
Lively Knight	5	1	1	0	3	3,550
Scoresheet	1	1	0	0	0	3,233
Headwind	3	1	1	0	1	3,020
Maestro Paul	8	1	1	0	6	2,969
Pa D'Or	7	1	0	2	4	2,828
Grooving	4	1	0	0	3	2,734
'Iggins	2	1	0	0	1	2,705
Antonio Mariano	3	1	0	0	2	2,098
Nasone	2	1	0	0	1	1,522
Boardroom Shuffle	1	1	0	0	0	1,459
Supreme Kellycarra	3	1	1	0	1	1,329

WINNING OWNERS

	Races Won	Value £		Races Won	Value £
Bill Naylor	4	25,790	Mrs S N J Embiricos	1	4,965
Pell-Mell Partners	5	23,864	Felix Rosenstiel's Widow & Son	1	4,401
A D Weller	5	20,693	Mrs Angela Brodie	1	3,998
John Plackett	4	16,333	Mrs Anthony Andrews	1	3,822
Mrs Tracy Brown	3	13,400	H T Pelham	1	2,969
The Marvellous Partnership	3	11,489	The Peoples Express P'ship	1	2,828
Mrs C Houston	3	11,362	Miss Monica Campbell	1	2,098
W E Gale	2	7,033	Mrs Davina Whiteman	1	1,445
Findon Cricket Racing Club	2	7,002	N C Rolfe	1	1,329

No of horses racing for the stable		78	Total winning prize-money	£164,821

Favourites	16-36	44.4%	+ 8.46	Average SP of winner	4.6/1
Longest win seq	3	Longest losing seq	34	Return on stakes invested	-15.5%

1994/95 Form	47-281	16.7%	- 48.42	1992/93 Form	49-300	16.3%	- 42.05
1993/94 Form	51-326	15.6%	- 38.72	1991/92 Form	49-389	12.6%	-150.20

S J GILMORE (Brackley, Northants)

	Races Run	1st	2nd	3rd	Unpl	Per cent	£1 Level Stake
Hurdles	0	0	0	0	0	–	0.00
Chases	14	2	0	1	11	14.3	– 3.50
Totals	14	2	0	1	11	14.3	– 3.50

Mr A Lay	2-11	– 0.50	Hereford	2-4	+ 6.50

No of horses racing for the stable   3   Total winning prize-money   £3,815

J A GLOVER (Carburton, Notts)

	Races Run	1st	2nd	3rd	Unpl	Per cent	£1 Level Stake
Hurdles	20	3	3	0	14	15.0	– 4.20
Chases	12	0	2	1	9	–	– 12.00
Totals	32	3	5	1	23	9.4	– 16.20

T Eley	2-5	+ 9.00	A S Smith	1-7	– 5.20
Towcester	1-2	– 0.20	Uttoxeter	1-3	0.00
Ludlow	1-2	+ 9.00			

No of horses racing for the stable   8   Total winning prize-money   £7,535

J S GOLDIE (Uplawmoor, Strathclyde)

	Races Run	1st	2nd	3rd	Unpl	Per cent	£1 Level Stake
Hurdles	65	2	3	7	53	3.1	– 52.00
Chases	0	0	0	0	0	–	0.00
Totals	65	2	3	7	53	3.1	– 52.00

P G Cahill	2-7	+ 6.00			
Hexham	1-3	+ 5.00	Perth	1-7	– 2.00

No of horses racing for the stable   11   Total winning prize-money   £4,793

R H GOLDIE (Dundonald, Strathclyde)

	Races Run	1st	2nd	3rd	Unpl	Per cent	£1 Level Stake
Hurdles	1	0	0	0	1	-	- 1.00
Chases	9	1	0	0	8	11.1	+ 8.00
Totals	10	1	0	0	9	10.0	+ 7.00

P G Cahill	1-1	+ 16.00	Kelso	1-3	+ 14.00

No of horses racing for the stable   4   Total winning prize-money   £4,221

D T GOLDSWORTHY (Bridgend, Mid Glamorgan)

	Races Run	1st	2nd	3rd	Unpl	Per cent	£1 Level Stake
Hurdles	0	0	0	0	0	-	0.00
Chases	2	1	0	0	1	50.0	+ 8.00
Totals	2	1	0	0	1	50.0	+ 8.00

Mr E Williams	1-1	+ 9.00	Chepstow	1-1	+ 9.00

No of horses racing for the stable   1   Total winning prize-money   £3,571

S GOLLINGS (Scamblesby, Lincs)

	Races Run	1st	2nd	3rd	Unpl	Per cent	£1 Level Stake
Hurdles	38	1	7	1	29	2.6	- 30.00
Chases	0	0	0	0	0	-	0.00
Totals	38	1	7	1	29	2.6	- 30.00

A Dobbin	1-7	+ 1.00	Market Rasen	1-10	- 2.00

No of horses racing for the stable   7   Total winning prize-money   £2,565

MRS J GOODFELLOW (Earlston, Borders)

	Races Run	1st	2nd	3rd	Unpl	Per cent	£1 Level Stake
Hurdles	20	3	1	3	13	15.0	- 0.38
Chases	11	2	2	1	6	18.2	- 7.10
Totals	31	5	3	4	19	16.1	- 7.48

Mr R Hale	2-5	+ 2.10	P G Cahill	1-1	+ 12.00
B Storey	2-15	- 11.58			
Kelso	3-11	- 2.10	Newcastle	1-5	- 3.38
Ayr	1-1	+ 12.00			

No of horses racing for the stable   8   Total winning prize-money   £15,035

N A GRAHAM (Newmarket, Suffolk)

	Races Run	1st	2nd	3rd	Unpl	Per cent	£1 Level Stake
Hurdles	21	3	4	4	10	14.3	- 12.62
Chases	0	0	0	0	0	-	0.00
Totals	21	3	4	4	10	14.3	- 12.62

L Wyer	3-8	+ 0.38	Wincanton	3-3	+ 5.38

No of horses racing for the stable   6   Total winning prize-money   £6,838

MRS P GRAINGER (Kidderminster, H'ford & Worcs)

	Races Run	1st	2nd	3rd	Unpl	Per cent	£1 Level Stake
Hurdles	0	0	0	0	0	-	0.00
Chases	3	1	1	1	0	33.3	+ 1.50
Totals	3	1	1	1	0	33.3	+ 1.50

Mr A J Phillips	1-3	+ 1.50	Hereford	1-1	+ 3.50

No of horses racing for the stable   1   Total winning prize-money   £1,725

V G GREENWAY (Lydeard St Lawrence, Somerset)

	Races Run	1st	2nd	3rd	Unpl	Per cent	£1 Level Stake
Hurdles	5	0	0	0	5	-	- 5.00
Chases	2	1	0	1	0	50.0	+ 8.00
Totals	7	1	0	1	5	14.3	+ 3.00

Mr Richard White	1-2	+ 8.00	Taunton	1-1	+ 9.00

No of horses racing for the stable   2   Total winning prize-money   £1,173

P GREENWOOD (Malmesbury, Wilts)

	Races Run	1st	2nd	3rd	Unpl	Per cent	£1 Level Stake
Hurdles	0	0	0	0	0	-	0.00
Chases	1	1	0	0	0	100.0	+ 2.25
Totals	1	1	0	0	0	100.0	+ 2.25

Mr A Charles-Jones	1-1	+ 2.25	Folkestone	1-1	+ 2.25

No of horses racing for the stable   1   Total winning prize-money   £1,800

S G GRIFFITHS (Nantgaredig, Dyfed)

	Races Run	1st	2nd	3rd	Unpl	Per cent	£1 Level Stake
Hurdles	12	3	2	1	6	25.0	+ 20.00
Chases	2	0	0	0	2	-	- 2.00
Totals	14	3	2	1	8	21.4	+ 18.00

Mr J Jukes	3-6	+ 26.00			
Hereford	1-1	+ 8.00	Chepstow	1-3	+ 3.00
Haydock	1-1	+ 16.00			

No of horses racing for the stable   3   Total winning prize-money   £13,443

D M GRISSELL (Brightling Park, East Sussex)

	Races Run	1st	2nd	3rd	Unpl	Per cent	£1 Level Stake
Hurdles	44	6	7	7	24	13.6	+ 3.88
Chases	26	2	2	4	18	7.7	- 10.25
Totals	70	8	9	11	42	11.4	- 6.37

BY MONTH

	W-R	Per cent	£1 Level Stake		W-R	Per cent	£1 Level Stake
June	0-2	-	- 2.00	December	2-7	28.6	+ 8.75
July	0-1	-	- 1.00	January	0-12	-	- 12.00
August	0-0	-	0.00	February	0-6	-	- 6.00
September	1-1	100.0	+ 9.00	March	1-13	7.7	- 10.62
October	0-7	-	- 7.00	April	2-10	20.0	- 2.50
November	1-7	14.3	+ 19.00	May	1-4	25.0	- 2.00

DISTANCE

	W-R	Per cent	£1 Level Stake		W-R	Per cent	£1 Level Stake
Hurdles				Chases			
2m-2m 3f	3-21	14.3	+ 12.50	2m-2m 3f	2-11	18.2	+ 4.75
2m 4f-2m 7f	3-19	15.8	- 4.62	2m 4f-2m 7f	0-8	-	- 8.00
3m +	0-4	-	- 4.00	3m +	0-7	-	- 7.00

TYPE OF RACE

	W-R	Per cent	£1 Level Stake		W-R	Per cent	£1 Level Stake
Novice hurdles	4-27	14.8	+ 5.88	Selling	0-1	-	- 1.00
H'cap hurdles	2-16	12.5	- 1.00	Amateur	0-2	-	- 2.00
Novice chases	0-2	-	- 2.00	Hunter chases	0-0	-	0.00
H'cap chases	2-21	9.5	- 5.25	N H Flat	0-1	-	- 1.00

COURSE GRADE

	W-R	Per cent	£1 Level Stake
Group 1	1-12	8.3	- 2.00
Group 2	0-20	-	- 20.00
Group 3	6-33	18.2	+ 18.63
Group 4	1-5	20.0	- 3.00

FIRST TIME OUT

	W-R	Per cent	£1 Level Stake
Hurdles	1-13	7.7	+ 13.00
Chases	1-7	14.3	+ 6.00
Totals	2-20	10.0	+ 19.00

JOCKEYS RIDING

	W-R	Per cent	£1 Level Stake		W-R	Per cent	£1 Level Stake
J R Kavanagh	3-20	15.0	- 13.12	D Bridgwater	1-7	14.3	+ 6.00
B Fenton	2-13	15.4	- 5.25	Peter Hobbs	1-11	9.1	+ 15.00
N Williamson	1-1	100.0	+ 9.00				

Grissell D M

M Richards	0-5	A Maguire	0-2	Mr M Armytage	0-1
D Morris	0-3	G Hogan	0-1	Mr M Phillips	0-1
J Railton	0-3	J Osborne	0-1	P McLoughlin	0-1

COURSE RECORD

	Total W-R	Nov Hdles	H'cap Hdles	Nov Chses	H'cap Chses	Hunter Chses	N H Flat	£1 Level Stake
Plumpton	3-11	2-4	0-1	0-0	1-6	0-0	0-0	+ 6.88
Folkestone	3-13	1-5	1-3	0-1	1-3	0-0	0-1	+ 20.75
Fakenham	1-1	1-1	0-0	0-0	0-0	0-0	0-0	+ 1.00
Cheltenham	1-2	0-0	1-1	0-0	0-1	0-0	0-0	+ 8.00

Fontwell	0-11	Kempton	0-3	Uttoxeter	0-2
Lingfield	0-9	Sandown	0-3	Newbury	0-1
Windsor	0-4	Towcester	0-3	Southwell	0-1
Ascot	0-3	Huntingdon	0-2	Stratford	0-1

WINNING HORSES

	Races Run	1st	2nd	3rd	Unpl	Win £
Le Chat Noir	5	2	0	0	3	6,081
Bon Voyage	7	2	3	1	1	5,283
Hurricane Blake	2	1	0	0	1	3,501
Buckland Lad	6	1	1	1	3	2,678
Jojo	6	1	0	1	4	2,406
Envopakleada	3	1	2	0	0	2,301

WINNING OWNERS

	Races Won	Value £		Races Won	Value £
F J T Parsons	2	6,081	Mrs R M Hepburn	1	2,678
Hon Mrs C Yeates	2	5,283	John Grist	1	2,406
Exors of the Late P D Rylands	1	3,501	Frank Arthur	1	2,301

No of horses racing for the stable	20	Total winning prize-money	£22,250

Favourites	5-9	55.6%	+ 5.63	Average SP of winner		7.0/1
Longest win seq	2	Longest losing seq	32	Return on stakes invested		-9.1%

1994/95 Form	5-84	6.0%	- 67.87	1992/93 Form	18-70	25.7%	+ 75.59
1993/94 Form	12-101	11.9%	- 54.35	1991/92 Form	5-77	6.5%	- 47.92

MRS D M GRISSELL (Robertsbridge, East Sussex)

	Races Run	1st	2nd	3rd	Unpl	Per cent	£1 Level Stake
Hurdles	0	0	0	0	0	-	0.00
Chases	8	3	1	0	4	37.5	+ 0.51
Totals	8	3	1	0	4	37.5	+ 0.51

Mr P Hacking	2-5	- 0.24	Mr J Culloty	1-1	+ 2.75
Newbury	1-1	+ 1.38	Southwell	1-1	+ 1.38
Ascot	1-1	+ 2.75			

No of horses racing for the stable	4	Total winning prize-money	£5,550

W J HAGGAS (Newmarket, Suffolk)

	Races Run	1st	2nd	3rd	Unpl	Per cent	£1 Level Stake
Hurdles	8	1	1	0	6	12.5	- 5.50
Chases	0	0	0	0	0	-	0.00
Totals	8	1	1	0	6	12.5	- 5.50

T Jenks	1-3	- 0.50	Fakenham	1-2	+ 0.50

No of horses racing for the stable	1	Total winning prize-money	£2,552

W W HAIGH (Norton, North Yorks)

	Races Run	1st	2nd	3rd	Unpl	Per cent	£1 Level Stake
Hurdles	16	2	5	3	6	12.5	- 12.32
Chases	0	0	0	0	0	-	0.00
Totals	16	2	5	3	6	12.5	- 12.32

D Gallagher	1-1	+ 0.30	D Byrne	1-10	- 7.62
Doncaster	1-1	+ 1.38	Carlisle	1-1	+ 0.30

No of horses racing for the stable	4	Total winning prize-money	£5,842

MRS D HAINE (Newmarket, Suffolk)

	Races Run	1st	2nd	3rd	Unpl	Per cent	£1 Level Stake
Hurdles	35	5	3	1	26	14.3	- 11.62
Chases	24	2	3	5	14	8.3	- 1.27
Totals	59	7	6	6	40	11.9	- 12.89

BY MONTH

	W-R	Per cent	£1 Level Stake		W-R	Per cent	£1 Level Stake
June	0-0	-	0.00	December	0-6	-	- 6.00
July	0-0	-	0.00	January	0-8	-	- 8.00
August	0-0	-	0.00	February	0-8	-	- 8.00
September	0-0	-	0.00	March	2-10	20.0	- 0.77
October	0-1	-	- 1.00	April	1-8	12.5	+ 13.00
November	3-8	37.5	+ 4.13	May	1-10	10.0	- 6.25

DISTANCE

	W-R	Per cent	£1 Level Stake		W-R	Per cent	£1 Level Stake
Hurdles				Chases			
2m-2m 3f	5-19	26.3	+ 4.38	2m-2m 3f	1-13	7.7	- 11.27
2m 4f-2m 7f	0-14	-	- 14.00	2m 4f-2m 7f	1-6	16.7	+ 15.00
3m +	0-2	-	- 2.00	3m +	0-5	-	- 5.00

TYPE OF RACE

	W-R	Per cent	£1 Level Stake		W-R	Per cent	£1 Level Stake
Novice hurdles	1-20	5.0	- 12.50	Selling	0-0	-	0.00
H'cap hurdles	2-13	15.4	- 4.92	Amateur	0-1	-	- 1.00
Novice chases	1-11	9.1	+ 10.00	Hunter chases	0-0	-	0.00
H'cap chases	1-12	8.3	- 10.27	N H Flat	2-2	100.0	+ 5.80

COURSE GRADE

	W-R	Per cent	£1 Level Stake
Group 1	1-15	6.7	- 7.50
Group 2	0-3	-	- 3.00
Group 3	3-26	11.5	- 16.47
Group 4	3-15	20.0	+ 14.08

FIRST TIME OUT

	W-R	Per cent	£1 Level Stake
Hurdles	3-10	30.0	+ 2.13
Chases	0-6	-	- 6.00
Totals	3-16	18.8	- 3.87

JOCKEYS RIDING

	W-R	Per cent	£1 Level Stake		W-R	Per cent	£1 Level Stake
J Titley	3-21	14.3	- 13.14	Mr R Wakley	1-4	25.0	+ 17.00
G Hogan	2-15	13.3	- 1.50	T J Murphy	1-4	25.0	- 0.25

G Bradley	0-5	A S Smith	0-1	Miss P Jones	0-1
B Fenton	0-3	D McCain	0-1	R Massey	0-1
A Maguire	0-1	M A Fitzgerald	0-1	S Curran	0-1

COURSE RECORD

	Total W–R	Nov Hdles	H'cap Hdles	Nov Chses	H'cap Chses	Hunter Chses	N H Flat	£1 Level Stake
Folkestone	2-7	0-2	0-1	0-2	1-1	0-0	1-1	- 3.47
Market Rasen	1-1	0-0	0-0	0-0	0-0	0-0	1-1	+ 5.00
Sandown	1-1	1-1	0-0	0-0	0-0	0-0	0-0	+ 6.50
Hereford	1-4	0-1	1-2	0-0	0-1	0-0	0-0	- 0.25
Fakenham	1-4	0-0	0-1	1-2	0-1	0-0	0-0	+ 17.00
Towcester	1-7	0-4	1-2	0-1	0-0	0-0	0-0	- 2.67

Newbury	0-5	Leicester	0-2	Fontwell	0-1
Huntingdon	0-4	Uttoxeter	0-2	Warwick	0-1
Plumpton	0-4	Wetherby	0-2	Windsor	0-1
Cheltenham	0-3	Aintree	0-1	Worcester	0-1
Kempton	0-3	Ascot	0-1		
Nottingham	0-3	Doncaster	0-1		

WINNING HORSES

	Races Run	1st	2nd	3rd	Unpl	Win £
Henrietta Howard	6	2	1	0	3	4,901
Crackling Frost	9	1	0	2	6	4,660
Mill O'The Rags	5	2	0	0	3	4,250
Peaceman	3	1	1	1	0	3,496
Peace Lord	4	1	1	0	2	1,287

WINNING OWNERS

	Races Won	Value £		Races Won	Value £
Mrs Solna Thomson Jones	2	4,901	The Unlucky For Some P'ship	1	4,660
Sir Peter Gibbings	2	4,783	E J Fenaroli	2	4,250

No of horses racing for the stable	16	Total winning prize-money	£18,594

Favourites	3-7	42.9%	+ 0.28	Average SP of winner		5.6/1
Longest win seq	2	Longest losing seq	27	Return on stakes invested		-21.8%

1994/95 Form	13-78	16.7%	- 14.76	1992/93 Form	6-58	10.3%	- 22.82
1993/94 Form	15-92	16.3%	+ 18.17	1991/92 Form	6-91	6.6%	- 70.84

J S HALDANE (Kelso, Borders)

	Races Run	1st	2nd	3rd	Unpl	Per cent	£1 Level Stake
Hurdles	16	1	0	0	15	6.3	- 7.00
Chases	10	0	1	0	9	-	- 10.00
Totals	26	1	1	0	24	3.8	- 17.00

B Harding	1-15	- 6.00	Newcastle	1-4	+ 5.00

No of horses racing for the stable	9	Total winning prize-money	£2,005

MISS S E HALL (Coverham, North Yorks)

	Races Run	1st	2nd	3rd	Unpl	Per cent	£1 Level Stake
Hurdles	16	5	2	0	9	31.3	+ 19.55
Chases	0	0	0	0	0	-	0.00
Totals	16	5	2	0	9	31.3	+ 19.55

N Bentley	2-5	+ 12.30	D Thomas	1-2	+ 8.00
P Carberry	2-6	+ 2.25			

Ayr	1-1	+ 2.00	Newcastle	1-3	+ 7.00
Carlisle	1-2	+ 12.30	Doncaster	1-3	+ 3.00
Market Rasen	1-2	+ 0.25			

No of horses racing for the stable 6   Total winning prize-money £10,811

G A HAM (Rooks Bridge, Somerset)

	Races Run	1st	2nd	3rd	Unpl	Per cent	£1 Level Stake
Hurdles	39	1	1	1	36	2.6	- 28.00
Chases	16	0	1	2	13	-	- 16.00
Totals	55	1	2	3	49	1.8	- 44.00

R Massey	1-4	+ 7.00	Hereford	1-4	+ 7.00

No of horses racing for the stable 16   Total winning prize-money £2,332

M D HAMMOND (Coverham, North Yorks)

	Races Run	1st	2nd	3rd	Unpl	Per cent	£1 Level Stake
Hurdles	196	22	33	26	115	11.2	- 84.50
Chases	103	12	30	12	49	11.7	- 48.93
Totals	299	34	63	38	164	11.4	-133.43

BY MONTH

	W-R	Per cent	£1 Level Stake		W-R	Per cent	£1 Level Stake
June	0-4	-	- 4.00	December	2-36	5.6	- 27.50
July	3-6	50.0	+ 9.75	January	5-46	10.9	- 23.50
August	2-8	25.0	- 3.56	February	7-39	17.9	+ 19.00
September	1-12	8.3	- 9.37	March	5-57	8.8	- 30.79
October	0-7	-	- 7.00	April	5-35	14.3	- 16.96
November	1-30	3.3	- 26.75	May	3-19	15.8	- 12.75

DISTANCE

Hurdles	W-R	Per cent	£1 Level Stake	Chases	W-R	Per cent	£1 Level Stake
2m-2m 3f	15-128	11.7	- 66.33	2m-2m 3f	5-32	15.6	- 14.62
2m 4f-2m 7f	6-50	12.0	- 6.67	2m 4f-2m 7f	6-26	23.1	+ 7.69
3m +	1-18	5.6	- 11.50	3m +	1-45	2.2	- 42.00

TYPE OF RACE

	W-R	Per cent	£1 Level Stake		W-R	Per cent	£1 Level Stake
Novice hurdles	14-112	12.5	- 59.75	Selling	1-7	14.3	- 1.50
H'cap hurdles	6-53	11.3	- 4.25	Amateur	1-14	7.1	- 10.75
Novice chases	1-29	3.4	- 25.00	Hunter chases	0-7	-	- 7.00
H'cap chases	10-62	16.1	- 15.18	N H Flat	1-15	6.7	- 10.00

COURSE GRADE

	W-R	Per cent	£1 Level Stake
Group 1	10-81	12.3	- 21.62
Group 2	0-22	-	- 22.00
Group 3	3-57	5.3	- 40.25
Group 4	21-139	15.1	- 49.56

FIRST TIME OUT

	W-R	Per cent	£1 Level Stake
Hurdles	2-58	3.4	- 50.37
Chases	0-21	-	- 21.00
Totals	2-79	2.5	- 71.37

JOCKEYS RIDING

	W-R	Per cent	£1 Level Stake		W-R	Per cent	£1 Level Stake
R Garrity	12-47	25.5	+ 7.17	C F Swan	1-3	33.3	+ 7.00
Mr C Bonner	7-98	7.1	- 64.56	M Foster	1-4	25.0	- 1.00
P Niven	6-23	26.1	+ 4.25	R Dunwoody	1-6	16.7	- 2.50
A Maguire	2-5	40.0	- 0.12	L Wyer	1-6	16.7	- 1.67
A Thornton	1-1	100.0	+ 3.50	B Storey	1-14	7.1	+ 3.00
O Pears	1-2	50.0	+ 1.50				

R P Burns	0-29	R Murphy	0-3	B Powell	0-1
A Dobbin	0-12	B Harding	0-2	E O'Riordan	0-1
D Bentley	0-9	D Parker	0-2	F Perratt	0-1
Mr J J Davies	0-6	Kate Sellars	0-2	G Bradley	0-1
J Callaghan	0-5	P Carberry	0-2	Mr M Hammond	0-1
D Bridgwater	0-4	R Supple	0-2	Mr T Whitaker	0-1
M Dwyer	0-4	A P McCoy	0-1	Richard Guest	0-1

COURSE RECORD

	Total W-R	Nov Hdles	H'cap Hdles	Nov Chses	H'cap Chses	Hunter Chses	N H Flat	£1 Level Stake
Musselburgh	8-23	3-10	2-3	1-6	1-3	0-0	1-1	+ 23.75
Ayr	3-11	1-2	1-5	0-1	1-2	0-1	0-0	+ 1.75
Haydock	3-15	0-7	2-3	0-2	1-3	0-0	0-0	+ 5.25
Kelso	3-22	2-9	0-4	0-3	1-4	0-2	0-0	- 8.42
Southwell	2-2	0-0	0-0	0-0	2-2	0-0	0-0	+ 4.94
Market Rasen	2-9	1-5	0-2	0-0	1-1	0-0	0-1	+ 0.75
Cartmel	2-9	1-4	0-1	0-1	1-3	0-0	0-0	- 3.75

Doncaster	2-10	1-5	0-0	0-1	1-3	0-0	0-1	- 3.62
Hexham	2-19	2-10	0-2	0-1	0-3	0-1	0-2	- 14.32
Perth	2-21	2-8	0-5	0-1	0-5	0-0	0-2	- 13.59
Worcester	1-1	0-0	0-0	0-0	1-1	0-0	0-0	+ 6.00
Aintree	1-9	0-1	1-2	0-0	0-6	0-0	0-0	- 1.00
Sedgefield	1-16	1-7	0-3	0-3	0-2	0-0	0-1	- 13.80
Carlisle	1-22	1-7	0-5	0-2	0-5	0-0	0-3	- 19.37
Newcastle	1-29	0-14	0-7	0-2	1-3	0-1	0-2	- 17.00

Catterick	0-17	Leicester	0-5	Ludlow	0-2
Wetherby	0-17	Sandown	0-5	Ascot	0-1
Nottingham	0-9	Lingfield	0-3	Kempton	0-1
Warwick	0-9	Bangor	0-2	Towcester	0-1
Huntingdon	0-6	Chepstow	0-2	Uttoxeter	0-1

WINNING HORSES

	Races Run	1st	2nd	3rd	Unpl	Win £
Outset	5	2	0	1	2	18,478
Valiant Warrior	5	2	2	0	1	18,043
Elpidos	6	3	0	0	3	10,487
Palmrush	5	3	0	0	2	9,935
Marchant Ming	5	3	0	0	2	9,918
Ham N'Eggs	5	3	0	1	1	7,867
Clay County	5	1	0	0	4	7,626
Ralitsa	10	2	2	2	4	5,537
Dominant Serenade	3	1	2	0	0	4,706
Port In A Storm	9	1	3	0	5	3,696
Wise Advice	8	1	2	2	3	3,389
Pagliaccio	12	1	5	1	5	3,124
Choice Challange	3	1	0	1	1	3,077
Eight Sharp	6	1	0	0	5	2,957
Master Ofthe House	7	1	1	0	5	2,853
Uk Hygiene	6	1	2	0	3	2,763
Alcian Blue	3	1	0	0	2	2,756
Campaign	4	1	0	1	2	2,696
Allimac Nomis	3	1	0	1	1	2,684
Eurolink The Rebel	4	1	0	1	2	2,679
Royal Crimson	3	1	0	0	2	2,154
Recluse	2	1	1	0	0	1,800
Lord Fortune	2	1	0	0	1	1,446

WINNING OWNERS

	Races Won	Value £		Races Won	Value £
Mark Kilner	2	18,478	D F Sills	1	3,077
P Sellars	2	18,043	The Gemini P'ship 3	1	2,957
Mrs Margi Winter	3	10,487	Allerton Racing Club	1	2,853
Mrs L M Carr-Walker	3	9,935	Wetherby Racing Bureau 25	1	2,814
Roland Roper	3	9,918	A J Peake	1	2,763
M H O G Racing	3	7,867	Rykneld Thoroughbred Co Ltd	1	2,756
The County Set	1	7,626	Spectrum	1	2,696
Wetherby Racing Bureau Plc	2	5,407	Megan Dennis-Craig Shields	1	2,679
North Briton Racing Club	1	4,706	Mrs W A Beaumont	1	2,154
John Doyle Construction Ltd	1	3,696	Million in Mind P'ship (4)	1	1,800
A G Chappell	1	3,389	Trevor Hemmings	1	1,446
A D Stewart	1	3,124			

No of horses racing for the stable	81	Total winning prize-money	£130,671

Favourites	11-40	27.5%	- 12.76	Average SP of winner		3.9/1
Longest win seq	2	Longest losing seq	38	Return on stakes invested		-44.6%

1994/95 Form	42-278	15.1%	- 78.37	1992/93 Form	51-271	18.8%	- 45.77
1993/94 Form	44-321	13.7%	- 87.24	1991/92 Form	35-228	15.4%	- 79.16

R HANNON (East Everleigh, Wilts)

	Races Run	1st	2nd	3rd	Unpl	Per cent	£1 Level Stake
Hurdles	9	1	0	0	8	11.1	- 4.00
Chases	0	0	0	0	0	-	0.00
Totals	9	1	0	0	8	11.1	- 4.00

G McCourt	1-7	- 2.00	Sandown		1-1	+ 4.00

No of horses racing for the stable	5	Total winning prize-money	£16,075

MRS C HARDINGE (Hereford, H'ford & Worcs)

	Races Run	1st	2nd	3rd	Unpl	Per cent	£1 Level Stake
Hurdles	0	0	0	0	0	-	0.00
Chases	7	3	1	1	2	42.9	+ 2.95
Totals	7	3	1	1	2	42.9	+ 2.95

Mr D Jones	3-7	+ 2.95

Leicester	1-1	+ 1.20	Hereford	1-2	+ 1.25
Warwick	1-1	+ 3.50			

No of horses racing for the stable	2	Total winning prize-money	£5,367

J A HARRIS (Bottesford, Leics)

	Races Run	1st	2nd	3rd	Unpl	Per cent	£1 Level Stake
Hurdles	41	3	4	5	29	7.3	- 21.75
Chases	7	0	1	2	4	-	- 7.00
Totals	48	3	5	7	33	6.3	- 28.75

T Dascombe	2-18	- 8.75		A P McCoy	1-6	+ 4.00
Hexham	1-3	+ 3.00		Ludlow	1-13	- 3.00
Southwell	1-5	- 1.75				

No of horses racing for the stable   11   Total winning prize-money   £6,022

J L HARRIS (Eastwell, Leics)

	Races Run	1st	2nd	3rd	Unpl	Per cent	£1 Level Stake
Hurdles	52	8	6	6	32	15.4	+ 16.50
Chases	5	0	0	0	5	-	- 5.00
Totals	57	8	6	6	37	14.0	+ 11.50

BY MONTH

	W-R	Per cent	£1 Level Stake		W-R	Per cent	£1 Level Stake
June	0-3	-	- 3.00	December	0-5	-	- 5.00
July	0-3	-	- 3.00	January	0-2	-	- 2.00
August	0-2	-	- 2.00	February	0-4	-	- 4.00
September	0-0	-	0.00	March	2-8	25.0	+ 10.25
October	2-4	50.0	+ 14.00	April	1-5	20.0	+ 12.00
November	3-9	33.3	+ 6.25	May	0-12	-	- 12.00

DISTANCE

	W-R	Per cent	£1 Level Stake		W-R	Per cent	£1 Level Stake
Hurdles				Chases			
2m-2m 3f	8-43	18.6	+ 25.50	2m-2m 3f	0-1	-	- 1.00
2m 4f-2m 7f	0-8	-	- 8.00	2m 4f-2m 7f	0-4	-	- 4.00
3m +	0-1	-	- 1.00	3m +	0-0	-	0.00

TYPE OF RACE

	W-R	Per cent	£1 Level Stake		W-R	Per cent	£1 Level Stake
Novice hurdles	1-11	9.1	- 5.00	Selling	2-15	13.3	- 1.50
H'cap hurdles	5-25	20.0	+ 24.00	Amateur	0-1	-	- 1.00
Novice chases	0-2	-	- 2.00	Hunter chases	0-0	-	0.00
H'cap chases	0-3	-	- 3.00	N H Flat	0-0	-	0.00

Harris J L

<table>
<tr><th colspan="4">COURSE GRADE</th><th colspan="4">FIRST TIME OUT</th></tr>
<tr><th></th><th>W-R</th><th>Per cent</th><th>£1 Level Stake</th><th></th><th>W-R</th><th>Per cent</th><th>£1 Level Stake</th></tr>
<tr><td>Group 1</td><td>2-11</td><td>18.2</td><td>+ 6.75</td><td>Hurdles</td><td>1-12</td><td>8.3</td><td>- 5.00</td></tr>
<tr><td>Group 2</td><td>0-0</td><td>-</td><td>0.00</td><td>Chases</td><td>0-1</td><td>-</td><td>- 1.00</td></tr>
<tr><td>Group 3</td><td>3-24</td><td>12.5</td><td>- 0.50</td><td></td><td></td><td></td><td></td></tr>
<tr><td>Group 4</td><td>3-22</td><td>13.6</td><td>+ 5.25</td><td>Totals</td><td>1-13</td><td>7.7</td><td>- 6.00</td></tr>
</table>

JOCKEYS RIDING

<table>
<tr><th></th><th>W-R</th><th>Per cent</th><th>£1 Level Stake</th><th></th><th>W-R</th><th>Per cent</th><th>£1 Level Stake</th></tr>
<tr><td>A S Smith</td><td>3-8</td><td>37.5</td><td>+ 7.25</td><td>P McLoughlin</td><td>2-8</td><td>25.0</td><td>+ 10.00</td></tr>
<tr><td>D Gallagher</td><td>2-7</td><td>28.6</td><td>+ 11.25</td><td>Mr J Culloty</td><td>1-3</td><td>33.3</td><td>+ 14.00</td></tr>
</table>

<table>
<tr><td>J Lodder</td><td>0-4</td><td>A P McCoy</td><td>0-2</td><td>D Bridgwater</td><td>0-1</td></tr>
<tr><td>R Dunwoody</td><td>0-4</td><td>P Carberry</td><td>0-2</td><td>D Walsh</td><td>0-1</td></tr>
<tr><td>Richard Guest</td><td>0-4</td><td>T Dascombe</td><td>0-2</td><td>G Bradley</td><td>0-1</td></tr>
<tr><td>B Dalton</td><td>0-3</td><td>A Maguire</td><td>0-1</td><td>Gary Lyons</td><td>0-1</td></tr>
<tr><td>J Supple</td><td>0-3</td><td>B Fenton</td><td>0-1</td><td>Mrs M Morris</td><td>0-1</td></tr>
</table>

COURSE RECORD

<table>
<tr><th></th><th>Total W-R</th><th>Nov Hdles</th><th>H'cap Hdles</th><th>Nov Chses</th><th>H'cap Chses</th><th>Hunter Chses</th><th>N H Flat</th><th>£1 Level Stake</th></tr>
<tr><td>Warwick</td><td>1-1</td><td>0-0</td><td>1-1</td><td>0-0</td><td>0-0</td><td>0-0</td><td>0-0</td><td>+ 10.00</td></tr>
<tr><td>Fakenham</td><td>1-1</td><td>0-0</td><td>1-1</td><td>0-0</td><td>0-0</td><td>0-0</td><td>0-0</td><td>+ 6.00</td></tr>
<tr><td>Carlisle</td><td>1-1</td><td>0-0</td><td>1-1</td><td>0-0</td><td>0-0</td><td>0-0</td><td>0-0</td><td>+ 2.25</td></tr>
<tr><td>Cheltenham</td><td>1-1</td><td>0-0</td><td>1-1</td><td>0-0</td><td>0-0</td><td>0-0</td><td>0-0</td><td>+ 14.00</td></tr>
<tr><td>Newcastle</td><td>1-1</td><td>0-0</td><td>1-1</td><td>0-0</td><td>0-0</td><td>0-0</td><td>0-0</td><td>+ 1.75</td></tr>
<tr><td>Catterick</td><td>1-2</td><td>1-1</td><td>0-1</td><td>0-0</td><td>0-0</td><td>0-0</td><td>0-0</td><td>+ 4.00</td></tr>
<tr><td>Towcester</td><td>1-3</td><td>0-1</td><td>1-2</td><td>0-0</td><td>0-0</td><td>0-0</td><td>0-0</td><td>+ 14.00</td></tr>
<tr><td>Market Rasen</td><td>1-12</td><td>0-5</td><td>1-5</td><td>0-2</td><td>0-0</td><td>0-0</td><td>0-0</td><td>- 5.50</td></tr>
</table>

<table>
<tr><td>Southwell</td><td>0-7</td><td>Haydock</td><td>0-2</td><td>Leicester</td><td>0-1</td></tr>
<tr><td>Bangor</td><td>0-4</td><td>Hereford</td><td>0-2</td><td>Newbury</td><td>0-1</td></tr>
<tr><td>Doncaster</td><td>0-4</td><td>Nottingham</td><td>0-2</td><td>Plumpton</td><td>0-1</td></tr>
<tr><td>Huntingdon</td><td>0-4</td><td>Aintree</td><td>0-1</td><td>Uttoxeter</td><td>0-1</td></tr>
<tr><td>Ludlow</td><td>0-4</td><td>Ascot</td><td>0-1</td><td></td><td></td></tr>
</table>

WINNING HORSES

<table>
<tr><th></th><th>Races Run</th><th>1st</th><th>2nd</th><th>3rd</th><th>Unpl</th><th>Win £</th></tr>
<tr><td>Star Rage</td><td>11</td><td>4</td><td>1</td><td>3</td><td>3</td><td>34,154</td></tr>
<tr><td>Wordsmith</td><td>5</td><td>2</td><td>0</td><td>1</td><td>2</td><td>5,042</td></tr>
<tr><td>Rain-N-Sun</td><td>8</td><td>1</td><td>1</td><td>0</td><td>6</td><td>2,688</td></tr>
<tr><td>Little Blackfoot</td><td>4</td><td>1</td><td>0</td><td>0</td><td>3</td><td>1,891</td></tr>
</table>

WINNING OWNERS

<table>
<tr><th></th><th>Races Won</th><th>Value £</th><th></th><th>Races Won</th><th>Value £</th></tr>
<tr><td>J David Abell</td><td>4</td><td>34,154</td><td>Mrs M Bostock</td><td>1</td><td>2,688</td></tr>
<tr><td>A K Collins</td><td>2</td><td>5,042</td><td>J L Harris</td><td>1</td><td>1,891</td></tr>
</table>

No of horses racing for the stable			14	Total winning prize-money			£43,775

| Favourites | 1-9 | 11.1% | - 5.75 | Average SP of winner | | | 7.6/1 |
| Longest win seq | 2 | Longest losing seq | 15 | Return on stakes invested | | | 20.2% |

| 1994/95 Form | 2-35 | 5.7% | - 16.00 | 1992/93 Form | 7-77 | 9.1% | - 34.12 |
| 1993/94 Form | 14-92 | 15.2% | - 0.94 | 1991/92 Form | 6-84 | 7.1% | - 41.00 |

R HARRIS (Exning, Suffolk)

	Races Run	1st	2nd	3rd	Unpl	Per cent	£1 Level Stake
Hurdles	23	1	1	2	19	4.3	- 17.50
Chases	1	0	0	0	1	-	- 1.00
Totals	24	1	1	2	20	4.2	- 18.50

L Aspell	1-3	+ 2.50	Wetherby	1-1	+ 4.50

No of horses racing for the stable	9	Total winning prize-money	£2,285

A HARRISON (Middleham, North Yorks)

	Races Run	1st	2nd	3rd	Unpl	Per cent	£1 Level Stake
Hurdles	13	3	1	0	9	23.1	+ 14.83
Chases	6	0	1	0	5	-	- 6.00
Totals	19	3	2	0	14	15.8	+ 8.83

D Bentley	3-7	+ 20.83

Southwell	2-3	+ 20.50	Market Rasen	1-1	+ 3.33

No of horses racing for the stable	8	Total winning prize-money	£6,495

G HARWOOD (Pulborough, West Sussex)

	Races Run	1st	2nd	3rd	Unpl	Per cent	£1 Level Stake
Hurdles	40	4	8	2	26	10.0	- 8.14
Chases	13	2	1	0	10	15.4	- 2.75
Totals	53	6	9	2	36	11.3	- 10.89

R Dunwoody	2-9	+ 1.25	M Richards	1-9	+ 8.00
Mrs A Perratt	1-3	+ 4.50	M Perrett	1-18	- 16.64
M A Fitzgerald	1-3	+ 3.00			
Plumpton	2-6	+ 12.36	Windsor	1-3	+ 4.50
Sandown	1-2	+ 4.00	Fontwell	1-12	- 4.50
Warwick	1-2	+ 0.75			

No of horses racing for the stable   12   Total winning prize-money   £34,944

P C HASLAM (Middleham. North Yorks)

	Races Run	1st	2nd	3rd	Unpl	Per cent	£1 Level Stake
Hurdles	13	3	1	0	9	23.1	+ 0.25
Chases	0	0	0	0	0	-	0.00
Totals	13	3	1	0	9	23.1	+ 0.25

M Foster	3-6	+ 7.25			
Uttoxeter	1-1	+ 2.25	Leicester	1-2	+ 3.50
Fakenham	1-1	+ 3.50			

No of horses racing for the stable   7   Total winning prize-money   £7,666

M J HAYNES (Epsom, Surrey)

	Races Run	1st	2nd	3rd	Unpl	Per cent	£1 Level Stake
Hurdles	21	4	2	2	13	19.0	- 2.67
Chases	0	0	0	0	0	-	0.00
Totals	21	4	2	2	13	19.0	- 2.67

D Skyrme	4-20	- 1.67			
Newbury	2-2	+ 9.50	Windsor	1-1	+ 3.33
Huntingdon	1-1	+ 1.50			

No of horses racing for the stable   4   Total winning prize-money   £18,582

P HAYWARD (Haxton, Wilts)

	Races Run	1st	2nd	3rd	Unpl	Per cent	£1 Level Stake
Hurdles	18	1	1	1	15	5.6	- 3.00
Chases	2	0	0	0	2	-	- 2.00
Totals	20	1	1	1	17	5.0	- 5.00

B Fenton	1-3	+ 12.00	Hereford	1-1	+ 14.00

No of horses racing for the stable	7	Total winning prize-money	£2,346

MRS E H HEATH (Kelshall, Herts)

	Races Run	1st	2nd	3rd	Unpl	Per cent	£1 Level Stake
Hurdles	23	0	2	1	20	-	- 23.00
Chases	8	1	2	0	5	12.5	+ 1.00
Totals	31	1	4	1	25	3.2	- 22.00

A Thornton	1-5	+ 4.00	Warwick	1-1	+ 8.00

No of horses racing for the stable	5	Total winning prize-money	£3,530

P R HEDGER (Eastergate, West Sussex)

	Races Run	1st	2nd	3rd	Unpl	Per cent	£1 Level Stake
Hurdles	43	6	7	6	24	14.0	- 15.11
Chases	23	2	4	4	13	8.7	- 15.25
Totals	66	8	11	10	37	12.1	- 30.36

BY MONTH

	W-R	Per cent	£1 Level Stake		W-R	Per cent	£1 Level Stake
June	0-1	-	- 1.00	December	0-4	-	- 4.00
July	0-0	-	0.00	January	0-4	-	- 4.00
August	2-2	100.0	+ 2.76	February	0-6	-	- 6.00
September	0-2	-	- 2.00	March	0-10	-	- 10.00
October	2-8	25.0	+ 1.75	April	1-8	12.5	- 3.00
November	2-12	16.7	- 4.87	May	1-9	11.1	0.00

DISTANCE

Hurdles	W-R	Per cent	£1 Level Stake	Chases	W-R	Per cent	£1 Level Stake
2m-2m 3f	4-32	12.5	- 11.24	2m-2m 3f	1-6	16.7	- 3.25
2m 4f-2m 7f	2-10	20.0	- 2.87	2m 4f-2m 7f	1-8	12.5	- 3.00
3m +	0-1	-	- 1.00	3m +	0-9	-	- 9.00

TYPE OF RACE

	W-R	Per cent	£1 Level Stake		W-R	Per cent	£1 Level Stake
Novice hurdles	3-18	16.7	- 4.24	Selling	0-5	-	- 5.00
H'cap hurdles	3-19	15.8	- 4.87	Amateur	0-0	-	0.00
Novice chases	1-11	9.1	- 6.00	Hunter chases	0-0	-	0.00
H'cap chases	1-11	9.1	- 8.25	N H Flat	0-2	-	- 2.00

COURSE GRADE

	W-R	Per cent	£1 Level Stake
Group 1	1-10	10.0	- 7.37
Group 2	1-16	6.3	- 13.62
Group 3	5-33	15.2	- 9.37
Group 4	1-7	14.3	0.00

FIRST TIME OUT

	W-R	Per cent	£1 Level Stake
Hurdles	3-14	21.4	- 0.12
Chases	0-5	-	- 5.00
Totals	3-19	15.8	- 5.12

JOCKEYS RIDING

	W-R	Per cent	£1 Level Stake		W-R	Per cent	£1 Level Stake
M Richards	4-21	19.0	- 8.99	M A Fitzgerald	1-8	12.5	- 3.00
M Clinton	3-18	16.7	+ 0.63				

I Lawrence	0-7	D O'Sullivan	0-2	M Perrett	0-1
G Bradley	0-3	A P McCoy	0-1	R Dunwoody	0-1
B Powell	0-2	J R Kavanagh	0-1	T Dascombe	0-1

COURSE RECORD

	Total W-R	Nov Hdles	H'cap Hdles	Nov Chses	H'cap Chses	Hunter Chses	N H Flat	£1 Level Stake
Plumpton	2-9	1-3	0-1	0-1	1-4	0-0	0-0	- 3.87
Cheltenham	1-1	0-0	1-1	0-0	0-0	0-0	0-0	+ 1.63
Worcester	1-2	0-0	0-0	1-1	0-1	0-0	0-0	+ 3.00
Newton Abbot	1-4	1-2	0-1	0-0	0-1	0-0	0-0	- 1.62
Huntingdon	1-4	1-2	0-1	0-0	0-1	0-0	0-0	+ 5.00
Taunton	1-4	0-1	1-3	0-0	0-0	0-0	0-0	+ 3.00
Windsor	1-6	0-2	1-2	0-1	0-1	0-0	0-0	- 1.50

Fontwell	0-11	Newbury	0-2	Lingfield	0-1
Wincanton	0-5	Sandown	0-2	Market Rasen	0-1
Kempton	0-4	Ascot	0-1	Towcester	0-1
Folkestone	0-3	Exeter	0-1		
Warwick	0-3	Hereford	0-1		

WINNING HORSES

	Races Run	1st	2nd	3rd	Unpl	Win £
Wave Hill	8	3	1	2	2	7,323
Ginger Jim	4	2	0	0	2	5,558
Super Gossip	4	1	1	1	1	4,499
General Shirley	6	1	2	1	2	2,705
Darzee	4	1	1	1	1	2,136

WINNING OWNERS

	Races Won	Value £		Races Won	Value £
J J Whelan	3	7,323	Mrs Gina Webster	2	5,558
P R Hedger	2	7,204	Tony Walsh	1	2,136

No of horses racing for the stable	19	Total winning prize-money	£22,221

Favourites	4-8	50.0%	+	4.39	Average SP of winner	3.5/1
Longest win seq	2	Longest losing seq		29	Return on stakes invested	-46.0%

1994/95 Form	4-61	6.6%	- 45.87	1992/93 Form	8-66	12.1%	- 30.50
1993/94 Form	5-54	9.3%	- 40.67	1991/92 Form	8-73	11.0%	- 28.95

J A HELLENS (Chester Moor, Co Durham)

	Races Run	1st	2nd	3rd	Unpl	Per cent	£1 Level Stake
Hurdles	52	2	2	4	44	3.8	- 39.25
Chases	40	4	4	3	29	10.0	- 15.62
Totals	92	6	6	7	73	6.5	- 54.87

T Reed	2-17	- 1.50	A Dobbin	1-8	- 5.12
M Dwyer	1-2	+ 4.00	Scott Taylor	1-25	- 21.25
L Wyer	1-2	+ 7.00			

Sedgefield	5-29	- 0.87	Perth	1-9	0.00

No of horses racing for the stable	22	Total winning prize-money	£19,686

N J HENDERSON (Lambourn, Berks)

	Races Run	1st	2nd	3rd	Unpl	Per cent	£1 Level Stake
Hurdles	163	24	21	17	101	14.7	- 34.70
Chases	115	23	20	15	57	20.0	- 17.57
Totals	278	47	41	32	158	16.9	- 52.27

BY MONTH

	W-R	Per cent	£1 Level Stake		W-R	Per cent	£1 Level Stake
June	0-3	-	- 3.00	December	7-26	26.9	+ 9.16
July	0-0	-	0.00	January	1-34	2.9	- 25.00
August	1-2	50.0	+ 0.38	February	9-41	22.0	+ 23.38
September	1-3	33.3	+ 0.75	March	5-54	9.3	- 24.95
October	2-12	16.7	- 7.82	April	5-40	12.5	- 25.88
November	11-38	28.9	+ 1.96	May	5-25	20.0	- 1.25

DISTANCE

Hurdles	W-R	Per cent	£1 Level Stake	Chases	W-R	Per cent	£1 Level Stake
2m-2m 3f	15-115	13.0	- 41.88	2m-2m 3f	12-45	26.7	- 2.54
2m 4f-2m 7f	8-37	21.6	+ 16.38	2m 4f-2m 7f	6-36	16.7	- 0.63
3m +	1-11	9.1	- 9.20	3m +	5-34	14.7	- 14.40

TYPE OF RACE

	W-R	Per cent	£1 Level Stake		W-R	Per cent	£1 Level Stake
Novice hurdles	12-81	14.8	- 29.61	Selling	0-0	-	0.00
H'cap hurdles	8-56	14.3	- 0.17	Amateur	0-5	-	- 5.00
Novice chases	10-36	27.8	- 4.11	Hunter chases	0-1	-	- 1.00
H'cap chases	13-74	17.6	- 8.46	N H Flat	4-25	16.0	- 3.92

COURSE GRADE | FIRST TIME OUT

	W-R	Per cent	£1 Level Stake		W-R	Per cent	£1 Level Stake
Group 1	17-131	13.0	- 41.38	Hurdles	8-51	15.7	- 16.71
Group 2	1-21	4.8	- 11.00	Chases	3-21	14.3	- 10.50
Group 3	22-84	26.2	+ 23.39				
Group 4	7-42	16.7	- 23.28	Totals	11-72	15.3	- 27.21

JOCKEYS RIDING

	W-R	Per cent	£1 Level Stake		W-R	Per cent	£1 Level Stake
M A Fitzgerald	25-164	15.2	- 58.71	M Lane	2-12	16.7	+ 0.83
J R Kavanagh	13-68	19.1	+ 5.06	A P McCoy	1-1	100.0	+ 6.00
J Osborne	3-5	60.0	+ 11.80	T Hagger	1-3	33.3	+ 2.00
R Dunwoody	2-4	50.0	+ 1.75				

Mr C Vigors	0-15	D Kiernan	0-1	R Johnson	0-1
B Powell	0-1	G Bradley	0-1	
C Llewellyn	0-1	J A McCarthy	0-1	

COURSE RECORD

	Total W-R	Nov Hdles	H'cap Hdles	Nov Chses	H'cap Chses	Hunter Chses	N H Flat	£1 Level Stake
Newbury	4-22	2-6	0-4	1-4	1-5	0-0	0-3	- 0.58
Leicester	3-8	0-2	2-3	1-2	0-1	0-0	0-0	+ 10.50
Huntingdon	3-9	0-1	1-4	1-1	0-1	0-0	1-2	+ 0.66
Worcester	3-12	0-0	0-2	1-2	0-5	0-0	2-3	- 1.50
Sandown	3-20	1-5	0-3	1-4	1-6	0-0	0-2	- 3.50
Cheltenham	3-28	1-8	1-8	0-5	1-6	0-0	0-1	- 18.80
Stratford	2-3	1-1	0-0	0-0	1-2	0-0	0-0	+ 3.75
Folkestone	2-3	0-0	0-0	2-2	0-0	0-0	0-1	+ 0.72
Hereford	2-5	1-3	0-1	1-1	0-0	0-0	0-0	- 0.59
Exeter	2-6	0-1	0-1	1-3	1-1	0-0	0-0	- 1.82
Windsor	2-6	1-2	0-0	0-1	1-3	0-0	0-0	+ 0.13
Uttoxeter	2-7	0-1	1-4	0-0	0-0	0-0	1-2	+ 6.00
Ascot	2-27	0-6	0-7	1-2	1-9	0-0	0-3	- 15.00

Henderson N J

Doncaster	1-1	0-0	1-1	0-0	0-0	0-0	0-0	+ 3.00
Fakenham	1-2	1-1	0-0	0-1	0-0	0-0	0-0	+ 0.88
Southwell	1-3	0-0	0-0	0-1	1-2	0-0	0-0	- 0.25
Ayr	1-3	0-0	0-0	0-0	1-1	0-0	0-2	+ 0.50
Plumpton	1-4	0-1	0-0	0-1	1-2	0-0	0-0	- 1.25
Market Rasen	1-5	0-0	0-0	0-0	1-5	0-0	0-0	- 2.62
Haydock	1-6	1-4	0-1	0-0	0-1	0-0	0-0	+ 4.00
Warwick	1-8	0-2	1-3	0-1	0-1	0-0	0-1	+ 13.00
Nottingham	1-9	1-5	0-1	0-1	0-1	0-0	0-1	- 7.00
Wincanton	1-10	0-4	0-0	0-1	1-5	0-0	0-0	+ 1.00
Towcester	1-11	0-2	0-1	0-1	1-4	0-1	0-2	- 6.50
Aintree	1-11	1-4	0-3	0-2	0-2	0-0	0-0	- 6.00
Kempton	1-13	1-6	0-2	0-1	0-3	0-0	0-1	- 5.00
Chepstow	1-14	0-6	1-4	0-0	0-3	0-0	0-1	- 4.00

Taunton	0-9	Newton Abbot	0-3	Wetherby	0-1
Bangor	0-3	Fontwell	0-2		
Ludlow	0-3	Lingfield	0-1		

WINNING HORSES

	Races Run	1st	2nd	3rd	Unpl	Win £
Travado	7	2	2	2	1	31,475
Big Matt	6	1	2	1	2	25,975
Amtrak Express	7	1	1	1	4	20,581
Dear Do	11	4	3	1	3	13,883
Conquering Leader	2	1	1	0	0	11,180
Cheryl's Lad	5	3	0	0	2	11,026
Tudor Fable	7	2	0	1	4	9,325
Kimanicky	4	1	1	1	1	8,918
Wonder Man	3	1	0	0	2	8,310
Sorbiere	7	2	0	0	5	7,726
Golden Spinner	5	2	1	1	1	7,631
Our Kris	6	2	1	1	2	7,588
Thinking Twice	6	1	0	1	4	7,103
Philip's Woody	12	2	6	2	2	6,336
Plunder Bay	8	2	0	0	6	5,952
Pashto	5	1	0	0	4	5,605
Braes of Mar	6	2	0	2	2	5,484
Ebullient Equiname	5	2	1	0	2	4,753
Journeys Friend	4	1	1	0	2	4,395
Castle Blue	2	1	0	1	0	3,470
Hunting Lore	2	1	0	1	0	3,248
Whattabob	6	1	3	1	1	3,178
Airtrak	9	1	1	0	7	3,052
Sovereigns Parade	3	1	0	0	2	2,957
Allez Wijins	4	1	0	0	3	2,829
Garnwin	7	1	1	0	5	2,775
Hooded Hawk	6	1	1	0	4	2,759
Nova Run	5	1	2	1	1	2,735
Elflaa	7	1	1	2	3	2,624
Litening Conductor	1	1	0	0	0	2,080
Pointed Remark	2	1	0	0	1	1,774
Salmon Breeze	3	1	0	0	2	1,385
Friendship	1	1	0	0	0	1,333

WINNING OWNERS

	Races Won	Value £		Races Won	Value £
Mrs P Sherwood	2	31,475	Queen Elizabeth	2	5,484
T Benfield and W Brown	2	27,308	Lynn Wilson	2	4,753
Amtrak Express Parcels Ltd	2	23,633	Peter S Winfield	1	4,395
Mrs Elaine Baines	4	19,944	R J Parish	1	3,470
Mrs R A Proctor	3	18,906	Milton Ritzenberg	1	3,248
C J Edwards	4	13,883	Mrs Margaret Turner	1	3,178
Raymond Tooth	3	11,186	Mrs Christopher Hanbury	1	2,829
J E H Collins	2	9,325	Pioneer Heat-Treatment	1	2,775
Mrs Shirley Robins	1	8,310	C M Hamer	1	2,759
Sir Peter Miller	2	7,631	S Keeling	1	2,735
Million in Mind P'ship (5)	2	7,588	Count K Goess-Saurau	1	2,080
Ed McGrath	1	7,103	Mrs Michael Ennever	1	1,774
B R Wilsdon	2	6,336	The Salmon Racing P'ship	1	1,385
E S & W V Robins	2	5,952			

No of horses racing for the stable		73	Total winning prize-money		£239,445
Favourites	22-72	30.6% - 16.26	Average SP of winner		3.8/1
Longest win seq 3	Longest losing seq	21	Return on stakes invested		-18.8%
1994/95 Form	45-211	21.3% + 24.68	1992/93 Form	53-289	18.3% - 61.67
1993/94 Form	48-270	17.8% - 71.48	1991/92 Form	52-251	20.7% - 58.96

W R HERN (Lambourn, Berks)

	Races Run	1st	2nd	3rd	Unpl	Per cent	£1 Level Stake
Hurdles	9	3	0	0	6	33.3	+ 6.44
Chases	0	0	0	0	0	-	0.00
Totals	9	3	0	0	6	33.3	+ 6.44

R Farrant	3-8	+ 7.44				
Market Rasen	1-1	+ 0.44	Wincanton		1-2	+ 7.00
Ludlow	1-1	+ 4.00				

No of horses racing for the stable   4   Total winning prize-money   £7,684

LADY HERRIES (Angmering Park, West Sussex)

	Races Run	1st	2nd	3rd	Unpl	Per cent	£1 Level Stake
Hurdles	38	7	10	3	18	18.4	- 0.62
Chases	1	0	0	0	1	-	- 1.00
Totals	39	7	10	3	19	17.9	- 1.62

BY MONTH

	W-R	Per cent	£1 Level Stake		W-R	Per cent	£1 Level Stake
June	0-0	-	0.00	December	1-3	33.3	+ 1.00
July	0-0	-	0.00	January	1-8	12.5	- 3.50
August	0-0	-	0.00	February	1-6	16.7	- 3.62
September	0-1	-	- 1.00	March	2-6	33.3	+ 7.50
October	1-3	33.3	+ 8.00	April	0-5	-	- 5.00
November	1-6	16.7	- 4.00	May	0-1	-	- 1.00

DISTANCE

Hurdles	W-R	Per cent	£1 Level Stake	Chases	W-R	Per cent	£1 Level Stake
2m-2m 3f	7-32	21.9	+ 5.38	2m-2m 3f	0-0	-	0.00
2m 4f-2m 7f	0-3	-	- 3.00	2m 4f-2m 7f	0-1	-	- 1.00
3m +	0-3	-	- 3.00	3m +	0-0	-	0.00

TYPE OF RACE

	W-R	Per cent	£1 Level Stake		W-R	Per cent	£1 Level Stake
Novice hurdles	3-21	14.3	- 9.00	Selling	0-1	-	- 1.00
H'cap hurdles	2-10	20.0	+ 11.00	Amateur	0-0	-	0.00
Novice chases	0-0	-	0.00	Hunter chases	0-0	-	0.00
H'cap chases	0-1	-	- 1.00	N H Flat	2-6	33.3	- 1.62

COURSE GRADE / FIRST TIME OUT

	W-R	Per cent	£1 Level Stake		W-R	Per cent	£1 Level Stake
Group 1	5-22	22.7	+ 7.88	Hurdles	2-13	15.4	+ 2.00
Group 2	0-3	-	- 3.00	Chases	0-0	-	0.00
Group 3	2-13	15.4	- 5.50				
Group 4	0-1	-	- 1.00	Totals	2-13	15.4	+ 2.00

JOCKEYS RIDING

	W-R	Per cent	£1 Level Stake		W-R	Per cent	£1 Level Stake
E Murphy	4-30	13.3	- 8.00	J Osborne	1-2	50.0	+ 0.38
Mr P P-Gordon	2-3	66.7	+ 10.00				

R Dunwoody 0-2   D Bridgwater 0-1   L Aspell 0-1

COURSE RECORD

	Total W-R	Nov Hdles	H'cap Hdles	Nov Chses	H'cap Chses	Hunter Chses	N H Flat	£1 Level Stake
Newbury	2-3	0-1	1-1	0-0	0-0	0-0	1-1	+ 10.38
Sandown	2-4	1-2	1-1	0-0	0-0	0-0	0-1	+ 10.50
Uttoxeter	1-3	1-2	0-1	0-0	0-0	0-0	0-0	+ 1.00
Plumpton	1-4	1-4	0-0	0-0	0-0	0-0	0-0	- 0.50
Kempton	1-6	0-5	0-0	0-0	0-0	0-0	1-1	- 4.00

Herries Lady

Ascot	0-5	Cheltenham	0-2	Doncaster		0-1
Fontwell	0-3	Huntingdon	0-2	Fakenham		0-1
Worcester	0-3	Aintree	0-1	Warwick		0-1

WINNING HORSES

	Races Run	1st	2nd	3rd	Unpl	Win £
Andanito	5	3	1	0	1	8,756
Tibetan	2	1	1	0	0	4,241
Amaze	6	1	3	0	2	3,039
Meant To Be	4	1	2	0	1	2,637
Serious	1	1	0	0	0	2,334

WINNING OWNERS

	Races Won	Value £		Races Won	Value £
Bonusprint	3	8,756	Lady Mary Mumford	1	2,637
Lady Herries	1	4,241	Mrs Denis Haynes	1	2,334
Lady Katharine Phillips	1	3,039			

No of horses racing for the stable	13		Total winning prize-money	£21,007

Favourites	3-11	27.3%	- 2.62	Average SP of winner		4.3/1
Longest win seq	2	Longest losing seq	10	Return on stakes invested		-4.2%

1994/95 Form	2-16	12.5%	+ 2.50	1992/93 Form	9-23	39.1%	+ 37.43
1993/94 Form	11-27	40.7%	+ 11.97	1991/92 Form	2-23	8.7%	- 12.00

J HETHERTON (Malton, North Yorks)

	Races Run	1st	2nd	3rd	Unpl	Per cent	£1 Level Stake
Hurdles	29	4	3	3	19	13.8	- 3.00
Chases	1	0	0	0	1	-	- 1.00
Totals	30	4	3	3	20	13.3	- 4.00

R Marley	2-16	+ 1.50	D Byrne		1-7	- 3.00
G E Tormey	1-4	+ 0.50				
Ludlow	1-2	+ 2.50	Uttoxeter		1-4	+ 2.50
Southwell	1-4	+ 7.00	Sedgefield		1-5	- 1.00

No of horses racing for the stable	5		Total winning prize-money	£9,324

D HIATT (Leamington Spa, Warwicks)

	Races Run	1st	2nd	3rd	Unpl	Per cent	£1 Level Stake
Hurdles	0	0	0	0	0	-	0.00
Chases	1	1	0	0	0	100.0	+ 10.00
Totals	1	1	0	0	0	100.0	+ 10.00

Miss C Townsley	1-1	+ 10.00	Huntingdon	1-1	+ 10.00

No of horses racing for the stable   1   Total winning prize-money   £1,648

P W HIATT (Hook Norton, Oxon)

	Races Run	1st	2nd	3rd	Unpl	Per cent	£1 Level Stake
Hurdles	34	3	4	1	26	8.8	- 9.00
Chases	0	0	0	0	0	-	0.00
Totals	34	3	4	1	26	8.8	- 9.00

E Husband	3-15	+ 10.00			
Warwick	1-1	+ 3.00	Stratford	1-3	+ 1.00
Newton Abbot	1-3	+ 14.00			

No of horses racing for the stable   6   Total winning prize-money   £7,041

MRS C HICKS (Cheltenham, Glos)

	Races Run	1st	2nd	3rd	Unpl	Per cent	£1 Level Stake
Hurdles	0	0	0	0	0	-	0.00
Chases	24	3	4	3	14	12.5	- 3.50
Totals	24	3	4	3	14	12.5	- 3.50

Mr R Hicks	3-24	- 3.50			
Nottingham	1-1	+ 8.00	Warwick	1-2	+ 4.00
Leicester	1-1	+ 4.50			

No of horses racing for the stable   5   Total winning prize-money   £4,447

A HIDE (Newmarket, Suffolk)

	Races Run	1st	2nd	3rd	Unpl	Per cent	£1 Level Stake
Hurdles	4	1	0	0	3	25.0	- 1.25
Chases	0	0	0	0	0	-	0.00
Totals	4	1	0	0	3	25.0	- 1.25

P Hide	1-3	- 0.25	Hereford	1-1	+ 1.75

No of horses racing for the stable   1   Total winning prize-money   £1,492

J W HILLS (Lambourn, Berks)

	Races Run	1st	2nd	3rd	Unpl	Per cent	£1 Level Stake
Hurdles	15	3	4	0	8	20.0	- 6.37
Chases	0	0	0	0	0	-	0.00
Totals	15	3	4	0	8	20.0	- 6.37

C Llewellyn	3-7	+ 1.63			
Bangor	1-1	+ 1.63	Worcester	1-3	+ 0.25
Hereford	1-1	+ 1.75			

No of horses racing for the stable   4   Total winning prize-money   £7,425

R P C HOAD (Lewes, East Sussex)

	Races Run	1st	2nd	3rd	Unpl	Per cent	£1 Level Stake
Hurdles	44	3	3	5	33	6.8	- 14.75
Chases	9	0	3	1	5	-	- 9.00
Totals	53	3	6	6	38	5.7	- 23.75

G Bradley	2-18	- 5.75	J Titley	1-1	+ 16.00
Newbury	1-1	+ 16.00	Fontwell	1-9	0.00
Plumpton	1-3	+ 0.25			

No of horses racing for the stable   14   Total winning prize-money   £5,713

P J HOBBS (Bilbrook, Somerset)

	Races Run	1st	2nd	3rd	Unpl	Per cent	£1 Level Stake
Hurdles	225	42	29	24	130	18.7	- 7.86
Chases	150	35	18	18	79	23.3	- 25.87
Totals	375	77	47	42	209	20.5	- 33.73

BY MONTH

	W-R	Per cent	£1 Level Stake		W-R	Per cent	£1 Level Stake
June	1-6	16.7	- 3.00	December	5-28	17.9	+ 11.50
July	6-15	40.0	- 0.70	January	4-41	9.8	- 18.00
August	14-24	58.3	+ 4.99	February	5-36	13.9	- 9.84
September	8-24	33.3	+ 7.31	March	9-60	15.0	- 0.50
October	6-23	26.1	- 1.12	April	8-41	19.5	- 4.68
November	6-44	13.6	- 10.75	May	5-33	15.2	- 8.94

DISTANCE

	W-R	Per cent	£1 Level Stake		W-R	Per cent	£1 Level Stake
Hurdles				Chases			
2m-2m 3f	24-131	18.3	- 12.73	2m-2m 3f	11-47	23.4	- 9.72
2m 4f-2m 7f	11-70	15.7	- 25.63	2m 4f-2m 7f	7-39	17.9	- 18.31
3m +	7-24	29.2	+ 30.50	3m +	17-64	26.6	+ 2.16

TYPE OF RACE

	W-R	Per cent	£1 Level Stake		W-R	Per cent	£1 Level Stake
Novice hurdles	23-116	19.8	+ 2.03	Selling	2-8	25.0	+ 2.75
H'cap hurdles	15-70	21.4	+ 8.53	Amateur	1-7	14.3	- 4.37
Novice chases	10-40	25.0	- 18.68	Hunter chases	0-0	-	0.00
H'cap chases	24-104	23.1	- 3.82	N H Flat	2-30	6.7	- 20.17

COURSE GRADE

	W-R	Per cent	£1 Level Stake
Group 1	9-98	9.2	- 34.00
Group 2	27-78	34.6	+ 38.28
Group 3	20-105	19.0	- 38.38
Group 4	21-94	22.3	+ 0.37

FIRST TIME OUT

	W-R	Per cent	£1 Level Stake
Hurdles	9-64	14.1	+ 3.37
Chases	9-24	37.5	+ 3.11
Totals	18-88	20.5	+ 6.48

JOCKEYS RIDING

	W–R	Per cent	£1 Level Stake		W–R	Per cent	£1 Level Stake
G E Tormey	19-113	16.8	- 22.47	D Bridgwater	2-7	28.6	- 1.00
Peter Hobbs	18-70	25.7	- 9.34	B Powell	2-8	25.0	+ 0.08
G McCourt	9-40	22.5	- 6.71	Mr Richard White	1-3	33.3	- 1.56
A P McCoy	8-38	21.1	- 7.04	W Marston	1-3	33.3	+ 4.00
C Maude	6-15	40.0	+ 17.87	M Moran	1-6	16.7	- 4.75
R Dunwoody	4-19	21.1	- 1.17	Mr S Mulcaire	1-7	14.3	- 4.37
R Farrant	2-3	66.7	+ 13.73	A Maguire	1-8	12.5	- 3.00
P Carberry	2-6	33.3	+ 21.00				

B M Clifford	0-5	A Dobbin	0-1	Mr J Creighton	0-1
M A Fitzgerald	0-4	C Llewellyn	0-1	Mr J Culloty	0-1
J R Kavanagh	0-3	G Bradley	0-1	P Hobbs	0-1
G Hogan	0-2	G Upton	0-1	Richard Davis	0-1
J Osborne	0-2	J Titley	0-1	T J Murphy	0-1
L Harvey	0-2	M Richards	0-1		

COURSE RECORD

	Total W–R	Nov Hdles	H'cap Hdles	Nov Chses	H'cap Chses	Hunter Chses	N H Flat	£1 Level Stake
Newton Abbot	16-39	5-11	2-4	3-8	5-11	0-0	1-5	+ 18.03
Taunton	8-21	3-8	1-3	2-3	2-7	0-0	0-0	+ 23.21
Chepstow	7-24	2-11	2-4	0-2	3-7	0-0	0-0	+ 26.80
Wincanton	5-21	2-8	0-4	1-1	2-7	0-0	0-1	- 5.92
Perth	4-4	0-0	2-2	1-1	1-1	0-0	0-0	+ 3.18
Fontwell	4-11	0-2	1-2	1-1	2-6	0-0	0-0	- 2.55
Ascot	4-16	2-6	1-2	0-1	1-3	0-0	0-4	+ 11.75
Uttoxeter	4-21	0-5	1-5	1-3	2-7	0-0	0-1	- 11.42
Worcester	4-25	2-9	2-8	0-1	0-6	0-0	0-1	- 15.29
Exeter	4-29	0-7	2-9	0-5	2-6	0-0	0-2	- 12.50
Nottingham	2-3	1-1	0-0	0-0	0-0	0-0	1-2	+ 10.50
Warwick	2-11	1-1	1-3	0-2	0-3	0-0	0-2	- 1.75
Stratford	2-12	0-3	0-2	0-2	2-5	0-0	0-0	- 7.00
Ludlow	2-16	1-5	0-4	0-0	1-6	0-0	0-1	+ 0.73
Cheltenham	2-22	0-7	1-5	0-1	1-7	0-0	0-2	- 6.50
Newbury	2-22	1-11	0-5	0-0	1-4	0-0	0-2	- 16.25
Folkestone	1-2	1-1	0-0	0-0	0-0	0-0	0-1	+ 2.50
Bangor	1-5	0-2	0-0	1-2	0-1	0-0	0-0	- 1.25
Hereford	1-8	1-3	0-1	0-2	0-1	0-0	0-1	- 5.75
Aintree	1-9	1-3	0-2	0-0	0-4	0-0	0-0	+ 6.00
Towcester	1-11	1-6	0-1	0-0	0-3	0-0	0-1	- 7.25

Kempton	0-15	Windsor	0-5	Leicester	0-1
Sandown	0-8	Lingfield	0-4		
Haydock	0-6	Plumpton	0-4		

WINNING HORSES

	Races Run	1st	2nd	3rd	Unpl	Win £
Kibreet	6	3	1	0	2	45,742
Pleasure Shared	6	4	0	0	2	45,551
Bells Life	9	4	1	0	4	15,515
Greenhil Tare Away	3	2	0	1	0	14,288
Muskora	8	4	1	0	3	13,069
Samlee	8	3	3	0	2	11,472
Certain Angle	11	3	2	1	5	10,596
Henley Wood	5	3	0	0	2	8,920
Mutual Trust	8	2	0	3	3	8,487
Faustino	8	3	0	1	4	8,036
Violet's Boy	2	2	0	0	0	7,575
Distant Memory	10	3	1	1	5	7,104
Charged	7	2	0	1	4	6,965
Blue Raven	9	3	0	1	5	6,663
Keano	8	2	1	3	2	6,629
Ashwell Boy	7	2	1	0	4	6,432
Bankroll	7	2	0	0	5	6,295
Sparkling Yasmin	8	2	2	2	2	6,256
Crack On	5	2	1	1	1	5,895
Badastan	5	2	2	1	0	5,615
The Country Trader	4	2	1	0	1	5,435
The Bobtail Fox	6	2	0	0	4	5,360
Clifton Beat	8	1	2	1	4	5,030
Amlah	9	2	2	1	4	4,758
Mr Devious	3	2	1	0	0	4,578
Shirley's Train	11	2	2	2	5	3,973
Ramstar	6	1	1	1	3	3,701
Aal El Aal	6	1	3	0	2	3,685
Lucky Eddie	3	1	0	0	2	3,648
Warner's Sports	4	1	0	0	3	3,152
Millies Own	4	1	1	1	1	2,514
Mellion Pride	5	1	0	1	3	2,482
Royal Ag Nag	5	1	2	1	1	2,448
Nordic Mine	4	1	0	0	3	2,416
Roi Du Nord	3	1	1	0	1	2,346
Jenzsoph	9	1	2	0	6	2,284
Winsford Hill	2	1	0	0	1	2,122
Warner For Players	3	1	0	2	0	1,313
Saxon Duke	3	1	0	0	2	1,236

WINNING OWNERS

	Races Won	Value £		Races Won	Value £
Tony Eaves	4	45,551	P J Hobbs	3	6,319
Terry Warner	1	28,179	Ian S Steers	2	6,295
Salvo Giannini	6	17,948	Victor G Palmer	2	6,256
Mrs Jill Emery	2	17,563	D R Peppiatt	2	5,895
R Gibbs	4	15,515	D B O'Connor	1	5,030
N C Savery	5	15,485	R W Devlin	2	4,578
Mrs P F Payne	2	14,288	Terry Warner Sports	2	4,465
Racing Club of Wales	4	10,795	S Martin	1	3,912
The Plyform Syndicate	3	10,596	A Loze	1	3,701
A J Scrimgeour	3	8,920	Six Horse Power	1	3,685
Mark Bowling	2	8,487	I L Shaw	1	3,648
The Bilbrook 4	3	8,036	Huntsman 4	1	2,514
White Lion Partnership	2	7,560	St Mellion Estates Ltd	1	2,482
Mrs Ann Weston	3	7,104	Royal Agricultural College	1	2,448
Brian Cooper	2	6,965	Superset Two	1	2,284
David Brace	3	6,663	A L Hobbs	1	2,122
Midavon Partnership	2	6,629	Saxon Duke Partnership	1	1,236
A B S Racing	2	6,432			

No of horses racing for the stable	89		Total winning prize-money	£309,586
Favourites	42-90	46.7%	+ 4.94	Average SP of winner	3.4/1
Longest win seq	5 Longest losing seq	22		Return on stakes invested	-9.0%
1994/95 Form	86-382	22.5%	- 27.03	1992/93 Form 37-305 12.1%	- 64.87
1993/94 Form	64-306	20.9%	+ 94.22	1991/92 Form 51-283 18.0%	- 31.00

R J HODGES (Charlton Adam, Somerset)

	Races Run	1st	2nd	3rd	Unpl	Per cent	£1 Level Stake
Hurdles	122	11	12	12	87	9.0	- 36.50
Chases	95	14	16	13	52	14.7	- 21.79
Totals	217	25	28	25	139	11.5	- 58.29

BY MONTH

	W-R	Per cent	£1 Level Stake		W-R	Per cent	£1 Level Stake
June	0-3	-	- 3.00	December	5-20	25.0	+ 30.50
July	0-3	-	- 3.00	January	2-35	5.7	- 24.00
August	0-2	-	- 2.00	February	1-27	3.7	- 20.00
September	0-4	-	- 4.00	March	5-34	14.7	- 3.25
October	1-20	5.0	- 17.00	April	4-26	15.4	- 11.29
November	3-28	10.7	- 5.50	May	4-15	26.7	+ 4.25

DISTANCE

	W-R	Per cent	£1 Level Stake		W-R	Per cent	£1 Level Stake
Hurdles				Chases			
2m-2m 3f	11-107	10.3	- 21.50	2m-2m 3f	12-63	19.0	+ 0.71
2m 4f-2m 7f	0-11	-	- 11.00	2m 4f-2m 7f	2-17	11.8	- 7.50
3m +	0-4	-	- 4.00	3m +	0-15	-	- 15.00

TYPE OF RACE

	W-R	Per cent	£1 Level Stake		W-R	Per cent	£1 Level Stake
Novice hurdles	0-14	-	- 14.00	Selling	4-38	10.5	- 8.00
H'cap hurdles	7-71	9.9	- 15.50	Amateur	0-3	-	- 3.00
Novice chases	4-25	16.0	- 14.04	Hunter chases	0-0	-	0.00
H'cap chases	10-63	15.9	- 0.75	N H Flat	0-3	-	- 3.00

COURSE GRADE

	W-R	Per cent	£1 Level Stake
Group 1	4-25	16.0	- 2.75
Group 2	2-28	7.1	- 17.75
Group 3	3-67	4.5	- 48.00
Group 4	16-97	16.5	+ 10.21

FIRST TIME OUT

	W-R	Per cent	£1 Level Stake
Hurdles	0-29	-	- 29.00
Chases	1-16	6.3	- 9.00
Totals	1-45	2.2	- 38.00

JOCKEYS RIDING

	W-R	Per cent	£1 Level Stake		W-R	Per cent	£1 Level Stake
T Dascombe	13-109	11.9	- 25.92	A Tory	2-27	7.4	- 10.75
R Dunwoody	5-22	22.7	+ 3.00	W McFarland	1-10	10.0	- 7.62
J Harris	4-23	17.4	+ 9.00				

J Frost	0-4	Mr C Ward Thomas	0-2	J Titley	0-1
A P McCoy	0-3	P Holley	0-2	Mr G Baines	0-1
B Powell	0-3	A Maguire	0-1	Mr P Henley	0-1
M A Fitzgerald	0-2	D Gallagher	0-1	P Carberry	0-1
Major G F Wheeler	0-2	I Lawrence	0-1	T Jenks	0-1

COURSE RECORD

	Total W-R	Nov Hdles	H'cap Hdles	Nov Chses	H'cap Chses	Hunter Chses	N H Flat	£1 Level Stake
Taunton	6-42	0-6	3-20	2-7	1-9	0-0	0-0	- 7.67
Hereford	4-15	0-1	3-9	0-2	1-3	0-0	0-0	+ 21.50
Sandown	3-11	0-2	0-1	0-1	3-7	0-0	0-0	+ 5.75
Bangor	2-5	0-0	0-2	1-1	1-2	0-0	0-0	- 0.12
Ludlow	2-9	1-1	0-3	0-0	1-5	0-0	0-0	+ 0.50
Newton Abbot	2-17	0-1	0-7	1-1	1-7	0-0	0-1	- 6.75
Exeter	2-24	0-3	2-11	0-3	0-7	0-0	0-0	- 2.00
Uttoxeter	1-3	0-0	1-3	0-0	0-0	0-0	0-0	+ 7.00
Worcester	1-5	0-0	0-2	0-0	1-3	0-0	0-0	- 2.50
Ascot	1-5	0-0	0-1	0-0	1-4	0-0	0-0	+ 0.50
Plumpton	1-9	0-1	1-3	0-1	0-4	0-0	0-0	- 2.50

Wincanton	0-17	Cheltenham	0-4	Newbury	0-2
Warwick	0-10	Catterick	0-3	Southwell	0-2
Fontwell	0-9	Folkestone	0-3	Chepstow	0-1
Windsor	0-8	Leicester	0-3	Haydock	0-1
Stratford	0-6	Kempton	0-2	Lingfield	0-1

WINNING HORSES

	Races Run	1st	2nd	3rd	Unpl	Win £
Jurz	5	4	0	0	1	13,994
Northern Saddler	8	3	1	2	2	13,173
High Baron	5	1	0	1	3	6,873
Hightown Cavalier	7	3	0	1	3	6,615
Fenwick	11	2	3	0	6	6,345
Corrin Hill	12	2	1	2	7	4,664
Medinas Swan Song	7	1	2	2	2	4,372
Indian Run	4	1	1	1	1	3,855
Take A Flyer	8	2	0	2	4	3,853
Smiling Chief	10	1	1	2	6	3,534
Dawn Chance	5	1	1	1	2	2,808
Northern Singer	7	1	1	0	5	2,379
Urban Lily	11	1	2	0	8	2,306
Persistent Gunner	12	1	1	2	8	2,274
Beyond Our Reach	4	1	1	0	2	2,103

WINNING OWNERS

	Races Won	Value £		Races Won	Value £
P Slade	6	20,123	Ron Osborne	2	3,853
Richard J Evans	3	13,173	Mrs E A Tucker	1	3,534
Miss C A James	1	6,873	G Small	1	2,808
Miss R Dobson	3	6,615	Joe Panes	1	2,379
A W C Pearn	2	6,345	Mrs C J Cole	1	2,306
Bob Froome	2	4,664	Hunt & Co (Bournemouth) Ltd	1	2,103
C A G Perry	1	4,372			

No of horses racing for the stable		46	Total winning prize-money	£79,148

Favourites	9-28	32.1%	+ 2.96	Average SP of winner		5.3/1
Longest win seq	3	Longest losing seq	32	Return on stakes invested		-26.9%

1994/95 Form	23-250	9.2%	- 74.43	1992/93 Form	32-258	12.4%	- 48.35
1993/94 Form	36-283	12.7%	- 49.57	1991/92 Form	21-260	8.1%	-179.99

K W HOGG (Isle of Man)

	Races Run	1st	2nd	3rd	Unpl	Per cent	£1 Level Stake
Hurdles	13	3	1	1	8	23.1	+ 13.00
Chases	0	0	0	0	0	-	0.00
Totals	13	3	1	1	8	23.1	+ 13.00

M A Fitzgerald	2-3	+ 12.00	S Wynne	1-8	+ 3.00
Sedgefield	1-1	+ 4.00	Catterick	1-3	+ 8.00
Towcester	1-2	+ 8.00			

No of horses racing for the stable   4   Total winning prize-money   £7,125

G HOLMES (Newton-on-Rawcliffe, North Yorks)

	Races Run	1st	2nd	3rd	Unpl	Per cent	£1 Level Stake
Hurdles	20	2	1	2	15	10.0	- 5.25
Chases	0	0	0	0	0	-	0.00
Totals	20	2	1	2	15	10.0	- 5.25

A Maguire	1-2	+ 1.75	M Dwyer	1-5	+ 6.00
Sedgefield	1-3	+ 8.00	Market Rasen	1-4	- 0.25

No of horses racing for the stable   6   Total winning prize-money   £3,512

MISS C HORLER (Hemington, Somerset)

	Races Run	1st	2nd	3rd	Unpl	Per cent	£1 Level Stake
Hurdles	11	2	0	0	9	18.2	- 1.00
Chases	3	0	0	0	3		- 3.00
Totals	14	2	0	0	12	14.3	- 4.00

C Maude	1-2	+ 3.00	G Upton	1-7	- 2.00
Exeter	1-2	+ 3.00	Hereford	1-2	+ 3.00

No of horses racing for the stable   4   Total winning prize-money   £4,679

G F JOHNSON HOUGHTON (Newmarket, Suffolk)

	Races Run	1st	2nd	3rd	Unpl	Per cent	£1 Level Stake
Hurdles	19	1	2	2	14	5.3	- 6.00
Chases	1	0	0	0	1	-	- 1.00
Totals	20	1	2	2	15	5.0	- 7.00

A Thornton	1-6	+ 7.00	Market Rasen	1-3	+ 10.00

No of horses racing for the stable   6   Total winning prize-money   £3,116

H S HOWE (Oakfordbridge, Devon)

	Races Run	1st	2nd	3rd	Unpl	Per cent	£1 Level Stake
Hurdles	22	2	1	1	18	9.1	- 2.67
Chases	12	0	1	0	11	-	- 12.00
Totals	34	2	2	1	29	5.9	- 14.67

A P McCoy	1-4	+ 0.33	D Bridgwater	1-5	+ 10.00
Uttoxeter	1-3	+ 1.33	Newton Abbot	1-5	+ 10.00

No of horses racing for the stable   7   Total winning prize-money   £4,377

G A HUBBARD (Worlingworth, Suffolk)

	Races Run	1st	2nd	3rd	Unpl	Per cent	£1 Level Stake
Hurdles	47	8	6	6	27	17.0	+ 1.00
Chases	25	1	5	1	18	4.0	- 21.00
Totals	72	9	11	7	45	12.5	- 20.00

BY MONTH

	W-R	Per cent	£1 Level Stake		W-R	Per cent	£1 Level Stake
June	0-0	-	0.00	December	0-9	-	- 9.00
July	0-0	-	0.00	January	0-15	-	- 15.00
August	0-0	-	0.00	February	0-5	-	- 5.00
September	0-0	-	0.00	March	1-13	7.7	- 4.50
October	3-11	27.3	+ 2.50	April	1-8	12.5	- 4.25
November	4-9	44.4	+ 17.25	May	0-2	-	- 2.00

DISTANCE

Hurdles	W-R	Per cent	£1 Level Stake	Chases	W-R	Per cent	£1 Level Stake
2m-2m 3f	3-21	14.3	- 5.50	2m-2m 3f	0-0	-	0.00
2m 4f-2m 7f	4-20	20.0	+ 4.00	2m 4f-2m 7f	0-15	-	- 15.00
3m +	1-6	16.7	+ 2.50	3m +	1-10	10.0	- 6.00

TYPE OF RACE

	W-R	Per cent	£1 Level Stake		W-R	Per cent	£1 Level Stake
Novice hurdles	5-24	20.8	+ 8.00	Selling	0-0	-	0.00
H'cap hurdles	3-20	15.0	- 4.00	Amateur	0-0	-	0.00
Novice chases	0-4	-	- 4.00	Hunter chases	0-0	-	0.00
H'cap chases	1-21	4.8	- 17.00	N H Flat	0-3	-	- 3.00

COURSE GRADE

	W-R	Per cent	£1 Level Stake
Group 1	1-23	4.3	- 17.00
Group 2	0-6	-	- 6.00
Group 3	5-30	16.7	- 2.50
Group 4	3-13	23.1	+ 5.50

FIRST TIME OUT

	W-R	Per cent	£1 Level Stake
Hurdles	2-11	18.2	- 1.50
Chases	1-8	12.5	- 4.00
Totals	3-19	15.8	- 5.50

JOCKEYS RIDING

	W-R	Per cent	£1 Level Stake
K P Gaule	9-67	13.4	- 15.00

A Thornton	0-2	D J Murphy	0-1
A P McCoy	0-1	M A Fitzgerald	0-1

COURSE RECORD

	Total W-R	Nov Hdles	H'cap Hdles	Nov Chses	H'cap Chses	Hunter Chses	N H Flat	£1 Level Stake
Folkestone	2-6	1-2	1-2	0-1	0-1	0-0	0-0	+ 10.75
Towcester	2-9	1-4	1-4	0-0	0-1	0-0	0-0	+ 5.50
Huntingdon	2-10	1-5	1-3	0-1	0-1	0-0	0-0	- 2.75
Plumpton	1-1	1-1	0-0	0-0	0-0	0-0	0-0	+ 2.50
Fakenham	1-4	0-1	0-0	0-0	1-3	0-0	0-0	0.00
Ascot	1-4	1-2	0-0	0-0	0-2	0-0	0-0	+ 2.00

Sandown	0-9	Nottingham	0-4	Worcester	0-2
Fontwell	0-5	Warwick	0-3	Aintree	0-1
Newbury	0-5	Cheltenham	0-2	Lingfield	0-1
Market Rasen	0-4	Kempton	0-2		

WINNING HORSES

	Races Run	1st	2nd	3rd	Unpl	Win £
Strong Promise	9	2	2	1	4	6,408
Pettaugh	8	2	0	2	4	5,351
Dennington	2	1	0	0	1	3,007
Merilena	5	1	0	0	4	2,495
Hi Hedley	6	1	1	1	3	2,343
Strong John	8	1	0	1	6	2,129
Run For Dante	5	1	2	0	2	2,108

WINNING OWNER

	Races Won	Value £
G A Hubbard	9	23,841

No of horses racing for the stable	19	Total winning prize-money	£23,841

Favourites	0-4		Average SP of winner	4.8/1
Longest win seq	3	Longest losing seq 30	Return on stakes invested	-27.8%

1994/95 Form	9-108	8.3%	- 24.79	1992/93 Form	0-2	
1993/94 Form	1-10	10.0%	- 1.00	1991/92 Form	1-4	25.0% + 63.00

J S HUBBUCK (Hexham, Northumberland)

	Races Run	1st	2nd	3rd	Unpl	Per cent	£1 Level Stake
Hurdles	0	0	0	0	0	-	0.00
Chases	17	1	0	2	14	5.9	0.00
Totals	17	1	0	2	14	5.9	0.00

B Storey	1-10	+ 7.00	Cartmel	1-2	+ 15.00

No of horses racing for the stable	2	Total winning prize-money	£3,481

J W HUGHES (Galashiels, Selkirks)

	Races Run	1st	2nd	3rd	Unpl	Per cent	£1 Level Stake
Hurdles	0	0	0	0	0	-	0.00
Chases	1	1	0	0	0	100.0	+ 5.00
Totals	1	1	0	0	0	100.0	+ 5.00

Mr M Bradburne	1-1	+ 5.00	Kelso	1-1	+ 5.00

No of horses racing for the stable	1	Total winning prize-money	£2,285

P HUTCHINSON (Lutterworth, Leics)

	Races Run	1st	2nd	3rd	Unpl	Per cent	£1 Level Stake
Hurdles	0	0	0	0	0	-	0.00
Chases	4	1	0	0	3	25.0	+ 9.00
Totals	4	1	0	0	3	25.0	+ 9.00

Mr P Hutchinson	1-4	+ 9.00	Huntingdon	1-1	+ 12.00

No of horses racing for the stable   1   Total winning prize-money   £1,637

C JAMES (East Garston, Berks)

	Races Run	1st	2nd	3rd	Unpl	Per cent	£1 Level Stake
Hurdles	29	4	2	2	21	13.8	+ 4.25
Chases	2	0	1	0	1	-	- 2.00
Totals	31	4	3	2	22	12.9	+ 2.25

Mr E James	3-15	+ 1.25	I Lawrence	1-2	+ 15.00
Hereford	1-2	+ 2.00	Towcester	1-4	+ 13.00
Leicester	1-2	+ 1.75	Worcester	1-5	+ 3.50

No of horses racing for the stable   6   Total winning prize-money   £9,630

A P JARVIS (Aston Upthorpe, Oxon)

	Races Run	1st	2nd	3rd	Unpl	Per cent	£1 Level Stake
Hurdles	37	4	3	3	27	10.8	- 23.12
Chases	15	2	4	2	7	13.3	+ 4.33
Totals	52	6	7	5	34	11.5	- 18.79

A Maguire	2-10	- 4.25	P Morris	1-10	- 4.50
N Williamson	1-1	+ 14.00	A Larnach	1-15	- 10.67
A P McCoy	1-4	- 1.37			
Cheltenham	3-12	+ 11.75	Newbury	1-2	+ 0.63
Chepstow	1-1	+ 1.50	Uttoxeter	1-3	+ 1.33

No of horses racing for the stable   17   Total winning prize-money   £20,611

J M JEFFERSON (Norton, North Yorks)

	Races Run	1st	2nd	3rd	Unpl	Per cent	£1 Level Stake
Hurdles	78	10	7	10	51	12.8	+ 35.70
Chases	12	4	1	0	7	33.3	+ 32.83
Totals	90	14	8	10	58	15.6	+ 68.53

BY MONTH

	W-R	Per cent	£1 Level Stake		W-R	Per cent	£1 Level Stake
June	1-2	50.0	+ 24.00	December	0-7	-	- 7.00
July	0-1	-	- 1.00	January	2-10	20.0	+ 66.00
August	2-2	100.0	+ 12.50	February	2-15	13.3	- 11.05
September	1-3	33.3	+ 1.33	March	2-12	16.7	+ 6.00
October	0-4	-	- 4.00	April	2-13	15.4	- 6.00
November	1-7	14.3	- 3.25	May	1-14	7.1	- 9.00

DISTANCE

Hurdles	W-R	Per cent	£1 Level Stake	Chases	W-R	Per cent	£1 Level Stake
2m-2m 3f	4-48	8.3	+ 27.57	2m-2m 3f	0-0	-	0.00
2m 4f-2m 7f	5-21	23.8	+ 10.13	2m 4f-2m 7f	2-7	28.6	+ 24.50
3m +	1-9	11.1	- 2.00	3m +	2-5	40.0	+ 8.33

TYPE OF RACE

	W-R	Per cent	£1 Level Stake		W-R	Per cent	£1 Level Stake
Novice hurdles	6-27	22.2	+ 62.70	Selling	0-2	-	- 2.00
H'cap hurdles	3-21	14.3	0.00	Amateur	0-0	-	0.00
Novice chases	2-4	50.0	+ 27.50	Hunter chases	0-0	-	0.00
H'cap chases	2-8	25.0	+ 5.33	N H Flat	1-28	3.6	- 25.00

COURSE GRADE

	W-R	Per cent	£1 Level Stake
Group 1	4-22	18.2	- 3.87
Group 2	1-6	16.7	- 4.43
Group 3	4-21	19.0	+ 23.50
Group 4	5-41	12.2	+ 53.33

FIRST TIME OUT

	W-R	Per cent	£1 Level Stake
Hurdles	2-21	9.5	+ 47.57
Chases	1-4	25.0	+ 22.00
Totals	3-25	12.0	+ 69.57

JOCKEYS RIDING

	W-R	Per cent	£1 Level Stake		W-R	Per cent	£1 Level Stake
L Wyer	6-19	31.6	+ 44.50	Richard Davis	1-12	8.3	- 7.67
M Dwyer	5-30	16.7	+ 47.70	M Newton	1-20	5.0	- 11.00
Richard Guest	1-1	100.0	+ 3.00				

A Dobbin	0-4	F Leahy	0-1	Mr J Culloty	0-1
D Bentley	0-1	J H Burke	0-1		

COURSE RECORD

	Total W-R	Nov Hdles	H'cap Hdles	Nov Chses	H'cap Chses	Hunter Chses	N H Flat	£1 Level Stake
Newcastle	3-8	2-4	1-3	0-0	0-0	0-0	0-1	+ 5.13
Market Rasen	3-11	1-2	0-0	2-3	0-2	0-0	0-4	+ 24.50
Perth	1-2	0-0	0-1	0-0	0-0	0-0	1-1	+ 1.00
Nottingham	1-2	0-0	1-2	0-0	0-0	0-0	0-0	+ 7.00
Southwell	1-3	0-0	0-1	0-0	1-1	0-0	0-1	+ 6.00
Bangor	1-5	0-1	0-2	0-0	1-1	0-0	0-1	- 0.67
Wetherby	1-6	1-2	0-3	0-0	0-0	0-0	0-1	- 4.43
Haydock	1-6	0-3	1-1	0-0	0-1	0-0	0-1	- 1.00
Carlisle	1-7	1-3	0-1	0-0	0-0	0-0	0-3	+ 4.00
Towcester	1-9	1-5	0-1	0-0	0-1	0-0	0-2	+ 58.00

Hexham	0-11	Leicester	0-2	Kelso	0-1
Ayr	0-5	Sedgefield	0-2	Musselburgh	0-1
Uttoxeter	0-3	Worcester	0-2	Stratford	0-1
Doncaster	0-2	Cheltenham	0-1		

WINNING HORSES

	Races Run	1st	2nd	3rd	Unpl	Win £
Magic Bloom	8	4	1	0	3	14,073
Tullymurry Toff	8	3	0	2	3	11,127
Dato Star	2	1	0	0	1	7,582
Go-Informal	5	2	1	0	2	5,018
Danbys Gorse	7	1	0	0	6	2,898
Strathmore Lodge	3	1	0	1	1	2,565
Northern Fusilier	2	1	0	0	1	2,490
Northern Squire	7	1	0	0	6	2,369

WINNING OWNERS

	Races Won	Value £		Races Won	Value £
Peter Nelson	4	14,073	D T Todd	1	2,898
John H Wilson & J H Riley	3	11,127	J M Jefferson	1	2,565
Mrs Kath Riley	1	7,582	Joe Donald	1	2,490
R G Marshall	2	5,018	Mrs J M Davenport	1	2,369

No of horses racing for the stable		25	Total winning prize-money	£48,122

Favourites	4-16	25.0%	- 4.05	Average SP of winner		10.3/1
Longest win seq	3	Longest losing seq	12	Return on stakes invested		76.1%

1994/95 Form	16-90	17.8%	+ 11.88	1992/93 Form	14-65	21.5%	- 1.85
1993/94 Form	11-68	16.2%	+ 47.40	1991/92 Form	3-37	8.1%	- 6.00

J R JENKINS (Royston, Herts)

	Races Run	1st	2nd	3rd	Unpl	Per cent	£1 Level Stake
Hurdles	236	25	28	37	146	10.6	- 94.99
Chases	42	3	9	4	26	7.1	- 29.00
Totals	278	28	37	41	172	10.1	-123.99

BY MONTH

	W-R	Per cent	£1 Level Stake		W-R	Per cent	£1 Level Stake
June	0-5	-	- 5.00	December	5-30	16.7	+ 10.38
July	0-10	-	- 10.00	January	1-19	5.3	- 14.50
August	8-20	40.0	+ 2.30	February	0-17	-	- 17.00
September	2-21	9.5	- 5.50	March	3-34	8.8	+ 6.00
October	0-24	-	- 24.00	April	4-24	16.7	- 7.92
November	3-38	7.9	- 29.25	May	2-36	5.6	- 29.50

DISTANCE

Hurdles	W-R	Per cent	£1 Level Stake	Chases	W-R	Per cent	£1 Level Stake
2m-2m 3f	11-136	8.1	- 57.75	2m-2m 3f	2-16	12.5	- 5.75
2m 4f-2m 7f	13-80	16.3	- 38.24	2m 4f-2m 7f	1-9	11.1	- 6.25
3m +	1-20	5.0	+ 1.00	3m +	0-17	-	- 17.00

TYPE OF RACE

	W-R	Per cent	£1 Level Stake		W-R	Per cent	£1 Level Stake
Novice hurdles	11-116	9.5	- 66.04	Selling	1-24	4.2	- 21.37
H'cap hurdles	11-88	12.5	- 9.08	Amateur	1-2	50.0	+ 1.00
Novice chases	2-27	7.4	- 17.75	Hunter chases	0-1	-	- 1.00
H'cap chases	1-14	7.1	- 10.25	N H Flat	1-6	16.7	+ 0.50

COURSE GRADE

	W-R	Per cent	£1 Level Stake
Group 1	2-71	2.8	- 47.25
Group 2	3-26	11.5	- 13.17
Group 3	12-125	9.6	- 80.70
Group 4	11-56	19.6	+ 17.13

FIRST TIME OUT

	W-R	Per cent	£1 Level Stake
Hurdles	4-40	10.0	- 15.00
Chases	0-6	-	- 6.00
Totals	4-46	8.7	- 21.00

JOCKEYS RIDING

	W-R	Per cent	£1 Level Stake		W-R	Per cent	£1 Level Stake
C Rae	9-47	19.1	- 1.45	R Supple	1-5	20.0	+ 2.00
S Fox	4-53	7.5	- 26.92	N Williamson	1-6	16.7	+ 3.00
A P McCoy	3-16	18.8	+ 13.25	D Walsh	1-7	14.3	- 3.75
Mr J Connolly	2-2	100.0	+ 3.50	J Titley	1-10	10.0	- 5.50
G Bradley	2-18	11.1	- 10.75	J Railton	1-13	7.7	- 6.50
Richard Guest	1-2	50.0	+ 1.00	J Osborne	1-30	3.3	- 27.37
D Skyrme	1-2	50.0	+ 2.50				

A Maguire	0-10	E Murphy	0-2	D O'Sullivan	0-1
R Dunwoody	0-9	M Dwyer	0-2	L Wyer	0-1
P Carberry	0-8	M Perrett	0-2	Miss E Tomlinson	0-1
D Yellowlees	0-7	W Marston	0-2	Mr R Wakley	0-1
B Powell	0-4	A Tory	0-1	Mr T McCarthy	0-1
R Hughes	0-3	B Fenton	0-1	S McNeill	0-1
C O'Dwyer	0-2	B Harding	0-1	S Smith Eccles	0-1
D Bridgwater	0-2	D Fortt	0-1		
E Husband	0-2	D Gallagher	0-1		

COURSE RECORD

	Total W-R	Nov Hdles	H'cap Hdles	Nov Chses	H'cap Chses	Hunter Chses	N H Flat	£1 Level Stake
Fakenham	5-18	3-7	2-7	0-1	0-2	0-1	0-0	+ 15.75
Fontwell	3-13	1-4	2-7	0-1	0-1	0-0	0-0	- 0.17
Southwell	3-20	1-6	0-8	1-2	1-2	0-0	0-2	- 7.12
Plumpton	3-24	1-11	2-10	0-2	0-1	0-0	0-0	- 18.57
Huntingdon	3-29	1-12	0-10	1-3	0-1	0-0	1-3	- 18.13
Bangor	2-5	1-2	1-2	0-1	0-0	0-0	0-0	+ 0.50
Worcester	2-16	0-6	2-8	0-1	0-1	0-0	0-0	- 10.50
Aintree	1-5	0-3	1-1	0-0	0-1	0-0	0-0	+ 16.00
Warwick	1-7	1-4	0-0	0-3	0-0	0-0	0-0	- 2.50
Windsor	1-8	0-3	1-3	0-2	0-0	0-0	0-0	- 3.50
Folkestone	1-8	1-3	0-3	0-1	0-1	0-0	0-0	- 3.50
Towcester	1-9	0-4	1-4	0-0	0-1	0-0	0-0	+ 12.00
Stratford	1-14	0-8	1-6	0-0	0-0	0-0	0-0	- 5.00
Ascot	1-28	1-14	0-8	0-4	0-2	0-0	0-0	- 25.25

Kempton	0-12	Sandown	0-6	Exeter	0-1
Cheltenham	0-7	Doncaster	0-5	Haydock	0-1
Newbury	0-7	Market Rasen	0-5	Hereford	0-1
Newton Abbot	0-7	Uttoxeter	0-5	Sedgefield	0 1
Leicester	0-6	Nottingham	0-3		
Lingfield	0-6	Cartmel	0-1		

WINNING HORSES

	Races Run	1st	2nd	3rd	Unpl	Win £
Gone By	14	5	4	3	2	11,707
Top Spin	11	1	0	1	9	11,576
Arctic Life	14	4	3	0	7	11,221
Viceroy Ruler	9	2	0	1	6	7,001
Djais	11	2	1	3	5	6,420
Tim	13	3	4	2	4	6,386

Jenkins J R

Stoney Valley	4	2	0	1	1	6,216
Circus Colours	7	2	1	0	4	5,098
Thane	8	2	0	1	5	4,648
Fierce	12	1	4	3	4	3,080
Last Spin	8	1	0	0	7	2,545
Durshan	8	1	2	0	5	2,303
Lucky Tucky	3	1	0	0	2	2,216
Omidjoy	13	1	6	3	3	1,790

WINNING OWNERS

	Races Won	Value £		Races Won	Value £
Mrs T McCoubrey	11	27,576	Ellis & Partners (Stockbrokers)	2	6,216
Mrs Eliza Long	2	14,121	S Powell	2	5,098
P W Piper	4	9,466	Oliver Donnelly	1	2,303
J McBarron	2	7,001	L E Tuckwell Ltd	1	2,216
T Long	2	6,420	R M Ellis	1	1,790

No of horses racing for the stable	47	Total winning prize-money	£82,207

Favourites	11-30	36.7% - 0.99	Average SP of winner		4.5/1
Longest win seq	4	Longest losing seq 39	Return on stakes invested		-44.6%

1994/95 Form	13-210	6.2%	-124.65	1992/93 Form	15-213	7.0%	-141.04
1993/94 Form	19-200	9.5%	- 72.00	1991/92 Form	20-244	8.2%	-120.30

W JENKS (Glazeley, Salop)

	Races Run	1st	2nd	3rd	Unpl	Per cent	£1 Level Stake
Hurdles	54	7	6	7	34	13.0	+ 2.25
Chases	12	0	1	0	11	-	- 12.00
Totals	66	7	7	7	45	10.6	- 9.75

BY MONTH

	W-R	Per cent	£1 Level Stake		W-R	Per cent	£1 Level Stake
June	0-0	-	0.00	December	0-8	-	- 8.00
July	0-0	-	0.00	January	1-13	7.7	- 4.00
August	0-0	-	0.00	February	2-7	28.6	+ 12.00
September	0-4	-	- 4.00	March	0-7	-	- 7.00
October	0-2	-	- 2.00	April	0-7	-	- 7.00
November	3-15	20.0	+ 8.75	May	1-3	33.3	+ 1.50

DISTANCE

	W-R	Per cent	£1 Level Stake	Chases	W-R	Per cent	£1 Level Stake
Hurdles							
2m-2m 3f	1-33	3.0	- 28.50	2m-2m 3f	0-3	-	- 3.00
2m 4f-2m 7f	5-19	26.3	+ 23.75	2m 4f-2m 7f	0-4	-	- 4.00
3m +	1-2	50.0	+ 7.00	3m +	0-5	-	- 5.00

TYPE OF RACE

	W-R	Per cent	£1 Level Stake		W-R	Per cent	£1 Level Stake
Novice hurdles	3-22	13.6	- 2.25	Selling	1-11	9.1	+ 6.00
H'cap hurdles	2-11	18.2	+ 4.00	Amateur	0-1	-	- 1.00
Novice chases	0-8	-	- 8.00	Hunter chases	0-0	-	0.00
H'cap chases	0-3	-	- 3.00	N H Flat	1-10	10.0	- 5.50

COURSE GRADE

	W-R	Per cent	£1 Level Stake
Group 1	1-9	11.1	- 5.00
Group 2	0-1	-	- 1.00
Group 3	3-25	12.0	- 0.75
Group 4	3-31	9.7	- 3.00

FIRST TIME OUT

	W-R	Per cent	£1 Level Stake
Hurdles	2-11	18.2	- 3.75
Chases	0-4	-	- 4.00
Totals	2-15	13.3	- 7.75

JOCKEYS RIDING

	W-R	Per cent	£1 Level Stake		W-R	Per cent	£1 Level Stake
S Wynne	3-10	30.0	+ 9.75	Mr R Burton	1-8	12.5	+ 9.00
A Dobbin	1-1	100.0	+ 8.00	T Jenks	1-28	3.6	- 22.00
R Johnson	1-2	50.0	+ 2.50				

G Hogan	0-3	J Railton	0-2	A Tory		0-1
R Bellamy	0-3	S Curran	0-2	D Walsh		0-1
C Llewellyn	0-2	W Marston	0-2	Martin Brennan		0-1

COURSE RECORD

	Total W-R	Nov Hdles	H'cap Hdles	Nov Chses	H'cap Chses	Hunter Chses	N H Flat	£1 Level Stake
Ludlow	3-12	1-4	2-6	0-0	0-1	0-0	0-1	+ 16.00
Leicester	1-2	0-1	1-1	0-0	0-0	0-0	0-0	+ 15.00
Warwick	1-5	0-2	0-2	0-0	0-0	0-0	1-1	- 0.50
Nottingham	1-5	1-2	0-0	0-2	0-0	0-0	0-1	- 2.25
Haydock	1-6	1-4	0-0	0-0	0-0	0-0	0-2	- 2.00

Bangor	0-11	Worcester	0-3	Towcester	0-2
Uttoxeter	0-8	Doncaster	0-2	Aintree	0-1
Hereford	0-6	Huntingdon	0-2	Chepstow	0-1

WINNING HORSES

	Races Run	1st	2nd	3rd	Unpl	Win £
Hoodwinker	7	3	0	3	1	9,446
Danzig Island	5	2	0	1	2	5,003
Edward Seymour	9	1	1	1	6	2,075
Kailash	1	1	0	0	0	1,700

WINNING OWNERS

	Races Won	Value £			Races Won	Value £
P A Howell	3	9,446	W Jenks		2	3,775
The Glazeley P'ship	2	5,003				

No of horses racing for the stable	15	Total winning prize-money	£18,224

Favourites	3-6	50.0%	+ 7.25	Average SP of winner		7.0/1
Longest win seq	2	Longest losing seq	17	Return on stakes invested		-14.8%

1994/95 Form	4-36	11.1%	- 8.00	1992/93 Form	1-16	6.3%	- 13.12
1993/94 Form	0-11			1991/92 Form	0-17		

MRS L C JEWELL (Sutton Valence, Kent)

	Races Run	1st	2nd	3rd	Unpl	Per cent	£1 Level Stake
Hurdles	50	1	2	5	42	2.0	- 46.50
Chases	8	1	0	2	5	12.5	0.00
Totals	58	2	2	7	47	3.4	- 46.50

D Gallagher	1-5	- 1.50	J Railton	1-12	- 4.00
Huntingdon	1-5	- 1.50	Fontwell	1-9	- 1.00

No of horses racing for the stable	21	Total winning prize-money	£4,718

MISS C JOHNSEY (Devauden, Gwent)

	Races Run	1st	2nd	3rd	Unpl	Per cent	£1 Level Stake
Hurdles	18	1	1	2	14	5.6	- 12.50
Chases	2	0	0	0	2	-	- 2.00
Totals	20	1	1	2	16	5.0	- 14.50

W Marston	1-1	+ 4.50	Uttoxeter	1-1	+ 4.50

No of horses racing for the stable	10	Total winning prize-money	£2,773

J H JOHNSON (Crook, Co Durham)

	Races Run	1st	2nd	3rd	Unpl	Per cent	£1 Level Stake
Hurdles	112	13	14	11	74	11.6	- 52.23
Chases	104	22	15	21	46	21.2	+ 28.72
Totals	216	35	29	32	120	16.2	- 23.51

BY MONTH

	W-R	Per cent	£1 Level Stake		W-R	Per cent	£1 Level Stake
June	0-0	-	0.00	December	3-19	15.8	- 4.92
July	0-0	-	0.00	January	3-20	15.0	- 10.00
August	0-0	-	0.00	February	8-33	24.2	- 8.24
September	2-9	22.2	- 3.37	March	2-24	8.3	+ 16.00
October	3-24	12.5	- 8.00	April	1-31	3.2	- 23.00
November	5-28	17.9	- 15.48	May	8-28	28.6	+ 33.50

DISTANCE

Hurdles	W-R	Per cent	£1 Level Stake	Chases	W-R	Per cent	£1 Level Stake
2m-2m 3f	10-70	14.3	- 32.43	2m-2m 3f	3-14	21.4	+ 3.50
2m 4f-2m 7f	1-23	4.3	- 8.00	2m 4f-2m 7f	13-42	31.0	+ 51.76
3m +	2-19	10.5	- 11.80	3m +	6-48	12.5	- 26.54

TYPE OF RACE

	W-R	Per cent	£1 Level Stake		W-R	Per cent	£1 Level Stake
Novice hurdles	7-56	12.5	- 20.61	Selling	0-3	-	- 3.00
H'cap hurdles	4-35	11.4	- 16.00	Amateur	1-4	25.0	+ 3.00
Novice chases	9-37	24.3	+ 6.46	Hunter chases	0-0	-	0.00
H'cap chases	12-63	19.0	+ 19.26	N H Flat	2-18	11.1	- 12.62

COURSE GRADE / FIRST TIME OUT

	W-R	Per cent	£1 Level Stake		W-R	Per cent	£1 Level Stake
Group 1	5-43	11.6	+ 4.11	Hurdles	1-35	2.9	- 32.00
Group 2	4-24	16.7	- 0.50	Chases	3-16	18.8	- 3.87
Group 3	5-27	18.5	+ 3.21				
Group 4	21-122	17.2	- 30.33	Totals	4-51	7.8	- 35.87

JOCKEYS RIDING

	W-R	Per cent	£1 Level Stake		W-R	Per cent	£1 Level Stake
P Carberry	17-78	21.8	+ 43.91	Miss P Jones	1-1	100.0	+ 6.00
A Maguire	5-16	31.3	+ 3.83	A Dobbin	1-1	100.0	+ 5.00
J Titley	3-22	13.6	- 12.14	Mr J Culloty	1-2	50.0	+ 6.00
M A Fitzgerald	2-7	28.6	- 0.87	D Bridgwater	1-3	33.3	+ 0.25
Mr C Bonner	2-22	9.1	- 16.62	M Foster	1-10	10.0	- 7.62
J Osborne	1-1	100.0	+ 1.75				

H Taylor	0-7	B Fenton	0-2	D Parker	0-1
T J Murphy	0-5	B Harding	0-2	M Moloney	0-1
R Johnson	0-4	G Upton	0-2	N Bentley	0-1
Richard Guest	0-4	K Johnson	0-2	N Williamson	0-1
A S Smith	0-3	Mr T McCarthy	0-2	P G Cahill	0-1
D J Moffatt	0-3	R Dunwoody	0-2	R Supple	0-1
Scott Taylor	0-3	W Marston	0-2	S Haworth	0-1
A Larnach	0-2	D Byrne	0-1		

Johnson J H

COURSE RECORD

	Total W-R	Nov Hdles	H'cap Hdles	Nov Chses	H'cap Chses	Hunter Chses	N H Flat	£1 Level Stake
Musselburgh	7-20	1-4	0-2	3-5	3-7	0-0	0-2	+ 7.13
Sedgefield	6-36	1-7	0-7	2-7	3-13	0-0	0-2	- 14.99
Wetherby	4-24	0-7	3-6	0-1	1-9	0-0	0-1	- 0.50
Hexham	3-21	2-8	0-3	0-4	1-4	0-0	0-2	+ 4.83
Uttoxeter	2-4	0-0	0-0	1-1	1-3	0-0	0-0	+ 4.50
Carlisle	2-13	1-3	0-3	0-1	0-4	0-0	1-2	- 8.80
Kelso	2-14	0-4	1-2	0-4	1-4	0-0	0-0	- 6.50
Catterick	2-16	0-4	0-2	1-4	0-3	0-0	1-3	- 9.29
Newcastle	2-27	2-13	0-4	0-3	0-5	0-0	0-2	- 23.14
Ascot	1-3	0-0	0-1	0-0	1-2	0-0	0-0	+ 5.00
Haydock	1-3	0-0	0-1	1-1	0-1	0-0	0-0	- 1.75
Aintree	1-5	0-0	0-1	0-0	1-4	0-0	0-0	+ 29.00
Market Rasen	1-7	0-2	0-2	1-2	0-0	0-0	0-1	+ 8.00
Perth	1-17	0-4	0-3	1-4	0-3	0-0	0-3	- 11.00

Cheltenham	0-3	Cartmel	0-1
Ayr	0-1	Sandown	0-1

WINNING HORSES

	Races Run	1st	2nd	3rd	Unpl	Win £
Joe White	8	3	1	1	3	29,625
Morceli	7	2	0	0	5	16,910
Aly Daley	9	3	2	2	2	9,618
Tom Brodie	8	3	1	1	3	7,512
Direct Route	8	4	3	1	0	7,479
Over The Island	6	2	2	0	2	7,149
Gnome's Tycoon	4	1	0	1	2	6,772
His Way	8	2	2	3	1	5,811
Grand Scenery	9	2	2	1	4	5,566
Abercromby Chief	3	1	0	0	2	4,931
Abbeylands	5	1	0	1	3	4,115
Down The Fell	9	1	1	2	5	3,652
Thunderstruck	2	1	0	1	0	3,395
Morning In May	7	1	1	0	5	3,028
Beckley Fountain	6	1	0	0	5	3,022
Killbally Boy	6	1	0	0	5	2,880
Houghton	10	1	3	2	4	2,815
Andros Gale	10	1	3	2	4	2,627
Daisy Days	5	1	0	1	3	2,532
Abbey Lamp	6	1	0	1	4	2,513
Duke of Perth	7	1	2	1	3	2,285
Mister Muddypaws	2	1	1	0	0	2,136

WINNING OWNERS

	Races Won	Value £		Races Won	Value £
J Howard Johnson	8	43,085	Ian Davidson	1	4,931
Mrs J M Corbett	2	16,910	Chris Heron	1	4,115
Michael Tobitt	3	9,618	D Thomas Sheridan	1	3,395
Mrs M W Bird	3	7,512	Maurice Hutchinson	1	3,028
T Harty	4	7,479	J Henderson (Co Durham)	1	3,022
The Braw Partnership	2	7,149	Everaldo Partnership	1	2,880
Flibbertigibbet	1	6,772	Gordon Brown	1	2,815
Mrs M Humble	2	5,811	W M G Black	1	2,285
The Scottish Steeplechasing	2	5,566			

No of horses racing for the stable		51	Total winning prize-money	£136,373

Favourites	14-35	40.0%	- 0.59	Average SP of winner		4.5/1
Longest win seq	3	Longest losing seq	25	Return on stakes invested		-10.9%

1994/95 Form	32-253	12.6%	- 78.19	1992/93 Form	19-176	10.8%	- 85.84
1993/94 Form	32-214	15.0%	+ 43.58	1991/92 Form	21-131	16.0%	+ 12.88

A P JONES (Eastbury, Berks)

	Races Run	1st	2nd	3rd	Unpl	Per cent	£1 Level Stake
Hurdles	62	2	3	11	46	3.2	- 38.37
Chases	22	2	2	1	17	9.1	- 14.00
Totals	84	4	5	12	63	4.8	- 52.37

L Aspell	1-4	- 2.50	S McNeill	1-19	- 12.50
Gary Brown	1-7	- 4.37	S Curran	1-34	- 13.00
Huntingdon	2-11	- 3.00	Exeter	1-6	- 3.37
Leicester	1-1	+ 20.00			

No of horses racing for the stable		18	Total winning prize-money	£10,967

I R JONES (Croesyceiliog, Gwent)

	Races Run	1st	2nd	3rd	Unpl	Per cent	£1 Level Stake
Hurdles	15	2	2	0	11	13.3	- 2.00
Chases	0	0	0	0	0	-	0.00
Totals	15	2	2	0	11	13.3	- 2.00

R Johnson	1-1	+ 7.00	Miss E Jones	1-12	- 7.00
Lingfield	1-1	+ 4.00	Newton Abbot	1-4	+ 4.00

No of horses racing for the stable		5	Total winning prize-money	£3,924

MRS LYNNE JONES (Taunton, Somerset)

	Races Run	1st	2nd	3rd	Unpl	Per cent	£1 Level Stake
Hurdles	0	0	0	0	0	-	0.00
Chases	1	1	0	0	0	100.0	+ 3.00
Totals	1	1	0	0	0	100.0	+ 3.00

Miss L Blackford	1-1	+ 3.00	Newton Abbot	1-1	+ 3.00

No of horses racing for the stable   1   Total winning prize-money   £1,031

MRS M A JONES (Lambourn, Berks)

	Races Run	1st	2nd	3rd	Unpl	Per cent	£1 Level Stake
Hurdles	41	7	5	1	28	17.1	+ 21.75
Chases	13	2	3	1	7	15.4	+ 9.00
Totals	54	9	8	2	35	16.7	+ 30.75

BY MONTH

	W-R	Per cent	£1 Level Stake		W-R	Per cent	£1 Level Stake
June	0-0	-	0.00	December	0-1	-	- 1.00
July	0-0	-	0.00	January	2-6	33.3	+ 18.00
August	0-0	-	0.00	February	1-7	14.3	- 4.25
September	0-2	-	- 2.00	March	1-13	7.7	- 9.00
October	0-1	-	- 1.00	April	3-12	25.0	+ 29.50
November	1-6	16.7	+ 1.00	May	1-6	16.7	- 0.50

DISTANCE

Hurdles	W-R	Per cent	£1 Level Stake	Chases	W-R	Per cent	£1 Level Stake
2m-2m 3f	5-29	17.2	+ 13.25	2m-2m 3f	0-1	-	- 1.00
2m 4f-2m 7f	1-9	11.1	- 3.50	2m 4f-2m 7f	1-4	25.0	+ 11.00
3m +	1-3	33.3	+ 12.00	3m +	1-8	12.5	- 1.00

TYPE OF RACE

	W-R	Per cent	£1 Level Stake		W-R	Per cent	£1 Level Stake
Novice hurdles	3-13	23.1	+ 2.00	Selling	0-1	-	- 1.00
H'cap hurdles	4-19	21.1	+ 28.75	Amateur	0-0	-	0.00
Novice chases	0-5	-	- 5.00	Hunter chases	0-0	-	0.00
H'cap chases	2-8	25.0	+ 14.00	N H Flat	0-8	-	- 8.00

COURSE GRADE

	W-R	Per cent	£1 Level Stake
Group 1	2-12	16.7	+ 8.50
Group 2	2-7	28.6	+ 2.50
Group 3	4-21	19.0	+ 31.00
Group 4	1-14	7.1	- 11.25

FIRST TIME OUT

	W-R	Per cent	£1 Level Stake
Hurdles	0-12	-	- 12.00
Chases	1-2	50.0	+ 5.00
Totals	1-14	7.1	- 7.00

JOCKEYS RIDING

	W-R	Per cent	£1 Level Stake		W-R	Per cent	£1 Level Stake
D Byrne	7-37	18.9	+ 33.25	D Bridgwater	1-3	33.3	+ 2.50
J Titley	1-2	50.0	+ 7.00				

J Cooke	0-7	G Bradley	0-4	P G Cahill	0-1		

COURSE RECORD

	Total W-R	Nov Hdles	H'cap Hdles	Nov Chses	H'cap Chses	Hunter Chses	N H Flat	£1 Level Stake
Windsor	1-1	0-0	0-0	0-0	1-1	0-0	0-0	+ 6.00
Lingfield	1-1	1-1	0-0	0-0	0-0	0-0	0-0	+ 3.00
Warwick	1-2	0-0	1-2	0-0	0-0	0-0	0-0	+ 7.00
Fakenham	1-2	0-0	1-1	0-0	0-1	0-0	0-0	+ 0.75
Ascot	1-2	0-0	1-1	0-1	0-0	0-0	0-0	+ 13.00
Folkestone	1-2	0-0	1-2	0-0	0-0	0-0	0-0	+ 19.00
Haydock	1-3	1-2	0-1	0-0	0-0	0-0	0-0	+ 2.50
Chepstow	1-4	1-2	0-2	0-0	0-0	0-0	0-0	+ 1.50
Worcester	1-5	0-1	0-1	0-1	1-1	0-0	0-1	+ 10.00

Ludlow	0-5	Leicester	0-2	Kempton	0-1
Newbury	0-4	Aintree	0-1	Newton Abbot	0-1
Nottingham	0-3	Cheltenham	0-1	Stratford	0-1
Towcester	0-3	Exeter	0-1	Taunton	0-1
Uttoxeter	0-3	Fontwell	0-1	Wincanton	0-1
Hereford	0-2	Huntingdon	0-1		

WINNING HORSES

	Races Run	1st	2nd	3rd	Unpl	Win £
Treasure Again	5	2	1	0	2	19,776
Zambezi Spirit	4	2	1	0	1	7,475
Manolete	6	2	2	0	2	6,491
Tarrock	5	2	0	0	3	4,228
Rosgill	5	1	1	0	3	2,924

WINNING OWNERS

	Races Won	Value £		Races Won	Value £
John Hugo Gwynne	2	19,776	F J Sainsbury	2	4,228
P C Townsend	2	7,475	Brigadier Racing	1	2,924
C Flear	2	6,491			

No of horses racing for the stable	16	Total winning prize-money	£40,894

Favourites	1-7	14.3%	- 4.25	Average SP of winner	8.4/1
Longest win seq	2	Longest losing seq	8	Return on stakes invested	56.9%

1994/95 Form	7-44	15.9%	- 11.18	1992/93 Form	6-9	66.7%	+ 5.28
1993/94 Form	2-15	13.3%	0.00	1991/92 Form	3-6	50.0%	+ 6.50

T THOMSON JONES (Upper Lambourn, Berks)

	Races Run	1st	2nd	3rd	Unpl	Per cent	£1 Level Stake
Hurdles	41	8	4	6	23	19.5	+ 11.13
Chases	25	6	4	4	11	24.0	+ 16.38
Totals	66	14	8	10	34	21.2	+ 27.51

BY MONTH

	W-R	Per cent	£1 Level Stake		W-R	Per cent	£1 Level Stake
June	0-1	-	- 1.00	December	0-6	-	- 6.00
July	0-1	-	- 1.00	January	4-11	36.4	+ 42.00
August	0-0	-	0.00	February	1-7	14.3	- 2.00
September	0-0	-	0.00	March	2-10	20.0	- 4.33
October	2-2	100.0	+ 8.83	April	3-7	42.9	+ 6.76
November	1-17	5.9	- 13.75	May	1-4	25.0	- 2.00

DISTANCE

Hurdles	W-R	Per cent	£1 Level Stake	Chases	W-R	Per cent	£1 Level Stake
2m-2m 3f	5-24	20.8	+ 7.38	2m-2m 3f	3-10	30.0	+ 4.71
2m 4f-2m 7f	1-6	16.7	+ 0.50	2m 4f-2m 7f	0-5	-	- 5.00
3m +	2-11	18.2	+ 3.25	3m +	3-10	30.0	+ 16.67

TYPE OF RACE

	W-R	Per cent	£1 Level Stake		W-R	Per cent	£1 Level Stake
Novice hurdles	5-14	35.7	+ 9.63	Selling	0-2	-	- 2.00
H'cap hurdles	3-20	15.0	+ 8.50	Amateur	1-4	25.0	0.00
Novice chases	2-7	28.6	- 1.00	Hunter chases	0-0	-	0.00
H'cap chases	3-16	18.8	+ 15.38	N H Flat	0-3	-	- 3.00

COURSE GRADE

	W-R	Per cent	£1 Level Stake
Group 1	6-22	27.3	+ 2.75
Group 2	3-9	33.3	+ 15.00
Group 3	3-17	17.6	+ 17.38
Group 4	2-18	11.1	- 7.62

FIRST TIME OUT

	W-R	Per cent	£1 Level Stake
Hurdles	1-11	9.1	- 4.50
Chases	1-5	20.0	- 0.67
Totals	2-16	12.5	- 5.17

JOCKEYS RIDING

	W-R	Per cent	£1 Level Stake		W-R	Per cent	£1 Level Stake
G McCourt	3-9	33.3	+ 26.25	A Thornton	1-2	50.0	0.00
M A Fitzgerald	3-14	21.4	+ 1.83	A P McCoy	1-3	33.3	- 0.62
Mr J Culloty	2-3	66.7	+ 8.38	B Powell	1-4	25.0	+ 4.00
Maj O Ellwood	2-3	66.7	+ 2.67	G E Tormey	1-9	11.1	+ 4.00

D Gallagher	0-3	C Llewellyn	0-1	J R Kavanagh	0-1
A Bates	0-2	C Maude	0-1	J Titley	0-1
Miss V Haigh	0-2	D Bridgwater	0-1	L Wyer	0-1
A Dobbin	0-1	G Bradley	0-1	P Niven	0-1
A Tory	0-1	Guy Lewis	0-1	W Marston	0-1

COURSE RECORD

	Total W-R	Nov Hdles	H'cap Hdles	Nov Chses	H'cap Chses	Hunter Chses	N H Flat	£1 Level Stake
Wincanton	2-4	1-2	0-0	0-0	1-2	0-0	0-0	+ 19.38
Ascot	2-5	0-2	1-2	1-1	0-0	0-0	0-0	+ 5.83
Sandown	2-5	0-1	0-2	1-1	1-1	0-0	0-0	+ 0.67
Towcester	2-8	0-1	0-2	0-0	2-5	0-0	0-0	+ 2.38
Aintree	1-1	1-1	0-0	0-0	0-0	0-0	0-0	+ 2.25
Lingfield	1-1	0-0	1-1	0-0	0-0	0-0	0-0	+ 12.00
Fontwell	1-2	0-0	1-2	0-0	0-0	0-0	0-0	+ 7.00
Kempton	1-3	1-2	0-1	0-0	0-0	0-0	0-0	+ 2.00
Newton Abbot	1-4	1-2	0-1	0-0	0-1	0-0	0-0	- 2.00
Nottingham	1-6	1-1	0-1	0-3	0-1	0-0	0-0	+ 5.00

Haydock	0-3	Exeter	0-2	Huntingdon	0-1
Leicester	0-3	Ludlow	0-2	Newcastle	0-1
Newbury	0-3	Southwell	0-2	Uttoxeter	0-1
Taunton	0-3	Doncaster	0-1	Warwick	0-1
Chepstow	0-2	Fakenham	0-1	Worcester	0-1

WINNING HORSES

	Races Run	1st	2nd	3rd	Unpl	Win £
Norman Conqueror	4	3	0	0	1	12,754
Decide Yourself	7	3	0	0	4	8,194
Sartorius	11	2	3	2	4	7,637
Take The Buckskin	4	2	1	0	1	6,447
Jackson Flint	7	1	0	2	4	4,464
Drummond Warrior	2	1	0	0	1	3,550
Blazon of Troy	7	1	2	2	2	2,918
Keel Row	5	1	0	0	4	2,532

WINNING OWNERS

	Races Won	Value £		Races Won	Value £
David F Wilson	7	21,109	M Popham	2	7,637
Queen Elizabeth	4	15,286	Mrs L G Turner	1	4,464

No of horses racing for the stable		16	Total winning prize-money		£48,496

Favourites	3-13	23.1%	- 6.95	Average SP of winner			5.7/1
Longest win seq	2	Longest losing seq	12	Return on stakes invested			41.7%

1994/95 Form	14-93	15.1%	- 23.69	1992/93 Form	14-137	10.2%	- 56.55
1993/94 Form	17-107	15.9%	- 28.25	1991/92 Form	23-130	17.7%	- 18.42

F JORDAN (Risbury, H'ford & Worcs)

	Races Run	1st	2nd	3rd	Unpl	Per cent	£1 Level Stake
Hurdles	98	4	5	9	80	4.1	- 72.50
Chases	23	3	4	6	10	13.0	- 10.43
Totals	121	7	9	15	90	5.8	- 82.93

BY MONTH

	W-R	Per cent	£1 Level Stake		W-R	Per cent	£1 Level Stake
June	0-1	-	- 1.00	December	0-6	-	- 6.00
July	1-7	14.3	+ 1.00	January	0-11	-	- 11.00
August	2-9	22.2	- 1.93	February	1-11	9.1	- 8.00
September	0-7	-	- 7.00	March	0-12	-	- 12.00
October	1-16	6.3	- 8.00	April	0-13	-	- 13.00
November	1-11	9.1	- 8.00	May	1-17	5.9	- 8.00

DISTANCE

Hurdles	W-R	Per cent	£1 Level Stake	Chases	W-R	Per cent	£1 Level Stake
2m-2m 3f	3-69	4.3	- 51.50	2m-2m 3f	0-4	-	- 4.00
2m 4f-2m 7f	1-21	4.8	- 13.00	2m 4f-2m 7f	1-11	9.1	- 8.00
3m +	0-8	-	- 8.00	3m +	2-8	25.0	+ 1.57

TYPE OF RACE

	W-R	Per cent	£1 Level Stake		W-R	Per cent	£1 Level Stake
Novice hurdles	1-32	3.1	- 26.50	Selling	2-25	8.0	- 8.00
H'cap hurdles	1-32	3.1	- 29.00	Amateur	0-2	-	- 2.00
Novice chases	2-8	25.0	- 3.43	Hunter chases	0-0	-	0.00
H'cap chases	1-15	6.7	- 7.00	N H Flat	0-7	-	- 7.00

COURSE GRADE

	W-R	Per cent	£1 Level Stake
Group 1	1-6	16.7	- 3.00
Group 2	1-12	8.3	- 6.50
Group 3	2-50	4.0	- 40.43
Group 4	3-53	5.7	- 33.00

FIRST TIME OUT

	W-R	Per cent	£1 Level Stake
Hurdles	1-24	4.2	- 16.00
Chases	0-4	-	- 4.00
Totals	1-28	3.6	- 20.00

JOCKEYS RIDING

	W-R	Per cent	£1 Level Stake
J Lodder	7-89	7.9	- 50.93

A Larnach	0-3	W Marston	0-2	R Bellamy	0-1
Mr M Jackson	0-3	A P McCoy	0-1	R Greene	0-1
S Curran	0-3	A Tory	0-1	R Massey	0-1
T Eley	0-3	B Powell	0-1	S Righton	0-1
Miss E Jones	0-2	D Bridgwater	0-1	Sophie Mitchell	0-1
Mr G Shenkin	0-2	D Leahy	0-1	T Jenks	0-1
R Painter	0-2	Mr S Blackwell	0-1		

COURSE RECORD

	Total W-R	Nov Hdles	H'cap Hdles	Nov Chses	H'cap Chses	Hunter Chses	N H Flat	£1 Level Stake
Ludlow	2-18	0-4	1-8	1-3	0-2	0-0	0-1	- 7.00
Huntingdon	1-4	0-0	0-1	1-2	0-1	0-0	0-0	- 2.43
Haydock	1-4	0-1	1-2	0-0	0-0	0-0	0-1	- 1.00
Newton Abbot	1-7	1-2	0-4	0-0	0-1	0-0	0-0	- 1.50
Stratford	1-8	0-3	0-1	0-1	1-3	0-0	0-0	0.00
Hereford	1-14	0-4	1-8	0-1	0-1	0-0	0-0	- 5.00

Uttoxeter	0-9	Leicester	0-4	Towcester	0-2
Bangor	0-8	Catterick	0-3	Fontwell	0-1
Exeter	0-7	Chepstow	0-3	Southwell	0-1
Worcester	0-7	Taunton	0-3	Wetherby	0-1
Nottingham	0-6	Cheltenham	0-2	Wincanton	0-1
Warwick	0-6	Plumpton	0-2		

WINNING HORSES

	Races Run	1st	2nd	3rd	Unpl	Win £
Golden Madjambo	9	2	3	4	0	5,287
Saraville	8	1	1	1	5	4,648
Saint Ciel	9	1	1	0	7	2,983
Pant Llin	4	1	1	0	2	2,912
Shifting Moon	7	1	1	0	5	2,533
George Lane	11	1	1	2	7	1,725

WINNING OWNERS

	Races Won	Value £		Races Won	Value £
T P Roberts-Hindle	2	5,287	David Martin	1	2,912
R V Cliff	1	4,648	Mrs K Roberts-Hindle	1	2,533
Tam Racing	1	2,983	Amtrak Express Parcels Ltd	1	1,725

No of horses racing for the stable		34	Total winning prize-money	£20,088

Favourites	1-8	12.5%	- 6.43	Average SP of winner		4.4/1
Longest win seq	1	Longest losing seq	35	Return on stakes invested		-68.5%

1994/95 Form	9-98	9.2%	- 65.95	1992/93 Form	3-131	2.3%	- 82.50
1993/94 Form	4-67	6.0%	- 31.00	1991/92 Form	5-136	3.7%	- 66.50

J JOSEPH (Coleshill, Bucks)

	Races Run	1st	2nd	3rd	Unpl	Per cent	£1 Level Stake
Hurdles	13	1	1	0	11	7.7	- 1.00
Chases	0	0	0	0	0	-	0.00
Totals	13	1	1	0	11	7.7	- 1.00

C Llewellyn	1-5	+ 7.00	Worcester	1-5	+ 7.00

No of horses racing for the stable   4   Total winning prize-money   £2,714

MISS GAY KELLEWAY (Whitcombe, Dorset)

	Races Run	1st	2nd	3rd	Unpl	Per cent	£1 Level Stake
Hurdles	13	1	0	0	12	7.7	- 10.90
Chases	0	0	0	0	0	-	0.00
Totals	13	1	0	0	12	7.7	- 10.90

D O'Sullivan	1-1	+ 1.10	Chepstow	1-1	+ 1.10

No of horses racing for the stable   8   Total winning prize-money   £1,641

P A KELLEWAY (Newmarket, Suffolk)

	Races Run	1st	2nd	3rd	Unpl	Per cent	£1 Level Stake
Hurdles	9	2	0	0	7	22.2	+ 6.00
Chases	0	0	0	0	0	-	0.00
Totals	9	2	0	0	7	22.2	+ 6.00

J Ryan	1-3	+ 6.00	A Bates	1-4	+ 2.00
Windsor	1-1	+ 5.00	Market Rasen	1-2	+ 7.00

No of horses racing for the stable   1   Total winning prize-money   £5,285

W T KEMP (Duns, Borders)

	Races Run	1st	2nd	3rd	Unpl	Per cent	£1 Level Stake
Hurdles	48	5	3	5	35	10.4	+ 52.00
Chases	4	0	0	1	3	-	- 4.00
Totals	52	5	3	6	38	9.6	+ 48.00

Mr M H Naughton	1-1	+ 3.50	B Storey	1-8	- 1.50
P G Cahill	1-2	+ 65.00	S McDougall	1-30	- 15.00
S Haworth	1-3	+ 4.00			
Perth	2-7	+ 6.50	Ayr	1-1	+ 66.00
Market Rasen	1-1	+ 3.50	Sedgefield	1-8	+ 7.00

No of horses racing for the stable   14   Total winning prize-money   £13,453

S E KETTLEWELL (Middleham, North Yorks)

	Races Run	1st	2nd	3rd	Unpl	Per cent	£1 Level Stake
Hurdles	38	1	4	1	32	2.6	- 29.50
Chases	18	7	0	1	10	38.9	+ 7.65
Totals	56	8	4	2	42	14.3	- 21.85

BY MONTH

	W-R	Per cent	£1 Level Stake		W-R	Per cent	£1 Level Stake
June	0-2	-	- 2.00	December	1-3	33.3	- 0.90
July	2-5	40.0	+ 10.50	January	0-5	-	- 5.00
August	0-1	-	- 1.00	February	1-6	16.7	- 3.00
September	0-0	-	0.00	March	1-9	11.1	- 6.62
October	0-0	-	0.00	April	0-10	-	- 10.00
November	2-11	18.2	- 4.33	May	1-4	25.0	+ 0.50

DISTANCE

Hurdles	W-R	Per cent	£1 Level Stake	Chases	W-R	Per cent	£1 Level Stake
2m-2m 3f	1-30	3.3	- 21.50	2m-2m 3f	0-5	-	- 5.00
2m 4f-2m 7f	0-6	-	- 6.00	2m 4f-2m 7f	6-10	60.0	+ 13.55
3m +	0-2	-	- 2.00	3m +	1-3	33.3	- 0.90

TYPE OF RACE

	W-R	Per cent	£1 Level Stake		W-R	Per cent	£1 Level Stake
Novice hurdles	0-11	-	- 11.00	Selling	0-0	-	0.00
H'cap hurdles	1-15	6.7	- 6.50	Amateur	0-4	-	- 4.00
Novice chases	2-4	50.0	+ 7.50	Hunter chases	0-0	-	0.00
H'cap chases	5-13	38.5	+ 1.15	N H Flat	0-9	-	- 9.00

Kettlewell S E

<table>
<tr><th colspan="4">COURSE GRADE</th><th colspan="4">FIRST TIME OUT</th></tr>
<tr><td></td><td>W-R</td><td>Per cent</td><td>£1 Level Stake</td><td></td><td>W-R</td><td>Per cent</td><td>£1 Level Stake</td></tr>
<tr><td>Group 1</td><td>1-7</td><td>14.3</td><td>- 5.33</td><td>Hurdles</td><td>0-14</td><td>-</td><td>- 14.00</td></tr>
<tr><td>Group 2</td><td>2-7</td><td>28.6</td><td>- 1.62</td><td>Chases</td><td>2-3</td><td>66.7</td><td>+ 9.00</td></tr>
<tr><td>Group 3</td><td>1-16</td><td>6.3</td><td>- 9.00</td><td></td><td></td><td></td><td></td></tr>
<tr><td>Group 4</td><td>4-26</td><td>15.4</td><td>- 5.90</td><td>Totals</td><td>2-17</td><td>11.8</td><td>- 5.00</td></tr>
</table>

JOCKEYS RIDING

<table>
<tr><td></td><td>W-R</td><td>Per cent</td><td>£1 Level Stake</td><td></td><td>W-R</td><td>Per cent</td><td>£1 Level Stake</td></tr>
<tr><td>P Niven</td><td>3-5</td><td>60.0</td><td>+ 1.77</td><td>Mr C Bonner</td><td>1-3</td><td>33.3</td><td>+ 2.00</td></tr>
<tr><td>M A Fitzgerald</td><td>1-1</td><td>100.0</td><td>+ 1.38</td><td>R Supple</td><td>1-4</td><td>25.0</td><td>+ 4.50</td></tr>
<tr><td>R Johnson</td><td>1-1</td><td>100.0</td><td>+ 3.50</td><td>R Garrity</td><td>1-5</td><td>20.0</td><td>+ 2.00</td></tr>
</table>

<table>
<tr><td>S Porritt</td><td>0-7</td><td>Mr S Swiers</td><td>0-2</td><td>Mr S Walker</td><td>0-1</td></tr>
<tr><td>B Storey</td><td>0-5</td><td>Sophie Mitchell</td><td>0-2</td><td>N Williamson</td><td>0-1</td></tr>
<tr><td>Mrs D Kettlewell</td><td>0-4</td><td>A S Smith</td><td>0-1</td><td>P McLoughlin</td><td>0-1</td></tr>
<tr><td>Scott Taylor</td><td>0-4</td><td>G Hogan</td><td>0-1</td><td>R Dunwoody</td><td>0-1</td></tr>
<tr><td>G Lee</td><td>0-3</td><td>J R Kavanagh</td><td>0-1</td><td></td><td></td></tr>
<tr><td>J Callaghan</td><td>0-2</td><td>K P Gaule</td><td>0-1</td><td></td><td></td></tr>
</table>

COURSE RECORD

<table>
<tr><td></td><td>Total W-R</td><td>Nov Hdles</td><td>H'cap Hdles</td><td>Nov Chses</td><td>H'cap Chses</td><td>Hunter Chses</td><td>N H Flat</td><td>£1 Level Stake</td></tr>
<tr><td>Hexham</td><td>2-3</td><td>0-0</td><td>0-1</td><td>0-0</td><td>2-2</td><td>0-0</td><td>0-0</td><td>+ 4.10</td></tr>
<tr><td>Newcastle</td><td>1-2</td><td>0-0</td><td>0-0</td><td>0-0</td><td>1-2</td><td>0-0</td><td>0-0</td><td>- 0.33</td></tr>
<tr><td>Lingfield</td><td>1-2</td><td>0-0</td><td>0-1</td><td>0-0</td><td>1-1</td><td>0-0</td><td>0-0</td><td>+ 0.38</td></tr>
<tr><td>Cartmel</td><td>1-4</td><td>0-1</td><td>0-1</td><td>1-2</td><td>0-0</td><td>0-0</td><td>0-0</td><td>+ 0.50</td></tr>
<tr><td>Southwell</td><td>1-5</td><td>0-0</td><td>1-1</td><td>0-0</td><td>0-4</td><td>0-0</td><td>0-0</td><td>+ 3.50</td></tr>
<tr><td>Wetherby</td><td>1-5</td><td>0-1</td><td>0-1</td><td>0-0</td><td>1-3</td><td>0-0</td><td>0-0</td><td>- 2.00</td></tr>
<tr><td>Market Rasen</td><td>1-7</td><td>0-1</td><td>0-1</td><td>1-1</td><td>0-1</td><td>0-0</td><td>0-3</td><td>0.00</td></tr>
</table>

<table>
<tr><td>Catterick</td><td>0-6</td><td>Musselburgh</td><td>0-2</td><td>Cheltenham</td><td>0-1</td></tr>
<tr><td>Sedgefield</td><td>0-6</td><td>Perth</td><td>0-2</td><td>Doncaster</td><td>0-1</td></tr>
<tr><td>Ayr</td><td>0-3</td><td>Warwick</td><td>0-2</td><td>Stratford</td><td>0-1</td></tr>
<tr><td>Kelso</td><td>0-3</td><td>Carlisle</td><td>0-1</td><td></td><td></td></tr>
</table>

WINNING HORSES

<table>
<tr><td></td><td>Races Run</td><td>1st</td><td>2nd</td><td>3rd</td><td>Unpl</td><td>Win £</td></tr>
<tr><td>Easby Joker</td><td>10</td><td>5</td><td>0</td><td>0</td><td>5</td><td>18,470</td></tr>
<tr><td>Yaakum</td><td>1</td><td>1</td><td>0</td><td>0</td><td>0</td><td>3,496</td></tr>
<tr><td>Old Money</td><td>2</td><td>1</td><td>0</td><td>1</td><td>0</td><td>2,937</td></tr>
<tr><td>Hostile Act</td><td>7</td><td>1</td><td>0</td><td>1</td><td>5</td><td>1,942</td></tr>
</table>

WINNING OWNERS

<table>
<tr><td></td><td>Races Won</td><td>Value £</td><td></td><td>Races Won</td><td>Value £</td></tr>
<tr><td>G R Orchard</td><td>5</td><td>18,470</td><td>Uncle Jack's Pub</td><td>1</td><td>2,937</td></tr>
<tr><td>Ian Thompson</td><td>1</td><td>3,496</td><td>J E Titley</td><td>1</td><td>1,942</td></tr>
</table>

| No of horses racing for the stable | 18 | Total winning prize-money | £26,845 |

| Favourites | 4-9 | 44.4% | + 0.15 | Average SP of winner | | 3.3/1 |
| Longest win seq | 2 | Longest losing seq | 16 | Return on stakes invested | | -39.0% |

| 1994/95 Form | 4-44 | 9.1% | - 24.59 | 1992/93 Form | 7-51 | 13.7% | + 10.89 |
| 1993/94 Form | 3-40 | 7.5% | - 27.00 | 1991/92 Form | 9-47 | 19.1% | - 3.10 |

J S KING (Broad Hinton, Wilts)

	Races Run	1st	2nd	3rd	Unpl	Per cent	£1 Level Stake
Hurdles	76	4	7	6	59	5.3	- 52.83
Chases	65	9	10	10	36	13.8	- 13.90
Totals	141	13	17	16	95	9.2	- 66.73

BY MONTH

	W-R	Per cent	£1 Level Stake		W-R	Per cent	£1 Level Stake
June	0-0	-	0.00	December	0-9	-	- 9.00
July	0-3	-	- 3.00	January	0-17	-	- 17.00
August	1-2	50.0	+ 0.10	February	2-13	15.4	- 5.75
September	0-6	-	- 6.00	March	4-27	14.8	- 1.25
October	0-7	-	- 7.00	April	1-22	4.5	- 16.50
November	5-19	26.3	+ 14.67	May	0-16	-	- 16.00

DISTANCE

Hurdles	W-R	Per cent	£1 Level Stake	Chases	W-R	Per cent	£1 Level Stake
2m-2m 3f	2-50	4.0	- 43.33	2m-2m 3f	6-23	26.1	+ 2.35
2m 4f-2m 7f	1-18	5.6	- 11.50	2m 4f-2m 7f	3-30	10.0	- 4.25
3m +	1-8	12.5	+ 2.00	3m +	0-12	-	- 12.00

TYPE OF RACE

	W-R	Per cent	£1 Level Stake		W-R	Per cent	£1 Level Stake
Novice hurdles	0-34	-	- 34.00	Selling	1-11	9.1	- 8.90
H'cap hurdles	4-27	14.8	- 3.83	Amateur	0-4	-	- 4.00
Novice chases	3-20	15.0	- 4.25	Hunter chases	0-0	-	0.00
H'cap chases	5-39	12.8	- 5.75	N H Flat	0-6	-	- 6.00

COURSE GRADE

	W-R	Per cent	£1 Level Stake
Group 1	5-30	16.7	+ 2.75
Group 2	1-19	5.3	- 14.00
Group 3	4-52	7.7	- 36.58
Group 4	3-40	7.5	- 18.90

FIRST TIME OUT

	W-R	Per cent	£1 Level Stake
Hurdles	2-22	9.1	- 10.50
Chases	1-9	11.1	- 1.50
Totals	3-31	9.7	- 12.00

JOCKEYS RIDING

	W–R	Per cent	£1 Level Stake		W–R	Per cent	£1 Level Stake
G Upton	7–78	9.0	– 37.73	J R Kavanagh	1–5	20.0	+ 4.00
Mr J Culloty	2–11	18.2	– 5.25	M A Fitzgerald	1–7	14.3	– 1.50
R Dunwoody	1–3	33.3	+ 0.75	T Dascombe	1–7	14.3	+ 3.00

T Jenks	0–8	A P McCoy	0–1	Miss P Jones	0–1
S Curran	0–3	B Harding	0–1	Mr L Baker	0–1
W Marston	0–3	Christopher Webb	0–1	Mr M Rimell	0–1
A Maguire	0–2	D Gallagher	0–1	P Carberry	0–1
S McNeill	0–2	D Walsh	0–1	T J Murphy	0–1
A Larnach	0–1	J Titley	0–1		

COURSE RECORD

	Total W–R	Nov Hdles	H'cap Hdles	Nov Chses	H'cap Chses	Hunter Chses	N H Flat	£1 Level Stake
Cheltenham	2–5	0–0	0–1	0–1	2–3	0–0	0–0	+ 13.50
Hereford	2–6	0–0	1–2	0–0	1–3	0–0	0–1	+ 6.10
Catterick	1–1	0–0	0–0	1–1	0–0	0–0	0–0	+ 3.50
Kempton	1–4	0–0	0–1	1–3	0–0	0–0	0–0	+ 3.50
Leicester	1–4	0–1	0–0	0–0	1–3	0–0	0–0	– 1.25
Chepstow	1–5	0–2	1–3	0–0	0–0	0–0	0–0	0.00
Newbury	1–6	0–4	0–0	0–0	1–1	0–0	0–1	– 3.00
Sandown	1–6	0–0	0–1	1–2	0–1	0–0	0–2	– 2.25
Ludlow	1–7	0–2	0–2	0–1	1–2	0–0	0–0	+ 2.00
Windsor	1–7	0–4	1–1	0–1	0–1	0–0	0–0	– 0.50
Wincanton	1–12	0–3	1–4	0–2	0–3	0–0	0–0	– 10.33

Exeter	0–11	Newton Abbot	0–5	Folkestone	0–2
Ascot	0–9	Lingfield	0–4	Stratford	0–2
Taunton	0–8	Plumpton	0–4	Towcester	0–2
Worcester	0–8	Bangor	0–3	Warwick	0–2
Uttoxeter	0–7	Huntingdon	0–3		
Fontwell	0–5	Southwell	0–3		

WINNING HORSES

	Races Run	1st	2nd	3rd	Unpl	Win £
Mister Oddy	10	3	0	4	3	12,300
Inchcailloch	8	2	2	0	4	8,433
Lightening Lad	2	2	0	0	0	6,437
Fortunes Course	6	2	1	1	2	5,948
Rivage Bleu	5	1	1	1	2	3,388
Little Tom	6	1	0	0	5	3,144
Turpin's Green	10	1	1	3	5	2,736
Akulite	5	1	0	0	4	2,346

WINNING OWNERS

	Races Won	Value £		Races Won	Value £
Mrs R M Hill	3	12,300	C D King	1	3,388
F J Carter	2	8,433	Mark O'Connor	1	3,144
Richard Peterson	2	6,437	Mrs P M King	1	2,736
Mrs A J Garrett	2	5,948	S Clough	1	2,346

No of horses racing for the stable		32	Total winning prize-money	£44,732
Favourites	4-16	25.0% - 6.48	Average SP of winner	4.7/1
Longest win seq	3	Longest losing seq 41	Return on stakes invested	-47.3%
1994/95 Form	17-127	13.4% - 38.82	1992/93 Form 11-121	9.1% + 20.25
1993/94 Form	19-144	13.2% - 26.87	1991/92 Form 5-128	3.9% - 68.00

MISS H C KNIGHT (Lockinge, Oxon)

	Races Run	1st	2nd	3rd	Unpl	Per cent	£1 Level Stake
Hurdles	212	36	25	32	119	17.0	- 38.24
Chases	100	23	11	10	56	23.0	+ 12.77
Totals	312	59	36	42	175	18.9	- 25.47

BY MONTH

	W-R	Per cent	£1 Level Stake		W-R	Per cent	£1 Level Stake
June	0-0	-	0.00	December	6-28	21.4	+ 13.37
July	0-2	-	- 2.00	January	13-47	27.7	+ 13.33
August	0-1	-	- 1.00	February	2-29	6.9	- 19.83
September	2-12	16.7	- 6.75	March	9-47	19.1	- 5.83
October	4-27	14.8	- 12.87	April	8-40	20.0	+ 5.35
November	6-40	15.0	- 14.23	May	9-39	23.1	+ 4.99

DISTANCE

	W-R	Per cent	£1 Level Stake		W-R	Per cent	£1 Level Stake
Hurdles				Chases			
2m-2m 3f	29-165	17.6	- 24.87	2m-2m 3f	8-20	40.0	+ 1.09
2m 4f-2m 7f	4-38	10.5	- 18.25	2m 4f-2m 7f	6-44	13.6	+ 7.18
3m +	3-9	33.3	+ 4.88	3m +	9-36	25.0	+ 4.50

TYPE OF RACE

	W-R	Per cent	£1 Level Stake		W-R	Per cent	£1 Level Stake
Novice hurdles	19-97	19.6	- 7.37	Selling	1-6	16.7	- 2.50
H'cap hurdles	10-63	15.9	- 12.62	Amateur	2-5	40.0	+ 3.25
Novice chases	10-43	23.3	+ 1.56	Hunter chases	0-1	-	- 1.00
H'cap chases	12-55	21.8	+ 8.21	N H Flat	5-42	11.9	- 15.00

Knight Miss H C

<table>
<tr><td colspan="4">COURSE GRADE</td><td colspan="4">FIRST TIME OUT</td></tr>
<tr><td></td><td>W-R</td><td>Per cent</td><td>£1 Level Stake</td><td></td><td>W-R</td><td>Per cent</td><td>£1 Level Stake</td></tr>
<tr><td>Group 1</td><td>13-75</td><td>17.3</td><td>+ 4.51</td><td>Hurdles</td><td>9-57</td><td>15.8</td><td>- 4.50</td></tr>
<tr><td>Group 2</td><td>2-21</td><td>9.5</td><td>- 15.00</td><td>Chases</td><td>2-25</td><td>8.0</td><td>- 19.12</td></tr>
<tr><td>Group 3</td><td>28-114</td><td>24.6</td><td>+ 12.61</td><td></td><td></td><td></td><td></td></tr>
<tr><td>Group 4</td><td>16-102</td><td>15.7</td><td>- 27.59</td><td>Totals</td><td>11-82</td><td>13.4</td><td>- 23.62</td></tr>
</table>

JOCKEYS RIDING

<table>
<tr><td></td><td>W-R</td><td>Per cent</td><td>£1 Level Stake</td><td></td><td>W-R</td><td>Per cent</td><td>£1 Level Stake</td></tr>
<tr><td>J Titley</td><td>31-137</td><td>22.6</td><td>- 6.07</td><td>M A Fitzgerald</td><td>3-8</td><td>37.5</td><td>+ 13.39</td></tr>
<tr><td>Mr J Culloty</td><td>18-75</td><td>24.0</td><td>+ 6.21</td><td>J Osborne</td><td>2-16</td><td>12.5</td><td>- 7.25</td></tr>
<tr><td>G Ryan</td><td>5-55</td><td>9.1</td><td>- 10.75</td><td></td><td></td><td></td><td></td></tr>
</table>

R Farrant	0-4	A Dowling	0-1	Mr G F Ryan	0-1
R Dunwoody	0-3	A P McCoy	0-1	Mrs M Tingey	0-1
G Bradley	0-2	J R Kavanagh	0-1	R Johnson	0-1
Miss J Brackenbury	0-2	L Aspell	0-1		
P Niven	0-2	Mr C Storey	0-1		

COURSE RECORD

	Total W-R	Nov Hdles	H'cap Hdles	Nov Chses	H'cap Chses	Hunter Chses	N H Flat	£1 Level Stake
Exeter	9-39	4-15	2-13	1-5	1-3	0-0	1-3	+ 7.36
Market Rasen	5-16	1-3	2-5	0-1	1-2	0-0	1-5	+ 6.98
Warwick	4-13	1-3	0-2	0-2	3-5	0-0	0-1	+ 9.00
Worcester	4-14	2-4	1-2	1-1	0-3	0-0	0-4	+ 9.50
Uttoxeter	4-21	2-9	1-4	1-3	0-3	0-0	0-2	- 6.95
Ludlow	4-23	1-7	1-4	1-3	0-5	0-0	1-4	- 6.08
Plumpton	3-3	2-2	0-0	1-1	0-0	0-0	0-0	+ 10.13
Kempton	3-11	1-3	0-1	0-0	1-3	0-0	1-4	+ 6.00
Huntingdon	2-5	0-0	0-0	2-4	0-0	0-0	0-1	+ 3.50
Wincanton	2-8	1-4	0-2	0-0	1-2	0-0	0-0	- 2.55
Leicester	2-8	1-4	0-1	0-1	1-2	0-0	0-0	+ 0.25
Sandown	2-9	1-3	0-1	0-2	1-2	0-1	0-0	+ 3.50
Haydock	2-10	0-2	0-5	0-0	2-3	0-0	0-0	- 7.24
Cheltenham	2-15	1-6	0-2	0-1	1-3	0-0	0-3	+ 4.75
Newbury	2-18	0-5	2-8	0-2	0-2	0-0	0-1	- 6.50
Stratford	1-4	0-2	0-0	1-2	0-0	0-0	0-0	- 1.75
Aintree	1-4	0-1	1-1	0-0	0-2	0-0	0-0	+ 5.00
Fontwell	1-5	1-3	0-0	0-1	0-1	0-0	0-0	- 2.25
Southwell	1-7	1-1	0-1	0-1	0-4	0-0	0-0	- 4.37
Ascot	1-7	0-2	0-3	0-0	0-1	0-0	1-1	0.00
Newton Abbot	1-9	0-3	0-2	0-1	1-2	0-0	0-1	- 5.75
Bangor	1-10	0-1	0-3	1-2	0-1	0-0	0-3	- 7.50
Towcester	1-11	1-5	0-0	0-0	0-2	0-0	0-4	- 5.00
Windsor	1-12	0-5	0-2	1-4	0-1	0-0	0-0	- 5.50

Taunton	0-7	Hereford	0-4	Doncaster	0-1
Folkestone	0-6	Nottingham	0-4	Fakenham	0-1
Chepstow	0-4	Lingfield	0-2	Wetherby	0-1

WINNING HORSES

	Races Run	1st	2nd	3rd	Unpl	Win £
Easthorpe	8	6	1	0	1	41,843
Yes Man	8	5	1	1	1	22,310
Full of Oats	5	3	0	1	1	21,799
Stompin	8	1	1	2	4	19,188
Grey Smoke	5	3	1	0	1	11,885
Debutante Days	5	2	0	0	3	9,388
Mim-Lou-And	8	3	2	0	3	7,287
Master Orchestra	5	2	1	0	2	7,273
Factor Ten	4	2	0	0	2	6,987
Tricksome	6	2	0	0	4	6,456
Perhaps	8	2	2	2	2	6,335
Tight Fist	8	2	2	0	4	6,135
Supreme Lady	6	2	1	3	0	6,061
Oban	4	2	0	0	2	5,578
Karshi	4	2	0	1	1	5,534
Wild West Wind	5	2	1	0	2	5,419
Bishops Island	10	1	1	2	6	5,296
Toureen Prince	6	1	2	1	2	4,811
Lessons Lass	2	2	0	0	0	4,396
The Padre	2	1	1	0	0	3,556
Slingsby	7	1	2	2	2	3,556
Grouseman	3	1	0	1	1	3,058
Too Sharp	5	1	0	3	1	2,879
Kindle's Delight	1	1	0	0	0	2,840
Serious Danger	2	1	0	0	1	2,612
Queenford Belle	4	1	0	1	2	2,520
Gone For Lunch	7	1	1	0	5	2,268
Wade Road	1	1	0	0	0	2,229
Coxwell Steptoe	8	1	2	0	5	1,930
Sounds Like Fun	4	1	1	1	1	1,828
Colonel Blazer	3	1	0	1	1	1,581
Barrier Express	1	1	0	0	0	1,448
Darakshan	2	1	0	0	1	1,434

WINNING OWNERS

	Races Won	Value £		Races Won	Value £
Martin Broughton	6	41,843	Lord Hartington	2	5,578
Azzmok Winton Wright	5	22,310	T H Shrimpton	2	5,137
I D Macdonald	3	21,799	Executive Racing	2	5,132
The Voice Group Ltd	1	19,188	Paul Stamp	1	4,811
Lord Vestey	5	16,249	V McCalla	2	4,396
Lord Chelsea	4	14,114	Mrs Linda McCalla	1	3,556
Mrs Shirley Brasher	2	9,388	Aquarius	1	3,058
J D Martin	3	7,287	Sir Anthony Scott	1	2,879
The Hatchet P'ship	2	7,273	Castle Farm Stud	1	2,840
Premier Crops Ltd	2	6,987	Gradely Partners	1	2,268
The Lady Vestey	2	6,456	M E R Allsopp	1	1,930
Harold Winton	2	6,335	Mrs H Brown	1	1,828
Mrs A M Davis	2	6,135	Allsport Barrier Systems Ltd	1	1,448
The Supreme Lady P'ship	2	6,061	Michael Watt	1	1,434

Knight Miss H C

No of horses racing for the stable		85	Total winning prize-money		£237,720

| Favourites | 26-61 | 42.6% | + 7.14 | Average SP of winner | | 3.9/1 |
| Longest win seq | 4 | Longest losing seq | 25 | Return on stakes invested | | -8.2% |

| 1994/95 Form | 44-221 | 19.9% | + 10.69 | 1992/93 Form | 37-152 | 24.3% | + 36.22 |
| 1993/94 Form | 25-156 | 16.0% | - 31.78 | 1991/92 Form | 14-171 | 8.2% | -102.85 |

S G KNIGHT (West Hatch, Somerset)

	Races Run	1st	2nd	3rd	Unpl	Per cent	£1 Level Stake
Hurdles	28	0	1	0	27	-	- 28.00
Chases	32	1	3	4	24	3.1	- 28.50
Totals	60	1	4	4	51	1.7	- 56.50

G Upton	1-17	- 13.50	Newton Abbot	1-14	- 10.50

No of horses racing for the stable	10	Total winning prize-money	£3,696

H W LAVIS (Haverfordwest, Dyfed)

	Races Run	1st	2nd	3rd	Unpl	Per cent	£1 Level Stake
Hurdles	0	0	0	0	0	-	0.00
Chases	7	2	0	1	4	28.6	+ 4.50
Totals	7	2	0	1	4	28.6	+ 4.50

Mr J Jukes	2-4	+ 7.50

Stratford	1-1	+ 6.00	Uttoxeter	1-2	+ 2.50

No of horses racing for the stable	6	Total winning prize-money	£4,871

C LAWSON (Beverley, North Humberside)

	Races Run	1st	2nd	3rd	Unpl	Per cent	£1 Level Stake
Hurdles	0	0	0	0	0	-	0.00
Chases	3	1	0	0	2	33.3	+ 1.50
Totals	3	1	0	0	2	33.3	+ 1.50

Mr C Mulhall	1-3	+ 1.50	Hexham	1-1	+ 3.50

No of horses racing for the stable	1	Total winning prize-money	£2,447

S J LEADBETTER (Ladykirk, Borders)

	Races Run	1st	2nd	3rd	Unpl	Per cent	£1 Level Stake
Hurdles	8	1	0	2	5	12.5	+ 3.00
Chases	0	0	0	0	0	-	0.00
Totals	8	1	0	2	5	12.5	+ 3.00

N Leach	1-8	+ 3.00	Hexham	1-3	+ 8.00

No of horses racing for the stable   2   Total winning prize-money   £1,688

R R LEDGER (Borden, Kent)

	Races Run	1st	2nd	3rd	Unpl	Per cent	£1 Level Stake
Hurdles	6	1	0	0	5	16.7	+ 4.00
Chases	13	0	1	2	10	-	- 13.00
Totals	19	1	1	2	15	5.3	- 9.00

Mrs N Ledger	1-18	- 8.00	Plumpton	1-5	+ 5.00

No of horses racing for the stable   2   Total winning prize-money   £2,266

R LEE (Byton, Salop)

	Races Run	1st	2nd	3rd	Unpl	Per cent	£1 Level Stake
Hurdles	46	1	5	6	34	2.2	- 41.50
Chases	23	2	1	3	17	8.7	- 7.50
Totals	69	3	6	9	51	4.3	- 49.00

R Johnson	1-6	+ 6.00	P McLoughlin	1-12	- 7.50
C Llewellyn	1-7	- 3.50			
Haydock	1-1	+ 3.50	Hereford	1-13	- 9.50
Market Rasen	1-1	+ 11.00			

No of horses racing for the stable   21   Total winning prize-money   £10,926

J P LEIGH (Willoughton, Lincs)

	Races Run	1st	2nd	3rd	Unpl	Per cent	£1 Level Stake
Hurdles	6	1	1	0	4	16.7	− 3.00
Chases	18	1	0	2	15	5.6	− 5.00
Totals	24	2	1	2	19	8.3	− 8.00

A Tory	1−3	+ 10.00	Mr W Morgan	1−8	− 5.00
Perth	1−1	+ 2.00	Uttoxeter	1−3	+ 10.00

No of horses racing for the stable   4   Total winning prize-money   £5,628

G W LEWIS (Llanelli, Dyfed)

	Races Run	1st	2nd	3rd	Unpl	Per cent	£1 Level Stake
Hurdles	0	0	0	0	0	−	0.00
Chases	6	1	1	0	4	16.7	− 2.00
Totals	6	1	1	0	4	16.7	− 2.00

Mr M Rimell	1−2	+ 2.00	Hereford	1−2	+ 2.00

No of horses racing for the stable   1   Total winning prize-money   £1,456

N P LITTMODEN (Wolverhampton, West Midlands)

	Races Run	1st	2nd	3rd	Unpl	Per cent	£1 Level Stake
Hurdles	17	3	0	3	11	17.6	+ 22.00
Chases	8	1	0	0	7	12.5	+ 7.00
Totals	25	4	0	3	18	16.0	+ 29.00

P Niven	1−2	+ 7.00	J Titley	1−2	+ 13.00
N Williamson	1−2	+ 13.00	Martin Brennan	1−3	+ 12.00
Cartmel	1−1	+ 8.00	Taunton	1−3	+ 12.00
Worcester	1−2	+ 13.00	Ludlow	1−3	+ 12.00

No of horses racing for the stable   6   Total winning prize-money   £12,604

B J LLEWELLYN (Bargoed, Mid Glamorgan)

	Races Run	1st	2nd	3rd	Unpl	Per cent	£1 Level Stake
Hurdles	100	5	15	8	72	5.0	- 77.75
Chases	17	1	2	3	11	5.9	- 9.00
Totals	117	6	17	11	83	5.1	- 86.75

Mr J L Llewellyn	3-65	- 51.50		Guy Lewis	1-16	- 13.25
A P McCoy	2-5	+ 9.00				
Stratford	3-10	+ 6.25		Plumpton	1-4	- 1.00
Aintree	1-1	+ 5.00		Bangor	1-6	- 1.00

No of horses racing for the stable	29	Total winning prize-money	£18,020

L R LLOYD-JAMES (Malton, North Yorks)

	Races Run	1st	2nd	3rd	Unpl	Per cent	£1 Level Stake
Hurdles	19	1	5	2	11	5.3	- 15.25
Chases	1	0	0	1	0	-	- 1.00
Totals	20	1	5	3	11	5.0	- 16.25

E Callaghan	1-5	- 1.25	Musselburgh	1-2	+ 1.75

No of horses racing for the stable	5	Total winning prize-money	£2,233

J E LONG (Plumpton Green, East Sussex)

	Races Run	1st	2nd	3rd	Unpl	Per cent	£1 Level Stake
Hurdles	23	1	1	0	21	4.3	- 13.00
Chases	0	0	0	0	0	-	0.00
Totals	23	1	1	0	21	4.3	- 13.00

B Fenton	1-6	+ 4.00	Towcester	1-4	+ 6.00

No of horses racing for the stable	7	Total winning prize-money	£2,192

MRS M E LONG (Woldingham, Surrey)

	Races Run	1st	2nd	3rd	Unpl	Per cent	£1 Level Stake
Hurdles	21	4	1	4	12	19.0	+ 3.50
Chases	2	0	0	1	1	-	- 2.00
Totals	23	4	1	5	13	17.4	+ 1.50

B Fenton	3-15	+ 3.00		D Gallagher	1-6	+ 0.50
Towcester	2-4	+ 10.00		Folkestone	1-5	+ 1.00
Lingfield	1-1	+ 3.50				

No of horses racing for the stable   7   Total winning prize-money   £9,732

L LUNGO (Carrutherstown, Dumfries)

	Races Run	1st	2nd	3rd	Unpl	Per cent	£1 Level Stake
Hurdles	122	10	7	8	97	8.2	- 41.02
Chases	16	4	2	0	10	25.0	- 9.30
Totals	138	14	9	8	107	10.1	- 50.32

BY MONTH

	W-R	Per cent	£1 Level Stake		W-R	Per cent	£1 Level Stake
June	0-0	-	0.00	December	4-19	21.1	+ 31.75
July	0-0	-	0.00	January	1-22	4.5	- 20.09
August	0-0	-	0.00	February	1-17	5.9	- 15.43
September	0-3	-	- 3.00	March	1-23	4.3	- 14.00
October	1-3	33.3	- 1.60	April	2-24	8.3	- 16.00
November	3-21	14.3	- 11.45	May	1-6	16.7	- 0.50

DISTANCE

Hurdles	W-R	Per cent	£1 Level Stake	Chases	W-R	Per cent	£1 Level Stake
2m-2m 3f	4-68	5.9	- 10.09	2m-2m 3f	3-5	60.0	+ 0.45
2m 4f-2m 7f	4-36	11.1	- 20.43	2m 4f-2m 7f	0-3	-	- 3.00
3m +	2-18	11.1	- 10.50	3m +	1-8	12.5	- 6.75

TYPE OF RACE

	W-R	Per cent	£1 Level Stake		W-R	Per cent	£1 Level Stake
Novice hurdles	5-52	9.6	- 35.02	Selling	0-7	-	- 7.00
H'cap hurdles	3-37	8.1	- 20.00	Amateur	0-2	-	- 2.00
Novice chases	3-11	27.3	- 6.68	Hunter chases	0-0	-	0.00
H'cap chases	1-4	25.0	- 1.62	N H Flat	2-25	8.0	+ 22.00

COURSE GRADE					FIRST TIME OUT			
	W-R	Per cent	£1 Level Stake			W-R	Per cent	£1 Level Stake
Group 1	2-50	4.0	- 19.00	Hurdles		3-36	8.3	+ 12.91
Group 2	1-9	11.1	- 7.60	Chases		1-5	20.0	- 3.60
Group 3	2-8	25.0	- 4.25					
Group 4	9-71	12.7	- 19.47	Totals		4-41	9.8	+ 9.31

JOCKEYS RIDING

	W-R	Per cent	£1 Level Stake		W-R	Per cent	£1 Level Stake
T Reed	8-65	12.3	- 43.23	L O'Hara	1-4	25.0	+ 22.00
F Perratt	4-45	8.9	- 10.59	M Foster	1-5	20.0	+ 0.50

I Jardine	0-8	E Husband	0-2	Mr K Anderson		0-1
A Dobbin	0-2	A P McCoy	0-1	Mr P Johnson		0-1
B Harding	0-2	Mr C Bonner	0-1	R Dunwoody		0-1

COURSE RECORD

	Total W-R	Nov Hdles	H'cap Hdles	Nov Chses	H'cap Chses	Hunter Chses	N H Flat	£1 Level Stake
Hexham	6-23	2-8	1-7	1-2	1-3	0-0	1-3	+ 16.05
Catterick	2-7	0-2	1-2	1-1	0-1	0-0	0-1	- 3.25
Carlisle	2-14	1-6	1-2	0-3	0-0	0-0	0-3	- 3.09
Wetherby	1-9	0-6	0-1	1-1	0-0	0-0	0-1	- 7.60
Kelso	1-16	1-10	0-4	0-2	0-0	0-0	0-0	- 14.43
Haydock	1-16	0-5	0-7	0-0	0-0	0-0	1-4	+ 10.00
Ayr	1-22	1-9	0-6	0-0	0-1	0-0	0-6	- 17.00

Newcastle	0-11	Bangor	0-4	Market Rasen	0-1
Perth	0-5	Musselburgh	0-4		
Sedgefield	0-5	Cheltenham	0-1		

WINNING HORSES

	Races Run	1st	2nd	3rd	Unpl	Win £
Supertop	3	2	0	0	1	6,706
Forbidden Time	3	2	1	0	0	5,692
Santa Concerto	3	2	0	1	0	5,252
Swanbister	5	2	0	0	3	4,773
Celtic Giant	3	1	1	0	1	3,123
The Stitcher	8	1	3	2	2	2,889
Livio	7	1	1	1	4	2,461
Kirstenbosch	3	1	0	0	2	2,290
Corston Rambo	3	1	0	0	2	2,231
River Nith	2	1	0	0	1	1,298

WINNING OWNERS

	Races Won	Value £		Races Won	Value £
R J Gilbert	3	9,829	The Low Flyers (Th'breds) Ltd	1	2,461
Mrs J K Peutherer	2	5,692	Mrs S J Matthews	1	2,290
John Corr	2	5,252	A S Lyburn	1	2,231
D C Greig	2	4,773	Mrs A G Martin	1	1,298
J K Huddleston	1	2,889			

No of horses racing for the stable		41	Total winning prize-money	£36,715

Favourites	8-19	42.1%	- 0.82	Average SP of winner		5.3/1
Longest win seq	2	Longest losing seq	24	Return on stakes invested		-36.5%

1994/95 Form	28-189	14.8%	- 17.01	1992/93 Form	22-91	24.2%	- 3.50
1993/94 Form	27-127	21.3%	+ 59.09	1991/92 Form	8-69	11.6%	- 27.77

MRS N MACAULEY (Sproxton, Leics)

	Races Run	1st	2nd	3rd	Unpl	Per cent	£1 Level Stake
Hurdles	43	4	3	6	30	9.3	- 8.25
Chases	0	0	0	0	0	-	0.00
Totals	43	4	3	6	30	9.3	- 8.25

P Hide	2-6	+ 2.75	R Johnson	1-11	- 2.00
Mr J Culloty	1-1	+ 16.00			

Ascot	2-4	+ 18.00	Uttoxeter	1-6	+ 3.00
Fontwell	1-4	- 0.25			

No of horses racing for the stable	15	Total winning prize-money	£16,000

J MACKIE (Church Broughton, Derbys)

	Races Run	1st	2nd	3rd	Unpl	Per cent	£1 Level Stake
Hurdles	80	12	7	5	56	15.0	+ 6.73
Chases	10	1	1	0	8	10.0	- 1.00
Totals	90	13	8	5	64	14.4	+ 5.73

BY MONTH

	W-R	Per cent	£1 Level Stake		W-R	Per cent	£1 Level Stake
June	0-3	-	- 3.00	December	1-9	11.1	- 6.62
July	0-1	-	- 1.00	January	1-8	12.5	- 5.62
August	0-1	-	- 1.00	February	0-14	-	- 14.00
September	1-4	25.0	+ 2.60	March	1-5	20.0	+ 1.00
October	2-11	18.2	+ 4.00	April	0-9	-	- 9.00
November	6-17	35.3	+ 37.37	May	1-8	12.5	+ 1.00

DISTANCE

	W-R	Per cent	£1 Level Stake		W-R	Per cent	£1 Level Stake
Hurdles				Chases			
2m-2m 3f	7-39	17.9	+ 22.75	2m-2m 3f	0-1	-	- 1.00
2m 4f-2m 7f	1-29	3.4	- 22.40	2m 4f-2m 7f	1-6	16.7	+ 3.00
3m +	4-12	33.3	+ 6.38	3m +	0-3	-	- 3.00

TYPE OF RACE

	W-R	Per cent	£1 Level Stake		W-R	Per cent	£1 Level Stake
Novice hurdles	4-31	12.9	+ 12.50	Selling	0-6	-	- 6.00
H'cap hurdles	8-36	22.2	+ 7.23	Amateur	0-0	-	0.00
Novice chases	0-0	-	0.00	Hunter chases	0-0	-	0.00
H'cap chases	1-10	10.0	- 1.00	N H Flat	0-7	-	- 7.00

COURSE GRADE

	W-R	Per cent	£1 Level Stake
Group 1	0-13	-	- 13.00
Group 2	2-10	20.0	+ 11.00
Group 3	5-43	11.6	- 3.63
Group 4	6-24	25.0	+ 11.36

FIRST TIME OUT

	W-R	Per cent	£1 Level Stake
Hurdles	3-19	15.8	+ 11.00
Chases	0-2	-	- 2.00
Totals	3-21	14.3	+ 9.00

JOCKEYS RIDING

	W-R	Per cent	£1 Level Stake		W-R	Per cent	£1 Level Stake
E Husband	7-32	21.9	+ 18.38	W Marston	1-7	14.3	+ 2.00
T Eley	4-32	12.5	- 2.25	R Supple	1-10	10.0	- 3.40

W McFarland	0-2	D Webb	0-1	R Dunwoody	0-1
A Dobbin	0-1	G Hogan	0-1	T Jenks	0-1
B Powell	0-1	G Lee	0-1		

COURSE RECORD

	Total W-R	Nov Hdles	H'cap Hdles	Nov Chses	H'cap Chses	Hunter Chses	N H Flat	£1 Level Stake
Bangor	3-11	0-2	2-5	0-0	1-4	0-0	0-0	+ 13.00
Musselburgh	2-2	0-0	2-2	0-0	0-0	0-0	0-0	+ 2.76
Leicester	2-5	1-3	1-1	0-0	0-1	0-0	0-0	+ 15.25
Market Rasen	2-7	1-4	1-2	0-0	0-0	0-0	0-1	+ 10.50
Catterick	1-1	0-0	1-1	0-0	0-0	0-0	0-0	+ 0.62
Sedgefield	1-3	0-1	1-2	0-0	0-0	0-0	0-0	+ 3.60
Chepstow	1-3	1-2	0-0	0-0	0-1	0-0	0-0	+ 3.00
Wetherby	1-7	1-3	0-3	0-0	0-0	0-0	0-1	+ 8.00

Uttoxeter	0-12	Doncaster	0-4	Huntingdon	0-1
Nottingham	0-6	Warwick	0-4	Kempton	0-1
Haydock	0-5	Cheltenham	0-2	Newbury	0-1
Southwell	0-5	Ludlow	0-2	Stratford	0-1
Worcester	0-5	Carlisle	0-1	Windsor	0-1

WINNING HORSES

	Races Run	1st	2nd	3rd	Unpl	Win £
Divertimiento	10	2	1	3	4	16,970
Master of The Rock	8	5	1	0	2	12,906
Nahri	6	2	1	0	3	8,290
Absalom's Pillar	2	1	0	0	1	3,267
Andermatt	4	1	1	0	2	3,160
Ciracusa	5	1	0	0	4	3,071
Trecento	1	1	0	0	0	2,879

WINNING OWNERS

	Races Won	Value £		Races Won	Value £
Mrs Sue Adams	7	21,196	The Marston Sept	1	3,160
B J Wood	2	16,970	Tim Kelly	1	3,071
Peter C Sherlock	1	3,267	F A Dickinson	1	2,879

No of horses racing for the stable	22	Total winning prize-money	£50,543
Favourites	4-11 36.4% - 1.37	Average SP of winner	6.4/1
Longest win seq 2 Longest losing seq 17		Return on stakes invested	6.4%
1994/95 Form 7-111 6.3% - 82.44		1992/93 Form 10-109 9.2% - 40.95	
1993/94 Form 10-95 10.5% + 20.13		1991/92 Form 11-155 7.1% - 90.50	

JOHN MACKLEY (Billingham, Co Cleveland)

	Races Run	1st	2nd	3rd	Unpl	Per cent	£1 Level Stake
Hurdles	0	0	0	0	0	-	0.00
Chases	1	1	0	0	0	100.0	+ 1.50
Totals	1	1	0	0	0	100.0	+ 1.50

Mr M Haigh	1-1	+ 1.50	Newcastle	1-1	+ 1.50

No of horses racing for the stable	1	Total winning prize-money	£1,402

B MACTAGGART (Hawick, Borders)

	Races Run	1st	2nd	3rd	Unpl	Per cent	£1 Level Stake
Hurdles	39	6	1	4	28	15.4	- 8.53
Chases	4	1	1	0	2	25.0	+ 11.00
Totals	43	7	2	4	30	16.3	+ 2.47

BY MONTH

	W-R	Per cent	£1 Level Stake		W-R	Per cent	£1 Level Stake
June	0-2	-	- 2.00	December	0-2	-	- 2.00
July	0-0	-	0.00	January	0-1	-	- 1.00
August	0-0	-	0.00	February	0-5	-	- 5.00
September	1-1	100.0	+ 14.00	March	2-9	22.2	+ 8.00
October	0-8	-	- 8.00	April	3-6	50.0	+ 5.80
November	0-3	-	- 3.00	May	1-6	16.7	- 4.33

DISTANCE

Hurdles	W-R	Per cent	£1 Level Stake	Chases	W-R	Per cent	£1 Level Stake
2m-2m 3f	3-27	11.1	- 6.00	2m-2m 3f	0-2	-	- 2.00
2m 4f-2m 7f	2-10	20.0	- 6.53	2m 4f-2m 7f	0-0	-	0.00
3m +	1-2	50.0	+ 4.00	3m +	1-2	50.0	+ 13.00

TYPE OF RACE

	W-R	Per cent	£1 Level Stake		W-R	Per cent	£1 Level Stake
Novice hurdles	3-19	15.8	- 9.53	Selling	0-3	-	- 3.00
H'cap hurdles	3-16	18.8	+ 5.00	Amateur	0-1	-	- 1.00
Novice chases	0-0	-	0.00	Hunter chases	0-0	-	0.00
H'cap chases	1-4	25.0	+ 11.00	N H Flat	0-0	-	0.00

COURSE GRADE / FIRST TIME OUT

	W-R	Per cent	£1 Level Stake		W-R	Per cent	£1 Level Stake
Group 1	1-10	10.0	- 4.00	Hurdles	0-8	-	- 8.00
Group 2	1-2	50.0	- 0.33	Chases	1-2	50.0	+ 13.00
Group 3	0-1	-	- 1.00				
Group 4	5-30	16.7	+ 7.80	Totals	1-10	10.0	+ 5.00

JOCKEYS RIDING

	W-R	Per cent	£1 Level Stake		W-R	Per cent	£1 Level Stake
B Storey	4-14	28.6	- 0.03	F Perratt	1-5	20.0	+ 0.50
S Melrose	1-3	33.3	+ 8.00	G Lee	1-15	6.7	0.00

A Dobbin	0-1	D Parker	0-1	M Dwyer	0-1
B Harding	0-1	L Wyer	0-1	Mr R Hale	0-1

COURSE RECORD

	Total W-R	Nov Hdles	H'cap Hdles	Nov Chses	H'cap Chses	Hunter Chses	N H Flat	£1 Level Stake
Carlisle	2-6	1-3	1-3	0-0	0-0	0-0	0-0	+ 1.30
Perth	1-2	0-0	1-1	0-0	0-1	0-0	0-0	+ 2.50
Wetherby	1-2	1-1	0-1	0-0	0-0	0-0	0-0	- 0.33
Hexham	1-3	0-1	1-2	0-0	0-0	0-0	0-0	+ 8.00
Ayr	1-7	1-4	0-3	0-0	0-0	0-0	0-0	- 1.00
Kelso	1-13	0-7	0-4	0-0	1-2	0-0	0-0	+ 2.00

Mactaggart B

Musselburgh	0-4	Sedgefield	0-2	Newcastle	0-1
Aintree	0-2	Market Rasen	0-1		

WINNING HORSES

	Races Run	1st	2nd	3rd	Unpl	Win £
Master Sandy	8	3	1	2	2	8,608
Merry Mermaid	4	2	0	0	2	6,614
Side of Hill	2	1	1	0	0	2,892
Well Appointed	5	1	0	1	3	2,066

WINNING OWNERS

	Races Won	Value £		Races Won	Value £
Miss I Forrest	3	8,608	J M Rudkin	1	2,892
Miss J Campbell	2	6,614	Drumlanrig Racing	1	2,066

No of horses racing for the stable   12   Total winning prize-money   £20,180

Favourites	3-6	50.0%	+ 1.97	Average SP of winner	5.5/1
Longest win seq	2	Longest losing seq 24		Return on stakes invested	5.7%

1994/95 Form	1-46	2.2%	- 31.00	1992/93 Form	3-47	6.4%	- 16.00
1993/94 Form	2-55	3.6%	- 48.67	1991/92 Form	1-36	2.8%	- 28.00

M MADGWICK (Denmead, Hants)

	Races Run	1st	2nd	3rd	Unpl	Per cent	£1 Level Stake
Hurdles	32	2	0	2	28	6.3	- 23.50
Chases	13	0	2	2	9	-	- 13.00
Totals	45	2	2	4	37	4.4	- 36.50

B Fenton   2-16   - 7.50   Lingfield   2-6   + 2.50

No of horses racing for the stable   17   Total winning prize-money   £4,836

P J MAKIN (Ogbourne Maisey, Wilts)

	Races Run	1st	2nd	3rd	Unpl	Per cent	£1 Level Stake
Hurdles	5	2	0	1	2	40.0	+ 2.50
Chases	1	0	0	0	1	-	- 1.00
Totals	6	2	0	1	3	33.3	+ 1.50

J R Kavanagh   1-2   + 1.00   M A Fitzgerald   1-3   + 1.50

Market Rasen   1-1   + 3.50   Warwick   1-1   + 2.00

No of horses racing for the stable   4   Total winning prize-money   £4,694

C J MANN (Upper Lambourn, Berks)

	Races Run	1st	2nd	3rd	Unpl	Per cent	£1 Level Stake
Hurdles	101	13	15	19	54	12.9	- 19.84
Chases	27	4	3	2	18	14.8	- 12.00
Totals	128	17	18	21	72	13.3	- 31.84

BY MONTH

	W-R	Per cent	£1 Level Stake		W-R	Per cent	£1 Level Stake
June	1-2	50.0	+ 4.50	December	1-10	10.0	- 1.50
July	1-6	16.7	+ 11.00	January	0-8	-	- 8.00
August	2-6	33.3	+ 1.50	February	0-12	-	- 12.00
September	3-10	30.0	- 0.50	March	1-20	5.0	- 14.00
October	2-11	18.2	- 6.09	April	3-15	20.0	- 3.50
November	2-19	10.5	+ 3.00	May	1-9	11.1	- 6.25

DISTANCE

Hurdles	W-R	Per cent	£1 Level Stake	Chases	W-R	Per cent	£1 Level Stake
2m-2m 3f	9-70	12.9	- 16.34	2m-2m 3f	0-1	-	- 1.00
2m 4f-2m 7f	2-20	10.0	+ 0.50	2m 4f-2m 7f	1-9	11.1	- 6.25
3m +	2-11	18.2	- 4.00	3m +	3-17	17.6	- 4.75

TYPE OF RACE

	W-R	Per cent	£1 Level Stake		W-R	Per cent	£1 Level Stake
Novice hurdles	6-45	13.3	- 20.59	Selling	1-3	33.3	+ 14.00
H'cap hurdles	4-40	10.0	- 20.25	Amateur	0-2	-	- 2.00
Novice chases	1-9	11.1	- 6.25	Hunter chases	0-0	-	0.00
H'cap chases	3-18	16.7	- 5.75	N H Flat	2-11	18.2	+ 9.00

COURSE GRADE

	W-R	Per cent	£1 Level Stake
Group 1	3-37	8.1	- 23.59
Group 2	1-12	8.3	- 8.50
Group 3	7-47	14.9	+ 7.50
Group 4	6-32	18.8	- 7.25

FIRST TIME OUT

	W-R	Per cent	£1 Level Stake
Hurdles	5-22	22.7	+ 27.00
Chases	0-7	-	- 7.00
Totals	5-29	17.2	+ 20.00

JOCKEYS RIDING

	W-R	Per cent	£1 Level Stake		W-R	Per cent	£1 Level Stake
R Dunwoody	6-37	16.2	- 19.09	A Thornton	1-2	50.0	+ 1.50
Muredach Kelly	3-18	16.7	+ 12.50	J R Kavanagh	1-2	50.0	+ 4.00
J Railton	3-42	7.1	- 28.75	C Llewellyn	1-3	33.3	+ 14.00
J Magee	1-1	100.0	+ 2.00	A P McCoy	1-6	16.7	- 1.00

Mann C J

W Marston	0-3	D Bridgwater	0-1	Mr E James	0-1
Mr J Culloty	0-2	D Gallagher	0-1	R Greene	0-1
A Larnach	0-1	G Bradley	0-1	T Reed	0-1
A Maguire	0-1	M A Fitzgerald	0-1	W McFarland	0-1
B Powell	0-1	M Perrett	0-1		

COURSE RECORD

	Total W-R	Nov Hdles	H'cap Hdles	Nov Chses	H'cap Chses	Hunter Chses	N H Flat	£1 Level Stake
Hereford	2-3	1-2	0-0	0-0	1-1	0-0	0-0	+ 7.00
Ludlow	2-8	1-5	1-3	0-0	0-0	0-0	0-0	- 1.75
Worcester	2-9	0-1	0-2	1-3	0-1	0-0	1-2	+ 10.75
Uttoxeter	2-10	1-5	0-2	0-0	1-3	0-0	0-0	- 1.75
Southwell	1-2	1-2	0-0	0-0	0-0	0-0	0-0	+ 1.50
Towcester	1-3	0-0	1-1	0-0	0-2	0-0	0-0	+ 2.00
Kempton	1-3	0-1	0-1	0-0	1-1	0-0	0-0	0.00
Haydock	1-3	0-1	1-2	0-0	0-0	0-0	0-0	+ 5.50
Market Rasen	1-4	0-1	0-1	0-1	0-0	0-0	1-1	- 1.00
Newton Abbot	1-4	0-1	1-2	0-0	0-1	0-0	0-0	- 0.50
Stratford	1-4	1-1	0-1	0-2	0-0	0-0	0-0	+ 2.50
Warwick	1-5	0-1	1-3	0-0	0-0	0-0	0-1	+ 12.00
Cheltenham	1-8	1-4	0-2	0-1	0-1	0-0	0-0	- 6.09

Ascot	0-9	Chepstow	0-3	Fakenham	0-1
Newbury	0-7	Huntingdon	0-3	Leicester	0-1
Bangor	0-6	Sandown	0-3	Lingfield	0-1
Wincanton	0-6	Windsor	0-3	Musselburgh	0-1
Exeter	0-4	Perth	0-2	Nottingham	0-1
Fontwell	0-4	Taunton	0-2	Plumpton	0-1
Aintree	0-3	Doncaster	0-1		

WINNING HORSES

	Races Run	1st	2nd	3rd	Unpl	Win £
General Rusty	7	3	1	1	2	21,167
Celibate	10	2	2	0	6	6,485
Multy	9	2	2	1	4	5,345
Its A Snip	8	1	1	1	5	3,193
Clifton Set	10	1	1	3	5	2,596
Injunction	5	1	1	0	3	2,515
Indie Rock	5	1	1	2	1	2,360
Yacht	7	1	1	1	4	2,220
Watermead	3	1	0	1	1	1,994
Nescaf	3	1	0	1	1	1,942
Convoy	7	1	1	1	4	1,794
Rangitikei	4	1	2	0	1	1,385
My Old China	1	1	0	0	0	1,329

WINNING OWNERS

	Races Won	Value £		Races Won	Value £
Michael Watt	4	23,109	Trevor Phillips	1	2,360
Stamford Bridge P'ship	2	6,485	C R Nugent	1	2,220
The Izz That Right Partnership	2	5,345	J E Brown	1	1,994
The Icy Fire Partnership	1	3,193	U K Home Computers	1	1,794
Mrs Christine Fennell	1	2,596	Mrs J M Mayo	1	1,385
Miss R I Still	1	2,515	Mrs Gertrude M Foster	1	1,329
No of horses racing for the stable		30	Total winning prize-money		£54,325

Favourites	6-29	20.7%	- 12.34	Average SP of winner			4.7/1
Longest win seq	2	Longest losing seq	38	Return on stakes invested			-24.9%
1994/95 Form	16-123	13.0%	- 47.22	1993/94 Form	15-49	30.6%	+ 17.13

H J MANNERS (Highworth, Wilts)

	Races Run	1st	2nd	3rd	Unpl	Per cent	£1 Level Stake
Hurdles	59	5	5	3	46	8.5	- 8.50
Chases	44	4	5	8	27	9.1	+ 39.00
Totals	103	9	10	11	73	8.7	+ 30.50

BY MONTH

	W-R	Per cent	£1 Level Stake		W-R	Per cent	£1 Level Stake
June	0-3	-	- 3.00	December	1-4	25.0	+ 17.00
July	0-10	-	- 10.00	January	2-9	22.2	+ 9.00
August	0-13	-	- 13.00	February	2-4	50.0	+ 12.00
September	0-8	-	- 8.00	March	3-11	27.3	+ 41.50
October	0-9	-	- 9.00	April	0-9	-	- 9.00
November	1-10	10.0	+ 16.00	May	0-13	-	- 13.00

DISTANCE

Hurdles	W-R	Per cent	£1 Level Stake	Chases	W-R	Per cent	£1 Level Stake
2m-2m 3f	3-44	6.8	- 23.50	2m-2m 3f	2-18	11.1	+ 42.00
2m 4f-2m 7f	2-13	15.4	+ 17.00	2m 4f-2m 7f	0-11	-	- 11.00
3m +	0-2	-	- 2.00	3m +	2-15	13.3	+ 8.00

TYPE OF RACE

	W-R	Per cent	£1 Level Stake		W-R	Per cent	£1 Level Stake
Novice hurdles	0-9	-	- 9.00	Selling	4-34	11.8	+ 7.00
H'cap hurdles	1-13	7.7	- 3.50	Amateur	0-7	-	- 7.00
Novice chases	1-17	5.9	+ 9.00	Hunter chases	1-4	25.0	+ 30.00
H'cap chases	2-15	13.3	+ 8.00	N H Flat	0-4	-	- 4.00

COURSE GRADE				FIRST TIME OUT			
	W-R	Per cent	£1 Level Stake		W-R	Per cent	£1 Level Stake
Group 1	1-6	16.7	+ 4.00	Hurdles	0-13	-	- 13.00
Group 2	3-32	9.4	+ 24.50	Chases	0-5	-	- 5.00
Group 3	3-35	8.6	+ 13.00				
Group 4	2-30	6.7	- 11.00	Totals	0-18	-	- 18.00

JOCKEYS RIDING

	W-R	Per cent	£1 Level Stake		W-R	Per cent	£1 Level Stake
S Curran	3-7	42.9	+ 21.00	M Bosley	1-4	25.0	+ 2.00
Mr A Charles-Jones	2-38	5.3	+ 22.00	Mr A Wintle	1-5	20.0	+ 4.00
J R Kavanagh	1-1	100.0	+ 20.00	A Dowling	1-15	6.7	- 5.50

Gary Brown	0-14	D Walsh	0-1	T Eley	0-1
M Appleby	0-13	Mr G Brown	0-1	X Aizpuru	0-1
Arnold Garvey	0-1	Sophie Mitchell	0-1		

COURSE RECORD

	Total W-R	Nov Hdles	H'cap Hdles	Nov Chses	H'cap Chses	Hunter Chses	N H Flat	£1 Level Stake
Leicester	2-3	0-0	1-2	0-0	0-0	1-1	0-0	+ 36.00
Fontwell	2-8	0-3	1-1	1-3	0-1	0-0	0-0	+ 27.50
Taunton	2-9	0-3	1-4	0-0	1-2	0-0	0-0	+ 10.00
Newcastle	1-1	0-0	0-0	0-0	1-1	0-0	0-0	+ 9.00
Huntingdon	1-4	0-1	1-1	0-2	0-0	0-0	0-0	+ 5.00
Chepstow	1-9	1-5	0-1	0-1	0-2	0-0	0-0	+ 12.00

Newton Abbot	0-14	Cheltenham	0-5	Warwick	0-2
Stratford	0-9	Ludlow	0-4	Windsor	0-2
Hereford	0-7	Plumpton	0-4	Lingfield	0-1
Towcester	0-7	Exeter	0-3	Uttoxeter	0-1
Worcester	0-7	Folkestone	0-2	Wincanton	0-1

WINNING HORSES

	Races Run	1st	2nd	3rd	Unpl	Win £
Killeshin	8	2	1	1	4	29,760
Touch Silver	11	3	2	0	6	7,018
Candle King	4	1	0	1	2	3,548
Cavalero	9	1	0	0	8	2,220
Halham Tarn	11	1	2	4	4	2,040
Il Bambino	8	1	1	1	5	2,003

WINNING OWNER

	Races Won	Value £
H J Manners	9	46,589

194

No of horses racing for the stable	19	Total winning prize-money	£46,589

| Favourites | 1-4 | 25.0% | + 2.00 | Average SP of winner | 13.8/1 |
| Longest win seq | 2 | Longest losing seq | 46 | Return on stakes invested | 29.6% |

| 1994/95 Form | 5-70 | 7.1% | - 33.25 | 1992/93 Form | 0-43 |
| 1993/94 Form | 6-53 | 11.3% | + 87.75 | | |

D MARKS (Upper Lambourn, Berks)

	Races Run	1st	2nd	3rd	Unpl	Per cent	£1 Level Stake
Hurdles	32	5	8	1	18	15.6	+ 14.00
Chases	2	0	2	0	0	-	- 2.00
Totals	34	5	10	1	18	14.7	+ 12.00

J A McCarthy	4-20	+ 22.00	A P McCoy	1-3	+ 1.00

Hereford	1-2	+ 2.00	Stratford	1-5	- 2.00
Leicester	1-2	+ 8.00	Chepstow	1-6	+ 11.00
Southwell	1-2	+ 10.00			

No of horses racing for the stable	6	Total winning prize-money	£12,018

I M MASON (Malton, North Yorks)

	Races Run	1st	2nd	3rd	Unpl	Per cent	£1 Level Stake
Hurdles	0	0	0	0	0	-	0.00
Chases	2	1	0	0	1	50.0	+ 3.00
Totals	2	1	0	0	1	50.0	+ 3.00

Mr S Swiers	1-2	+ 3.00	Uttoxeter	1-1	+ 4.00

No of horses racing for the stable	1	Total winning prize-money	£2,710

N B MASON (Crook, Co Durham)

	Races Run	1st	2nd	3rd	Unpl	Per cent	£1 Level Stake
Hurdles	13	2	4	2	5	15.4	- 2.00
Chases	4	1	1	0	2	25.0	+ 6.00
Totals	17	3	5	2	7	17.6	+ 4.00

S Haworth	2-14	+ 1.50	J Supple	1-1	+ 4.50

| Huntingdon | 1-1 | + 9.00 | Catterick | 1-6 | - 0.50 |
| Perth | 1-6 | - 0.50 | | | |

No of horses racing for the stable	9	Total winning prize-money	£7,860

D MCCAIN (Cholmondeley Castle, Cheshire)

	Races Run	1st	2nd	3rd	Unpl	Per cent	£1 Level Stake
Hurdles	57	2	3	2	50	3.5	- 8.00
Chases	42	2	8	5	27	4.8	- 13.00
Totals	99	4	11	7	77	4.0	- 21.00

D McCain	3-78	- 34.00	A Maguire	1-2	+ 32.00
Market Rasen	1-1	+ 11.00	Sedgefield	1-8	+ 9.00
Warwick	1-3	+ 31.00	Bangor	1-16	- 1.00

No of horses racing for the stable	26	Total winning prize-money	£11,750

J C MCCONNOCHIE (Wilmcote, Warwicks)

	Races Run	1st	2nd	3rd	Unpl	Per cent	£1 Level Stake
Hurdles	13	0	0	2	11	-	- 13.00
Chases	38	3	3	6	26	7.9	- 8.00
Totals	51	3	3	8	37	5.9	- 21.00

A P McCoy	1-1	+ 4.00	S McNeill	1-27	- 14.00
A Maguire	1-2	+ 10.00			
Southwell	1-3	+ 10.00	Newton Abbot	1-5	0.00
Warwick	1-4	+ 8.00			

No of horses racing for the stable	12	Total winning prize-money	£12,270

M MCCORMACK (Sparsholt, Oxon)

	Races Run	1st	2nd	3rd	Unpl	Per cent	£1 Level Stake
Hurdles	17	2	3	5	7	11.8	+ 14.00
Chases	1	0	0	0	1	-	- 1.00
Totals	18	2	3	5	8	11.1	+ 13.00

A Thornton	2-9	+ 22.00			
Wincanton	1-1	+ 25.00	Towcester	1-3	+ 2.00

No of horses racing for the stable	3	Total winning prize-money	£5,904

G M MCCOURT (Letcombe Regis, Oxon)

	Races Run	1st	2nd	3rd	Unpl	Per cent	£1 Level Stake
Hurdles	13	0	0	1	12	-	- 13.00
Chases	22	9	2	3	8	40.9	+ 21.69
Totals	35	9	2	4	20	25.7	+ 8.69

BY MONTH

	W-R	Per cent	£1 Level Stake		W-R	Per cent	£1 Level Stake
June	0-0	-	0.00	December	0-0	-	0.00
July	0-0	-	0.00	January	0-0	-	0.00
August	0-0	-	0.00	February	2-7	28.6	+ 16.00
September	0-0	-	0.00	March	5-14	35.7	- 2.81
October	0-0	-	0.00	April	2-7	28.6	+ 2.50
November	0-0	-	0.00	May	0-7	-	- 7.00

DISTANCE

	W-R	Per cent	£1 Level Stake		W-R	Per cent	£1 Level Stake
Hurdles				Chases			
2m-2m 3f	0-11	-	- 11.00	2m-2m 3f	3-9	33.3	+ 14.25
2m 4f-2m 7f	0-2	-	- 2.00	2m 4f-2m 7f	4-6	66.7	+ 6.69
3m +	0-0	-	0.00	3m +	2-7	28.6	+ 0.75

TYPE OF RACE

	W-R	Per cent	£1 Level Stake		W-R	Per cent	£1 Level Stake
Novice hurdles	0-5	-	- 5.00	Selling	0-4	-	- 4.00
H'cap hurdles	0-3	-	- 3.00	Amateur	0-0	-	0.00
Novice chases	3-8	37.5	+ 0.69	Hunter chases	1-2	50.0	+ 2.00
H'cap chases	5-12	41.7	+ 19.00	N H Flat	0-1	-	- 1.00

COURSE GRADE

	W-R	Per cent	£1 Level Stake
Group 1	0-1	-	- 1.00
Group 2	4-7	57.1	+ 5.00
Group 3	2-10	20.0	- 2.56
Group 4	3-17	17.6	+ 7.25

FIRST TIME OUT

	W-R	Per cent	£1 Level Stake
Hurdles	0-2	-	- 2.00
Chases	1-1	100.0	+ 3.00
Totals	1-3	33.3	+ 1.00

JOCKEYS RIDING

	W-R	Per cent	£1 Level Stake		W-R	Per cent	£1 Level Stake
G McCourt	3-5	60.0	+ 4.69	Mr M Armytage	1-2	50.0	+ 2.00
D Fortt	2-8	25.0	- 1.75	R Dunwoody	1-3	33.3	- 1.75
B M Clifford	2-13	15.4	+ 9.50				

G Bradley	0-1	S Ryan	0-1
Mr A Lay	0-1	T J Murphy	0-1

COURSE RECORD

	Total W-R	Nov Hdles	H'cap Hdles	Nov Chses	H'cap Chses	Hunter Chses	N H Flat	£1 Level Stake
Fontwell	2-2	0-0	0-0	0-0	2-2	0-0	0-0	+ 6.50
Taunton	2-4	0-1	0-1	0-0	2-2	0-0	0-0	+ 16.25
Newton Abbot	1-1	0-0	0-0	1-1	0-0	0-0	0-0	+ 0.25
Fakenham	1-2	0-0	0-0	0-1	0-0	1-1	0-0	+ 2.00
Windsor	1-2	0-1	0-0	1-1	0-0	0-0	0-0	+ 4.00
Plumpton	1-4	0-1	0-1	1-2	0-0	0-0	0-0	- 2.56
Chepstow	1-4	0-2	0-0	0-0	1-2	0-0	0-0	- 1.75

Southwell	0-5	Towcester		0-2	Sandown	0-1
Hereford	0-3	Bangor		0-1	Worcester	0-1
Stratford	0-2	Huntingdon		0-1		

WINNING HORSES

	Races Run	1st	2nd	3rd	Unpl	Win £
Uncle Bert	6	3	0	1	2	8,858
Sister Stephanie	4	2	1	0	1	7,030
Lance Armstrong	3	2	0	0	1	6,576
Donna Del Lago	3	1	0	0	2	3,098
Prinzal	2	1	0	1	0	2,434

WINNING OWNERS

	Races Won	Value £		Races Won	Value £
Alec Tuckerman	3	8,858	M Maccarthy	1	3,098
The Antwick Partnership	2	7,030	Mrs Pam Froud	1	2,434
G L Porter	2	6,576			

No of horses racing for the stable	13	Total winning prize-money	£27,996

Favourites	6-11	54.5%	+ 5.69	Average SP of winner	3.9/1
Longest win seq	2	Longest losing seq	11	Return on stakes invested	24.8%

MRS M MCCOURT (Letcombe Regis, Oxon)

	Races Run	1st	2nd	3rd	Unpl	Per cent	£1 Level Stake
Hurdles	40	4	2	5	29	10.0	- 29.06
Chases	10	2	3	1	4	20.0	- 5.70
Totals	50	6	5	6	33	12.0	- 34.76

E Husband	2-4	- 0.56	B M Clifford	1-15	- 11.50
J Titley	1-2	+ 0.63	G McCourt	1-17	- 13.00
R Dunwoody	1-3	- 1.33			

Southwell	2-8	- 2.47	Fakenham	1-1	+ 1.63
Newton Abbot	2-8	- 2.83	Worcester	1-6	- 4.09

No of horses racing for the stable	18	Total winning prize-money	£16,081

T P MCGOVERN (Lewes, East Sussex)

	Races Run	1st	2nd	3rd	Unpl	Per cent	£1 Level Stake
Hurdles	38	8	6	6	18	21.1	+ 6.50
Chases	5	0	0	0	5	-	- 5.00
Totals	43	8	6	6	23	18.6	+ 1.50

BY MONTH

	W-R	Per cent	£1 Level Stake		W-R	Per cent	£1 Level Stake
June	0-0	-	0.00	December	2-5	40.0	+ 7.00
July	0-0	-	0.00	January	1-4	25.0	+ 5.00
August	2-2	100.0	+ 5.75	February	0-6	-	- 6.00
September	0-2	-	- 2.00	March	1-6	16.7	+ 1.00
October	1-7	14.3	- 3.25	April	0-1	-	- 1.00
November	1-5	20.0	0.00	May	0-5	-	- 5.00

DISTANCE

Hurdles	W-R	Per cent	£1 Level Stake	Chases	W-R	Per cent	£1 Level Stake
2m-2m 3f	2-22	9.1	- 12.25	2m-2m 3f	0-1	-	- 1.00
2m 4f-2m 7f	6-16	37.5	+ 18.75	2m 4f-2m 7f	0-2	-	- 2.00
3m +	0-0	-	0.00	3m +	0-2	-	- 2.00

TYPE OF RACE

	W-R	Per cent	£1 Level Stake		W-R	Per cent	£1 Level Stake
Novice hurdles	3-12	25.0	+ 4.50	Selling	3-11	27.3	+ 8.75
H'cap hurdles	2-16	12.5	- 7.75	Amateur	0-0	-	0.00
Novice chases	0-1	-	- 1.00	Hunter chases	0-0	-	0.00
H'cap chases	0-3	-	- 3.00	N H Flat	0-0	-	0.00

COURSE GRADE / FIRST TIME OUT

	W-R	Per cent	£1 Level Stake		W-R	Per cent	£1 Level Stake
Group 1	0-1	-	- 1.00	Hurdles	4-8	50.0	+ 16.25
Group 2	1-9	11.1	- 5.25	Chases	0-2	-	- 2.00
Group 3	5-25	20.0	+ 3.75				
Group 4	2-8	25.0	+ 4.00	Totals	4-10	40.0	+ 14.25

JOCKEYS RIDING

	W-R	Per cent	£1 Level Stake		W-R	Per cent	£1 Level Stake
A P McCoy	5-21	23.8	+ 5.00	D Bridgwater	1-4	25.0	+ 1.50
T J Murphy	1-3	33.3	+ 3.00	J R Kavanagh	1-6	16.7	+ 1.00

D Finnegan	0-2	D Gallagher	0-1	W Marston	0-1
A Maguire	0-1	G Hogan	0-1	W McFarland	0-1
B Fenton	0-1	R Johnson	0-1		

COURSE RECORD

	Total W-R	Nov Hdles	H'cap Hdles	Nov Chses	H'cap Chses	Hunter Chses	N H Flat	£1 Level Stake
Plumpton	3-8	2-4	1-3	0-0	0-1	0-0	0-0	+ 4.75
Southwell	2-3	1-2	1-1	0-0	0-0	0-0	0-0	+ 9.00
Windsor	1-4	0-0	1-2	0-0	0-2	0-0	0-0	+ 3.00
Folkestone	1-5	0-1	1-3	0-1	0-0	0-0	0-0	+ 4.00
Fontwell	1-8	0-2	1-5	0-0	0-1	0-0	0-0	- 4.25

Stratford	0-3	Warwick	0-2	Lingfield	0-1
Towcester	0-3	Cheltenham	0-1	Ludlow	0-1
Leicester	0-2	Fakenham	0-1	Wincanton	0-1

WINNING HORSES

	Races Run	1st	2nd	3rd	Unpl	Win £
Walking Tall	8	2	2	2	2	4,653
Riva Rock	2	2	0	0	0	4,354
North Bannister	5	2	0	2	1	4,159
Simply	6	1	1	0	4	2,881
Lord Glenvara	7	1	0	2	4	1,925

WINNING OWNERS

	Races Won	Value £		Races Won	Value £
Phil Collins	4	9,007	Liam Ogs Racing	2	4,159
Paul Gibbons	2	4,806			

No of horses racing for the stable	11	Total winning prize-money	£17,972

Favourites	1-5	20.0%	- 1.25	Average SP of winner		4.6/1
Longest win seq	2	Longest losing seq	11	Return on stakes invested		3.5%

1994/95 Form	4-33	12.1%	- 16.65	1992/93 Form	4-32	12.5%	+ 27.58
1993/94 Form	3-38	7.9%	- 17.12	1991/92 Form	0-39		

W MCKEOWN (Wide Open, Tyne & Wear)

	Races Run	1st	2nd	3rd	Unpl	Per cent	£1 Level Stake
Hurdles	27	4	2	0	21	14.8	+155.00
Chases	20	0	3	4	13	-	- 20.00
Totals	47	4	5	4	34	8.5	+135.00

P G Cahill	2-20	- 6.00	A Stanford	1-10	+ 91.00
Mr K Whelan	1-6	+ 61.00			

Catterick	2-4	+ 69.00	Hexham	1-9	- 1.00
Ayr	1-3	+ 98.00			

No of horses racing for the stable	11	Total winning prize-money	£6,426

MRS I MCKIE (Twyford, Bucks)

	Races Run	1st	2nd	3rd	Unpl	Per cent	£1 Level Stake
Hurdles	34	2	2	3	27	5.9	- 17.50
Chases	8	2	1	0	5	25.0	+ 9.50
Totals	42	4	3	3	32	9.5	- 8.00

L Harvey	4-31	+ 3.00			
Towcester	3-8	+ 13.00	Nottingham	1-2	+ 11.00

No of horses racing for the stable	14	Total winning prize-money	£14,147

B A MCMAHON (Hopwas, Staffs)

	Races Run	1st	2nd	3rd	Unpl	Per cent	£1 Level Stake
Hurdles	6	1	0	1	4	16.7	+ 11.00
Chases	0	0	0	0	0	-	0.00
Totals	6	1	0	1	4	16.7	+ 11.00

M W Martin	1-2	+ 15.00	Leicester	1-2	+ 15.00

No of horses racing for the stable	2	Total winning prize-money	£1,994

M D MCMILLAN (Bibury, Glos)

	Races Run	1st	2nd	3rd	Unpl	Per cent	£1 Level Stake
Hurdles	0	0	0	0	0	-	0.00
Chases	11	3	1	5	2	27.3	+ 1.75
Totals	11	3	1	5	2	27.3	+ 1.75

J R Kavanagh	2-10	- 1.75	L Wyer	1-1	+ 3.50
Hereford	2-2	+ 6.25	Market Rasen	1-1	+ 3.50

No of horses racing for the stable	1	Total winning prize-money	£9,534

M G MEAGHER (Westhead, Lancs)

	Races Run	1st	2nd	3rd	Unpl	Per cent	£1 Level Stake
Hurdles	25	2	2	2	19	8.0	+ 7.00
Chases	0	0	0	0	0	-	0.00
Totals	25	2	2	2	19	8.0	+ 7.00

D Byrne	1-7	+ 14.00	B Harding	1-8	+ 3.00
Catterick	1-3	+ 18.00	Bangor	1-5	+ 6.00

No of horses racing for the stable   8   Total winning prize-money   £4,194

S MELLOR (Wanborough, Wilts)

	Races Run	1st	2nd	3rd	Unpl	Per cent	£1 Level Stake
Hurdles	140	12	18	10	100	8.6	- 49.75
Chases	45	9	6	4	26	20.0	+ 8.43
Totals	185	21	24	14	126	11.4	- 41.32

BY MONTH

	W-R	Per cent	£1 Level Stake		W-R	Per cent	£1 Level Stake
June	3-6	50.0	+ 1.30	December	3-21	14.3	+ 8.25
July	0-7	-	- 7.00	January	0-23	-	- 23.00
August	0-2	-	- 2.00	February	0-17	-	- 17.00
September	1-6	16.7	- 3.25	March	3-32	9.4	+ 4.25
October	2-12	16.7	- 0.50	April	4-22	18.2	+ 12.38
November	5-28	17.9	- 5.75	May	0-9	-	- 9.00

DISTANCE

Hurdles	W-R	Per cent	£1 Level Stake	Chases	W-R	Per cent	£1 Level Stake
2m-2m 3f	11-108	10.2	- 21.00	2m-2m 3f	6-20	30.0	+ 1.68
2m 4f-2m 7f	1-24	4.2	- 20.75	2m 4f-2m 7f	2-14	14.3	+ 14.75
3m +	0-8	-	- 8.00	3m +	1-11	9.1	- 8.00

TYPE OF RACE

	W-R	Per cent	£1 Level Stake		W-R	Per cent	£1 Level Stake
Novice hurdles	3-59	5.1	- 38.50	Selling	3-10	30.0	+ 29.50
H'cap hurdles	5-60	8.3	- 33.25	Amateur	1-4	25.0	- 0.50
Novice chases	7-24	29.2	+ 0.68	Hunter chases	0-0	-	0.00
H'cap chases	2-19	10.5	+ 9.75	N H Flat	0-9	-	- 9.00

COURSE GRADE					FIRST TIME OUT			
	W–R	Per cent	£1 Level Stake			W–R	Per cent	£1 Level Stake
Group 1	5-35	14.3	- 15.50	Hurdles		2-26	7.7	- 20.50
Group 2	1-23	4.3	- 8.00	Chases		2-5	40.0	+ 5.80
Group 3	6-77	7.8	- 34.25					
Group 4	9-50	18.0	+ 16.43	Totals		4-31	12.9	- 14.70

JOCKEYS RIDING

	W–R	Per cent	£1 Level Stake			W–R	Per cent	£1 Level Stake
Christopher Webb	11-76	14.5	- 12.70	C Maude		1-2	50.0	+ 24.00
N Mann	7-73	9.6	- 27.62	M Perrett		1-19	5.3	- 13.50
Mr P Scott	1-2	50.0	+ 1.50					

A Thornton	0-2		D Bridgwater	0-1		Mr D Alers-Hankey	0-1
J Lodder	0-2		G Bradley	0-1		Mr G Elliott	0-1
A Procter	0-1		Miss E Joyce	0-1		R Dunwoody	0-1
C Llewellyn	0-1		Miss P Jones	0-1			

COURSE RECORD

	Total W–R	Nov Hdles	H'cap Hdles	Nov Chses	H'cap Chses	Hunter Chses	N H Flat	£1 Level Stake
Perth	3-6	1-2	1-2	1-1	0-1	0-0	0-0	+ 1.30
Cheltenham	2-4	0-0	0-1	1-1	1-2	0-0	0-0	+ 1.25
Aintree	2-4	0-0	1-1	1-2	0-1	0-0	0-0	+ 7.00
Market Rasen	2-5	0-0	1-2	1-2	0-0	0-0	0-1	+ 18.75
Exeter	2-7	0-2	1-3	0-0	1-2	0-0	0-0	+ 26.50
Hereford	2-11	1-3	0-4	1-2	0-1	0-0	0-1	+ 2.38
Windsor	2-18	1-9	1-4	0-1	0-4	0-0	0-0	- 8.00
Huntingdon	1-3	1-2	0-1	0-0	0-0	0-0	0-0	+ 0.50
Ludlow	1-3	0-1	0-0	1-1	0-1	0-0	0-0	+ 0.25
Fakenham	1-8	0-2	0-5	1-1	0-0	0-0	0-0	+ 1.00
Newbury	1-8	0-5	1-2	0-0	0-0	0-0	0-1	- 4.75
Lingfield	1-12	1-7	0-2	0-1	0-1	0-0	0-1	+ 3.00
Warwick	1-13	0-8	1-2	0-1	0-0	0-0	0-2	- 7.50

Stratford	0-11	Plumpton	0-5		Uttoxeter	0-3
Chepstow	0-7	Sandown	0-5		Southwell	0-2
Worcester	0-7	Ascot	0-4		Wincanton	0-2
Bangor	0-5	Nottingham	0-4		Fontwell	0-1
Folkestone	0-5	Taunton	0-4		Leicester	0-1
Haydock	0-5	Towcester	0-4			
Kempton	0-5	Newton Abbot	0-3			

WINNING HORSES

	Races Run	1st	2nd	3rd	Unpl	Win £
Bone Setter	12	4	2	1	5	12,317
Storm Falcon	4	3	0	1	0	11,893
Seod Rioga	8	2	1	1	4	7,507
Court Nap	8	2	2	0	4	5,043

Mellor S

Anlace	10	2	1	1	6	4,932
Titan Empress	10	1	1	1	7	3,398
Harding	10	1	2	3	4	2,801
Frankus	7	1	1	0	5	2,736
Oldhill Wood	10	1	1	0	8	2,520
Nessun Doro	9	1	2	0	6	2,339
Mason	8	1	0	1	6	1,989
Erlking	9	1	0	1	7	1,982
Hullo Mary Doll	9	1	1	1	6	1,902

WINNING OWNERS

	Races Won	Value £		Races Won	Value £
S P Tindall	5	14,279	T D J Syder	1	3,398
Lord Leverhulme	4	12,317	Jack Woodward & Partners	1	2,736
E R Dalby	3	11,893	David Mullen	1	2,520
Sir Michael Connell	2	5,043	Paul Porter & Partners	1	2,339
The Felix Bowness P'ship	2	4,932	Plough Jumpers (Ashton Keynes)	1	1,902

No of horses racing for the stable	31	Total winning prize-money		£61,359

Favourites	10-29	34.5%	+ 2.05	Average SP of winner	5.8/1
Longest win seq 3	Longest losing seq	46		Return on stakes invested	-22.3%

1994/95 Form	11-82	13.4%	+ 31.38	1992/93 Form	4-98	4.1%	- 74.62
1993/94 Form	9-110	8.2%	- 48.30	1991/92 Form	8-145	5.5%	- 87.92

MRS SALLY MESSER-BENNETTS (Wadebridge, Cornwall)

	Races Run	1st	2nd	3rd	Unpl	Per cent	£1 Level Stake
Hurdles	0	0	0	0	0	-	0.00
Chases	5	1	0	0	4	20.0	+ 1.00
Totals	5	1	0	0	4	20.0	+ 1.00

A P McCoy	1-2	+ 4.00	Exeter	1-3	+ 3.00

No of horses racing for the stable	1	Total winning prize-money	£3,496

MISS M K MILLIGAN (Middleham, North Yorks)

	Races Run	1st	2nd	3rd	Unpl	Per cent	£1 Level Stake
Hurdles	57	2	7	8	40	3.5	- 49.33
Chases	9	1	1	2	5	11.1	- 6.00
Totals	66	3	8	10	45	4.5	- 55.33

Richard Guest	3-27	- 16.33			
Leicester	1-2	+ 4.00	Hexham	1-12	- 9.00
Catterick	1-5	- 3.33			

No of horses racing for the stable 20 Total winning prize-money £7,182

B R MILLMAN (Kentisbeare, Devon)

	Races Run	1st	2nd	3rd	Unpl	Per cent	£1 Level Stake
Hurdles	39	4	5	4	26	10.3	- 21.59
Chases	10	0	2	0	8	-	- 10.00
Totals	49	4	7	4	34	8.2	- 31.59

D Salter	3-38	- 26.09	J R Kavanagh	1-2	+ 3.50
Windsor	1-2	+ 2.50	Exeter	1-10	- 4.50
Hereford	1-2	- 0.09	Taunton	1-11	- 5.50

No of horses racing for the stable 14 Total winning prize-money £9,677

T G MILLS (Headley, Surrey)

	Races Run	1st	2nd	3rd	Unpl	Per cent	£1 Level Stake
Hurdles	9	1	2	1	5	11.1	- 5.25
Chases	0	0	0	0	0	-	0.00
Totals	9	1	2	1	5	11.1	- 5.25

Christopher Webb	1-3	+ 0.75	Plumpton	1-1	+ 2.75

No of horses racing for the stable 3 Total winning prize-money £2,364

C W MITCHELL (Buckland Newton, Dorset)

	Races Run	1st	2nd	3rd	Unpl	Per cent	£1 Level Stake
Hurdles	7	0	0	0	7	-	- 7.00
Chases	6	1	1	0	4	16.7	0.00
Totals	13	1	1	0	11	7.7	- 7.00

S McNeill	1-1	+ 5.00	Chepstow	1-2	+ 4.00

No of horses racing for the stable   5   Total winning prize-money   £3,894

N R MITCHELL (Piddletrenthide, Dorset)

	Races Run	1st	2nd	3rd	Unpl	Per cent	£1 Level Stake
Hurdles	37	4	1	2	30	10.8	- 0.50
Chases	19	2	2	3	12	10.5	- 11.42
Totals	56	6	3	5	42	10.7	- 11.92

D Skyrme	2-15	- 2.50	G Upton	1-5	- 2.00
A P McCoy	1-1	+ 2.25	Sophie Mitchell	1-16	+ 5.00
K P Gaule	1-4	+ 0.33			

Wincanton	2-7	+ 4.33	Newton Abbot	1-6	- 0.50
Fontwell	1-1	+ 2.00	Exeter	1-16	- 12.75
Taunton	1-4	+ 17.00			

No of horses racing for the stable   12   Total winning prize-money   £16,408

D MOFFATT (Cartmel, Cumbria)

	Races Run	1st	2nd	3rd	Unpl	Per cent	£1 Level Stake
Hurdles	59	2	6	6	45	3.4	- 47.00
Chases	2	0	0	0	2	-	- 2.00
Totals	61	2	6	6	47	3.3	- 49.00

D J Moffatt	2-51	- 39.00

Haydock	1-6	- 1.00	Cartmel	1-7	0.00

No of horses racing for the stable   15   Total winning prize-money   £9,823

P MONTEITH (Rosewell, Lothian)

	Races Run	1st	2nd	3rd	Unpl	Per cent	£1 Level Stake
Hurdles	78	11	14	11	42	14.1	- 41.64
Chases	63	13	16	10	24	20.6	- 14.51
Totals	141	24	30	21	66	17.0	- 56.15

BY MONTH

	W-R	Per cent	£1 Level Stake		W-R	Per cent	£1 Level Stake
June	1-3	33.3	+ 4.00	December	1-6	16.7	- 1.00
July	0-3	-	- 3.00	January	2-18	11.1	- 8.00
August	0-2	-	- 2.00	February	1-14	7.1	- 11.50
September	3-15	20.0	- 8.48	March	4-22	18.2	- 7.27
October	5-14	35.7	+ 4.69	April	1-19	5.3	- 16.00
November	4-19	21.1	- 7.50	May	2-6	33.3	- 0.09

DISTANCE

	W-R	Per cent	£1 Level Stake		W-R	Per cent	£1 Level Stake
Hurdles				Chases			
2m-2m 3f	8-65	12.3	- 35.06	2m-2m 3f	8-33	24.2	- 12.51
2m 4f-2m 7f	2-10	20.0	- 5.83	2m 4f-2m 7f	2-13	15.4	- 0.50
3m +	1-3	33.3	- 0.75	3m +	3-17	17.6	- 1.50

TYPE OF RACE

	W-R	Per cent	£1 Level Stake		W-R	Per cent	£1 Level Stake
Novice hurdles	6-37	16.2	- 17.83	Selling	4-15	26.7	+ 1.94
H'cap hurdles	2-22	9.1	- 17.25	Amateur	0-2	-	- 2.00
Novice chases	3-19	15.8	- 11.77	Hunter chases	0-0	-	0.00
H'cap chases	9-42	21.4	- 5.24	N H Flat	0-4	-	- 4.00

COURSE GRADE / FIRST TIME OUT

	W-R	Per cent	£1 Level Stake		W-R	Per cent	£1 Level Stake
Group 1	6-39	15.4	- 20.27	Hurdles	1-19	5.3	- 16.00
Group 2	0-1	-	- 1.00	Chases	2-8	25.0	+ 1.60
Group 3	2-6	33.3	+ 3.00				
Group 4	16-95	16.8	- 37.88	Totals	3-27	11.1	- 14.40

JOCKEYS RIDING

	W-R	Per cent	£1 Level Stake		W-R	Per cent	£1 Level Stake
A Dobbin	13-50	26.0	- 6.80	B Harding	3-21	14.3	- 12.08
P G Cahill	7-41	17.1	- 15.27	T Jenks	1-9	11.1	- 2.00

D Parker	0-4	L O'Hara	0-2	D Bridgwater	0-1
R Supple	0-3	Mr R Hale	0-2	M Foster	0-1
A Thornton	0-2	P Carberry	0-2		
J Titley	0-2	A S Smith	0-1		

COURSE RECORD

	Total W-R	Nov Hdles	H'cap Hdles	Nov Chses	H'cap Chses	Hunter Chses	N H Flat	£1 Level Stake
Kelso	6-34	3-14	0-8	0-3	3-9	0-0	0-0	- 6.56
Newcastle	3-11	2-7	0-1	1-2	0-1	0-0	0-0	+ 0.50
Hexham	3-12	1-4	1-3	0-1	1-4	0-0	0-0	- 5.33
Perth	3-13	0-2	0-4	1-3	2-3	0-0	0-1	- 3.90
Ayr	3-26	2-9	0-4	1-3	0-8	0-0	0-2	- 18.77
Carlisle	2-11	0-1	1-2	0-1	1-7	0-0	0-0	- 4.00
Market Rasen	1-3	1-1	0-1	0-1	0-0	0-0	0-0	+ 4.00
Cartmel	1-3	0-0	0-0	0-2	1-1	0-0	0-0	- 1.09
Catterick	1-3	0-0	0-1	0-0	1-2	0-0	0-0	- 1.00
Sedgefield	1-11	0-1	0-2	0-1	1-7	0-0	0-0	- 6.00

Musselburgh	0-9	Doncaster	0-1	Wetherby	0-1
Southwell	0-2	Haydock	0-1		

WINNING HORSES

	Races Run	1st	2nd	3rd	Unpl	Win £
Emerald Storm	7	3	1	0	3	12,979
Flash of Realm	14	3	2	2	7	7,440
Grouse-N-Heather	6	2	1	0	3	6,701
Wild Rose of York	13	3	2	3	5	6,332
Beldine	8	2	2	0	4	5,959
Aragon Ayr	3	2	1	0	0	4,590
Done Well	5	2	1	1	1	4,415
Unor	2	1	1	0	0	4,358
Killimor Lad	8	1	2	2	3	4,160
Montrave	8	1	3	2	2	3,223
Juke Box Billy	8	1	4	1	2	2,861
Electric Committee	7	1	1	2	3	2,373
Rallegio	5	1	1	1	2	2,155
Master Bavard	3	1	1	0	1	1,976

WINNING OWNERS

	Races Won	Value £		Races Won	Value £
T P Finch	3	12,979	C Jenkins	1	4,160
W L Monteith	5	12,291	D St Clair	1	3,223
Allan W Melville	5	11,855	Everaldo Partnership	1	2,861
D J Fairbairn	2	6,701	Mrs Maud Monteith	1	2,373
Kelso Members Lowflyers Club	2	4,590	Guthrie Robertson	1	2,155
Miss H B Hamilton	1	4,358	P Monteith	1	1,976

No of horses racing for the stable	27	Total winning prize-money	£69,522

Favourites	14-43	32.6%	- 8.15	Average SP of winner	2.5/1
Longest win seq	2	Longest losing seq	18	Return on stakes invested	-39.8%

1994/95 Form	18-148	12.2%	- 6.34	1992/93 Form	14-131	10.7%	- 75.56
1993/94 Form	20-146	13.7%	+131.71	1991/92 Form	23-107	21.5%	+ 13.29

G L MOORE (Epsom, Surrey)

	Races Run	1st	2nd	3rd	Unpl	Per cent	£1 Level Stake
Hurdles	45	8	4	2	31	17.8	+ 6.92
Chases	0	0	0	0	0	-	0.00
Totals	45	8	4	2	31	17.8	+ 6.92

BY MONTH

	W-R	Per cent	£1 Level Stake		W-R	Per cent	£1 Level Stake
June	0-0	-	0.00	December	0-5	-	- 5.00
July	0-0	-	0.00	January	2-7	28.6	+ 18.50
August	0-1	-	- 1.00	February	1-4	25.0	+ 2.00
September	0-0	-	0.00	March	3-13	23.1	+ 4.25
October	2-4	50.0	- 0.83	April	0-2	-	- 2.00
November	0-9	-	- 9.00	May	0-0	-	0.00

DISTANCE

Hurdles	W-R	Per cent	£1 Level Stake	Chases	W-R	Per cent	£1 Level Stake
2m-2m 3f	6-39	15.4	+ 9.75	2m-2m 3f	0-0	-	0.00
2m 4f-2m 7f	2-6	33.3	- 2.83	2m 4f-2m 7f	0-0	-	0.00
3m +	0-0	-	0.00	3m +	0-0	-	0.00

TYPE OF RACE

	W-R	Per cent	£1 Level Stake		W-R	Per cent	£1 Level Stake
Novice hurdles	1-19	5.3	- 17.33	Selling	0-3	-	- 3.00
H'cap hurdles	7-22	31.8	+ 28.25	Amateur	0-0	-	0.00
Novice chases	0-0	-	0.00	Hunter chases	0-0	-	0.00
H'cap chases	0-0	-	0.00	N H Flat	0-1	-	- 1.00

COURSE GRADE / FIRST TIME OUT

	W-R	Per cent	£1 Level Stake		W-R	Per cent	£1 Level Stake
Group 1	1-13	7.7	+ 8.00	Hurdles	2-16	12.5	+ 6.67
Group 2	5-18	27.8	+ 9.75	Chases	0-0	-	0.00
Group 3	2-12	16.7	- 8.83				
Group 4	0-2	-	- 2.00	Totals	2-16	12.5	+ 6.67

JOCKEYS RIDING

	W-R	Per cent	£1 Level Stake			W-R	Per cent	£1 Level Stake
A P McCoy	5-10	50.0	+ 29.42	M Attwater		3-12	25.0	+ 0.50
E Murphy	0-5			D Gallagher	0-2	Peter Hobbs		0-1
A Thornton	0-4			G Upton	0-1	R Dunwoody		0-1
M A Fitzgerald	0-4			J Osborne	0-1			
M Richards	0-3			L Wyer	0-1			

COURSE RECORD

	Total W-R	Nov Hdles	H'cap Hdles	Nov Chses	H'cap Chses	Hunter Chses	N H Flat	£1 Level Stake
Lingfield	4-11	0-5	4-6	0-0	0-0	0-0	0-0	+ 4.75
Plumpton	2-7	1-4	1-3	0-0	0-0	0-0	0-0	- 3.83
Kempton	1-3	0-1	1-2	0-0	0-0	0-0	0-0	+ 18.00
Fontwell	1-6	0-4	1-2	0-0	0-0	0-0	0-0	+ 6.00
Newbury	0-5	Aintree			0-1	Taunton		0-1
Windsor	0-3	Ascot			0-1	Towcester		0-1
Folkestone	0-2	Cheltenham			0-1			
Sandown	0-2	Chepstow			0-1			

WINNING HORSES

	Races Run	1st	2nd	3rd	Unpl	Win £
Warm Spell	3	1	0	0	2	17,125
Tickerty's Gift	10	4	1	2	3	11,855
Call Me Albi	3	2	0	0	1	4,751
Sophie May	8	1	1	0	6	2,511

WINNING OWNERS

	Races Won	Value £		Races Won	Value £
K Higson	5	28,980	J Daniels	1	2,511
Mrs Rita Bates	2	4,751			

No of horses racing for the stable		16	Total winning prize-money		£36,242
Favourites	4-7	57.1% + 1.42	Average SP of winner		5.5/1
Longest win seq	2	Longest losing seq 15	Return on stakes invested		15.4%
1994/95 Form	6-43	14.0% - 18.17	1993/94 Form	2-21	9.5% - 12.75

G M MOORE (Middleham, North Yorks)

	Races Run	1st	2nd	3rd	Unpl	Per cent	£1 Level Stake
Hurdles	127	12	13	16	86	9.4	- 56.00
Chases	21	5	2	1	13	23.8	- 9.33
Totals	148	17	15	17	99	11.5	- 65.33

BY MONTH

	W-R	Per cent	£1 Level Stake		W-R	Per cent	£1 Level Stake
June	0-1	-	- 1.00	December	0-13	-	- 13.00
July	0-2	-	- 2.00	January	0-8	-	- 8.00
August	0-2	-	- 2.00	February	0-21	-	- 21.00
September	1-4	25.0	0.00	March	3-27	11.1	- 16.00
October	3-9	33.3	- 2.71	April	1-18	5.6	- 14.50
November	2-21	9.5	+ 7.50	May	7-22	31.8	+ 7.38

DISTANCE

Hurdles	W-R	Per cent	£1 Level Stake	Chases	W-R	Per cent	£1 Level Stake
2m-2m 3f	8-75	10.7	- 34.25	2m-2m 3f	2-9	22.2	- 3.25
2m 4f-2m 7f	1-34	2.9	- 30.75	2m 4f-2m 7f	0-4	-	- 4.00
3m +	3-18	16.7	+ 9.00	3m +	3-8	37.5	- 2.08

TYPE OF RACE

	W-R	Per cent	£1 Level Stake		W-R	Per cent	£1 Level Stake
Novice hurdles	6-56	10.7	- 18.00	Selling	0-7	-	- 7.00
H'cap hurdles	6-49	12.2	- 16.00	Amateur	0-0	-	0.00
Novice chases	2-11	18.2	- 7.46	Hunter chases	0-0	-	0.00
H'cap chases	3-10	30.0	- 1.87	N H Flat	0-15	-	- 15.00

COURSE GRADE / FIRST TIME OUT

	W-R	Per cent	£1 Level Stake		W-R	Per cent	£1 Level Stake
Group 1	3-41	7.3	- 9.50	Hurdles	3-30	10.0	+ 2.50
Group 2	1-15	6.7	- 13.71	Chases	1-2	50.0	+ 0.75
Group 3	1-12	8.3	- 9.25				
Group 4	12-80	15.0	- 32.87	Totals	4-32	12.5	+ 3.25

JOCKEYS RIDING

	W-R	Per cent	£1 Level Stake		W-R	Per cent	£1 Level Stake
N Bentley	9-60	15.0	- 7.58	E Callaghan	1-1	100.0	+ 4.00
J Callaghan	6-77	7.8	- 54.00	T Hogg	1-5	20.0	- 2.75

P Walsh	0-2	P Carberry	0-1
N Williamson	0-1	R Garrity	0-1

COURSE RECORD

	Total W-R	Nov Hdles	H'cap Hdles	Nov Chses	H'cap Chses	Hunter Chses	N H Flat	£1 Level Stake
Sedgefield	5-22	3-7	2-12	0-2	0-0	0-0	0-1	- 2.25
Cartmel	3-6	1-2	1-3	0-0	1-1	0-0	0-0	+ 1.38
Kelso	3-14	1-5	1-5	1-4	0-0	0-0	0-0	+ 2.25
Newbury	1-1	0-0	0-0	0-0	1-1	0-0	0-0	+ 2.00
Worcester	1-2	0-1	0-0	0-0	1-1	0-0	0-0	+ 0.75
Southwell	1-5	0-1	1-3	0-0	0-1	0-0	0-0	- 1.25
Ayr	1-12	0-6	1-3	0-0	0-1	0-0	0-2	- 4.50
Wetherby	1-15	0-7	0-4	1-1	0-2	0-0	0-1	- 13.71
Newcastle	1-16	1-8	0-6	0-1	0-0	0-0	0-1	+ 5.00

Carlisle	0-10	Catterick	0-6	Market Rasen	0-2
Haydock	0-10	Musselburgh	0-5	Leicester	0-1
Hexham	0-8	Bangor	0-3	Nottingham	0-1
Perth	0-7	Doncaster	0-2		

WINNING HORSES

	Races Run	1st	2nd	3rd	Unpl	Win £
Glenugie	10	3	0	2	5	10,999
Gale Ahead	6	3	1	0	2	10,118
Wee River	6	2	1	1	2	7,814
Tallywagger	8	2	2	2	2	5,338
House of Dreams	5	2	0	0	3	5,184
Devilry	7	1	1	0	5	3,566
Classic Crest	10	1	3	0	6	2,863
Bold Account	4	1	1	1	1	2,754
Xaipete	7	1	0	1	5	2,373
Nonios	9	1	1	3	4	1,814

WINNING OWNERS

	Races Won	Value £		Races Won	Value £
John Robson	4	12,872	Richard Johnson	1	3,566
Frazer Hines	3	10,999	G B A & G Peacock	1	2,863
S Graham	2	7,814	Mrs Susan Moore	1	2,373
J R Featherstone	2	5,338	B R A T S	1	1,814
J & M Leisure Ltd	2	5,184			

No of horses racing for the stable		32	Total winning prize-money	£52,823

Favourites	10-25	40.0%	+ 1.17	Average SP of winner		3.9/1
Longest win seq	3	Longest losing seq	71	Return on stakes invested		-44.1%

1994/95 Form	28-167	16.8%	- 48.01	1992/93 Form	29-200	14.5%	- 72.75
1993/94 Form	26-164	15.9%	- 25.64	1991/92 Form	38-240	15.8%	- 71.40

J S MOORE (East Garston, Berks)

	Races Run	1st	2nd	3rd	Unpl	Per cent	£1 Level Stake
Hurdles	31	3	1	3	24	9.7	- 20.50
Chases	0	0	0	0	0	-	0.00
Totals	31	3	1	3	24	9.7	- 20.50

W McFarland	3-26	- 15.50			
Hereford	1-2	+ 1.25	Towcester	1-4	- 0.25
Fontwell	1-4	- 0.50			

No of horses racing for the stable	9	Total winning prize-money	£7,265

K A MORGAN (Waltham-on-the-Wolds, Leics)

	Races Run	1st	2nd	3rd	Unpl	Per cent	£1 Level Stake
Hurdles	106	16	5	14	71	15.1	- 10.14
Chases	8	0	0	0	8	-	- 8.00
Totals	114	16	5	14	79	14.0	- 18.14

BY MONTH

	W-R	Per cent	£1 Level Stake		W-R	Per cent	£1 Level Stake
June	0-6	-	- 6.00	December	0-7	-	- 7.00
July	1-3	33.3	+ 2.50	January	1-11	9.1	+ 6.00
August	1-2	50.0	+ 4.00	February	2-14	14.3	+ 3.00
September	2-6	33.3	+ 5.00	March	0-14	-	- 14.00
October	3-10	30.0	- 1.37	April	2-9	22.2	+ 4.00
November	3-16	18.8	- 2.02	May	1-16	6.3	- 12.25

DISTANCE

	W-R	Per cent	£1 Level Stake		W-R	Per cent	£1 Level Stake
Hurdles				Chases			
2m-2m 3f	10-83	12.0	- 15.74	2m-2m 3f	0-2	-	- 2.00
2m 4f-2m 7f	4-12	33.3	+ 7.60	2m 4f-2m 7f	0-5	-	- 5.00
3m +	2-11	18.2	- 2.00	3m +	0-1	-	- 1.00

TYPE OF RACE

	W-R	Per cent	£1 Level Stake		W-R	Per cent	£1 Level Stake
Novice hurdles	7-22	31.8	+ 20.73	Selling	3-11	27.3	+ 5.25
H'cap hurdles	6-52	11.5	- 15.12	Amateur	0-1	-	- 1.00
Novice chases	0-2	-	- 2.00	Hunter chases	0-0	-	0.00
H'cap chases	0-6	-	- 6.00	N H Flat	0-20	-	- 20.00

Morgan K A

<table>
<tr><th colspan="4">COURSE GRADE</th><th colspan="4">FIRST TIME OUT</th></tr>
<tr><th></th><th>W-R</th><th>Per cent</th><th>£1 Level Stake</th><th></th><th>W-R</th><th>Per cent</th><th>£1 Level Stake</th></tr>
<tr><td>Group 1</td><td>0-8</td><td>-</td><td>- 8.00</td><td>Hurdles</td><td>2-27</td><td>7.4</td><td>- 15.00</td></tr>
<tr><td>Group 2</td><td>0-11</td><td>-</td><td>- 11.00</td><td>Chases</td><td>0-1</td><td>-</td><td>- 1.00</td></tr>
<tr><td>Group 3</td><td>12-74</td><td>16.2</td><td>+ 4.13</td><td></td><td></td><td></td><td></td></tr>
<tr><td>Group 4</td><td>4-21</td><td>19.0</td><td>- 3.27</td><td>Totals</td><td>2-28</td><td>7.1</td><td>- 16.00</td></tr>
</table>

JOCKEYS RIDING

<table>
<tr><th></th><th>W-R</th><th>Per cent</th><th>£1 Level Stake</th><th></th><th>W-R</th><th>Per cent</th><th>£1 Level Stake</th></tr>
<tr><td>A S Smith</td><td>12-85</td><td>14.1</td><td>- 15.39</td><td>W Fry</td><td>1-1</td><td>100.0</td><td>+ 4.50</td></tr>
<tr><td>R Dunwoody</td><td>2-4</td><td>50.0</td><td>+ 5.75</td><td>R Massey</td><td>1-15</td><td>6.7</td><td>- 4.00</td></tr>
</table>

E Callaghan	0-2	M Dwyer	0-1	P Niven	0-1
G Ryan	0-1	Miss Joanna Holmes	0-1	S Ryan	0-1
Gary Lyons	0-1	Mr J Culloty	0-1		

COURSE RECORD

<table>
<tr><th></th><th>Total W-R</th><th>Nov Hdles</th><th>H'cap Hdles</th><th>Nov Chses</th><th>H'cap Chses</th><th>Hunter Chses</th><th>N H Flat</th><th>£1 Level Stake</th></tr>
<tr><td>Catterick</td><td>3-7</td><td>2-3</td><td>1-2</td><td>0-1</td><td>0-0</td><td>0-0</td><td>0-1</td><td>+ 30.00</td></tr>
<tr><td>Huntingdon</td><td>3-15</td><td>0-2</td><td>3-9</td><td>0-0</td><td>0-2</td><td>0-0</td><td>0-2</td><td>- 4.12</td></tr>
<tr><td>Market Rasen</td><td>3-21</td><td>0-2</td><td>3-11</td><td>0-1</td><td>0-1</td><td>0-0</td><td>0-6</td><td>- 6.50</td></tr>
<tr><td>Stratford</td><td>2-4</td><td>1-1</td><td>1-2</td><td>0-0</td><td>0-1</td><td>0-0</td><td>0-0</td><td>+ 5.75</td></tr>
<tr><td>Hexham</td><td>1-1</td><td>1-1</td><td>0-0</td><td>0-0</td><td>0-0</td><td>0-0</td><td>0-0</td><td>+ 1.10</td></tr>
<tr><td>Perth</td><td>1-4</td><td>1-2</td><td>0-1</td><td>0-0</td><td>0-0</td><td>0-0</td><td>0-1</td><td>+ 2.00</td></tr>
<tr><td>Sedgefield</td><td>1-4</td><td>1-1</td><td>0-1</td><td>0-0</td><td>0-1</td><td>0-0</td><td>0-1</td><td>- 1.37</td></tr>
<tr><td>Southwell</td><td>1-6</td><td>1-2</td><td>0-3</td><td>0-0</td><td>0-0</td><td>0-0</td><td>0-1</td><td>+ 1.00</td></tr>
<tr><td>Nottingham</td><td>1-8</td><td>1-4</td><td>0-3</td><td>0-0</td><td>0-0</td><td>0-0</td><td>0-1</td><td>- 2.00</td></tr>
</table>

Uttoxeter	0-10	Hereford	0-2	Kempton	0-1
Wetherby	0-9	Leicester	0-2	Sandown	0-1
Worcester	0-5	Newcastle	0-2	Warwick	0-1
Chepstow	0-2	Towcester	0-2	Windsor	0-1
Doncaster	0-2	Ayr	0-1		
Fakenham	0-2	Cheltenham	0-1		

WINNING HORSES

<table>
<tr><th></th><th>Races Run</th><th>1st</th><th>2nd</th><th>3rd</th><th>Unpl</th><th>Win £</th></tr>
<tr><td>Moobakkr</td><td>11</td><td>4</td><td>0</td><td>2</td><td>5</td><td>10,195</td></tr>
<tr><td>Wamdha</td><td>10</td><td>3</td><td>0</td><td>3</td><td>4</td><td>8,226</td></tr>
<tr><td>King Athelstan</td><td>7</td><td>1</td><td>0</td><td>1</td><td>5</td><td>3,136</td></tr>
<tr><td>Wisdom</td><td>8</td><td>1</td><td>0</td><td>3</td><td>4</td><td>2,677</td></tr>
<tr><td>Nocatchim</td><td>8</td><td>1</td><td>1</td><td>2</td><td>4</td><td>2,460</td></tr>
<tr><td>Tonnerre</td><td>2</td><td>1</td><td>0</td><td>0</td><td>1</td><td>2,453</td></tr>
<tr><td>George Ashford</td><td>7</td><td>1</td><td>0</td><td>1</td><td>5</td><td>2,422</td></tr>
<tr><td>Opera Fan</td><td>2</td><td>1</td><td>0</td><td>0</td><td>1</td><td>2,339</td></tr>
<tr><td>Phalarope</td><td>3</td><td>1</td><td>2</td><td>0</td><td>0</td><td>2,206</td></tr>
<tr><td>Sylvan Sabre</td><td>4</td><td>1</td><td>0</td><td>0</td><td>3</td><td>2,128</td></tr>
<tr><td>Wassl Street</td><td>2</td><td>1</td><td>0</td><td>0</td><td>1</td><td>2,108</td></tr>
</table>

WINNING OWNERS

	Races Won	Value £		Races Won	Value £
Ian Guise	5	12,648	R E Gray	1	2,460
T R Pryke	4	10,903	R D Piper	1	2,339
B Leatherday	2	4,530	Foreneish Racing	1	2,206
Rex Norton	1	3,136	J C Fretwell	1	2,128

No of horses racing for the stable		30	Total winning prize-money	£40,350

Favourites	6-19	31.6%	- 0.64	Average SP of winner		5.0/1
Longest win seq	1	Longest losing seq	19	Return on stakes invested		-15.9%

1994/95 Form	16-114	14.0%	- 14.78	1992/93 Form	13-126	10.3%	- 52.15
1993/94 Form	12-102	11.8%	- 20.25	1991/92 Form	8-114	7.0%	- 30.50

M P MUGGERIDGE (East Garston, Berks)

	Races Run	1st	2nd	3rd	Unpl	Per cent	£1 Level Stake
Hurdles	17	0	2	2	13	–	- 17.00
Chases	7	2	0	3	2	28.6	+ 1.25
Totals	24	2	2	5	15	8.3	- 15.75

B Powell	2-8	+ 0.25	Plumpton	2-4	+ 4.25

No of horses racing for the stable		8	Total winning prize-money	£7,328

W R MUIR (Lambourn, Berks)

	Races Run	1st	2nd	3rd	Unpl	Per cent	£1 Level Stake
Hurdles	45	2	6	6	31	4.4	- 28.17
Chases	2	0	0	0	2	–	- 2.00
Totals	47	2	6	6	33	4.3	- 30.17

M Richards	2-24	- 7.17

Newton Abbot	1-1	+ 14.00	Fontwell	1-2	- 0.17

No of horses racing for the stable		9	Total winning prize-money	£4,156

J W MULLINS (Wilsford-cum-Lake, Wilts)

	Races Run	1st	2nd	3rd	Unpl	Per cent	£1 Level Stake
Hurdles	66	4	2	6	54	6.1	+ 16.50
Chases	45	2	7	1	35	4.4	- 39.00
Totals	111	6	9	7	89	5.4	- 22.50

S Curran	5-70	+ 1.50	R Greene	1-13	+ 4.00
Taunton	2-5	+ 15.25	Newton Abbot	1-6	+ 5.00
Hereford	2-12	+ 42.50	Huntingdon	1-11	- 8.25

No of horses racing for the stable   24   Total winning prize-money   £13,168

F MURPHY (Middleham, North Yorks)

	Races Run	1st	2nd	3rd	Unpl	Per cent	£1 Level Stake
Hurdles	73	12	7	5	49	16.4	- 23.20
Chases	44	7	5	9	23	15.9	+ 12.82
Totals	117	19	12	14	72	16.2	- 10.38

BY MONTH

	W-R	Per cent	£1 Level Stake		W-R	Per cent	£1 Level Stake
June	0-2	-	- 2.00	December	0-7	-	- 7.00
July	1-3	33.3	+ 0.50	January	2-15	13.3	- 7.27
August	0-1	-	- 1.00	February	2-21	9.5	- 15.75
September	0-4	-	- 4.00	March	5-30	16.7	+ 4.32
October	0-2	-	- 2.00	April	1-12	8.3	- 6.50
November	5-12	41.7	+ 7.75	May	3-8	37.5	+ 22.57

DISTANCE

Hurdles	W-R	Per cent	£1 Level Stake	Chases	W-R	Per cent	£1 Level Stake
2m-2m 3f	10-51	19.6	- 4.57	2m-2m 3f	3-13	23.1	- 5.68
2m 4f-2m 7f	1-12	8.3	- 10.20	2m 4f-2m 7f	1-16	6.3	- 12.50
3m +	1-10	10.0	- 8.43	3m +	3-15	20.0	+ 31.00

TYPE OF RACE

	W-R	Per cent	£1 Level Stake		W-R	Per cent	£1 Level Stake
Novice hurdles	6-33	18.2	- 2.32	Selling	1-4	25.0	+ 1.50
H'cap hurdles	3-25	12.0	- 15.63	Amateur	1-5	20.0	+ 12.00
Novice chases	3-21	14.3	- 13.68	Hunter chases	0-0	-	0.00
H'cap chases	3-20	15.0	+ 12.50	N H Flat	2-9	22.2	- 4.75

COURSE GRADE					FIRST TIME OUT			
	W-R	Per cent	£1 Level Stake			W-R	Per cent	£1 Level Stake
Group 1	5-40	12.5	- 1.43	Hurdles		4-28	14.3	- 14.57
Group 2	2-5	40.0	+ 27.00	Chases		1-11	9.1	- 7.50
Group 3	4-34	11.8	- 21.18					
Group 4	8-38	21.1	- 14.77	Totals		5-39	12.8	- 22.07

JOCKEYS RIDING

	W-R	Per cent	£1 Level Stake		W-R	Per cent	£1 Level Stake
P Carberry	7-43	16.3	+ 4.05	K P Gaule	1-2	50.0	+ 3.50
R Dunwoody	2-3	66.7	+ 11.50	A Maguire	1-3	33.3	- 1.20
Mr K Whelan	2-3	66.7	+ 16.00	L Wyer	1-5	20.0	+ 2.00
B Fenton	2-7	28.6	- 2.43	D J Kavanagh	1-13	7.7	- 11.43
M Dwyer	1-2	50.0	+ 0.88	M Foster	1-13	7.7	- 10.25

A P McCoy	0-4	R Supple	0-2	Mr B R Hamilton	0-1
R Johnson	0-3	A Thornton	0-1	Mr P Matthias	0-1
Capt A Ogden	0-2	B Powell	0-1	N Bentley	0-1
D Gallagher	0-2	J Titley	0-1	S Porritt	0-1
Miss E Doyle	0-2	M A Fitzgerald	0-1		

COURSE RECORD

	Total W-R	Nov Hdles	H'cap Hdles	Nov Chses	H'cap Chses	Hunter Chses	N H Flat	£1 Level Stake
Hereford	3-5	0-0	0-2	3-3	0-0	0-0	0-0	+ 2.32
Sedgefield	3-8	1-3	1-1	0-2	1-2	0-0	0-0	- 0.32
Wetherby	2-5	0-2	1-1	0-0	1-2	0-0	0-0	+ 27.00
Kelso	2-8	2-4	0-1	0-1	0-2	0-0	0-0	+ 0.23
Cheltenham	2-10	1-1	0-5	0-1	1-3	0-0	0-0	+ 18.00
Huntingdon	1-3	0-1	1-1	0-0	0-0	0-0	0-1	+ 2.50
Ascot	1-3	1-1	0-1	0-0	0-1	0-0	0-0	+ 4.00
Newcastle	1-4	1-2	0-0	0-2	0-0	0-0	0-0	- 2.43
Market Rasen	1-5	0-1	0-0	0-0	1-3	0-0	0-1	- 1.50
Newbury	1-5	0-1	0-1	0-1	0-1	0-0	1-1	- 3.00
Uttoxeter	1-6	0-3	0-1	0-1	0-0	0-0	1-1	- 3.75
Catterick	1-6	0-3	1-2	0-1	0-0	0-0	0-0	- 4.43

Carlisle	0-7	Worcester	0-4	Leicester	0-2
Warwick	0-6	Bangor	0-3	Windsor	0-2
Sandown	0-5	Haydock	0-3	Doncaster	0-1
Aintree	0-4	Musselburgh	0-3	Kempton	0-1
Ayr	0-4	Towcester	0-3	Perth	0-1

WINNING HORSES

	Races Run	1st	2nd	3rd	Unpl	Win £
Paddy's Return	5	3	2	0	0	51,114
Stop The Waller	5	2	2	0	1	25,712
Oscail An Doras	11	3	1	4	3	8,615
Colonel In Chief	3	2	0	0	1	5,614

Murphy F

Adrien	1	1	0	0	0	4,497
French Holly	2	2	0	0	0	4,086
Rich Desire	2	2	0	0	0	3,960
Frickley	6	1	1	0	4	3,945
Andrelot	3	1	0	1	1	3,910
Edelweiss Du Moulin	4	1	1	0	2	2,463
General Jimbo	5	1	0	1	3	1,989

WINNING OWNERS

	Races Won	Value £		Races Won	Value £
P O'Donnell	3	51,114	K Flood	2	4,086
R Burgan	2	25,712	Miss Marie Kearns	2	3,960
R Ogden	4	12,022	H Jones	1	3,910
Rhys Thomas Williams	3	8,615	R E Baskerville	1	1,989
Miss K S Bramall	1	4,497			

No of horses racing for the stable	42	Total winning prize-money	£115,905

Favourites	10-23	43.5%	- 1.88	Average SP of winner		4.6/1
Longest win seq	2	Longest losing seq	18	Return on stakes invested		-8.9%

1994/95 Form	12-91	13.2%	- 31.90	1992/93 Form	23-141	16.3%	+ 23.51
1993/94 Form	8-127	6.3%	- 68.50	1991/92 Form	19-133	14.3%	- 41.38

MRS L A MURPHY (Newport, Gwent)

	Races Run	1st	2nd	3rd	Unpl	Per cent	£1 Level Stake
Hurdles	26	5	3	4	14	19.2	+ 30.58
Chases	2	1	0	0	1	50.0	+ 2.00
Totals	28	6	3	4	15	21.4	+ 32.58

W Marston	2-11	+ 6.33	M Richards	1-2	+ 2.00
D Bridgwater	1-1	+ 33.00	R Farrant	1-2	0.00
J Osborne	1-1	+ 2.25			
Warwick	2-2	+ 4.00	Bangor	1-1	+ 33.00
Worcester	2-6	+ 11.33	Newbury	1-1	+ 2.25

No of horses racing for the stable	13	Total winning prize-money	£19,924

P G MURPHY (Portbury, Avon)

	Races Run	1st	2nd	3rd	Unpl	Per cent	£1 Level Stake
Hurdles	40	1	3	3	33	2.5	- 32.00
Chases	2	0	0	0	2	-	- 2.00
Totals	42	1	3	3	35	2.4	- 34.00

J R Kavanagh	1-2	+ 6.00	Doncaster	1-2	+ 6.00

No of horses racing for the stable   13   Total winning prize-money   £2,532

F P MURTAGH (Carlisle, Cumbria)

	Races Run	1st	2nd	3rd	Unpl	Per cent	£1 Level Stake
Hurdles	43	1	2	3	37	2.3	- 32.00
Chases	4	0	0	0	4	-	- 4.00
Totals	47	1	2	3	41	2.1	- 36.00

B Harding	1-10	+ 1.00	Musselburgh	1-2	+ 9.00

No of horses racing for the stable   13   Total winning prize-money   £2,026

C T NASH (Kingston Lisle, Oxon)

	Races Run	1st	2nd	3rd	Unpl	Per cent	£1 Level Stake
Hurdles	54	5	5	1	43	9.3	- 25.75
Chases	10	0	1	4	5	-	- 10.00
Totals	64	5	6	5	48	7.8	- 35.75

J R Kavanagh	2-28	- 15.75	G Hogan	1-8	- 5.00
D Gallagher	1-3	+ 2.00	C Maude	1-10	- 2.00
Huntingdon	3-7	+ 4.25	Fontwell	1-5	+ 3.00
Worcester	1-3	+ 6.00			

No of horses racing for the stable   21   Total winning prize-money   £13,848

MRS A M NAUGHTON (Richmond, North Yorks)

	Races Run	1st	2nd	3rd	Unpl	Per cent	£1 Level Stake
Hurdles	28	0	2	2	24	-	- 28.00
Chases	14	1	2	1	10	7.1	- 10.75
Totals	42	1	4	3	34	2.4	- 38.75

M Foster	1-19	- 15.75	Ayr		1-6	- 2.75

No of horses racing for the stable   14   Total winning prize-money   £3,558

T J NAUGHTON (Epsom, Surrey)

	Races Run	1st	2nd	3rd	Unpl	Per cent	£1 Level Stake
Hurdles	26	4	2	1	19	15.4	- 9.75
Chases	0	0	0	0	0	-	0.00
Totals	26	4	2	1	19	15.4	- 9.75

D Fortt	1-1	+ 2.50	A P McCoy	1-4	+ 0.50
C Llewellyn	1-1	+ 4.00	D Gallagher	1-10	- 6.75
Fontwell	1-2	+ 1.25	Chepstow	1-2	+ 2.50
Fakenham	1-2	+ 1.50	Stratford	1-4	+ 1.00

No of horses racing for the stable   8   Total winning prize-money   £10,300

J L NEEDHAM (Ludlow, Salop)

	Races Run	1st	2nd	3rd	Unpl	Per cent	£1 Level Stake
Hurdles	12	0	0	1	11	-	- 12.00
Chases	27	1	0	3	23	3.7	- 16.00
Totals	39	1	0	4	34	2.6	- 28.00

G Hogan	1-15	- 4.00	Hereford	1-7	+ 4.00

No of horses racing for the stable   12   Total winning prize-money   £2,671

J NEVILLE (Newport, Gwent)

	Races Run	1st	2nd	3rd	Unpl	Per cent	£1 Level Stake
Hurdles	36	5	3	3	25	13.9	- 7.75
Chases	2	0	0	0	2	-	- 2.00
Totals	38	5	3	3	27	13.2	- 9.75

R Farrant	2-4	+ 3.75	D Bridgwater	1-1	+ 6.00
Mr J Culloty	2-9	+ 4.50			
Plumpton	3-5	+ 15.50	Exeter	1-3	+ 0.25
Taunton	1-3	+ 1.50			

No of horses racing for the stable   13   Total winning prize-money   £12,108

A G NEWCOMBE (Huntshaw, Devon)

	Races Run	1st	2nd	3rd	Unpl	Per cent	£1 Level Stake
Hurdles	34	6	3	2	23	17.6	+ 12.00
Chases	11	5	1	1	4	45.5	+ 3.14
Totals	45	11	4	3	27	24.4	+ 15.14

BY MONTH

	W-R	Per cent	£1 Level Stake		W-R	Per cent	£1 Level Stake
June	0-0	-	0.00	December	0-1	-	- 1.00
July	1-1	100.0	+ 4.00	January	0-6	-	- 6.00
August	0-0	-	0.00	February	1-3	33.3	+ 3.00
September	0-3	-	- 3.00	March	4-10	40.0	+ 10.54
October	0-1	-	- 1.00	April	2-8	25.0	+ 10.50
November	0-5	-	- 5.00	May	3-7	42.9	+ 3.10

DISTANCE

Hurdles	W-R	Per cent	£1 Level Stake	Chases	W-R	Per cent	£1 Level Stake
2m-2m 3f	2-23	8.7	- 12.00	2m-2m 3f	2-2	100.0	+ 4.63
2m 4f-2m 7f	3-10	30.0	+ 10.00	2m 4f-2m 7f	2-4	50.0	+ 1.60
3m +	1-1	100.0	+ 14.00	3m +	1-5	20.0	- 3.09

TYPE OF RACE

	W-R	Per cent	£1 Level Stake		W-R	Per cent	£1 Level Stake
Novice hurdles	0-5	-	- 5.00	Selling	0-8	-	- 8.00
H'cap hurdles	6-18	33.3	+ 28.00	Amateur	0-0	-	0.00
Novice chases	0-0	-	0.00	Hunter chases	0-0	-	0.00
H'cap chases	5-11	45.5	+ 3.14	N H Flat	0-3	-	- 3.00

Newcombe A G

<table>
<tr><td colspan="4" align="center">COURSE GRADE</td><td colspan="4" align="center">FIRST TIME OUT</td></tr>
<tr><td></td><td>W-R</td><td>Per cent</td><td>£1 Level Stake</td><td></td><td>W-R</td><td>Per cent</td><td>£1 Level Stake</td></tr>
<tr><td>Group 1</td><td>0-0</td><td>-</td><td>0.00</td><td>Hurdles</td><td>0-6</td><td>-</td><td>- 6.00</td></tr>
<tr><td>Group 2</td><td>7-24</td><td>29.2</td><td>+ 7.51</td><td>Chases</td><td>0-1</td><td>-</td><td>- 1.00</td></tr>
<tr><td>Group 3</td><td>1-14</td><td>7.1</td><td>- 9.00</td><td></td><td></td><td></td><td></td></tr>
<tr><td>Group 4</td><td>3-7</td><td>42.9</td><td>+ 16.63</td><td>Totals</td><td>0-7</td><td>-</td><td>- 7.00</td></tr>
</table>

JOCKEYS RIDING

<table>
<tr><td></td><td>W-R</td><td>Per cent</td><td>£1 Level Stake</td><td></td><td>W-R</td><td>Per cent</td><td>£1 Level Stake</td></tr>
<tr><td>A Thornton</td><td>8-21</td><td>38.1</td><td>+ 25.51</td><td>P McLoughlin</td><td>1-3</td><td>33.3</td><td>+ 2.00</td></tr>
<tr><td>A P McCoy</td><td>1-2</td><td>50.0</td><td>+ 4.00</td><td>D Gallagher</td><td>1-4</td><td>25.0</td><td>- 1.37</td></tr>
<tr><td>B Fenton</td><td>0-2</td><td></td><td>B Clarke</td><td>0-1</td><td>L Wyer</td><td></td><td>0-1</td></tr>
<tr><td>J R Kavanagh</td><td>0-2</td><td></td><td>D Bentley</td><td>0-1</td><td>M Griffiths</td><td></td><td>0-1</td></tr>
<tr><td>N Mann</td><td>0-2</td><td></td><td>D Finnegan</td><td>0-1</td><td>P Holley</td><td></td><td>0-1</td></tr>
<tr><td>A Dicken</td><td>0-1</td><td></td><td>J Railton</td><td>0-1</td><td>R Johnson</td><td></td><td>0-1</td></tr>
</table>

COURSE RECORD

	Total W-R	Nov Hdles	H'cap Hdles	Nov Chses	H'cap Chses	Hunter Chses	N H Flat	£1 Level Stake
Newton Abbot	7-23	0-3	3-10	0-0	4-8	0-0	0-2	+ 8.51
Bangor	1-1	0-0	1-1	0-0	0-0	0-0	0-0	+ 14.00
Hereford	1-2	0-0	0-0	0-0	1-1	0-0	0-1	+ 0.63
Taunton	1-2	0-0	1-2	0-0	0-0	0-0	0-0	+ 4.00
Stratford	1-3	0-0	1-3	0-0	0-0	0-0	0-0	+ 2.00

Warwick	0-5	Chepstow	0-1	Windsor 0-1
Nottingham	0-3	Exeter	0-1	
Worcester	0-2	Towcester	0-1	

WINNING HORSES

	Races Run	1st	2nd	3rd	Unpl	Win £
Allo George	11	5	1	1	4	18,086
Marine Society	9	4	0	0	5	14,129
Nine O Three	3	1	0	0	2	2,285
Missed The Boat	2	1	0	1	0	2,220

WINNING OWNERS

	Races Won	Value £		Races Won	Value £
Lavis Medical Systems	5	18,086	R Harding	1	2,220
Bideford Tool Ltd	5	16,414			

No of horses racing for the stable	11	Total winning prize-money	£36,720

Favourites	4-6	66.7%	+ 4.14	Average SP of winner	4.5/1
Longest win seq	3	Longest losing seq	17	Return on stakes invested	33.6%

1994/95 Form	4-20	20.0%	+ 25.00	1993/94 Form	0-2

D E NICHOLLS (Overton-on-Dee, Clwyd)

	Races Run	1st	2nd	3rd	Unpl	Per cent	£1 Level Stake
Hurdles	0	0	0	0	0	-	0.00
Chases	7	3	0	2	2	42.9	+ 13.25
Totals	7	3	0	2	2	42.9	+ 13.25

Mr A Griffith	3-6	+ 14.25			
Cheltenham	1-1	+ 9.00	Bangor	1-2	+ 5.00
Uttoxeter	1-1	+ 2.25			

No of horses racing for the stable	1	Total winning prize-money	£6,092

P F NICHOLLS (Ditcheat, Somerset)

	Races Run	1st	2nd	3rd	Unpl	Per cent	£1 Level Stake
Hurdles	82	14	12	13	43	17.1	- 26.83
Chases	183	39	40	17	87	21.3	- 21.72
Totals	265	53	52	30	130	20.0	- 48.55

BY MONTH

	W-R	Per cent	£1 Level Stake		W-R	Per cent	£1 Level Stake
June	0-1	-	- 1.00	December	8-28	28.6	+ 2.96
July	0-0	-	0.00	January	2-24	8.3	- 11.50
August	0-0	-	0.00	February	3-25	12.0	- 3.93
September	5-13	38.5	+ 4.38	March	5-55	9.1	- 29.75
October	7-24	29.2	- 1.01	April	6-30	20.0	- 7.74
November	10-43	23.3	+ 5.10	May	7-22	31.8	- 6.06

DISTANCE

Hurdles	W-R	Per cent	£1 Level Stake	Chases	W-R	Per cent	£1 Level Stake
2m-2m 3f	8-49	16.3	- 25.61	2m-2m 3f	12-63	19.0	- 9.14
2m 4f-2m 7f	5-25	20.0	- 0.22	2m 4f-2m 7f	12-40	30.0	+ 9.48
3m +	1-8	12.5	- 1.00	3m +	15-80	18.8	- 22.06

TYPE OF RACE

	W-R	Per cent	£1 Level Stake		W-R	Per cent	£1 Level Stake
Novice hurdles	10-43	23.3	- 9.33	Selling	2-2	100.0	+ 4.50
H'cap hurdles	2-24	8.3	- 9.00	Amateur	1-9	11.1	- 4.50
Novice chases	13-56	23.2	- 3.23	Hunter chases	0-1	-	- 1.00
H'cap chases	25-118	21.2	- 13.99	N H Flat	0-12	-	- 12.00

COURSE GRADE

	W-R	Per cent	£1 Level Stake
Group 1	12-65	18.5	- 10.94
Group 2	15-73	20.5	- 6.38
Group 3	15-64	23.4	- 6.94
Group 4	11-63	17.5	- 24.29

FIRST TIME OUT

	W-R	Per cent	£1 Level Stake
Hurdles	5-23	21.7	+ 1.13
Chases	6-28	21.4	- 8.42
Totals	11-51	21.6	- 7.29

JOCKEYS RIDING

	W-R	Per cent	£1 Level Stake		W-R	Per cent	£1 Level Stake
A P McCoy	42-146	28.8	+ 21.41	Miss P Curling	1-3	33.3	+ 1.50
P Hide	3-16	18.8	+ 1.41	Mr J Culloty	1-7	14.3	- 3.50
Guy Lewis	2-16	12.5	- 10.37	T Dascombe	1-9	11.1	- 6.25
G Bradley	1-1	100.0	+ 1.25	M Griffiths	1-13	7.7	- 5.00
Sophie Mitchell	1-1	100.0	+ 4.00				

J R Kavanagh	0-8	A Maguire	0-1	Miss T Spearing	0-1
M A Fitzgerald	0-8	B M Clifford	0-1	Mr D Pipe	0-1
C Maude	0-7	D Gallagher	0-1	Mr M Armytage	0-1
R Dunwoody	0-6	D Meredith	0-1	Mr R Nuttall	0-1
D Bridgwater	0-3	G Hogan	0-1	Mr R Thornton	0-1
A Thornton	0-2	G Supple	0-1	Mr Richard White	0-1
R Johnson	0-2	J Frost	0-1	Mr Tim Mitchell	0-1
A Dobbin	0-1	J Titley	0-1	R Farrant	0-1

COURSE RECORD

	Total W-R	Nov Hdles	H'cap Hdles	Nov Chses	H'cap Chses	Hunter Chses	N H Flat	£1 Level Stake
Newton Abbot	7-43	0-8	0-9	2-10	5-14	0-0	0-2	- 13.17
Wincanton	6-25	1-8	1-2	2-3	2-11	0-0	0-1	+ 0.91
Chepstow	4-22	3-6	0-4	0-4	1-8	0-0	0-0	- 1.62
Taunton	4-28	1-5	1-3	0-5	2-14	0-1	0-0	- 15.50
Southwell	3-5	0-1	0-0	0-0	3-4	0-0	0-0	+ 4.13
Fontwell	3-7	0-0	0-1	3-3	0-3	0-0	0-0	+ 5.41
Kempton	3-8	1-1	0-1	1-2	1-3	0-0	0-1	- 0.70
Sandown	3-9	2-2	0-1	0-1	1-5	0-0	0-0	- 0.62
Hereford	3-13	1-1	0-1	1-4	1-7	0-0	0-0	+ 1.20
Worcester	3-14	0-4	0-0	2-5	1-2	0-0	0-3	+ 3.00
Stratford	2-3	0-0	0-0	1-1	1-2	0-0	0-0	+ 0.46
Uttoxeter	2-6	1-1	0-0	0-0	1-5	0-0	0-0	- 1.81
Ascot	2-9	1-1	0-1	0-4	1-3	0-0	0-0	- 3.37
Newbury	2-12	0-1	0-0	0-2	2-8	0-0	0-1	+ 4.75
Warwick	2-14	0-0	0-0	0-3	2-9	0-0	0-2	- 7.50
Lingfield	1-1	0-0	0-0	0-0	1-1	0-0	0-0	+ 3.00
Bangor	1-2	0-0	0-0	0-0	1-2	0-0	0-0	+ 0.88
Ayr	1-2	0-0	1-1	0-0	0-1	0-0	0-0	+ 5.00
Cheltenham	1-16	0-3	0-2	1-6	0-5	0-0	0-0	- 7.00

Exeter	0-9	Haydock	0-2	Newcastle	0-1
Aintree	0-6	Ludlow	0-2	Plumpton	0-1
Towcester	0-4	Leicester	0-1		

WINNING HORSES

	Races Run	1st	2nd	3rd	Unpl	Win £
Straight Talk	10	4	1	0	5	27,385
General Crack	10	5	0	1	4	19,127
Call Equiname	7	4	1	0	2	18,070
Captain Khedive	9	3	2	0	4	17,965
See More Business	3	3	0	0	0	16,127
James The First	12	3	1	2	6	12,817
Sunley Bay	11	2	2	2	5	11,450
Larry's Lord	7	3	2	1	1	11,398
Childhay Chocolate	5	3	1	0	1	11,188
Herbert Buchanan	14	3	5	1	5	10,789
Court Melody	12	3	3	0	6	10,222
Bramblehill Buck	9	3	1	1	4	8,730
Coolree	8	2	3	1	2	6,664
Beau Babillard	10	2	2	0	6	6,508
Ottowa	8	1	3	2	2	5,443
What's In Orbit	4	1	2	0	1	4,351
Cherrynut	4	1	1	1	1	4,276
Northern Starlight	2	2	0	0	0	4,062
Stoney Burke	1	1	0	0	0	2,916
Myblackthorn	11	1	2	2	6	2,626
Lansdowne	6	1	1	3	1	2,478
Iktasab	5	1	1	2	1	2,402
Supreme Music	5	1	0	0	4	2,276

WINNING OWNERS

	Races Won	Value £		Races Won	Value £
Mrs C I A Paterson	6	33,893	Marten Julian Turf Club Ltd	2	6,793
Paul K Barber	9	33,300	B T R Weston	2	6,664
M Coburn, P K Barber, C Lewis	4	18,070	J Blackwell, T Curry, D Nichols	1	4,605
Khedive Partnership	3	17,965	C I A Paterson	1	4,351
J A Keighley	3	16,127	Hunt & Co (Bournemouth) Ltd	1	4,276
Mrs Marianne G Barber	3	14,366	Richard Castle	2	4,062
B L Blinman	3	12,817	Mrs Mary Coburn	1	2,626
T C Frost	3	11,188	R F Denmead	1	2,478
Five For Fun	3	10,789	T & J A Curry	1	2,402
Mick Coburn	3	10,222	Russell Dennis	1	2,276

No of horses racing for the stable		55	Total winning prize-money	£219,270

Favourites	22-60	36.7%	- 9.89	Average SP of winner		3.1/1
Longest win seq	4	Longest losing seq	25	Return on stakes invested		-18.3%

1994/95 Form	28-168	16.7%	- 33.02	1992/93 Form	20-132	15.2%	- 49.80
1993/94 Form	29-164	17.7%	- 16.03	1991/92 Form	10-100	10.0%	- 47.54

D NICHOLSON (Temple Guiting, Glos)

	Races Run	1st	2nd	3rd	Unpl	Per cent	£1 Level Stake
Hurdles	261	54	56	31	120	20.7	- 18.33
Chases	116	32	28	16	40	27.6	+ 7.64
Totals	377	86	84	47	160	22.8	- 10.69

BY MONTH

	W-R	Per cent	£1 Level Stake		W-R	Per cent	£1 Level Stake
June	0-1	-	- 1.00	December	10-44	22.7	- 1.37
July	0-0	-	0.00	January	19-72	26.4	+ 0.90
August	3-3	100.0	+ 5.23	February	14-58	24.1	+ 1.94
September	1-5	20.0	- 2.50	March	8-67	11.9	- 37.51
October	1-12	8.3	- 10.47	April	9-40	22.5	+ 19.75
November	11-51	21.6	- 11.82	May	10-24	41.7	+ 26.16

DISTANCE

Hurdles	W-R	Per cent	£1 Level Stake	Chases	W-R	Per cent	£1 Level Stake
2m-2m 3f	36-164	22.0	+ 1.90	2m-2m 3f	8-32	25.0	- 2.87
2m 4f-2m 7f	11-63	17.5	- 17.11	2m 4f-2m 7f	8-32	25.0	- 8.21
3m +	7-34	20.6	- 3.12	3m +	16-52	30.8	+ 18.72

TYPE OF RACE

	W-R	Per cent	£1 Level Stake		W-R	Per cent	£1 Level Stake
Novice hurdles	32-136	23.5	+ 2.61	Selling	0-0	-	0.00
H'cap hurdles	10-68	14.7	- 17.89	Amateur	0-1	-	- 1.00
Novice chases	24-66	36.4	- 1.47	Hunter chases	0-0	-	0.00
H'cap chases	8-49	16.3	+ 10.11	N H Flat	12-57	21.1	- 3.05

COURSE GRADE

	W-R	Per cent	£1 Level Stake
Group 1	29-152	19.1	+ 1.75
Group 2	15-48	31.3	- 4.84
Group 3	22-106	20.8	- 15.03
Group 4	20-71	28.2	+ 7.43

FIRST TIME OUT

	W-R	Per cent	£1 Level Stake
Hurdles	11-63	17.5	+ 3.48
Chases	8-25	32.0	+ 5.91
Totals	19-88	21.6	+ 9.39

JOCKEYS RIDING

	W-R	Per cent	£1 Level Stake		W-R	Per cent	£1 Level Stake
A Maguire	32-119	26.9	- 15.15	Mr F Hutsby	2-4	50.0	+ 10.25
R Johnson	26-95	27.4	+ 40.36	P Niven	2-6	33.3	- 2.76
R Dunwoody	6-25	24.0	- 5.76	M Dwyer	1-1	100.0	+ 20.00
R Massey	6-35	17.1	- 13.87	D Bridgwater	1-5	20.0	- 1.75
W Marston	6-41	14.6	- 20.76	G Hogan	1-5	20.0	- 2.75
A P McCoy	3-11	27.3	+ 11.50				

X Aizpuru	0-8	C F Swan	0-2	J R Kavanagh	0-1
R Bellamy	0-7	D Gallagher	0-2	J Titley	0-1
Mr G Smith	0-3	C Maude	0-1	Mr A J Martin	0-1
B Powell	0-2	G Bradley	0-1	R Farrant	0-1

COURSE RECORD

	Total W-R	Nov Hdles	H'cap Hdles	Nov Chses	H'cap Chses	Hunter Chses	N H Flat	£1 Level Stake
Towcester	8-22	3-12	0-0	1-2	1-2	0-0	3-6	+ 23.64
Kempton	5-11	4-4	0-1	1-2	0-2	0-0	0-2	+ 12.25
Nottingham	5-14	2-7	0-1	2-3	0-0	0-0	1-3	+ 5.29
Wetherby	5-15	2-8	0-1	2-3	1-2	0-0	0-1	- 3.65
Worcester	5-17	1-4	1-1	1-3	1-2	0-0	1-7	+ 1.13
Newbury	5-19	3-6	0-5	2-3	0-2	0-0	0-3	- 2.64
Uttoxeter	5-21	1-7	2-5	1-2	0-2	0-0	1-5	- 0.95
Sandown	5-23	0-4	0-3	2-5	2-8	0-0	1-3	+ 9.88
Ascot	5-26	0-6	2-7	2-5	1-7	0-0	0-1	- 3.62
Stratford	4-8	3-6	1-1	0-0	0-1	0-0	0-0	+ 4.50
Newton Abbot	4-11	0-2	1-4	1-1	0-0	0-0	2-4	- 0.44
Ludlow	4-13	1-4	0-3	1-1	1-2	0-0	1-3	- 2.27
Hereford	3-8	2-3	0-0	0-1	0-1	0-0	1-3	+ 0.13
Lingfield	3-8	0-2	0-1	3-3	0-0	0-0	0-2	0.00
Chepstow	3-14	1-4	0-5	2-3	0-1	0-0	0-1	- 0.75
Haydock	3-15	3-9	0-1	0-2	0-2	0-0	0-1	- 4.75
Bangor	3-18	2-8	1-3	0-2	0-1	0-0	0-4	- 9.12
Cheltenham	3-40	1-12	1-9	1-7	0-9	0-0	0-3	- 24.87
Aintree	2-10	1-6	0-1	1-3	0-0	0-0	0-0	+ 2.50
Warwick	2-19	1-6	1-6	0-4	0-2	0-0	0-1	- 9.00
Southwell	1-2	0-0	0-0	1-2	0-0	0-0	0-0	- 0.20
Huntingdon	1-4	0-0	0-1	0-1	0-0	0-0	1-2	+ 7.00
Ayr	1-6	0-3	0-1	0-0	1-2	0-0	0-0	+ 15.00
Exeter	1-8	1-3	0-1	0-4	0-0	0-0	0-0	- 4.75

Leicester	0-13	Wincanton	0-5
Market Rasen	0-5	Newcastle	0-2

Nicholson D

WINNING HORSES

	Races Run	1st	2nd	3rd	Unpl	Win £
Viking Flagship	7	3	2	1	1	75,555
Zabadi	6	3	0	0	3	40,487
Moorcroft Boy	5	1	0	1	3	38,590
Hill of Tullow	4	3	0	0	1	34,120
Certainly Strong	3	2	1	0	0	26,723
Miss Optimist	7	3	0	1	3	21,942
Barton Bank	6	1	1	0	4	20,581
Newton Point	6	4	1	1	0	17,317
Pharanear	7	3	0	2	2	16,161
St Mellion Fairway	4	3	0	0	1	15,240
Arthur's Minstrel	7	2	0	3	2	14,136
Percy Smollet	4	1	2	0	1	12,346
Castle Sweep	6	4	0	2	0	10,385
Turning Trix	5	2	1	1	1	8,370
Chicodari	8	3	3	0	2	8,096
King Lucifer	6	2	2	1	1	7,388
Air Shot	7	2	3	1	1	7,118
Billygoat Gruff	4	2	1	0	1	7,036
Shankar	5	2	1	1	1	6,669
Call It A Day	6	2	4	0	0	6,511
Baronet	6	2	1	0	3	6,207
Dream Ride	10	2	5	2	1	6,177
Buttercup Joe	7	2	2	0	3	5,557
Blucanoo	3	2	0	0	1	5,500
Potter's Bay	8	2	2	1	3	5,289
Sounds Strong	2	1	0	0	1	5,159
Rolfe	8	2	1	2	3	4,988
Belstone Fox	3	1	0	1	1	4,650
Sonic Star	5	2	1	1	1	4,484
Hatta Breeze	3	1	0	1	1	4,120
Fixturessecretary	6	1	2	1	2	3,768
Boss's Bank	3	2	0	0	1	3,700
Musthaveaswig	1	1	0	0	0	3,443
Mighty Moss	4	2	1	1	0	3,443
Shining Light	7	1	1	2	3	3,420
Goldwyn	3	1	0	0	2	3,305
The Captain's Wish	5	1	1	0	3	3,269
Hebridean	6	1	0	0	5	3,155
Hatcham Boy	4	1	1	0	2	3,035
What's Your Story	5	1	3	0	1	3,035
Simple Simon	5	1	1	2	1	2,794
Jathib	10	1	5	1	3	2,558
Hurricane Lamp	2	1	0	0	1	2,304
Potter's Gale	3	1	1	1	0	1,721
Sutherland Moss	5	1	2	0	2	1,572
Forest Ivory	4	1	2	0	1	1,455
Johnny-K	3	1	1	0	1	1,410
In The Rough	1	1	0	0	0	1,347
Dublin Freddy	2	1	0	0	1	1,341

WINNING OWNERS

	Races Won	Value £		Races Won	Value £
Roach Foods Limited	3	75,555	J C Collett	2	5,500
Lady Harris	6	74,607	Mrs J E Potter	2	5,289
K G Manley	2	42,358	Stanley W Clarke	2	4,988
Mrs J Mould	4	28,401	Mrs R J Skan	1	4,650
Nick Skelton	2	26,723	R F Nutland	2	4,484
The Plough P'ship	3	21,942	P R D Fasteners Ltd	1	3,488
Miss C C & Mrs E W Pegna	4	17,317	K Hutsby	2	3,443
Stainless Threaded Fasteners Ltd	3	16,161	The Deeley Partnership	1	3,420
St Mellion Estates Ltd	3	15,240	Crown Pkg & Mailing Svs Ltd	1	3,305
Bernard Hathaway	2	14,136	Miss A J Murray	1	3,269
R G Murray	1	12,346	P A Deal	1	3,155
Mrs David Thompson	3	11,366	Jerry Wright	1	3,035
Lord Vestey	4	10,385	Robert Benton	1	3,035
Mel Davies	2	8,370	Mrs Claire Smith	2	2,913
C B Harvey	3	8,096	Mrs M A Powis	1	2,794
J A H West	2	7,388	Lou Giaracuni	1	2,558
Mrs Peter Prowting	2	7,118	F C & Mrs Welch & R A Barrs	1	2,304
Peter D Cooper	2	7,036	J E Potter	1	1,721
International Plywood Plc	2	6,669	The Old Foresters Partnership	1	1,455
Mrs Jane Lane	2	6,511	Norwood Partners	1	1,410
G Mordaunt & C Clarke	2	6,177	Mrs L R Lovell	1	1,347
R C F Faiers	2	5,557			

No of horses racing for the stable	90		Total winning prize-money	£497,022

Favourites	52-126	41.3%	+ 8.60	Average SP of winner			3.3/1
Longest win seq	4	Longest losing seq	28	Return on stakes invested			-2.8%

1994/95 Form	96-390	24.6%	+ 26.03	1992/93 Form	100-366	27.3%	+147.92
1993/94 Form	81-341	23.8%	+ 35.43	1991/92 Form	63-329	19.1%	- 41.37

R NIXON (Ettrickbridge End, Borders)

	Races Run	1st	2nd	3rd	Unpl	Per cent	£1 Level Stake
Hurdles	7	1	0	0	6	14.3	+ 0.50
Chases	8	3	2	0	3	37.5	+ 9.00
Totals	15	4	2	0	9	26.7	+ 9.50

A Dobbin	2-3	+ 5.00		N Bentley	1-5	+ 2.50
T Reed	1-5	+ 4.00				

Perth	1-1	+ 2.00		Kelso	1-3	+ 4.50
Wetherby	1-2	+ 3.00		Ayr	1-4	+ 5.00

No of horses racing for the stable	2	Total winning prize-money	£18,666

MRS SUSAN NOCK (Icomb, Glos)

	Races Run	1st	2nd	3rd	Unpl	Per cent	£1 Level Stake
Hurdles	9	1	0	1	7	11.1	+ 8.00
Chases	8	3	1	0	4	37.5	+ 68.50
Totals	17	4	1	1	11	23.5	+ 76.50

G Bradley	4-13	+ 80.50		
Ascot	2-2	+ 68.00	Sandown	1-3	+ 3.50
Worcester	1-1	+ 16.00		

No of horses racing for the stable   3   Total winning prize-money   £41,943

J NORTON (High Hoyland, South Yorks)

	Races Run	1st	2nd	3rd	Unpl	Per cent	£1 Level Stake
Hurdles	50	3	4	1	42	6.0	- 25.00
Chases	5	0	0	1	4	-	- 5.00
Totals	55	3	4	2	46	5.5	- 30.00

W Fry	2-35	- 25.00	E Callaghan	1-13	+ 2.00
Southwell	1-5	+ 10.00	Sedgefield	1-11	- 6.50
Catterick	1-6	- 0.50		

No of horses racing for the stable   21   Total winning prize-money   £7,603

D C O'BRIEN (Capel, Kent)

	Races Run	1st	2nd	3rd	Unpl	Per cent	£1 Level Stake
Hurdles	28	1	3	2	22	3.6	- 21.00
Chases	6	0	0	0	6	-	- 6.00
Totals	34	1	3	2	28	2.9	- 27.00

C Llewellyn	1-9	- 2.00	Windsor	1-7	0.00

No of horses racing for the stable   10   Total winning prize-money   £2,513

J G O'NEILL (Stratton Audley, Oxon)

	Races Run	1st	2nd	3rd	Unpl	Per cent	£1 Level Stake
Hurdles	4	0	0	1	3	–	– 4.00
Chases	6	1	0	2	3	16.7	+ 3.00
Totals	10	1	0	3	6	10.0	– 1.00

S Curran	1-7	+ 2.00	Windsor	1-1	+ 8.00

No of horses racing for the stable	2	Total winning prize-money	£4,500

J J O'NEILL (Skelton Wood End, Cumbria)

	Races Run	1st	2nd	3rd	Unpl	Per cent	£1 Level Stake
Hurdles	122	17	9	16	80	13.9	– 56.94
Chases	44	1	4	11	28	2.3	– 33.00
Totals	166	18	13	27	108	10.8	– 89.94

BY MONTH

	W-R	Per cent	£1 Level Stake		W-R	Per cent	£1 Level Stake
June	0-3	–	– 3.00	December	2-13	15.4	– 0.47
July	1-3	33.3	– 0.50	January	1-22	4.5	– 20.09
August	1-3	33.3	– 1.09	February	2-34	5.9	– 26.00
September	0-5	–	– 5.00	March	2-19	10.5	– 7.50
October	4-11	36.4	+ 7.83	April	1-17	5.9	– 11.00
November	4-32	12.5	– 19.12	May	0-4	–	– 4.00

DISTANCE

Hurdles	W-R	Per cent	£1 Level Stake	Chases	W-R	Per cent	£1 Level Stake
2m-2m 3f	9-62	14.5	– 22.92	2m-2m 3f	0-1	–	– 1.00
2m 4f-2m 7f	5-37	13.5	– 16.57	2m 4f-2m 7f	1-20	5.0	– 9.00
3m +	3-23	13.0	– 17.45	3m +	0-23	–	– 23.00

TYPE OF RACE

	W-R	Per cent	£1 Level Stake		W-R	Per cent	£1 Level Stake
Novice hurdles	7-47	14.9	– 30.43	Selling	1-5	20.0	– 1.75
H'cap hurdles	4-55	7.3	– 33.59	Amateur	0-2	–	– 2.00
Novice chases	0-17	–	– 17.00	Hunter chases	0-0	–	0.00
H'cap chases	1-26	3.8	– 15.00	N H Flat	5-14	35.7	+ 9.83

O'Neill J J

<table>
<tr><th colspan="4">COURSE GRADE</th><th colspan="4">FIRST TIME OUT</th></tr>
<tr><th></th><th>W-R</th><th>Per cent</th><th>£1 Level Stake</th><th></th><th>W-R</th><th>Per cent</th><th>£1 Level Stake</th></tr>
<tr><td>Group 1</td><td>4-45</td><td>8.9</td><td>- 29.59</td><td>Hurdles</td><td>3-32</td><td>9.4</td><td>- 15.00</td></tr>
<tr><td>Group 2</td><td>1-12</td><td>8.3</td><td>- 7.00</td><td>Chases</td><td>0-8</td><td>-</td><td>- 8.00</td></tr>
<tr><td>Group 3</td><td>4-35</td><td>11.4</td><td>- 12.77</td><td></td><td></td><td></td><td></td></tr>
<tr><td>Group 4</td><td>9-74</td><td>12.2</td><td>- 40.58</td><td>Totals</td><td>3-40</td><td>7.5</td><td>- 23.00</td></tr>
</table>

JOCKEYS RIDING

<table>
<tr><th></th><th>W-R</th><th>Per cent</th><th>£1 Level Stake</th><th></th><th>W-R</th><th>Per cent</th><th>£1 Level Stake</th></tr>
<tr><td>A J Roche</td><td>14-98</td><td>14.3</td><td>- 38.08</td><td>A P McCoy</td><td>1-4</td><td>25.0</td><td>+ 2.00</td></tr>
<tr><td>M Dwyer</td><td>2-36</td><td>5.6</td><td>- 27.77</td><td>R McGrath</td><td>1-17</td><td>5.9</td><td>- 15.09</td></tr>
</table>

<table>
<tr><td>L Wyer</td><td>0-2</td><td>G Bradley</td><td>0-1</td><td>P Carberry</td><td>0-1</td></tr>
<tr><td>Mr L Corcoran</td><td>0-2</td><td>G McCourt</td><td>0-1</td><td>R Dunwoody</td><td>0-1</td></tr>
<tr><td>P Niven</td><td>0-2</td><td>M Moloney</td><td>0-1</td><td></td><td></td></tr>
</table>

COURSE RECORD

	Total W-R	Nov Hdles	H'cap Hdles	Nov Chses	H'cap Chses	Hunter Chses	N H Flat	£1 Level Stake
Uttoxeter	3-8	1-3	1-3	0-0	1-1	0-0	0-1	+ 11.73
Sedgefield	3-10	2-5	0-1	0-1	0-2	0-0	1-1	- 5.99
Ayr	3-24	3-11	0-8	0-1	0-4	0-0	0-0	- 14.59
Bangor	2-12	1-2	0-4	0-1	0-3	0-0	1-2	+ 1.25
Ludlow	1-1	0-0	0-0	0-0	0-0	0-0	1-1	+ 3.50
Cartmel	1-2	0-0	1-1	0-1	0-0	0-0	0-0	- 0.09
Cheltenham	1-4	0-1	1-2	0-0	0-0	0-0	0-1	+ 2.00
Market Rasen	1-7	1-2	0-1	0-3	0-1	0-0	0-0	- 4.50
Kelso	1-11	0-4	1-4	0-1	0-2	0-0	0-0	- 4.50
Wetherby	1-12	0-1	0-4	0-3	0-3	0-0	1-1	- 7.00
Carlisle	1-15	0-4	0-5	0-2	0-1	0-0	1-3	- 11.75

<table>
<tr><td>Perth</td><td>0-13</td><td>Leicester</td><td>0-6</td><td>Worcester</td><td>0-3</td></tr>
<tr><td>Haydock</td><td>0-10</td><td>Newcastle</td><td>0-4</td><td>Aintree</td><td>0-2</td></tr>
<tr><td>Hexham</td><td>0-7</td><td>Musselburgh</td><td>0-3</td><td>Warwick</td><td>0-2</td></tr>
<tr><td>Catterick</td><td>0-6</td><td>Nottingham</td><td>0-3</td><td>Doncaster</td><td>0-1</td></tr>
</table>

WINNING HORSES

	Races Run	1st	2nd	3rd	Unpl	Win £
Magslad	8	5	0	1	2	8,659
Uncle Keeny	9	2	2	3	2	5,034
Riverdale Boy	3	2	0	0	1	3,380
Valley Garden	6	1	1	0	4	3,217
Naughty Future	8	1	0	3	4	2,742
East Houston	12	1	4	4	3	2,660
Give Best	4	1	1	1	1	2,621
Jymjam Johnny	5	1	0	0	4	2,584
General Chaos	2	1	0	0	1	2,320
Lord of The West	7	1	0	0	6	2,274
Glandalane Lady	5	1	0	1	3	2,217
Steadfast Elite	8	1	3	1	3	1,973

WINNING OWNERS

	Races Won	Value £		Races Won	Value £
David Alan Harrison	5	8,659	Miss Jacqueline Bellamy	1	2,621
Richard Seed	2	5,034	Allan J Schaverien	1	2,584
G & P Barker Ltd Globe Eng.	2	3,380	C H Stevens	1	2,320
The Motley Crew	1	3,217	Anne Duchess of Westminster	1	2,274
A K Collins	1	2,742	Mrs M O'Neill	1	2,217
Highgreen Partnership	1	2,660	J Clayton	1	1,973

No of horses racing for the stable	41	Total winning prize-money	£39,681

Favourites	9-21	42.9%	- 0.94	Average SP of winner		3.2/1
Longest win seq	2	Longest losing seq	31	Return on stakes invested		-54.2%

1994/95 Form	26-189	13.8%	- 42.09	1992/93 Form	21-151	13.9%	- 19.74
1993/94 Form	19-179	10.6%	- 56.38	1991/92 Form	26-155	16.8%	- 55.88

O O'NEILL (Cleeve Hill, Glos)

	Races Run	1st	2nd	3rd	Unpl	Per cent	£1 Level Stake
Hurdles	20	0	1	1	18	-	- 20.00
Chases	19	3	0	3	13	15.8	+ 1.00
Totals	39	3	1	4	31	7.7	- 19.00

G Hogan	2-10	+ 1.00		V Slattery	1-10	- 1.00
Warwick	1-3	+ 3.50		Stratford	1-6	+ 3.00
Ludlow	1-5	- 0.50				

No of horses racing for the stable	9	Total winning prize-money	£10,208

J G M O'SHEA (Redditch, H'ford & Worcs)

	Races Run	1st	2nd	3rd	Unpl	Per cent	£1 Level Stake
Hurdles	76	9	6	9	52	11.8	- 12.89
Chases	32	3	9	3	17	9.4	- 18.75
Totals	108	12	15	12	69	11.1	- 31.64

BY MONTH

	W-R	Per cent	£1 Level Stake		W-R	Per cent	£1 Level Stake
June	1-3	33.3	+ 10.00	December	0-5	-	- 5.00
July	1-10	10.0	- 4.00	January	0-1	-	- 1.00
August	0-13	-	- 13.00	February	0-5	-	- 5.00
September	4-10	40.0	+ 2.98	March	0-6	-	- 6.00
October	2-14	14.3	+ 6.50	April	2-14	14.3	+ 4.25
November	0-11	-	- 11.00	May	2-16	12.5	- 10.37

DISTANCE

Hurdles	W-R	Per cent	£1 Level Stake	Chases	W-R	Per cent	£1 Level Stake
2m-2m 3f	7-62	11.3	- 19.39	2m-2m 3f	0-13	-	- 13.00
2m 4f-2m 7f	1-11	9.1	- 3.50	2m 4f-2m 7f	0-9	-	- 9.00
3m +	1-3	33.3	+ 10.00	3m +	3-10	30.0	+ 3.25

TYPE OF RACE

	W-R	Per cent	£1 Level Stake		W-R	Per cent	£1 Level Stake
Novice hurdles	3-32	9.4	- 14.52	Selling	2-17	11.8	- 9.62
H'cap hurdles	4-16	25.0	+ 22.25	Amateur	0-0	-	0.00
Novice chases	2-19	10.5	- 9.75	Hunter chases	0-0	-	0.00
H'cap chases	1-11	9.1	- 7.00	N H Flat	0-13	-	- 13.00

COURSE GRADE / FIRST TIME OUT

	W-R	Per cent	£1 Level Stake		W-R	Per cent	£1 Level Stake
Group 1	1-15	6.7	- 11.75	Hurdles	2-23	8.7	- 2.50
Group 2	0-2	-	- 2.00	Chases	0-4	-	- 4.00
Group 3	4-49	8.2	- 21.89				
Group 4	7-42	16.7	+ 4.00	Totals	2-27	7.4	- 6.50

JOCKEYS RIDING

	W-R	Per cent	£1 Level Stake		W-R	Per cent	£1 Level Stake
M A Fitzgerald	6-27	22.2	- 3.27	Michael Brennan	2-28	7.1	- 10.25
A P McCoy	3-10	30.0	+ 11.88	G Lee	1-5	20.0	+ 8.00

B Fenton	0-6	N Williamson	0-2	J Osborne	0-1
S A Quilty	0-6	A Maguire	0-1	M Dwyer	0-1
R Supple	0-5	C O'Dwyer	0-1	R Dunwoody	0-1
D Bentley	0-2	Christopher Webb	0-1	R McGrath	0-1
D Byrne	0-2	D Finnegan	0-1	V Slattery	0-1
J R Kavanagh	0-2	D Walsh	0-1	
Mr M Brennan	0-2	G Hogan	0-1	

COURSE RECORD

	Total W-R	Nov Hdles	H'cap Hdles	Nov Chses	H'cap Chses	Hunter Chses	N H Flat	£1 Level Stake
Hexham	3-6	1-2	1-2	0-1	1-1	0-0	0-0	+ 5.25
Southwell	3-7	1-2	1-1	1-1	0-2	0-0	0-1	+ 14.75
Worcester	3-24	1-10	2-5	0-2	0-4	0-0	0-3	+ 0.23
Warwick	1-2	1-2	0-0	0-0	0-0	0-0	0-0	+ 0.88
Ascot	1-5	0-0	0-1	1-4	0-0	0-0	0-0	- 1.75
Bangor	1-17	1-7	0-5	0-4	0-0	0-0	0-1	- 4.00

Uttoxeter	0-10	Newbury	0-3	Doncaster	0-1
Ludlow	0-7	Towcester	0-3	Haydock	0-1
Huntingdon	0-6	Fontwell	0-2	Leicester	0-1
Cheltenham	0-4	Taunton	0-2	Market Rasen	0-1
Stratford	0-4	Aintree	0-1	Plumpton	0-1

WINNING HORSES

	Races Run	1st	2nd	3rd	Unpl	Win £
Go Ballistic	11	2	2	0	7	14,881
Trumpet	7	3	0	2	2	8,182
Red Valerian	7	3	1	1	2	7,596
Scorched Air	6	2	0	1	3	4,801
Governor Daniel	6	1	0	1	4	2,658
Boltrose	3	1	1	0	1	1,695

WINNING OWNERS

	Races Won	Value £		Races Won	Value £
Mrs B J Lockhart	2	14,881	Gary Roberts	3	6,496
Costas Andreou	3	8,182	Patrick Kelly	1	2,658
Mrs Alurie O'Sullivan	3	7,596			

No of horses racing for the stable	28		Total winning prize-money			£39,813
Favourites	4-17	23.5% - 6.39	Average SP of winner			5.4/1
Longest win seq	3	Longest losing seq 30	Return on stakes invested			-29.3%
1994/95 Form	8-53	15.1% - 15.62	1992/93 Form	3-28	10.7%	- 22.34
1993/94 Form	11-56	19.6% - 20.25	1991/92 Form	5-38	13.2%	- 25.44

R J O'SULLIVAN (Whitcombe, Dorset)

	Races Run	1st	2nd	3rd	Unpl	Per cent	£1 Level Stake
Hurdles	76	10	6	5	55	13.2	+ 9.25
Chases	17	0	3	1	13	-	- 17.00
Totals	93	10	9	6	68	10.8	- 7.75

BY MONTH

	W-R	Per cent	£1 Level Stake		W-R	Per cent	£1 Level Stake
June	0-4	-	- 4.00	December	0-6	-	- 6.00
July	0-7	-	- 7.00	January	2-12	16.7	+ 7.50
August	3-8	37.5	+ 21.75	February	0-9	-	- 9.00
September	0-5	-	- 5.00	March	1-8	12.5	- 1.50
October	1-10	10.0	+ 5.00	April	3-9	33.3	+ 5.50
November	0-8	-	- 8.00	May	0-7	-	- 7.00

DISTANCE

Hurdles	W-R	Per cent	£1 Level Stake	Chases	W-R	Per cent	£1 Level Stake
2m-2m 3f	7-52	13.5	+ 18.25	2m-2m 3f	0-6	-	- 6.00
2m 4f-2m 7f	3-20	15.0	- 5.00	2m 4f-2m 7f	0-8	-	- 8.00
3m +	0-4	-	- 4.00	3m +	0-3	-	- 3.00

TYPE OF RACE

	W-R	Per cent	£1 Level Stake		W-R	Per cent	£1 Level Stake
Novice hurdles	5-38	13.2	+ 23.00	Selling	0-4	-	- 4.00
H'cap hurdles	5-31	16.1	- 6.75	Amateur	0-0	-	0.00
Novice chases	0-2	-	- 2.00	Hunter chases	0-0	-	0.00
H'cap chases	0-15	-	- 15.00	N H Flat	0-3	-	- 3.00

COURSE GRADE

	W-R	Per cent	£1 Level Stake
Group 1	1-8	12.5	+ 7.00
Group 2	3-26	11.5	- 5.00
Group 3	4-42	9.5	- 2.75
Group 4	2-17	11.8	- 7.00

FIRST TIME OUT

	W-R	Per cent	£1 Level Stake
Hurdles	1-19	5.3	- 4.00
Chases	0-2	-	- 2.00
Totals	1-21	4.8	- 6.00

JOCKEYS RIDING

	W-R	Per cent	£1 Level Stake		W-R	Per cent	£1 Level Stake
D O'Sullivan	5-46	10.9	+ 11.00	M A Fitzgerald	1-3	33.3	+ 3.50
S Curran	3-14	21.4	- 0.75	D Bridgwater	1-4	25.0	+ 4.50

B Powell	0-7	M Richards	0-2	M Perrett	0-1
A Procter	0-5	D Morris	0-1	N Williamson	0-1
C Llewellyn	0-3	D Skyrme	0-1	N Wilmington	0-1
A P McCoy	0-2	I Lawrence	0-1	T Grantham	0-1

COURSE RECORD

	Total W-R	Nov Hdles	H'cap Hdles	Nov Chses	H'cap Chses	Hunter Chses	N H Flat	£1 Level Stake
Newton Abbot	2-8	1-3	1-3	0-0	0-2	0-0	0-0	+ 7.50
Plumpton	2-18	0-9	2-5	0-1	0-3	0-0	0-0	- 8.25
Warwick	1-1	1-1	0-0	0-0	0-0	0-0	0-0	+ 7.50
Kempton	1-2	1-2	0-0	0-0	0-0	0-0	0-0	+ 13.00
Exeter	1-3	0-1	1-2	0-0	0-0	0-0	0-0	+ 3.00
Ludlow	1-4	0-2	1-2	0-0	0-0	0-0	0-0	0.00
Worcester	1-8	1-2	0-1	0-0	0-5	0-0	0-0	+ 13.00
Fontwell	1-15	1-6	0-8	0-0	0-1	0-0	0-0	- 9.50

Taunton	0-7	Hereford	0-2	Ascot	0-1
Sandown	0-4	Huntingdon	0-2	Cheltenham	0-1
Stratford	0-4	Market Rasen	0-2	Towcester	0-1
Lingfield	0-3	Uttoxeter	0-2		
Windsor	0-3	Wincanton	0-2		

WINNING HORSES

	Races Run	1st	2nd	3rd	Unpl	Win £
Jovial Man	5	3	0	0	2	8,010
Volunteer	4	2	1	0	1	5,795
Ikhtiraa	10	2	1	0	7	3,889
Smuggler's Point	9	1	1	2	5	3,350
United Front	4	1	0	0	3	2,369
Pie Hatch	3	1	0	0	2	2,178

WINNING OWNERS

	Races Won	Value £		Races Won	Value £
Mrs Barbara Marchant	3	8,010	Martin Hickey	1	3,350
M J Marchant	2	5,795	T Beresford	1	2,369
I Kerman	2	3,889	Mrs June Peters	1	2,178

No of horses racing for the stable	23	Total winning prize-money	£25,591

Favourites	1-12	8.3%	- 7.50	Average SP of winner	7.5/1
Longest win seq	2	Longest losing seq	20	Return on stakes invested	-8.3%

1994/95 Form	15-73	20.5%	- 19.66	1992/93 Form	13-87	14.9%	- 30.19
1993/94 Form	11-79	13.9%	- 29.52	1991/92 Form	14-56	25.0%	+ 0.94

MRS S M ODELL (Little Tew, Oxon)

	Races Run	1st	2nd	3rd	Unpl	Per cent	£1 Level Stake
Hurdles	1	0	0	0	1	-	- 1.00
Chases	5	1	0	0	4	20.0	- 1.75
Totals	6	1	0	0	5	16.7	- 2.75

B Fenton	1-2	+ 1.25	Plumpton	1-1	+ 2.25

No of horses racing for the stable	3	Total winning prize-money	£2,448

J A B OLD (Wroughton, Wilts)

	Races Run	1st	2nd	3rd	Unpl	Per cent	£1 Level Stake
Hurdles	118	13	18	10	77	11.0	- 41.44
Chases	28	4	4	1	19	14.3	- 8.62
Totals	146	17	22	11	96	11.6	- 50.06

BY MONTH

	W-R	Per cent	£1 Level Stake		W-R	Per cent	£1 Level Stake
June	0-0	-	0.00	December	2-11	18.2	+ 2.00
July	0-0	-	0.00	January	1-19	5.3	+ 7.00
August	0-0	-	0.00	February	4-29	13.8	- 11.50
September	0-1	-	- 1.00	March	8-39	20.5	- 7.94
October	0-1	-	- 1.00	April	1-23	4.3	- 20.12
November	1-14	7.1	- 8.50	May	0-9	-	- 9.00

DISTANCE

Hurdles	W-R	Per cent	£1 Level Stake	Chases	W-R	Per cent	£1 Level Stake
2m-2m 3f	12-66	18.2	+ 6.06	2m-2m 3f	3-8	37.5	+ 4.88
2m 4f-2m 7f	1-29	3.4	- 24.50	2m 4f-2m 7f	1-12	8.3	- 5.50
3m +	0-23	-	- 23.00	3m +	0-8	-	- 8.00

TYPE OF RACE

	W-R	Per cent	£1 Level Stake		W-R	Per cent	£1 Level Stake
Novice hurdles	8-57	14.0	- 23.19	Selling	0-0	-	0.00
H'cap hurdles	1-36	2.8	- 10.00	Amateur	0-1	-	- 1.00
Novice chases	2-6	33.3	+ 4.00	Hunter chases	0-0	-	0.00
H'cap chases	2-21	9.5	- 11.62	N H Flat	4-25	16.0	- 8.25

COURSE GRADE

	W-R	Per cent	£1 Level Stake
Group 1	4-64	6.3	- 18.00
Group 2	4-25	16.0	- 9.75
Group 3	4-36	11.1	- 18.75
Group 4	5-21	23.8	- 3.56

FIRST TIME OUT

	W-R	Per cent	£1 Level Stake
Hurdles	5-33	15.2	+ 11.66
Chases	0-3	-	- 3.00
Totals	5-36	13.9	+ 8.66

JOCKEYS RIDING

	W-R	Per cent	£1 Level Stake		W-R	Per cent	£1 Level Stake
G Upton	7-59	11.9	- 39.69	M A Fitzgerald	2-7	28.6	+ 2.38
G Bradley	3-3	100.0	+ 36.25	Mr J Smyth-Osbourne	1-9	11.1	- 2.50
J Osborne	3-13	23.1	+ 0.50	T Grantham	1-35	2.9	- 27.00

C Llewellyn	0-6		A Maguire	0-1		L Harvey	0-1
S McNeill	0-6		J A McCarthy	0-1		Mr G Baines	0-1
D Creech	0-2		J R Kavanagh	0-1		P Niven	0-1

COURSE RECORD

	Total W-R	Nov Hdles	H'cap Hdles	Nov Chses	H'cap Chses	Hunter Chses	N H Flat	£1 Level Stake
Uttoxeter	4-13	2-4	0-4	0-0	1-3	0-0	1-2	+ 4.25
Taunton	3-7	3-6	0-1	0-0	0-0	0-0	0-0	- 0.44
Chepstow	2-9	0-2	0-2	2-2	0-3	0-0	0-0	+ 1.00
Lingfield	1-3	0-2	0-0	0-0	0-0	0-0	1-1	+ 0.25
Exeter	1-5	0-1	0-3	0-0	1-1	0-0	0-0	- 2.12
Towcester	1-8	0-2	0-1	0-1	0-3	0-0	1-1	0.00
Sandown	1-8	0-4	1-2	0-0	0-0	0-0	0-2	+ 18.00
Ascot	1-9	1-5	0-3	0-0	0-0	0-0	0-1	- 4.50
Newton Abbot	1-12	0-2	0-3	0-2	0-1	0-0	1-4	- 10.00
Cheltenham	1-13	1-7	0-4	0-0	0-0	0-0	0-2	- 3.00
Newbury	1-14	1-7	0-2	0-0	0-3	0-0	0-2	- 8.50

Ayr	0-7	Leicester	0-3	Fontwell	0-1
Haydock	0-6	Warwick	0-3	Hereford	0-1
Nottingham	0-6	Wincanton	0-3	Huntingdon	0-1
Kempton	0-5	Aintree	0-2	Windsor	0-1
Folkestone	0-3	Plumpton	0-2	Worcester	0-1

WINNING HORSES

	Races Run	1st	2nd	3rd	Unpl	Win £
Collier Bay	2	2	0	0	0	138,470
Killone Abbot	4	1	0	1	2	10,820
Mole Board	6	1	2	0	3	10,114
Pete The Parson	7	3	1	1	2	9,909
Backgammon	6	2	1	0	3	5,495
Chai-Yo	6	2	2	0	2	4,008
Corrarder	8	1	0	0	7	3,550
Jefferies	2	1	0	0	1	2,542
Frys No Fool	2	1	0	1	0	1,785
Boxgrove Man	3	1	0	0	2	1,553
Wise King	3	1	1	0	1	1,551
Three Farthings	3	1	1	0	1	1,544

WINNING OWNERS

	Races Won	Value £		Races Won	Value £
W E Sturt	8	163,988	R P Fry	1	1,785
Lady Lloyd Webber	1	10,820	Sir Andrew Lloyd Webber	1	1,553
Nick Viney	2	4,008	J A B Old	1	1,551
Mrs E T Smyth-Osbourne	1	3,550	K R Britten	1	1,544
Miss S Blumberg	1	2,542			

No of horses racing for the stable	36	Total winning prize-money £191,341

Favourites	8-22	36.4%	- 1.56	Average SP of winner		4.6/1
Longest win seq	2	Longest losing seq	31	Return on stakes invested		-34.3%

1994/95 Form	10-85	11.8%	- 40.36	1992/93 Form	19-92	20.7%	+ 58.76
1993/94 Form	22-93	23.7%	+ 33.58	1991/92 Form	21-75	28.0%	+ 66.73

H OLIVER (Elton, Glos)

	Races Run	1st	2nd	3rd	Unpl	Per cent	£1 Level Stake
Hurdles	55	4	1	4	46	7.3	- 35.25
Chases	14	2	3	0	9	14.3	- 8.65
Totals	69	6	4	4	55	8.7	- 43.90

Jacqui Oliver	4-39	- 26.40	Philip Hughes	1-9	- 4.50
Mr Nigel Oliver	1-1	+ 7.00			
Southwell	1-2	+ 2.50	Huntingdon	1-5	- 2.90
Newton Abbot	1-4	- 0.75	Ludlow	1-6	- 2.75
Sedgefield	1-5	- 1.00	Worcester	1-10	- 2.00

No of horses racing for the stable　　16　　Total winning prize-money　　£15,216

J K M OLIVER (Hawick, Borders)

	Races Run	1st	2nd	3rd	Unpl	Per cent	£1 Level Stake
Hurdles	11	1	2	1	7	9.1	- 5.00
Chases	14	3	6	1	4	21.4	+ 1.50
Totals	25	4	8	2	11	16.0	- 3.50

B Storey	3-16	- 0.50	S Melrose	1-8	- 2.00
Wetherby	1-2	+ 3.50	Carlisle	1-4	+ 2.00
Perth	1-4	+ 1.00	Kelso	1-7	- 2.00

No of horses racing for the stable　　7　　Total winning prize-money　　£19,643

IAN PARK (Eaglescliffe, Co Cleveland)

	Races Run	1st	2nd	3rd	Unpl	Per cent	£1 Level Stake
Hurdles	15	1	1	4	9	6.7	- 12.37
Chases	0	0	0	0	0	-	0.00
Totals	15	1	1	4	9	6.7	- 12.37

N Smith	1-13	- 10.37	Sedgefield	1-8	- 5.37

No of horses racing for the stable　　4　　Total winning prize-money　　£2,198

C PARKER (Kettleholm, Dumfries)

	Races Run	1st	2nd	3rd	Unpl	Per cent	£1 Level Stake
Hurdles	61	3	3	3	52	4.9	- 26.00
Chases	57	11	9	8	29	19.3	- 20.12
Totals	118	14	12	11	81	11.9	- 46.12

BY MONTH

	W-R	Per cent	£1 Level Stake		W-R	Per cent	£1 Level Stake
June	0-1	-	- 1.00	December	0-10	-	- 10.00
July	0-0	-	0.00	January	2-17	11.8	- 10.77
August	0-1	-	- 1.00	February	3-16	18.8	+ 7.00
September	1-4	25.0	- 1.90	March	3-20	15.0	- 6.70
October	1-5	20.0	- 3.00	April	1-11	9.1	- 7.75
November	3-24	12.5	- 2.00	May	0-9	-	- 9.00

DISTANCE

Hurdles	W-R	Per cent	£1 Level Stake	Chases	W-R	Per cent	£1 Level Stake
2m-2m 3f	1-34	2.9	- 29.00	2m-2m 3f	1-11	9.1	- 6.50
2m 4f-2m 7f	2-23	8.7	+ 7.00	2m 4f-2m 7f	4-17	23.5	- 3.77
3m +	0-4	-	- 4.00	3m +	6-29	20.7	- 9.85

TYPE OF RACE

	W-R	Per cent	£1 Level Stake		W-R	Per cent	£1 Level Stake
Novice hurdles	0-26	-	- 26.00	Selling	2-4	50.0	+ 7.50
H'cap hurdles	2-24	8.3	+ 6.00	Amateur	0-2	-	- 2.00
Novice chases	5-20	25.0	- 3.45	Hunter chases	0-0	-	0.00
H'cap chases	5-36	13.9	- 22.17	N H Flat	0-6	-	- 6.00

COURSE GRADE

	W-R	Per cent	£1 Level Stake
Group 1	6-46	13.0	- 15.47
Group 2	1-5	20.0	+ 10.00
Group 3	0-4	-	- 4.00
Group 4	7-63	11.1	- 36.65

FIRST TIME OUT

	W-R	Per cent	£1 Level Stake
Hurdles	1-21	4.8	- 6.00
Chases	1-9	11.1	- 5.50
Totals	2-30	6.7	- 11.50

JOCKEYS RIDING

	W-R	Per cent	£1 Level Stake		W-R	Per cent	£1 Level Stake
B Storey	9-50	18.0	- 11.37	Mr A Parker	1-4	25.0	+ 2.50
D Parker	4-60	6.7	- 33.25				

A Dobbin	0-2	F Leahy	0-1	R Supple	0-1

COURSE RECORD

	Total W-R	Nov Hdles	H'cap Hdles	Nov Chses	H'cap Chses	Hunter Chses	N H Flat	£1 Level Stake
Ayr	5-24	0-8	1-4	2-6	2-5	0-0	0-1	+ 3.03
Carlisle	4-18	0-2	0-6	1-2	3-6	0-0	0-2	- 6.15
Wetherby	1-5	0-0	1-1	0-0	0-4	0-0	0-0	+ 10.00
Musselburgh	1-5	0-1	1-2	0-1	0-1	0-0	0-0	0.00
Sedgefield	1-6	0-0	0-1	1-4	0-1	0-0	0-0	- 3.00
Newcastle	1-9	0-3	0-2	1-1	0-2	0-0	0-1	- 5.50
Hexham	1-10	0-3	0-1	0-2	1-4	0-0	0-0	- 3.50

Kelso	0-16	Doncaster		0-4	Cheltenham			0-1
Haydock	0-8	Cartmel		0-2	Market Rasen			0-1
Perth	0-6	Catterick		0-2	Worcester			0-1

WINNING HORSES

	Races Run	1st	2nd	3rd	Unpl	Win £
Solba	9	3	2	2	2	10,655
Stormy Coral	5	3	1	1	0	9,724
Kushbaloo	4	2	1	1	0	7,143
Lie Detector	7	2	0	1	4	5,801
Sparky Gale	5	1	1	1	2	3,615
Trump	8	1	0	1	6	3,020
Lupy Minstrel	9	1	1	1	6	2,658
Latin Leader	4	1	0	0	3	2,469

WINNING OWNER

	Races Won	Value £
Raymond Anderson Green	14	45,085

No of horses racing for the stable	31	Total winning prize-money	£45,085

Favourites	5-15	33.3%	- 4.37	Average SP of winner	4.1/1
Longest win seq	1	Longest losing seq	19	Return on stakes invested	-39.1%

1994/95 Form	13-129	10.1%	- 66.72	1992/93 Form	14-85	16.5%	- 10.34
1993/94 Form	12-91	13.2%	+ 6.29	1991/92 Form	7-116	6.0%	- 67.40

MRS H PARROTT (Abenhall, Glos)

	Races Run	1st	2nd	3rd	Unpl	Per cent	£1 Level Stake
Hurdles	26	2	4	2	18	7.7	- 2.25
Chases	4	0	0	0	4	-	- 4.00
Totals	30	2	4	2	22	6.7	- 6.25

C Llewellyn	1-1	+ 1.75	S Curran	1-10	+ 11.00
Hereford	1-3	- 0.25	Bangor	1-3	+ 18.00

No of horses racing for the stable	8	Total winning prize-money	£4,617

R E PEACOCK (Chedglow, Wilts)

	Races Run	1st	2nd	3rd	Unpl	Per cent	£1 Level Stake
Hurdles	13	1	0	2	10	7.7	- 9.25
Chases	1	0	0	0	1	-	- 1.00
Totals	14	1	0	2	11	7.1	- 10.25

Christopher Webb	1-8	- 4.25	Exeter	1-3	+ 0.75

No of horses racing for the stable	3	Total winning prize-money	£2,193

J PEARCE (Newmarket, Suffolk)

	Races Run	1st	2nd	3rd	Unpl	Per cent	£1 Level Stake
Hurdles	46	7	6	1	32	15.2	+ 5.75
Chases	10	1	2	0	7	10.0	- 8.27
Totals	56	8	8	1	39	14.3	- 2.52

BY MONTH

	W-R	Per cent	£1 Level Stake		W-R	Per cent	£1 Level Stake
June	0-3	-	- 3.00	December	0-7	-	- 7.00
July	0-0	-	0.00	January	0-4	-	- 4.00
August	0-0	-	0.00	February	1-7	14.3	+ 2.00
September	1-1	100.0	+ 14.00	March	1-8	12.5	+ 0.50
October	1-6	16.7	+ 1.00	April	0-4	-	- 4.00
November	4-11	36.4	+ 2.98	May	0-5	-	- 5.00

DISTANCE

Hurdles	W-R	Per cent	£1 Level Stake	Chases	W-R	Per cent	£1 Level Stake
2m-2m 3f	6-38	15.8	+ 9.75	2m-2m 3f	0-4	-	- 4.00
2m 4f-2m 7f	1-8	12.5	- 4.00	2m 4f-2m 7f	1-2	50.0	- 0.27
3m +	0-0	-	0.00	3m +	0-4	-	- 4.00

TYPE OF RACE

	W-R	Per cent	£1 Level Stake		W-R	Per cent	£1 Level Stake
Novice hurdles	1-10	10.0	- 5.00	Selling	1-14	7.1	- 5.00
H'cap hurdles	4-14	28.6	+ 15.25	Amateur	0-1	-	- 1.00
Novice chases	0-4	-	- 4.00	Hunter chases	0-0	-	0.00
H'cap chases	1-6	16.7	- 4.27	N H Flat	1-7	14.3	+ 1.50

Pearce J

COURSE GRADE

	W-R	Per cent	£1 Level Stake
Group 1	2-11	18.2	+ 0.75
Group 2	0-2	-	- 2.00
Group 3	5-27	18.5	+ 5.73
Group 4	1-16	6.3	- 7.00

FIRST TIME OUT

	W-R	Per cent	£1 Level Stake
Hurdles	1-12	8.3	+ 3.00
Chases	1-2	50.0	- 0.27
Totals	2-14	14.3	+ 2.73

JOCKEYS RIDING

	W-R	Per cent	£1 Level Stake
P Hide	4-8	50.0	+ 20.73
L Aspell	3-9	33.3	+ 6.75
M Dwyer	1-5	20.0	+ 4.00

J McLaughlin	0-17	D Skyrme	0-1	Miss P Robson	0-1
Martin Brennan	0-5	E Callaghan	0-1	P Niven	0-1
P McLoughlin	0-3	G Bradley	0-1	R Dunwoody	0-1
Arnold Garvey	0-1	Miss P Jones	0-1	T Dascombe	0-1

COURSE RECORD

	Total W-R	Nov Hdles	H'cap Hdles	Nov Chses	H'cap Chses	Hunter Chses	N H Flat	£1 Level Stake
Market Rasen	3-9	1-3	2-5	0-1	0-0	0-0	0-0	+ 18.00
Kempton	1-1	0-0	1-1	0-0	0-0	0-0	0-0	+ 2.25
Aintree	1-2	0-1	0-0	0-0	0-0	0-0	1-1	+ 6.50
Uttoxeter	1-4	0-0	1-4	0-0	0-0	0-0	0-0	0.00
Huntingdon	1-5	0-0	0-2	0-0	1-1	0-0	0-2	- 3.27
Fakenham	1-8	0-1	1-6	0-1	0-0	0-0	0-0	+ 1.00

Cheltenham	0-4	Lingfield	0-2	Ludlow	0-1
Nottingham	0-4	Towcester	0-2	Newbury	0-1
Musselburgh	0-3	Haydock	0-1	Southwell	0-1
Stratford	0-3	Hereford	0-1	Worcester	0-1
Ascot	0-2	Leicester	0-1		

WINNING HORSES

	Races Run	1st	2nd	3rd	Unpl	Win £
Can Can Charlie	7	3	0	0	4	7,322
Burn Out	3	1	1	0	1	6,960
Kilfinny Cross	5	1	1	0	3	4,533
Lambson	11	1	2	0	8	2,714
Aviator's Dream	3	1	0	0	2	2,408
Lucy Tufty	6	1	3	0	2	1,994

WINNING OWNERS

	Races Won	Value £
G H Tufts	4	9,316
The Al Yancy P'ship	1	6,960
A J Thompson	1	4,533
Ian Hall	1	2,714
P Bottomley	1	2,408

No of horses racing for the stable		14		Total winning prize-money			£25,931

Favourites	2-6	33.3%	- 1.02	Average SP of winner			5.7/1
Longest win seq	1	Longest losing seq	14	Return on stakes invested			-4.5%

1994/95 Form	6-36	16.7%	+ 13.75	1992/93 Form	2-14	14.3%	+ 3.00
1993/94 Form	1-16	6.3%	- 5.00	1991/92 Form	4-23	17.4%	- 4.24

KEITH R PEARCE (Carmarthen, Dyfed)

	Races Run	1st	2nd	3rd	Unpl	Per cent	£1 Level Stake
Hurdles	0	0	0	0	0	-	0.00
Chases	3	1	1	0	1	33.3	+ 5.00
Totals	3	1	1	0	1	33.3	+ 5.00

Mr D Jones	1-3	+ 5.00	Bangor	1-1	+ 7.00

No of horses racing for the stable	2	Total winning prize-money	£1,659

MISS L A PERRATT (Ayr, Strathclyde)

	Races Run	1st	2nd	3rd	Unpl	Per cent	£1 Level Stake
Hurdles	23	1	1	2	19	4.3	- 16.00
Chases	4	0	0	1	3	-	- 4.00
Totals	27	1	1	3	22	3.7	- 20.00

P Niven	1-6	+ 1.00	Sedgefield	1-2	+ 5.00

No of horses racing for the stable	8	Total winning prize-money	£2,425

R T PHILLIPS (Lambourn, Berks)

	Races Run	1st	2nd	3rd	Unpl	Per cent	£1 Level Stake
Hurdles	18	4	3	1	10	22.2	+ 4.63
Chases	30	4	3	0	23	13.3	- 18.90
Totals	48	8	6	1	33	16.7	- 14.27

BY MONTH

	W-R	Per cent	£1 Level Stake		W-R	Per cent	£1 Level Stake
June	0-3	-	- 3.00	December	1-3	33.3	- 0.90
July	0-0	-	0.00	January	1-7	14.3	- 3.75
August	0-2	-	- 2.00	February	1-2	50.0	+ 5.50
September	0-0	-	0.00	March	2-9	22.2	+ 3.50
October	1-3	33.3	+ 0.25	April	1-8	12.5	- 5.37
November	1-3	33.3	- 0.50	May	0-8	-	- 8.00

DISTANCE

Hurdles	W-R	Per cent	£1 Level Stake	Chases	W-R	Per cent	£1 Level Stake
2m-2m 3f	4-14	28.6	+ 8.63	2m-2m 3f	4-15	26.7	- 3.90
2m 4f-2m 7f	0-2	-	- 2.00	2m 4f-2m 7f	0-7	-	- 7.00
3m +	0-2	-	- 2.00	3m +	0-8	-	- 8.00

TYPE OF RACE

	W-R	Per cent	£1 Level Stake		W-R	Per cent	£1 Level Stake
Novice hurdles	2-7	28.6	+ 4.00	Selling	0-7	-	- 7.00
H'cap hurdles	2-4	50.0	+ 7.63	Amateur	0-0	-	0.00
Novice chases	0-12	-	- 12.00	Hunter chases	0-0	-	0.00
H'cap chases	4-17	23.5	- 5.90	N H Flat	0-1	-	- 1.00

COURSE GRADE

	W-R	Per cent	£1 Level Stake
Group 1	5-14	35.7	+ 10.35
Group 2	1-8	12.5	- 5.37
Group 3	2-15	13.3	- 8.25
Group 4	0-11	-	- 11.00

FIRST TIME OUT

	W-R	Per cent	£1 Level Stake
Hurdles	0-8	-	- 8.00
Chases	0-5	-	- 5.00
Totals	0-13	-	- 13.00

JOCKEYS RIDING

	W-R	Per cent	£1 Level Stake
J Railton	8-37	21.6	- 3.27

S Curran	0-4	G Crone	0-1	S McNeill	0-1
A Thornton	0-1	J A McCarthy	0-1	W Marston	0-1
C Maude	0-1	R Bellamy	0-1		

COURSE RECORD

	Total W-R	Nov Hdles	H'cap Hdles	Nov Chses	H'cap Chses	Hunter Chses	N H Flat	£1 Level Stake
Haydock	1-1	0-0	0-0	0-0	1-1	0-0	0-0	+ 1.50
Kempton	1-2	0-1	0-0	0-0	1-1	0-0	0-0	+ 1.25
Sandown	1-2	1-1	0-0	0-0	0-1	0-0	0-0	+ 5.50
Doncaster	1-2	0-0	0-0	0-1	1-1	0-0	0-0	+ 0.10
Newton Abbot	1-3	0-0	1-1	0-2	0-0	0-0	0-0	- 0.37
Newbury	1-3	0-0	1-2	0-0	0-1	0-0	0-0	+ 6.00
Windsor	1-3	1-1	0-0	0-2	0-0	0-0	0-0	+ 0.50
Stratford	1-4	0-0	0-0	0-1	1-3	0-0	0-0	- 0.75

Ludlow	0-4	Fontwell		0-2	Ascot	0-1
Hereford	0-3	Leicester		0-2	Exeter	0-1
Southwell	0-3	Uttoxeter		0-2	Plumpton	0-1
Cheltenham	0-2	Worcester		0-2	Warwick	0-1
Chepstow	0-2	Aintree		0-1	Wetherby	0-1

WINNING HORSES

	Races Run	1st	2nd	3rd	Unpl	Win £
Time Won't Wait	12	4	2	0	6	18,513
Frogmarch	6	4	1	0	1	12,797

WINNING OWNERS

	Races Won	Value £		Races Won	Value £
Old Berks Partnership	4	18,513	Mrs Helen Mills	4	12,797

No of horses racing for the stable	13	Total winning prize-money	£31,310
Favourites	6-9 66.7% + 8.23	Average SP of winner	3.2/1
Longest win seq 1 Longest losing seq 15		Return on stakes invested	-29.7%
1994/95 Form	7-41 17.1% - 16.24	1992/93 Form 0-4	
1993/94 Form	4-34 11.8% + 6.25		

J A PICKERING (Sharnford, Leics)

	Races Run	1st	2nd	3rd	Unpl	Per cent	£1 Level Stake
Hurdles	32	2	1	2	27	6.3	- 14.25
Chases	17	1	0	1	15	5.9	- 9.50
Totals	49	3	1	3	42	6.1	- 23.75

Miss J Wormall	1-4 - 1.25	M Sharratt	1-16	- 8.50
T Dascombe	1-7 + 8.00			
Towcester	2-9 + 1.25	Bangor	1-6	+ 9.00

No of horses racing for the stable	15	Total winning prize-money	£7,778

MISS J PIDGEON (Northampton, Northants)

	Races Run	1st	2nd	3rd	Unpl	Per cent	£1 Level Stake
Hurdles	0	0	0	0	0	-	0.00
Chases	6	3	1	1	1	50.0	- 0.19
Totals	6	3	1	1	1	50.0	- 0.19

Mr Richard White	3-5	+ 0.81

Ludlow	2-2	+ 2.08	Huntingdon	1-1	+ 0.73

No of horses racing for the stable   2   Total winning prize-money   £5,535

S L PIKE (Sidbury, Devon)

	Races Run	1st	2nd	3rd	Unpl	Per cent	£1 Level Stake
Hurdles	0	0	0	0	0	-	0.00
Chases	18	2	3	3	10	11.1	- 10.75
Totals	18	2	3	3	10	11.1	- 10.75

M A Fitzgerald	1-1	+ 3.50	Mr J Culloty	1-2	+ 0.75
Stratford	1-2	+ 0.75	Cheltenham	1-3	+ 1.50

No of horses racing for the stable   4   Total winning prize-money   £16,066

M C PIPE (Nicholashayne, Devon)

	Races Run	1st	2nd	3rd	Unpl	Per cent	£1 Level Stake
Hurdles	555	124	73	59	299	22.3	- 29.17
Chases	215	52	43	23	97	24.2	- 31.84
Totals	770	176	116	82	396	22.9	- 61.01

BY MONTH

	W-R	Per cent	£1 Level Stake		W-R	Per cent	£1 Level Stake
June	6-19	31.6	- 2.69	December	14-63	22.2	+ 5.43
July	11-29	37.9	+ 5.82	January	16-93	17.2	- 7.83
August	13-29	44.8	+ 8.36	February	9-65	13.8	- 23.11
September	16-36	44.4	+ 5.45	March	15-122	12.3	+ 0.48
October	13-51	25.5	- 16.15	April	15-72	20.8	- 14.07
November	13-61	21.3	- 15.61	May	35-130	26.9	- 7.09

DISTANCE

Hurdles	W-R	Per cent	£1 Level Stake	Chases	W-R	Per cent	£1 Level Stake
2m-2m 3f	81-372	21.8	- 34.09	2m-2m 3f	13-52	25.0	- 8.28
2m 4f-2m 7f	29-124	23.4	+ 6.25	2m 4f-2m 7f	20-73	27.4	+ 1.40
3m +	14-59	23.7	- 1.33	3m +	19-90	21.1	- 24.96

TYPE OF RACE

	W-R	Per cent	£1 Level Stake		W-R	Per cent	£1 Level Stake
Novice hurdles	56-210	26.7	+ 12.08	Selling	23-90	25.6	- 4.84
H'cap hurdles	35-200	17.5	- 26.33	Amateur	4-9	44.4	+ 2.76
Novice chases	25-76	32.9	- 4.12	Hunter chases	1-6	16.7	- 2.50
H'cap chases	25-122	20.5	- 20.72	N H Flat	7-57	12.3	- 17.34

COURSE GRADE

	W-R	Per cent	£1 Level Stake
Group 1	19-171	11.1	- 39.63
Group 2	46-177	26.0	- 8.36
Group 3	56-210	26.7	- 20.22
Group 4	55-212	25.9	+ 7.20

FIRST TIME OUT

	W-R	Per cent	£1 Level Stake
Hurdles	22-117	18.8	- 8.89
Chases	8-40	20.0	- 7.98
Totals	30-157	19.1	- 16.87

JOCKEYS RIDING

	W-R	Per cent	£1 Level Stake		W-R	Per cent	£1 Level Stake
D Bridgwater	111-428	25.9	- 38.80	R Dunwoody	1-1	100.0	+ 1.38
J Lower	19-117	16.2	- 5.03	R Cochrane	1-1	100.0	+ 3.50
C Maude	9-51	17.6	- 4.51	Jeff King	1-1	100.0	+ 9.00
O Burrows	9-55	16.4	- 4.40	E Husband	1-1	100.0	+ 4.00
A P McCoy	7-11	63.6	+ 8.10	S Wynne	1-2	50.0	+ 2.00
Mr A Farrant	5-9	55.6	+ 6.26	R Bellamy	1-2	50.0	+ 2.50
D Walsh	3-12	25.0	- 3.89	R Farrant	1-3	33.3	- 0.90
J Osborne	2-7	28.6	- 1.12	D Leahy	1-3	33.3	- 1.60
Jamie Evans	2-29	6.9	- 7.50	B Moore	1-11	9.1	- 4.00

C F Swan	0-4	G Bradley	0-1	Mr J P Dempsey	0-1
M Richards	0-2	G McCourt	0-1	Mr J P Durkan	0-1
R Johnson	0-2	M Dwyer	0-1	Mr L Jefford	0-1
R Massey	0-2	Mike Gallemore	0-1	Mr P Fenton	0-1
A Maguire	0-1	Miss A Plunkett	0-1	P Holley	0-1
B Powell	0-1	Miss S Vickery	0-1	V Slattery	0-1
F Leahy	0-1	Mr J Evans	0-1		

COURSE RECORD

	Total W-R	Nov Hdles	H'cap Hdles	Nov Chses	H'cap Chses	Hunter Chses	N H Flat	£1 Level Stake
Newton Abbot	21-98	6-22	3-34	5-10	5-19	1-2	1-11	- 22.45
Exeter	20-64	7-22	6-22	3-6	4-10	0-0	0-4	+ 24.68
Chepstow	13-38	4-12	6-14	0-1	1-7	0-0	2-4	+ 11.36
Uttoxeter	9-29	3-12	2-8	1-3	3-5	0-0	0-1	- 5.01
Taunton	9-43	5-13	3-21	1-3	0-6	0-0	0-0	- 17.00
Wincanton	7-27	4-11	2-7	1-2	0-5	0-0	0-2	- 7.34

Pipe M C

Hereford	7-29	6-11	0-6	1-2	0-5	0-1	0-4	− 8.71
Fontwell	6-19	3-7	1-6	2-5	0-1	0-0	0-0	− 4.90
Market Rasen	6-21	2-5	2-8	2-3	0-3	0-0	0-2	+ 2.66
Worcester	6-21	3-7	2-6	0-2	1-6	0-0	0-0	− 2.36
Lingfield	6-22	3-6	1-5	0-3	1-1	0-0	1-7	+ 7.63
Warwick	6-26	3-5	1-11	1-1	1-7	0-0	0-2	+ 1.04
Stratford	6-29	1-14	1-5	1-2	3-6	0-2	0-0	− 4.96
Haydock	6-36	4-12	2-13	0-1	0-6	0-0	0-4	− 11.52
Perth	5-6	1-2	2-2	1-1	0-0	0-0	1-1	+ 11.13
Plumpton	5-8	3-4	0-1	1-1	1-2	0-0	0-0	+ 7.34
Bangor	5-24	1-6	2-10	0-2	2-5	0-0	0-1	+ 10.13
Huntingdon	4-9	1-1	2-5	0-2	1-1	0-0	0-0	+ 3.79
Leicester	4-12	2-6	1-3	1-2	0-1	0-0	0-0	+ 5.30
Southwell	4-13	4-5	0-4	0-2	0-2	0-0	0-0	− 3.00
Cheltenham	4-47	1-18	0-11	2-8	1-7	0-1	0-2	− 23.44
Ludlow	3-17	1-11	2-4	0-0	0-1	0-0	0-1	+ 2.91
Aintree	3-22	2-7	0-5	0-0	1-9	0-0	0-1	+ 24.00
Folkestone	2-9	0-3	1-3	0-0	0-1	0-0	1-2	− 5.18
Kempton	2-13	1-4	0-5	1-4	0-0	0-0	0-0	− 9.17
Ascot	2-16	1-5	1-7	0-1	0-3	0-0	0-0	− 0.50
Cartmel	1-2	0-1	0-0	1-1	0-0	0-0	0-0	− 0.67
Towcester	1-11	0-4	1-2	0-2	0-1	0-0	0-2	− 9.27
Sandown	1-12	0-3	1-6	0-0	0-3	0-0	0-0	− 3.00
Nottingham	1-14	0-6	0-3	0-0	0-1	0-0	1-4	− 10.50
Newbury	1-19	0-5	0-4	0-2	1-6	0-0	0-2	− 10.00

Ayr	0-5	Fakenham	0-2	Newcastle	0-1
Windsor	0-5	Kelso	0-1		

WINNING HORSES

	Races Run	1st	2nd	3rd	Unpl	Win £
Cyborgo	1	1	0	0	0	53,585
Challenger Du Luc	8	3	3	2	0	41,928
Tragic Hero	7	3	2	0	2	39,974
James Pigg	15	6	3	1	5	26,826
Preenka Girl	11	7	1	0	3	21,359
Draborgie	3	2	0	0	1	20,994
Runaway Pete	12	6	2	1	3	17,877
Silver Shred	5	2	1	1	1	17,439
Elite Reg	13	5	2	2	4	17,227
Terao	6	3	0	0	3	15,985
All For Luck	9	2	2	2	3	15,719
Lemon's Mill	8	4	1	0	3	14,054
Tonys Gift	11	5	0	3	3	13,474
First Century	8	4	1	2	1	12,264
Errant Knight	4	3	0	0	1	11,473
Nordic Valley	16	5	3	5	3	11,103
Banntown Bill	18	3	7	2	6	10,789
Evangelica	11	3	2	0	6	10,656
Gysart	8	4	0	1	3	10,211
Pridwell	11	2	2	2	5	10,087
Shikaree	7	4	1	0	2	10,063
Glengarrif Girl	8	4	1	1	2	9,853
Indian Jockey	10	4	3	0	3	9,447

Sohrab	8	2	3	0	3	8,844
Most Equal	13	3	4	1	5	8,821
Dominion's Dream	6	4	1	1	0	8,670
Ever Smile	7	3	0	1	3	8,487
Potentate	4	3	0	0	1	8,486
Make A Stand	4	3	0	0	1	7,823
Crosula	8	2	0	1	5	6,889
Yubralee	9	3	2	1	3	6,631
Out Ranking	9	3	1	3	2	6,622
Peter Monamy	4	3	1	0	0	6,347
Chaprassi	3	3	0	0	0	6,282
Superior Risk	5	2	2	0	1	5,844
Seasonal Splendour	5	2	0	1	2	5,769
Belmore Cloud	5	2	0	0	3	5,658
Toomuch Toosoon	5	2	2	0	1	5,576
Cool Clown	5	2	0	0	3	5,320
Vario	3	2	0	1	0	5,126
Celcius	14	2	0	1	11	4,877
All Clear	8	2	1	1	4	4,680
Tipping The Line	7	2	2	0	3	4,307
The Black Monk	13	2	3	1	7	4,228
Toute Bagaille	6	2	0	0	4	4,209
Nordic Crown	8	2	0	0	6	4,125
Morning Blush	5	2	0	0	3	4,121
Crosa's Delight	5	2	1	0	2	4,106
Escartefigue	4	1	1	1	1	4,013
Hamilton Silk	7	1	3	1	2	3,556
Big Strand	7	1	1	1	4	3,037
Robert's Toy	8	1	2	1	4	2,970
Arctic Maid	2	1	0	0	1	2,910
St Mellion Drive	4	2	0	0	2	2,851
Born To Be Wild	4	1	0	0	3	2,810
Mack The Knife	4	1	2	0	1	2,808
Lisotho	2	1	0	0	1	2,738
Norse Raider	2	1	0	1	0	2,723
Political Panto	5	1	0	0	4	2,705
Habasha	9	1	1	3	4	2,696
Pond House	6	1	1	2	2	2,632
Damas	8	1	1	1	5	2,626
Sozzled	4	1	2	1	0	2,564
Sophism	11	1	2	1	7	2,496
Mr Bureaucrat	3	1	0	0	2	2,484
Diamond Cut	6	1	2	0	3	2,320
Jennyellen	1	1	0	0	0	2,318
Belmore Rock	1	1	0	0	0	2,276
Valiant Toski	8	1	0	4	3	2,206
Friendly House	3	1	0	1	1	2,206
Kiniohio	1	1	0	0	0	2,187
Balasani	5	1	0	0	4	2,180
Palosanto	5	1	3	1	0	2,094
Irkutsk	3	1	0	1	1	2,044
St Mellion Green	3	1	1	0	1	1,862
Norman's Convinced	3	1	0	1	1	1,760
Indian Tracker	3	1	1	0	1	1,152
Southerly Gale	4	1	1	0	2	1,138

WINNING OWNERS

	Races Won	Value £		Races Won	Value £
Martin Pipe Racing Club	20	60,209	A J Lomas	3	7,176
Knight Hawks Partnership	11	58,557	Richard Green (Fine Paintings)	3	6,347
County Stores (Somerset) Holdings	1	53,585	The Sun Punters Club	3	6,226
D A Johnson	6	45,120	J D Smeadon	2	6,189
Bisgrove Partnership	12	41,942	L G Kennard	2	5,576
Darren C Mercer	9	40,298	Mrs P B Browne	2	5,320
B A Kilpatrick	7	24,361	C R Fleet	2	4,819
David L'Estrange	7	18,340	Elite Racing Club	1	3,556
D M Beresford	2	17,439	E C Jones	1	3,037
Pond House Racing Ltd	7	15,957	Clive D Smith	1	2,970
B J Craig	2	15,719	Steve Jones Partnership	1	2,910
Perran Associates	5	14,252	St Mellion Estates Ltd	2	2,851
Stuart M Mercer	4	14,054	Mrs L M Sewell	1	2,826
The Blue Chip Group	5	13,474	D & G Mercer	1	2,808
Merthyr Motor Auctions	4	12,264	S Nelson	1	2,738
Mrs N J Bird	3	11,473	Peter Fyvie	1	2,723
Eric Scarth	3	10,789	Sean Lucey	1	2,705
Mrs R Cobbold	4	10,211	Terry Neill	1	2,696
Malcolm B Jones	2	10,087	Stanley W Clarke	1	2,484
The Baad Boys	4	10,063	0336 405200 Racing	1	2,444
Mrs Joanne Richards	3	9,996	Liam Mulryan	1	2,318
J & J Securities Limited	2	9,208	Sir John Swaine	1	2,206
Heeru Kirpalani	3	8,821	Mrs Sarah Buckley	1	2,206
Jim Weeden	3	8,486	M D Smith	1	2,180
Mrs Audrey J Hartnett	3	7,934	Somerset White Lining Ltd	1	1,760
P A Deal	3	7,823	0336 405200 Pipeline	1	1,481
405200 Racing	4	7,583			

No of horses racing for the stable	159	Total winning prize-money	£648,597

Favourites	102-231	44.2% – 6.01	Average SP of winner		3.0/1
Longest win seq 5	Longest losing seq	20	Return on stakes invested		-7.9%

1994/95 Form	137-602	22.8% – 58.65	1992/93 Form	194-769	25.2%	– 84.21
1993/94 Form	127-572	22.2% – 78.28	1991/92 Form	224-839	26.7%	– 60.90

MRS J PITMAN (Upper Lambourn, Berks)

	Races Run	1st	2nd	3rd	Unpl	Per cent	£1 Level Stake
Hurdles	125	21	15	9	80	16.8	+ 46.75
Chases	131	27	16	20	68	20.6	+ 0.85
Totals	256	48	31	29	148	18.8	+ 47.60

BY MONTH

	W-R	Per cent	£1 Level Stake		W-R	Per cent	£1 Level Stake
June	0-0	-	0.00	December	2-23	8.7	- 9.00
July	0-0	-	0.00	January	11-49	22.4	- 1.97
August	0-0	-	0.00	February	6-32	18.8	+ 10.41
September	1-8	12.5	0.00	March	5-39	12.8	+ 14.00
October	3-20	15.0	- 7.50	April	3-22	13.6	- 13.49
November	13-39	33.3	+ 59.85	May	4-24	16.7	- 4.70

DISTANCE

Hurdles	W-R	Per cent	£1 Level Stake	Chases	W-R	Per cent	£1 Level Stake
2m-2m 3f	10-69	14.5	+ 22.50	2m-2m 3f	3-11	27.3	+ 7.50
2m 4f-2m 7f	8-41	19.5	+ 31.75	2m 4f-2m 7f	9-42	21.4	- 1.83
3m +	3-15	20.0	- 7.50	3m +	15-78	19.2	- 4.82

TYPE OF RACE

	W-R	Per cent	£1 Level Stake		W-R	Per cent	£1 Level Stake
Novice hurdles	11-66	16.7	+ 5.00	Selling	0-3	-	- 3.00
H'cap hurdles	5-29	17.2	+ 24.25	Amateur	0-0	-	0.00
Novice chases	9-51	17.6	- 9.31	Hunter chases	0-0	-	0.00
H'cap chases	18-78	23.1	+ 12.16	N H Flat	5-29	17.2	+ 18.50

COURSE GRADE

	W-R	Per cent	£1 Level Stake
Group 1	21-97	21.6	+ 35.16
Group 2	4-22	18.2	+ 39.50
Group 3	17-105	16.2	- 22.44
Group 4	6-32	18.8	- 4.62

FIRST TIME OUT

	W-R	Per cent	£1 Level Stake
Hurdles	8-42	19.0	+ 51.50
Chases	4-21	19.0	+ 5.50
Totals	12-63	19.0	+ 57.00

JOCKEYS RIDING

	W-R	Per cent	£1 Level Stake		W-R	Per cent	£1 Level Stake
W Marston	30-143	21.0	+ 14.88	A P McCoy	1-1	100.0	+ 4.00
R Farrant	10-54	18.5	+ 31.79	R Dunwoody	1-3	33.3	- 1.20
A Bates	4-13	30.8	+ 22.63	S Knott	1-7	14.3	+ 2.00
A Maguire	1-1	100.0	+ 7.50				

Mr M McGrath	0-9	G Bradley	0-2	J Magee	0-1
G Hogan	0-5	A Thornton	0-1	J Osborne	0-1
I Lawrence	0-4	B Powell	0-1	K Brown	0-1
R Bellamy	0-4	C Maude	0-1		
L Wyer	0-3	D Bridgwater	0-1		

Pitman Mrs J

COURSE RECORD

	Total W-R	Nov Hdles	H'cap Hdles	Nov Chses	H'cap Chses	Hunter Chses	N H Flat	£1 Level Stake
Cheltenham	5-14	1-2	2-3	1-2	1-6	0-0	0-1	+ 32.00
Warwick	5-16	0-0	0-3	3-5	1-5	0-0	1-3	+ 5.62
Ascot	4-15	0-5	1-2	0-1	2-6	0-0	1-1	+ 16.25
Newbury	4-17	3-5	0-2	0-1	1-7	0-0	0-2	- 1.00
Uttoxeter	4-21	0-5	0-4	0-5	4-6	0-0	0-1	- 3.47
Chepstow	3-9	1-4	1-2	0-0	1-3	0-0	0-0	+ 46.50
Leicester	3-9	2-3	0-0	1-4	0-2	0-0	0-0	+ 3.91
Haydock	3-14	0-5	1-1	1-2	1-5	0-0	0-1	- 5.59
Worcester	3-17	0-2	0-1	1-6	1-5	0-0	1-3	+ 0.50
Hereford	2-4	0-1	0-0	0-0	2-3	0-0	0-0	+ 7.63
Kempton	2-10	1-3	0-1	0-0	1-3	0-0	0-3	- 2.00
Towcester	2-11	1-6	0-0	1-2	0-2	0-0	0-1	- 5.25
Sandown	2-13	0-1	0-2	0-2	2-7	0-0	0-1	+ 0.50
Ludlow	1-3	1-2	0-0	0-0	0-1	0-0	0-0	+ 1.00
Doncaster	1-3	0-1	0-1	1-1	0-0	0-0	0-0	+ 6.00
Newton Abbot	1-7	0-1	0-1	0-0	0-2	0-0	1-3	- 1.00
Exeter	1-7	0-1	0-1	0-2	0-1	0-0	1-2	- 1.00
Nottingham	1-8	1-4	0-1	0-1	0-1	0-0	0-1	- 5.00
Wincanton	1-10	0-3	0-2	0-3	1-2	0-0	0-0	0.00

Aintree	0-9	Plumpton	0-4	Lingfield	0-1
Windsor	0-9	Huntingdon	0-3	Market Rasen	0-1
Bangor	0-5	Fakenham	0-2	Newcastle	0-1
Stratford	0-5	Folkestone	0-2	Wetherby	0-1
Fontwell	0-4	Ayr	0-1		

WINNING HORSES

	Races Run	1st	2nd	3rd	Unpl	Win £
Nahthen Lad	6	4	2	0	0	65,354
Indefence	5	3	0	1	1	50,892
Jibber The Kibber	8	3	0	1	4	25,567
Superior Finish	6	1	0	3	2	21,300
Smith's Band	5	3	1	0	1	18,064
Wrekengale	7	4	0	0	3	17,447
Willsford	8	2	1	2	3	17,115
Egypt Mill Prince	8	1	2	2	3	16,856
Jet Rules	6	2	1	0	3	12,652
Idiot's Lady	5	3	0	0	2	12,497
Gilpa Valu	7	3	2	0	2	11,561
Arithmetic	5	2	0	1	2	6,854
Master Tribe	5	2	0	0	3	6,780
Cantoris Frater	5	2	2	0	1	6,458
Smith Too	8	2	0	1	5	6,204
Tennessee Twist	4	2	1	0	1	6,057
Magellan Bay	5	1	0	0	4	3,600
File Concord	2	1	1	0	0	3,556
Do Be Brief	5	1	1	0	3	3,535

Ever Blessed	2	1	1	0	0	2,852
Celtic Laird	6	1	0	1	4	2,811
Buster Bob	6	1	1	0	4	2,166
Mentmore Towers	1	1	0	0	0	1,459
Silver Thyne	1	1	0	0	0	1,369
Princeful	1	1	0	0	0	1,333

WINNING OWNERS

	Races Won	Value £		Races Won	Value £
J Shaw	4	65,354	Miss N F Thesiger	3	11,561
Indef Limited	3	50,892	Jebel Ali Racing Stables	2	6,780
Robert & Elizabeth Hitchins	10	31,980	The Ley Partnership	2	6,458
J Hitchins	3	25,567	Smith Mansfield Meat Co Ltd	2	6,204
G Henfrey	1	21,300	Halewood Int'l Ltd	2	6,057
Arthur Smith	3	18,064	Autofour Engineering	1	3,600
Arnie Kaplan	2	17,115	Errol Brown	1	3,535
S R Webb	1	16,856	The Ever Blessed P'ship	1	2,852
The Jet Stationery Co Ltd	3	16,208	Philip Matton	1	1,459
Mrs J Ollivant	3	12,497			

No of horses racing for the stable	64	Total winning prize-money	£324,339
Favourites	20-51	39.2%	+ 5.85	Average SP of winner	5.3/1
Longest win seq	2	Longest losing seq	19	Return on stakes invested	18.6%
1994/95 Form	36-219	16.4%	+ 24.70	1992/93 Form	36-242	14.9%	- 26.07
1993/94 Form	26-221	11.8%	- 74.69	1991/92 Form	50-333	15.0%	- 69.40

C L POPHAM (West Bagborough, Somerset)

	Races Run	1st	2nd	3rd	Unpl	Per cent	£1 Level Stake
Hurdles	78	6	9	11	52	7.7	- 22.50
Chases	40	2	4	6	28	5.0	- 21.50
Totals	118	8	13	17	80	6.8	- 44.00

BY MONTH

	W-R	Per cent	£1 Level Stake		W-R	Per cent	£1 Level Stake
June	0-1	-	- 1.00	December	1-13	7.7	- 5.00
July	0-2	-	- 2.00	January	2-10	20.0	+ 10.00
August	0-0	-	0.00	February	1-13	7.7	0.00
September	0-7	-	- 7.00	March	1-17	5.9	- 11.50
October	2-13	15.4	+ 9.00	April	0-14	-	- 14.00
November	1-16	6.3	- 10.50	May	0-12	-	- 12.00

DISTANCE

Hurdles	W-R	Per cent	£1 Level Stake	Chases	W-R	Per cent	£1 Level Stake
2m-2m 3f	6-62	9.7	- 6.50	2m-2m 3f	1-23	4.3	- 10.00
2m 4f-2m 7f	0-13	-	- 13.00	2m 4f-2m 7f	1-9	11.1	- 3.50
3m +	0-3	-	- 3.00	3m +	0-8	-	- 8.00

TYPE OF RACE

	W-R	Per cent	£1 Level Stake		W-R	Per cent	£1 Level Stake
Novice hurdles	2-34	5.9	- 20.00	Selling	3-20	15.0	+ 21.00
H'cap hurdles	2-27	7.4	- 13.50	Amateur	0-1	-	- 1.00
Novice chases	0-8	-	- 8.00	Hunter chases	0-0	-	0.00
H'cap chases	1-26	3.8	- 20.50	N H Flat	0-2	-	- 2.00

COURSE GRADE

	W-R	Per cent	£1 Level Stake
Group 1	0-6	-	- 6.00
Group 2	2-24	8.3	- 5.50
Group 3	5-31	16.1	+ 17.50
Group 4	1-57	1.8	- 50.00

FIRST TIME OUT

	W-R	Per cent	£1 Level Stake
Hurdles	2-19	10.5	+ 3.00
Chases	0-5	-	- 5.00
Totals	2-24	8.3	- 2.00

JOCKEYS RIDING

	W-R	Per cent	£1 Level Stake		W-R	Per cent	£1 Level Stake
T Dascombe	7-68	10.3	- 1.00	M A Fitzgerald	1-16	6.3	- 9.00

	W-R		W-R		W-R
G E Tormey	0-5	R Dunwoody	0-2	J Harris	0-1
A Thornton	0-3	R Johnson	0-2	J Titley	0-1
W Marston	0-3	T Murphy	0-2	M Bosley	0-1
A Dobbin	0-2	Christopher Webb	0-1	P Holley	0-1
A P McCoy	0-2	D Bentley	0-1	S McNeill	0-1
B Powell	0-2	D Gallagher	0-1		
Mr J Culloty	0-2	G Supple	0-1		

COURSE RECORD

	Total W-R	Nov Hdles	H'cap Hdles	Nov Chses	H'cap Chses	Hunter Chses	N H Flat	£1 Level Stake
Plumpton	2-4	0-1	1-1	0-0	1-2	0-0	0-0	+ 16.50
Newton Abbot	2-15	0-5	1-3	0-0	1-7	0-0	0-0	+ 3.50
Folkestone	1-3	0-0	1-1	0-0	0-2	0-0	0-0	+ 5.00
Catterick	1-4	0-0	1-2	0-1	0-1	0-0	0-0	+ 9.00
Wincanton	1-11	1-6	0-2	0-2	0-1	0-0	0-0	- 4.00
Taunton	1-28	1-12	0-9	0-1	0-6	0-0	0-0	- 21.00

Exeter	0-13	Cheltenham	0-3	Warwick	0-2
Ludlow	0-9	Hereford	0-3	Bangor	0-1
Chepstow	0-5	Ascot	0-2	Sandown	0-1
Fontwell	0-4	Southwell	0-2	Towcester	0-1
Worcester	0-4	Stratford	0-2	Uttoxeter	0-1

Popham C L

WINNING HORSES

	Races Run	1st	2nd	3rd	Unpl	Win £
Robins Pride	6	2	2	0	2	5,208
Dontdressfordinner	8	2	1	2	3	4,184
Lucky Again	9	1	1	1	6	3,800
Emral Miss	10	1	2	1	6	2,857
He's A King	10	1	1	1	7	2,264
Queens Contractor	5	1	0	0	4	2,108

WINNING OWNERS

	Races Won	Value £		Races Won	Value £
M A Long	2	5,208	Mrs Jonathan Bennett	1	2,857
The Dontdressfordinner P'ship	2	4,184	Mrs Jill Emery	1	2,264
Richard Weeks	1	3,800	A G Fear	1	2,108

No of horses racing for the stable		28	Total winning prize-money		£20,421
Favourites	0-7		Average SP of winner		8.3/1
Longest win seq	1	Longest losing seq 30	Return on stakes invested		-37.3%

1994/95 Form	8-85	9.4%	- 33.25	1992/93 Form	8-118	6.8%	- 54.54
1993/94 Form	7-109	6.4%	- 75.50	1991/92 Form	3-100	3.0%	- 87.46

B PREECE (Uppington, Salop)

	Races Run	1st	2nd	3rd	Unpl	Per cent	£1 Level Stake
Hurdles	83	2	6	3	72	2.4	- 64.00
Chases	6	0	0	1	5	-	- 6.00
Totals	89	2	6	4	77	2.2	- 70.00

G Hogan	2-38	- 19.00			
Stratford	1-4	+ 8.00	Worcester	1-11	- 4.00

No of horses racing for the stable	28	Total winning prize-money	£4,703

G M PRICE (Brecon, Powys)

	Races Run	1st	2nd	3rd	Unpl	Per cent	£1 Level Stake
Hurdles	15	2	5	0	8	13.3	- 2.50
Chases	0	0	0	0	0	-	0.00
Totals	15	2	5	0	8	13.3	- 2.50

J R Kavanagh	1-1	+ 7.00	A P McCoy	1-2	+ 2.50
Warwick	2-3	+ 9.50			

No of horses racing for the stable	3	Total winning prize-money	£7,171

R J PRICE (Leominster, H'ford & Worcs)

	Races Run	1st	2nd	3rd	Unpl	Per cent	£1 Level Stake
Hurdles	66	7	3	5	51	10.6	- 9.00
Chases	22	1	3	1	17	4.5	- 18.50
Totals	88	8	6	6	68	9.1	- 27.50

BY MONTH

	W-R	Per cent	£1 Level Stake		W-R	Per cent	£1 Level Stake
June	0-3	-	- 3.00	December	0-4	-	- 4.00
July	0-3	-	- 3.00	January	1-2	50.0	+ 4.00
August	2-6	33.3	- 0.50	February	0-8	-	- 8.00
September	0-7	-	- 7.00	March	1-10	10.0	- 1.00
October	0-10	-	- 10.00	April	2-8	25.0	+ 10.50
November	0-12	-	- 12.00	May	2-15	13.3	+ 6.50

DISTANCE

Hurdles	W-R	Per cent	£1 Level Stake	Chases	W-R	Per cent	£1 Level Stake
2m-2m 3f	6-53	11.3	- 11.00	2m-2m 3f	0-5	-	- 5.00
2m 4f-2m 7f	0-9	-	- 9.00	2m 4f-2m 7f	0-6	-	- 6.00
3m +	1-4	25.0	+ 11.00	3m +	1-11	9.1	- 7.50

TYPE OF RACE

	W-R	Per cent	£1 Level Stake		W-R	Per cent	£1 Level Stake
Novice hurdles	3-26	11.5	- 5.50	Selling	1-10	10.0	- 4.00
H'cap hurdles	3-19	15.8	+ 11.50	Amateur	0-4	-	- 4.00
Novice chases	0-5	-	- 5.00	Hunter chases	0-0	-	0.00
H'cap chases	1-13	7.7	- 9.50	N H Flat	0-11	-	- 11.00

COURSE GRADE					FIRST TIME OUT			
	W-R	Per cent	£1 Level Stake			W-R	Per cent	£1 Level Stake
Group 1	0-9	-	- 9.00	Hurdles		0-19	-	- 19.00
Group 2	0-5	-	- 5.00	Chases		0-3	-	- 3.00
Group 3	3-32	9.4	- 19.75					
Group 4	5-42	11.9	+ 6.25	Totals		0-22	-	- 22.00

JOCKEYS RIDING

	W-R	Per cent	£1 Level Stake			W-R	Per cent	£1 Level Stake
A P McCoy	4-14	28.6	+ 7.00	Richard Davis		1-4	25.0	+ 11.00
D Bentley	1-1	100.0	+ 14.00	B Fenton		1-7	14.3	- 3.50
A Maguire	1-2	50.0	+ 4.00					

A Thornton	0-7	Mr J Culloty	0-2	Mr R Thornton	0-1
P McLoughlin	0-7	Mr M Jackson	0-2	N Williamson	0-1
T Jenks	0-7	C Maude	0-1	Philip Hughes	0-1
R Johnson	0-6	D Bridgwater	0-1	R Greene	0-1
Miss E Jones	0-4	D Finnegan	0-1	R Supple	0-1
R Dunwoody	0-4	G Hogan	0-1	S Wynne	0-1
Jodie Mogford	0-3	G Upton	0-1	T Dascombe	0-1
Guy Lewis	0-2	J A McCarthy	0-1		
J R Kavanagh	0-2	J Osborne	0-1		

COURSE RECORD

	Total W-R	Nov Hdles	H'cap Hdles	Nov Chses	H'cap Chses	Hunter Chses	N H Flat	£1 Level Stake
Bangor	2-11	1-2	1-4	0-0	0-2	0-0	0-3	+ 19.00
Worcester	2-13	1-4	1-4	0-0	0-4	0-0	0-1	- 4.25
Plumpton	1-1	0-0	0-0	0-0	1-1	0-0	0-0	+ 2.50
Taunton	1-1	0-0	1-1	0-0	0-0	0-0	0-0	+ 8.00
Ludlow	1-12	0-5	1-3	0-2	0-2	0-0	0-0	- 6.00
Hereford	1-14	1-5	0-6	0-0	0-2	0-0	0-1	- 10.75

Uttoxeter	0-5	Haydock	0-2	Doncaster	0-1
Cheltenham	0-4	Hexham	0-2	Fontwell	0-1
Chepstow	0-3	Leicester	0-2	Newbury	0-1
Stratford	0-3	Nottingham	0-2	Newton Abbot	0-1
Warwick	0-3	Southwell	0-2	Wincanton	0-1
Catterick	0-2	Ascot	0-1		

WINNING HORSES

	Races Run	1st	2nd	3rd	Unpl	Win £
Pridewood Picker	8	3	0	1	4	7,235
Little Gunner	5	2	0	0	3	6,365
Taahhub	8	2	2	1	3	4,442
Foxgrove	12	1	3	0	8	3,240

WINNING OWNERS

	Races Won	Value £		Races Won	Value £
Mrs B Morris	3	7,235	A E Price	2	4,442
A W Bailey	2	6,365	Mrs C W Middleton	1	3,240

No of horses racing for the stable	23	Total winning prize-money	£21,282

Favourites	2-7	28.6%	+ 1.25	Average SP of winner		6.6/1
Longest win seq	1	Longest losing seq	36	Return on stakes invested		-31.3%

1994/95 Form	1-80	1.3%	- 77.00	1992/93 Form	10-85	11.8%	- 13.27
1993/94 Form	9-59	15.3%	+ 9.88	1991/92 Form	8-67	11.9%	+ 12.30

GEORGE PRODROMOU (East Harling, Norfolk)

	Races Run	1st	2nd	3rd	Unpl	Per cent	£1 Level Stake
Hurdles	0	0	0	0	0	-	0.00
Chases	4	1	0	0	3	25.0	- 0.25
Totals	4	1	0	0	3	25.0	- 0.25

Mr A Coe	1-3	+ 0.75	Fakenham	1-3	+ 0.75

No of horses racing for the stable	2	Total winning prize-money	£2,753

J J QUINN (Settrington, North Yorks)

	Races Run	1st	2nd	3rd	Unpl	Per cent	£1 Level Stake
Hurdles	53	5	7	7	34	9.4	- 20.67
Chases	10	2	3	1	4	20.0	- 4.09
Totals	63	7	10	8	38	11.1	- 24.76

BY MONTH

	W-R	Per cent	£1 Level Stake		W-R	Per cent	£1 Level Stake
June	1-1	100.0	+ 3.50	December	0-8	-	- 8.00
July	0-0	-	0.00	January	2-13	15.4	+ 6.00
August	0-0	-	0.00	February	0-7	-	- 7.00
September	0-0	-	0.00	March	1-9	11.1	- 5.00
October	0-1	-	- 1.00	April	2-5	40.0	+ 3.83
November	1-14	7.1	- 12.09	May	0-5	-	- 5.00

DISTANCE

Hurdles	W-R	Per cent	£1 Level Stake	Chases	W-R	Per cent	£1 Level Stake
2m-2m 3f	4-44	9.1	- 20.67	2m-2m 3f	2-5	40.0	+ 0.91
2m 4f-2m 7f	1-4	25.0	+ 5.00	2m 4f-2m 7f	0-5	-	- 5.00
3m +	0-5	-	- 5.00	3m +	0-0	-	0.00

TYPE OF RACE

	W-R	Per cent	£1 Level Stake		W-R	Per cent	£1 Level Stake
Novice hurdles	2-25	8.0	- 11.50	Selling	1-10	10.0	0.00
H'cap hurdles	1-14	7.1	- 9.67	Amateur	0-1	-	- 1.00
Novice chases	1-1	100.0	+ 3.00	Hunter chases	0-0	-	0.00
H'cap chases	1-9	11.1	- 7.09	N H Flat	1-3	33.3	+ 1.50

COURSE GRADE

	W-R	Per cent	£1 Level Stake
Group 1	0-8	-	- 8.00
Group 2	0-5	-	- 5.00
Group 3	2-26	7.7	- 20.09
Group 4	5-24	20.8	+ 8.33

FIRST TIME OUT

	W-R	Per cent	£1 Level Stake
Hurdles	2-13	15.4	- 4.00
Chases	0-2	-	- 2.00
Totals	2-15	13.3	- 6.00

JOCKEYS RIDING

	W-R	Per cent	£1 Level Stake		W-R	Per cent	£1 Level Stake
E Callaghan	2-8	25.0	+ 0.33	L Wyer	1-7	14.3	- 2.50
A S Smith	1-2	50.0	- 0.09	D Byrne	1-8	12.5	+ 1.00
R Marley	1-3	33.3	+ 1.50	M Dwyer	1-22	4.5	- 12.00

B Harding	0-3	J R Kavanagh	0-1	W J Dwan	0-1
F Leahy	0-2	Mr S Swiers	0-1	W Marston	0-1
D J Kavanagh	0-1	P Niven	0-1	
G McCourt	0-1	Richard Guest	0-1	

COURSE RECORD

	Total W-R	Nov Hdles	H'cap Hdles	Nov Chses	H'cap Chses	Hunter Chses	N H Flat	£1 Level Stake
Hexham	2-7	0-1	1-4	0-0	0-1	0-0	1-1	+ 1.83
Sedgefield	2-11	1-4	1-5	0-0	0-2	0-0	0-0	+ 8.00
Catterick	2-11	0-4	0-4	1-1	1-1	0-0	0-1	- 5.09
Perth	1-1	1-1	0-0	0-0	0-0	0-0	0-0	+ 3.50

Wetherby	0-5	Newcastle	0-3	Carlisle	0-1
Bangor	0-3	Nottingham	0-3	Doncaster	0-1
Haydock	0-3	Warwick	0-3	Huntingdon	0-1
Leicester	0-3	Uttoxeter	0-2	Musselburgh	0-1
Market Rasen	0-3	Ascot	0-1		

Quinn J J

WINNING HORSES

	Races Run	1st	2nd	3rd	Unpl	Win £
The Toaster	7	2	3	1	1	4,955
Eriny	9	2	2	1	4	4,785
High Penhowe	4	1	0	1	2	2,157
Orchidarma	9	1	0	0	8	2,122
B The One	1	1	0	0	0	1,301

WINNING OWNERS

	Races Won	Value £		Races Won	Value £
Mrs Kay Owens	2	4,955	C R Galloway	1	2,122
Lady Anne Bentinck	2	4,785	Andrew Page & John Pollard	1	1,301
M J Buck	1	2,157			

No of horses racing for the stable	15	Total winning prize-money	£15,320

Favourites	1-7	14.3%	- 5.09	Average SP of winner	4.5/1
Longest win seq	2	Longest losing seq	13	Return on stakes invested	-39.3%

1994/95 Form	8-40	20.0%	- 8.89

MAJ-GEN C A RAMSAY (Coldstream, Berwicks)

	Races Run	1st	2nd	3rd	Unpl	Per cent	£1 Level Stake
Hurdles	0	0	0	0	0	-	0.00
Chases	2	1	0	1	0	50.0	+ 3.50
Totals	2	1	0	1	0	50.0	+ 3.50

Capt W B Ramsay	1-2	+ 3.50	Hexham	1-1	+ 4.50

No of horses racing for the stable	1	Total winning prize-money	£1,114

MRS J R RAMSDEN (Sandhutton, North Yorks)

	Races Run	1st	2nd	3rd	Unpl	Per cent	£1 Level Stake
Hurdles	28	4	5	6	13	14.3	- 16.77
Chases	0	0	0	0	0	-	0.00
Totals	28	4	5	6	13	14.3	- 16.77

R Garrity	3-16	- 7.52	D Thomas	1-7	- 4.25
Market Rasen	2-8	- 3.52	Wetherby	1-3	+ 0.25
Aintree	1-2	+ 1.50			

No of horses racing for the stable	11	Total winning prize-money	£14,268

W G REED (Haydon Bridge, Northumberland)

	Races Run	1st	2nd	3rd	Unpl	Per cent	£1 Level Stake
Hurdles	32	1	4	2	25	3.1	- 26.00
Chases	26	0	2	4	20	-	- 26.00
Totals	58	1	6	6	45	1.7	- 52.00

T Reed	1-44	- 38.00	Sedgefield	1-8	- 2.00

No of horses racing for the stable   14   Total winning prize-money   £2,635

MRS J RENFREE-BARONS (Broughton, Hants)

	Races Run	1st	2nd	3rd	Unpl	Per cent	£1 Level Stake
Hurdles	16	0	1	4	11	-	- 16.00
Chases	16	1	3	4	8	6.3	- 11.50
Totals	32	1	4	8	19	3.1	- 27.50

R Greene	1-27	- 22.50	Ludlow	1-2	+ 2.50

No of horses racing for the stable   17   Total winning prize-money   £3,074

MRS J G RETTER (Whitestone, Devon)

	Races Run	1st	2nd	3rd	Unpl	Per cent	£1 Level Stake
Hurdles	29	2	0	2	25	6.9	- 13.00
Chases	8	0	1	1	6	-	- 8.00
Totals	37	2	1	3	31	5.4	- 21.00

R Dunwoody	1-3	+ 2.00	A P McCoy	1-9	+ 2.00
Exotor	2-17	- 1.00			

No of horses racing for the stable   10   Total winning prize-money   £4,706

MRS M REVELEY (Lingdale Saltburn, Co Cleveland)

	Races Run	1st	2nd	3rd	Unpl	Per cent	£1 Level Stake
Hurdles	313	72	42	30	169	23.0	- 44.58
Chases	84	14	12	8	50	16.7	- 27.33
Totals	397	86	54	38	219	21.7	- 71.91

BY MONTH

	W-R	Per cent	£1 Level Stake		W-R	Per cent	£1 Level Stake
June	2-10	20.0	- 2.59	December	6-41	14.6	- 16.35
July	0-5	-	- 5.00	January	10-46	21.7	- 0.64
August	3-5	60.0	- 0.74	February	7-44	15.9	- 18.00
September	1-10	10.0	- 8.09	March	12-63	19.0	+ 25.88
October	11-28	39.3	+ 0.53	April	11-44	25.0	- 16.47
November	16-74	21.6	- 24.88	May	7-27	25.9	- 5.56

DISTANCE

Hurdles	W-R	Per cent	£1 Level Stake	Chases	W-R	Per cent	£1 Level Stake
2m-2m 3f	41-189	21.7	- 25.39	2m-2m 3f	5-17	29.4	+ 11.80
2m 4f-2m 7f	24-83	28.9	+ 5.84	2m 4f-2m 7f	5-31	16.1	- 12.07
3m +	7-41	17.1	- 25.03	3m +	4-36	11.1	- 27.06

TYPE OF RACE

	W-R	Per cent	£1 Level Stake		W-R	Per cent	£1 Level Stake
Novice hurdles	24-115	20.9	- 46.70	Selling	5-22	22.7	+ 0.85
H'cap hurdles	35-133	26.3	+ 16.06	Amateur	3-7	42.9	- 0.29
Novice chases	4-23	17.4	- 14.44	Hunter chases	0-0	-	0.00
H'cap chases	10-60	16.7	- 11.89	N H Flat	5-37	13.5	- 15.50

COURSE GRADE / FIRST TIME OUT

	W-R	Per cent	£1 Level Stake		W-R	Per cent	£1 Level Stake
Group 1	28-158	17.7	- 50.67	Hurdles	16-80	20.0	- 27.24
Group 2	12-39	30.8	- 10.13	Chases	3-16	18.8	- 6.34
Group 3	10-57	17.5	- 9.79				
Group 4	36-143	25.2	- 1.32	Totals	19-96	19.8	- 33.58

JOCKEYS RIDING

	W-R	Per cent	£1 Level Stake		W-R	Per cent	£1 Level Stake
P Niven	55-227	24.2	- 15.20	C McCormack	2-21	9.5	- 14.50
P G Cahill	12-44	27.3	+ 3.98	A Dobbin	1-1	100.0	+ 1.75
G Lee	6-25	24.0	- 5.40	L Wyer	1-4	25.0	- 0.25
R Hodge	4-19	21.1	- 1.75	M Herrington	1-12	8.3	- 8.75
Mr M H Naughton	3-16	18.8	- 9.29	N Smith	1-15	6.7	- 9.50

T Comerford	0-4	D Bridgwater	0-1	Peter Hobbs	0-1
G Bradley	0-3	G McCourt	0-1	Sarah Bainbridge	0-1
Capt A Ogden	0-1	Mr N Wilson	0-1		

COURSE RECORD

	Total W-R	Nov Hdles	H'cap Hdles	Nov Chses	H'cap Chses	Hunter Chses	N H Flat	£1 Level Stake
Wetherby	12-39	5-16	7-17	0-1	0-4	0-0	0-1	- 10.13
Newcastle	10-50	2-17	5-18	1-5	2-7	0-0	0-3	- 12.38
Ayr	9-44	2-11	3-13	1-4	2-8	0-0	1-8	- 19.12
Sedgefield	9-48	2-14	4-19	1-5	2-9	0-0	0-1	- 12.58
Kelso	7-27	2-10	5-10	0-2	0-5	0-0	0-0	+ 0.99
Carlisle	6-25	1-8	3-9	0-1	2-4	0-0	0-3	+ 1.50
Perth	5-13	4-7	0-3	0-0	1-2	0-0	0-1	- 4.81
Huntingdon	3-5	0-1	2-2	0-0	0-0	0-0	1-2	+ 10.25
Musselburgh	3-8	1-2	2-3	0-0	0-1	0-0	0-2	+ 10.00
Catterick	3-10	0-4	3-4	0-0	0-1	0-0	0-1	+ 2.13
Doncaster	3-17	1-2	0-5	0-2	1-5	0-0	1-3	+ 13.00
Haydock	3-17	1-7	2-9	0-0	0-0	0-0	0-1	- 9.20
Southwell	2-3	0-0	1-2	0-0	0-0	0-0	1-1	+ 5.25
Uttoxeter	2-9	0-2	2-6	0-0	0-0	0-0	0-1	+ 0.50
Hexham	2-10	1-2	1-4	0-2	0-1	0-0	0-1	+ 3.00
Cartmel	1-1	1-1	0-0	0-0	0-0	0-0	0-0	+ 0.33
Bangor	1-2	0-0	0-1	0-0	0-0	0-0	1-1	+ 1.00
Kempton	1-3	0-1	1-1	0-0	0-1	0-0	0-0	- 0.75
Newbury	1-4	1-2	0-2	0-0	0-0	0-0	0-0	- 0.75
Nottingham	1-5	1-2	0-1	0-0	0-0	0-0	0-2	+ 1.00
Cheltenham	1-9	0-2	0-5	1-1	0-1	0-0	0-0	- 7.47
Market Rasen	1-21	1-5	0-6	0-0	0-8	0-0	0-2	- 16.67

Aintree	0-7	Fakenham	0-2	Hereford	0-1
Sandown	0-7	Ludlow	0-2	Towcester	0-1
Leicester	0-4	Stratford	0-2	Worcester	0-1

WINNING HORSES

	Races Run	1st	2nd	3rd	Unpl	Win £
Penny A Day	4	4	0	0	0	23,001
Executive Design	6	3	1	0	2	17,059
Seven Towers	6	4	0	0	2	16,642
Turnpole	4	3	0	0	1	16,563
Erzadjan	6	4	0	0	2	14,742
South Westerly	8	5	0	0	3	13,426
Hit The Canvas	5	4	1	0	0	9,580
Cab On Target	4	1	1	0	2	9,240
Linlathen	6	3	1	0	2	9,097
Sword Beach	12	2	3	1	6	9,024
Highbank	9	3	1	1	4	6,824
Lochnagrain	5	2	2	0	1	6,745
Just Frankie	4	2	0	0	2	6,527
Stay Awake	8	2	1	1	4	5,504
Cutthroat Kid	6	2	0	1	3	5,493

Broctune Bay	3	2	0	0	1	5,476
Once More For Luck	5	2	0	3	0	5,452
Desert Fighter	7	2	1	1	3	5,414
Moonshine Dancer	5	2	0	1	2	5,410
Viardot	5	2	1	2	0	5,384
Eden Dancer	6	2	2	1	1	5,366
Welsh Mill	6	2	3	0	1	5,335
Sedvicta	6	2	0	0	4	5,304
Barton Heights	6	2	1	0	3	5,224
Bayrouge	3	1	0	0	2	5,175
Mill Thyme	8	2	2	0	4	4,930
Keep Your Distance	3	1	0	0	2	4,825
Jalcanto	3	1	0	0	2	4,811
Kimberley Boy	6	2	1	1	2	4,625
Royal Expression	7	2	3	0	2	4,546
Son of Iris	5	1	0	0	4	4,115
Uron V	7	1	2	0	4	4,007
Rhossili Bay	4	1	2	0	1	3,785
Mr Woodcock	3	1	1	0	1	3,371
Marello	2	2	0	0	0	3,316
Highbeath	7	1	0	1	5	3,164
Bark'N'Bite	5	1	0	0	4	2,979
Wynyard Lady	3	2	1	0	0	2,970
Fearless Wonder	3	1	1	0	1	2,879
Star Performer	5	1	2	0	2	2,828
Srivijaya	4	1	0	2	1	2,140
Jomove	7	1	1	1	4	1,968
Suffolk Girl	1	1	0	0	0	1,291

WINNING OWNERS

	Races Won	Value £		Races Won	Value £
Mrs E A Murray	5	25,882	Malcolm Bailey	2	5,476
P D Savill	8	23,067	A Frame	2	5,414
J Good	4	23,001	Peter Colquhoun	2	5,410
D S Hall	6	20,077	Ashley Graham	2	5,366
W H Strawson	6	17,072	Miss C J Raines	2	5,224
W J Williams	3	16,563	Mrs Brigitte Pollard	2	4,930
The Mary Reveley Racing Club	6	16,140	Jeremy Mitchell	2	4,818
L T Foster	2	13,413	Mrs Susan McDonald	2	4,625
Mrs J A Niven	3	9,097	M H G Systems Ltd	1	4,115
Mrs S J Mason	2	9,024	Guy Faber and Peter Ambler	1	4,007
A Sharratt	2	8,339	P A Tylor	1	3,371
William A Davies	2	7,690	Lady Mae Hall	2	2,970
Mrs M Williams	3	7,101	Les De La Haye	1	2,366
Peter M Dodd	3	6,824	K Holder	1	2,140
Lightbody of Hamilton Ltd	2	6,745	Raby Racing	1	1,968
Lady Susan Watson	2	6,527	Lucayan Stud	1	1,291
Austin Donnellon	2	5,504			

| No of horses racing for the stable | 96 | Total winning prize-money | £285,557 |

| Favourites | 55–121 | 45.5% | + 9.26 | Average SP of winner | 2.8/1 |
| Longest win seq | 4 | Longest losing seq | 17 | Return on stakes invested | -18.1% |

| 1994/95 Form | 100–373 | 26.8% | - 20.41 | 1992/93 Form | 90–341 | 26.4% | - 73.32 |
| 1993/94 Form | 103–403 | 25.6% | - 23.40 | 1991/92 Form | 99–323 | 30.7% | - 0.88 |

E RHODES (Llandysul, Dyfed)

	Races Run	1st	2nd	3rd	Unpl	Per cent	£1 Level Stake
Hurdles	0	0	0	0	0	-	0.00
Chases	2	2	0	0	0	100.0	+ 8.00
Totals	2	2	0	0	0	100.0	+ 8.00

| Mr J Jukes | 2–2 | + 8.00 | | | |

| Wincanton | 1–1 | + 6.00 | Ludlow | 1–1 | + 2.00 |

| No of horses racing for the stable | 1 | Total winning prize-money | £3,148 |

P M RICH (Llangovan, Gwent)

	Races Run	1st	2nd	3rd	Unpl	Per cent	£1 Level Stake
Hurdles	17	4	1	1	11	23.5	+ 14.75
Chases	0	0	0	0	0	-	0.00
Totals	17	4	1	1	11	23.5	+ 14.75

| D Finnegan | 2–2 | + 22.75 | W Marston | 2–4 | + 3.00 |

| Wincanton | 1–1 | + 2.75 | Newton Abbot | 1–3 | + 0.25 |
| Uttoxeter | 1–2 | + 1.75 | Bangor | 1–3 | + 18.00 |

| No of horses racing for the stable | 4 | Total winning prize-money | £11,033 |

G RICHARDS (Greystoke, Cumbria)

	Races Run	1st	2nd	3rd	Unpl	Per cent	£1 Level Stake
Hurdles	89	19	13	6	51	21.3	+ 2.54
Chases	136	50	23	14	49	36.8	+ 16.11
Totals	225	69	36	20	100	30.7	+ 18.65

BY MONTH

	W-R	Per cent	£1 Level Stake		W-R	Per cent	£1 Level Stake
June	0-3	-	- 3.00	December	5-21	23.8	- 4.96
July	0-0	-	0.00	January	5-21	23.8	- 5.89
August	1-2	50.0	+ 1.75	February	8-25	32.0	- 6.54
September	3-12	25.0	+ 1.67	March	10-42	23.8	+ 4.40
October	14-24	58.3	+ 27.38	April	5-20	25.0	- 2.00
November	15-39	38.5	+ 8.72	May	3-16	18.8	- 2.88

DISTANCE

	W-R	Per cent	£1 Level Stake		W-R	Per cent	£1 Level Stake
Hurdles				Chases			
2m-2m 3f	10-52	19.2	+ 3.40	2m-2m 3f	9-26	34.6	- 1.27
2m 4f-2m 7f	5-27	18.5	- 12.07	2m 4f-2m 7f	18-54	33.3	- 0.19
3m +	4-10	40.0	+ 11.21	3m +	23-56	41.1	+ 17.57

TYPE OF RACE

	W-R	Per cent	£1 Level Stake		W-R	Per cent	£1 Level Stake
Novice hurdles	9-43	20.9	- 3.53	Selling	0-2	-	- 2.00
H'cap hurdles	10-39	25.6	+ 13.07	Amateur	0-0	-	0.00
Novice chases	30-63	47.6	+ 14.76	Hunter chases	3-7	42.9	+ 1.05
H'cap chases	17-66	25.8	+ 0.30	N H Flat	0-5	-	- 5.00

COURSE GRADE

FIRST TIME OUT

	W-R	Per cent	£1 Level Stake		W-R	Per cent	£1 Level Stake
Group 1	33-85	38.8	+ 45.51	Hurdles	2-22	9.1	- 1.00
Group 2	8-27	29.6	- 0.77	Chases	10-25	40.0	+ 6.14
Group 3	2-14	14.3	- 4.50				
Group 4	26-99	26.3	- 21.59	Totals	12-47	25.5	+ 5.14

JOCKEYS RIDING

	W-R	Per cent	£1 Level Stake		W-R	Per cent	£1 Level Stake
A Dobbin	35-105	33.3	+ 19.13	M Dwyer	3-6	50.0	+ 3.93
B Harding	15-60	25.0	- 9.82	Capt A Ogden	3-7	42.9	+ 1.05
P Carberry	6-19	31.6	+ 7.58	J Railton	2-6	33.3	+ 1.80
R Dunwoody	5-15	33.3	+ 1.98				

L O'Hara	0-2	M Moloney	0-1	N Leach		0-1
B Storey	0-1	Mr R Hale	0-1	W Marston		0-1

COURSE RECORD

	Total W-R	Nov Hdles	H'cap Hdles	Nov Chses	H'cap Chses	Hunter Chses	N H Flat	£1 Level Stake
Carlisle	10-33	4-8	0-5	5-7	1-9	0-0	0-4	+ 0.27
Wetherby	8-25	1-3	1-4	2-7	3-9	1-2	0-0	+ 1.23
Newcastle	7-12	1-3	2-3	3-5	1-1	0-0	0-0	+ 16.80
Haydock	7-18	1-5	1-4	5-6	0-2	0-1	0-0	+ 0.58
Kelso	6-16	0-3	2-6	2-4	2-3	0-0	0-0	+ 0.09
Ayr	5-22	0-6	1-4	2-4	2-8	0-0	0-0	- 0.77
Bangor	4-15	1-5	0-1	2-5	1-4	0-0	0-0	- 8.04
Cheltenham	3-8	0-2	1-1	1-2	1-3	0-0	0-0	+ 0.27
Doncaster	3-8	0-0	1-2	1-2	1-3	0-0	0-1	+ 14.38
Aintree	3-9	0-1	0-0	2-4	1-3	0-1	0-0	+ 3.62
Perth	3-15	1-5	0-4	1-2	1-4	0-0	0-0	+ 0.75
Newbury	2-2	0-0	0-0	1-1	1-1	0-0	0-0	+ 5.50
Sandown	2-4	0-0	0-0	1-2	0-0	1-2	0-0	+ 2.63
Stratford	1-1	0-0	0-0	0-0	1-1	0-0	0-0	+ 5.00
Musselburgh	1-1	0-0	0-0	0-0	0-0	1-1	0-0	+ 0.67
Ascot	1-2	0-0	0-0	0-0	1-2	0-0	0-0	+ 2.50
Market Rasen	1-3	0-0	1-1	0-1	0-1	0-0	0-0	+ 0.50
Sedgefield	1-6	0-0	0-0	1-3	0-3	0-0	0-0	- 4.33
Hexham	1-9	0-1	0-2	1-5	0-1	0-0	0-0	- 7.00

Uttoxeter	0-7	Chepstow	0-2	Warwick	0-2
Cartmel	0-2	Southwell	0-2	Catterick	0-1

WINNING HORSES

	Races Run	1st	2nd	3rd	Unpl	Win £
One Man	4	3	0	0	1	84,258
Addington Boy	8	6	1	0	1	68,777
Unguided Missile	7	3	3	1	0	47,849
Better Times Ahead	5	4	0	0	1	26,417
The Grey Monk	6	6	0	0	0	24,818
Spanish Light	9	4	2	0	3	17,791
Parsons Boy	8	4	1	1	2	14,108
McGregor The Third	7	3	1	0	3	13,123
Ninfa	8	3	1	2	2	11,621
Dancing Dove	13	4	2	0	7	10,642
General Command	6	3	2	0	1	10,630
Earlymorning Light	9	3	4	0	2	9,925
Wind Force	13	2	0	1	10	9,889
Whaat Fettle	3	2	0	0	1	9,059
Elation	5	3	1	0	1	8,447
Buckboard Bounce	2	1	0	0	1	7,249
Carley Lad	4	2	2	0	0	5,780
Lansborough	4	2	2	0	0	5,544
Jocks Cross	7	2	2	0	3	4,888
Scilly Cay	4	2	1	0	1	4,442
The Major General	3	2	0	0	1	4,172
Thistle Princess	2	1	0	0	1	4,065
Clever Folly	3	1	1	0	1	3,598
Tartan Tradewinds	6	1	0	0	5	3,551
Real Tonic	4	1	0	1	2	2,952
On The Other Hand	4	1	1	0	2	1,534

WINNING OWNERS

	Races Won	Value £		Races Won	Value £
J Hales	3	84,258	Dr Kenneth S Fraser	4	10,642
Gott Foods Limited	6	68,777	Mrs Ann Starkie	3	9,925
D E Harrison	3	47,849	J N G Moreton	2	9,889
R Ogden	10	32,081	N B Mason (Farms) Ltd	3	9,378
E Briggs	4	26,417	Mackinnon Mills	2	9,059
Alistair Duff	6	24,818	R Tyrer	3	8,447
Sir John Barlow	4	17,791	Mrs Gill Harrison	2	4,888
Mrs D A Whitaker	5	17,565	Joseph A Gordon	1	4,065
B Ridge	4	14,108	Mackinnon Mills	1	3,551
Lord Cavendish	3	11,621			

No of horses racing for the stable		47	Total winning prize-money	£415,129

Favourites	39-75	52.0%	+ 10.09	Average SP of winner		2.5/1
Longest win seq	8	Longest losing seq	16	Return on stakes invested		8.3%

1994/95 Form	43-279	15.4%	- 76.59	1992/93 Form	104-459	22.7%	- 52.27
1993/94 Form	48-302	15.9%	- 96.91	1991/92 Form	67-409	16.4%	- 90.01

MRS L RICHARDS (Yapton, West Sussex)

	Races Run	1st	2nd	3rd	Unpl	Per cent	£1 Level Stake
Hurdles	25	1	2	2	20	4.0	- 8.00
Chases	33	3	3	8	19	9.1	+ 6.50
Totals	58	4	5	10	39	6.9	- 1.50

M Richards	3-29	+ 18.50	J Osborne	1-2	+ 7.00

Fontwell	2-9	+ 17.00	Lingfield	1-8	- 3.50
Windsor	1-7	+ 19.00			

No of horses racing for the stable	11	Total winning prize-money	£13,554

P C RITCHENS (Shipton Bellinger, Hants)

	Races Run	1st	2nd	3rd	Unpl	Per cent	£1 Level Stake
Hurdles	36	2	4	2	28	5.6	- 22.00
Chases	24	3	6	5	10	12.5	- 11.59
Totals	60	5	10	7	38	8.3	- 33.59

A Tory	3-27	- 14.59	D Gallagher	1-4	+ 2.00
C Maude	1-1	+ 7.00			

Fontwell	2-8	- 0.09	Plumpton	1-3	+ 5.00
Southwell	1-2	+ 0.50	Uttoxeter	1-6	+ 2.00

No of horses racing for the stable	14	Total winning prize-money	£16,404

MRS P ROBESON (Tyringham, Bucks)

	Races Run	1st	2nd	3rd	Unpl	Per cent	£1 Level Stake
Hurdles	11	1	2	2	6	9.1	+ 10.00
Chases	5	0	2	0	3	-	- 5.00
Totals	16	1	4	2	9	6.3	+ 5.00

M Richards	1-9	+ 12.00	Worcester	1-1	+ 20.00

No of horses racing for the stable 5   Total winning prize-money £2,653

P R RODFORD (Ash, Somerset)

	Races Run	1st	2nd	3rd	Unpl	Per cent	£1 Level Stake
Hurdles	17	0	2	0	15	-	- 17.00
Chases	43	2	6	5	30	4.7	- 37.45
Totals	60	2	8	5	45	3.3	- 54.45

S Burrough	2-57	- 51.45			
Hereford	1-1	+ 2.75	Wincanton	1-6	- 4.20

No of horses racing for the stable 18   Total winning prize-money £6,448

MISS A S ROSS (Yelverton, Devon)

	Races Run	1st	2nd	3rd	Unpl	Per cent	£1 Level Stake
Hurdles	0	0	0	0	0	-	0.00
Chases	3	1	1	1	0	33.3	+ 2.00
Totals	3	1	1	1	0	33.3	+ 2.00

Mr G Penfold	1-2	+ 3.00	Hereford	1-1	+ 4.00

No of horses racing for the stable 1   Total winning prize-money £1,506

B S ROTHWELL (Malton, North Yorks)

	Races Run	1st	2nd	3rd	Unpl	Per cent	£1 Level Stake
Hurdles	40	1	1	0	38	2.5	- 38.33
Chases	31	4	4	5	18	12.9	- 14.37
Totals	71	5	5	5	56	7.0	- 52.70

R Supple	5-38	- 19.70	

Stratford	2-5	+ 1.13	Southwell	1-4	+ 4.00
Haydock	1-1	+ 0.67	Worcester	1-5	- 2.50

No of horses racing for the stable   21   Total winning prize-money   £15,960

R ROWE (Storrington, West Sussex)

	Races Run	1st	2nd	3rd	Unpl	Per cent	£1 Level Stake
Hurdles	105	11	9	11	74	10.5	- 40.84
Chases	50	6	3	10	31	12.0	- 1.12
Totals	155	17	12	21	105	11.0	- 41.96

BY MONTH

	W-R	Per cent	£1 Level Stake		W-R	Per cent	£1 Level Stake
June	2-5	40.0	+ 23.00	December	0-13	-	- 13.00
July	0-0	-	0.00	January	1-20	5.0	- 9.00
August	0-0	-	0.00	February	1-23	4.3	- 19.75
September	0-5	-	- 5.00	March	2-22	9.1	- 10.00
October	4-13	30.8	+ 4.51	April	3-20	15.0	- 3.12
November	3-24	12.5	- 2.10	May	1-10	10.0	- 7.50

DISTANCE

Hurdles	W-R	Per cent	£1 Level Stake	Chases	W-R	Per cent	£1 Level Stake
2m-2m 3f	2-45	4.4	- 28.00	2m-2m 3f	2-11	18.2	- 0.62
2m 4f-2m 7f	8-45	17.8	- 10.84	2m 4f-2m 7f	2-15	13.3	+ 9.00
3m +	1-15	6.7	- 2.00	3m +	2-24	8.3	- 9.50

TYPE OF RACE

	W-R	Per cent	£1 Level Stake		W-R	Per cent	£1 Level Stake
Novice hurdles	1-35	2.9	- 33.60	Selling	1-7	14.3	0.00
H'cap hurdles	8-52	15.4	- 6.24	Amateur	0-4	-	- 4.00
Novice chases	3-14	21.4	+ 12.88	Hunter chases	0-1	-	- 1.00
H'cap chases	2-28	7.1	- 13.00	N H Flat	2-14	14.3	+ 3.00

COURSE GRADE					FIRST TIME OUT			
	W-R	Per cent	£1 Level Stake			W-R	Per cent	£1 Level Stake
Group 1	1-27	3.7	- 22.00	Hurdles		1-23	4.3	- 12.00
Group 2	7-47	14.9	- 0.87	Chases		3-12	25.0	+ 4.88
Group 3	7-71	9.9	- 18.97					
Group 4	2-10	20.0	- 0.12	Totals		4-35	11.4	- 7.12

JOCKEYS RIDING

	W-R	Per cent	£1 Level Stake			W-R	Per cent	£1 Level Stake
D O'Sullivan	16-126	12.7	- 23.96	J Railton		1-2	50.0	+ 9.00
D Carson	0-5			P Hide		0-3		T Grantham 0-1
Mr J Luck	0-5			E Murphy		0-2		W Marston 0-1
L Aspell	0-3			I Lawrence		0-2		
Mr A Kinane	0-3			Mr P O'Keeffe		0-2		

COURSE RECORD

	Total W-R	Nov Hdles	H'cap Hdles	Nov Chses	H'cap Chses	Hunter Chses	N H Flat	£1 Level Stake
Fontwell	4-27	0-8	4-10	0-1	0-7	0-0	0-1	- 4.75
Chepstow	3-10	0-2	2-4	0-1	1-3	0-0	0-0	+ 13.88
Worcester	3-14	0-2	1-5	1-3	0-2	0-0	1-2	+ 16.63
Towcester	2-5	0-1	0-1	2-2	0-1	0-0	0-0	+ 4.88
Plumpton	2-20	0-7	0-4	0-0	2-9	0-0	0-0	- 6.00
Sandown	1-6	0-1	1-2	0-1	0-0	0-0	0-2	- 1.00
Huntingdon	1-9	1-3	0-3	0-0	0-1	0-0	0-2	- 7.60
Folkestone	1-13	0-1	0-4	0-2	0-3	0-0	1-3	- 7.00

Kempton	0-8	Warwick	0-4	Exeter	0-2
Lingfield	0-7	Windsor	0-4	Taunton	0-2
Newbury	0-5	Leicester	0-3	Bangor	0-1
Ascot	0-4	Newton Abbot	0-3	Stratford	0-1
Cheltenham	0-4	Uttoxeter	0-3		

WINNING HORSES

	Races Run	1st	2nd	3rd	Unpl	Win £
Lead Vocalist	8	3	0	4	1	12,095
Black Church	5	2	0	1	2	6,673
Fresh Choice	9	2	1	2	4	5,705
Punch's Hotel	5	2	0	0	3	4,875
Suffolk Road	3	1	0	2	0	3,833
Karar	8	1	2	0	5	3,583
Merivel	3	1	1	0	1	3,020
Hawaiian Youth	2	1	0	0	1	2,793
Green Walk	9	1	1	2	5	2,467
Clowater Lady	6	1	2	1	2	2,163
Sir Turtle	1	1	0	0	0	1,674
Sir Dante	4	1	0	0	3	1,317

273

WINNING OWNERS

	Races Won	Value £		Races Won	Value £
Captain A Pratt	3	12,095	Faulkner West & Co Ltd	1	3,020
Dr B Alexander	2	6,673	Peter R Wilby	2	2,991
I Kerman	2	5,705	G Redford	1	2,793
Mrs A E Dawes	2	4,875	C Cornwell	1	2,467
Alpha Financial Futures	1	3,833	The Paclin P'ship	1	2,163
Mrs Margaret Sampson	1	3,583			

No of horses racing for the stable	35		Total winning prize-money	£50,198

Favourites	4-15	26.7%	- 2.47	Average SP of winner		5.6/1
Longest win seq	2	Longest losing seq	28	Return on stakes invested		-27.1%

1994/95 Form	17-142	12.0%	- 46.84	1992/93 Form	23-167	13.8%	- 31.10
1993/94 Form	12-202	5.9%	-106.32	1991/92 Form	7-96	7.3%	- 59.50

MISS M ROWLAND (Lower Blidworth, Notts)

	Races Run	1st	2nd	3rd	Unpl	Per cent	£1 Level Stake
Hurdles	30	1	2	1	26	3.3	- 18.00
Chases	8	0	0	1	7	-	- 8.00
Totals	38	1	2	2	33	2.6	- 26.00

Gary Lyons	1-37	- 25.00	Stratford	1-2	+ 10.00

No of horses racing for the stable	9	Total winning prize-money	£3,136

MISS L V RUSSELL (Milnathort, Tayside)

	Races Run	1st	2nd	3rd	Unpl	Per cent	£1 Level Stake
Hurdles	18	0	0	3	15	-	- 18.00
Chases	62	12	17	5	28	19.4	- 0.12
Totals	80	12	17	8	43	15.0	- 18.12

BY MONTH

	W-R	Per cent	£1 Level Stake		W-R	Per cent	£1 Level Stake
June	0-0	-	0.00	December	1-9	11.1	- 5.50
July	0-0	-	0.00	January	1-11	9.1	- 5.50
August	0-0	-	0.00	February	1-7	14.3	- 3.75
September	2-3	66.7	+ 12.00	March	1-12	8.3	- 1.00
October	2-7	28.6	- 1.37	April	1-15	6.7	- 12.50
November	1-11	9.1	- 3.00	May	2-5	40.0	+ 2.50

DISTANCE

Hurdles	W-R	Per cent	£1 Level Stake	Chases	W-R	Per cent	£1 Level Stake
2m-2m 3f	0-5	-	- 5.00	2m-2m 3f	0-9	-	- 9.00
2m 4f-2m 7f	0-3	-	- 3.00	2m 4f-2m 7f	6-17	35.3	+ 11.00
3m +	0-10	-	- 10.00	3m +	6-36	16.7	- 2.12

TYPE OF RACE

	W-R	Per cent	£1 Level Stake		W-R	Per cent	£1 Level Stake
Novice hurdles	0-5	-	- 5.00	Selling	0-5	-	- 5.00
H'cap hurdles	0-7	-	- 7.00	Amateur	1-3	33.3	+ 8.00
Novice chases	4-31	12.9	- 10.50	Hunter chases	0-0	-	0.00
H'cap chases	7-28	25.0	+ 2.38	N H Flat	0-1	-	- 1.00

COURSE GRADE

	W-R	Per cent	£1 Level Stake
Group 1	3-16	18.8	+ 3.75
Group 2	1-2	50.0	+ 0.88
Group 3	0-2	-	- 2.00
Group 4	8-60	13.3	- 20.75

FIRST TIME OUT

	W-R	Per cent	£1 Level Stake
Hurdles	0-5	-	- 5.00
Chases	2-8	25.0	+ 7.00
Totals	2-13	15.4	+ 2.00

JOCKEYS RIDING

	W-R	Per cent	£1 Level Stake		W-R	Per cent	£1 Level Stake
A Thornton	8-40	20.0	- 0.50	Mr P Henley	1-1	100.0	+ 10.00
P Niven	2-7	28.6	+ 1.88	M Foster	1-14	7.1	- 11.50

G Lee	0-5	B Harding	0-1	Richard Davis	0-1
F Leahy	0-3	Miss P Robson	0-1	T Reed	0-1
Mr C Storey	0-2	Miss S Forster	0-1		
Mr K Anderson	0-2	Mr J McGurgan	0-1		

COURSE RECORD

	Total W-R	Nov Hdles	H'cap Hdles	Nov Chses	H'cap Chses	Hunter Chses	N H Flat	£1 Level Stake
Hexham	2-12	0-0	0-2	1-5	1-5	0-0	0-0	- 6.25
Kelso	2-12	0-1	0-0	2-7	0-4	0-0	0-0	+ 2.00
Perth	2-13	0-1	0-3	0-6	2-3	0-0	0-0	+ 0.50
Wetherby	1-2	0-0	0-0	0-1	1-1	0-0	0-0	+ 0.88
Aintree	1-2	0-0	0-0	0-0	1-2	0-0	0-0	+ 9.00
Newcastle	1-5	0-0	0-1	0-1	1-3	0-0	0-0	+ 0.50
Carlisle	1-6	0-1	0-0	0-3	1-2	0-0	0-0	- 3.50
Ayr	1-8	0-1	0-0	0-3	1-4	0-0	0-0	- 4.75
Musselburgh	1-14	0-0	0-5	1-4	0-4	0-0	0-1	- 10.50

Sedgefield	0-3	Catterick	0-2	Cheltenham	0-1

WINNING HORSES

	Races Run	1st	2nd	3rd	Unpl	Win £
Fiveleigh Builds	12	5	3	2	2	19,411
Rocket Run	9	4	4	0	1	18,596
Vavasir	6	2	1	0	3	5,871
Movac	1	1	0	0	0	2,678

WINNING OWNERS

	Races Won	Value £		Races Won	Value £
Miss Lucinda V Russell	5	19,411	M F B Nicholson	2	5,871
Peter J S Russell	4	18,596	Green For Glory	1	2,678

No of horses racing for the stable		16	Total winning prize-money	£46,556

Favourites	4-13	30.8%	- 1.37	Average SP of winner	4.2/1
Longest win seq	2	Longest losing seq	17	Return on stakes invested	-22.7%

1994/95 Form	1-4	25.0%	- 1.25	1992/93 Form	1-3	33.3%	- 0.62
1993/94 Form	0-5			1991/92 Form	0-2		

B J M RYALL (Rimpton, Somerset)

	Races Run	1st	2nd	3rd	Unpl	Per cent	£1 Level Stake
Hurdles	16	2	1	2	11	12.5	+ 23.00
Chases	3	0	0	0	3	-	- 3.00
Totals	19	2	1	2	14	10.5	+ 20.00

T Dascombe	1-5	0.00	G Upton	1-7	+ 27.00
Newton Abbot	1-3	+ 31.00	Fontwell	1-5	0.00

No of horses racing for the stable		5	Total winning prize-money	£5,034

M J RYAN (Newmarket, Suffolk)

	Races Run	1st	2nd	3rd	Unpl	Per cent	£1 Level Stake
Hurdles	33	1	5	3	24	3.0	+ 18.00
Chases	0	0	0	0	0	-	0.00
Totals	33	1	5	3	24	3.0	+ 18.00

K P Gaule	1-2	+ 49.00	Fontwell	1-6	+ 45.00

No of horses racing for the stable		12	Total winning prize-money	£2,427

MISS B SANDERS (Epsom, Surrey)

	Races Run	1st	2nd	3rd	Unpl	Per cent	£1 Level Stake
Hurdles	14	2	1	1	10	14.3	- 6.00
Chases	1	0	0	0	1	-	- 1.00
Totals	15	2	1	1	11	13.3	- 7.00

N Williamson	1-2	+ 4.00		A Maguire	1-3	- 1.00
Cheltenham	1-1	+ 1.00		Fontwell	1-4	+ 2.00

No of horses racing for the stable   7   Total winning prize-money   £5,483

MISS C SAUNDERS (Northampton, Northants)

	Races Run	1st	2nd	3rd	Unpl	Per cent	£1 Level Stake
Hurdles	0	0	0	0	0	-	0.00
Chases	19	7	3	2	7	36.8	- 2.15
Totals	19	7	3	2	7	36.8	- 2.15

BY MONTH

	W-R	Per cent	£1 Level Stake		W-R	Per cent	£1 Level Stake
June	0-0	-	0.00	December	0-0	-	0.00
July	0-0	-	0.00	January	0-0	-	0.00
August	0-0	-	0.00	February	1-3	33.3	0.00
September	0-0	-	0.00	March	2-7	28.6	- 2.31
October	0-0	-	0.00	April	2-4	50.0	- 0.97
November	0-0	-	0.00	May	2-5	40.0	+ 1.13

DISTANCE

	W-R	Per cent	£1 Level Stake		W-R	Per cent	£1 Level Stake
Hurdles				Chases			
2m-2m 3f	0-0	-	0.00	2m-2m 3f	1-1	100.0	+ 2.75
2m 4f-2m 7f	0-0	-	0.00	2m 4f-2m 7f	2-7	28.6	- 3.26
3m +	0-0	-	0.00	3m +	4-11	36.4	- 1.64

TYPE OF RACE

	W-R	Per cent	£1 Level Stake		W-R	Per cent	£1 Level Stake
Novice hurdles	0-0	-	0.00	Selling	0-0	-	0.00
H'cap hurdles	0-0	-	0.00	Amateur	0-0	-	0.00
Novice chases	0-0	-	0.00	Hunter chases	7-19	36.8	- 2.15
H'cap chases	0-0	-	0.00	N H Flat	0-0	-	0.00

COURSE GRADE

	W–R	Per cent	£1 Level Stake
Group 1	0–4	–	– 4.00
Group 2	1–1	100.0	+ 2.00
Group 3	1–3	33.3	+ 0.25
Group 4	5–11	45.5	– 0.40

FIRST TIME OUT

	W–R	Per cent	£1 Level Stake
Hurdles	0–0	–	0.00
Chases	2–5	40.0	+ 1.25
Totals	2–5	40.0	+ 1.25

JOCKEYS RIDING

	W–R	Per cent	£1 Level Stake		W–R	Per cent	£1 Level Stake
Mr B Pollock	5–12	41.7	– 1.28	Mr T Marks	2–7	28.6	– 0.87

COURSE RECORD

	Total W–R	Nov Hdles	H'cap Hdles	Nov Chses	H'cap Chses	Hunter Chses	N H Flat	£1 Level Stake
Towcester	4–6	0–0	0–0	0–0	0–0	4–6	0–0	+ 2.93
Wetherby	1–1	0–0	0–0	0–0	0–0	1–1	0–0	+ 2.00
Leicester	1–1	0–0	0–0	0–0	0–0	1–1	0–0	+ 2.25
Bangor	1–2	0–0	0–0	0–0	0–0	1–2	0–0	– 0.33

Aintree	0–1	Hereford	0–1	Southwell	0–1
Cheltenham	0–1	Kempton	0–1	Uttoxeter	0–1
Fakenham	0–1	Sandown	0–1	Windsor	0–1

WINNING HORSES

	Races Run	1st	2nd	3rd	Unpl	Win £
Teaplanter	7	4	2	0	1	6,092
Ryde Again	4	1	0	1	2	3,870
Beau Dandy	4	2	0	0	2	2,498

WINNING OWNERS

	Races Won	Value £		Races Won	Value £
R G Russell	4	6,092	C C Shand Kydd	2	2,498
Miss J E Hayward	1	3,870			

No of horses racing for the stable	5	Total winning prize-money	£12,460

Favourites	5–8	62.5%	+ 2.60	Average SP of winner	1.4/1
Longest win seq	2	Longest losing seq	4	Return on stakes invested	–11.3%

1994/95 Form	8–27	29.6%	– 7.88	1992/93 Form	13–40	32.5%	– 7.88
1993/94 Form	19–45	42.2%	+ 9.07	1991/92 Form	9–35	25.7%	+ 19.83

DR J D SCARGILL (Newmarket, Suffolk)

	Races Run	1st	2nd	3rd	Unpl	Per cent	£1 Level Stake
Hurdles	3	1	1	0	1	33.3	- 0.62
Chases	0	0	0	0	0	-	0.00
Totals	3	1	1	0	1	33.3	- 0.62

N Mann	1-3	- 0.62		Ludlow	1-1	+ 1.38

No of horses racing for the stable   1   Total winning prize-money   £2,584

M SHEPPARD (Eastnor, H'ford & Worcs)

	Races Run	1st	2nd	3rd	Unpl	Per cent	£1 Level Stake
Hurdles	31	1	1	4	25	3.2	+ 3.00
Chases	6	1	0	1	4	16.7	+ 28.00
Totals	37	2	1	5	29	5.4	+ 31.00

P Carberry	1-2	+ 32.00		B Powell	1-18	+ 16.00
Newbury	1-1	+ 33.00		Chepstow	1-6	+ 28.00

No of horses racing for the stable   11   Total winning prize-money   £13,696

O SHERWOOD (Upper Lambourn, Berks)

	Races Run	1st	2nd	3rd	Unpl	Per cent	£1 Level Stake
Hurdles	148	30	16	17	85	20.3	+ 14.20
Chases	94	16	17	16	45	17.0	- 39.27
Totals	242	46	33	33	130	19.0	- 25.07

BY MONTH

	W-R	Per cent	£1 Level Stake		W-R	Per cent	£1 Level Stake
June	0-1	-	- 1.00	December	5-27	18.5	+ 9.25
July	0-0	-	0.00	January	1-29	3.4	- 26.50
August	0-0	-	0.00	February	6-28	21.4	+ 23.00
September	0-3	-	- 3.00	March	11-46	23.9	+ 9.04
October	8-17	47.1	+ 5.08	April	4-30	13.3	- 15.31
November	10-39	25.6	- 7.63	May	1-22	4.5	- 18.00

DISTANCE

	W-R	Per cent	£1 Level Stake		W-R	Per cent	£1 Level Stake
Hurdles				Chases			
2m-2m 3f	21-96	21.9	+ 24.29	2m-2m 3f	8-36	22.2	- 13.14
2m 4f-2m 7f	6-40	15.0	- 18.59	2m 4f-2m 7f	2-25	8.0	- 19.75
3m +	3-12	25.0	+ 8.50	3m +	6-33	18.2	- 6.38

TYPE OF RACE

	W-R	Per cent	£1 Level Stake		W-R	Per cent	£1 Level Stake
Novice hurdles	24-90	26.7	+ 20.95	Selling	0-1	-	- 1.00
H'cap hurdles	4-37	10.8	+ 3.25	Amateur	0-2	-	- 2.00
Novice chases	12-46	26.1	- 4.89	Hunter chases	0-0	-	0.00
H'cap chases	4-46	8.7	- 32.38	N H Flat	2-20	10.0	- 9.00

COURSE GRADE

	W-R	Per cent	£1 Level Stake
Group 1	17-91	18.7	- 20.12
Group 2	2-25	8.0	- 20.81
Group 3	18-83	21.7	+ 11.14
Group 4	9-43	20.9	+ 4.72

FIRST TIME OUT

	W-R	Per cent	£1 Level Stake
Hurdles	10-42	23.8	+ 14.54
Chases	5-20	25.0	- 8.84
Totals	15-62	24.2	+ 5.70

JOCKEYS RIDING

	W-R	Per cent	£1 Level Stake		W-R	Per cent	£1 Level Stake
J A McCarthy	21-95	22.1	+ 24.47	P Niven	1-1	100.0	+ 0.62
J Osborne	17-83	20.5	- 22.10	C Maude	1-1	100.0	+ 0.44
M Richards	3-26	11.5	+ 1.00	R Dunwoody	1-3	33.3	- 1.00
G Bradley	2-3	66.7	+ 1.50				

D Thomas	0-18	G Hogan	0-1	P Carberry	0-1
Mr A Harvey	0-6	Mr J P Durkan	0-1		
B Powell	0-2	Mr P Scott	0-1		

COURSE RECORD

	Total W-R	Nov Hdles	H'cap Hdles	Nov Chses	H'cap Chses	Hunter Chses	N H Flat	£1 Level Stake
Uttoxeter	5-13	2-6	0-1	3-3	0-1	0-0	0-2	+ 7.34
Wincanton	4-11	2-5	0-0	0-1	1-4	0-0	1-1	+ 1.17
Sandown	4-15	3-7	0-2	1-2	0-4	0-0	0-0	+ 2.57
Ascot	4-24	3-12	0-3	0-2	1-5	0-0	0-2	- 1.97
Taunton	3-7	1-3	0-0	1-1	1-3	0-0	0-0	+ 5.75
Huntingdon	3-14	1-4	1-2	1-4	0-2	0-0	0-2	+ 11.25
Newbury	3-15	3-7	0-4	0-2	0-1	0-0	0-1	- 4.00
Exeter	2-4	2-2	0-1	0-0	0-0	0-0	0-1	+ 15.25
Windsor	2-4	1-2	1-1	0-0	0-1	0-0	0-0	+ 18.00
Newton Abbot	2-6	1-2	1-2	0-1	0-0	0-0	0-1	- 1.81

Doncaster	2-8	0-2	0-1	2-2	0-2	0-0	0-1	-	3.75
Cheltenham	2-9	2-4	0-1	0-2	0-2	0-0	0-0	-	1.59
Newcastle	1-1	0-0	0-0	0-0	1-1	0-0	0-0	+	0.62
Bangor	1-2	1-1	0-0	0-0	0-0	0-0	0-1	-	0.78
Stratford	1-5	0-2	1-1	0-0	0-2	0-0	0-0	-	1.50
Fakenham	1-5	0-0	0-2	1-1	0-2	0-0	0-0	-	2.00
Worcester	1-6	0-0	0-1	0-3	0-0	0-0	1-2		0.00
Southwell	1-6	0-0	0-0	1-3	0-3	0-0	0-0	-	2.00
Warwick	1-7	1-3	0-3	0-1	0-0	0-0	0-0	-	4.62
Kempton	1-7	0-2	0-2	1-1	0-2	0-0	0-0		0.00
Folkestone	1-9	0-3	0-3	1-3	0-0	0-0	0-0	-	6.50
Ludlow	1-10	1-6	0-0	0-1	0-2	0-0	0-1	-	2.50

Aintree	0-9	Towcester	0-6	Ayr	0-2
Nottingham	0-8	Fontwell	0-4	Plumpton	0-2
Chepstow	0-7	Leicester	0-4	Haydock	0-1
Wetherby	0-7	Hereford	0-3	Lingfield	0-1

WINNING HORSES

	Races Run	1st	2nd	3rd	Unpl	Win £
Coulton	8	2	0	1	5	27,509
Silver Wedge	5	1	0	1	3	25,996
Large Action	2	2	0	0	0	17,944
Father Sky	7	3	1	0	3	14,034
Abbey Street	4	3	0	0	1	12,359
Callisoe Bay	7	3	1	1	2	12,279
Alltime Dancer	9	4	1	1	3	11,944
Celtic Town	6	2	0	3	1	7,084
Myland	4	2	0	0	2	6,949
Early Drinker	8	2	2	1	3	6,406
Zephyrus	5	2	1	0	2	6,340
Merlins Dream	7	2	2	0	3	5,684
Keep It Zipped	8	2	2	0	4	5,531
Copper Mine	1	1	0	0	0	5,398
High Learie	5	1	0	0	4	4,258
Charming Girl	5	2	1	0	2	4,091
Foxbow	5	1	0	1	3	3,583
Butler's Twitch	4	1	0	0	3	3,535
Real Glee	5	1	1	1	2	3,410
Lyme Gold	7	1	1	2	3	3,398
The Bounder	11	1	2	4	4	3,335
Welcome Call	1	1	0	0	0	3,225
Him of Praise	1	1	0	0	0	2,983
Layham Low	4	1	0	1	2	2,635
Dark Nightingale	7	1	1	2	3	2,514
Menelave	3	1	0	1	1	2,248
Dawn Leader	1	1	0	0	0	2,094
Aerion	1	1	0	0	0	1,448

WINNING OWNERS

	Races Won	Value £		Races Won	Value £
B T Stewart-Brown	7	36,863	Mrs Luisa Stewart-Brown	2	5,531
M G St Quinton	3	30,492	J Dougall	1	5,398
E S & W V Robins	2	29,741	Edward Harvey	1	4,258
Kenneth Kornfeld	3	14,034	C Coxen	2	4,091
R Waters	3	12,279	Christopher Heath	1	3,535
H M Heyman	4	11,944	John Stone	1	3,410
Bonusprint	3	9,043	Nigel Chamberlain	1	3,398
Lady Helen Smith	2	7,084	I A Low	1	2,635
S Channing-Williams	2	6,406	Miss Liz Clark	1	2,514
Mrs Shirley Robins	2	6,178	R B Holt	1	2,248
W S Watt	2	5,684	P Chamberlain, D Addiscott	1	1,448

No of horses racing for the stable	63	Total winning prize-money	£208,214

Favourites	25-61	41.0%	- 3.07	Average SP of winner		3.7/1
Longest win seq	4	Longest losing seq	30	Return on stakes invested		-10.4%

1994/95 Form	48-216	22.2%	- 46.60	1992/93 Form	37-203	18.2%	- 38.47
1993/94 Form	41-208	19.7%	- 12.41	1991/92 Form	48-227	21.1%	- 69.45

S SHERWOOD (East Ilsley, Berks)

	Races Run	1st	2nd	3rd	Unpl	Per cent	£1 Level Stake
Hurdles	50	3	5	11	31	6.0	- 38.63
Chases	32	7	5	0	20	21.9	- 9.27
Totals	82	10	10	11	51	12.2	- 47.90

BY MONTH

	W-R	Per cent	£1 Level Stake		W-R	Per cent	£1 Level Stake
June	0-0	-	0.00	December	1-5	20.0	- 2.62
July	0-0	-	0.00	January	1-17	5.9	- 15.38
August	0-0	-	0.00	February	1-14	7.1	- 7.50
September	0-0	-	0.00	March	0-18	-	- 18.00
October	3-4	75.0	+ 8.75	April	0-10	-	- 10.00
November	2-6	33.3	- 1.65	May	2-8	25.0	- 1.50

DISTANCE

Hurdles	W-R	Per cent	£1 Level Stake	Chases	W-R	Per cent	£1 Level Stake
2m-2m 3f	3-30	10.0	- 18.63	2m-2m 3f	5-11	45.5	+ 3.73
2m 4f-2m 7f	0-13	-	- 13.00	2m 4f-2m 7f	2-12	16.7	- 4.00
3m +	0-7	-	- 7.00	3m +	0-9	-	- 9.00

TYPE OF RACE

	W-R	Per cent	£1 Level Stake		W-R	Per cent	£1 Level Stake
Novice hurdles	2-24	8.3	- 15.88	Selling	0-0	-	0.00
H'cap hurdles	0-16	-	- 16.00	Amateur	0-3	-	- 3.00
Novice chases	2-10	20.0	- 2.75	Hunter chases	0-0	-	0.00
H'cap chases	5-20	25.0	- 4.52	N H Flat	1-9	11.1	- 5.75

COURSE GRADE / FIRST TIME OUT

	W-R	Per cent	£1 Level Stake		W-R	Per cent	£1 Level Stake
Group 1	3-28	10.7	- 17.02	Hurdles	1-18	5.6	- 14.75
Group 2	0-7	-	- 7.00	Chases	3-9	33.3	+ 2.75
Group 3	3-33	9.1	- 20.25				
Group 4	4-14	28.6	- 3.63	Totals	4-27	14.8	- 12.00

JOCKEYS RIDING

	W-R	Per cent	£1 Level Stake		W-R	Per cent	£1 Level Stake
J Osborne	4-17	23.5	- 5.90	G Bradley	1-6	16.7	- 1.50
G Upton	3-18	16.7	- 9.25	S Curran	1-13	7.7	- 9.75
C Maude	1-4	25.0	+ 2.50				

M Richards	0-7	Mr M Fitzgerald	0-2	D Walsh	0-1
C Llewellyn	0-3	O Evans	0-2	Mr E James	0-1
A P McCoy	0-2	D Fortt	0-1	Richard Davis	0-1
J A McCarthy	0-2	D Gallagher	0-1	S McNeill	0-1

COURSE RECORD

	Total W-R	Nov Hdles	H'cap Hdles	Nov Chses	H'cap Chses	Hunter Chses	N H Flat	£1 Level Stake
Exeter	1-2	0-0	0-0	0-1	1-1	0-0	0-0	+ 1.50
Worcester	1-2	0-0	0-0	1-1	0-1	0-0	0-0	+ 3.00
Southwell	1-2	0-0	0-0	0-0	1-1	0-0	0-1	+ 1.00
Stratford	1-3	0-0	0-0	0-0	1-3	0-0	0-0	+ 1.50
Ludlow	1-3	1-3	0-0	0-0	0-0	0-0	0-0	- 1.38
Taunton	1-4	0-1	0-2	1-1	0-0	0-0	0-0	- 1.75
Ascot	1-5	0-2	0-0	0-0	1-3	0-0	0-0	- 2.62
Sandown	1-5	1-2	0-0	0-3	0-0	0-0	0-0	+ 1.50
Warwick	1-8	0-2	0-2	0-1	0-2	0-0	1-1	- 4.75
Newbury	1-11	0-2	0-4	0-0	1-3	0-0	0-2	- 8.90

Cheltenham	0-5	Leicester	0-2	Lingfield	0-1
Chepstow	0-5	Market Rasen	0-2	Newton Abbot	0-1
Folkestone	0-4	Windsor	0-2	Nottingham	0-1
Wincanton	0-4	Aintree	0-1	Plumpton	0-1
Uttoxeter	0-3	Doncaster	0-1	Towcester	0-1
Bangor	0-2	Huntingdon	0-1		

WINNING HORSES

	Races Run	1st	2nd	3rd	Unpl	Win £
Front Street	6	3	0	0	3	21,739
The Mine Captain	6	2	2	0	2	6,676
Falmouth Bay	6	1	1	0	4	4,691
Sir Leonard	4	1	1	1	1	3,550
Rocco	6	1	1	0	4	2,843
Danjing	6	1	2	2	1	2,668
Kilcarne Bay	2	1	0	0	1	1,350

WINNING OWNERS

	Races Won	Value £		Races Won	Value £
Mrs Jean R Bishop	4	25,289	M L Oberstein	1	2,843
Gerald W Evans	2	6,676	Richard Green (Fine Paintings)	1	2,668
James Morton	1	4,691	The Compass Partnership	1	1,350

No of horses racing for the stable	27	Total winning prize-money	£43,517

Favourites	6-18	33.3%	- 3.40	Average SP of winner	2.4/1
Longest win seq	2	Longest losing seq	36	Return on stakes invested	-58.4%

1994/95 Form	8-95	8.4%	- 68.75	1992/93 Form	30-175	17.1%	+ 8.36
1993/94 Form	24-144	16.7%	- 23.93	1991/92 Form	17-125	13.6%	+ 8.11

S H SHIRLEY-BEAVAN (Hawick, Borders)

	Races Run	1st	2nd	3rd	Unpl	Per cent	£1 Level Stake
Hurdles	0	0	0	0	0	-	0.00
Chases	4	1	0	1	2	25.0	+ 4.00
Totals	4	1	0	1	2	25.0	+ 4.00

Miss S Forster	1-4	+ 4.00	Kelso	1-1	+ 7.00

No of horses racing for the stable	3	Total winning prize-money	£2,433

MISS L C SIDDALL (Colton, North Yorks)

	Races Run	1st	2nd	3rd	Unpl	Per cent	£1 Level Stake
Hurdles	67	5	11	5	46	7.5	- 39.50
Chases	7	1	1	3	2	14.3	- 1.50
Totals	74	6	12	8	48	8.1	- 41.00

A Thornton	3-27	-	8.50	E Husband		1-11	- 6.50
R Dunwoody	2-7	+	3.00				
Market Rasen	3-17	-	1.50	Worcester		1-5	- 0.50
Hexham	2-5	+	8.00				

No of horses racing for the stable   13   Total winning prize-money   £16,355

MRS EVELYN SLACK (Hilton, Cumbria)

	Races Run	1st	2nd	3rd	Unpl	Per cent	£1 Level Stake
Hurdles	18	1	2	2	13	5.6	- 11.00
Chases	0	0	0	0	0	-	0.00
Totals	18	1	2	2	13	5.6	- 11.00

F Perratt	1-9	-	2.00	Kelso	1-4	+ 3.00

No of horses racing for the stable   4   Total winning prize-money   £3,209

MRS P SLY (Thorney, Cambs)

	Races Run	1st	2nd	3rd	Unpl	Per cent	£1 Level Stake
Hurdles	36	1	6	2	27	2.8	- 30.50
Chases	5	1	1	1	2	20.0	+ 4.00
Totals	41	2	7	3	29	4.9	- 26.50

B Harding	1-1	+	4.50	R Marley	1-33	- 24.00
Sedgefield	1-5	+	0.50	Leicester	1-6	+ 3.00

No of horses racing for the stable   12   Total winning prize-money   £6,890

B SMART (Lambourn, Berks)

	Races Run	1st	2nd	3rd	Unpl	Per cent	£1 Level Stake
Hurdles	34	1	3	3	27	2.9	- 28.50
Chases	1	0	0	0	1	-	- 1.00
Totals	35	1	3	3	28	2.9	- 29.50

D Gallagher	1-2	+ 3.50	Windsor	1-2	+ 3.50

No of horses racing for the stable   12   Total winning prize-money   £2,425

D J G MURRAY SMITH (Lambourn, Berks)

	Races Run	1st	2nd	3rd	Unpl	Per cent	£1 Level Stake
Hurdles	4	2	0	0	2	50.0	+ 43.00
Chases	0	0	0	0	0	-	0.00
Totals	4	2	0	0	2	50.0	+ 43.00

R Painter	1-1	+ 25.00	D Gallagher	1-2	+ 19.00
Towcester	1-1	+ 20.00	Ludlow	1-2	+ 24.00

No of horses racing for the stable   3   Total winning prize-money   £5,044

DENYS SMITH (Bishop Auckland, Co Durham)

	Races Run	1st	2nd	3rd	Unpl	Per cent	£1 Level Stake
Hurdles	50	7	5	3	35	14.0	- 10.25
Chases	11	4	0	1	6	36.4	+ 1.25
Totals	61	11	5	4	41	18.0	- 9.00

BY MONTH

	W-R	Per cent	£1 Level Stake		W-R	Per cent	£1 Level Stake
June	0-4	-	- 4.00	December	0-0	-	0.00
July	0-0	-	0.00	January	0-7	-	- 7.00
August	0-0	-	0.00	February	2-7	28.6	+ 4.75
September	4-8	50.0	+ 4.50	March	0-6	-	- 6.00
October	2-5	40.0	+ 0.75	April	1-7	14.3	+ 6.00
November	1-10	10.0	- 7.00	May	1-7	14.3	- 1.00

DISTANCE

	W-R	Per cent	£1 Level Stake		W-R	Per cent	£1 Level Stake
Hurdles	4-39	10.3	- 9.00	Chases	0-0	-	0.00
2m-2m 3f	4-39	10.3	- 9.00	2m-2m 3f	0-0	-	0.00
2m 4f-2m 7f	3-11	27.3	- 1.25	2m 4f-2m 7f	2-4	50.0	+ 0.25
3m +	0-0	-	0.00	3m +	2-7	28.6	+ 1.00

TYPE OF RACE

	W-R	Per cent	£1 Level Stake		W-R	Per cent	£1 Level Stake
Novice hurdles	0-16	-	- 16.00	Selling	1-5	20.0	+ 3.00
H'cap hurdles	5-28	17.9	- 9.25	Amateur	0-0	-	0.00
Novice chases	2-4	50.0	+ 3.75	Hunter chases	0-0	-	0.00
H'cap chases	2-7	28.6	- 2.50	N H Flat	1-1	100.0	+ 12.00

COURSE GRADE

	W-R	Per cent	£1 Level Stake
Group 1	0-8	-	- 8.00
Group 2	0-0	-	0.00
Group 3	0-6	-	- 6.00
Group 4	11-47	23.4	+ 5.00

FIRST TIME OUT

	W-R	Per cent	£1 Level Stake
Hurdles	2-10	20.0	+ 5.50
Chases	2-3	66.7	+ 1.25
Totals	4-13	30.8	+ 6.75

JOCKEYS RIDING

	W-R	Per cent	£1 Level Stake		W-R	Per cent	£1 Level Stake
P Niven	6-18	33.3	+ 1.00	B Storey	2-12	16.7	- 6.00
Richard Guest	2-3	66.7	+ 16.00	B Harding	1-7	14.3	+ 1.00

L Wyer	0-5	T Reed	0-2	Mr N Wilson	0-1
R P Burns	0-3	A Charlton	0-1	P Carberry	0-1
A Thornton	0-2	F Leahy	0-1	R Johnson	0-1
G Lee	0-2	J Callaghan	0-1	S Haworth	0-1

COURSE RECORD

	Total W-R	Nov Hdles	H'cap Hdles	Nov Chses	H'cap Chses	Hunter Chses	N H Flat	£1 Level Stake
Sedgefield	8-22	0-4	4-12	1-1	2-4	0-0	1-1	+ 15.50
Cartmel	1-1	0-0	1-1	0-0	0-0	0-0	0-0	+ 5.00
Hexham	1-4	0-0	1-4	0-0	0-0	0-0	0-0	- 1.00
Carlisle	1-9	0-3	0-4	1-1	0-1	0-0	0-0	- 3.50

Perth	0-5	Market Rasen	0-4	Musselburgh	0-2
Ayr	0-4	Newcastle	0-4		
Kelso	0-4	Catterick	0-2		

WINNING HORSES

	Races Run	1st	2nd	3rd	Unpl	Win £
Val De Rama	14	3	1	1	9	7,498
Staigue Fort	7	2	0	1	4	4,533
Cadeaux Premiere	12	2	3	1	6	4,391
Cornet	2	1	0	0	1	4,088
Oakley	1	1	0	0	0	2,975
Reve De Valse	9	1	0	0	8	1,947
Duraid	1	1	0	0	0	1,385

WINNING OWNERS

	Races Won	Value £		Races Won	Value £
D Morland	3	7,498	Lumsden & Carroll Construction	2	4,391
Duke of Sutherland	2	7,063	K Higson	1	1,947
Denys Smith	2	4,533	A Suddes	1	1,385

No of horses racing for the stable	13	Total winning prize-money	£26,817

Favourites	5-12	41.7%	+ 1.75	Average SP of winner	3.7/1
Longest win seq	3	Longest losing seq	14	Return on stakes invested	-14.8%

1994/95 Form	5-73	6.8%	- 33.50	1992/93 Form	14-119	11.8%	- 34.39
1993/94 Form	3-95	3.2%	- 84.30	1991/92 Form	19-129	14.7%	- 51.07

J S SMITH (Tirley, Glos)

	Races Run	1st	2nd	3rd	Unpl	Per cent	£1 Level Stake
Hurdles	18	1	1	2	14	5.6	- 5.00
Chases	3	0	0	1	2	-	- 3.00
Totals	21	1	1	3	16	4.8	- 8.00

T J Murphy	1-2	+ 11.00	Worcester	1-2	+ 11.00

No of horses racing for the stable	9	Total winning prize-money	£2,390

M SMITH (Thornaby-on-Tees, Co Cleveland)

	Races Run	1st	2nd	3rd	Unpl	Per cent	£1 Level Stake
Hurdles	12	1	3	1	7	8.3	+ 39.00
Chases	3	0	0	1	2	-	- 3.00
Totals	15	1	3	2	9	6.7	+ 36.00

G Harker	1-11	+ 40.00	Catterick	1-2	+ 49.00

No of horses racing for the stable	3	Total winning prize-money	£2,226

N A SMITH (Upton Snodsbury, H'ford & Worcs)

	Races Run	1st	2nd	3rd	Unpl	Per cent	£1 Level Stake
Hurdles	33	1	1	1	30	3.0	- 28.50
Chases	1	0	0	0	1	-	- 1.00
Totals	34	1	1	1	31	2.9	- 29.50

Mr J Culloty	1-2	+ 2.50		Lingfield	1-2	+ 2.50

No of horses racing for the stable	8	Total winning prize-money	£2,024

MRS S J SMITH (High Eldwick, West Yorks)

	Races Run	1st	2nd	3rd	Unpl	Per cent	£1 Level Stake
Hurdles	137	9	11	13	104	6.6	- 83.75
Chases	110	16	7	15	72	14.5	+ 54.39
Totals	247	25	18	28	176	10.1	- 29.36

BY MONTH

	W-R	Per cent	£1 Level Stake		W-R	Per cent	£1 Level Stake
June	0-4	-	- 4.00	December	1-22	4.5	- 17.50
July	1-5	20.0	+ 0.50	January	2-22	9.1	- 9.00
August	5-17	29.4	- 1.86	February	0-23	-	- 23.00
September	3-16	18.8	+ 1.50	March	3-36	8.3	- 15.75
October	3-17	17.6	+ 56.50	April	2-20	10.0	+ 12.00
November	3-41	7.3	- 14.00	May	2-24	8.3	- 14.75

DISTANCE

Hurdles	W-R	Per cent	£1 Level Stake	Chases	W-R	Per cent	£1 Level Stake
2m-2m 3f	4-78	5.1	- 59.25	2m-2m 3f	5-24	20.8	+ 8.14
2m 4f-2m 7f	4-40	10.0	- 15.50	2m 4f-2m 7f	4-31	12.9	+ 14.50
3m +	1-19	5.3	- 9.00	3m +	7-55	12.7	+ 31.75

TYPE OF RACE

	W-R	Per cent	£1 Level Stake		W-R	Per cent	£1 Level Stake
Novice hurdles	4-64	6.3	- 47.00	Selling	0-16	-	- 16.00
H'cap hurdles	5-39	12.8	- 2.75	Amateur	0-6	-	- 6.00
Novice chases	4-45	8.9	- 25.75	Hunter chases	0-0	-	0.00
H'cap chases	12-60	20.0	+ 85.14	N H Flat	0-17	-	- 17.00

Smith Mrs S J

COURSE GRADE

	W-R	Per cent	£1 Level Stake
Group 1	2-42	4.8	- 24.00
Group 2	2-20	10.0	- 10.00
Group 3	7-68	10.3	- 25.80
Group 4	14-117	12.0	+ 30.44

FIRST TIME OUT

	W-R	Per cent	£1 Level Stake
Hurdles	2-33	6.1	- 20.00
Chases	2-17	11.8	+ 39.50
Totals	4-50	8.0	+ 19.50

JOCKEYS RIDING

	W-R	Per cent	£1 Level Stake		W-R	Per cent	£1 Level Stake
Richard Guest	20-145	13.8	+ 3.64	Mr P Murray	2-27	7.4	+ 27.75
R Wilkinson	3-32	9.4	- 17.75				

L Donnelly	0-19	L Wyer	0-2	P Niven	0-1
L McGrath	0-9	R Supple	0-2	Richard Davis	0-1
R Garrity	0-3	J Callaghan	0-1	T Eley	0-1
A Thornton	0-2	Miss V Haigh	0-1	W McFarland	0-1

COURSE RECORD

	Total W-R	Nov Hdles	H'cap Hdles	Nov Chses	H'cap Chses	Hunter Chses	N H Flat	£1 Level Stake
Worcester	3-10	0-2	0-1	1-3	2-3	0-0	0-1	- 0.30
Catterick	3-19	0-4	0-3	0-2	3-7	0-0	0-3	+ 2.50
Bangor	3-20	1-6	1-4	0-5	1-4	0-0	0-1	- 4.31
Cartmel	2-5	1-2	0-0	1-2	0-1	0-0	0-0	+ 4.50
Carlisle	2-10	0-2	0-3	1-2	1-1	0-0	0-2	+ 19.75
Kelso	2-13	1-5	0-3	0-2	1-3	0-0	0-0	+ 39.50
Hexham	2-20	0-5	0-2	0-4	2-8	0-0	0-1	+ 7.00
Perth	1-4	1-1	0-0	0-1	0-2	0-0	0-0	- 1.50
Chepstow	1-5	0-2	1-1	0-0	0-2	0-0	0-0	- 1.00
Haydock	1-8	0-3	1-3	0-0	0-1	0-0	0-1	0.00
Towcester	1-10	0-4	0-3	1-2	0-1	0-0	0-0	- 4.00
Wetherby	1-15	0-5	0-5	0-3	1-2	0-0	0-0	- 9.00
Newcastle	1-16	0-6	1-5	0-2	0-2	0-0	0-1	- 6.00
Market Rasen	1-17	0-2	1-5	0-4	0-4	0-0	0-2	- 6.00
Southwell	1-19	0-7	0-2	0-3	1-7	0-0	0-0	- 14.50

Sedgefield	0-7	Musselburgh	0-5	Aintree	0-2
Uttoxeter	0-6	Nottingham	0-5	Cheltenham	0-2
Ayr	0-5	Ascot	0-4	Newbury	0-1
Huntingdon	0-5	Doncaster	0-4	Stratford	0-1
Leicester	0-5	Hereford	0-4		

WINNING HORSES

	Races Run	1st	2nd	3rd	Unpl	Win £
The Last Fling	8	5	1	0	2	17,199
Peruvian Gale	13	4	0	4	5	12,600
Regal Romper	9	4	3	0	2	11,980
Celtic Silver	6	2	0	1	3	6,258
Supposin	9	2	0	1	6	5,981
Reapers Rock	4	1	0	0	3	3,712
Mony-Skip	10	1	1	0	8	3,059

Nova Champ	10	1	2	3	4	3,051
Brambleberry	12	1	0	3	8	2,997
Fruhman	3	1	0	0	2	2,786
Ten Mile Hill	3	1	2	0	0	2,710
Exemplar	13	1	2	1	9	2,513
Hard Try	3	1	0	0	2	2,268

WINNING OWNERS

	Races Won	Value £		Races Won	Value £
Mrs S Smith	13	37,660	A Baylis	1	3,712
J L Walbank	4	12,600	Trevor Hemmings	1	3,059
R Waterson	2	8,054	Mrs C E Van Praagh	1	3,051
J Kemp	2	5,981	Hampers Racing	1	2,997

No of horses racing for the stable		51	Total winning prize-money	£77,114

Favourites	7-19	36.8%	- 2.61	Average SP of winner		7.7/1
Longest win seq	2	Longest losing seq	31	Return on stakes invested		-11.9%

1994/95 Form	22-229	9.6%	+ 2.48	1992/93 Form	6-200	3.0%	-153.75
1993/94 Form	22-198	11.1%	- 41.87	1991/92 Form	12-108	11.1%	+113.50

W J SMITH (Richmond, North Yorks)

	Races Run	1st	2nd	3rd	Unpl	Per cent	£1 Level Stake
Hurdles	30	2	2	2	24	6.7	+ 30.00
Chases	0	0	0	0	0	-	0.00
Totals	30	2	2	2	24	6.7	+ 30.00

S Porritt	1-3	+ 48.00	Scott Taylor	1-22	- 13.00
Cartmel	1-1	+ 8.00	Sedgefield	1-7	+ 44.00

No of horses racing for the stable	4	Total winning prize-money	£4,743

W M SMITH (Hambledon, Hants)

	Races Run	1st	2nd	3rd	Unpl	Per cent	£1 Level Stake
Hurdles	0	0	0	0	0	-	0.00
Chases	1	1	0	0	0	100.0	+ 1.00
Totals	1	1	0	0	0	100.0	+ 1.00

Mr J Culloty	1-1	+ 1.00	Huntingdon	1-1	+ 1.00

No of horses racing for the stable	1	Total winning prize-money	£2,320

J L SPEARING (Wixford, Warwicks)

	Races Run	1st	2nd	3rd	Unpl	Per cent	£1 Level Stake
Hurdles	81	6	7	13	55	7.4	- 40.75
Chases	8	0	0	0	8	-	- 8.00
Totals	89	6	7	13	63	6.7	- 48.75

D Bridgwater	2-8	+ 3.00	L Wyer	1-4	+ 13.00
N Williamson	1-2	+ 2.50	R Johnson	1-8	- 4.00
A P McCoy	1-4	- 0.25			
Market Rasen	1-3	+ 3.00	Haydock	1-4	+ 13.00
Newbury	1-3	+ 2.00	Uttoxeter	1-7	- 2.50
Chepstow	1-3	+ 0.75	Warwick	1-7	- 3.00

No of horses racing for the stable   18   Total winning prize-money   £20,812

S R SPORBORG (Ware, Herts)

	Races Run	1st	2nd	3rd	Unpl	Per cent	£1 Level Stake
Hurdles	0	0	0	0	0	-	0.00
Chases	5	2	0	1	2	40.0	+ 1.63
Totals	5	2	0	1	2	40.0	+ 1.63

Mr S Sporborg	2-5	+ 1.63			
Folkestone	1-1	+ 1.88	Sandown	1-2	+ 1.75

No of horses racing for the stable   2   Total winning prize-money   £4,235

P SPOTTISWOOD (Greenhaugh, Northumberland)

	Races Run	1st	2nd	3rd	Unpl	Per cent	£1 Level Stake
Hurdles	8	1	0	0	7	12.5	+ 7.00
Chases	2	0	0	0	2	-	- 2.00
Totals	10	1	0	0	9	10.0	+ 5.00

P Waggott	1-2	+ 13.00	Wetherby	1-1	+ 14.00

No of horses racing for the stable   2   Total winning prize-money   £2,548

J SQUIRE (Torrington, Devon)

	Races Run	1st	2nd	3rd	Unpl	Per cent	£1 Level Stake
Hurdles	0	0	0	0	0	–	0.00
Chases	2	1	0	0	1	50.0	+ 1.75
Totals	2	1	0	0	1	50.0	+ 1.75

Miss L Blackford	1-2	+ 1.75	Cheltenham	1-1	+ 2.75

No of horses racing for the stable — 1 — Total winning prize-money — £1,854

MISS V A STEPHENS (Taunton, Somerset)

	Races Run	1st	2nd	3rd	Unpl	Per cent	£1 Level Stake
Hurdles	0	0	0	0	0	–	0.00
Chases	3	1	0	0	2	33.3	+ 1.00
Totals	3	1	0	0	2	33.3	+ 1.00

Miss V Stephens	1-3	+ 1.00	Taunton	1-1	+ 3.00

No of horses racing for the stable — 2 — Total winning prize-money — £1,235

MRS M K STIRK (Laverton, North Yorks)

	Races Run	1st	2nd	3rd	Unpl	Per cent	£1 Level Stake
Hurdles	5	1	2	1	1	20.0	+ 46.00
Chases	0	0	0	0	0	–	0.00
Totals	5	1	2	1	1	20.0	+ 46.00

Mr S Swiers	1-5	+ 46.00	Hexham	1-2	+ 49.00

No of horses racing for the stable — 1 — Total winning prize-money — £2,128

F S STOREY (Kirklinton, Cumbria)

	Races Run	1st	2nd	3rd	Unpl	Per cent	£1 Level Stake
Hurdles	18	2	1	3	12	11.1	+ 6.00
Chases	0	0	0	0	0	–	0.00
Totals	18	2	1	3	12	11.1	+ 6.00

B Storey	2-17	+ 7.00			
Cartmel	1-3	+ 14.00	Sedgefield	1-6	+ 1.00

No of horses racing for the stable — 4 — Total winning prize-money — £4,552

MRS JANE STOREY (Kelso, Borders)

	Races Run	1st	2nd	3rd	Unpl	Per cent	£1 Level Stake
Hurdles	0	0	0	0	0	-	0.00
Chases	20	6	3	2	9	30.0	- 5.25
Totals	20	6	3	2	9	30.0	- 5.25

Mr C Storey	6-14	+ 0.75

Kelso	2-6	- 0.70	Ayr	1-1	+ 2.50
Catterick	1-1	+ 0.50	Newcastle	1-3	- 1.43
Aintree	1-1	+ 1.88			

No of horses racing for the stable	4	Total winning prize-money	£19,403

W STOREY (Muggleswick, Co Durham)

	Races Run	1st	2nd	3rd	Unpl	Per cent	£1 Level Stake
Hurdles	67	11	10	4	42	16.4	- 6.95
Chases	10	1	2	1	6	10.0	- 7.00
Totals	77	12	12	5	48	15.6	- 13.95

BY MONTH

	W-R	Per cent	£1 Level Stake		W-R	Per cent	£1 Level Stake
June	0-2	-	- 2.00	December	1-4	25.0	+ 4.00
July	0-0	-	0.00	January	1-8	12.5	0.00
August	0-0	-	0.00	February	0-8	-	- 8.00
September	2-10	20.0	- 5.00	March	5-13	38.5	+ 15.30
October	0-4	-	- 4.00	April	0-2	-	- 2.00
November	1-21	4.8	- 17.50	May	2-5	40.0	+ 5.25

DISTANCE

Hurdles	W-R	Per cent	£1 Level Stake	Chases	W-R	Per cent	£1 Level Stake
2m-2m 3f	2-32	6.3	- 26.00	2m-2m 3f	0-4	-	- 4.00
2m 4f-2m 7f	6-21	28.6	+ 11.05	2m 4f-2m 7f	0-2	-	- 2.00
3m +	3-14	21.4	+ 8.00	3m +	1-4	25.0	- 1.00

TYPE OF RACE

	W-R	Per cent	£1 Level Stake		W-R	Per cent	£1 Level Stake
Novice hurdles	0-14	-	- 14.00	Selling	3-11	27.3	+ 1.75
H'cap hurdles	8-42	19.0	+ 5.30	Amateur	0-0	-	0.00
Novice chases	0-4	-	- 4.00	Hunter chases	0-0	-	0.00
H'cap chases	1-6	16.7	- 3.00	N H Flat	0-0	-	0.00

COURSE GRADE

	W-R	Per cent	£1 Level Stake
Group 1	7-31	22.6	+ 13.30
Group 2	0-2	-	- 2.00
Group 3	0-8	-	- 8.00
Group 4	5-36	13.9	- 17.25

FIRST TIME OUT

	W-R	Per cent	£1 Level Stake
Hurdles	1-16	6.3	- 13.50
Chases	0-1	-	- 1.00
Totals	1-17	5.9	- 14.50

JOCKEYS RIDING

	W-R	Per cent	£1 Level Stake		W-R	Per cent	£1 Level Stake
R McGrath	7-26	26.9	+ 19.55	R Dunwoody	1-1	100.0	+ 2.00
J Supple	2-32	6.3	- 26.00	P Carberry	1-6	16.7	0.00
A Maguire	1-1	100.0	+ 1.50				

M Moloney	0-7	B Harding	0-1
R Supple	0-2	E Callaghan	0-1

COURSE RECORD

	Total W-R	Nov Hdles	H'cap Hdles	Nov Chses	H'cap Chses	Hunter Chses	N H Flat	£1 Level Stake
Sedgefield	3-12	0-3	3-7	0-2	0-0	0-0	0-0	+ 0.75
Ayr	2-8	0-2	2-6	0-0	0-0	0-0	0-0	+ 3.30
Cheltenham	1-1	0-0	1-1	0-0	0-0	0-0	0-0	+ 7.00
Newbury	1-1	0-0	0-0	0-0	1-1	0-0	0-0	+ 2.00
Doncaster	1-1	0-0	1-1	0-0	0-0	0-0	0-0	+ 5.00
Kempton	1-2	0-0	1-2	0-0	0-0	0-0	0-0	+ 6.00
Haydock	1-2	0-0	1-2	0-0	0-0	0-0	0-0	+ 6.00
Carlisle	1-4	0-0	1-3	0-0	0-1	0-0	0-0	- 1.50
Kelso	1-7	0-1	1-6	0-0	0-0	0-0	0-0	- 3.50

Newcastle	0-15	Hexham	0-4	Aintree	0-1
Catterick	0-7	Musselburgh	0-3	Cartmel	0-1
Perth	0-5	Wetherby	0-2	Uttoxeter	0-1

WINNING HORSES

	Races Run	1st	2nd	3rd	Unpl	Win £
Great Easeby	5	3	1	0	1	34,836
Karaylar	6	2	0	0	4	9,104
Zamhareer	7	1	2	0	4	5,114
Izza	10	2	2	1	5	5,109
Master Hyde	2	2	0	0	0	5,063
Northants	6	1	1	1	3	5,020
King of The Horse	7	1	2	1	3	1,856

WINNING OWNERS

	Races Won	Value £		Races Won	Value £
D C Batey	8	54,163	C B Rennison	1	5,020
D Callaghan	2	5,063	Alan Crook	1	1,856

No of horses racing for the stable		17		Total winning prize-money			£66,102

Favourites	6-9	66.7%	+ 9.75	Average SP of winner			4.3/1
Longest win seq	3	Longest losing seq	21	Return on stakes invested			-18.1%

1994/95 Form	10-69	14.5%	+ 33.81	1992/93 Form	3-43	7.0%	- 21.56
1993/94 Form	4-55	7.3%	- 24.00	1991/92 Form	6-76	7.9%	- 42.03

A STREETER (Stramshall, Staffs)

	Races Run	1st	2nd	3rd	Unpl	Per cent	£1 Level Stake
Hurdles	50	10	9	6	25	20.0	+ 19.35
Chases	6	4	1	0	1	66.7	+ 8.33
Totals	56	14	10	6	26	25.0	+ 27.68

BY MONTH

	W-R	Per cent	£1 Level Stake		W-R	Per cent	£1 Level Stake
June	0-0	-	0.00	December	1-8	12.5	- 3.67
July	0-0	-	0.00	January	2-7	28.6	+ 1.25
August	2-3	66.7	+ 2.85	February	2-7	28.6	+ 2.75
September	0-3	-	- 3.00	March	2-10	20.0	+ 4.00
October	1-4	25.0	+ 1.50	April	0-5	-	- 5.00
November	2-4	50.0	+ 7.00	May	2-5	40.0	+ 20.00

DISTANCE

Hurdles	W-R	Per cent	£1 Level Stake	Chases	W-R	Per cent	£1 Level Stake
2m-2m 3f	9-40	22.5	+ 14.35	2m-2m 3f	4-6	66.7	+ 8.33
2m 4f-2m 7f	1-8	12.5	+ 7.00	2m 4f-2m 7f	0-0	-	0.00
3m +	0-2	-	- 2.00	3m +	0-0	-	0.00

TYPE OF RACE

	W-R	Per cent	£1 Level Stake		W-R	Per cent	£1 Level Stake
Novice hurdles	1-10	10.0	- 4.00	Selling	3-10	30.0	+ 10.50
H'cap hurdles	6-26	23.1	+ 16.85	Amateur	0-0	-	0.00
Novice chases	0-0	-	0.00	Hunter chases	0-0	-	0.00
H'cap chases	4-6	66.7	+ 8.33	N H Flat	0-4	-	- 4.00

COURSE GRADE

	W-R	Per cent	£1 Level Stake		W-R	Per cent	£1 Level Stake
Group 1	1-7	14.3	+ 1.00	Hurdles	1-11	9.1	- 5.50
Group 2	0-4	-	- 4.00	Chases	0-0	-	0.00
Group 3	11-36	30.6	+ 34.33				
Group 4	2-9	22.2	- 3.65	Totals	1-11	9.1	- 5.50

FIRST TIME OUT

JOCKEYS RIDING

	W-R	Per cent	£1 Level Stake			W-R	Per cent	£1 Level Stake
T Eley	11-41	26.8	+ 30.10	A Larnach		1-1	100.0	+ 4.00
A S Smith	1-1	100.0	+ 3.33	Gary Lyons		1-2	50.0	+ 1.25
W Humphreys	0-3			C Rae	0-2	P Carey		0-2
B Harding	0-2			L Aspell	0-2			

COURSE RECORD

	Total W-R	Nov Hdles	H'cap Hdles	Nov Chses	H'cap Chses	Hunter Chses	N H Flat	£1 Level Stake
Catterick	5-9	1-2	2-5	0-0	2-2	0-0	0-0	+ 16.08
Stratford	3-4	2-2	1-2	0-0	0-0	0-0	0-0	+ 15.25
Perth	1-1	0-0	1-1	0-0	0-0	0-0	0-0	+ 1.10
Newbury	1-1	0-0	1-1	0-0	0-0	0-0	0-0	+ 7.00
Warwick	1-2	0-0	1-2	0-0	0-0	0-0	0-0	+ 13.00
Ludlow	1-3	0-0	0-0	0-0	1-1	0-0	0-2	+ 0.25
Worcester	1-4	0-1	0-2	0-0	1-1	0-0	0-0	- 1.00
Uttoxeter	1-9	0-5	1-4	0-0	0-0	0-0	0-0	- 1.00

Market Rasen	0-4	Bangor	0-1	Leicester	0-1
Wetherby	0-4	Carlisle	0-1	Newcastle	0-1
Doncaster	0-3	Cheltenham	0-1	Taunton	0-1
Nottingham	0-2	Haydock	0-1		
Southwell	0-2	Huntingdon	0-1		

WINNING HORSES

	Races Run	1st	2nd	3rd	Unpl	Win £
Newhall Prince	8	5	2	0	1	15,675
Centaur Express	9	3	2	2	2	8,162
Classic Exhibit	3	2	0	1	0	5,500
Bossymoss	4	1	1	0	2	2,637
Preston Guild	4	1	1	0	2	2,556
Jemima Puddleduck	8	1	1	1	5	2,241
Legatee	5	1	1	0	3	2,227

WINNING OWNERS

	Races Won	Value £		Races Won	Value £
R W Trubshaw	5	15,675	Mrs Margaret James	1	2,637
Centaur Racing	3	8,162	The Fiveways Partnership	1	2,556
Principal Racing	3	7,741	South Normanton Racing	1	2,227

No of horses racing for the stable	13	Total winning prize-money	£38,998

Favourites	4-8	50.0%	+ 4.10	Average SP of winner	5.0/1
Longest win seq	2	Longest losing seq	8	Return on stakes invested	49.4%

C J R SWEETING (Chipping Norton, Oxon)

	Races Run	1st	2nd	3rd	Unpl	Per cent	£1 Level Stake
Hurdles	0	0	0	0	0	–	0.00
Chases	4	2	0	1	1	50.0	+ 27.50
Totals	4	2	0	1	1	50.0	+ 27.50

Mr R Sweeting	2-4	+ 27.50				
Southwell	1-1	+ 25.00	Stratford	1-2	+ 3.50	

No of horses racing for the stable	3	Total winning prize-money	£4,373

MRS A SWINBANK (Melsonby, North Yorks)

	Races Run	1st	2nd	3rd	Unpl	Per cent	£1 Level Stake
Hurdles	44	5	3	4	32	11.4	– 9.75
Chases	4	0	2	1	1	–	– 4.00
Totals	48	5	5	5	33	10.4	– 13.75

J Railton	3-26	+ 0.25	P Carberry	1-2	0.00	
Mr A Parker	1-1	+ 5.00				
Ayr	2-5	+ 18.00	Aintree	1-1	+ 5.00	
Carlisle	2-7	– 1.75				

No of horses racing for the stable	15	Total winning prize-money	£12,053

G J TARRY (Daventry, Northants)

	Races Run	1st	2nd	3rd	Unpl	Per cent	£1 Level Stake
Hurdles	0	0	0	0	0	–	0.00
Chases	3	1	0	1	1	33.3	– 0.25
Totals	3	1	0	1	1	33.3	– 0.25

Mr G Tarry	1-3	– 0.25	Uttoxeter	1-2	+ 0.75

No of horses racing for the stable	2	Total winning prize-money	£1,817

R TATE (Thirsk, North Yorks)

	Races Run	1st	2nd	3rd	Unpl	Per cent	£1 Level Stake
Hurdles	8	1	1	0	6	12.5	- 1.00
Chases	7	0	2	1	4	-	- 7.00
Totals	15	1	3	1	10	6.7	- 8.00

Mr C Bonner	1-3	+ 4.00	Sedgefield	1-3	+ 4.00

No of horses racing for the stable	6	Total winning prize-money	£2,530

T P TATE (Tadcaster, North Yorks)

	Races Run	1st	2nd	3rd	Unpl	Per cent	£1 Level Stake
Hurdles	23	2	2	1	18	8.7	- 4.00
Chases	22	6	4	3	9	27.3	+ 16.20
Totals	45	8	6	4	27	17.8	+ 12.20

BY MONTH

	W-R	Per cent	£1 Level Stake		W-R	Per cent	£1 Level Stake
June	0-3	-	- 3.00	December	2-5	40.0	+ 12.00
July	0-0	-	0.00	January	1-7	14.3	- 4.80
August	0-0	-	0.00	February	1-7	14.3	- 2.50
September	0-0	-	0.00	March	1-7	14.3	+ 4.00
October	0-2	-	- 2.00	April	1-6	16.7	- 2.50
November	2-5	40.0	+ 14.00	May	0-3	-	- 3.00

DISTANCE

Hurdles	W-R	Per cent	£1 Level Stake	Chases	W-R	Per cent	£1 Level Stake
2m-2m 3f	2-18	11.1	+ 1.00	2m-2m 3f	3-8	37.5	+ 11.20
2m 4f-2m 7f	0-4	-	- 4.00	2m 4f-2m 7f	0-3	-	- 3.00
3m +	0-1	-	- 1.00	3m +	3-11	27.3	+ 8.00

TYPE OF RACE

	W-R	Per cent	£1 Level Stake		W-R	Per cent	£1 Level Stake
Novice hurdles	0-9	-	- 9.00	Selling	0-0	-	0.00
H'cap hurdles	0-2	-	- 2.00	Amateur	0-2	-	- 2.00
Novice chases	3-13	23.1	+ 6.20	Hunter chases	0-0	-	0.00
H'cap chases	3-8	37.5	+ 11.00	N H Flat	2-11	18.2	+ 8.00

Tate T P

<table>
<tr><th colspan="4">COURSE GRADE</th><th colspan="4">FIRST TIME OUT</th></tr>
<tr><th></th><th>W-R</th><th>Per cent</th><th>£1 Level Stake</th><th></th><th>W-R</th><th>Per cent</th><th>£1 Level Stake</th></tr>
<tr><td>Group 1</td><td>3-13</td><td>23.1</td><td>+ 4.70</td><td>Hurdles</td><td>1-9</td><td>11.1</td><td>+ 4.00</td></tr>
<tr><td>Group 2</td><td>2-7</td><td>28.6</td><td>+ 7.50</td><td>Chases</td><td>2-5</td><td>40.0</td><td>+ 12.00</td></tr>
<tr><td>Group 3</td><td>2-14</td><td>14.3</td><td>+ 5.00</td><td></td><td></td><td></td><td></td></tr>
<tr><td>Group 4</td><td>1-11</td><td>9.1</td><td>- 5.00</td><td>Totals</td><td>3-14</td><td>21.4</td><td>+ 16.00</td></tr>
</table>

JOCKEYS RIDING

<table>
<tr><th></th><th>W-R</th><th>Per cent</th><th>£1 Level Stake</th><th></th><th>W-R</th><th>Per cent</th><th>£1 Level Stake</th></tr>
<tr><td>R Garrity</td><td>4-23</td><td>17.4</td><td>+ 4.20</td><td>P Niven</td><td>1-3</td><td>33.3</td><td>+ 8.00</td></tr>
<tr><td>C F Swan</td><td>1-1</td><td>100.0</td><td>+ 3.50</td><td>Mr S Swiers</td><td>1-6</td><td>16.7</td><td>+ 5.00</td></tr>
<tr><td>J Callaghan</td><td>1-3</td><td>33.3</td><td>+ 0.50</td><td></td><td></td><td></td><td></td></tr>
</table>

<table>
<tr><td>Mr W Burnell</td><td>0-4</td><td>G Bradley</td><td>0-2</td></tr>
<tr><td>B Harding</td><td>0-2</td><td>Mr R Ford</td><td>0-1</td></tr>
</table>

COURSE RECORD

<table>
<tr><th></th><th>Total W-R</th><th>Nov Hdles</th><th>H'cap Hdles</th><th>Nov Chses</th><th>H'cap Chses</th><th>Hunter Chses</th><th>N H Flat</th><th>£1 Level Stake</th></tr>
<tr><td>Haydock</td><td>2-3</td><td>0-0</td><td>0-0</td><td>1-2</td><td>1-1</td><td>0-0</td><td>0-0</td><td>+ 3.70</td></tr>
<tr><td>Wetherby</td><td>2-7</td><td>0-1</td><td>0-0</td><td>0-2</td><td>2-3</td><td>0-0</td><td>0-1</td><td>+ 7.50</td></tr>
<tr><td>Aintree</td><td>1-1</td><td>0-0</td><td>0-0</td><td>1-1</td><td>0-0</td><td>0-0</td><td>0-0</td><td>+ 10.00</td></tr>
<tr><td>Nottingham</td><td>1-2</td><td>0-1</td><td>0-0</td><td>1-1</td><td>0-0</td><td>0-0</td><td>0-0</td><td>+ 4.00</td></tr>
<tr><td>Hexham</td><td>1-4</td><td>0-2</td><td>0-0</td><td>0-0</td><td>0-1</td><td>0-0</td><td>1-1</td><td>+ 2.00</td></tr>
<tr><td>Worcester</td><td>1-6</td><td>0-1</td><td>0-1</td><td>0-0</td><td>0-1</td><td>0-0</td><td>1-3</td><td>+ 7.00</td></tr>
</table>

<table>
<tr><td>Sedgefield</td><td>0-5</td><td>Cheltenham</td><td>0-2</td><td>Newcastle</td><td>0-1</td></tr>
<tr><td>Doncaster</td><td>0-4</td><td>Carlisle</td><td>0-1</td><td>Uttoxeter</td><td>0-1</td></tr>
<tr><td>Catterick</td><td>0-3</td><td>Kelso</td><td>0-1</td><td>Warwick</td><td>0-1</td></tr>
<tr><td>Ayr</td><td>0-2</td><td>Market Rasen</td><td>0-1</td><td></td><td></td></tr>
</table>

WINNING HORSES

<table>
<tr><th></th><th>Races Run</th><th>1st</th><th>2nd</th><th>3rd</th><th>Unpl</th><th>Win £</th></tr>
<tr><td>Lo Stregone</td><td>4</td><td>2</td><td>1</td><td>0</td><td>1</td><td>58,660</td></tr>
<tr><td>Ask Tom</td><td>4</td><td>3</td><td>0</td><td>0</td><td>1</td><td>31,783</td></tr>
<tr><td>Rualmit</td><td>8</td><td>1</td><td>2</td><td>1</td><td>4</td><td>3,665</td></tr>
<tr><td>Nordic Prince</td><td>2</td><td>2</td><td>0</td><td>0</td><td>0</td><td>3,423</td></tr>
</table>

WINNING OWNERS

<table>
<tr><th></th><th>Races Won</th><th>Value £</th><th></th><th>Races Won</th><th>Value £</th></tr>
<tr><td>Mrs Sylvia Clegg</td><td>2</td><td>58,660</td><td>T P Tate</td><td>3</td><td>7,088</td></tr>
<tr><td>B T Stewart-Brown</td><td>3</td><td>31,783</td><td></td><td></td><td></td></tr>
</table>

| No of horses racing for the stable | | 14 | Total winning prize-money | | | £97,531 |

| Favourites | 2-7 | 28.6% | - 1.30 | Average SP of winner | | | 6.2/1 |
| Longest win seq | 2 | Longest losing seq | 9 | Return on stakes invested | | | 27.1% |

| 1994/95 Form | 4-44 | 9.1% | - 26.83 | 1992/93 Form | 12-69 | 17.4% | - 23.55 |
| 1993/94 Form | 11-79 | 13.9% | - 28.62 | 1991/92 Form | 8-67 | 11.9% | - 23.62 |

MRS L C TAYLOR (Chipping Warden, Northants)

	Races Run	1st	2nd	3rd	Unpl	Per cent	£1 Level Stake
Hurdles	9	0	1	1	7	-	- 9.00
Chases	13	1	3	2	7	7.7	- 8.50
Totals	22	1	4	3	14	4.5	- 17.50

| R Supple | 1-13 | - 8.50 | Hereford | 1-2 | + 2.50 |

| No of horses racing for the stable | 7 | Total winning prize-money | £3,620 |

D T THOM (Exning, Suffolk)

	Races Run	1st	2nd	3rd	Unpl	Per cent	£1 Level Stake
Hurdles	15	1	2	0	12	6.7	- 10.50
Chases	0	0	0	0	0	-	0.00
Totals	15	1	2	0	12	6.7	- 10.50

| S McNeill | 1-5 | - 0.50 | Towcester | 1-2 | + 2.50 |

| No of horses racing for the stable | 7 | Total winning prize-money | £2,110 |

RONALD THOMPSON (Stainforth, South Yorks)

	Races Run	1st	2nd	3rd	Unpl	Per cent	£1 Level Stake
Hurdles	22	1	2	3	16	4.5	- 20.09
Chases	0	0	0	0	0	-	0.00
Totals	22	1	2	3	16	4.5	- 20.09

| W Fry | 1-15 | - 13.09 | Hexham | 1-6 | - 4.09 |

| No of horses racing for the stable | 7 | Total winning prize-money | £1,316 |

V THOMPSON (Embleton, Northumberland)

	Races Run	1st	2nd	3rd	Unpl	Per cent	£1 Level Stake
Hurdles	1	0	0	0	1	–	– 1.00
Chases	37	1	0	4	32	2.7	– 30.00
Totals	38	1	0	4	33	2.6	– 31.00

Mr N Wilson	1-1	+ 6.00	Sedgefield	1-17	– 10.00

No of horses racing for the stable	11	Total winning prize-money	£2,180

MRS D THOMSON (Milnathort, Tayside)

	Races Run	1st	2nd	3rd	Unpl	Per cent	£1 Level Stake
Hurdles	50	1	4	9	36	2.0	– 44.50
Chases	11	1	2	1	7	9.1	– 8.90
Totals	61	2	6	10	43	3.3	– 53.40

L O'Hara	2-30	– 22.40	Sedgefield	2-8	– 0.40

No of horses racing for the stable	13	Total winning prize-money	£5,032

N B THOMSON (Shaftesbury, Dorset)

	Races Run	1st	2nd	3rd	Unpl	Per cent	£1 Level Stake
Hurdles	33	1	1	2	29	3.0	– 18.00
Chases	5	0	0	0	5	–	– 5.00
Totals	38	1	1	2	34	2.6	– 23.00

J Titley	1-3	+ 12.00	Exeter	1-3	+ 12.00

No of horses racing for the stable	8	Total winning prize-money	£4,083

G THORNER (Letcombe Regis, Oxon)

	Races Run	1st	2nd	3rd	Unpl	Per cent	£1 Level Stake
Hurdles	34	0	1	2	31	-	- 34.00
Chases	24	3	6	3	12	12.5	- 13.12
Totals	58	3	7	5	43	5.2	- 47.12

Mr J Culloty	1-2	+ 2.50	M A Fitzgerald	1-4	- 1.12
I Lawrence	1-3	+ 0.50			
Towcester	1-4	- 0.50	Ludlow	1-6	- 1.50
Taunton	1-5	- 2.12			

No of horses racing for the stable   16   Total winning prize-money   £9,280

C W THORNTON (Middleham, North Yorks)

	Races Run	1st	2nd	3rd	Unpl	Per cent	£1 Level Stake
Hurdles	35	4	6	6	19	11.4	- 0.67
Chases	13	3	2	1	7	23.1	- 0.75
Totals	48	7	8	7	26	14.6	- 1.42

BY MONTH

	W-R	Per cent	£1 Level Stake		W-R	Per cent	£1 Level Stake
June	0-5	-	- 5.00	December	1-3	33.3	+ 3.00
July	0-0	-	0.00	January	2-5	40.0	+ 1.75
August	0-3	-	- 3.00	February	0-3	-	- 3.00
September	0-3	-	- 3.00	March	1-7	14.3	- 2.67
October	0-1	-	- 1.00	April	3-8	37.5	+ 21.50
November	0-6	-	- 6.00	May	0-4	-	- 4.00

DISTANCE

Hurdles	W-R	Per cent	£1 Level Stake	Chases	W-R	Per cent	£1 Level Stake
2m-2m 3f	4-29	13.8	+ 5.33	2m-2m 3f	2-4	50.0	+ 2.75
2m 4f-2m 7f	0-4	-	- 4.00	2m 4f-2m 7f	1-6	16.7	- 0.50
3m +	0-2	-	- 2.00	3m +	0-3	-	- 3.00

TYPE OF RACE

	W-R	Per cent	£1 Level Stake		W-R	Per cent	£1 Level Stake
Novice hurdles	1-8	12.5	+ 5.00	Selling	0-3	-	- 3.00
H'cap hurdles	1-10	10.0	- 4.00	Amateur	0-1	-	- 1.00
Novice chases	2-4	50.0	+ 2.75	Hunter chases	0-0	-	0.00
H'cap chases	1-8	12.5	- 2.50	N H Flat	2-14	14.3	+ 1.33

Thornton C W

<table>
<tr><th colspan="5">COURSE GRADE</th><th colspan="5">FIRST TIME OUT</th></tr>
<tr><th></th><th>W-R</th><th>Per cent</th><th>£1 Level Stake</th><th></th><th></th><th>W-R</th><th>Per cent</th><th>£1 Level Stake</th></tr>
<tr><td>Group 1</td><td>4-15</td><td>26.7</td><td>+ 11.08</td><td>Hurdles</td><td></td><td>0-12</td><td>-</td><td>- 12.00</td></tr>
<tr><td>Group 2</td><td>0-2</td><td>-</td><td>- 2.00</td><td>Chases</td><td></td><td>0-3</td><td>-</td><td>- 3.00</td></tr>
<tr><td>Group 3</td><td>0-9</td><td>-</td><td>- 9.00</td><td></td><td></td><td></td><td></td><td></td></tr>
<tr><td>Group 4</td><td>3-22</td><td>13.6</td><td>- 1.50</td><td>Totals</td><td></td><td>0-15</td><td>-</td><td>- 15.00</td></tr>
</table>

JOCKEYS RIDING

<table>
<tr><th></th><th>W-R</th><th>Per cent</th><th>£1 Level Stake</th><th></th><th>W-R</th><th>Per cent</th><th>£1 Level Stake</th></tr>
<tr><td>N Horrocks</td><td>3-15</td><td>20.0</td><td>+ 6.33</td><td>A Dobbin</td><td>1-2</td><td>50.0</td><td>+ 1.50</td></tr>
<tr><td>P Carberry</td><td>2-4</td><td>50.0</td><td>+ 4.75</td><td>M Foster</td><td>1-5</td><td>20.0</td><td>+ 8.00</td></tr>
</table>

<table>
<tr><td>D Wilkinson</td><td>0-11</td><td>Mark Roberts</td><td>0-1</td><td>Richard Guest</td><td>0-1</td></tr>
<tr><td>P Niven</td><td>0-2</td><td>Mr C Bonner</td><td>0-1</td><td>Scott Taylor</td><td>0-1</td></tr>
<tr><td>B D Grattan</td><td>0-1</td><td>Mr S Swiers</td><td>0-1</td><td>W Marston</td><td>0-1</td></tr>
<tr><td>E Callaghan</td><td>0-1</td><td>N Williamson</td><td>0-1</td><td></td><td></td></tr>
</table>

COURSE RECORD

<table>
<tr><th></th><th>Total W-R</th><th>Nov Hdles</th><th>H'cap Hdles</th><th>Nov Chses</th><th>H'cap Chses</th><th>Hunter Chses</th><th>N H Flat</th><th>£1 Level Stake</th></tr>
<tr><td>Newcastle</td><td>2-4</td><td>0-0</td><td>0-1</td><td>1-1</td><td>0-0</td><td>0-0</td><td>1-2</td><td>+ 3.58</td></tr>
<tr><td>Musselburgh</td><td>2-4</td><td>0-0</td><td>1-2</td><td>1-1</td><td>0-0</td><td>0-0</td><td>0-1</td><td>+ 5.50</td></tr>
<tr><td>Hexham</td><td>1-1</td><td>0-0</td><td>0-0</td><td>0-0</td><td>0-0</td><td>0-0</td><td>1-1</td><td>+ 10.00</td></tr>
<tr><td>Cheltenham</td><td>1-1</td><td>0-0</td><td>0-0</td><td>0-0</td><td>1-1</td><td>0-0</td><td>0-0</td><td>+ 4.50</td></tr>
<tr><td>Ayr</td><td>1-7</td><td>1-3</td><td>0-1</td><td>0-0</td><td>0-2</td><td>0-0</td><td>0-1</td><td>+ 6.00</td></tr>
</table>

<table>
<tr><td>Carlisle</td><td>0-4</td><td>Perth</td><td>0-3</td><td>Kelso</td><td>0-1</td></tr>
<tr><td>Catterick</td><td>0-4</td><td>Wetherby</td><td>0-2</td><td>Sandown</td><td>0-1</td></tr>
<tr><td>Sedgefield</td><td>0-4</td><td>Aintree</td><td>0-1</td><td>Uttoxeter</td><td>0-1</td></tr>
<tr><td>Southwell</td><td>0-4</td><td>Cartmel</td><td>0-1</td><td>Worcester</td><td>0-1</td></tr>
<tr><td>Market Rasen</td><td>0-3</td><td>Doncaster</td><td>0-1</td><td></td><td></td></tr>
</table>

WINNING HORSES

<table>
<tr><th></th><th>Races Run</th><th>1st</th><th>2nd</th><th>3rd</th><th>Unpl</th><th>Win £</th></tr>
<tr><td>Five To Seven</td><td>8</td><td>3</td><td>2</td><td>0</td><td>3</td><td>10,614</td></tr>
<tr><td>Cittadino</td><td>6</td><td>1</td><td>1</td><td>1</td><td>3</td><td>3,591</td></tr>
<tr><td>Chantry Beath</td><td>7</td><td>1</td><td>1</td><td>1</td><td>4</td><td>2,211</td></tr>
<tr><td>Sioux To Speak</td><td>2</td><td>1</td><td>0</td><td>0</td><td>1</td><td>1,439</td></tr>
<tr><td>War Whoop</td><td>4</td><td>1</td><td>0</td><td>1</td><td>2</td><td>1,312</td></tr>
</table>

WINNING OWNERS

<table>
<tr><th></th><th>Races Won</th><th>Value £</th><th></th><th>Races Won</th><th>Value £</th></tr>
<tr><td>The Five To Seven P'ship</td><td>3</td><td>10,614</td><td>Racegoers Club Spigot</td><td></td><td></td></tr>
<tr><td>D B Dennison</td><td>1</td><td>3,591</td><td>Lodge Owners Group</td><td>1</td><td>2,211</td></tr>
<tr><td>Guy Reed</td><td>2</td><td>2,751</td><td></td><td></td><td></td></tr>
</table>

Thornton C W

No of horses racing for the stable	15	Total winning prize-money	£19,167

Favourites	0-6		Average SP of winner	5.7/1
Longest win seq	2	Longest losing seq 18	Return on stakes invested	-3.0%

1994/95 Form	7-42	16.7%	+ 22.50	1992/93 Form	11-38	28.9%	+ 17.47
1993/94 Form	6-49	12.2%	- 28.45	1991/92 Form	10-47	21.3%	+ 4.55

N TINKLER (Langton, North Yorks)

	Races Run	1st	2nd	3rd	Unpl	Per cent	£1 Level Stake
Hurdles	61	6	5	5	45	9.8	- 27.87
Chases	38	8	9	5	16	21.1	- 13.74
Totals	99	14	14	10	61	14.1	- 41.61

BY MONTH

	W-R	Per cent	£1 Level Stake		W-R	Per cent	£1 Level Stake
June	1-3	33.3	+ 1.50	December	2-14	14.3	- 3.37
July	0-2	-	- 2.00	January	1-12	8.3	- 8.50
August	0-3	-	- 3.00	February	1-12	8.3	- 9.00
September	1-5	20.0	- 0.50	March	1-8	12.5	- 0.50
October	2-10	20.0	- 3.87	April	0-6	-	- 6.00
November	4-18	22.2	- 3.62	May	1-6	16.7	- 2.75

DISTANCE

	W-R	Per cent	£1 Level Stake		W-R	Per cent	£1 Level Stake
Hurdles				Chases			
2m-2m 3f	5-46	10.9	- 19.87	2m-2m 3f	6-25	24.0	- 6.87
2m 4f-2m 7f	0-11	-	- 11.00	2m 4f-2m 7f	2-8	25.0	- 1.87
3m +	1-4	25.0	+ 3.00	3m +	0-5	-	- 5.00

TYPE OF RACE

	W-R	Per cent	£1 Level Stake		W-R	Per cent	£1 Level Stake
Novice hurdles	0-17	-	- 17.00	Selling	3-16	18.8	+ 1.38
H'cap hurdles	3-28	10.7	- 12.25	Amateur	0-2	-	- 2.00
Novice chases	1-1	100.0	+ 3.50	Hunter chases	0-0	-	0.00
H'cap chases	7-35	20.0	- 15.24	N H Flat	0-0	-	0.00

COURSE GRADE

	W-R	Per cent	£1 Level Stake
Group 1	2-26	7.7	- 19.25
Group 2	0-6	-	- 6.00
Group 3	8-33	24.2	- 0.61
Group 4	4-34	11.8	- 15.75

FIRST TIME OUT

	W-R	Per cent	£1 Level Stake
Hurdles	0-15	-	- 15.00
Chases	1-5	20.0	- 0.50
Totals	1-20	5.0	- 15.50

JOCKEYS RIDING

	W-R	Per cent	£1 Level Stake		W-R	Per cent	£1 Level Stake
Miss P Jones	3-6	50.0	+ 7.50	Mrs A Perratt	1-1	100.0	+ 2.25
G McCourt	3-7	42.9	+ 0.38	N Williamson	1-2	50.0	+ 0.88
A S Smith	2-12	16.7	+ 0.50	R Dunwoody	1-5	20.0	- 1.75
M Dwyer	2-15	13.3	- 7.87	G Bradley	1-6	16.7	+ 1.50

E Husband	0-25	A Thornton	0-1	J Titley	0-1
J Railton	0-4	C Llewellyn	0-1	L Wyer	0-1
B Storey	0-3	D Gallagher	0-1	P Niven	0-1
P Carberry	0-2	J Callaghan	0-1	R Garrity	0-1
W Marston	0-2	J Osborne	0-1		

COURSE RECORD

	Total W-R	Nov Hdles	H'cap Hdles	Nov Chses	H'cap Chses	Hunter Chses	N H Flat	£1 Level Stake
Nottingham	3-7	0-1	1-4	0-0	2-2	0-0	0-0	+ 4.63
Market Rasen	3-15	1-5	1-6	1-1	0-3	0-0	0-0	- 0.12
Hereford	1-1	0-0	0-0	0-0	1-1	0-0	0-0	+ 2.25
Perth	1-2	0-0	1-2	0-0	0-0	0-0	0-0	+ 2.50
Stratford	1-2	0-0	1-2	0-0	0-0	0-0	0-0	+ 1.25
Catterick	1-2	0-0	0-1	0-0	1-1	0-0	0-0	+ 0.63
Sedgefield	1-6	0-0	1-4	0-0	0-2	0-0	0-0	+ 1.00
Newcastle	1-7	0-3	0-3	0-0	1-1	0-0	0-0	- 3.25
Doncaster	1-7	0-2	0-1	0-0	1-4	0-0	0-0	- 4.00
Musselburgh	1-9	0-1	0-2	0-0	1-6	0-0	0-0	- 5.50

Wetherby	0-6	Southwell	0-3	Hexham	0-1
Carlisle	0-5	Cartmel	0-2	Kempton	0-1
Ayr	0-4	Cheltenham	0-2	Leicester	0-1
Uttoxeter	0-4	Huntingdon	0-2	Ludlow	0-1
Haydock	0-3	Aintree	0-1	Sandown	0-1
Kelso	0-3	Bangor	0-1		

WINNING HORSES

	Races Run	1st	2nd	3rd	Unpl	Win £
Rodeo Star	11	2	2	0	7	10,480
Judicial Field	12	3	5	2	2	8,342
Puritan	7	2	2	0	3	6,696
Pleasure Trick	5	2	1	2	0	4,481
Rawaan	1	1	0	0	0	4,276
Vain Prince	6	1	2	1	2	3,404
Fox Sparrow	3	1	0	0	2	2,832
Elite Justice	7	1	0	0	6	1,977
Balzino	12	1	2	2	7	1,814

WINNING OWNERS

	Races Won	Value £		Races Won	Value £
J C Bradbury	2	10,480	A C Findlay	1	3,404
Mrs E E Newbould	3	8,342	B Todd	1	2,832
J Parks	2	6,696	Elite Racing Club	1	1,977
J D Gordon	2	4,481	G N Jackson	1	1,814
The Full Circle Racing Club	1	4,276			

No of horses racing for the stable	21	Total winning prize-money	£44,302

Favourites	7-12	58.3%	+ 9.14	Average SP of winner		3.1/1
Longest win seq	2	Longest losing seq	13	Return on stakes invested		-41.5%

1994/95 Form	16-155	10.3%	- 78.98	1992/93 Form	25-139	18.0%	- 64.33
1993/94 Form	23-152	15.1%	- 83.66	1991/92 Form	38-163	23.3%	- 12.15

W H TINNING (Kirkby Overblow, North Yorks)

	Races Run	1st	2nd	3rd	Unpl	Per cent	£1 Level Stake
Hurdles	10	1	3	3	3	10.0	- 5.00
Chases	5	0	2	1	2	-	- 5.00
Totals	15	1	5	4	5	6.7	- 10.00

D Parker	1-13	- 8.00	Carlisle	1-1	+ 4.00

No of horses racing for the stable	2	Total winning prize-money	£2,178

C TIZZARD (Sherborne, Dorset)

	Races Run	1st	2nd	3rd	Unpl	Per cent	£1 Level Stake
Hurdles	0	0	0	0	0	-	0.00
Chases	2	2	0	0	0	100.0	+ 4.63
Totals	2	2	0	0	0	100.0	+ 4.63

Mr J Tizzard	2-2	+ 4.63

Wincanton	1-1	+ 3.00	Chepstow	1-1	+ 1.63

No of horses racing for the stable	1	Total winning prize-money	£3,280

D M TODHUNTER (Ulverston, Cumbria)

	Races Run	1st	2nd	3rd	Unpl	Per cent	£1 Level Stake
Hurdles	29	3	4	5	17	10.3	- 19.09
Chases	5	0	0	0	5	-	- 5.00
Totals	34	3	4	5	22	8.8	- 24.09

M Dwyer	2-5	-	0.09	R Garrity	1-14	- 9.00
Hexham	1-2	-	0.09	Kelso	1-6	- 1.00
Carlisle	1-5	-	2.00			

No of horses racing for the stable	8	Total winning prize-money	£8,393

M H TOMPKINS (Newmarket, Suffolk)

	Races Run	1st	2nd	3rd	Unpl	Per cent	£1 Level Stake
Hurdles	49	5	1	6	37	10.2	- 26.45
Chases	0	0	0	0	0	-	0.00
Totals	49	5	1	6	37	10.2	- 26.45

D Gallagher	3-17	-	2.75	D Bridgwater	1-3	- 1.20
K P Gaule	1-2	+	4.50			
Fakenham	2-6	+	4.50	Fontwell	1-2	+ 1.75
Uttoxeter	2-8	+	0.30			

No of horses racing for the stable	16	Total winning prize-money	£12,809

M J TRICKEY (South Molton, Devon)

	Races Run	1st	2nd	3rd	Unpl	Per cent	£1 Level Stake
Hurdles	0	0	0	0	0	-	0.00
Chases	2	1	0	0	1	50.0	+ 6.00
Totals	2	1	0	0	1	50.0	+ 6.00

Mr Richard White	1-2	+	6.00	Cheltenham	1-1	+ 7.00

No of horses racing for the stable	1	Total winning prize-money	£4,280

J C TUCK (Oldbury-on-the-Hill, Glos)

	Races Run	1st	2nd	3rd	Unpl	Per cent	£1 Level Stake
Hurdles	43	1	1	3	38	2.3	- 35.00
Chases	7	0	1	0	6	-	- 7.00
Totals	50	1	2	3	44	2.0	- 42.00

S McNeill	1-31	- 23.00		Ludlow	1-6	+ 2.00

No of horses racing for the stable   10   Total winning prize-money   £2,360

ANDREW TURNELL (East Hendred, Oxon)

	Races Run	1st	2nd	3rd	Unpl	Per cent	£1 Level Stake
Hurdles	73	9	3	8	53	12.3	- 26.25
Chases	55	6	6	7	36	10.9	- 15.00
Totals	128	15	9	15	89	11.7	- 41.25

BY MONTH

	W-R	Per cent	£1 Level Stake		W-R	Per cent	£1 Level Stake
June	0-0	-	0.00	December	1-12	8.3	- 4.00
July	0-0	-	0.00	January	1-27	3.7	- 25.00
August	0-0	-	0.00	February	4-21	19.0	+ 6.00
September	0-0	-	0.00	March	3-28	10.7	- 1.50
October	2-8	25.0	+ 2.00	April	1-11	9.1	- 7.75
November	3-20	15.0	- 10.00	May	0-1	-	- 1.00

DISTANCE

Hurdles	W-R	Per cent	£1 Level Stake	Chases	W-R	Per cent	£1 Level Stake
2m-2m 3f	9-60	15.0	- 13.25	2m-2m 3f	0-18	-	- 18.00
2m 4f-2m 7f	0-13	-	- 13.00	2m 4f-2m 7f	3-21	14.3	+ 3.50
3m	0-0	-	0.00	3m +	3-16	18.8	- 0.50

TYPE OF RACE

	W-R	Per cent	£1 Level Stake		W-R	Per cent	£1 Level Stake
Novice hurdles	5-51	9.8	- 30.00	Selling	0-0	-	0.00
H'cap hurdles	2-20	10.0	- 6.00	Amateur	2-3	66.7	+ 8.75
Novice chases	3-22	13.6	- 6.50	Hunter chases	0-0	-	0.00
H'cap chases	3-32	9.4	- 7.50	N H Flat	0-0	-	0.00

COURSE GRADE

	W-R	Per cent	£1 Level Stake
Group 1	7-46	15.2	+ 7.50
Group 2	2-28	7.1	- 23.00
Group 3	5-36	13.9	- 11.25
Group 4	1-18	5.6	- 14.50

FIRST TIME OUT

	W-R	Per cent	£1 Level Stake
Hurdles	3-24	12.5	- 5.50
Chases	1-9	11.1	- 5.50
Totals	4-33	12.1	- 11.00

JOCKEYS RIDING

	W-R	Per cent	£1 Level Stake		W-R	Per cent	£1 Level Stake
P Carberry	5-29	17.2	- 5.00	Mr J Rees	1-2	50.0	+ 1.25
L Harvey	4-33	12.1	- 15.00	J Titley	1-2	50.0	+ 6.00
G Crone	2-18	11.1	+ 3.00	S McNeill	1-28	3.6	- 24.00
Capt A Ogden	1-1	100.0	+ 7.50				

C Rae	0-7	J Leech	0-1	W McFarland	0-1
N Wilmington	0-3	R Dunwoody	0-1		
B M Clifford	0-1	S Fox	0-1		

COURSE RECORD

	Total W-R	Nov Hdles	H'cap Hdles	Nov Chses	H'cap Chses	Hunter Chses	N H Flat	£1 Level Stake
Newbury	3-15	0-6	2-4	1-2	0-3	0-0	0-0	+ 2.50
Windsor	2-7	2-4	0-0	0-1	0-2	0-0	0-0	- 0.50
Lingfield	2-11	1-3	0-1	1-6	0-1	0-0	0-0	- 6.00
Ascot	1-1	1-1	0-0	0-0	0-0	0-0	0-0	+ 3.50
Bangor	1-2	0-0	0-0	0-1	1-1	0-0	0-0	+ 1.50
Haydock	1-2	1-2	0-0	0-0	0-0	0-0	0-0	+ 6.00
Worcester	1-4	0-2	1-2	0-0	0-0	0-0	0-0	- 0.75
Warwick	1-4	0-1	0-1	0-1	1-1	0-0	0-0	+ 2.00
Nottingham	1-4	0-1	0-1	1-1	0-1	0-0	0-0	+ 5.00
Cheltenham	1-5	0-3	0-0	0-0	1-2	0-0	0-0	+ 10.00
Sandown	1-7	0-3	1-2	0-1	0-1	0-0	0-0	+ 1.50

Kempton	0-10	Newton Abbot	0-4	Ayr	0-1
Leicester	0-8	Wincanton	0-4	Exeter	0-1
Towcester	0-8	Hereford	0-3	Fakenham	0-1
Fontwell	0-7	Stratford	0-2	Ludlow	0-1
Chepstow	0-6	Taunton	0-2	Market Rasen	0-1
Aintree	0-5	Uttoxeter	0-2		

WINNING HORSES

	Races Run	1st	2nd	3rd	Unpl	Win £
Squire Silk	6	2	0	0	4	60,764
Old Bridge	6	2	1	1	2	36,488
Society Guest	6	2	1	2	1	7,142
Kingdom of Shades	4	2	1	1	0	6,695
Giventime	6	2	0	0	4	6,226

Act The Wag	6	1	1	2	2	4,533
Too Plush	6	1	0	0	5	4,260
Crown Equerry	5	1	1	1	2	2,808
Hawaiian Sam	9	1	2	1	5	2,320
Relkowen	5	1	0	0	4	2,320

WINNING OWNERS

	Races Won	Value £		Races Won	Value £
R Ogden	6	74,800	Mrs C C Williams	1	4,260
K C B Mackenzie	2	36,488	Mrs M I Barton	1	2,320
Robinson Webster (Holdings) Ltd	2	7,142	Robert K Russell	1	2,320
L G Kimber	2	6,226			

No of horses racing for the stable		33	Total winning prize-money	£133,556
Favourites	5-17	29.4% − 1.75	Average SP of winner	4.8/1
Longest win seq	2	Longest losing seq 25	Return on stakes invested	−32.2%
1994/95 Form	20-118	16.9% − 22.01	1992/93 Form 37-157 23.6%	+ 13.99
1993/94 Form	21-123	17.1% − 13.11	1991/92 Form 18-113 15.9%	+ 10.82

J M TURNER (Bury St Edmunds, Suffolk)

	Races Run	1st	2nd	3rd	Unpl	Per cent	£1 Level Stake
Hurdles	0	0	0	0	0	-	0.00
Chases	10	1	0	1	8	10.0	− 6.00
Totals	10	1	0	1	8	10.0	− 6.00

Miss L Hollis	1-4	0.00	Folkestone	1-3	+ 1.00
No of horses racing for the stable		6	Total winning prize-money		£2,180

J R TURNER (Norton-le-Clay, North Yorks)

	Races Run	1st	2nd	3rd	Unpl	Per cent	£1 Level Stake
Hurdles	25	0	1	1	23	-	− 25.00
Chases	10	1	0	2	7	10.0	− 3.50
Totals	35	1	1	3	30	2.9	− 28.50

M Dwyer	1-2	+ 4.50	Catterick	1-5	+ 1.50
No of horses racing for the stable		7	Total winning prize-money		£2,898

W G M TURNER (Corton Denham, Somerset)

	Races Run	1st	2nd	3rd	Unpl	Per cent	£1 Level Stake
Hurdles	74	7	12	9	46	9.5	- 41.75
Chases	6	4	0	0	2	66.7	+ 23.63
Totals	80	11	12	9	48	13.8	- 18.12

BY MONTH

	W-R	Per cent	£1 Level Stake		W-R	Per cent	£1 Level Stake
June	1-2	50.0	+ 1.50	December	2-10	20.0	+ 1.50
July	0-2	-	- 2.00	January	2-12	16.7	+ 0.25
August	2-3	66.7	+ 2.75	February	1-8	12.5	- 5.62
September	0-5	-	- 5.00	March	2-11	18.2	- 1.50
October	0-8	-	- 8.00	April	0-4	-	- 4.00
November	1-10	10.0	+ 7.00	May	0-5	-	- 5.00

DISTANCE

Hurdles	W-R	Per cent	£1 Level Stake	Chases	W-R	Per cent	£1 Level Stake
2m-2m 3f	5-45	11.1	- 23.25	2m-2m 3f	0-0	-	0.00
2m 4f-2m 7f	2-18	11.1	- 7.50	2m 4f-2m 7f	0-0	-	0.00
3m +	0-11	-	- 11.00	3m +	4-6	66.7	+ 23.63

TYPE OF RACE

	W-R	Per cent	£1 Level Stake		W-R	Per cent	£1 Level Stake
Novice hurdles	1-38	2.6	- 33.50	Selling	2-10	20.0	- 4.25
H'cap hurdles	4-21	19.0	+ 1.00	Amateur	0-2	-	- 2.00
Novice chases	0-0	-	0.00	Hunter chases	0-0	-	0.00
H'cap chases	4-5	80.0	+ 24.63	N H Flat	0-4	-	- 4.00

COURSE GRADE

	W-R	Per cent	£1 Level Stake
Group 1	0-1	-	- 1.00
Group 2	5-20	25.0	+ 8.38
Group 3	2-24	8.3	- 8.00
Group 4	4-35	11.4	- 17.50

FIRST TIME OUT

	W-R	Per cent	£1 Level Stake
Hurdles	1-23	4.3	- 19.50
Chases	1-1	100.0	+ 16.00
Totals	2-24	8.3	- 3.50

JOCKEYS RIDING

	W-R	Per cent	£1 Level Stake		W-R	Per cent	£1 Level Stake
R Dunwoody	3-7	42.9	+ 15.63	T Murphy	1-5	20.0	- 2.25
T C Murphy	2-13	15.4	- 6.00	A Thornton	1-10	10.0	- 3.00
J Power	2-14	14.3	+ 2.00	M Griffiths	1-15	6.7	- 11.50
Mr E James	1-1	100.0	+ 2.00				

P Holley	0-3	C Maude	0-1	Mr M Rimell	0-1
A P McCoy	0-2	G E Tormey	0-1	P McLoughlin	0-1
R Greene	0-2	G Upton	0-1	S Burrough	0-1
B Powell	0-1	Mr M Daly	0-1		

COURSE RECORD

	Total W-R	Nov Hdles	H'cap Hdles	Nov Chses	H'cap Chses	Hunter Chses	N H Flat	£1 Level Stake
Fontwell	3-6	1-3	0-1	0-0	2-2	0-0	0-0	+ 2.38
Newton Abbot	2-8	0-2	1-5	0-0	1-1	0-0	0-0	+ 12.00
Hereford	1-2	0-1	1-1	0-0	0-0	0-0	0-0	+ 0.50
Southwell	1-2	0-1	1-1	0-0	0-0	0-0	0-0	+ 1.50
Bangor	1-3	0-2	0-0	0-0	1-1	0-0	0-0	+ 4.00
Warwick	1-3	0-0	1-2	0-0	0-1	0-0	0-0	+ 4.00
Exeter	1-5	1-4	0-0	0-0	0-0	0-0	0-1	- 0.50
Wincanton	1-6	0-5	1-1	0-0	0-0	0-0	0-0	+ 3.00

Taunton	0-13	Uttoxeter		0-3	Worcester	0-2
Ludlow	0-6	Folkestone		0-2	Doncaster	0-1
Plumpton	0-5	Huntingdon		0-2	Leicester	0-1
Chepstow	0-3	Musselburgh		0-2		
Lingfield	0-3	Towcester		0-2		

WINNING HORSES

	Races Run	1st	2nd	3rd	Unpl	Win £
Nazzaro	6	4	0	0	2	17,691
Lying Eyes	9	3	1	1	4	11,053
Reach For Glory	6	3	1	0	2	5,589
Fleur De Tal	8	1	0	1	6	2,246

WINNING OWNERS

	Races Won	Value £		Races Won	Value £
A Morrish	4	17,691	O J Stokes	3	5,589
A K Holbrook	3	11,053	John Woods	1	2,246

No of horses racing for the stable			24	Total winning prize-money		£36,579

Favourites	5-9	55.6%	+ 5.38	Average SP of winner			4.6/1
Longest win seq	2	Longest losing seq	16	Return on stakes invested			-22.7%

1994/95 Form	15-131	11.5%	- 3.62	1992/93 Form	5-104	4.8%	- 66.84
1993/94 Form	10-112	8.9%	- 59.38	1991/92 Form	8-110	7.3%	+ 1.50

313

N A TWISTON-DAVIES (Naunton, Glos)

	Races Run	1st	2nd	3rd	Unpl	Per cent	£1 Level Stake
Hurdles	318	51	39	33	195	16.0	- 43.45
Chases	176	23	20	23	110	13.1	- 60.86
Totals	494	74	59	56	305	15.0	-104.31

BY MONTH

	W-R	Per cent	£1 Level Stake		W-R	Per cent	£1 Level Stake
June	2-11	18.2	- 2.50	December	4-36	11.1	- 11.50
July	2-7	28.6	+ 6.50	January	8-65	12.3	- 13.32
August	2-9	22.2	- 4.88	February	4-63	6.3	- 41.65
September	5-27	18.5	- 7.10	March	7-73	9.6	- 42.57
October	8-36	22.2	+ 20.33	April	4-40	10.0	- 1.00
November	17-83	20.5	- 22.04	May	11-44	25.0	+ 15.42

DISTANCE

	W-R	Per cent	£1 Level Stake	Chases	W-R	Per cent	£1 Level Stake
Hurdles							
2m-2m 3f	23-185	12.4	- 56.07	2m-2m 3f	8-35	22.9	+ 0.13
2m 4f-2m 7f	17-81	21.0	+ 10.34	2m 4f-2m 7f	7-47	14.9	- 15.37
3m +	11-52	21.2	+ 2.28	3m +	8-94	8.5	- 45.62

TYPE OF RACE

	W-R	Per cent	£1 Level Stake		W-R	Per cent	£1 Level Stake
Novice hurdles	22-111	19.8	- 3.88	Selling	5-23	21.7	- 2.50
H'cap hurdles	17-107	15.9	+ 0.93	Amateur	3-19	15.8	- 7.50
Novice chases	9-65	13.8	- 31.12	Hunter chases	3-16	18.8	- 3.62
H'cap chases	9-87	10.3	- 25.62	N H Flat	6-66	9.1	- 31.00

COURSE GRADE / FIRST TIME OUT

	W-R	Per cent	£1 Level Stake		W-R	Per cent	£1 Level Stake
Group 1	21-159	13.2	- 56.33	Hurdles	15-79	19.0	- 1.77
Group 2	5-63	7.9	- 22.50	Chases	7-32	21.9	- 8.72
Group 3	28-141	19.9	+ 3.87				
Group 4	20-131	15.3	- 29.35	Totals	22-111	19.8	- 10.49

JOCKEYS RIDING

	W-R	Per cent	£1 Level Stake		W-R	Per cent	£1 Level Stake
C Llewellyn	37-208	17.8	- 23.14	G E Tormey	1-1	100.0	+ 10.00
C Maude	11-54	20.4	+ 2.20	A Shakespeare	1-4	25.0	+ 13.00
T Jenks	8-72	11.1	- 32.75	Mr D Drinkwater	1-4	25.0	- 1.00
Mr M Rimell	6-41	14.6	- 15.12	Miss A Plunkett	1-5	20.0	- 2.50
D Walsh	5-40	12.5	- 3.00	M Keighley	1-14	7.1	- 10.50
G Bradley	1-1	100.0	+ 2.00	S Joynes	1-25	4.0	- 18.50

Twiston-Davies N A

Mr A Balding	0-4	W Marston	0-2	M Richards	0-1
D Bridgwater	0-3	A Maguire	0-1	Mr G Elliott	0-1
L Harvey	0-3	D Leahy	0-1	P Hide	0-1
Mr C Bonner	0-2	J Frost	0-1	P Scudamore	0-1
Mr J Goldstein	0-2	M Moloney	0-1	R Johnson	0-1

COURSE RECORD

	Total W-R	Nov Hdles	H'cap Hdles	Nov Chses	H'cap Chses	Hunter Chses	N H Flat	£1 Level Stake
Uttoxeter	8-31	2-9	2-5	1-6	1-6	0-0	2-5	+ 8.29
Hereford	7-28	2-7	4-9	0-2	1-7	0-0	0-3	- 0.45
Cheltenham	5-42	2-12	2-10	1-8	0-10	0-2	0-0	- 23.20
Wincanton	4-9	2-2	1-2	1-1	0-3	0-0	0-1	+ 9.92
Aintree	4-14	1-5	0-1	0-1	2-4	0-1	1-2	+ 3.00
Chepstow	4-25	0-7	1-7	0-5	2-4	0-1	1-1	+ 10.50
Ascot	4-27	3-8	0-4	0-6	1-6	0-1	0-2	+ 11.50
Worcester	4-28	3-7	0-8	0-2	1-4	0-0	0-7	- 12.20
Leicester	3-8	1-3	0-0	2-3	0-2	0-0	0-0	+ 7.38
Stratford	3-11	2-3	0-5	1-1	0-1	0-1	0-0	+ 11.50
Haydock	3-16	0-2	0-1	1-3	1-5	1-1	0-4	- 8.96
Warwick	3-18	1-4	1-4	1-3	0-4	0-0	0-3	+ 0.60
Bangor	3-19	0-4	2-6	0-2	0-2	0-0	1-5	+ 0.50
Towcester	3-23	2-5	1-6	0-5	0-3	0-1	0-3	- 0.50
Market Rasen	2-8	0-1	0-4	1-1	0-0	1-1	0-1	- 2.62
Perth	2-10	1-3	1-3	0-2	0-1	0-0	0-1	- 2.90
Kempton	2-14	2-6	0-3	0-1	0-1	0-0	0-3	- 8.50
Exeter	2-15	0-4	1-4	1-1	0-2	0-1	0-3	- 6.50
Newbury	2-23	0-8	1-8	0-1	1-3	0-0	0-3	- 14.17
Doncaster	1-3	0-0	0-0	0-0	0-1	1-1	0-1	+ 4.00
Carlisle	1-4	0-2	1-2	0-0	0-0	0-0	0-0	+ 2.00
Lingfield	1-7	0-1	0-0	0-1	0-0	0-2	1-3	- 2.00
Taunton	1-12	0-3	1-6	0-0	0-3	0-0	0-0	- 4.00
Nottingham	1-12	0-4	1-4	0-0	0-0	0-1	0-3	- 3.00
Ludlow	1-18	1-3	0-5	0-2	0-5	0-1	0-2	- 15.50

Newton Abbot	0-22	Wetherby	0-5	Southwell	0-2
Sandown	0-17	Fontwell	0-4	Ayr	0-1
Huntingdon	0-7	Catterick	0-3		
Windsor	0-6	Newcastle	0-2		

WINNING HORSES

	Races Run	1st	2nd	3rd	Unpl	Win £
Arctic Kinsman	6	3	1	1	1	42,895
Young Hustler	9	1	1	1	6	24,508
Grange Brake	12	1	1	2	8	19,678
Wisley Wonder	7	4	0	0	3	18,222
Easy Buck	4	2	1	0	1	17,498
Haile Derring	6	4	0	0	2	10,870
Buckhouse Boy	8	3	1	1	3	9,706
Flapjack Lad	11	2	0	3	6	7,056
Romancer	6	1	2	1	2	6,908
San Giorgio	7	2	1	0	4	6,852
Percy Thrower	8	3	0	0	5	6,809
Speedwell Prince	9	2	2	0	5	6,404
Star Market	8	2	0	0	6	6,096
Guinda	5	2	1	0	2	6,033
Ocean Hawk	11	2	3	2	4	6,008
Exterior Profiles	8	2	1	1	4	5,651
Chief Rager	5	1	0	2	2	5,634
Gala's Pride	6	2	2	1	1	5,430
Ramsdens	6	1	1	2	2	5,199
Pimberley Place	7	1	2	0	4	5,132
Great Marquess	3	1	1	1	0	4,958
Freddie Muck	6	2	2	1	1	4,734
Blustery Fellow	7	1	0	0	6	4,707
Country Picture	3	1	1	0	1	4,624
Mistinguett	5	1	2	0	2	4,572
Beatson	5	1	2	1	1	4,182
Holy Sting	8	1	1	1	5	4,145
Mister Morose	5	2	1	1	1	4,129
Tothewoods	7	1	1	1	4	3,650
Paris Fashion	3	1	0	0	2	3,626
Gospel	2	1	0	1	0	3,496
Chief Joseph	2	1	0	1	0	3,266
French Buck	7	1	0	2	4	3,074
Just One Canaletto	9	1	1	0	7	3,032
Huge Mistake	1	1	0	0	0	2,814
Rocktor	5	1	0	0	4	2,618
Swing Quartet	7	1	2	0	4	2,507
Dajraan	6	1	1	0	4	2,348
Hot Breeze	5	1	1	0	3	2,346
Much Sought After	3	1	0	1	1	2,163
Better Bythe Glass	7	1	0	0	6	2,150
Poetic Fancy	10	1	1	1	7	2,094
Blessed Oliver	8	1	0	2	5	2,094
Dictum	3	1	0	0	2	1,996
La Bella Villa	4	1	0	0	3	1,882
Zamirah	11	1	4	1	5	1,877
Spring Double	4	1	0	1	2	1,763
Queen of Spades	2	1	1	0	0	1,669
Clare Man	6	1	0	1	4	1,495
Ganpati	3	1	1	0	1	1,494
Tipping Tim	5	1	0	1	3	1,152

WINNING OWNERS

	Races Won	Value £		Races Won	Value £
Mrs R E Hambro	3	42,895	Mrs C Twiston-Davies	2	4,734
Gavin Macechern	2	28,653	R D Russell	1	4,624
Mrs J Mould	4	24,959	Mrs E B Gardiner	1	4,182
The Wisley Golf Partnership	4	18,222	N A Twiston-Davies	2	4,027
J P M & J W Cook	2	17,498	Mrs M Scott & R Cooper	1	3,650
Mrs V Stockdale	4	10,870	J O'Gorman	1	3,266
Peter Kelsall	3	10,478	Mrs C M Scott	1	3,074
John Duggan	2	9,771	Farmers Racing P'ship	1	3,032
The Bawtry Boys	3	9,706	Windrush Racing	1	2,814
Mrs J K Powell	3	9,529	Mrs L J Griffiths	1	2,618
H B Shouler	2	7,056	A M Armitage	1	2,507
Matt Archer	1	6,908	The Great Marquess P'ship	1	2,348
The Double Octagon P'ship	3	6,809	The Wrinkly Tin P'ship	1	2,346
Mrs R A Humphries	2	6,703	The MSA Partnership	1	2,163
The Bar Fixtures Partnership	2	6,404	Mrs David Plunkett	1	2,094
Mrs P Joynes	2	6,096	Oxbridge Fanciers	1	2,094
Miss Jean Broadhurst	2	6,008	P C J F Bloodstock	1	1,882
Exterior Profiles Ltd	2	5,651	Mrs Lorna Berryman	1	1,763
James Cheetham	1	5,634	Mrs R Vaughan	1	1,669
Audley Twiston-Davies	2	5,430	M P Wareing	1	1,495
A J Cresser	1	5,132	The Oriental Partnership	1	1,494
The Great Marquess Partnership	1	4,958			

No of horses racing for the stable		112	Total winning prize-money		£313,246
Favourites	29-77	37.7% + 4.61	Average SP of winner		4.3/1
Longest win seq 4	Longest losing seq	59	Return on stakes invested		-21.1%
1994/95 Form	81-509	15.9% - 80.26	1992/93 Form 76-317	24.0%	+ 81.67
1993/94 Form	72-447	16.1% - 63.82	1991/92 Form 31-224	13.8%	- 31.90

J R UPSON (Adstone, Northants)

	Races Run	1st	2nd	3rd	Unpl	Per cent	£1 Level Stake
Hurdles	70	6	5	8	51	8.6	- 30.42
Chases	14	1	4	3	6	7.1	- 8.00
Totals	84	7	9	11	57	8.3	- 38.42

BY MONTH

	W-R	Per cent	£1 Level Stake		W-R	Per cent	£1 Level Stake
June	0-2	-	- 2.00	December	0-6	-	- 6.00
July	2-6	33.3	+ 5.50	January	0-13	-	- 13.00
August	1-7	14.3	- 2.67	February	0-9	-	- 9.00
September	0-1	-	- 1.00	March	2-14	14.3	+ 7.00
October	0-6	-	- 6.00	April	0-7	-	- 7.00
November	0-2	-	- 2.00	May	2-11	18.2	- 2.25

DISTANCE

Hurdles	W-R	Per cent	£1 Level Stake	Chases	W-R	Per cent	£1 Level Stake
2m-2m 3f	2-30	6.7	- 21.50	2m-2m 3f	0-8	-	- 8.00
2m 4f-2m 7f	1-26	3.8	- 23.25	2m 4f-2m 7f	1-5	20.0	+ 1.00
3m +	3-14	21.4	+ 14.33	3m +	0-1	-	- 1.00

TYPE OF RACE

	W-R	Per cent	£1 Level Stake		W-R	Per cent	£1 Level Stake
Novice hurdles	0-37	-	- 37.00	Selling	2-8	25.0	+ 0.50
H'cap hurdles	4-23	17.4	+ 8.08	Amateur	0-0	-	0.00
Novice chases	0-4	-	- 4.00	Hunter chases	0-0	-	0.00
H'cap chases	1-10	10.0	- 4.00	N H Flat	0-2	-	- 2.00

COURSE GRADE

	W-R	Per cent	£1 Level Stake
Group 1	0-9	-	- 9.00
Group 2	0-9	-	- 9.00
Group 3	3-29	10.3	- 2.50
Group 4	4-37	10.8	- 17.92

FIRST TIME OUT

	W-R	Per cent	£1 Level Stake
Hurdles	0-17	-	- 17.00
Chases	0-4	-	- 4.00
Totals	0-21	-	- 21.00

JOCKEYS RIDING

	W-R	Per cent	£1 Level Stake		W-R	Per cent	£1 Level Stake
R Supple	3-25	12.0	+ 5.00	J Ryan	1-2	50.0	+ 0.75
J Supple	2-26	7.7	- 19.17	C Maude	1-6	16.7	0.00

Mr T Byrne	0-10	C Llewellyn	0-1	L Harvey	0-1
C Davies	0-3	D Finnegan	0-1	M A Fitzgerald	0-1
A Dobbin	0-2	G Supple	0-1	Mr P Scott	0-1
S Curran	0-2	J Osborne	0-1	R Johnson	0-1

COURSE RECORD

	Total W-R	Nov Hdles	H'cap Hdles	Nov Chses	H'cap Chses	Hunter Chses	N H Flat	£1 Level Stake
Stratford	2-5	1-3	1-1	0-0	0-1	0-0	0-0	+ 6.50
Towcester	2-21	0-10	1-4	0-2	1-3	0-0	0-2	- 12.25
Fakenham	1-3	0-1	1-1	0-1	0-0	0-0	0-0	+ 3.00
Hereford	1-4	0-0	1-3	0-0	0-1	0-0	0-0	+ 0.33
Huntingdon	1-6	0-4	1-1	0-0	0-1	0-0	0-0	+ 9.00

Worcester	0-6	Newton Abbot	0-2	Folkestone	0-1
Sedgefield	0-4	Nottingham	0-2	Fontwell	0-1
Kempton	0-3	Sandown	0-2	Haydock	0-1
Uttoxeter	0-3	Warwick	0-2	Leicester	0-1
Wetherby	0-3	Aintree	0-1	Lingfield	0-1
Chepstow	0-2	Ayr	0-1	Southwell	0-1
Ludlow	0-2	Carlisle	0-1	Taunton	0-1
Market Rasen	0-2	Doncaster	0-1	Windsor	0-1

WINNING HORSES

	Races Run	1st	2nd	3rd	Unpl	Win £
Cats Run	9	4	1	0	4	10,648
Truss	4	1	1	1	1	3,082
Blown A Fuse	6	1	0	1	4	2,727
Lady Confess	7	1	2	0	4	2,024

WINNING OWNERS

	Races Won	Value £		Races Won	Value £
Mrs Ann Key	4	10,648	Mrs Diane Upson	1	2,727
The Three Horseshoes			Mrs R E Tate	1	2,024
Sporting Club	1	3,082			

No of horses racing for the stable	21	Total winning prize-money	£18,481

Favourites	2-8	25.0%	- 2.75	Average SP of winner	5.5/1
Longest win seq	2	Longest losing seq	43	Return on stakes invested	-45.7%

1994/95 Form	7-72	9.7%	- 8.75	1992/93 Form	31-186	16.7%	+ 39.14
1993/94 Form	7-135	5.2%	-103.92	1991/92 Form	24-161	14.9%	- 40.70

M D I USHER (Wanborough, Wilts)

	Races Run	1st	2nd	3rd	Unpl	Per cent	£1 Level Stake
Hurdles	14	2	0	2	10	14.3	+ 1.50
Chases	0	0	0	0	0	-	0.00
Totals	14	2	0	2	10	14.3	+ 1.50

W Marston	1-2	+ 2.50	W McFarland	1-8	+ 3.00
Fontwell	2-5	+ 10.50			

No of horses racing for the stable	5	Total winning prize-money	£4,390

J WADE (Mordan, Co Durham)

	Races Run	1st	2nd	3rd	Unpl	Per cent	£1 Level Stake
Hurdles	46	2	4	2	38	4.3	- 32.00
Chases	69	7	10	6	46	10.1	- 37.71
Totals	115	9	14	8	84	7.8	- 69.71

BY MONTH

	W-R	Per cent	£1 Level Stake		W-R	Per cent	£1 Level Stake
June	0-0	-	0.00	December	1-13	7.7	- 7.00
July	0-0	-	0.00	January	2-8	25.0	- 2.37
August	0-0	-	0.00	February	0-8	-	- 8.00
September	0-14	-	- 14.00	March	0-10	-	- 10.00
October	1-14	7.1	- 9.00	April	2-17	11.8	- 6.09
November	0-19	-	- 19.00	May	3-12	25.0	+ 5.75

DISTANCE

Hurdles	W-R	Per cent	£1 Level Stake	Chases	W-R	Per cent	£1 Level Stake
2m-2m 3f	0-19	-	- 19.00	2m-2m 3f	0-16	-	- 16.00
2m 4f-2m 7f	2-23	8.7	- 9.00	2m 4f-2m 7f	1-27	3.7	- 24.25
3m +	0-4	-	- 4.00	3m +	6-26	23.1	+ 2.54

TYPE OF RACE

	W-R	Per cent	£1 Level Stake		W-R	Per cent	£1 Level Stake
Novice hurdles	0-21	-	- 21.00	Selling	1-8	12.5	- 3.00
H'cap hurdles	1-8	12.5	+ 1.00	Amateur	0-0	-	0.00
Novice chases	6-46	13.0	- 17.96	Hunter chases	0-0	-	0.00
H'cap chases	1-22	4.5	- 18.75	N H Flat	0-10	-	- 10.00

COURSE GRADE

	W-R	Per cent	£1 Level Stake
Group 1	0-9	-	- 9.00
Group 2	0-9	-	- 9.00
Group 3	1-21	4.8	- 18.25
Group 4	8-76	10.5	- 33.46

FIRST TIME OUT

	W-R	Per cent	£1 Level Stake
Hurdles	0-12	-	- 12.00
Chases	0-13	-	- 13.00
Totals	0-25	-	- 25.00

JOCKEYS RIDING

	W-R	Per cent	£1 Level Stake		W-R	Per cent	£1 Level Stake
K Jones	4-77	5.2	- 60.71	D Ryan	1-13	7.7	- 8.00
A Thornton	2-3	66.7	+ 9.25	A S Smith	1-16	6.3	- 13.25
P Carberry	1-1	100.0	+ 8.00				

F Perratt	0-1	M Dwyer	0-1	P McLoughlin	0-1
G Bradley	0-1	Mr S Swiers	0-1		

COURSE RECORD

	Total W-R	Nov Hdles	H'cap Hdles	Nov Chses	H'cap Chses	Hunter Chses	N H Flat	£1 Level Stake
Sedgefield	6-44	0-10	1-10	4-13	1-8	0-0	0-3	- 19.46
Hexham	2-22	0-4	1-2	1-8	0-5	0-0	0-3	- 4.00
Market Rasen	1-10	0-0	0-0	1-8	0-2	0-0	0-0	- 7.25

Wetherby	0-9	Kelso	0-2	Haydock	0-1
Catterick	0-8	Uttoxeter	0-2	Musselburgh	0-1
Carlisle	0-7	Ascot	0-1	Nottingham	0-1
Newcastle	0-6	Ayr	0-1		

WINNING HORSES

	Races Run	1st	2nd	3rd	Unpl	Win £
Russian Castle	10	3	3	2	2	9,279
Overflowing River	4	2	0	0	2	7,335
Chief Raider	7	1	1	2	3	3,910
Call The Shots	4	1	1	0	2	3,647
Shelton Abbey	9	1	0	1	7	2,266
Souson	6	1	2	0	3	1,772

WINNING OWNER

	Races Won	Value £
John Wade	9	28,209

No of horses racing for the stable			25	Total winning prize-money			£28,209

Favourites	4-7	57.1%	+ 3.79	Average SP of winner			4.0/1
Longest win seq	1	Longest losing seq	33	Return on stakes invested			-60.6%

1994/95 Form	3-77	3.9%	- 55.00	1992/93 Form	7-77	9.1%	- 6.25
1993/94 Form	10-112	8.9%	- 53.24	1991/92 Form	0-42		

MRS LUCY WADHAM (Newmarket, Suffolk)

	Races Run	1st	2nd	3rd	Unpl	Per cent	£1 Level Stake
Hurdles	5	2	0	1	2	40.0	+ 3.50
Chases	1	0	0	0	1	-	- 1.00
Totals	6	2	0	1	3	33.3	+ 2.50

G Hogan	2-5	+ 3.50			

Windsor	1-1	+ 5.00	Lingfield	1-2	+ 0.50

No of horses racing for the stable		2	Total winning prize-money	£4,965

A J WALKER (Beverley, North Humberside)

	Races Run	1st	2nd	3rd	Unpl	Per cent	£1 Level Stake
Hurdles	0	0	0	0	0	-	0.00
Chases	2	1	1	0	0	50.0	+ 4.00
Totals	2	1	1	0	0	50.0	+ 4.00

Mr S Walker	1-2	+ 4.00	Aintree	1-1	+ 5.00

No of horses racing for the stable	1	Total winning prize-money	£1,764

N J H WALKER (Kingston Lisle, Oxon)

	Races Run	1st	2nd	3rd	Unpl	Per cent	£1 Level Stake
Hurdles	28	0	2	1	25	-	- 28.00
Chases	11	1	4	1	5	9.1	- 8.25
Totals	39	1	6	2	30	2.6	- 36.25

N Williamson	1-2	+ 0.75	Newton Abbot	1-2	+ 0.75

No of horses racing for the stable	15	Total winning prize-money	£2,710

J WALL (Cheltenham, Glos)

	Races Run	1st	2nd	3rd	Unpl	Per cent	£1 Level Stake
Hurdles	0	0	0	0	0	-	0.00
Chases	5	1	1	1	2	20.0	+ 1.50
Totals	5	1	1	1	2	20.0	+ 1.50

Mr C Ward Thomas	1-5	+ 1.50	Ludlow	1-1	+ 5.50

No of horses racing for the stable	1	Total winning prize-money	£1,725

T WALL (Church Stretton, Salop)

	Races Run	1st	2nd	3rd	Unpl	Per cent	£1 Level Stake
Hurdles	29	1	1	3	24	3.4	- 21.00
Chases	5	0	0	2	3	-	- 5.00
Totals	34	1	1	5	27	2.9	- 26.00

R Massey	1-18	- 10.00	Worcester	1-4	+ 4.00

No of horses racing for the stable	11	Total winning prize-money	£2,600

F T WALTON (Thropton, Northumberland)

	Races Run	1st	2nd	3rd	Unpl	Per cent	£1 Level Stake
Hurdles	13	0	0	0	13	-	- 13.00
Chases	27	1	1	5	20	3.7	- 24.50
Totals	40	1	1	5	33	2.5	- 37.50

B Storey	1-16	- 13.50	Hexham	1-14	- 11.50

No of horses racing for the stable	9	Total winning prize-money	£2,135

MRS K WALTON (Middleham, North Yorks)

	Races Run	1st	2nd	3rd	Unpl	Per cent	£1 Level Stake
Hurdles	7	1	0	2	4	14.3	- 4.12
Chases	0	0	0	0	0	-	0.00
Totals	7	1	0	2	4	14.3	- 4.12

J Callaghan	1-6	- 3.12	Market Rasen	1-1	+ 1.88

No of horses racing for the stable	2	Total winning prize-money	£2,902

MARTYN WANE (Melsonby, North Yorks)

	Races Run	1st	2nd	3rd	Unpl	Per cent	£1 Level Stake
Hurdles	9	1	1	2	5	11.1	- 7.67
Chases	1	1	0	0	0	100.0	+ 4.00
Totals	10	2	1	2	5	20.0	- 3.67

Mr S Swiers	1-2	+ 3.00	J Callaghan	1-7	- 5.67
Hexham	2-4	+ 2.33			

No of horses racing for the stable	5	Total winning prize-money	£5,918

MRS V C WARD (Aisby, Lincs)

	Races Run	1st	2nd	3rd	Unpl	Per cent	£1 Level Stake
Hurdles	16	2	0	1	13	12.5	- 5.75
Chases	28	3	1	4	20	10.7	- 10.50
Totals	44	5	1	5	33	11.4	- 16.25

Richard Davis	2-7	+ 5.50	J R Kavanagh	1-11	- 7.75
B Fenton	1-2	+ 5.00	D Parker	1-14	- 9.00
Southwell	3-10	+ 9.50	Catterick	1-3	+ 2.00
Plumpton	1-1	+ 2.25			

No of horses racing for the stable   7   Total winning prize-money   £11,593

MRS BARBARA WARING (Colerne, Wilts)

	Races Run	1st	2nd	3rd	Unpl	Per cent	£1 Level Stake
Hurdles	28	2	1	2	23	7.1	- 14.37
Chases	4	0	2	0	2	-	- 4.00
Totals	32	2	3	2	25	6.3	- 18.37

E Byrne	2-32	- 18.37	Worcester	2-8	+ 5.63

No of horses racing for the stable   8   Total winning prize-money   £4,325

W J WARNER (Northampton, Northants)

	Races Run	1st	2nd	3rd	Unpl	Per cent	£1 Level Stake
Hurdles	0	0	0	0	0	-	0.00
Chases	8	2	2	1	3	25.0	- 4.60
Totals	8	2	2	1	3	25.0	- 4.60

Mr A Hill	2-8	- 4.60	Fakenham	2-3	+ 0.40

No of horses racing for the stable   2   Total winning prize-money   £5,223

MRS S WEATHERLAKE (Taunton, Somerset)

	Races Run	1st	2nd	3rd	Unpl	Per cent	£1 Level Stake
Hurdles	0	0	0	0	0	-	0.00
Chases	2	1	0	0	1	50.0	+ 4.50
Totals	2	1	0	0	1	50.0	+ 4.50

Mr N Harris	1-2	+ 4.50		Taunton		1-1	+ 5.50

No of horses racing for the stable   1   Total winning prize-money   £3,501

P R WEBBER (Mollington, Oxon)

	Races Run	1st	2nd	3rd	Unpl	Per cent	£1 Level Stake
Hurdles	77	10	3	5	59	13.0	+ 59.00
Chases	31	3	3	7	18	9.7	- 22.23
Totals	108	13	6	12	77	12.0	+ 36.77

BY MONTH

	W-R	Per cent	£1 Level Stake		W-R	Per cent	£1 Level Stake
June	0-0	-	0.00	December	3-13	23.1	+ 6.83
July	0-0	-	0.00	January	0-13	-	- 13.00
August	0-0	-	0.00	February	2-20	10.0	+ 62.00
September	0-0	-	0.00	March	3-21	14.3	- 10.06
October	0-1	-	- 1.00	April	2-18	11.1	- 3.50
November	2-10	20.0	- 1.50	May	1-12	8.3	- 3.00

DISTANCE

	W-R	Per cent	£1 Level Stake		W-R	Per cent	£1 Level Stake
Hurdles				Chases			
2m-2m 3f	10-65	15.4	+ 71.00	2m-2m 3f	2-7	28.6	- 3.73
2m 4f-2m 7f	0-9	-	- 9.00	2m 4f-2m 7f	0-10	-	- 10.00
3m +	0-3	-	- 3.00	3m +	1-14	7.1	- 8.50

TYPE OF RACE

	W-R	Per cent	£1 Level Stake		W-R	Per cent	£1 Level Stake
Novice hurdles	5-34	14.7	+ 60.00	Selling	0-0	-	0.00
H'cap hurdles	1-19	5.3	- 14.50	Amateur	0-1	-	- 1.00
Novice chases	2-13	15.4	- 9.73	Hunter chases	0-4	-	- 4.00
H'cap chases	1-14	7.1	- 8.50	N H Flat	4-23	17.4	+ 14.50

COURSE GRADE

	W-R	Per cent	£1 Level Stake
Group 1	5-30	16.7	+ 13.00
Group 2	0-7	-	- 7.00
Group 3	7-51	13.7	+ 40.77
Group 4	1-20	5.0	- 10.00

FIRST TIME OUT

	W-R	Per cent	£1 Level Stake
Hurdles	3-24	12.5	+ 3.00
Chases	0-7	-	- 7.00
Totals	3-31	9.7	- 4.00

JOCKEYS RIDING

	W-R	Per cent	£1 Level Stake
Mr P Scott	4-31	12.9	+ 6.50
R Bellamy	4-33	12.1	- 18.67
G McCourt	3-20	15.0	+ 53.94
M Dwyer	1-5	20.0	+ 4.00
Mr J R Lawther	1-5	20.0	+ 5.00

A P McCoy	0-3	R Garrity	0-2	Mr S Swiers	0-1
M A Fitzgerald	0-3	J Osborne	0-1	T J Murphy	0-1
G Bradley	0-2	Mr J P Durkan	0-1		

COURSE RECORD

	Total W-R	Nov Hdles	H'cap Hdles	Nov Chses	H'cap Chses	Hunter Chses	N H Flat	£1 Level Stake
Uttoxeter	3-19	2-8	0-3	1-2	0-3	0-0	0-3	+ 54.83
Doncaster	2-2	0-0	0-0	0-0	0-0	0-0	2-2	+ 16.00
Warwick	2-4	0-0	0-0	1-1	0-0	0-0	1-3	+ 1.94
Newbury	1-2	0-0	0-1	0-0	1-1	0-0	0-0	+ 3.50
Ascot	1-3	0-0	1-2	0-0	0-1	0-0	0-0	+ 1.50
Market Rasen	1-5	1-2	0-1	0-0	0-0	0-1	0-1	+ 4.00
Kempton	1-5	0-2	0-0	0-0	0-1	0-0	1-2	+ 10.00
Nottingham	1-6	1-2	0-0	0-2	0-1	0-0	0-1	- 3.00
Towcester	1-9	1-3	0-2	0-1	0-1	0-0	0-2	+ 1.00

Worcester	0-8	Plumpton	0-3	Wetherby	0-2
Cheltenham	0-6	Sandown	0-3	Ayr	0-1
Haydock	0-6	Aintree	0-2	Bangor	0-1
Ludlow	0-6	Huntingdon	0-2	Fakenham	0-1
Chepstow	0-4	Leicester	0-2	Lingfield	0-1
Hereford	0-3	Stratford	0-2		

WINNING HORSES

	Races Run	1st	2nd	3rd	Unpl	Win £
Flying Instructor	6	3	0	0	3	12,245
Jacob's Wife	4	2	0	1	1	7,712
Euro Singer	4	1	0	0	3	3,143
John Drumm	4	2	0	0	2	2,851
Mid Day Chaser	4	2	1	1	0	2,830
Cropredy Lad	6	1	0	1	4	2,785
Limited Liability	1	1	0	0	0	2,784
Brazil Or Bust	4	1	0	0	3	1,792

WINNING OWNERS

	Races Won	Value £		Races Won	Value £
Lady Lyell	3	12,245	Tavern Racing	2	2,830
The Black Sheep Flock	2	7,712	Richard Hall	1	2,785
Syndicate From Hell	1	3,143	Miss Elizabeth Aldous	1	2,784
Andrew Jenkins	2	2,851	Mrs C A Waters	1	1,792

No of horses racing for the stable	32	Total winning prize-money	£36,142

Favourites	4-12	33.3% - 1.23	Average SP of winner		10.1/1
Longest win seq	2	Longest losing seq 23	Return on stakes invested		34.0%

1994/95 Form   0-1

C WEEDON (Chiddingfold, Surrey)

	Races Run	1st	2nd	3rd	Unpl	Per cent	£1 Level Stake
Hurdles	45	3	6	4	32	6.7	+ 2.50
Chases	17	3	5	0	9	17.6	+ 0.50
Totals	62	6	11	4	41	9.7	+ 3.00

M Richards	3-10	+ 7.50	B Fenton	1-9	+ 25.00
J Osborne	1-1	+ 5.00	Peter Hobbs	1-16	- 8.50

Worcester	2-4	+ 10.50	Bangor	1-2	+ 4.50
Leicester	1-1	+ 5.00	Cheltenham	1-5	+ 29.00
Market Rasen	1-1	+ 3.00			

No of horses racing for the stable	20	Total winning prize-money	£43,939

L WELLS (Wisborough Green, West Sussex)

	Races Run	1st	2nd	3rd	Unpl	Per cent	£1 Level Stake
Hurdles	10	1	0	0	9	10.0	- 3.00
Chases	5	0	0	1	4	-	- 5.00
Totals	15	1	0	1	13	6.7	- 8.00

G Hogan	1-7	0.00	Plumpton	1-1	+ 6.00

No of horses racing for the stable	9	Total winning prize-money	£2,027

J WHARTON (Waltham-on-the-Wolds, Leics)

	Races Run	1st	2nd	3rd	Unpl	Per cent	£1 Level Stake
Hurdles	18	0	2	1	15	-	- 18.00
Chases	2	1	0	0	1	50.0	+ 6.00
Totals	20	1	2	1	16	5.0	- 12.00

B Dalton	1-15	- 7.00	Huntingdon	1-2	+ 6.00

No of horses racing for the stable	6	Total winning prize-money	£2,906

A C WHILLANS (Newmill-on-Slitrig, Borders)

	Races Run	1st	2nd	3rd	Unpl	Per cent	£1 Level Stake
Hurdles	30	4	10	4	12	13.3	- 5.75
Chases	7	4	0	0	3	57.1	+ 9.75
Totals	37	8	10	4	15	21.6	+ 4.00

BY MONTH

	W-R	Per cent	£1 Level Stake		W-R	Per cent	£1 Level Stake
June	0-0	-	0.00	December	0-2	-	- 2.00
July	0-0	-	0.00	January	1-4	25.0	+ 1.00
August	0-0	-	0.00	February	2-9	22.2	- 2.25
September	0-0	-	0.00	March	1-9	11.1	- 4.50
October	0-0	-	0.00	April	3-6	50.0	+ 15.75
November	0-2	-	- 2.00	May	1-5	20.0	- 2.00

DISTANCE

Hurdles	W-R	Per cent	£1 Level Stake	Chases	W-R	Per cent	£1 Level Stake
2m-2m 3f	4-22	18.2	+ 2.25	2m-2m 3f	0-0	-	0.00
2m 4f-2m 7f	0-7	-	- 7.00	2m 4f-2m 7f	2-2	100.0	+ 5.25
3m +	0-1	-	- 1.00	3m +	2-5	40.0	+ 4.50

TYPE OF RACE

	W-R	Per cent	£1 Level Stake		W-R	Per cent	£1 Level Stake
Novice hurdles	1-15	6.7	- 12.00	Selling	0-1	-	- 1.00
H'cap hurdles	3-15	20.0	+ 6.25	Amateur	0-0	-	0.00
Novice chases	1-3	33.3	+ 2.00	Hunter chases	0-0	-	0.00
H'cap chases	3-3	100.0	+ 8.75	N H Flat	0-0	-	0.00

COURSE GRADE				FIRST TIME OUT			
	W-R	Per cent	£1 Level Stake		W-R	Per cent	£1 Level Stake
Group 1	3-11	27.3	+ 1.25	Hurdles	0-7	-	- 7.00
Group 2	1-3	33.3	+ 1.50	Chases	1-2	50.0	+ 3.00
Group 3	0-0	-	0.00				
Group 4	4-23	17.4	+ 1.25	Totals	1-9	11.1	- 4.00

JOCKEYS RIDING

	W-R	Per cent	£1 Level Stake		W-R	Per cent	£1 Level Stake
M Moloney	3-17	17.6	- 4.00	B Harding	2-12	16.7	- 5.75
D Parker	2-4	50.0	+ 14.00	A Dobbin	1-1	100.0	+ 2.75

B Storey 0-1   E Callaghan   0-1   Mr M H Naughton   0-1

COURSE RECORD

	Total W-R	Nov Hdles	H'cap Hdles	Nov Chses	H'cap Chses	Hunter Chses	N H Flat	£1 Level Stake
Kelso	4-15	1-7	2-5	1-3	0-0	0-0	0-0	+ 9.25
Ayr	3-6	0-2	1-2	0-0	2-2	0-0	0-0	+ 6.25
Chepstow	1-1	0-0	0-0	0-0	1-1	0-0	0-0	+ 3.50

Carlisle	0-3	Newcastle		0-2	Perth			0-1
Haydock	0-3	Wetherby		0-2				
Hexham	0-3	Cartmel		0-1				

WINNING HORSES

	Races Run	1st	2nd	3rd	Unpl	Win £
Major Bell	4	4	0	0	0	29,327
Palacegate King	3	1	0	0	2	6,775
Miss Greenyards	4	2	0	1	1	5,623
Crystal Gift	6	1	3	1	1	3,053

WINNING OWNERS

	Races Won	Value £		Races Won	Value £
Ian T Middlemiss	4	29,327	J T Blacklock	2	5,623
Chas N Whillans	1	6,775	Mrs L M Whillans	1	3,053

No of horses racing for the stable			11	Total winning prize-money			£44,778
Favourites	5-8	62.5%	+ 10.50	Average SP of winner			4.1/1
Longest win seq	2	Longest losing seq	6	Return on stakes invested			10.8%
1994/95 Form	6-29	20.7%	+ 16.50	1992/93 Form	2-32	6.3%	+ 17.00
1993/94 Form	6-34	17.6%	+ 6.37	1991/92 Form	2-24	8.3%	- 2.00

D W WHILLANS (Hawick, Borders)

	Races Run	1st	2nd	3rd	Unpl	Per cent	£1 Level Stake
Hurdles	8	0	0	1	7	-	- 8.00
Chases	4	1	0	0	3	25.0	- 1.25
Totals	12	1	0	1	10	8.3	- 9.25

B Harding	1-11	- 8.25	Carlisle	1-2	+ 0.75

No of horses racing for the stable	5	Total winning prize-money	£3,087

MRS F E WHITE (Mayland, Essex)

	Races Run	1st	2nd	3rd	Unpl	Per cent	£1 Level Stake
Hurdles	3	1	0	0	2	33.3	+ 31.00
Chases	0	0	0	0	0	-	0.00
Totals	3	1	0	0	2	33.3	+ 31.00

Miss S White	1-3	+ 31.00	Market Rasen	1-2	+ 32.00

No of horses racing for the stable	1	Total winning prize-money	£2,425

J WHITE (Ashton Rowant, Oxon)

	Races Run	1st	2nd	3rd	Unpl	Per cent	£1 Level Stake
Hurdles	165	21	15	22	107	12.7	- 62.43
Chases	90	14	14	12	50	15.6	- 33.43
Totals	255	35	29	34	157	13.7	- 95.86

BY MONTH

	W-R	Per cent	£1 Level Stake		W-R	Per cent	£1 Level Stake
June	5-36	13.9	- 5.25	December	1-17	5.9	- 9.50
July	10-31	32.3	+ 12.85	January	0-13	-	- 13.00
August	10-29	34.5	+ 1.37	February	0-6	-	- 6.00
September	2-14	14.3	- 8.00	March	0-12	-	- 12.00
October	2-27	7.4	- 18.50	April	0-8	-	- 8.00
November	3-35	8.6	- 21.33	May	2-27	7.4	- 8.50

DISTANCE

Hurdles	W-R	Per cent	£1 Level Stake	Chases	W-R	Per cent	£1 Level Stake
2m-2m 3f	17-105	16.2	- 19.73	2m-2m 3f	9-39	23.1	+ 0.40
2m 4f-2m 7f	3-43	7.0	- 30.70	2m 4f-2m 7f	4-26	15.4	- 11.33
3m +	1-17	5.9	- 12.00	3m +	1-25	4.0	- 22.50

TYPE OF RACE

	W-R	Per cent	£1 Level Stake		W-R	Per cent	£1 Level Stake
Novice hurdles	7-63	11.1	- 43.40	Selling	9-37	24.3	+ 12.80
H'cap hurdles	4-59	6.8	- 32.83	Amateur	0-1	-	- 1.00
Novice chases	11-52	21.2	- 13.55	Hunter chases	0-0	-	0.00
H'cap chases	3-35	8.6	- 16.88	N H Flat	1-8	12.5	- 1.00

COURSE GRADE

	W-R	Per cent	£1 Level Stake
Group 1	1-30	3.3	- 28.33
Group 2	6-29	20.7	- 6.87
Group 3	20-148	13.5	- 49.19
Group 4	8-48	16.7	- 11.47

FIRST TIME OUT

	W-R	Per cent	£1 Level Stake
Hurdles	6-52	11.5	- 17.45
Chases	3-19	15.8	- 7.00
Totals	9-71	12.7	- 24.45

JOCKEYS RIDING

	W-R	Per cent	£1 Level Stake		W-R	Per cent	£1 Level Stake
A P McCoy	11-35	31.4	+ 0.85	L Wyer	1-5	20.0	- 1.00
P McLoughlin	7-53	13.2	- 7.00	J Titley	1-5	20.0	- 3.33
A Maguire	4-18	22.2	- 6.20	M A Fitzgerald	1-6	16.7	- 0.50
Richard Guest	3-15	20.0	- 7.85	R Greene	1-6	16.7	+ 7.00
S Earle	1-1	100.0	+ 6.00	D Bentley	1-12	8.3	- 7.00
B Fenton	1-1	100.0	+ 4.50	D Gallagher	1-13	7.7	- 2.00
D Matthews	1-3	33.3	- 1.33	N Williamson	1-18	5.6	- 14.00

D Bohan	0-22	A Bates	0-1	K P Gaule	0-1
W McFarland	0-16	C Llewellyn	0-1	M Payne	0-1
D Bridgwater	0-6	D Finnegan	0-1	Mr J Culloty	0-1
D Morris	0-4	D Skyrme	0-1	R Johnson	0-1
Mr J R Lawther	0-2	J R Kavanagh	0-1	Sophie Mitchell	0-1
R Dunwoody	0-2	Jacqui Oliver	0-1	W Marston	0-1

COURSE RECORD

	Total W-R	Nov Hdles	H'cap Hdles	Nov Chses	H'cap Chses	Hunter Chses	N H Flat	£1 Level Stake
Market Rasen	5-20	2-5	1-4	1-5	1-6	0-0	0-0	+ 6.05
Stratford	5-26	2-10	1-9	2-4	0-3	0-0	0-0	+ 0.17
Plumpton	4-19	2-7	1-7	0-2	1-3	0-0	0-0	- 10.41
Fontwell	3-15	1-6	1-4	1-2	0-3	0-0	0-0	- 0.50
Huntingdon	3-23	0-5	2-8	0-4	0-3	0-0	1-3	- 7.25
Newton Abbot	2-8	1-2	0-4	1-2	0-0	0-0	0-0	- 2.87
Southwell	2-8	1-3	0-2	1-2	0-1	0-0	0-0	- 2.20
Cartmel	1-1	0-0	0-0	1-1	0-0	0-0	0-0	+ 0.73
Exeter	1-4	0-1	1-2	0-1	0-0	0-0	0-0	+ 9.00

White J

Folkestone	1-4	1-1	0-1	0-1	0-1	0-0	0-0	+	3.50
Hereford	1-5	0-2	1-2	0-0	0-1	0-0	0-0	+	0.50
Chepstow	1-5	0-1	0-2	1-2	0-0	0-0	0-0	-	2.50
Bangor	1-6	0-3	0-0	1-2	0-1	0-0	0-0	-	2.50
Aintree	1-6	0-0	0-1	1-2	0-3	0-0	0-0	-	4.33
Perth	1-7	0-3	0-1	1-3	0-0	0-0	0-0	-	4.50
Towcester	1-7	1-3	0-2	0-1	0-0	0-0	0-1	-	2.50
Uttoxeter	1-14	1-5	0-4	0-3	0-1	0-0	0-1	-	10.25
Worcester	1-15	0-2	0-4	0-4	1-3	0-0	0-2	-	4.00

Windsor	0-12	Ludlow		0-4	Wincanton	0-2
Warwick	0-7	Leicester		0-3	Fakenham	0-1
Sandown	0-6	Newbury		0-3	Haydock	0-1
Cheltenham	0-5	Nottingham		0-3	Lingfield	0-1
Ascot	0-4	Taunton		0-3	Newcastle	0-1
Kempton	0-4	Hexham		0-2		

WINNING HORSES

	Races Run	1st	2nd	3rd	Unpl	Win £
Linden's Lotto	10	3	2	1	4	15,617
Simply George	10	4	5	0	1	11,954
Take Two	5	3	0	0	2	7,802
Come On Dancer	6	2	0	2	2	5,741
Ramallah	7	2	1	2	2	5,333
Flying Eagle	5	2	2	0	1	5,165
Captain Tandy	9	2	0	1	6	5,016
Couchant	7	2	1	0	4	4,761
Days of Thunder	8	2	1	1	4	4,758
Telmar Systems	7	2	0	0	5	4,220
Swedish Invader	4	2	0	0	2	3,861
Sohail	2	1	1	0	0	3,764
Googly	2	1	0	1	0	3,139
Miss Mah-Jong	4	1	1	1	1	2,200
Happy Hostage	3	1	0	0	2	2,194
Celestial Fire	1	1	0	0	0	2,167
Kings of Canvey Is	3	1	0	0	2	2,089
Doctor-J	1	1	0	0	0	1,968
Wakt	7	1	0	2	4	1,898
Lake Dominion	9	1	2	2	4	1,819

WINNING OWNERS

	Races Won	Value £		Races Won	Value £
Crocketts Racing Club	3	15,617	Richard Dodson	2	4,220
K Sturgis	4	11,954	Willwewontwe Club	2	3,861
Brian Gatensbury	3	7,802	Highbrook Racing	1	2,200
Ms M Horan	2	6,903	A J Allright	1	2,194
Mrs E Reid	2	5,741	E C Nott	1	2,167
Maidens Green Acres	2	5,333	Kings Bloodstock Ltd	1	2,089
T F Maycock	2	5,165	J T Morris	1	1,968
D Powell	2	5,016	B Whitehorn	1	1,898
Adrian Fitzpatrick	2	4,761	Mrs B Bate & Mr M Campbell	1	1,819
Mrs Joan Meredith	2	4,758			

No of horses racing for the stable		72	Total winning prize-money		£95,466

Favourites	16-42	38.1%	- 3.86	Average SP of winner		3.5/1
Longest win seq	4	Longest losing seq	49	Return on stakes invested		-37.6%

1994/95 Form	52-330	15.8%	- 45.38	1992/93 Form	38-252	15.1%	-103.79
1993/94 Form	53-279	19.0%	-123.81	1991/92 Form	39-183	21.3%	- 26.31

J W WHYTE (Ilketshall St Andrew, Suffolk)

	Races Run	1st	2nd	3rd	Unpl	Per cent	£1 Level Stake
Hurdles	21	2	5	1	13	9.5	- 14.50
Chases	5	0	0	0	5	-	- 5.00
Totals	26	2	5	1	18	7.7	- 19.50

R Dunwoody	1-2	+ 1.25	Mr M Gingell	1-3	+ 0.25
Plumpton	1-2	+ 1.25	Fakenham	1-7	- 3.75

No of horses racing for the stable	5	Total winning prize-money	£4,882

A J WIGHT (Cockburnspath, Borders)

	Races Run	1st	2nd	3rd	Unpl	Per cent	£1 Level Stake
Hurdles	0	0	0	0	0	-	0.00
Chases	4	1	0	1	2	25.0	+ 1.00
Totals	4	1	0	1	2	25.0	+ 1.00

Mr A Robson	1-4	+ 1.00	Ayr	1-1	+ 4.00

No of horses racing for the stable	2	Total winning prize-money	£1,844

C P WILDMAN (Larkhill, Wilts)

	Races Run	1st	2nd	3rd	Unpl	Per cent	£1 Level Stake
Hurdles	26	1	4	2	19	3.8	- 15.00
Chases	0	0	0	0	0	-	0.00
Totals	26	1	4	2	19	3.8	- 15.00

D Salter	1-17	- 6.00	Newton Abbot	1-10	+ 1.00

No of horses racing for the stable	5	Total winning prize-money	£5,810

R C WILKINS (Bath, Avon)

	Races Run	1st	2nd	3rd	Unpl	Per cent	£1 Level Stake
Hurdles	0	0	0	0	0	-	0.00
Chases	3	2	1	0	0	66.7	+ 1.01
Totals	3	2	1	0	0	66.7	+ 1.01

Mr R Treloggen	2-3	+ 1.01

Hereford	1-1	+ 1.10	Cheltenham	1-1	+ 0.91

No of horses racing for the stable   1   Total winning prize-money   £3,987

B E WILKINSON (Middleham, North Yorks)

	Races Run	1st	2nd	3rd	Unpl	Per cent	£1 Level Stake
Hurdles	12	0	0	1	11	-	- 12.00
Chases	10	2	2	2	4	20.0	+ 0.83
Totals	22	2	2	3	15	9.1	- 11.17

A Dobbin	1-1	+ 3.33	D Bentley	1-8	- 1.50
Market Rasen	1-4	+ 0.33	Catterick	1-6	+ 0.50

No of horses racing for the stable   6   Total winning prize-money   £6,069

M J WILKINSON (Edgcote, Northants)

	Races Run	1st	2nd	3rd	Unpl	Per cent	£1 Level Stake
Hurdles	66	4	3	4	55	6.1	- 45.00
Chases	33	5	4	5	19	15.2	- 3.25
Totals	99	9	7	9	74	9.1	- 48.25

BY MONTH

	W-R	Per cent	£1 Level Stake		W-R	Per cent	£1 Level Stake
June	0-0	-	0.00	December	1-11	9.1	0.00
July	0-0	-	0.00	January	1-14	7.1	- 10.00
August	0-0	-	0.00	February	1-15	6.7	- 8.00
September	0-0	-	0.00	March	2-12	16.7	- 3.50
October	0-6	-	- 6.00	April	1-13	7.7	- 9.75
November	1-15	6.7	- 11.50	May	2-13	15.4	+ 0.50

Wilkinson M J

DISTANCE

Hurdles	W-R	Per cent	£1 Level Stake	Chases	W-R	Per cent	£1 Level Stake
2m-2m 3f	2-37	5.4	- 23.50	2m-2m 3f	0-4	-	- 4.00
2m 4f-2m 7f	2-26	7.7	- 18.50	2m 4f-2m 7f	3-13	23.1	+ 5.25
3m +	0-3	-	- 3.00	3m +	2-16	12.5	- 4.50

TYPE OF RACE

	W-R	Per cent	£1 Level Stake		W-R	Per cent	£1 Level Stake
Novice hurdles	1-32	3.1	- 28.00	Selling	0-4	-	- 4.00
H'cap hurdles	3-25	12.0	- 8.00	Amateur	0-1	-	- 1.00
Novice chases	3-16	18.8	- 4.25	Hunter chases	0-0	-	0.00
H'cap chases	2-17	11.8	+ 1.00	N H Flat	0-4	-	- 4.00

COURSE GRADE

	W-R	Per cent	£1 Level Stake
Group 1	1-16	6.3	- 12.50
Group 2	2-19	10.5	- 10.50
Group 3	5-46	10.9	- 18.25
Group 4	1-18	5.6	- 7.00

FIRST TIME OUT

	W-R	Per cent	£1 Level Stake
Hurdles	0-23	-	- 23.00
Chases	1-4	25.0	+ 7.00
Totals	1-27	3.7	- 16.00

JOCKEYS RIDING

	W-R	Per cent	£1 Level Stake		W-R	Per cent	£1 Level Stake
P Crowley	4-38	10.5	- 18.75	M Dwyer	1-3	33.3	+ 3.00
C Llewellyn	2-8	25.0	+ 10.00	R Supple	1-24	4.2	- 20.50
A P McCoy	1-2	50.0	+ 2.00				

J Titley	0-6	D McCain	0-1	R Farrant	0-1
I Lawrence	0-5	G Hogan	0-1	R Massey	0-1
J R Kavanagh	0-2	G McCourt	0-1	T J Murphy	0-1
R Dunwoody	0-2	J Frost	0-1
B Powell	0-1	Mr P Scott	0-1

COURSE RECORD

	Total W-R	Nov Hdles	H'cap Hdles	Nov Chses	H'cap Chses	Hunter Chses	N H Flat	£1 Level Stake
Lingfield	2-6	0-1	0-1	2-3	0-1	0-0	0-0	+ 2.50
Plumpton	1-2	0-1	0-0	1-1	0-0	0-0	0-0	+ 1.25
Bangor	1-2	0-0	0-0	0-0	1-2	0-0	0-0	+ 9.00
Windsor	1-2	1-1	0-0	0-0	0-1	0-0	0-0	+ 2.00
Market Rasen	1-3	0-1	1-1	0-1	0-0	0-0	0-0	+ 3.00
Sandown	1-4	0-1	1-3	0-0	0-0	0-0	0-0	- 0.50
Huntingdon	1-5	0-0	1-2	0-2	0-1	0-0	0-0	+ 2.50
Leicester	1-7	0-2	0-1	0-2	1-2	0-0	0-0	0.00

Wilkinson M J

Warwick	0-10	Newbury	0-4	Southwell	0-2
Chepstow	0-8	Nottingham	0-4	Aintree	0-1
Towcester	0-8	Worcester	0-4	Cheltenham	0-1
Uttoxeter	0-6	Ascot	0-3	Doncaster	0-1
Wetherby	0-5	Stratford	0-3	Hereford	0-1
Exeter	0-4	Kempton	0-2	Ludlow	0-1

WINNING HORSES

	Races Run	1st	2nd	3rd	Unpl	Win £
Distinctive	7	2	1	1	3	7,274
Knockaverry	7	2	1	1	3	6,277
Mister Drum	8	2	1	2	3	6,041
Bendor Mark	7	1	0	2	4	3,234
No Fiddling	3	1	0	0	2	2,740
Coulin Loch	5	1	0	0	4	2,723

WINNING OWNERS

	Races Won	Value £		Races Won	Value £
Malcolm Batchelor	3	8,781	C J Courage	1	3,234
Jeremy Hancock	2	7,274	Mrs Leonie Harper	1	2,723
Mrs W Morrell	2	6,277			

No of horses racing for the stable		29	Total winning prize-money	£28,289
Favourites	2-6	33.3% + 2.00	Average SP of winner	4.6/1
Longest win seq	1	Longest losing seq 21	Return on stakes invested	-48.7%
1994/95 Form	4-103	3.9% - 58.25	1992/93 Form 10-83	12.0% + 8.84
1993/94 Form	8-82	9.8% - 10.75	1991/92 Form 4-71	5.6% - 34.50

D L WILLIAMS (Great Shefford, Berks)

	Races Run	1st	2nd	3rd	Unpl	Per cent	£1 Level Stake
Hurdles	45	2	1	3	39	4.4	- 27.67
Chases	41	5	6	7	23	12.2	0.00
Totals	86	7	7	10	62	8.1	- 27.67

BY MONTH

	W-R	Per cent	£1 Level Stake		W-R	Per cent	£1 Level Stake
June	0-1	-	- 1.00	December	0-3	-	- 3.00
July	0-3	-	- 3.00	January	1-4	25.0	+ 0.33
August	1-2	50.0	+ 4.00	February	0-9	-	- 9.00
September	0-1	-	- 1.00	March	2-16	12.5	+ 14.00
October	0-8	-	- 8.00	April	2-9	22.2	+ 6.75
November	0-12	-	- 12.00	May	1-18	5.6	- 15.75

DISTANCE

	W-R	Per cent	£1 Level Stake		W-R	Per cent	£1 Level Stake
Hurdles				Chases			
2m-2m 3f	1-38	2.6	- 33.67	2m-2m 3f	0-8	-	- 8.00
2m 4f-2m 7f	0-4	-	- 4.00	2m 4f-2m 7f	1-16	6.3	+ 5.00
3m +	1-3	33.3	+ 10.00	3m +	4-17	23.5	+ 3.00

TYPE OF RACE

	W-R	Per cent	£1 Level Stake		W-R	Per cent	£1 Level Stake
Novice hurdles	0-15	-	- 15.00	Selling	2-19	10.5	- 1.67
H'cap hurdles	0-6	-	- 6.00	Amateur	0-1	-	- 1.00
Novice chases	1-14	7.1	- 8.00	Hunter chases	3-15	20.0	+ 11.00
H'cap chases	1-9	11.1	0.00	N H Flat	0-7	-	- 7.00

COURSE GRADE

	W-R	Per cent	£1 Level Stake
Group 1	1-18	5.6	- 9.00
Group 2	0-10	-	- 10.00
Group 3	1-23	4.3	- 18.67
Group 4	5-35	14.3	+ 10.00

FIRST TIME OUT

	W-R	Per cent	£1 Level Stake
Hurdles	0-10	-	- 10.00
Chases	0-6	-	- 6.00
Totals	0-16	-	- 16.00

JOCKEYS RIDING

	W-R	Per cent	£1 Level Stake		W-R	Per cent	£1 Level Stake
Mr J Culloty	1-1	100.0	+ 1.75	A P McCoy	1-9	11.1	- 4.67
Mr C Bonner	1-5	20.0	- 2.75	Miss S Higgins	1-9	11.1	+ 12.00
P Holley	1-5	20.0	+ 4.00	M Clarke	1-20	5.0	- 7.00
C Llewellyn	1-6	16.7	0.00				

G Hogan	0-5	D Bridgwater	0-1	Mr A Brown	0-1
A Larnach	0-4	D McCain	0-1	Mr K Goble	0-1
Mr A Balding	0-3	G Bradley	0-1	Mr M Fitzgerald	0-1
R Johnson	0-3	J Osborne	0-1	R Dunwoody	0-1
A Thornton	0-1	K Nakatake	0-1	R J Beggan	0-1
B Powell	0-1	L Harvey	0-1	T Dascombe	0-1
Capt S Robinson	0-1	Maj O Ellwood	0-1		

COURSE RECORD

	Total W-R	Nov Hdles	H'cap Hdles	Nov Chses	H'cap Chses	Hunter Chses	N H Flat	£1 Level Stake
Hereford	2-7	1-2	0-1	1-2	0-1	0-1	0-0	+ 12.00
Towcester	2-11	0-4	0-0	0-0	0-1	2-4	0-2	- 6.00
Nottingham	1-1	1-1	0-0	0-0	0-0	0-0	0-0	+ 3.33
Ludlow	1-4	0-0	0-0	0-0	0-2	1-1	0-1	+ 17.00
Newbury	1-4	0-2	0-0	0-0	1-2	0-0	0-0	+ 5.00

Williams D L

Cheltenham	0-5	Leicester	0-3	Plumpton	0-2
Taunton	0-5	Stratford	0-3	Windsor	0-2
Bangor	0-4	Uttoxeter	0-3	Lingfield	0-1
Newton Abbot	0-4	Worcester	0-3	Southwell	0-1
Sandown	0-4	Ascot	0-2	Warwick	0-1
Fakenham	0-3	Catterick	0-2	Wincanton	0-1
Fontwell	0-3	Chepstow	0-2		
Haydock	0-3	Market Rasen	0-2		

WINNING HORSES

	Races Run	1st	2nd	3rd	Unpl	Win £
Danger Baby	4	1	0	2	1	4,541
Hermes Harvest	8	2	2	1	3	3,317
Taurean Tycoon	11	1	1	1	8	3,276
Amber Valley	7	1	1	1	4	2,449
Toskano	9	1	0	0	8	2,080
Hickelton Lad	6	1	0	0	5	1,954

WINNING OWNERS

	Races Won	Value £		Races Won	Value £
Miss B W Palmer	3	5,271	D L Williams	1	3,276
Mouse Racing	1	4,541			
Berkshire Commercial Components	2	4,529			

No of horses racing for the stable	18	Total winning prize-money	£17,617

Favourites	1-5	20.0% - 2.75	Average SP of winner		7.3/1
Longest win seq	1	Longest losing seq 25	Return on stakes invested		-32.2%

1994/95 Form	9-65	13.8% - 27.58	1992/93 Form	3-63	4.8% - 39.00
1993/94 Form	1-69	1.4% - 52.00	1991/92 Form	2-51	3.9% - 31.00

R J R WILLIAMS (Newmarket, Suffolk)

	Races Run	1st	2nd	3rd	Unpl	Per cent	£1 Level Stake
Hurdles	9	1	2	1	5	11.1	- 6.25
Chases	0	0	0	0	0	-	0.00
Totals	9	1	2	1	5	11.1	- 6.25

B Powell	1-1	+ 1.75	Hereford	1-3	- 0.25

No of horses racing for the stable	3	Total winning prize-money	£1,440

MRS S D WILLIAMS (Mariansleigh, Devon)

	Races Run	1st	2nd	3rd	Unpl	Per cent	£1 Level Stake
Hurdles	48	4	4	4	36	8.3	- 25.04
Chases	5	0	0	0	5	-	- 5.00
Totals	53	4	4	4	41	7.5	- 30.04

R Dunwoody	1-2	+	2.33	S McNeill	1-8	-	5.00
A P McCoy	1-2	+	0.63	A Tory	1-9	+	4.00
Wincanton	2-7	-	1.37	Taunton	1-5	+	8.00
Chepstow	1-4	+	0.33				

No of horses racing for the stable	15	Total winning prize-money	£10,743

MISS V WILLIAMS (Kings Caple, H'ford & Worcs)

	Races Run	1st	2nd	3rd	Unpl	Per cent	£1 Level Stake
Hurdles	25	4	2	4	15	16.0	+ 17.25
Chases	27	3	10	6	8	11.1	- 3.50
Totals	52	7	12	10	23	13.5	+ 13.75

BY MONTH

	W-R	Per cent	£1 Level Stake		W-R	Per cent	£1 Level Stake
June	0-0	-	0.00	December	0-4	-	- 4.00
July	0-0	-	0.00	January	1-4	25.0	+ 11.00
August	0-0	-	0.00	February	0-5	-	- 5.00
September	0-0	-	0.00	March	2-12	16.7	+ 0.50
October	0-0	-	0.00	April	2-8	25.0	+ 5.75
November	1-5	20.0	+ 2.50	May	1-14	7.1	+ 3.00

DISTANCE

	W-R	Per cent	£1 Level Stake		W-R	Per cent	£1 Level Stake
Hurdles				Chases			
2m-2m 3f	2-11	18.2	+ 8.75	2m-2m 3f	0-6	-	- 6.00
2m 4f-2m 7f	1-11	9.1	- 3.50	2m 4f-2m 7f	0-11	-	- 11.00
3m +	1-3	33.3	+ 12.00	3m +	3-10	30.0	+ 13.50

TYPE OF RACE

	W-R	Per cent	£1 Level Stake		W-R	Per cent	£1 Level Stake
Novice hurdles	3-17	17.6	+ 10.25	Selling	0-0	-	0.00
H'cap hurdles	1-4	25.0	+ 11.00	Amateur	0-0	-	0.00
Novice chases	1-4	25.0	- 0.50	Hunter chases	0-0	-	0.00
H'cap chases	2-23	8.7	- 3.00	N H Flat	0-4	-	- 4.00

Williams Miss V

COURSE GRADE

	W-R	Per cent	£1 Level Stake
Group 1	1-10	10.0	+ 5.00
Group 2	2-14	14.3	+ 5.75
Group 3	1-13	7.7	- 5.50
Group 4	3-15	20.0	+ 8.50

FIRST TIME OUT

	W-R	Per cent	£1 Level Stake
Hurdles	1-11	9.1	- 3.50
Chases	2-6	33.3	+ 14.00
Totals	3-17	17.6	+ 10.50

JOCKEYS RIDING

	W-R	Per cent	£1 Level Stake
Richard Davis	5-21	23.8	+ 33.75
Chip Miller	1-1	100.0	+ 6.50

	W-R	Per cent	£1 Level Stake
R Farrant	1-4	25.0	- 0.50

R Greene	0-5	Michael Brennan	0-3	D Morris	0-1
R Johnson	0-5	R Dunwoody	0-2	J R Kavanagh	0-1
A Maguire	0-3	A P McCoy	0-1	T P Treacy	0-1
A Thornton	0-3	Blythe Miller	0-1		

COURSE RECORD

	Total W-R	Nov Hdles	H'cap Hdles	Nov Chses	H'cap Chses	Hunter Chses	N H Flat	£1 Level Stake
Taunton	1-1	0-0	0-0	0-0	1-1	0-0	0-0	+ 10.00
Towcester	1-2	0-1	0-0	0-0	1-1	0-0	0-0	+ 7.00
Fontwell	1-3	1-1	0-0	0-0	0-2	0-0	0-0	- 0.25
Hereford	1-3	0-1	0-0	1-1	0-0	0-0	0-1	+ 0.50
Ascot	1-3	0-1	1-2	0-0	0-0	0-0	0-0	+ 12.00
Worcester	1-4	1-1	0-0	0-1	0-1	0-0	0-1	+ 3.50
Chepstow	1-6	1-2	0-1	0-1	0-2	0-0	0-0	+ 11.00

Cheltenham	0-4	Southwell	0-2	Nottingham	0-1
Bangor	0-3	Doncaster	0-1	Stratford	0-1
Newton Abbot	0-3	Exeter	0-1	Uttoxeter	0-1
Windsor	0-3	Fakenham	0-1	Warwick	0-1
Aintree	0-2	Lingfield	0-1	Wetherby	0-1
Ludlow	0-2	Market Rasen	0-1	Wincanton	0-1

WINNING HORSES

	Races Run	1st	2nd	3rd	Unpl	Win £
Storm North	5	2	1	0	2	8,147
Channels Gate	1	1	0	0	0	3,810
Don't Light Up	3	1	0	0	2	3,563
Bally Clover	6	1	1	3	1	3,312
Rosencrantz	2	1	0	0	1	2,486
Raphael Bodine	5	1	1	1	2	2,119

WINNING OWNERS

	Races Won	Value £		Races Won	Value £
Irvin S Naylor	1	5,459	F Bruce Miller	1	2,688
Cabalva Racing Partnership	1	3,810	L J Fulford	1	2,486
Miss V M Williams	1	3,563	Howard Parker	1	2,119
James Williams	1	3,312			

No of horses racing for the stable	18	Total winning prize-money	£23,437

Favourites	1-4	25.0%	-	1.25	Average SP of winner	8.4/1
Longest win seq	1	Longest losing seq	9		Return on stakes invested	26.4%

A J WILSON (Ham, Glos)

	Races Run	1st	2nd	3rd	Unpl	Per cent	£1 Level Stake
Hurdles	84	2	4	5	73	2.4	- 75.27
Chases	4	0	0	0	4	-	- 4.00
Totals	88	2	4	5	77	2.3	- 79.27

D Bridgwater	1-2	- 0.27	L Harvey	1-29	- 22.00
Wetherby	1-1	+ 6.00	Uttoxeter	1-9	- 7.27

No of horses racing for the stable	26	Total winning prize-money	£10,139

CAPT J H WILSON (Sollom, Lancs)

	Races Run	1st	2nd	3rd	Unpl	Per cent	£1 Level Stake
Hurdles	15	1	1	4	9	6.7	- 4.00
Chases	4	0	0	1	3	-	- 4.00
Totals	19	1	1	5	12	5.3	- 8.00

Richard Guest	1-5	+ 6.00	Catterick	1-4	+ 7.00

No of horses racing for the stable	3	Total winning prize-money	£1,968

K G WINGROVE (Newmarket, Suffolk)

	Races Run	1st	2nd	3rd	Unpl	Per cent	£1 Level Stake
Hurdles	56	10	8	9	29	17.9	+ 32.13
Chases	10	0	0	0	10	-	- 10.00
Totals	66	10	8	9	39	15.2	+ 22.13

BY MONTH

	W-R	Per cent	£1 Level Stake		W-R	Per cent	£1 Level Stake
June	1-5	20.0	0.00	December	0-2	-	- 2.00
July	4-10	40.0	+ 4.63	January	0-0	-	0.00
August	1-15	6.7	- 12.00	February	0-3	-	- 3.00
September	0-6	-	- 6.00	March	0-3	-	- 3.00
October	2-5	40.0	+ 28.50	April	1-9	11.1	+ 12.00
November	0-2	-	- 2.00	May	1-6	16.7	+ 5.00

DISTANCE

Hurdles	W-R	Per cent	£1 Level Stake	Chases	W-R	Per cent	£1 Level Stake
2m-2m 3f	5-32	15.6	+ 13.00	2m-2m 3f	0-7	-	- 7.00
2m 4f-2m 7f	5-21	23.8	+ 22.13	2m 4f-2m 7f	0-2	-	- 2.00
3m +	0-3	-	- 3.00	3m +	0-1	-	- 1.00

TYPE OF RACE

	W-R	Per cent	£1 Level Stake		W-R	Per cent	£1 Level Stake
Novice hurdles	0-9	-	- 9.00	Selling	5-28	17.9	+ 31.00
H'cap hurdles	5-19	26.3	+ 10.13	Amateur	0-1	-	- 1.00
Novice chases	0-4	-	- 4.00	Hunter chases	0-0	-	0.00
H'cap chases	0-5	-	- 5.00	N H Flat	0-0	-	0.00

COURSE GRADE

	W-R	Per cent	£1 Level Stake
Group 1	0-4	-	- 4.00
Group 2	0-2	-	- 2.00
Group 3	8-44	18.2	+ 36.88
Group 4	2-16	12.5	- 8.75

FIRST TIME OUT

	W-R	Per cent	£1 Level Stake
Hurdles	2-11	18.2	+ 20.00
Chases	0-2	-	- 2.00
Totals	2-13	15.4	+ 18.00

JOCKEYS RIDING

	W-R	Per cent	£1 Level Stake		W-R	Per cent	£1 Level Stake
J Ryan	9-51	17.6	+ 32.13	G E Tormey	1-2	50.0	+ 3.00

	W-R			W-R			W-R
Mr A Wintle	0-6	K P Gaule	0-1	R Massey	0-1
D Fortt	0-1	M Berry	0-1	Richard Guest	0-1
J McLaughlin	0-1	Miss S Duckett	0-1		

COURSE RECORD

	Total W-R	Nov Hdles	H'cap Hdles	Nov Chses	H'cap Chses	Hunter Chses	N H Flat	£1 Level Stake
Worcester	4-17	1-6	3-9	0-1	0-1	0-0	0-0	+ 19.38
Uttoxeter	3-6	0-0	3-6	0-0	0-0	0-0	0-0	+ 31.00
Southwell	2-8	1-5	1-2	0-0	0-1	0-0	0-0	- 0.75
Stratford	1-1	0-0	1-1	0-0	0-0	0-0	0-0	+ 6.50

Market Rasen	0-11	Doncaster	0-2	Sandown	0-1
Huntingdon	0-6	Fontwell	0-2	Warwick	0-1
Fakenham	0-5	Nottingham	0-2		
Hereford	0-3	Cheltenham	0-1		

WINNING HORSES

	Races Run	1st	2nd	3rd	Unpl	Win £
Chicago's Best	15	6	4	3	2	14,884
Ray River	6	2	0	0	4	4,179
Noble Society	7	2	3	2	0	3,937

WINNING OWNERS

	Races Won	Value £		Races Won	Value £
Alan Bosley	6	14,884	M M Foulger	1	2,141
First In Racing Partnership	3	5,975			

No of horses racing for the stable	13	Total winning prize-money	£23,000

Favourites	5-8	62.5%	+ 10.63	Average SP of winner		7.8/1
Longest win seq	2	Longest losing seq	22	Return on stakes invested		33.5%

1994/95 Form	6-49	12.2%	+ 6.50	1992/93 Form	1-40	2.5%	- 37.00
1993/94 Form	4-26	15.4%	+ 38.25	1991/92 Form	0-24		

P L WINKWORTH (Dunsfold, Surrey)

	Races Run	1st	2nd	3rd	Unpl	Per cent	£1 Level Stake
Hurdles	13	0	2	1	10	-	- 13.00
Chases	5	2	1	0	2	40.0	+ 0.91
Totals	18	2	3	1	12	11.1	- 12.09

J R Kavanagh	1-4	0.00	P Hide		1-5	- 3.09
Windsor	1-1	+ 3.00	Fontwell		1-3	- 1.09

No of horses racing for the stable	4	Total winning prize-money	£7,800

R D E WOODHOUSE (Welburn, North Yorks)

	Races Run	1st	2nd	3rd	Unpl	Per cent	£1 Level Stake
Hurdles	53	4	1	4	44	7.5	- 18.00
Chases	20	5	2	1	12	25.0	+ 0.21
Totals	73	9	3	5	56	12.3	- 17.79

BY MONTH

	W-R	Per cent	£1 Level Stake		W-R	Per cent	£1 Level Stake
June	0-0	-	0.00	December	2-4	50.0	+ 7.33
July	0-0	-	0.00	January	2-11	18.2	- 4.62
August	1-3	33.3	+ 1.00	February	0-10	-	- 10.00
September	1-7	14.3	- 4.50	March	1-10	10.0	- 1.00
October	1-5	20.0	+ 2.00	April	1-8	12.5	+ 7.00
November	0-8	-	- 8.00	May	0-7	-	- 7.00

DISTANCE

Hurdles	W-R	Per cent	£1 Level Stake	Chases	W-R	Per cent	£1 Level Stake
2m-2m 3f	2-34	5.9	- 23.00	2m-2m 3f	1-5	20.0	- 2.50
2m 4f-2m 7f	0-9	-	- 9.00	2m 4f-2m 7f	4-9	44.4	+ 8.71
3m +	2-10	20.0	+ 14.00	3m +	0-6	-	- 6.00

TYPE OF RACE

	W-R	Per cent	£1 Level Stake		W-R	Per cent	£1 Level Stake
Novice hurdles	1-9	11.1	- 5.00	Selling	0-3	-	- 3.00
H'cap hurdles	2-26	7.7	- 10.00	Amateur	1-1	100.0	+ 14.00
Novice chases	0-3	-	- 3.00	Hunter chases	0-0	-	0.00
H'cap chases	5-17	29.4	+ 3.21	N H Flat	0-14	-	- 14.00

COURSE GRADE

	W-R	Per cent	£1 Level Stake
Group 1	2-24	8.3	- 13.00
Group 2	3-9	33.3	+ 4.71
Group 3	1-24	4.2	- 21.50
Group 4	3-16	18.8	+ 12.00

FIRST TIME OUT

	W-R	Per cent	£1 Level Stake
Hurdles	1-12	8.3	- 8.00
Chases	0-3	-	- 3.00
Totals	1-15	6.7	- 11.00

JOCKEYS RIDING

	W-R	Per cent	£1 Level Stake		W-R	Per cent	£1 Level Stake
L Wyer	4-10	40.0	+ 7.71	Mr S Swiers	1-2	50.0	+ 13.00
L O'Hara	2-21	9.5	- 10.00	M Dwyer	1-10	10.0	- 7.50
A S Smith	1-2	50.0	+ 7.00				

D J Kavanagh	0-15	A P McCoy	0-1	G Lee	0-1
D Gallagher	0-2	B Storey	0-1	Guy Lewis	0-1
F Leahy	0-2	C McCormack	0-1	R Dunwoody	0-1
P Niven	0-2	E Callaghan	0-1		

COURSE RECORD

	Total W-R	Nov Hdles	H'cap Hdles	Nov Chses	H'cap Chses	Hunter Chses	N H Flat	£1 Level Stake
Wetherby	3-9	0-1	1-4	0-0	2-4	0-0	0-0	+ 4.71
Huntingdon	1-2	0-0	0-0	0-0	1-1	0-0	0-1	+ 0.50
Kempton	1-2	0-0	0-0	0-0	1-1	0-0	0-1	+ 2.00
Cartmel	1-3	1-1	0-1	0-0	0-1	0-0	0-0	+ 1.00
Perth	1-3	0-0	1-1	0-0	0-1	0-0	0-1	+ 12.00
Bangor	1-5	0-1	1-2	0-0	0-2	0-0	0-0	+ 4.00
Haydock	1-6	0-0	0-3	0-0	1-1	0-0	0-2	+ 1.00

Ayr	0-5	Market Rasen	0-3	Doncaster	0-1
Catterick	0-5	Nottingham	0-3	Hexham	0-1
Worcester	0-5	Sedgefield	0-3	Musselburgh	0-1
Uttoxeter	0-4	Leicester	0-2	Newbury	0-1
Aintree	0-3	Newcastle	0-2		
Ascot	0-3	Cheltenham	0-1		

WINNING HORSES

	Races Run	1st	2nd	3rd	Unpl	Win £
Master Boston	10	4	1	0	5	21,963
Pharare	12	3	1	1	7	8,292
Shrewd John	6	1	1	0	4	3,823
Grace Card	9	1	0	2	6	3,402

WINNING OWNERS

	Races Won	Value £		Races Won	Value £
M K Oldham	4	21,963	R D E Woodhouse	1	3,823
C F Colquhoun	3	8,292	G A Farndon	1	3,402

No of horses racing for the stable		15	Total winning prize-money £37,480
Favourites	3-6	50.0% + 4.71	Average SP of winner 5.1/1
Longest win seq	1	Longest losing seq 20	Return on stakes invested -24.4%
1994/95 Form	7-51	13.7% - 4.87	1992/93 Form 2-51 3.9% - 31.00
1993/94 Form	3-63	4.8% - 30.00	1991/92 Form 6-67 9.0% - 41.12

S WOODMAN (East Lavant, West Sussex)

	Races Run	1st	2nd	3rd	Unpl	Per cent	£1 Level Stake
Hurdles	25	0	2	1	22	-	- 25.00
Chases	12	1	0	2	9	8.3	+ 5.00
Totals	37	1	2	3	31	2.7	- 20.00

A P McCoy	1-9	+ 8.00	Plumpton	1-3	+ 14.00

No of horses racing for the stable	7	Total winning prize-money	£3,671

G H YARDLEY (Newland, H'ford & Worcs)

	Races Run	1st	2nd	3rd	Unpl	Per cent	£1 Level Stake
Hurdles	18	1	1	4	12	5.6	- 11.00
Chases	1	0	0	0	1	-	- 1.00
Totals	19	1	1	4	13	5.3	- 12.00

B Fenton	1-3	+ 4.00	Hereford	1-3	+ 4.00

No of horses racing for the stable	6	Total winning prize-money	£1,982

MRS A YOUNG (Sherborne, Dorset)

	Races Run	1st	2nd	3rd	Unpl	Per cent	£1 Level Stake
Hurdles	0	0	0	0	0	-	0.00
Chases	4	2	0	0	2	50.0	+ 0.98
Totals	4	2	0	0	2	50.0	+ 0.98

Mr M Miller	2-4	+ 0.98

Cheltenham	1-1	+ 0.73	Uttoxeter	1-1	+ 2.25

No of horses racing for the stable	2	Total winning prize-money	£7,132

TRAINERS WITH NO WINNERS

	No. of Horses	Races Run	2nd	3rd	Unpl
Mrs V A Aconley	6	13	0	0	13
D S Alder	4	19	2	2	15
J Allen	1	10	2	1	7
J S Allen	1	1	0	0	1
S G Allen	1	5	0	1	4
R Allsop	7	26	1	2	23
K Anderson	1	1	0	0	1
J Andrews	1	3	0	0	3
S R Andrews	1	1	0	0	1
Mrs B Ansell	1	1	0	0	1
Michael Appleby	1	2	0	0	2
M Avison	3	5	0	0	5
N G Ayliffe	13	26	1	1	24
J W F Aynsley	3	7	0	0	7
Miss D J Baker	1	1	0	1	0
I Baker	1	1	0	0	1
S Baker	1	4	0	0	4
A J Balmer	1	1	1	0	0
J Barclay	8	30	2	4	24
H R Barker	1	2	1	0	1
D R Barnard	1	1	0	0	1
D H Barons	4	13	2	0	11
Mrs J O Barr	1	1	0	0	1
R Barr	2	4	0	0	4
R E Barr	9	27	3	4	20
L J Barratt	4	12	1	1	10
Mrs P Barthorpe	1	1	0	0	1
Mrs G Bartle	1	2	0	0	2
Ronnie A Bartlett	1	2	0	0	2
D F Bassett	3	3	0	0	3
R Bastiman	3	9	0	0	9
Miss D E Bastin	1	1	0	0	1
Mrs S L Bates	1	1	0	0	1
B P J Baugh	6	16	1	1	14
Mrs A M Bell	1	3	2	0	1
C J Benstead	1	1	1	0	0
J Berry	3	6	1	0	5
John Berry	12	24	2	3	19
N E Berry	4	6	0	0	6
J Best	4	5	1	0	4
E G Bevan	3	8	0	0	8
R J Bevis	2	2	1	0	1
J R Bewley	3	13	2	2	9
Mrs P Bickerton	2	4	0	0	4
M Biddick	1	1	0	0	1
M Bielby	6	13	0	0	13
E F Birchall	1	1	0	0	1
V R Bishop	1	1	0	0	1
Miss L Blackford	2	4	2	0	2
M Blanshard	4	21	4	2	15
M Bloom	1	1	0	1	0
D Bloomfield	3	4	0	0	4
C B Booth	1	1	0	0	1

	No. of Horses	Races Run	2nd	3rd	Unpl
J R Bosley	16	52	4	4	44
J R Bostock	2	3	0	0	3
B Bousfield	2	13	2	2	9
John Bowen	1	2	0	0	2
Mrs K Bowen	1	1	0	0	1
S A Bowen	1	2	0	0	2
Miss J Bower	6	12	0	1	11
Miss L Bower	7	30	0	2	28
Mrs Amanda Bowlby	4	7	1	0	6
Lee Bowles	5	8	1	1	6
F R Bown	1	1	0	0	1
David Brace	1	3	0	1	2
Miss M Bragg	2	2	0	0	2
Ms S Braithwaite	1	1	1	0	0
R G Brazington	4	13	2	2	9
S Breen	1	2	0	0	2
F J Brennan	1	1	0	0	1
G W Briscoe	2	5	0	2	3
Mrs B K Broad	1	8	0	2	6
J E Brockbank	1	2	0	0	2
Lady Susan Brooke	5	11	2	2	7
Mrs E M Brooks	1	7	1	1	5
Miss S Brotherton	1	1	0	0	1
I A Brown	1	2	1	1	0
I R Brown	5	11	0	1	10
J L Brown	2	2	0	0	2
M J Brown	1	1	0	0	1
Miss A E Broyd	3	6	0	0	6
Mrs J R Buckley	1	2	0	0	2
Miss Anna Bucknall	1	1	0	0	1
P Burgoyne	4	5	0	0	5
Mrs R J Burrow	1	3	0	0	3
Mrs J Bush	1	3	0	1	2
N Bycroft	9	17	0	1	16
E M Caine	4	17	0	1	16
T H Caldwell	9	20	1	0	19
I Campbell	3	4	1	0	3
A M Campion	10	30	2	2	26
T J Carr	10	23	1	1	21
O J Carter	4	12	1	0	11
J M Castle	1	1	0	0	1
Mrs C J Chadney	1	1	0	0	1
A J Chamberlain	10	24	1	0	23
G Chambers	1	1	0	0	1
D W Chapman	5	11	0	0	11
Dick Chapman	1	3	0	0	3
P W Chapple-Hyam	1	3	0	1	2
M R Churches	2	10	0	1	9
Mrs E Clark	1	1	0	0	1
Mrs Jane Clark	1	1	0	0	1
S Clark	1	1	0	0	1
S B Clark	6	13	1	3	9
Miss S Clarke	1	2	0	0	2
T T Clement	8	13	0	0	13
K F Clutterbuck	4	7	0	0	7
S Coathup	8	33	3	3	27

	No. of Horses	Races Run	2nd	3rd	Unpl
R G Cockburn	3	7	0	0	7
P F I Cole	2	3	0	1	2
Miss Y T Coleman	1	1	0	0	1
R R Collier	1	1	0	0	1
H J Collingridge	6	12	0	0	12
Mrs J Conway	2	3	0	0	3
Miss S E Cook	1	4	0	1	3
Frank Corbett	1	1	0	0	1
J Cornforth	2	2	0	0	2
J R Cornwall	2	10	0	0	10
D J S Cosgrove	1	1	0	0	1
F Coton	2	8	1	1	6
C Cottingham	1	1	0	0	1
L G Cottrell	8	17	2	0	15
Miss Nell Courtenay	1	1	1	0	0
C Cowley	3	5	0	0	5
C F Coyne	2	2	0	0	2
R W Crank	3	4	0	0	4
Miss J F Craze	2	6	1	0	5
Miss Scarlett Crew	1	1	0	0	1
R Crosby	1	3	1	1	1
A M Crow	3	12	0	0	12
A B Crozier	1	1	0	0	1
P D Cundell	4	10	0	1	9
Miss Polly Curling	1	4	0	1	3
C A Cyzer	1	1	0	0	1
Miss I Dady	2	3	0	0	3
T N Dalgetty	2	3	0	0	3
M R Daniell	1	1	0	0	1
A M Darlington	1	1	0	0	1
T R Darlington	1	1	0	0	1
D J Davies	2	3	0	0	3
G W J Davies	1	3	0	0	3
R B Davies	1	2	0	0	2
N J Dawe	3	3	0	0	3
Miss C E J Dawson	1	1	0	0	1
J A T De Giles	1	1	0	1	0
B De Haan	9	27	3	2	22
R Dean	3	9	0	2	7
M J Deasley	1	1	0	0	1
C P Dennis	1	1	0	0	1
P J Dennis	2	7	1	1	5
J J Dixon	1	1	0	0	1
J H Docker	1	2	2	0	0
J Dooler	2	7	0	1	6
J Dooner	1	1	0	0	1
S A Douch	2	4	0	0	4
B Dowling	1	2	0	0	2
Mrs H B Dowson	1	4	0	1	3
C J Drewe	5	10	0	0	10
K J Drewry	3	6	1	1	4
Miss J Du Plessis	2	8	2	1	5
J W Dufosse	13	39	3	9	27
J L Dunlop	1	1	0	0	1
Mrs D J Dyson	1	1	0	0	1
Mrs J E Eales	1	1	1	0	0

	No. of Horses	Races Run	2nd	3rd	Unpl
M W Eckley	2	5	0	0	5
E A Elliott	4	15	2	1	12
C C Elsey	3	8	0	0	8
C W C Elsey	2	3	0	0	3
Mrs Teresa Elwell	1	1	0	0	1
Miss E M England	2	4	0	0	4
A Eubank	3	8	2	0	6
G C Evans	1	2	1	0	1
J T Evans	2	8	0	0	8
Mrs Jane Evans	1	2	0	0	2
Mrs L T J Evans	1	5	2	0	3
R R Evans	1	2	0	0	2
J M I Evetts	1	1	0	0	1
Miss J A Ewer	3	13	1	1	11
R A Fahey	7	16	1	0	15
D J Fairbairn	3	4	1	0	3
Fred Farrow	1	5	1	0	4
Tony Fawcett	1	1	0	0	1
Mrs D Fell	1	1	0	0	1
M J Feth-Godley	1	1	0	0	1
Miss P Fitton	1	1	0	0	1
D E Fletcher	2	2	0	0	2
S M Flook	1	1	0	0	1
R M Flower	2	3	1	0	2
M J Footer	1	1	0	0	1
Mrs C T Forber	1	1	0	0	1
R A Ford	1	1	0	0	1
P Forster	1	1	0	0	1
A G Foster	9	22	0	0	22
Anthony Foster	3	7	0	2	5
K Frost	2	5	2	1	2
G A Fynn	1	1	0	0	1
R W Gardiner	1	1	0	0	1
Miss S Garratt	1	1	0	0	1
Mrs R Gee	1	1	0	0	1
Mrs Pauline Geering	1	2	1	0	1
G W Giddings	1	2	0	0	2
K D Giles	1	2	0	0	2
Mrs G M Gladders	2	2	0	0	2
J L Gledson	4	8	0	2	6
W G Gooden	1	4	0	2	2
Miss C Gordon	2	4	1	0	3
J L Goulding	3	11	0	2	9
P F Graffin	2	2	0	0	2
Mrs H O Graham	1	4	1	0	3
Chris Grant	1	1	0	0	1
L P Grassick	6	21	0	2	19
F Gray	3	5	0	0	5
T R Greathead	5	10	1	0	9
Miss A J Green	2	3	1	0	2
C A Green	1	2	0	0	2
R Green	1	2	0	1	1
Miss Z A Green	4	11	2	0	9
M Griffin	4	15	1	2	12
Mrs J G Griffith	1	2	0	0	2
J Groucott	1	2	0	0	2

	No. of Horses	Races Run	2nd	3rd	Unpl
Miss T Habgood	1	1	0	0	1
W P Hacking	1	1	0	0	1
E Haddock	1	2	0	0	2
M Haigh	1	1	0	0	1
L Montague Hall	1	2	0	2	0
W R Halliday	1	1	0	0	1
Mrs A Hamilton	1	1	0	0	1
Mrs Hamilton-Fairley	2	10	1	1	8
B Hanbury	1	2	0	0	2
Mrs Mandy Hand	1	1	0	0	1
Miss A V Handel	1	1	0	0	1
Mrs C Handel	2	6	0	2	4
J D Hankinson	1	1	0	0	1
Patrick J Hanly	1	2	0	0	2
J Harriman	1	8	0	1	7
Miss Helen Harris	1	1	0	0	1
S A Harris	3	12	0	1	11
D A Harrison	1	3	0	1	2
Mrs Helen Harvey	1	1	0	0	1
R Harvey	1	2	0	0	2
N J Hawke	6	12	0	1	11
R Hawker	2	6	0	0	6
Mrs A A Hawkins	1	1	0	0	1
Mrs J E Hawkins	2	3	0	0	3
Mrs G M Hay	1	1	0	0	1
William Hayes	1	1	0	0	1
H E Haynes	5	17	0	2	15
J C Haynes	3	9	0	0	9
Mrs K Heard	1	2	1	0	1
M J Heaton-Ellis	6	13	0	2	11
C J Hemsley	2	7	0	1	6
Mrs Mary Henderson	1	1	0	0	1
Mrs R G Henderson	9	26	0	1	25
C Henn	1	1	1	0	0
Mrs A R Hewitt	7	18	2	1	15
P S Hewitt	1	1	0	0	1
Mrs S J Hickman	3	3	0	1	2
M A Hill	1	2	0	0	2
Mrs T J Hill	3	3	0	0	3
B W Hills	1	1	0	0	1
T J Hills	1	1	0	0	1
T Hind	3	7	0	0	7
A H B Hodge	1	2	0	0	2
H B Hodge	1	1	0	0	1
W Hodge	1	2	0	0	2
T Holland-Martin	1	2	0	1	1
R Hollinshead	12	42	1	3	38
F G Hollis	2	4	0	0	4
J S Homewood	1	2	0	0	2
J W Hope	2	3	0	2	1
S C Horn	2	3	0	0	3
Miss S Horner	2	2	0	0	2
Miss Laura J Horsey	1	1	0	0	1
R F J Houghton	2	3	0	0	3
P Howling	1	1	0	0	1
J Hunt	1	1	0	0	1

	No. of Horses	Races Run	2nd	3rd	Unpl
Lord Huntingdon	1	3	1	2	0
Dennis Hutchinson	1	4	0	0	4
J Hutsby	1	7	0	0	7
D M Hyde	6	8	0	0	8
J Ibbott	2	2	0	0	2
T C Illsley	1	5	1	0	4
R Ingram	3	6	0	0	6
C F C Jackson	11	35	1	2	32
F S Jackson	2	7	0	0	7
A P James	13	34	0	2	32
M A Jarvis	1	1	0	0	1
W Jarvis	1	1	0	0	1
T E Jeffrey	2	3	0	0	3
Mrs S R Jeffries	1	1	0	0	1
A Jessop	4	8	0	0	8
F Jestin	1	1	0	0	1
C R Johnson	1	3	0	2	1
M A Johnson	1	2	0	0	2
P R Johnson	3	8	0	0	8
R W Johnson	6	18	3	4	11
Mrs S M Johnson	4	39	2	8	29
M Johnston	1	1	0	0	1
Mrs D B Johnstone	1	2	0	0	2
P Jonason	1	4	0	0	4
Bob Jones	6	9	1	0	8
C H Jones	10	34	2	0	32
D G Jones	2	7	1	0	6
G E Jones	1	2	0	0	2
G H Jones	3	8	1	0	7
John Jones	1	1	0	0	1
M P Jones	1	1	0	0	1
N B Jones	1	1	0	0	1
P D Jones	6	21	1	2	18
P J Jones	4	12	1	0	11
Paul Jones	1	2	0	0	2
R T Jones	1	1	0	0	1
T L Jones	1	2	0	0	2
T M Jones	3	4	0	0	4
Mrs J Jordan	2	3	0	1	2
R T Juckes	16	60	6	4	50
H M Kavanagh	5	15	0	1	14
Martyn R Keenor	3	3	0	0	3
G P Kelly	7	29	0	3	26
S Kelly	4	9	1	1	7
Mrs M A Kendall	4	11	0	1	10
T Kersey	4	7	0	0	7
Mrs A L M King	2	2	0	0	2
C O King	1	2	0	1	1
Neil King	1	2	0	0	2
Neville King	1	2	0	0	2
Peter King	1	1	0	0	1
T R Kinsey	3	9	2	0	7
Fred Kirby	2	6	0	0	6
J Kirby	1	2	0	1	1
Mrs A Knight	2	2	0	0	2
D G Knowles	1	1	0	0	1

	No. of Horses	Races Run	2nd	3rd	Unpl
R J Kyle	1	3	0	0	3
D A Lamb	20	119	0	15	104
Mrs K M Lamb	3	23	0	1	22
Mrs R M Lampard	2	2	0	0	2
N M Lampard	9	32	1	2	29
Mrs S Lamyman	7	21	0	3	18
Mrs P Laws	1	2	0	0	2
G Lewis	1	1	0	0	1
M Lewis	1	1	0	0	1
W D Lewis	1	1	0	0	1
R Light	1	2	0	0	2
R J S Linne	1	1	0	1	0
O A Little	1	3	0	0	3
Richard Livermore	1	1	1	0	0
D M Lloyd	3	7	0	0	7
F Lloyd	6	19	0	2	17
M A Lloyd	3	5	1	2	2
Mrs A Lockwood	1	1	0	0	1
Mrs F A Lockwood	1	1	0	0	1
I A Lockwood	1	2	1	0	1
M F Loggin	1	3	0	1	2
T Long	3	6	1	1	4
P D Luckin	2	6	0	1	5
S Lynch	1	1	0	0	1
J Mahon	1	2	1	0	1
W G Mann	6	13	1	0	12
Miss C S March	1	2	0	0	2
B Marley	1	1	0	0	1
Mrs L Marshall	4	29	1	1	27
Mrs Kit Martin	1	1	0	0	1
R F Marvin	1	1	0	0	1
Mrs R C Matheson	1	1	0	0	1
Robin Mathew	1	2	0	0	2
Richard Mathias	2	5	0	1	4
F L Matthews	4	10	0	0	10
Ms K Matthews	1	1	0	0	1
Mrs S Maude	2	2	1	0	1
A C Maylam	1	1	0	0	1
Lady E Mays-Smith	2	5	0	0	5
K W J McAuliffe	3	6	0	1	5
P J McBride	1	2	0	0	2
Mrs D H McCarthy	4	5	1	1	3
Mrs D McCormack	1	1	0	0	1
D McCune	5	20	0	1	19
R McDonald	2	4	0	0	4
R M McKellar	7	18	0	2	16
W G McKenzie-Coles	3	4	0	0	4
Miss F McLachlan	1	1	0	0	1
Ian McLaughlin	1	2	0	0	2
Paul McMahon	1	3	0	0	3
B J McMath	6	8	0	0	8
M Meade	3	8	0	0	8
B J Meehan	2	4	0	0	4
Mrs A Merriam	1	2	0	1	1
Mrs Janine M Mills	3	9	0	0	9
D J Minty	2	10	0	1	9

	No. of Horses	Races Run	2nd	3rd	Unpl
N Mitchell	1	2	0	0	2
P Mitchell	5	16	3	3	10
Pat Mitchell	1	1	0	0	1
A Moore	17	47	1	8	38
J A Moore	3	18	0	0	18
John Moore	1	1	0	0	1
Mrs K A Moore	1	2	1	0	1
D Morris	1	4	0	0	4
Mrs M Morris	2	5	1	0	4
P H Morris	3	4	0	1	3
Paul Morris	1	1	0	0	1
T Morton	3	13	0	0	13
Mrs E Moscrop	3	5	0	0	5
A B Mulholland	1	1	0	0	1
Michael Mullineaux	1	1	0	0	1
Mrs Sally Mullins	1	5	1	0	4
M Murphy	1	1	0	0	1
B W Murray	5	14	0	1	13
W J Musson	7	19	1	4	14
A S Neaves	4	17	0	0	17
Mrs F Needham	1	1	0	0	1
P Needham	1	1	0	0	1
D Nicholls	6	16	1	1	14
Miss Carron Nicol	1	1	0	0	1
C N Nimmo	2	6	0	1	5
D A Nolan	7	22	0	1	21
S G Norton	5	6	2	0	4
J O'Donoghue	2	2	0	0	2
F J O'Mahony	2	4	0	1	3
J J O'Shea	1	2	0	0	2
M B Ogle	2	7	0	0	7
G R Oldroyd	7	25	1	2	22
E H Owen	6	10	0	2	8
Mrs F M Owen	5	18	0	1	17
B Palling	8	20	0	0	20
J N Llewellen Palmer	1	3	0	0	3
J F Panvert	2	13	0	0	13
J Parkes	11	38	3	2	33
Miss R J Patman	4	7	0	0	7
Miss H Z Pavey	1	1	0	0	1
J R Payne	3	6	0	0	6
J S Payne	1	1	0	0	1
J W Payne	2	2	0	0	2
N Payne	1	1	0	0	1
A D Peachey	3	5	0	0	5
J H Peacock	9	21	0	1	20
T A Peake	1	2	1	0	1
Brian Arthur Pearce	3	11	1	0	10
Charlie Peckitt	1	3	0	0	3
M Pepper	1	2	0	0	2
N J Pewter	1	1	0	0	1
Miss C Phillips	2	8	0	2	6
R W Phizacklea	1	2	0	0	2
Mrs A R Piggott	1	2	0	0	2
Mrs P M Pile	2	4	0	0	4
Mrs T Pilkington	2	8	0	1	7

	No. of Horses	Races Run	2nd	3rd	Unpl
S I Pittendrigh	3	9	0	0	9
Miss L Plater	2	3	0	0	3
G W Plenderleith	1	2	0	0	2
R E Pocock	4	6	0	1	5
M J Polglase	1	1	0	0	1
N J Pomfret	3	6	2	1	3
J Porter	4	6	0	0	6
J Poulton	19	44	1	1	42
Miss S Prangley	1	1	0	0	1
Mrs A Price	5	17	0	1	16
C G Price	2	3	0	0	3
J K Price	1	4	0	0	4
Miss E J Pring	1	1	0	0	1
D Pritchard	1	3	0	0	3
Dr P Pritchard	6	20	1	4	15
P A Pritchard	10	51	1	2	48
R C Pugh	2	9	1	0	8
W Raw	4	16	1	2	13
Miss M Raymond	1	1	0	0	1
Mrs J Read	3	7	1	1	5
R A Read	1	1	0	0	1
Mrs L Redman	1	2	0	0	2
Miss M Ree	1	1	0	1	0
W J Reed	1	2	0	0	2
E Retter	1	2	0	0	2
Graham Richards	3	9	0	0	9
Miss Caro Richardson	2	3	0	0	3
Mrs S Richardson	1	1	0	1	0
B Richmond	2	4	0	0	4
J A Riddell	1	3	0	0	3
N T Ridout	1	6	0	1	5
Mrs T Ritson	1	2	1	0	1
Miss L Robbins	1	1	0	0	1
M J Roberts	9	31	1	0	30
D Robertson	2	15	1	2	12
Miss S Robertson	2	2	0	0	2
D T Robinson	2	5	0	1	4
S J Robinson	2	5	0	0	5
K Robson	2	6	0	1	5
Miss P Robson	1	1	1	0	0
T L A Robson	1	2	1	0	1
Miss S J Rodgers	1	2	2	0	0
G Roe	1	3	0	1	2
Graeme Roe	10	23	0	0	23
Joe Roper	1	2	0	0	2
Mrs P Rowe	1	1	1	0	0
H Rowsell	5	10	0	2	8
A G Russell	1	3	0	0	3
Mrs Ailsa Russell	4	4	0	0	4
Miss G A Russell	1	4	0	0	4
C J Sample	1	1	0	0	1
Mrs D C Samworth	2	2	0	0	2
L Saunders	4	4	0	0	4
M S Saunders	3	8	1	1	6
H Sawyer	1	3	0	0	3
Mrs E B Scott	1	1	0	0	1

	No. of Horses	Races Run	2nd	3rd	Unpl
Miss S J K Scott	1	1	0	0	1
B Scriven	2	9	0	0	9
Mrs J Scrivens	2	5	0	0	5
Mrs J Seymour	1	1	0	0	1
Miss Laura Shally	4	22	2	0	20
Mrs N S Sharpe	1	1	0	0	1
T S Sharpe	1	1	0	0	1
B Shaw	3	10	0	0	10
R V Shaw	3	3	1	0	2
J Shearer	1	2	0	1	1
J J Sheehan	2	3	1	0	2
Mrs M G Sheppard	1	2	1	0	1
Matthew Sheppard	1	2	0	0	1
Mrs Nicola Sheppard	1	1	0	0	1
R Shiels	2	3	0	0	3
Mrs J Sidebottom	2	13	1	2	10
Mrs D B A Silk	2	2	0	0	2
R Simpson	8	14	1	0	13
A G Sims	1	2	0	0	2
Mrs J A Skelton	1	1	0	1	0
Mrs T J M Skinner	2	15	1	1	13
A Smith	3	10	0	2	8
C Smith	12	27	0	2	25
C A Smith	7	14	0	3	11
Miss D Smith	1	4	0	0	4
David F Smith	1	2	0	0	2
G R Smith	2	6	0	0	6
J P Smith	4	11	0	1	10
Keith Smith	1	2	0	0	2
R Smith	2	3	0	1	2
R Michael Smith	1	2	0	0	2
Sidney J Smith	2	8	1	2	5
H Smyth	1	1	0	0	1
L A Snook	5	16	0	2	14
P L Southcombe	2	2	0	1	1
M E Sowersby	4	6	1	0	4
G M Spencer	1	1	0	0	1
R C Spicer	3	5	0	0	5
J G Staveley	1	1	1	0	0
Anthony M Steel	1	3	0	0	3
B Stevens	1	3	0	0	3
S R Stevens	3	7	0	0	7
D R Stoddart	1	1	0	0	1
Miss F M Stone	1	1	0	0	1
Mrs S Stratford	1	2	0	0	2
R M Stronge	16	55	2	3	50
B R Summers	1	2	0	1	1
F E Sutherland	1	2	0	0	2
J R Suthern	2	2	0	1	1
C R R Sweeting	1	1	0	0	1
J E Swiers	1	9	0	2	7
J S Swindells	2	8	3	1	4
D G Swindlehurst	3	15	0	2	13
Tim Tarratt	1	1	0	0	1
G B Tarry	1	2	1	1	0
M Tate	5	25	2	2	21

	No. of Horses	Races Run	2nd	3rd	Unpl
A G L Taylor	1	2	0	0	2
J Taylor	1	1	0	0	1
Ms M Teague	1	1	0	0	1
R Teague	1	3	0	0	3
W Tellwright	2	3	0	2	1
B M Temple	2	5	0	0	5
Cyrill Thomas	1	1	0	0	1
Mrs D Thomas	4	7	0	0	7
J D Thompson	1	1	0	0	1
R Thompson	1	1	0	0	1
A M Thomson	3	9	1	0	8
R W Thomson	1	4	0	0	4
G Thornton	1	1	0	0	1
Mrs Sally Thornton	1	2	1	0	1
J G Thorpe	2	5	0	0	5
J Tilley	1	2	0	0	2
D T Todd	2	2	0	0	2
K Tork	1	1	0	0	1
Mrs P Townsley	2	8	0	0	8
A Tredwell	1	3	0	1	2
J Tredwell	1	1	0	0	1
Jon Trice-Rolph	1	2	2	0	0
C C Trietline	2	3	0	0	3
A Trotman	1	1	0	0	1
D C Tucker	1	3	0	0	3
F G Tucker	3	14	1	0	13
E Tuer	1	1	0	1	0
J P Tulloch	1	2	0	0	2
W G Turner	7	17	2	0	15
P N Upson	1	1	0	0	1
P Venner	1	1	0	0	1
Mrs R A Vickery	1	1	0	0	1
K Vincent	1	2	0	0	2
N Waggott	3	8	0	1	7
J S Wainwright	9	35	1	4	30
R B Waley-Cohen	1	3	0	0	3
T D Walford	1	3	0	0	3
Ms Helen Wallis	1	2	0	0	2
J W Walmsley	1	1	0	0	1
P T Walwyn	1	2	0	0	2
A D Wardall	1	1	0	0	1
G Wareham	1	1	0	0	1
J S Warner	1	1	0	0	1
K O Warner	3	4	0	0	4
Noel Warner	1	1	0	0	1
P G Warner	1	1	0	1	0
Mrs S Warr	1	1	0	0	1
Miss S Waterman	1	3	0	0	3
Miss C Wates	1	2	0	0	2
P G Watkins	1	4	0	0	4
F Watson	4	12	1	0	11
T R Watson	8	23	4	1	18
Miss S Waugh	1	2	0	0	2
R J Weaver	6	22	0	3	19
H J M Webb	3	6	0	0	6
P Wegmann	7	43	0	3	40

	No. of Horses	Races Run	2nd	3rd	Unpl
Mrs R Welch	1	1	0	0	1
H Wellstead	2	2	0	1	1
M H Weston	1	8	1	2	5
E Weymes	2	4	0	0	4
P Whiston	2	3	0	0	3
R M Whitaker	3	7	0	0	7
D C White	1	1	0	0	1
G F White	4	4	0	0	4
Mrs T White	1	1	0	1	0
Mrs Kate Whitehead	1	1	0	0	1
Miss K Whitehouse	10	31	0	0	31
Miss P M Whittle	6	7	0	0	7
I J Widdicombe	1	3	1	0	2
S J Wiles	2	5	0	0	5
Mrs D Wilesmith	1	1	1	0	0
Mrs J V Wilkinson	2	7	0	1	6
A J Williams	3	8	0	0	8
Miss A L Williams	1	2	0	0	2
Denis Williams	1	1	0	0	1
R H P Williams	1	1	0	0	1
Mrs L Williamson	7	26	1	2	23
M Williamson	3	3	0	0	3
Miss S Williamson	7	16	2	0	14
C Wilson	1	4	0	2	2
Cooper Wilson	1	1	0	0	1
D A Wilson	3	7	1	1	5
Miss S J Wilton	11	33	3	4	26
R Winslade	1	4	0	1	3
A Witcomb	1	1	0	0	1
E Wonnacott	1	1	0	0	1
Miss L Wonnacott	2	6	0	1	5
R S Wood	2	3	0	0	3
Mrs A M Woodrow	2	9	1	1	7
L Woods	1	2	0	1	1
S P C Woods	2	3	0	0	3
L Wordingham	3	23	1	2	20
Miss Jill Wormall	1	3	2	1	0
Mrs G Worsley	1	1	0	0	1
Nigel Wrighton	1	2	1	0	1
Ian Wynne	1	1	0	0	1
F J Yardley	6	23	1	2	20
R H York	1	5	0	1	4
J Young	2	3	0	0	3
Mrs J A Young	2	4	0	0	4
Miss Susan Young	1	1	0	0	1
W G Young	5	31	1	0	30

WINNING OVERSEAS TRAINERS
E BOLGER (Ireland)

	Races Run	1st	2nd	3rd	Unpl	Per cent	£1 Level Stake
Hurdles	0	0	0	0	0	-	0.00
Chases	1	1	0	0	0	100.0	+ 3.00
Totals	1	1	0	0	0	100.0	+ 3.00

Mr E Bolger	1-1	+ 3.00		Cheltenham	1-1	+ 3.00

No of horses racing for the stable	1	Total winning prize-money	£19,364

F DOUMEN (France)

	Races Run	1st	2nd	3rd	Unpl	Per cent	£1 Level Stake
Hurdles	2	2	0	0	0	100.0	+ 4.17
Chases	6	0	1	0	5	-	- 6.00
Totals	8	2	1	0	5	25.0	- 1.83

A Kondrat	1-2	- 0.33		Mr T Doumen	1-3	+ 1.50
Fontwell	1-1	+ 0.67		Warwick	1-2	+ 2.50

No of horses racing for the stable	5	Total winning prize-money	£3,986

D MCBRATNEY (Ireland)

	Races Run	1st	2nd	3rd	Unpl	Per cent	£1 Level Stake
Hurdles	1	0	0	0	1	-	- 1.00
Chases	1	1	0	0	0	100.0	+ 2.50
Totals	2	1	0	0	1	50.0	+ 1.50

T Rudd	1-2	+ 1.50		Perth	1-2	+ 1.50

No of horses racing for the stable	2	Total winning prize-money	£4,065

A L T MOORE (Ireland)

	Races Run	1st	2nd	3rd	Unpl	Per cent	£1 Level Stake
Hurdles	3	0	0	0	3	–	– 3.00
Chases	13	1	1	0	11	7.7	– 3.00
Totals	16	1	1	0	14	6.3	– 6.00

F Woods	1-13	– 3.00	Cheltenham	1-6	+ 4.00

No of horses racing for the stable   11   Total winning prize-money   £82,085

W P MULLINS (Ireland)

	Races Run	1st	2nd	3rd	Unpl	Per cent	£1 Level Stake
Hurdles	1	1	0	0	0	100.0	+ 2.75
Chases	0	0	0	0	0	–	0.00
Totals	1	1	0	0	0	100.0	+ 2.75

Mr W Mullins	1-1	+ 2.75	Cheltenham	1-1	+ 2.75

No of horses racing for the stable   1   Total winning prize-money   £15,880

A P O'BRIEN (Ireland)

	Races Run	1st	2nd	3rd	Unpl	Per cent	£1 Level Stake
Hurdles	9	2	0	0	7	22.2	+ 3.93
Chases	5	1	0	0	4	20.0	+ 8.00
Totals	14	3	0	0	11	21.4	+ 11.93

C F Swan	3-11	+ 14.93

Sandown	1-1	+ 12.00	Cheltenham	1-9	– 0.40
Aintree	1-2	+ 2.33			

No of horses racing for the stable   11   Total winning prize-money   £141,352

E J O'GRADY (Ireland)

	Races Run	1st	2nd	3rd	Unpl	Per cent	£1 Level Stake
Hurdles	4	0	0	1	3	-	- 4.00
Chases	9	5	2	2	0	55.6	+ 15.13
Totals	13	5	2	3	3	38.5	+ 11.13

R Dunwoody	4-10	+ 3.13	Mr P Fenton	1-3	+ 8.00
Ascot	2-3	+ 0.30	Sandown	1-1	+ 0.83
Cheltenham	2-6	+ 13.00			

No of horses racing for the stable   7   Total winning prize-money   £161,144

E M O'SULLIVAN (Ireland)

	Races Run	1st	2nd	3rd	Unpl	Per cent	£1 Level Stake
Hurdles	0	0	0	0	0	-	0.00
Chases	3	1	0	1	1	33.3	+ 12.00
Totals	3	1	0	1	1	33.3	+ 12.00

B Powell	1-1	+ 14.00	Uttoxeter	1-1	+ 14.00

No of horses racing for the stable   1   Total winning prize-money   £32,810

W ROCK (Ireland)

	Races Run	1st	2nd	3rd	Unpl	Per cent	£1 Level Stake
Hurdles	2	1	0	0	1	50.0	+ 1.25
Chases	1	0	0	0	1	-	- 1.00
Totals	3	1	0	0	2	33.3	+ 0.25

A P McCoy	1-3	+ 0.25	Perth	1-3	+ 0.25

No of horses racing for the stable   3   Total winning prize-money   £2,571

F SUTHERLAND (Ireland)

	Races Run	1st	2nd	3rd	Unpl	Per cent	£1 Level Stake
Hurdles	0	0	0	0	0	–	0.00
Chases	1	1	0	0	0	100.0	+ 4.50
Totals	1	1	0	0	0	100.0	+ 4.50

C O'Dwyer	1-1	+ 4.50	Cheltenham	1-1	+ 4.50

No of horses racing for the stable   1   Total winning prize-money   £131,156

OVERSEAS TRAINERS WITH NO WINNERS

	No. of Horses	Races Run	2nd	3rd	Unpl
J S Bolger (Ire)	1	1	0	0	1
P O Brady (Ire)	1	1	0	0	1
P G Bruen (Ire)	1	1	0	0	1
P Burke (Ire)	2	2	0	0	2
P J Casserly (Ire)	1	2	1	1	0
M Cunningham (Ire)	4	6	1	1	4
H De Bromhead (Ire)	1	2	0	0	2
P M J Doyle (Ire)	1	2	0	0	2
J T Dreaper (Ire)	1	1	0	0	1
I R Ferguson (Ire)	6	6	0	1	5
P J Flynn (Ire)	1	1	0	0	1
T Foley (Ire)	2	3	0	1	2
J R H Fowler (Ire)	1	1	0	0	1
M J Grassick (Ire)	1	1	1	0	0
John Hackett (Ire)	1	1	0	0	1
Mrs Harrington (Ire)	3	3	0	0	3
D Hassett (Ire)	1	1	0	0	1
P Heffernan (Ire)	1	1	0	0	1
G Heymans (Bel)	1	1	0	0	1
M G Holden (Ire)	1	1	0	0	1
M Hourigan (Ire)	1	1	0	0	1
D T Hughes (Ire)	1	1	0	0	1
E J Kearns (Ire)	1	1	0	0	1
J E Kiely (Ire)	1	1	0	0	1
P D McCreery (Ire)	1	1	0	0	1
Miss A McMahon (Ire)	1	2	0	0	2
A J McNamara (Ire)	1	1	0	0	1
N Meade (Ire)	5	5	0	0	5
F Bruce Miller (USA)	1	2	0	1	1
M F Morris (Ire)	6	12	1	2	9
J E Mulhern (Ire)	1	1	0	0	1
P Mullins (Ire)	4	6	1	0	5
J O'Callaghan (Ire)	1	1	0	1	0
Pat O'Leary (Ire)	1	1	0	0	1
M O'Toole (Ire)	1	1	0	0	1
J Peromingo (Fra)	1	1	0	0	1
C Von De Recke (Ger)	2	3	0	1	2
D K Weld (Ire)	3	3	0	0	3

COURSE SECTION

AINTREE (Group 1)

Leading Trainers 1991-96

	Total W-R	Nov Hdles	H'cap Hdles	Nov Chses	H'cap Chses	Per cent	£1 Level Stake
D Nicholson	11-60	6-30	3-7	2-13	0-10	18.3	+ 14.00
M C Pipe	10-83	5-23	0-21	2-8	3-31	12.0	+ 8.00
N Twiston-Davies	9-51	2-18	0-8	1-6	6-19	17.6	- 2.63
G Richards	8-46	1-10	2-8	2-12	3-16	17.4	+ 26.12
K C Bailey	7-28	1-7	0-0	5-8	1-13	25.0	- 5.28
J T Gifford	4-14	1-2	0-2	3-7	0-3	28.6	+ 18.25
Mrs M Reveley	4-22	2-7	1-10	1-1	0-4	18.2	- 0.13
G B Balding	4-31	2-9	0-4	0-1	2-17	12.9	- 2.20
J G FitzGerald	3-22	1-7	0-3	0-4	2-8	13.6	- 2.50
J H Johnson	3-22	0-0	0-3	1-3	2-16	13.6	+ 23.25
N J Henderson	3-41	1-14	1-9	1-10	0-8	7.3	- 28.06
T Foley (Ire)	2-3	2-3	0-0	0-0	0-0	66.7	+ 5.50
J Pearce	2-3	2-3	0-0	0-0	0-0	66.7	+ 10.50
Miss J S Doyle	2-4	1-3	1-1	0-0	0-0	50.0	+ 26.00
S L Pike	2-4	0-0	0-0	2-3	0-1	50.0	+ 2.40
M W Easterby	2-9	1-2	0-0	1-1	0-6	22.2	+ 2.35
R Akehurst	2-10	1-3	1-6	0-0	0-1	20.0	- 2.75
Miss H C Knight	2-10	1-3	1-3	0-0	0-4	20.0	+ 9.00
T Thomson Jones	2-11	2-7	0-3	0-0	0-1	18.2	- 4.25
S Mellor	2-15	0-3	1-4	1-3	0-5	13.3	- 4.00

Leading Jockeys

	Total W-R	Per cent	£1 Level Stake	Best Trainer	W-R	Per cent	£1 Level Stake
R Dunwoody	10-80	12.5	- 3.76	M C Pipe	3-14	21.4	+ 14.50
N Williamson	7-36	19.4	- 4.03	K C Bailey	4-14	28.6	- 1.03
G Bradley	6-33	18.2	- 6.62	C P E Brooks	2-11	18.2	- 2.62
A Dobbin	5-19	26.3	+ 5.12	G Richards	4-7	57.1	+ 7.12
C Llewellyn	5-22	22.7	+ 28.21	N Twiston-Davies	2-15	13.3	- 5.12
A P McCoy	5-23	21.7	+ 21.00	D Nicholson	2-4	50.0	+ 8.50
P Niven	5-29	17.2	- 0.37	Mrs M Reveley	3-14	21.4	+ 0.88
C F Swan	5-32	15.6	+ 0.83	T Foley (Ire)	2-2	100.0	+ 6.50
J Osborne	5-35	14.3	- 7.80	K C Bailey	1-1	100.0	+ 1.50
A Maguire	5-49	10.2	- 4.50	D Nicholson	3-21	14.3	+ 1.50
J Lower	4-13	30.8	+ 35.75	M C Pipe	4-13	30.8	+ 35.75
S McNeill	4-24	16.7	+ 12.30	Andrew Turnell	2-8	25.0	+ 11.20

How the Favourites Fared

	W-R	Per cent	£1 Level Stake		W-R	Per cent	£1 Level Stake
Novice Hurdles	11-37	29.7	- 13.35	Novice Chases	14-29	48.3	+ 2.91
H'cap Hurdles	7-29	24.1	- 7.29	H'cap Chases	15-42	35.7	+ 11.41
N H Flat	0-6	-	- 6.00	Hunter Chases	5-9	55.6	+ 9.28
Totals	18-72	25.0	- 26.64	Totals	34-80	42.5	+ 23.60
All favourites	52-152	34.2	- 3.04				

LEADING TRAINERS BY MONTH AT AINTREE 1991-96

November	Total W-R	Nov Hdles	H'cap Hdles	Nov Chses	H'cap Chses	Per cent	£1 Level Stake
N Twiston-Davies	4-7	2-2	0-1	0-1	2-3	57.1	+ 7.50
D Nicholson	4-10	2-4	2-3	0-2	0-1	40.0	+ 5.00
K C Bailey	3-6	1-1	0-0	2-3	0-2	50.0	+ 4.87
J White	2-6	0-1	0-2	1-1	1-2	33.3	+ 3.17
S Mellor	2-7	0-3	1-2	1-2	0-0	28.6	+ 4.00

March	Total W-R	Nov Hdles	H'cap Hdles	Nov Chses	H'cap Chses	Per cent	£1 Level Stake
M C Pipe	3-20	2-7	0-4	0-0	1-9	15.0	+ 26.00
D Nicholson	2-10	1-6	0-1	1-3	0-0	20.0	+ 2.50
T Casey	1-1	0-0	0-0	0-0	1-1	100.0	+ 7.00
Mrs Jane Storey	1-1	0-0	0-0	1-1	0-0	100.0	+ 1.88
T P Tate	1-1	0-0	0-0	1-1	0-0	100.0	+ 10.00

April	Total W-R	Nov Hdles	H'cap Hdles	Nov Chses	H'cap Chses	Per cent	£1 Level Stake
M C Pipe	6-58	2-14	0-15	2-7	2-22	10.3	- 15.75
D Nicholson	5-40	3-20	1-3	1-8	0-9	12.5	+ 6.50
J T Gifford	4-14	1-2	0-2	3-7	0-3	28.6	+ 18.25
G B Balding	4-28	2-9	0-3	0-1	2-15	14.3	+ 0.80
Mrs M Reveley	3-11	2-4	0-4	1-1	0-2	27.3	+ 3.88

May	Total W-R	Nov Hdles	H'cap Hdles	Nov Chses	H'cap Chses	Per cent	£1 Level Stake
G Richards	2-6	0-3	0-0	1-1	1-2	33.3	+ 2.12
D W P Arbuthnot	1-1	1-1	0-0	0-0	0-0	100.0	+ 1.10
J F Bottomley	1-1	1-1	0-0	0-0	0-0	100.0	+ 1.00
J I A Charlton	1-1	0-0	0-0	0-0	1-1	100.0	+ 3.50
R Hollinshead	1-1	0-0	1-1	0-0	0-0	100.0	+ 3.50

ASCOT (Group 1)

Leading Trainers 1991-96

	Total W-R	Nov Hdles	H'cap Hdles	Nov Chses	H'cap Chses	Per cent	£1 Level Stake
M C Pipe	17-84	9-36	6-25	1-6	1-17	20.2	+ 11.22
N Twiston-Davies	17-103	8-34	1-16	5-22	3-31	16.5	+ 11.71
D Nicholson	16-66	6-22	3-13	4-13	3-18	24.2	- 8.98
O Sherwood	15-72	9-33	1-13	4-11	1-15	20.8	- 16.96
J T Gifford	15-135	3-50	1-24	5-30	6-31	11.1	- 58.02
N J Henderson	13-95	3-33	3-23	2-9	5-30	13.7	- 24.88
K C Bailey	9-54	0-14	2-5	2-8	5-27	16.7	- 13.43
G B Balding	9-71	2-27	3-19	1-5	3-20	12.7	+ 5.52
Mrs J Pitman	8-44	2-15	1-9	1-7	4-13	18.2	- 1.72
D R C Elsworth	7-50	5-24	1-9	1-9	0-8	14.0	- 19.41
P J Hobbs	7-50	3-20	1-10	1-6	2-14	14.0	- 2.25
S Dow	5-15	2-5	3-7	0-2	0-1	33.3	+ 9.74
I A Balding	5-20	3-12	0-3	0-3	2-2	25.0	- 1.80
Miss H C Knight	5-22	3-8	0-4	2-6	0-4	22.7	+ 0.82
R J Hodges	5-23	0-3	1-7	1-2	3-11	21.7	+ 9.50
R H Alner	5-27	0-9	1-6	1-4	3-8	18.5	+ 14.33
R Akehurst	5-34	4-14	1-16	0-2	0-2	14.7	- 14.22
Andrew Turnell	4-14	1-3	0-0	0-2	3-9	28.6	+ 0.50
S Sherwood	4-19	0-9	1-2	0-2	3-6	21.1	+ 4.88
F Murphy	4-37	2-11	0-3	1-5	1-18	10.8	- 11.40

Leading Jockeys

	Total W-R	Per cent	£1 Level Stake	Best Trainer	W-R	Per cent	£1 Level Stake
J Osborne	34-124	27.4	+ 47.72	O Sherwood	12-49	24.5	- 4.17
R Dunwoody	20-128	15.6	- 59.58	D Nicholson	5-16	31.3	- 0.14
A Maguire	17-96	17.7	- 21.70	D Nicholson	8-31	25.8	- 0.46
M A FitzGerald	15-93	16.1	+ 7.84	N J Henderson	9-38	23.7	+ 19.88
A P McCoy	13-55	23.6	+ 42.51	P J Hobbs	2-5	40.0	+ 3.75
C Llewellyn	10-66	15.2	+ 19.38	N Twiston-Davies	8-44	18.2	+ 8.38
C Maude	7-26	26.9	+ 34.00	N Twiston-Davies	3-11	27.3	+ 18.00
M Dwyer	7-38	18.4	- 16.01	F Murphy	2-3	66.7	+ 2.60
S McNeill	7-42	16.7	- 12.77	Andrew Turnell	3-11	27.3	- 1.00
W Marston	7-52	13.5	- 27.71	Mrs J Pitman	5-20	25.0	- 5.46
P Hide	6-63	9.5	- 44.55	J T Gifford	4-50	8.0	- 38.46
J Frost	5-30	16.7	- 5.36	G B Balding	3-11	27.3	+ 7.44

How the Favourites Fared

	W-R	Per cent	£1 Level Stake		W-R	Per cent	£1 Level Stake
Novice Hurdles	32-81	39.5	- 12.77	Novice Chases	21-53	39.6	- 1.53
H'cap Hurdles	23-70	32.9	- 7.73	H'cap Chases	29-80	36.3	- 9.41
N H Flat	3-11	27.3	- 0.55	Hunter Chases	7-10	70.0	+ 7.42
Totals	58-162	35.8	- 21.05	Totals	57-143	39.9	- 3.52
All favourites	115-305	37.7	- 24.57				

LEADING TRAINERS BY MONTH AT ASCOT 1991-96

October	Total W-R	Nov Hdles	H'cap Hdles	Nov Chses	H'cap Chses	Per cent	£1 Level Stake
Andrew Turnell	3-7	0-1	0-0	0-2	3-4	42.9	+ 3.00
N Twiston-Davies	3-8	2-4	0-0	1-1	0-3	37.5	+ 25.00
S Sherwood	2-2	0-0	0-0	0-0	2-2	100.0	+ 10.50
T Thomson Jones	2-3	0-0	1-2	1-1	0-0	66.7	+ 7.83

November	Total W-R	Nov Hdles	H'cap Hdles	Nov Chses	H'cap Chses	Per cent	£1 Level Stake
J T Gifford	6-17	2-5	0-3	0-2	4-7	35.3	+ 7.11
O Sherwood	3-8	2-5	0-1	1-1	0-1	37.5	+ 2.98
Mrs J Pitman	3-9	0-3	1-2	0-0	2-4	33.3	- 1.72
K C Bailey	3-13	0-3	0-0	0-0	3-10	23.1	- 2.00

December	Total W-R	Nov Hdles	H'cap Hdles	Nov Chses	H'cap Chses	Per cent	£1 Level Stake
N Twiston-Davies	3-10	1-3	0-0	0-2	2-5	30.0	+ 4.88
D Nicholson	3-12	3-5	0-0	0-3	0-4	25.0	- 5.01
M C Pipe	3-12	2-6	0-0	0-1	1-5	25.0	+ 9.00
O Sherwood	2-6	2-3	0-0	0-1	0-2	33.3	+ 3.91

January	Total W-R	Nov Hdles	H'cap Hdles	Nov Chses	H'cap Chses	Per cent	£1 Level Stake
D Nicholson	6-18	1-5	0-3	2-3	3-7	33.3	+ 11.13
M C Pipe	5-16	1-5	4-8	0-1	0-2	31.3	+ 17.57
N Twiston-Davies	3-16	2-3	0-5	1-4	0-4	18.8	+ 2.00
J T Gifford	3-37	0-18	1-7	2-6	0-6	8.1	- 15.25

February	Total W-R	Nov Hdles	H'cap Hdles	Nov Chses	H'cap Chses	Per cent	£1 Level Stake
M C Pipe	4-13	1-4	2-5	1-3	0-1	30.8	+ 6.67
Miss H C Knight	2-4	1-2	0-0	1-2	0-0	50.0	+ 8.00
C D Broad	2-5	0-1	2-3	0-1	0-0	40.0	+ 12.00
Mrs J Pitman	2-8	1-3	0-0	1-5	0-0	25.0	+ 16.00

March	Total W-R	Nov Hdles	H'cap Hdles	Nov Chses	H'cap Chses	Per cent	£1 Level Stake
R H Alner	2-3	0-1	1-1	1-1	0-0	66.7	+ 6.33
O Sherwood	2-5	2-2	0-2	0-1	0-0	40.0	+ 6.00
M C Pipe	2-6	2-6	0-0	0-0	0-0	33.3	+ 5.50
Mrs S A Bramall	1-1	0-0	0-0	1-1	0-0	100.0	+ 5.50

April	Total W-R	Nov Hdles	H'cap Hdles	Nov Chses	H'cap Chses	Per cent	£1 Level Stake
P J Hobbs	5-16	2-11	1-3	1-1	1-1	31.3	+ 17.50
N Twiston-Davies	5-35	1-11	1-7	2-7	1-10	14.3	- 1.00
N J Henderson	4-31	2-15	1-7	1-4	0-5	12.9	- 20.63
D Nicholson	3-13	1-5	2-4	0-1	0-3	23.1	- 0.42

May	Total W-R	Nov Hdles	H'cap Hdles	Nov Chses	H'cap Chses	Per cent	£1 Level Stake
N M Babbage	1-1	0-0	1-1	0-0	0-0	100.0	+ 66.00
N J Henderson	1-1	0-0	0-0	0-0	1-1	100.0	+ 4.00
W R Muir	1-1	0-0	1-1	0-0	0-0	100.0	+ 7.00
Mrs J G Retter	1-1	0-0	0-0	1-1	0-0	100.0	+ 5.50

AYR (Group 1)

Leading Trainers 1991-96

	Total W-R	Nov Hdles	H'cap Hdles	Nov Chses	H'cap Chses	Per cent	£1 Level Stake
G Richards	49-211	7-65	11-41	13-44	18-61	23.2	+ 0.67
Mrs M Reveley	42-159	16-65	14-46	8-20	4-28	26.4	- 59.65
J J O'Neill	19-92	9-38	8-36	1-5	1-13	20.7	+ 10.30
C Parker	15-117	2-43	5-28	3-19	5-27	12.8	- 33.11
Mrs S C Bradburne	13-124	2-30	2-27	3-31	6-36	10.5	- 27.15
M D Hammond	12-73	3-19	3-25	2-8	4-21	16.4	- 23.74
G M Moore	12-77	7-33	4-26	1-9	0-9	15.6	- 19.32
P Monteith	12-129	5-60	4-34	2-11	1-24	9.3	- 48.46
L Lungo	11-103	5-62	1-25	2-4	3-12	10.7	- 50.30
C W Thornton	7-26	7-18	0-5	0-1	0-2	26.9	+ 0.18
A C Whillans	6-25	2-12	2-10	0-1	2-2	24.0	+ 43.25
J T Gifford	5-19	1-2	0-4	2-6	2-7	26.3	- 5.66
N B Mason	5-20	3-9	0-3	1-6	1-2	25.0	+ 9.85
N Twiston-Davies	4-14	2-4	0-1	0-3	2-6	28.6	+ 31.00
J G FitzGerald	4-18	3-7	0-4	0-1	1-6	22.2	+ 5.50
Mrs J Goodfellow	4-28	0-4	2-11	1-8	1-5	14.3	- 5.20
P Cheesbrough	4-30	1-7	0-4	1-5	2-14	13.3	- 12.50
D Moffatt	4-36	3-20	1-14	0-1	0-1	11.1	- 21.45
J S Goldie	4-37	1-17	3-20	0-0	0-0	10.8	- 11.50
M A Barnes	4-53	0-26	1-6	0-6	3-15	7.5	- 38.75

Leading Jockeys

	Total W-R	Per cent	£1 Level Stake	Best Trainer	W-R	Per cent	£1 Level Stake
P Niven	38-157	24.2	- 54.53	Mrs M Reveley	27-97	27.8	- 35.35
A Dobbin	26-137	19.0	+ 23.61	G Richards	10-30	33.3	+ 14.10
B Storey	26-187	13.9	+ 6.43	C Parker	13-71	18.3	- 3.37
T Reed	17-147	11.6	- 64.81	L Lungo	9-45	20.0	- 8.79
M Dwyer	10-81	12.3	- 15.63	J J O'Neill	5-26	19.2	+ 4.87
A J Roche	9-37	24.3	+ 10.51	J J O'Neill	9-36	25.0	+ 11.51
P G Cahill	9-44	20.5	+ 54.21	Mrs M Reveley	4-8	50.0	+ 3.73
L Wyer	9-49	18.4	- 16.38	T D Easterby	3-7	42.9	+ 6.63
J Callaghan	9-80	11.3	- 24.08	G M Moore	5-40	12.5	- 5.15
M Moloney	8-77	10.4	- 4.95	A C Whillans	3-10	30.0	+ 36.50
Mr M Buckley	7-19	36.8	- 2.22	Mrs M Reveley	5-12	41.7	- 0.35
F Perratt	7-85	8.2	- 42.25	Miss L A Perratt	2-5	40.0	+ 5.50

How the Favourites Fared

	W-R	Per cent	£1 Level Stake		W-R	Per cent	£1 Level Stake
Novice Hurdles	46-88	52.3	+ 2.64	Novice Chases	32-57	56.1	- 2.84
H'cap Hurdles	33-90	36.7	- 4.16	H'cap Chases	32-89	36.0	- 20.09
N H Flat	8-20	40.0	- 2.13	Hunter Chases	5-9	55.6	+ 2.68
Totals	87-198	43.9	- 3.65	Totals	69-155	44.5	- 20.25
All favourites	156-353	44.2	- 23.90				

LEADING TRAINERS BY MONTH AT AYR 1991-96

October

	Total W-R	Nov Hdles	H'cap Hdles	Nov Chses	H'cap Chses	Per cent	£1 Level Stake
G Richards	5-8	2-3	1-1	1-1	1-3	62.5	+ 14.30
P Monteith	5-11	3-6	0-0	1-2	1-3	45.5	+ 9.31
Mrs M Reveley	5-11	1-4	2-3	2-3	0-1	45.5	+ 2.50
J S Goldie	2-5	1-3	1-2	0-0	0-0	40.0	+ 8.00
R Allan	1-1	0-0	0-0	1-1	0-0	100.0	+ 3.50

November

	Total W-R	Nov Hdles	H'cap Hdles	Nov Chses	H'cap Chses	Per cent	£1 Level Stake
G Richards	14-50	3-15	4-13	2-9	5-13	28.0	+ 2.13
Mrs M Reveley	8-42	4-20	3-12	1-6	0-4	19.0	- 26.56
J J O'Neill	5-22	2-9	1-7	1-2	1-4	22.7	- 4.98
M A Barnes	3-10	0-4	1-2	0-0	2-4	30.0	+ 0.75
G M Moore	3-20	1-12	2-6	0-1	0-1	15.0	- 2.75

December

	Total W-R	Nov Hdles	H'cap Hdles	Nov Chses	H'cap Chses	Per cent	£1 Level Stake
J Andrews	1-1	0-0	0-0	0-0	1-1	100.0	+ 4.00
T Dyer	1-1	0-0	1-1	0-0	0-0	100.0	+ 2.50
J K M Oliver	1-1	0-0	0-0	1-1	0-0	100.0	+ 6.00
D W Whillans	1-1	0-0	0-0	0-0	1-1	100.0	+ 3.50
N B Mason	1-2	1-1	0-0	0-1	0-0	50.0	+ 4.00

January

	Total W-R	Nov Hdles	H'cap Hdles	Nov Chses	H'cap Chses	Per cent	£1 Level Stake
G Richards	12-51	1-18	3-12	3-9	5-12	23.5	- 0.46
Mrs M Reveley	11-30	5-13	3-8	2-5	1-4	36.7	- 3.77
J J O'Neill	4-23	2-13	2-7	0-1	0-2	17.4	+ 5.41
Mrs S C Bradburne	4-26	0-4	1-3	1-10	2-9	15.4	+ 6.00
S Mellor	3-6	1-1	0-0	1-2	1-3	50.0	+ 13.33

February

	Total W-R	Nov Hdles	H'cap Hdles	Nov Chses	H'cap Chses	Per cent	£1 Level Stake
Mrs M Reveley	6-17	1-5	1-5	1-1	3-6	35.3	- 2.00
G Richards	4-21	0-7	1-3	1-4	2-7	19.0	- 10.90
L Lungo	3-8	1-4	0-1	0-0	2-3	37.5	+ 1.85
A C Whillans	2-8	1-7	0-0	0-0	1-1	25.0	+ 8.50
Mrs S C Bradburne	2-11	1-4	0-4	0-0	1-3	18.2	- 1.50

March

	Total W-R	Nov Hdles	H'cap Hdles	Nov Chses	H'cap Chses	Per cent	£1 Level Stake
G Richards	6-28	0-8	2-3	2-8	2-9	21.4	+ 5.31
Mrs M Reveley	5-20	3-9	2-7	0-2	0-2	25.0	- 8.01
C Parker	5-21	1-7	2-5	2-4	0-5	23.8	- 1.12
G M Moore	4-16	3-9	0-4	1-1	0-2	25.0	- 10.36
T D Easterby	3-4	1-2	2-2	0-0	0-0	75.0	+ 9.63

April

	Total W-R	Nov Hdles	H'cap Hdles	Nov Chses	H'cap Chses	Per cent	£1 Level Stake
G Richards	8-50	1-14	0-8	4-13	3-15	16.0	- 6.70
Mrs M Reveley	7-36	2-14	3-11	2-2	0-9	19.4	- 18.82
J T Gifford	5-19	1-2	0-4	2-6	2-7	26.3	- 5.66
M D Hammond	5-23	0-0	3-10	0-3	2-10	21.7	+ 1.75
N Twiston-Davies	4-14	2-4	0-1	0-3	2-6	28.6	+ 31.00

BANGOR (Group 4)

Leading Trainers 1991-96

	Total W-R	Nov Hdles	H'cap Hdles	Nov Chses	H'cap Chses	Per cent	£1 Level Stake
G Richards	29-122	6-36	2-16	11-25	10-45	23.8	- 36.17
M C Pipe	22-85	9-44	4-19	4-9	5-13	25.9	- 5.41
N Twiston-Davies	16-71	10-36	4-15	2-10	0-10	22.5	+ 10.25
J White	11-33	5-15	2-3	1-8	3-7	33.3	- 3.58
D Nicholson	11-40	6-23	2-5	1-4	2-8	27.5	- 0.82
J Mackie	10-64	0-19	4-16	2-7	4-22	15.6	- 2.63
R Dickin	8-31	0-3	4-10	2-5	2-13	25.8	+ 13.71
J J O'Neill	8-58	3-22	1-15	3-8	1-13	13.8	- 27.16
M D Hammond	7-19	1-5	2-8	1-2	3-4	36.8	+ 21.13
K C Bailey	7-32	4-11	0-8	0-6	3-7	21.9	+ 6.38
W Clay	7-92	3-52	3-25	1-8	0-7	7.6	- 44.75
C P E Brooks	6-17	2-6	0-2	2-5	2-4	35.3	+ 2.09
C D Broad	6-18	2-8	2-5	1-3	1-2	33.3	+ 14.58
D Burchell	6-25	3-12	3-10	0-1	0-2	24.0	+ 27.38
J M Bradley	6-29	0-10	2-7	1-5	3-7	20.7	+ 14.75
G M Moore	6-30	2-11	2-10	0-3	2-6	20.0	+ 5.25
R Lee	6-58	3-18	1-11	0-7	2-22	10.3	+ 15.13
Miss C Saunders	5-9	0-0	0-0	5-9	0-0	55.6	+ 1.54
O Sherwood	5-21	2-5	2-5	0-3	1-8	23.8	- 2.78
Capt T A Forster	5-37	1-9	1-5	2-6	1-17	13.5	- 17.97

Leading Jockeys

	Total W-R	Per cent	£1 Level Stake	Best Trainer	W-R	Per cent	£1 Level Stake
R Dunwoody	26-87	29.9	+ 21.01	M C Pipe	7-20	35.0	+ 0.09
A Maguire	13-76	17.1	- 13.44	J White	6-16	37.5	- 2.78
D Bridgwater	12-71	16.9	+ 14.23	N Twiston-Davies	4-12	33.3	+ 1.00
N Williamson	10-46	21.7	+ 1.75	K C Bailey	3-7	42.9	+ 3.00
C Llewellyn	10-48	20.8	+ 8.63	N Twiston-Davies	5-22	22.7	+ 3.00
M Dwyer	9-46	19.6	- 8.50	G M Moore	3-6	50.0	+ 11.75
W Marston	8-42	19.0	+ 1.46	D Nicholson	3-7	42.9	+ 5.13
A Dobbin	7-31	22.6	- 4.88	J J O'Neill	2-9	22.2	- 1.37
S Wynne	7-76	9.2	+ 14.75	R Hollinshead	4-20	20.0	+ 5.87
G Bradley	6-29	20.7	- 5.03	C P E Brooks	4-10	40.0	+ 2.34
R Garrity	6-31	19.4	- 4.23	G Richards	1-1	100.0	+ 3.00
D Meredith	6-31	19.4	- 6.12	R Dickin	5-15	33.3	- 0.12

How the Favourites Fared

	W-R	Per cent	£1 Level Stake		W-R	Per cent	£1 Level Stake
Novice Hurdles	45-115	39.1	- 9.44	Novice Chases	28-58	48.3	- 2.32
H'cap Hurdles	28-86	32.6	- 1.15	H'cap Chases	35-92	38.0	- 15.18
N H Flat	3-17	17.6	- 9.50	Hunter Chases	9-24	37.5	- 8.10
Totals	76-218	34.9	- 20.09	Totals	72-174	41.4	- 25.60
All favourites	148-392	37.8	- 45.69				

LEADING TRAINERS BY MONTH AT BANGOR 1991-96

July

	Total W-R	Nov Hdles	H'cap Hdles	Nov Chses	H'cap Chses	Per cent	£1 Level Stake
M C Pipe	3-4	2-2	0-0	0-1	1-1	75.0	+ 4.43
J White	3-12	2-7	0-0	0-4	1-1	25.0	- 6.83
G Richards	2-2	0-0	1-1	0-0	1-1	100.0	+ 9.13

August

	Total W-R	Nov Hdles	H'cap Hdles	Nov Chses	H'cap Chses	Per cent	£1 Level Stake
G Richards	5-9	1-3	0-1	1-1	3-4	55.6	- 0.52
J White	4-10	3-5	1-2	0-2	0-1	40.0	- 0.83
J R Jenkins	3-3	2-2	1-1	0-0	0-0	100.0	+ 5.25

September

	Total W-R	Nov Hdles	H'cap Hdles	Nov Chses	H'cap Chses	Per cent	£1 Level Stake
G Richards	3-8	1-3	1-3	0-1	1-1	37.5	- 2.81
N Twiston-Davies	3-8	2-4	0-2	1-1	0-1	37.5	+ 4.00
J M Jefferson	2-3	1-2	0-0	0-0	1-1	66.7	+ 4.58

October

	Total W-R	Nov Hdles	H'cap Hdles	Nov Chses	H'cap Chses	Per cent	£1 Level Stake
G Richards	5-17	0-2	0-2	2-4	3-9	29.4	+ 0.94
N Twiston-Davies	4-18	2-11	2-3	0-3	0-1	22.2	- 0.50
C P E Brooks	3-7	1-3	0-0	0-1	2-3	42.9	+ 2.24

November

	Total W-R	Nov Hdles	H'cap Hdles	Nov Chses	H'cap Chses	Per cent	£1 Level Stake
J J O'Neill	4-11	1-5	0-0	2-3	1-3	36.4	- 1.66
M C Pipe	3-8	1-4	1-2	0-1	1-1	37.5	+ 5.50
J T Gifford	2-3	0-0	0-0	0-1	2-2	66.7	+ 2.35

December

	Total W-R	Nov Hdles	H'cap Hdles	Nov Chses	H'cap Chses	Per cent	£1 Level Stake
M D Hammond	3-6	0-0	2-4	0-0	1-2	50.0	+ 21.00
D Nicholson	2-9	1-3	1-2	0-2	0-2	22.2	- 4.03
G Richards	2-13	0-2	0-1	2-4	0-6	15.4	- 6.25

February

	Total W-R	Nov Hdles	H'cap Hdles	Nov Chses	H'cap Chses	Per cent	£1 Level Stake
N Twiston-Davies	2-5	2-3	0-0	0-1	0-1	40.0	+ 2.25
R Lee	2-8	2-3	0-0	0-1	0-4	25.0	+ 23.50
D H Barons	1-1	0-0	0-0	0-0	1-1	100.0	+ 5.50

March

	Total W-R	Nov Hdles	H'cap Hdles	Nov Chses	H'cap Chses	Per cent	£1 Level Stake
G Richards	5-26	2-9	0-2	3-9	0-6	19.2	- 17.00
D Nicholson	4-7	1-3	0-1	1-1	2-2	57.1	+ 4.95
J Mackie	4-10	0-2	2-3	1-3	1-2	40.0	+ 5.38

April

	Total W-R	Nov Hdles	H'cap Hdles	Nov Chses	H'cap Chses	Per cent	£1 Level Stake
Miss C Saunders	4-6	0-0	0-0	4-6	0-0	66.7	+ 2.81
G Richards	4-10	2-3	0-2	1-1	1-4	40.0	+ 12.25
M C Pipe	3-9	1-2	0-3	1-1	1-3	33.3	- 0.83

May

	Total W-R	Nov Hdles	H'cap Hdles	Nov Chses	H'cap Chses	Per cent	£1 Level Stake
K C Bailey	4-17	3-7	0-5	0-4	1-1	23.5	+ 2.88
M C Pipe	4-17	1-5	2-7	0-1	1-4	23.5	- 2.88
J M Bradley	2-4	0-1	1-2	0-0	1-1	50.0	+ 17.00

CARLISLE (Group 4)

Leading Trainers 1991-96

	Total W-R	Nov Hdles	H'cap Hdles	Nov Chses	H'cap Chses	Per cent	£1 Level Stake
G Richards	32-192	11-67	3-28	9-36	9-61	16.7	- 56.78
Mrs M Reveley	27-93	10-45	10-28	2-8	5-12	29.0	+ 1.31
M D Hammond	17-123	7-48	1-26	2-17	7-32	13.8	- 20.88
C Parker	16-125	3-44	2-26	4-18	7-37	12.8	- 41.65
J M Jefferson	12-42	8-25	1-7	2-5	1-5	28.6	+ 51.15
J J O'Neill	12-109	7-42	1-30	3-16	1-21	11.0	- 32.94
J I A Charlton	10-68	3-33	0-3	1-12	6-20	14.7	- 13.47
G M Moore	10-69	7-32	1-16	2-10	0-11	14.5	- 10.27
L Lungo	10-78	6-45	2-17	0-12	2-4	12.8	- 29.26
Mrs S A Bramall	8-41	1-15	2-4	3-14	2-8	19.5	+ 54.50
J H Johnson	8-53	5-26	1-11	2-9	0-7	15.1	- 27.77
Mrs S J Smith	7-51	3-22	1-9	1-9	2-11	13.7	+ 38.10
J G FitzGerald	6-24	3-15	1-3	2-4	0-2	25.0	- 1.54
B Mactaggart	5-34	2-13	1-7	0-5	2-9	14.7	+ 6.30
W Storey	5-35	1-11	4-19	0-3	0-2	14.3	- 19.21
P Monteith	5-50	0-20	2-14	2-7	1-9	10.0	- 25.25
T W Donnelly	4-8	2-4	2-3	0-1	0-0	50.0	+ 17.00
W Bentley	4-11	1-2	3-7	0-1	0-1	36.4	+ 14.00
Mrs J Goodfellow	4-19	1-5	0-2	1-5	2-7	21.1	+ 11.00
Mrs A Swinbank	4-23	4-14	0-7	0-2	0-0	17.4	+ 6.00

Leading Jockeys

	Total W-R	Per cent	£1 Level Stake	Best Trainer	W-R	Per cent	£1 Level Stake
P Niven	34-125	27.2	+ 4.92	Mrs M Reveley	21-53	39.6	+ 19.77
B Storey	25-186	13.4	- 43.05	C Parker	12-69	17.4	- 5.39
A Dobbin	20-108	18.5	- 15.29	G Richards	10-33	30.3	+ 1.04
M Dwyer	16-87	18.4	- 13.90	J G FitzGerald	3-12	25.0	- 0.12
L Wyer	10-50	20.0	+ 9.18	J J O'Neill	2-9	22.2	+ 13.50
J Callaghan	9-58	15.5	- 13.98	G M Moore	5-23	21.7	+ 9.90
A Maguire	8-23	34.8	+ 1.65	J H Johnson	5-10	50.0	+ 7.95
D Bentley	8-53	15.1	+ 36.15	W M Nelson	3-4	75.0	+ 22.15
T Reed	8-102	7.8	- 51.67	L Lungo	4-31	12.9	- 14.42
P Williams	7-38	18.4	- 5.85	Mrs S C Bradburne	4-22	18.2	+ 3.50
F Perratt	7-62	11.3	- 12.09	L Lungo	5-28	17.9	+ 1.41
N Bentley	6-40	15.0	+ 11.80	G M Moore	3-24	12.5	- 5.50

How the Favourites Fared

	W-R	Per cent	£1 Level Stake		W-R	Per cent	£1 Level Stake
Novice Hurdles	48-95	50.5	+ 8.62	Novice Chases	24-52	46.2	+ 2.43
H'cap Hurdles	29-78	37.2	+ 3.05	H'cap Chases	26-72	36.1	- 8.57
N H Flat	4-21	19.0	- 10.20	Hunter Chases	4-5	80.0	+ 3.83
Totals	81-194	41.8	+ 1.47	Totals	54-129	41.9	- 2.31
All favourites	135-323	41.8	- 0.84				

LEADING TRAINERS BY MONTH AT CARLISLE 1991-96

September

	Total W-R	Nov Hdles	H'cap Hdles	Nov Chses	H'cap Chses	Per cent	£1 Level Stake
M D Hammond	5-15	3-8	1-4	0-0	1-3	33.3	- 1.13
G M Moore	4-17	2-9	1-3	1-3	0-2	23.5	- 1.50
Mrs M Reveley	3-4	2-3	1-1	0-0	0-0	75.0	+ 5.35
G Richards	3-8	1-2	0-0	1-4	1-2	37.5	- 1.27

October

	Total W-R	Nov Hdles	H'cap Hdles	Nov Chses	H'cap Chses	Per cent	£1 Level Stake
Mrs M Reveley	9-22	3-12	4-7	0-0	2-3	40.9	+ 3.08
G Richards	9-26	3-8	0-4	3-6	3-8	34.6	+ 15.02
J H Johnson	3-9	2-4	1-3	0-1	0-1	33.3	+ 4.25
G M Moore	3-13	2-7	0-4	1-2	0-0	23.1	- 6.77

November

	Total W-R	Nov Hdles	H'cap Hdles	Nov Chses	H'cap Chses	Per cent	£1 Level Stake
G Richards	6-41	4-19	0-6	1-6	1-10	14.6	- 6.32
J I A Charlton	5-18	1-11	0-1	0-2	4-4	27.8	- 3.47
Mrs M Reveley	5-26	1-14	2-8	0-1	2-3	19.2	- 7.58
W Storey	3-9	1-3	2-4	0-2	0-0	33.3	+ 1.42

December

	Total W-R	Nov Hdles	H'cap Hdles	Nov Chses	H'cap Chses	Per cent	£1 Level Stake
G Richards	3-12	0-2	2-2	0-2	1-6	25.0	+ 3.25
Mrs S A Bramall	1-1	0-0	0-0	0-0	1-1	100.0	+ 14.00
J M Jefferson	1-1	1-1	0-0	0-0	0-0	100.0	+ 16.00
Martyn Wane	1-1	0-0	1-1	0-0	0-0	100.0	+ 5.50

January

	Total W-R	Nov Hdles	H'cap Hdles	Nov Chses	H'cap Chses	Per cent	£1 Level Stake
G Richards	5-27	2-12	0-5	2-4	1-6	18.5	- 10.92
Mrs M Reveley	3-6	0-0	2-3	1-2	0-1	50.0	+ 11.50
L Lungo	3-13	2-7	0-2	0-3	1-1	23.1	+ 0.66
Mrs S A Bramall	2-7	1-2	0-0	1-4	0-1	28.6	+ 44.00

February

	Total W-R	Nov Hdles	H'cap Hdles	Nov Chses	H'cap Chses	Per cent	£1 Level Stake
J M Jefferson	3-6	2-4	1-2	0-0	0-0	50.0	+ 18.75
T W Donnelly	2-2	0-0	2-2	0-0	0-0	100.0	+ 14.50
Miss L A Perratt	2-3	0-0	2-3	0-0	0-0	66.7	+ 10.50
L Lungo	2-7	1-3	0-2	0-1	1-1	28.6	+ 1.00

March

	Total W-R	Nov Hdles	H'cap Hdles	Nov Chses	H'cap Chses	Per cent	£1 Level Stake
G Richards	4-28	1-10	1-3	1-7	1-8	14.3	- 14.87
J M Jefferson	3-10	2-7	0-2	1-1	0-0	30.0	+ 13.33
L Lungo	3-14	2-10	1-2	0-2	0-0	21.4	- 0.67
Mrs S C Bradburne	2-6	0-1	0-0	0-1	2-4	33.3	+ 7.00

April

	Total W-R	Nov Hdles	H'cap Hdles	Nov Chses	H'cap Chses	Per cent	£1 Level Stake
C Parker	6-26	2-10	1-5	1-4	2-7	23.1	+ 1.25
Mrs S J Smith	3-7	1-2	1-2	0-2	1-1	42.9	+ 27.35
B Mactaggart	3-11	2-5	1-2	0-1	0-3	27.3	+ 11.30
Mrs M Reveley	3-18	2-10	1-5	0-1	0-2	16.7	- 6.50

CARTMEL (Group 4)

Leading Trainers 1991–96

	Total W–R	Nov Hdles	H'cap Hdles	Nov Chses	H'cap Chses	Per cent	£1 Level Stake
J White	13-44	7-18	2-7	4-14	0-5	29.5	– 6.67
G Richards	13-51	1-18	1-11	4-9	7-13	25.5	– 15.34
M C Chapman	9-65	3-22	4-29	0-4	2-10	13.8	+ 0.25
D Moffatt	8-28	2-12	6-16	0-0	0-0	28.6	– 0.45
M A Barnes	7-18	1-4	4-7	1-2	1-5	38.9	+ 18.53
Mrs M Reveley	7-21	3-7	2-10	1-2	1-2	33.3	– 5.60
G M Moore	6-17	4-12	1-3	0-0	1-2	35.3	+ 6.54
Denys Smith	5-19	1-6	3-10	0-1	1-2	26.3	+ 10.46
J J O'Neill	4-19	0-5	3-8	1-2	0-4	21.1	– 3.37
M D Hammond	4-26	2-11	1-8	0-2	1-5	15.4	– 13.75
R D E Woodhouse	3-5	1-1	0-1	0-0	2-3	60.0	+ 11.50
D Burchell	3-8	0-4	2-2	1-2	0-0	37.5	+ 13.00
L Lungo	3-9	2-2	1-6	0-1	0-0	33.3	+ 2.75
M C Pipe	3-12	2-6	0-5	1-1	0-0	25.0	+ 2.71
P Beaumont	3-17	1-5	1-5	1-3	0-4	17.6	+ 0.50
G B Balding	2-3	0-0	1-1	1-1	0-1	66.7	+ 4.50
Paul Bradley	2-3	0-0	0-1	0-0	2-2	66.7	+ 4.50
S A Brookshaw	2-4	0-0	0-0	2-3	0-1	50.0	+ 2.50
J A C Edwards	2-5	1-3	0-0	1-1	0-1	40.0	– 1.36
F Jordan	2-5	1-2	1-2	0-1	0-0	40.0	+ 19.00

Leading Jockeys

	Total W–R	Per cent	£1 Level Stake	Best Trainer	W–R	Per cent	£1 Level Stake
P Niven	11-33	33.3	+ 10.80	Mrs M Reveley	5-12	41.7	– 3.70
Richard Guest	8-21	38.1	+ 8.15	J White	5-8	62.5	+ 5.65
A Dobbin	8-24	33.3	+ 14.44	M A Barnes	7-10	70.0	+ 26.53
D J Moffatt	8-31	25.8	– 3.45	D Moffatt	8-27	29.6	+ 0.55
M Dwyer	6-24	25.0	– 1.59	J J Quinn	1-1	100.0	+ 0.67
A Maguire	5-13	38.5	+ 1.91	G B Balding	1-1	100.0	+ 2.00
B Storey	5-29	17.2	+ 15.67	G Richards	2-2	100.0	+ 3.67
W Worthington	5-45	11.1	– 3.75	M C Chapman	5-45	11.1	– 3.75
N Bentley	4-7	57.1	+ 7.80	G M Moore	4-6	66.7	+ 8.80
R Dunwoody	4-18	22.2	+ 3.63	K R Burke	2-3	66.7	+ 14.00
J Railton	3-5	60.0	+ 4.30	J White	2-2	100.0	+ 2.80
D J Burchell	3-7	42.9	+ 14.00	D Burchell	3-7	42.9	+ 14.00

How the Favourites Fared

	W–R	Per cent	£1 Level Stake		W–R	Per cent	£1 Level Stake
Novice Hurdles	19-47	40.4	– 9.81	Novice Chases	14-25	56.0	– 2.96
H'cap Hurdles	17-47	36.2	+ 1.85	H'cap Chases	10-27	37.0	– 7.67
N H Flat	0-0	–	0.00	Hunter Chases	3-5	60.0	+ 5.50
Totals	36-94	38.3	– 7.96	Totals	27-57	47.4	– 5.13
All favourites	63-151	41.7	– 13.09				

LEADING TRAINERS BY MONTH AT CARTMEL 1991-96

August	Total W–R	Nov Hdles	H'cap Hdles	Nov Chses	H'cap Chses	Per cent	£1 Level Stake
J White	7–17	4–7	1–3	2–5	0–2	41.2	+ 2.08
M A Barnes	4–6	1–1	2–4	0–0	1–1	66.7	+ 13.73
D Moffatt	4–8	1–2	3–6	0–0	0–0	50.0	+ 4.35
M C Chapman	4–34	0–10	3–16	0–3	1–5	11.8	– 10.25
G M Moore	3–6	3–5	0–1	0–0	0–0	50.0	+ 10.17

May	Total W–R	Nov Hdles	H'cap Hdles	Nov Chses	H'cap Chses	Per cent	£1 Level Stake
G Richards	10–26	1–3	0–7	3–7	6–9	38.5	– 1.50
Mrs M Reveley	6–16	2–5	2–8	1–2	1–1	37.5	– 1.93
J White	6–27	3–11	1–4	2–9	0–3	22.2	– 8.75
M C Chapman	5–31	3–12	1–13	0–1	1–5	16.1	+ 10.50
Denys Smith	4–12	1–4	3–7	0–1	0–0	33.3	+ 8.96

CATTERICK (Group 3)

Leading Trainers 1991-96

	Total W-R	Nov Hdles	H'cap Hdles	Nov Chses	H'cap Chses	Per cent	£1 Level Stake
Mrs M Reveley	23-106	7-46	7-22	4-13	5-25	21.7	- 10.87
J G FitzGerald	14-65	8-40	2-13	3-7	1-5	21.5	- 5.85
K A Morgan	13-40	3-16	6-14	3-5	1-5	32.5	+ 50.47
M D Hammond	12-100	4-45	1-19	0-6	7-30	12.0	- 38.07
L Lungo	10-39	2-10	5-18	2-4	1-7	25.6	+ 40.50
J H Johnson	10-97	4-46	1-15	1-14	4-22	10.3	- 8.29
J I A Charlton	9-68	1-15	0-6	5-21	3-26	13.2	- 5.30
G M Moore	9-70	6-45	2-17	1-7	0-1	12.9	- 19.27
N Tinkler	8-35	3-15	2-8	2-9	1-3	22.9	- 5.73
P Beaumont	8-73	1-16	3-13	0-16	4-28	11.0	- 28.67
Mrs S J Smith	6-52	1-17	1-11	0-10	4-14	11.5	- 9.25
A Streeter	5-9	1-2	2-5	0-0	2-2	55.6	+ 16.08
J J Quinn	5-19	1-8	1-7	2-2	1-2	26.3	+ 2.33
Mrs V A Aconley	5-40	3-20	0-9	1-6	1-5	12.5	- 22.43
M A Barnes	5-48	0-10	0-6	3-13	2-19	10.4	- 3.00
M W Easterby	5-75	0-39	0-7	1-11	4-18	6.7	- 49.00
C W Thornton	4-11	3-9	1-1	0-1	0-0	36.4	+ 7.16
G Richards	4-54	0-20	0-6	1-13	3-15	7.4	- 43.97
M J Camacho	3-6	3-5	0-0	0-1	0-0	50.0	+ 14.50
S G Norton	3-10	2-9	1-1	0-0	0-0	30.0	+ 12.75

Leading Jockeys

	Total W-R	Per cent	£1 Level Stake	Best Trainer	W-R	Per cent	£1 Level Stake
M Dwyer	19-70	27.1	+ 4.22	J G FitzGerald	10-31	32.3	+ 7.40
P Niven	18-88	20.5	- 2.50	Mrs M Reveley	10-46	21.7	- 0.26
B Storey	15-148	10.1	- 24.72	J I A Charlton	7-55	12.7	- 2.30
A S Smith	14-44	31.8	+ 39.71	K A Morgan	10-27	37.0	+ 38.97
R Garrity	13-93	14.0	- 15.14	M W Easterby	4-25	16.0	- 3.50
A Dobbin	12-80	15.0	- 18.55	M A Barnes	3-16	18.8	+ 1.00
T Reed	12-87	13.8	+ 1.14	L Lungo	8-17	47.1	+ 51.51
L Wyer	10-102	9.8	+ 2.07	Mrs P Sly	1-1	100.0	+ 14.00
J Callaghan	9-81	11.1	- 13.00	G M Moore	4-23	17.4	- 3.50
D Byrne	7-46	15.2	+ 5.80	Mrs V A Aconley	2-3	66.7	+ 3.50
D Bentley	7-79	8.9	- 41.87	M D Hammond	3-19	15.8	- 6.87
R Hodge	6-32	18.8	- 2.05	Mrs M Reveley	4-16	25.0	- 0.05

How the Favourites Fared

	W-R	Per cent	£1 Level Stake		W-R	Per cent	£1 Level Stake
Novice Hurdles	32-92	34.8	- 21.44	Novice Chases	21-48	43.8	- 3.65
H'cap Hurdles	22-70	31.4	- 16.03	H'cap Chases	22-76	28.9	- 22.55
N H Flat	2-15	13.3	- 9.87	Hunter Chases	2-4	50.0	- 0.88
Totals	56-177	31.6	- 47.34	Totals	45-128	35.2	- 27.08
All favourites	101-305	33.1	- 74.42				

LEADING TRAINERS BY MONTH AT CATTERICK 1991-96

October

	Total W–R	Nov Hdles	H'cap Hdles	Nov Chses	H'cap Chses	Per cent	£1 Level Stake
N Tinkler	2–3	0–1	0–0	2–2	0–0	66.7	+ 1.50
Mrs V A Aconley	2–4	2–2	0–0	0–1	0–1	50.0	+ 4.75
Mrs M Reveley	2–7	0–2	0–1	1–2	1–2	28.6	+ 2.12
W Bentley	1–2	1–2	0–0	0–0	0–0	50.0	+ 2.00
G M Moore	1–2	1–1	0–0	0–1	0–0	50.0	– 0.27

November

	Total W–R	Nov Hdles	H'cap Hdles	Nov Chses	H'cap Chses	Per cent	£1 Level Stake
Mrs M Reveley	5–23	2–13	2–3	0–2	1–5	21.7	– 0.75
J H Johnson	4–13	1–7	1–2	1–2	1–2	30.8	+ 9.21
J G FitzGerald	4–15	3–9	0–4	0–1	1–1	26.7	– 0.58
M J Camacho	2–2	2–2	0–0	0–0	0–0	100.0	+ 6.50
A Harrison	2–5	0–1	2–3	0–0	0–1	40.0	+ 18.50

December

	Total W–R	Nov Hdles	H'cap Hdles	Nov Chses	H'cap Chses	Per cent	£1 Level Stake
Mrs M Reveley	6–19	1–7	2–6	1–1	2–5	31.6	– 0.16
L Lungo	5–12	1–1	3–7	1–1	0–3	41.7	+ 9.13
J G FitzGerald	5–18	3–12	0–1	2–2	0–3	27.8	– 0.03
G M Moore	5–19	2–12	2–6	1–1	0–0	26.3	+ 14.50
N Tinkler	3–9	2–3	0–3	0–1	1–2	33.3	– 2.98

January

	Total W–R	Nov Hdles	H'cap Hdles	Nov Chses	H'cap Chses	Per cent	£1 Level Stake
J I A Charlton	4–18	1–5	0–1	3–7	0–5	22.2	+ 25.25
Mrs M Reveley	4–30	1–11	2–8	0–4	1–7	13.3	– 14.50
J H Johnson	4–31	1–12	0–6	0–7	3–6	12.9	+ 10.50
J J Quinn	3–7	1–3	1–3	1–1	0–0	42.9	+ 8.43
K A Morgan	3–9	0–1	3–6	0–0	0–2	33.3	+ 23.00

February

	Total W–R	Nov Hdles	H'cap Hdles	Nov Chses	H'cap Chses	Per cent	£1 Level Stake
K A Morgan	6–18	1–10	3–4	1–2	1–2	33.3	+ 21.25
Mrs M Reveley	4–18	2–6	0–3	2–4	0–5	22.2	+ 6.45
M D Hammond	4–22	1–9	1–5	0–1	2–7	18.2	+ 6.63
Mrs J R Ramsden	2–3	0–0	1–2	1–1	0–0	66.7	+ 14.00
C W Thornton	2–3	1–2	1–1	0–0	0–0	66.7	+ 6.91

March

	Total W–R	Nov Hdles	H'cap Hdles	Nov Chses	H'cap Chses	Per cent	£1 Level Stake
J G FitzGerald	3–9	2–8	1–1	0–0	0–0	33.3	+ 7.50
Mrs M Reveley	2–9	1–7	1–1	0–0	0–1	22.2	– 4.03
T H Caldwell	1–1	0–0	0–0	1–1	0–0	100.0	+ 14.00
M J Camacho	1–1	1–1	0–0	0–0	0–0	100.0	+ 11.00
J M Carr	1–1	1–1	0–0	0–0	0–0	100.0	+ 6.00

CHELTENHAM (Group 1)

Leading Trainers 1991-96

	Total W-R	Nov Hdles	H'cap Hdles	Nov Chses	H'cap Chses	Per cent	£1 Level Stake
D Nicholson	37-195	12-70	3-25	8-38	14-62	19.0	- 8.56
M C Pipe	35-289	17-120	9-71	4-45	5-53	12.1	-102.80
N Twiston-Davies	33-226	12-74	7-47	7-49	7-56	14.6	- 16.28
K C Bailey	23-95	7-21	0-12	10-26	6-36	24.2	- 9.35
J T Gifford	20-135	5-32	1-28	6-28	8-47	14.8	+ 10.52
G B Balding	16-127	4-33	1-32	5-19	6-43	12.6	- 29.35
N J Henderson	16-133	3-40	5-34	4-22	4-37	12.0	- 53.13
Mrs J Pitman	13-98	2-16	2-22	3-24	6-36	13.3	- 6.17
O Sherwood	12-73	5-24	3-16	2-13	2-20	16.4	- 25.53
P J Hobbs	9-101	0-30	3-27	0-8	6-36	8.9	- 41.59
I A Balding	7-25	4-17	0-2	2-4	1-2	28.0	- 0.96
C P E Brooks	7-52	2-16	0-9	0-12	5-15	13.5	+ 4.50
R C Wilkins	6-7	0-0	0-0	6-7	0-0	85.7	+ 14.99
Capt T A Forster	5-27	0-3	1-3	0-6	4-15	18.5	+ 2.08
G Richards	5-36	0-7	1-5	1-10	3-14	13.9	- 21.47
M H Tompkins	5-38	5-28	0-9	0-1	0-0	13.2	- 12.07
R Dickin	5-43	0-11	4-17	0-3	1-12	11.6	- 12.17
F Murphy	5-44	1-8	0-6	1-8	3-22	11.4	+ 4.75
D R C Elsworth	5-68	2-36	1-17	0-6	2-9	7.4	- 47.25
N Tinkler	4-17	2-6	1-8	0-1	1-2	23.5	- 0.83

Leading Jockeys

	Total W-R	Per cent	£1 Level Stake	Best Trainer	W-R	Per cent	£1 Level Stake
R Dunwoody	46-236	19.5	+ 9.24	D Nicholson	16-59	27.1	+ 19.23
A Maguire	26-182	14.3	- 52.83	D Nicholson	10-49	20.4	- 21.12
J Osborne	24-173	13.9	- 64.81	O Sherwood	11-56	19.6	- 13.03
N Williamson	21-87	24.1	+ 33.53	K C Bailey	10-30	33.3	+ 13.65
W Marston	14-99	14.1	- 20.75	Mrs J Pitman	9-27	33.3	+ 30.75
D Bridgwater	14-112	12.5	- 13.87	N Twiston-Davies	7-40	17.5	- 5.81
C Llewellyn	14-129	10.9	- 4.36	N Twiston-Davies	14-93	15.1	+ 31.64
A P McCoy	11-55	20.0	+ 29.00	G B Balding	4-21	19.0	+ 6.00
M A FitzGerald	11-124	8.9	- 14.05	N J Henderson	4-45	8.9	- 33.05
A Tory	10-28	35.7	+ 13.47	K C Bailey	8-16	50.0	+ 10.97
C F Swan	10-71	14.1	+ 17.73	E J O'Grady (Ire)	2-9	22.2	+ 7.50
G Bradley	10-106	9.4	- 26.35	C P E Brooks	5-35	14.3	+ 9.75

How the Favourites Fared

	W-R	Per cent	£1 Level Stake		W-R	Per cent	£1 Level Stake
Novice Hurdles	48-112	42.9	- 3.59	Novice Chases	35-82	42.7	- 1.61
H'cap Hurdles	28-100	28.0	- 11.10	H'cap Chases	46-121	38.0	+ 2.81
N H Flat	2-18	11.1	- 10.75	Hunter Chases	17-35	48.6	+ 4.48
Totals	78-230	33.9	- 25.44	Totals	98-238	41.2	+ 5.68
All favourites	176-468	37.6	- 19.76				

LEADING TRAINERS BY MONTH AT CHELTENHAM 1991-96

September	Total W-R	Nov Hdles	H'cap Hdles	Nov Chses	H'cap Chses	Per cent	£1 Level Stake
M C Pipe	6-11	3-4	0-2	1-2	2-3	54.5	+ 12.26
O Sherwood	3-6	0-1	1-1	0-1	2-3	50.0	+ 6.08
N Twiston-Davies	3-14	1-5	1-3	1-2	0-4	21.4	- 3.94
D H Barons	2-2	0-0	0-0	1-1	1-1	100.0	+ 11.00

October	Total W-R	Nov Hdles	H'cap Hdles	Nov Chses	H'cap Chses	Per cent	£1 Level Stake
K C Bailey	5-15	2-2	0-3	2-3	1-7	33.3	+ 6.40
M C Pipe	5-25	3-10	1-6	0-4	1-5	20.0	- 10.42
N Twiston-Davies	5-27	2-12	0-4	2-4	1-7	18.5	- 11.80
A P Jarvis	4-16	1-7	2-5	1-3	0-1	25.0	+ 12.75

November	Total W-R	Nov Hdles	H'cap Hdles	Nov Chses	H'cap Chses	Per cent	£1 Level Stake
N Twiston-Davies	12-42	5-12	2-10	2-7	3-13	28.6	+ 12.13
D Nicholson	10-35	3-10	0-2	4-8	3-15	28.6	- 5.63
J T Gifford	8-21	1-1	1-4	2-6	4-10	38.1	+ 44.60
K C Bailey	5-13	2-3	0-0	3-5	0-5	38.5	- 1.11

December	Total W-R	Nov Hdles	H'cap Hdles	Nov Chses	H'cap Chses	Per cent	£1 Level Stake
D Nicholson	11-30	5-11	0-2	2-3	4-14	36.7	+ 26.44
M C Pipe	7-25	1-10	4-9	0-1	2-5	28.0	+ 15.60
K C Bailey	6-11	1-2	0-0	2-2	3-7	54.5	+ 9.90
N J Henderson	5-17	1-6	1-4	1-1	2-6	29.4	+ 4.17

January	Total W-R	Nov Hdles	H'cap Hdles	Nov Chses	H'cap Chses	Per cent	£1 Level Stake
D Nicholson	4-21	0-7	1-3	0-4	3-7	19.0	+ 2.25
G B Balding	3-18	2-5	0-2	0-2	1-9	16.7	+ 9.00
M C Pipe	3-19	2-7	1-6	0-2	0-4	15.8	- 1.13
C D Broad	2-3	1-2	1-1	0-0	0-0	66.7	+ 9.00

March	Total W-R	Nov Hdles	H'cap Hdles	Nov Chses	H'cap Chses	Per cent	£1 Level Stake
D Nicholson	8-75	3-30	0-9	2-18	3-18	10.7	- 22.00
M C Pipe	8-159	5-73	1-32	2-28	0-26	5.0	- 95.00
N J Henderson	5-59	1-16	1-15	3-15	0-13	8.5	- 23.75
E J O'Grady (Ire)	4-20	1-3	1-7	2-8	0-2	20.0	+ 15.50

April	Total W-R	Nov Hdles	H'cap Hdles	Nov Chses	H'cap Chses	Per cent	£1 Level Stake
N Twiston-Davies	6-32	1-8	3-12	0-5	2-7	18.8	- 3.50
G B Balding	5-25	1-3	0-15	2-2	2-5	20.0	- 0.58
R C Wilkins	2-2	0-0	0-0	2-2	0-0	100.0	+ 2.35
D R Gandolfo	2-3	0-0	0-1	2-2	0-0	66.7	+ 7.00

May	Total W-R	Nov Hdles	H'cap Hdles	Nov Chses	H'cap Chses	Per cent	£1 Level Stake
R C Wilkins	2-2	0-0	0-0	2-2	0-0	100.0	+ 1.24
I A Balding	1-1	0-0	0-0	1-1	0-0	100.0	+ 2.00
Miss J Eaton	1-1	0-0	0-0	1-1	0-0	100.0	+ 25.00
L P Grassick	1-1	0-0	0-0	1-1	0-0	100.0	+ 6.50

CHEPSTOW (Group 2)

Leading Trainers 1991-96

	Total W-R	Nov Hdles	H'cap Hdles	Nov Chses	H'cap Chses	Per cent	£1 Level Stake
M C Pipe	64-229	25-86	18-72	11-20	10-51	27.9	- 3.54
N Twiston-Davies	21-104	7-39	7-23	3-25	4-17	20.2	+ 18.17
P J Hobbs	19-82	5-27	4-19	2-11	8-25	23.2	+ 40.64
D Nicholson	12-43	6-20	2-11	4-7	0-5	27.9	- 0.82
Mrs J Pitman	10-71	4-20	2-14	3-19	1-18	14.1	+ 29.88
J A B Old	9-35	2-11	1-12	2-4	4-8	25.7	+ 2.37
Capt T A Forster	9-62	0-23	4-11	3-12	2-16	14.5	- 10.16
J T Gifford	9-79	1-23	0-14	2-14	6-28	11.4	- 35.58
J A C Edwards	7-29	1-13	1-4	1-4	4-8	24.1	+ 12.25
N J Henderson	7-46	2-18	2-10	2-8	1-10	15.2	- 11.33
G B Balding	7-65	1-14	0-21	3-11	3-19	10.8	- 18.50
Mrs J G Retter	6-28	0-6	3-13	0-2	3-7	21.4	- 10.28
R Rowe	6-28	1-6	3-9	0-5	2-8	21.4	+ 9.75
P F Nicholls	6-51	4-12	0-10	1-10	1-19	11.8	- 20.79
D Burchell	5-31	4-13	0-7	0-2	1-9	16.1	- 7.88
C P E Brooks	5-36	1-12	1-7	1-8	2-9	13.9	- 15.67
J White	4-18	1-7	1-7	2-3	0-1	22.2	- 4.25
D R C Elsworth	4-19	3-8	1-4	0-3	0-4	21.1	+ 0.63
J S King	4-24	1-8	2-8	0-4	1-4	16.7	+ 2.50
R H Buckler	4-27	2-13	1-8	1-3	0-3	14.8	+ 47.25

Leading Jockeys

	Total W-R	Per cent	£1 Level Stake	Best Trainer	W-R	Per cent	£1 Level Stake
R Dunwoody	32-125	25.6	- 22.96	M C Pipe	13-45	28.9	- 12.81
D Bridgwater	17-76	22.4	+ 8.48	M C Pipe	9-23	39.1	+ 9.23
C Llewellyn	17-100	17.0	- 17.24	N Twiston-Davies	12-51	23.5	+ 14.13
A Maguire	15-83	18.1	- 8.13	D Nicholson	4-12	33.3	+ 5.70
A P McCoy	12-52	23.1	- 5.57	P F Nicholls	4-12	33.3	+ 8.38
M A FitzGerald	11-72	15.3	- 16.38	Mrs J G Retter	3-9	33.3	- 2.21
G Bradley	9-42	21.4	+ 16.58	C P E Brooks	5-21	23.8	- 0.67
J Lower	8-40	20.0	+ 6.04	M C Pipe	8-38	21.1	+ 8.04
W Marston	8-51	15.7	+ 20.92	Mrs J Pitman	2-9	22.2	+ 5.50
P Hide	6-46	13.0	- 11.25	J T Gifford	4-36	11.1	- 10.75
N Williamson	5-25	20.0	- 3.25	C L Popham	1-1	100.0	+ 2.75
T Grantham	5-28	17.9	- 5.88	J A B Old	5-22	22.7	+ 0.12

How the Favourites Fared

	W-R	Per cent	£1 Level Stake		W-R	Per cent	£1 Level Stake
Novice Hurdles	47-98	48.0	+ 1.38	Novice Chases	27-54	50.0	+ 4.07
H'cap Hurdles	33-91	36.3	- 9.65	H'cap Chases	24-79	30.4	- 27.66
N H Flat	6-13	46.2	+ 0.26	Hunter Chases	6-14	42.9	+ 0.35
Totals	86-202	42.6	- 8.01	Totals	57-147	38.8	- 23.24
All favourites	143-349	41.0	- 31.25				

LEADING TRAINERS BY MONTH AT CHEPSTOW 1991-96

June

	Total W-R	Nov Hdles	H'cap Hdles	Nov Chses	H'cap Chses	Per cent	£1 Level Stake
J Etherington	1-1	1-1	0-0	0-0	0-0	100.0	+ 3.50
T G Mills	1-1	1-1	0-0	0-0	0-0	100.0	+ 6.50

September

	Total W-R	Nov Hdles	H'cap Hdles	Nov Chses	H'cap Chses	Per cent	£1 Level Stake
P F Nicholls	2-4	1-1	0-1	0-1	1-1	50.0	+ 3.88
A P Jarvis	1-1	0-0	1-1	0-0	0-0	100.0	+ 1.50
Mrs S J Smith	1-1	0-0	1-1	0-0	0-0	100.0	+ 3.00

October

	Total W-R	Nov Hdles	H'cap Hdles	Nov Chses	H'cap Chses	Per cent	£1 Level Stake
P J Hobbs	4-9	1-1	1-4	1-2	1-2	44.4	+ 10.17
M C Pipe	4-19	1-2	3-17	0-0	0-0	21.1	- 2.08
N Twiston-Davies	3-13	1-2	2-4	0-4	0-3	23.1	- 6.96

November

	Total W-R	Nov Hdles	H'cap Hdles	Nov Chses	H'cap Chses	Per cent	£1 Level Stake
M C Pipe	6-24	1-5	3-10	1-3	1-6	25.0	+ 0.58
D Nicholson	5-16	1-5	2-8	2-3	0-0	31.3	+ 7.58
N Twiston-Davies	4-20	2-10	1-6	1-4	0-0	20.0	- 1.75

December

	Total W-R	Nov Hdles	H'cap Hdles	Nov Chses	H'cap Chses	Per cent	£1 Level Stake
M C Pipe	15-47	5-17	2-6	3-5	5-19	31.9	+ 4.42
N Twiston-Davies	5-15	1-5	0-1	1-4	3-5	33.3	+ 18.63
J A C Edwards	2-4	0-1	0-0	0-1	2-2	50.0	+ 16.00

January

	Total W-R	Nov Hdles	H'cap Hdles	Nov Chses	H'cap Chses	Per cent	£1 Level Stake
M C Pipe	5-19	3-9	0-3	2-3	0-4	26.3	- 9.21
Mrs R Brackenbury	1-1	0-0	0-0	0-0	1-1	100.0	+ 6.00
C D Broad	1-1	0-0	0-0	1-1	0-0	100.0	+ 0.67

February

	Total W-R	Nov Hdles	H'cap Hdles	Nov Chses	H'cap Chses	Per cent	£1 Level Stake
J A B Old	3-8	1-1	0-4	1-1	1-2	37.5	+ 3.88
P J Hobbs	3-12	0-3	1-2	1-1	1-6	25.0	+ 12.00
J T Gifford	3-13	0-3	0-3	1-2	2-5	23.1	+ 4.25

March

	Total W-R	Nov Hdles	H'cap Hdles	Nov Chses	H'cap Chses	Per cent	£1 Level Stake
M C Pipe	9-36	5-17	2-13	1-2	1-4	25.0	- 10.36
D Nicholson	4-8	4-6	0-1	0-0	0-1	50.0	+ 3.75
P J Hobbs	4-9	1-3	0-2	0-1	3-3	44.4	+ 6.68

April

	Total W-R	Nov Hdles	H'cap Hdles	Nov Chses	H'cap Chses	Per cent	£1 Level Stake
M C Pipe	10-28	5-18	2-6	1-1	2-3	35.7	+ 22.22
N Twiston-Davies	3-7	1-3	1-2	0-0	1-2	42.9	+ 20.50
D R C Elsworth	2-2	2-2	0-0	0-0	0-0	100.0	+ 7.75

May

	Total W-R	Nov Hdles	H'cap Hdles	Nov Chses	H'cap Chses	Per cent	£1 Level Stake
M C Pipe	12-28	5-10	5-11	1-1	1-6	42.9	+ 10.65
N Twiston-Davies	3-8	1-2	1-2	1-4	0-0	37.5	+ 3.25
J S King	2-5	1-2	1-3	0-0	0-0	40.0	+ 6.50

DONCASTER (Group 1)

Leading Trainers 1991-96

	Total W-R	Nov Hdles	H'cap Hdles	Nov Chses	H'cap Chses	Per cent	£1 Level Stake
Mrs M Reveley	18-78	9-36	2-19	3-7	4-16	23.1	- 0.90
J G FitzGerald	10-66	5-30	1-16	1-7	3-13	15.2	- 28.78
D Nicholson	9-41	2-22	0-4	4-5	3-10	22.0	- 8.83
M C Pipe	7-17	3-6	2-3	0-0	2-8	41.2	+ 26.35
G Richards	7-38	2-10	2-10	2-8	1-10	18.4	+ 2.23
M D Hammond	7-44	3-19	1-10	1-3	2-12	15.9	- 9.88
N Twiston-Davies	6-16	3-8	0-1	2-2	1-5	37.5	+ 19.83
O Sherwood	6-36	3-14	0-3	3-9	0-10	16.7	- 14.81
N Tinkler	6-37	1-18	1-9	0-1	4-9	16.2	- 9.27
Mrs J R Ramsden	4-11	1-3	3-8	0-0	0-0	36.4	+ 9.63
P Cheesbrough	4-15	0-4	0-1	0-1	4-9	26.7	+ 6.80
C P E Brooks	4-16	1-10	0-0	2-3	1-3	25.0	+ 16.00
C W Thornton	3-7	3-4	0-1	0-1	0-1	42.9	+ 46.00
J Hanson	3-9	3-5	0-2	0-2	0-0	33.3	+ 6.25
N J Henderson	3-10	0-4	2-3	0-0	1-3	30.0	+ 4.33
R Lee	3-12	0-2	1-2	0-2	2-6	25.0	+ 2.75
O Brennan	3-42	2-24	1-8	0-3	0-7	7.1	- 12.00
P R Webber	2-2	2-2	0-0	0-0	0-0	100.0	+ 16.00
Mrs J Cecil	2-3	0-0	2-3	0-0	0-0	66.7	+ 9.00
P G Murphy	2-3	1-1	0-1	0-0	1-1	66.7	+ 16.00

Leading Jockeys

	Total W-R	Per cent	£1 Level Stake	Best Trainer	W-R	Per cent	£1 Level Stake
P Niven	17-62	27.4	+ 13.67	Mrs M Reveley	11-38	28.9	+ 12.32
L Wyer	11-59	18.6	- 22.36	Mrs M Reveley	3-6	50.0	+ 1.13
M Dwyer	9-59	15.3	- 21.02	J G FitzGerald	3-29	10.3	- 20.22
R Dunwoody	5-14	35.7	+ 8.55	D Nicholson	4-7	57.1	+ 12.05
J R Kavanagh	5-15	33.3	+ 13.33	N J Henderson	3-5	60.0	+ 9.33
A Maguire	5-17	29.4	+ 4.21	D Nicholson	2-5	40.0	+ 0.08
P Carberry	4-11	36.4	+ 16.88	G Richards	2-3	66.7	+ 12.88
G Bradley	4-20	20.0	- 10.22	O Sherwood	1-1	100.0	+ 0.25
W Marston	4-23	17.4	+ 24.30	D Nicholson	2-7	28.6	- 1.70
Mr M Rimell	3-7	42.9	+ 17.00	N Twiston-Davies	3-4	75.0	+ 20.00
C Llewellyn	3-8	37.5	+ 2.08	N A Gaselee	1-1	100.0	+ 4.00
W J Dwan	3-9	33.3	+ 4.00	J G FitzGerald	3-7	42.9	+ 6.00

How the Favourites Fared

	W-R	Per cent	£1 Level Stake		W-R	Per cent	£1 Level Stake
Novice Hurdles	21-49	42.9	- 5.28	Novice Chases	21-33	63.6	+ 7.35
H'cap Hurdles	17-37	45.9	+ 14.89	H'cap Chases	15-44	34.1	- 5.61
N H Flat	6-26	23.1	- 9.48	Hunter Chases	2-7	28.6	- 3.87
Totals	44-112	39.3	+ 0.13	Totals	38-84	45.2	- 2.13
All favourites	82-196	41.8	- 2.00				

LEADING TRAINERS BY MONTH AT DONCASTER 1991-96

December	Total W-R	Nov Hdles	H'cap Hdles	Nov Chses	H'cap Chses	Per cent	£1 Level Stake
Mrs M Reveley	9-33	5-15	1-8	1-4	2-6	27.3	- 4.18
J G FitzGerald	5-26	1-12	1-5	1-4	2-5	19.2	- 6.83
D Nicholson	4-14	1-8	0-1	2-3	1-2	28.6	- 4.70
M C Pipe	3-6	1-3	2-2	0-0	0-1	50.0	+ 15.00
G Richards	3-17	1-5	0-6	2-5	0-1	17.6	- 1.63

January	Total W-R	Nov Hdles	H'cap Hdles	Nov Chses	H'cap Chses	Per cent	£1 Level Stake
Mrs M Reveley	4-17	1-8	0-3	2-3	1-3	23.5	- 1.16
D Nicholson	3-10	1-4	0-0	1-1	1-5	30.0	+ 7.80
N Tinkler	2-4	1-3	0-0	0-0	1-1	50.0	+ 3.73
O Sherwood	2-11	2-5	0-0	0-2	0-4	18.2	+ 1.25
J F Bottomley	1-1	1-1	0-0	0-0	0-0	100.0	+ 4.00

February	Total W-R	Nov Hdles	H'cap Hdles	Nov Chses	H'cap Chses	Per cent	£1 Level Stake
C P E Brooks	3-6	1-4	0-0	2-2	0-0	50.0	+ 22.25
N J Henderson	2-2	0-0	2-2	0-0	0-0	100.0	+ 6.33
Miss L A Perratt	2-2	1-1	1-1	0-0	0-0	100.0	+ 3.33
P G Murphy	2-3	1-1	0-1	0-0	1-1	66.7	+ 16.00
R Lee	2-4	0-0	1-1	0-0	1-3	50.0	+ 4.75

March	Total W-R	Nov Hdles	H'cap Hdles	Nov Chses	H'cap Chses	Per cent	£1 Level Stake
Mrs M Reveley	5-17	3-7	1-5	0-0	1-5	29.4	+ 15.44
M D Hammond	4-19	2-7	0-3	1-2	1-7	21.1	+ 0.38
M C Pipe	3-5	2-3	0-0	0-0	1-2	60.0	+ 13.60
N Twiston-Davies	3-8	1-3	0-1	2-2	0-2	37.5	+ 4.83
O Sherwood	3-10	1-3	0-2	2-2	0-3	30.0	- 4.06

EXETER (Group 4)

Leading Trainers 1991-96

	Total W-R	Nov Hdles	H'cap Hdles	Nov Chses	H'cap Chses	Per cent	£1 Level Stake
M C Pipe	92-297	53-137	19-92	9-35	11-33	31.0	+ 10.44
Miss H C Knight	27-81	12-31	10-28	2-11	3-11	33.3	+ 56.98
P J Hobbs	25-137	5-41	6-45	2-23	12-28	18.2	- 19.08
Mrs J G Retter	14-90	4-26	5-41	2-9	3-14	15.6	+ 25.46
G B Balding	14-94	5-31	4-28	2-16	3-19	14.9	- 20.23
G F Edwards	10-43	2-10	5-22	0-3	3-8	23.3	+ 33.60
I A Balding	9-17	7-11	2-4	0-1	0-1	52.9	+ 3.66
R J Hodges	9-120	2-36	5-39	1-23	1-22	7.5	- 67.95
K C Bailey	8-44	4-16	1-8	2-10	1-10	18.2	- 11.38
R H Alner	8-55	0-14	2-8	3-13	3-20	14.5	- 13.15
D R C Elsworth	7-24	1-7	2-9	3-5	1-3	29.2	+ 2.57
N J Henderson	7-25	2-7	0-4	3-7	2-7	28.0	- 8.20
A J K Dunn	7-27	1-6	2-8	1-4	3-9	25.9	- 4.23
J White	7-34	3-21	1-5	3-6	0-2	20.6	+ 1.40
R G Frost	7-125	1-48	1-23	2-36	3-18	5.6	- 96.34
O Sherwood	6-21	4-8	1-4	0-3	1-6	28.6	+ 11.88
C James	6-25	1-8	4-14	1-2	0-1	24.0	+ 3.83
Mrs A Knight	6-82	0-46	6-31	0-5	0-0	7.3	- 53.62
Mrs P N Dutfield	5-24	0-7	1-5	1-5	3-7	20.8	- 3.05
B R Millman	5-37	1-12	2-13	2-4	0-8	13.5	- 0.13

Leading Jockeys

	Total W-R	Per cent	£1 Level Stake	Best Trainer	W-R	Per cent	£1 Level Stake
R Dunwoody	32-141	22.7	- 23.42	M C Pipe	8-57	14.0	- 23.48
J Osborne	21-70	30.0	- 0.41	Miss H C Knight	11-20	55.0	+ 27.16
M A FitzGerald	20-119	16.8	+ 21.26	Mrs J G Retter	9-32	28.1	+ 38.13
D Bridgwater	17-88	19.3	- 1.85	M C Pipe	13-40	32.5	+ 15.15
J Frost	15-143	10.5	- 90.07	R G Frost	7-98	7.1	- 69.34
J Lower	12-39	30.8	+ 4.17	M C Pipe	12-39	30.8	+ 4.17
P Holley	11-63	17.5	- 14.90	D R C Elsworth	5-17	29.4	+ 4.65
A P McCoy	11-64	17.2	+ 14.83	G B Balding	4-18	22.2	+ 4.58
L Harvey	9-64	14.1	+ 10.41	J Akehurst	2-9	22.2	+ 10.00
M Hourigan	7-32	21.9	+ 9.74	P J Hobbs	3-7	42.9	+ 5.24
M Foster	7-40	17.5	- 15.84	M C Pipe	7-30	23.3	- 5.84
Mr J Culloty	7-55	12.7	- 14.52	Miss H C Knight	4-16	25.0	- 3.77

How the Favourites Fared

	W-R	Per cent	£1 Level Stake		W-R	Per cent	£1 Level Stake
Novice Hurdles	73-154	47.4	- 12.30	Novice Chases	34-71	47.9	- 3.01
H'cap Hurdles	43-136	31.6	- 20.64	H'cap Chases	30-74	40.5	+ 1.54
N H Flat	6-13	46.2	+ 2.57	Hunter Chases	3-8	37.5	- 0.32
Totals	122-303	40.3	- 30.37	Totals	67-153	43.8	- 1.79
All favourites	189-456	41.4	- 32.16				

LEADING TRAINERS BY MONTH AT EXETER 1991-96

August	Total W-R	Nov Hdles	H'cap Hdles	Nov Chses	H'cap Chses	Per cent	£1 Level Stake
M C Pipe	14-37	7-13	2-11	3-8	2-5	37.8	+ 0.04
R J Hodges	5-13	1-4	2-4	1-4	1-1	38.5	+ 5.05
J White	3-11	1-6	0-2	2-2	0-1	27.3	− 3.10

September	Total W-R	Nov Hdles	H'cap Hdles	Nov Chses	H'cap Chses	Per cent	£1 Level Stake
M C Pipe	15-45	9-25	4-11	0-3	2-6	33.3	− 6.99
P J Hobbs	5-20	3-7	2-6	0-2	0-5	25.0	+ 6.71
K C Bailey	4-5	2-2	1-1	0-1	1-1	80.0	+ 13.05

October	Total W-R	Nov Hdles	H'cap Hdles	Nov Chses	H'cap Chses	Per cent	£1 Level Stake
M C Pipe	15-42	10-21	2-14	1-4	2-3	35.7	+ 0.52
Miss H C Knight	6-13	1-4	4-7	1-1	0-1	46.2	+ 6.04
P J Hobbs	6-19	0-2	0-6	1-6	5-5	31.6	+ 0.81

November	Total W-R	Nov Hdles	H'cap Hdles	Nov Chses	H'cap Chses	Per cent	£1 Level Stake
M C Pipe	8-17	5-10	2-4	1-1	0-2	47.1	+ 11.49
G B Balding	3-14	0-4	0-5	1-2	2-3	21.4	− 4.13
C J Mann	2-2	2-2	0-0	0-0	0-0	100.0	+ 12.00

December	Total W-R	Nov Hdles	H'cap Hdles	Nov Chses	H'cap Chses	Per cent	£1 Level Stake
Miss H C Knight	8-20	2-3	4-9	0-4	2-4	40.0	+ 45.91
D R C Elsworth	5-11	0-2	2-3	3-4	0-2	45.5	+ 7.90
M C Pipe	5-33	2-12	1-13	0-3	2-5	15.2	− 6.42

January	Total W-R	Nov Hdles	H'cap Hdles	Nov Chses	H'cap Chses	Per cent	£1 Level Stake
M C Pipe	11-25	5-10	4-11	2-4	0-0	44.0	+ 11.99
Mrs J G Retter	4-20	2-6	1-10	0-2	1-2	20.0	+ 18.38
R H Alner	2-8	0-1	1-2	0-4	1-1	25.0	+ 6.50

March	Total W-R	Nov Hdles	H'cap Hdles	Nov Chses	H'cap Chses	Per cent	£1 Level Stake
M C Pipe	8-28	5-10	1-9	0-1	2-8	28.6	+ 12.41
P J Hobbs	3-12	0-4	1-3	0-0	2-5	25.0	+ 21.00
Miss H C Knight	2-7	0-1	1-2	0-0	1-4	28.6	+ 0.75

April	Total W-R	Nov Hdles	H'cap Hdles	Nov Chses	H'cap Chses	Per cent	£1 Level Stake
Miss H C Knight	4-14	4-7	0-3	0-2	0-2	28.6	+ 0.25
P J Hobbs	4-18	0-7	1-6	0-1	3-4	22.2	− 7.00
M C Pipe	3-23	3-13	0-7	0-2	0-1	13.0	− 13.63

May	Total W-R	Nov Hdles	H'cap Hdles	Nov Chses	H'cap Chses	Per cent	£1 Level Stake
M C Pipe	13-48	7-23	3-13	2-9	1-3	27.1	+ 0.02
Miss H C Knight	6-21	5-14	0-5	1-2	0-0	28.6	+ 0.03
J White	3-8	1-3	1-3	1-2	0-0	37.5	+ 13.50

FAKENHAM (Group 4)

Leading Trainers 1991-96

	Total W-R	Nov Hdles	H'cap Hdles	Nov Chses	H'cap Chses	Per cent	£1 Level Stake
O Brennan	12-33	0-2	9-20	2-5	1-6	36.4	+ 27.43
J R Jenkins	12-50	4-12	7-28	1-7	0-3	24.0	+ 20.83
Miss C Saunders	6-7	0-0	0-0	6-7	0-0	85.7	+ 9.51
K C Bailey	6-26	1-4	0-5	3-9	2-8	23.1	- 7.89
D R Gandolfo	5-9	0-1	0-1	3-4	2-3	55.6	+ 8.60
O Sherwood	5-12	1-2	0-3	3-4	1-3	41.7	+ 6.74
Mrs D Haine	5-26	0-4	0-7	3-5	2-10	19.2	+ 7.91
M H Tompkins	5-28	1-6	4-19	0-2	0-1	17.9	- 2.80
J R Upson	4-10	0-3	2-2	1-2	1-3	40.0	+ 9.00
G C Bravery	4-16	0-3	2-8	0-0	2-5	25.0	- 0.50
D Nicholson	3-8	2-3	0-1	1-2	0-2	37.5	- 0.43
Mrs N Macauley	3-14	0-3	3-10	0-0	0-1	21.4	+ 10.25
M J Ryan	3-20	1-6	1-8	0-3	1-3	15.0	+ 1.50
K A Morgan	3-29	1-4	2-20	0-2	0-3	10.3	- 15.25
J M Turner	3-30	0-0	0-0	3-30	0-0	10.0	- 22.08
J W Whyte	3-36	0-1	3-19	0-11	0-5	8.3	- 18.25
C D Dawson	2-2	0-0	0-0	2-2	0-0	100.0	+ 16.00
P C Haslam	2-4	1-2	1-1	0-0	0-1	50.0	+ 4.00
P A Kelleway	2-4	2-2	0-2	0-0	0-0	50.0	+ 12.50
J T Gifford	2-5	0-0	0-0	1-3	1-2	40.0	- 0.51

Leading Jockeys

	Total W-R	Per cent	£1 Level Stake	Best Trainer	W-R	Per cent	£1 Level Stake
Martin Brennan	12-44	27.3	+ 16.43	O Brennan	12-32	37.5	+ 28.43
Mr M Armytage	6-12	50.0	+ 4.65	G M McCourt	1-1	100.0	+ 3.00
A Maguire	6-26	23.1	+ 23.88	D Nicholson	2-3	66.7	+ 2.38
J Ryan	4-38	10.5	- 8.50	M J Ryan	3-16	18.8	+ 5.50
J Osborne	3-7	42.9	+ 3.45	O Sherwood	2-3	66.7	+ 3.12
Mrs L Gibbon	3-10	30.0	+ 28.50	M H Tompkins	2-2	100.0	+ 10.50
T Jenks	3-10	30.0	- 1.50	W J Haggas	1-1	100.0	+ 1.50
J A McCarthy	3-11	27.3	+ 7.00	O Sherwood	2-3	66.7	+ 7.00
R Dunwoody	3-13	23.1	- 2.17	Mrs N Macauley	1-1	100.0	+ 2.25
M Ahern	3-13	23.1	- 0.25	J R Jenkins	3-8	37.5	+ 4.75
Richard Davis	3-14	21.4	- 1.37	Mrs L C Jewell	1-2	50.0	+ 0.88
R Farrant	3-17	17.6	- 2.70	L Wordingham	2-7	28.6	+ 5.50

How the Favourites Fared

	W-R	Per cent	£1 Level Stake		W-R	Per cent	£1 Level Stake
Novice Hurdles	8-27	29.6	- 8.35	Novice Chases	13-23	56.5	+ 0.62
H'cap Hurdles	24-67	35.8	- 0.81	H'cap Chases	9-33	27.3	- 9.06
N H Flat	0-0	-	0.00	Hunter Chases	15-30	50.0	+ 4.56
Totals	32-94	34.0	- 9.16	Totals	37-86	43.0	- 3.88
All favourites	69-180	38.3	- 13.04				

LEADING TRAINERS BY MONTH AT FAKENHAM 1991-96

October

	Total W-R	Nov Hdles	H'cap Hdles	Nov Chses	H'cap Chses	Per cent	£1 Level Stake
K C Bailey	3-5	1-1	0-0	0-1	2-3	60.0	+ 2.20
P A Kelleway	2-2	2-2	0-0	0-0	0-0	100.0	+ 14.50
O Sherwood	2-3	0-0	0-0	1-2	1-1	66.7	+ 3.12
M H Tompkins	2-4	1-2	1-2	0-0	0-0	50.0	+ 6.50
Mrs D Haine	2-6	0-1	0-1	1-1	1-3	33.3	+ 2.91

December

	Total W-R	Nov Hdles	H'cap Hdles	Nov Chses	H'cap Chses	Per cent	£1 Level Stake
J R Jenkins	4-7	2-3	2-4	0-0	0-0	57.1	+ 16.25
J T Gifford	2-3	0-0	0-0	1-1	1-2	66.7	+ 1.49
O Brennan	2-8	0-0	1-5	1-1	0-2	25.0	- 4.10
M Bradstock	1-1	0-0	1-1	0-0	0-0	100.0	+ 6.00
D R Gandolfo	1-1	0-0	0-0	1-1	0-0	100.0	+ 0.80

February

	Total W-R	Nov Hdles	H'cap Hdles	Nov Chses	H'cap Chses	Per cent	£1 Level Stake
D R Gandolfo	3-4	0-1	0-0	2-2	1-1	75.0	+ 4.80
Miss C Saunders	3-4	0-0	0-0	3-4	0-0	75.0	+ 4.73
D Nicholson	2-6	1-2	0-1	1-2	0-1	33.3	- 0.63
O Brennan	2-8	0-0	2-5	0-3	0-0	25.0	+ 1.83
N A Callaghan	1-1	1-1	0-0	0-0	0-0	100.0	+ 2.25

March

	Total W-R	Nov Hdles	H'cap Hdles	Nov Chses	H'cap Chses	Per cent	£1 Level Stake
O Brennan	3-6	0-0	2-3	0-0	1-3	50.0	+ 3.95
J R Jenkins	3-9	2-2	1-3	0-3	0-1	33.3	+ 13.25
S W Campion	2-2	0-0	1-1	0-0	1-1	100.0	+ 16.50
Miss C Saunders	2-2	0-0	0-0	2-2	0-0	100.0	+ 1.79
K A Morgan	2-7	0-0	2-5	0-0	0-2	28.6	+ 1.75

April

	Total W-R	Nov Hdles	H'cap Hdles	Nov Chses	H'cap Chses	Per cent	£1 Level Stake
G C Bravery	4-8	0-0	2-6	0-0	2-2	50.0	+ 7.50
J R Upson	3-5	0-0	1-1	1-2	1-2	60.0	+ 8.00
J R Jenkins	3-6	0-0	3-5	0-0	0-1	50.0	+ 8.00
M C Banks	1-1	0-0	1-1	0-0	0-0	100.0	+ 6.00
O Brennan	1-1	0-0	1-1	0-0	0-0	100.0	+ 2.00

May

	Total W-R	Nov Hdles	H'cap Hdles	Nov Chses	H'cap Chses	Per cent	£1 Level Stake
M H Tompkins	2-2	0-0	2-2	0-0	0-0	100.0	+ 10.50
O Brennan	2-3	0-1	2-2	0-0	0-0	66.7	+ 9.75
M C Pipe	2-4	0-1	1-2	1-1	0-0	50.0	- 0.72
K C Bailey	2-5	0-1	0-1	2-2	0-1	40.0	- 2.09
J M Turner	2-10	0-0	0-0	2-10	0-0	20.0	- 5.58

FOLKESTONE (Group 3)

Leading Trainers 1991-96

	Total W-R	Nov Hdles	H'cap Hdles	Nov Chses	H'cap Chses	Per cent	£1 Level Stake
J T Gifford	16-74	4-27	0-4	6-18	6-25	21.6	+ 8.36
R Rowe	10-60	3-13	4-14	2-13	1-20	16.7	- 4.68
D M Grissell	10-64	3-27	2-14	2-6	3-17	15.6	+ 5.58
M C Pipe	9-34	4-20	3-8	1-2	1-4	26.5	- 6.11
N J Henderson	7-19	1-5	2-5	3-6	1-3	36.8	+ 2.50
Capt T A Forster	5-16	2-5	0-0	1-4	2-7	31.3	+ 33.88
Miss H C Knight	5-18	0-8	1-2	1-3	3-5	27.8	- 0.97
R H Alner	5-19	0-4	0-0	1-3	4-12	26.3	+ 3.25
Mrs D Haine	5-25	2-13	0-2	0-6	3-4	20.0	- 13.19
A P Jones	4-12	1-3	1-4	1-2	1-3	33.3	+ 48.75
S Dow	4-20	2-9	1-9	1-1	0-1	20.0	- 5.29
R Akehurst	4-24	3-17	0-5	1-2	0-0	16.7	- 6.50
Andrew Turnell	3-9	1-2	0-1	1-4	1-2	33.3	+ 1.73
J R Upson	3-10	1-5	0-2	1-2	1-1	30.0	+ 23.50
C P E Brooks	3-14	1-6	1-2	0-4	1-2	21.4	+ 2.00
T Thomson Jones	3-14	0-2	1-1	0-2	2-9	21.4	- 3.53
D A Wilson	3-16	0-3	3-13	0-0	0-0	18.8	+ 16.00
N A Gaselee	3-19	1-9	0-1	2-7	0-2	15.8	+ 7.62
R Curtis	3-24	2-5	0-8	0-2	1-9	12.5	+ 6.75
J White	3-32	2-16	0-8	0-2	1-6	9.4	- 19.58

Leading Jockeys

	Total W-R	Per cent	£1 Level Stake	Best Trainer	W-R	Per cent	£1 Level Stake
A Maguire	12-69	17.4	- 19.99	D A Wilson	2-5	40.0	+ 6.00
R Dunwoody	10-52	19.2	- 12.73	N J Henderson	2-7	28.6	- 3.71
J Osborne	7-58	12.1	- 36.43	Miss H C Knight	4-9	44.4	+ 6.50
M Richards	6-30	20.0	+ 5.73	W R Muir	2-3	66.7	+ 12.50
P Hide	6-34	17.6	- 4.70	J T Gifford	6-30	20.0	- 0.70
E Murphy	5-19	26.3	+ 4.08	B J Curley	2-3	66.7	+ 4.50
S McNeill	5-23	21.7	+ 2.70	J T Gifford	2-2	100.0	+ 2.70
D Bridgwater	5-23	21.7	- 11.17	M C Pipe	2-6	33.3	- 2.18
M A FitzGerald	5-28	17.9	- 9.78	N J Henderson	5-11	45.5	+ 7.22
A P McCoy	4-27	14.8	- 1.50	J White	1-1	100.0	+ 6.50
B Powell	4-37	10.8	+ 0.25	R Akehurst	1-1	100.0	+ 1.00
Mr C Newport	3-9	33.3	+ 2.25	Mrs D M Grissell	1-2	50.0	+ 1.50

How the Favourites Fared

	W-R	Per cent	£1 Level Stake		W-R	Per cent	£1 Level Stake
Novice Hurdles	19-51	37.3	- 10.21	Novice Chases	17-30	56.7	+ 4.46
H'cap Hurdles	14-44	31.8	- 10.06	H'cap Chases	24-52	46.2	+ 9.46
N H Flat	4-7	57.1	+ 1.71	Hunter Chases	15-34	44.1	- 0.71
Totals	37-102	36.3	- 18.56	Totals	56-116	48.3	+ 13.21
All favourites	93-218	42.7	- 5.35				

LEADING TRAINERS BY MONTH AT FOLKESTONE 1991-96

November

	Total W-R	Nov Hdles	H'cap Hdles	Nov Chses	H'cap Chses	Per cent	£1 Level Stake
D M Grissell	3-10	2-5	0-0	0-0	1-5	30.0	+ 29.25
G A Hubbard	2-2	1-1	1-1	0-0	0-0	100.0	+ 14.75
R H Alner	2-3	0-1	0-0	0-0	2-2	66.7	+ 4.38
Mrs D Haine	2-9	2-7	0-1	0-1	0-0	22.2	- 5.29
J T Gifford	2-13	0-4	0-0	2-3	0-6	15.4	- 9.61

December

	Total W-R	Nov Hdles	H'cap Hdles	Nov Chses	H'cap Chses	Per cent	£1 Level Stake
M C Pipe	5-9	2-6	2-2	0-0	1-1	55.6	+ 4.27
J R Upson	3-5	1-3	0-0	1-1	1-1	60.0	+ 28.50
R Akehurst	3-9	2-6	0-2	1-1	0-0	33.3	+ 6.00
J T Gifford	3-15	0-4	0-0	2-6	1-5	20.0	- 3.63
R Rowe	3-15	0-3	1-4	1-3	1-5	20.0	+ 4.00

January

	Total W-R	Nov Hdles	H'cap Hdles	Nov Chses	H'cap Chses	Per cent	£1 Level Stake
M C Pipe	3-8	2-5	0-2	1-1	0-0	37.5	+ 4.12
N J Henderson	2-4	0-1	1-2	1-1	0-0	50.0	+ 2.17
J T Gifford	2-11	0-3	0-1	1-6	1-1	18.2	+ 17.00
R Rowe	2-12	0-0	2-6	0-3	0-3	16.7	- 0.50
T Casey	1-1	0-0	1-1	0-0	0-0	100.0	+ 2.50

February

	Total W-R	Nov Hdles	H'cap Hdles	Nov Chses	H'cap Chses	Per cent	£1 Level Stake
J T Gifford	5-19	1-7	0-1	1-2	3-9	26.3	+ 9.63
D M Grissell	4-14	1-4	1-3	2-2	0-5	28.6	- 0.42
R Rowe	3-19	2-4	1-4	0-3	0-8	15.8	- 1.63
P Mitchell	2-3	0-1	2-2	0-0	0-0	66.7	+ 3.70
Capt T A Forster	2-4	1-1	0-0	0-1	1-2	50.0	+ 1.88

March

	Total W-R	Nov Hdles	H'cap Hdles	Nov Chses	H'cap Chses	Per cent	£1 Level Stake
J T Gifford	4-12	3-7	0-0	0-1	1-4	33.3	- 1.02
B J Curley	2-2	0-0	2-2	0-0	0-0	100.0	+ 5.50
C P E Brooks	2-3	1-1	0-0	0-1	1-1	66.7	+ 5.50
N J Henderson	2-3	1-1	0-0	1-2	0-0	66.7	+ 0.72
N A Gaselee	2-5	1-3	0-0	1-2	0-0	40.0	+ 4.62

April

	Total W-R	Nov Hdles	H'cap Hdles	Nov Chses	H'cap Chses	Per cent	£1 Level Stake
Mrs J Cecil	1-1	1-1	0-0	0-0	0-0	100.0	+ 1.25
G F J Houghton	1-1	0-0	1-1	0-0	0-0	100.0	+ 10.00
Mrs M A Jones	1-1	0-0	1-1	0-0	0-0	100.0	+ 20.00
S Dow	1-2	0-0	1-2	0-0	0-0	50.0	- 0.09
N J Henderson	1-2	0-1	0-0	1-1	0-0	50.0	- 0.38

May

	Total W-R	Nov Hdles	H'cap Hdles	Nov Chses	H'cap Chses	Per cent	£1 Level Stake
H Wellstead	2-3	0-0	0-0	2-3	0-0	66.7	+ 3.00
Miss Newton-Smith	2-5	0-0	0-0	2-5	0-0	40.0	+ 2.00
J M Turner	2-16	0-0	0-0	2-16	0-0	12.5	- 8.75
G B Balding	1-1	0-0	0-0	1-1	0-0	100.0	+ 3.50
Mrs D Buckett	1-1	0-0	0-0	1-1	0-0	100.0	+ 12.00

FONTWELL (Group 2)

Leading Trainers 1991-96

	Total W-R	Nov Hdles	H'cap Hdles	Nov Chses	H'cap Chses	Per cent	£1 Level Stake
J T Gifford	29-151	10-58	6-24	5-30	8-39	19.2	- 29.74
M C Pipe	26-81	12-36	4-21	9-18	1-6	32.1	- 16.59
G B Balding	18-92	6-23	1-20	7-20	4-29	19.6	- 14.83
P J Hobbs	17-58	2-13	3-9	3-10	9-26	29.3	+ 2.21
J White	16-77	7-37	4-14	3-13	2-13	20.8	- 20.27
R Curtis	14-81	0-28	1-12	2-15	11-26	17.3	- 32.37
R Rowe	14-132	0-41	9-39	0-15	5-37	10.6	- 38.09
R H Alner	13-38	0-10	0-1	5-6	8-21	34.2	+ 3.46
G Harwood	13-43	3-13	9-23	1-4	0-3	30.2	- 4.39
K C Bailey	10-33	4-10	0-5	1-4	5-14	30.3	+ 4.21
R J O'Sullivan	10-57	6-22	0-20	2-7	2-8	17.5	- 24.46
D M Grissell	9-75	2-32	1-17	4-9	2-17	12.0	+ 9.54
R H Buckler	8-52	4-17	4-12	0-10	0-13	15.4	+ 8.35
J S Moore	7-32	4-18	3-12	0-0	0-2	21.9	+ 11.00
Miss B Sanders	7-33	2-14	5-13	0-4	0-2	21.2	- 6.66
T Casey	7-43	1-12	0-6	2-8	4-17	16.3	- 19.29
Mrs L Richards	6-25	0-5	2-6	1-7	3-7	24.0	+ 68.25
N J Henderson	6-31	3-12	0-2	0-6	3-11	19.4	- 7.03
S Dow	6-39	4-15	2-17	0-2	0-5	15.4	- 10.30
J R Jenkins	6-60	1-20	3-22	1-11	1-7	10.0	- 36.40

Leading Jockeys

	Total W-R	Per cent	£1 Level Stake		Best Trainer	W-R	Per cent	£1 Level Stake
A Maguire	25-151	16.6	- 72.28		J White	7-26	26.9	- 4.59
P Hide	19-88	21.6	+ 21.78		J T Gifford	13-60	21.7	+ 4.21
D Morris	16-105	15.2	- 38.85		R Curtis	14-65	21.5	- 16.35
R Dunwoody	16-126	12.7	- 64.04		M C Pipe	4-17	23.5	- 2.95
J Frost	15-82	18.3	+ 2.73		G B Balding	7-17	41.2	+ 12.23
J Osborne	14-52	26.9	- 0.56		S Sherwood	2-2	100.0	+ 3.25
A P McCoy	13-65	20.0	- 9.56		D L Williams	3-4	75.0	+ 4.75
M Richards	13-79	16.5	+ 37.46		Mrs L Richards	4-13	30.8	+ 64.75
D O'Sullivan	13-99	13.1	- 51.94		R J O'Sullivan	7-34	20.6	- 15.69
B Powell	13-103	12.6	+ 3.75		R H Buckler	5-17	29.4	+ 30.10
D Bridgwater	12-45	26.7	+ 15.35		M C Pipe	5-13	38.5	- 1.53
E Murphy	10-55	18.2	- 26.62		J T Gifford	4-22	18.2	- 11.75

How the Favourites Fared

	W-R	Per cent	£1 Level Stake		W-R	Per cent	£1 Level Stake
Novice Hurdles	67-146	45.9	- 2.96	Novice Chases	42-81	51.9	- 0.17
H'cap Hurdles	40-106	37.7	+ 6.99	H'cap Chases	59-116	50.9	+ 26.83
N H Flat	0-1	-	- 1.00	Hunter Chases	7-10	70.0	+ 4.90
Totals	107-253	42.3	+ 3.03	Totals	108-207	52.2	+ 31.56
All favourites	215-460	46.7	+ 34.59				

LEADING TRAINERS BY MONTH AT FONTWELL 1991-96

August	Total W-R	Nov Hdles	H'cap Hdles	Nov Chses	H'cap Chses	Per cent	£1 Level Stake
J White	9-17	2-4	2-4	3-5	2-4	52.9	+ 16.03
P J Hobbs	4-7	1-3	2-2	1-1	0-1	57.1	+ 1.36
R J O'Sullivan	3-4	3-3	0-0	0-0	0-1	75.0	+ 4.73

September	Total W-R	Nov Hdles	H'cap Hdles	Nov Chses	H'cap Chses	Per cent	£1 Level Stake
G Harwood	4-6	1-2	3-4	0-0	0-0	66.7	+ 5.76
P J Hobbs	4-7	1-4	0-0	1-1	2-2	57.1	+ 2.64
M D I Usher	3-7	0-0	3-7	0-0	0-0	42.9	+ 10.50

October	Total W-R	Nov Hdles	H'cap Hdles	Nov Chses	H'cap Chses	Per cent	£1 Level Stake
G B Balding	6-11	1-2	1-3	3-4	1-2	54.5	+ 5.24
R Rowe	5-16	0-4	3-5	0-3	2-4	31.3	+ 8.78
R H Alner	4-8	0-1	0-1	1-1	3-5	50.0	+ 3.86

November	Total W-R	Nov Hdles	H'cap Hdles	Nov Chses	H'cap Chses	Per cent	£1 Level Stake
J T Gifford	5-15	1-5	2-3	1-3	1-4	33.3	- 1.42
C Weedon	2-4	2-2	0-1	0-1	0-0	50.0	+ 10.50
S Dow	2-5	1-3	1-2	0-0	0-0	40.0	+ 2.07

December	Total W-R	Nov Hdles	H'cap Hdles	Nov Chses	H'cap Chses	Per cent	£1 Level Stake
J T Gifford	3-10	1-4	1-3	0-1	1-2	30.0	- 1.38
G B Balding	3-11	2-2	0-2	1-2	0-5	27.3	+ 2.91
Mrs J Pitman	2-4	0-0	1-2	0-0	1-2	50.0	+ 2.75

January	Total W-R	Nov Hdles	H'cap Hdles	Nov Chses	H'cap Chses	Per cent	£1 Level Stake
Capt T A Forster	3-3	1-1	0-0	1-1	1-1	100.0	+ 18.90
J A C Edwards	3-6	2-3	0-0	1-2	0-1	50.0	+ 5.45
J T Gifford	3-14	1-5	0-0	1-4	1-5	21.4	- 0.75

February	Total W-R	Nov Hdles	H'cap Hdles	Nov Chses	H'cap Chses	Per cent	£1 Level Stake
M C Pipe	6-17	3-8	0-4	2-3	1-2	35.3	- 4.92
P J Hobbs	3-4	0-0	0-0	1-1	2-3	75.0	+ 14.00
N J Henderson	3-6	2-3	0-1	0-0	1-2	50.0	+ 1.47

March	Total W-R	Nov Hdles	H'cap Hdles	Nov Chses	H'cap Chses	Per cent	£1 Level Stake
M C Pipe	4-7	2-3	0-1	2-2	0-1	57.1	+ 5.74
J T Gifford	4-17	2-7	0-4	1-3	1-3	23.5	- 0.70
R Curtis	3-9	0-4	1-1	0-1	2-3	33.3	+ 14.50

April	Total W-R	Nov Hdles	H'cap Hdles	Nov Chses	H'cap Chses	Per cent	£1 Level Stake
D M Grissell	4-17	1-8	1-3	1-1	1-5	23.5	+ 5.83
R H Buckler	3-9	2-6	1-3	0-0	0-0	33.3	+ 21.10
J T Gifford	3-22	3-11	0-1	0-3	0-7	13.6	- 3.50

May	Total W-R	Nov Hdles	H'cap Hdles	Nov Chses	H'cap Chses	Per cent	£1 Level Stake
M C Pipe	9-27	2-11	3-8	4-7	0-1	33.3	- 4.53
G Harwood	4-9	1-3	2-4	1-2	0-0	44.4	+ 2.13
G B Balding	4-14	1-2	0-3	2-3	1-6	28.6	- 7.48

HAYDOCK (Group 1)

Leading Trainers 1991-96

	Total W-R	Nov Hdles	H'cap Hdles	Nov Chses	H'cap Chses	Per cent	£1 Level Stake
G Richards	36-122	5-38	3-22	18-31	10-31	29.5	+ 4.12
M C Pipe	29-138	16-63	5-33	4-14	4-28	21.0	- 38.46
J G FitzGerald	15-57	6-23	3-13	2-6	4-15	26.3	+ 16.53
N Twiston-Davies	14-57	4-27	0-7	7-11	3-12	24.6	+ 7.22
Mrs M Reveley	11-46	4-20	6-22	0-1	1-3	23.9	- 4.58
D Nicholson	11-47	7-27	1-6	3-9	0-5	23.4	- 8.60
C P E Brooks	9-32	2-9	0-3	3-10	4-10	28.1	+ 4.58
M D Hammond	6-43	1-17	3-15	0-3	2-8	14.0	- 7.71
D McCain	6-67	1-26	0-3	1-20	4-18	9.0	- 8.65
T P Tate	5-19	3-9	0-4	1-4	1-2	26.3	- 7.70
Mrs J Pitman	5-28	1-9	1-5	1-4	2-10	17.9	- 11.51
J J O'Neill	5-48	0-17	3-19	1-8	1-4	10.4	- 27.90
J M Jefferson	4-18	2-10	2-5	0-1	0-2	22.2	+ 4.13
Mrs S A Bramall	4-23	0-3	0-4	0-6	4-10	17.4	+ 16.50
P J Bevan	3-6	3-4	0-1	0-0	0-1	50.0	+ 38.00
Capt T A Forster	3-6	1-2	0-1	0-1	2-2	50.0	- 0.07
P Cheesbrough	3-8	0-1	0-1	2-3	1-3	37.5	+ 8.75
F Jordan	3-10	0-5	3-5	0-0	0-0	30.0	+ 1.50
N J Henderson	3-12	1-6	1-3	0-0	1-3	25.0	+ 7.75
N A Gaselee	3-13	1-1	0-3	1-3	1-6	23.1	+ 7.66

Leading Jockeys

	Total W-R	Per cent	£1 Level Stake	Best Trainer	W-R	Per cent	£1 Level Stake
R Dunwoody	21-75	28.0	- 10.52	M C Pipe	9-29	31.0	- 3.48
M Dwyer	20-127	15.7	- 54.18	J G FitzGerald	9-32	28.1	+ 5.29
A Maguire	12-58	20.7	- 13.63	D Nicholson	5-20	25.0	- 8.05
D Bridgwater	11-37	29.7	+ 9.13	N Twiston-Davies	4-9	44.4	+ 7.99
L Wyer	11-65	16.9	+ 1.01	R D E Woodhouse	1-1	100.0	+ 6.00
G Bradley	10-40	25.0	+ 21.08	C P E Brooks	8-23	34.8	+ 8.08
A Dobbin	10-48	20.8	- 1.44	G Richards	9-30	30.0	+ 11.56
C Llewellyn	9-42	21.4	+ 12.31	N Twiston-Davies	5-21	23.8	+ 7.71
P Niven	8-61	13.1	- 36.00	Mrs M Reveley	6-28	21.4	- 9.25
R Garrity	6-32	18.8	- 5.67	M D Hammond	1-3	33.3	+ 5.00
C F Swan	5-17	29.4	+ 15.88	T P Tate	1-1	100.0	+ 3.50
M A FitzGerald	5-20	25.0	+ 48.43	Miss H C Knight	1-1	100.0	+ 0.14

How the Favourites Fared

	W-R	Per cent	£1 Level Stake		W-R	Per cent	£1 Level Stake
Novice Hurdles	41-93	44.1	- 12.37	Novice Chases	23-49	46.9	- 6.97
H'cap Hurdles	22-70	31.4	- 12.84	H'cap Chases	28-64	43.8	- 2.64
N H Flat	4-10	40.0	+ 0.16	Hunter Chases	3-4	75.0	+ 2.51
Totals	67-173	38.7	- 25.05	Totals	54-117	46.2	- 7.10
All favourites	121-290	41.7	- 32.15				

LEADING TRAINERS BY MONTH AT HAYDOCK 1991-96

November	Total W-R	Nov Hdles	H'cap Hdles	Nov Chses	H'cap Chses	Per cent	£1 Level Stake
G Richards	14-39	0-7	3-9	6-9	5-14	35.9	+ 5.56
Mrs M Reveley	10-18	4-7	5-9	0-0	1-2	55.6	+ 20.93
N Twiston-Davies	7-14	2-3	0-1	4-5	1-5	50.0	+ 14.48
J G FitzGerald	6-12	3-5	1-2	1-1	1-4	50.0	+ 9.01
D McCain	6-32	1-11	0-1	1-7	4-13	18.8	+ 26.35

December	Total W-R	Nov Hdles	H'cap Hdles	Nov Chses	H'cap Chses	Per cent	£1 Level Stake
G Richards	7-28	0-11	0-4	5-7	2-6	25.0	- 14.52
M C Pipe	4-22	3-12	0-3	1-3	0-4	18.2	- 13.66
C P E Brooks	3-10	0-1	0-0	1-5	2-4	30.0	+ 8.00
L Lungo	3-12	2-7	1-4	0-1	0-0	25.0	+ 36.00
D Nicholson	3-13	1-5	0-1	2-4	0-3	23.1	- 5.20

January	Total W-R	Nov Hdles	H'cap Hdles	Nov Chses	H'cap Chses	Per cent	£1 Level Stake
M C Pipe	10-39	6-21	1-3	2-6	1-9	25.6	- 9.78
G Richards	8-25	3-11	0-1	2-6	3-7	32.0	+ 8.95
T P Tate	3-3	2-2	0-0	1-1	0-0	100.0	+ 2.27
J G FitzGerald	3-11	1-4	0-0	1-2	1-5	27.3	+ 20.00
D Nicholson	3-12	3-10	0-0	0-2	0-0	25.0	- 2.58

February	Total W-R	Nov Hdles	H'cap Hdles	Nov Chses	H'cap Chses	Per cent	£1 Level Stake
M C Pipe	7-33	3-13	2-9	1-4	1-7	21.2	+ 3.68
G Richards	5-28	0-8	0-7	5-9	0-4	17.9	- 10.86
P Cheesbrough	3-6	0-1	0-1	2-2	1-2	50.0	+ 10.75
M W Easterby	2-2	0-0	1-1	0-0	1-1	100.0	+ 9.00
M J Wilkinson	2-2	1-1	1-1	0-0	0-0	100.0	+ 13.50

May	Total W-R	Nov Hdles	H'cap Hdles	Nov Chses	H'cap Chses	Per cent	£1 Level Stake
M C Pipe	3-17	2-8	1-9	0-0	0-0	17.6	- 3.33
G Richards	2-3	2-2	0-1	0-0	0-0	66.7	+ 14.00
D Nicholson	2-6	1-2	1-4	0-0	0-0	33.3	+ 9.50
M J Camacho	1-1	1-1	0-0	0-0	0-0	100.0	+ 1.10
S G Griffiths	1-1	0-0	1-1	0-0	0-0	100.0	+ 16.00

HEREFORD (Group 4)

Leading Trainers 1991-96

	Total W-R	Nov Hdles	H'cap Hdles	Nov Chses	H'cap Chses	Per cent	£1 Level Stake
M C Pipe	36-123	19-66	10-33	3-11	4-13	29.3	+ 11.83
N Twiston-Davies	26-91	10-36	7-26	2-7	7-22	28.6	+ 32.56
K C Bailey	17-80	7-35	3-17	5-14	2-14	21.3	+ 15.32
N J Henderson	14-30	4-12	1-5	4-5	5-8	46.7	+ 20.24
D Nicholson	12-43	10-24	0-2	2-7	0-10	27.9	- 5.96
P J Hobbs	11-54	6-18	2-15	2-10	1-11	20.4	- 12.54
R H Buckler	8-32	0-8	5-11	2-5	1-8	25.0	+116.38
P F Nicholls	8-40	4-10	0-6	2-10	2-14	20.0	- 7.57
D Burchell	8-53	5-28	2-15	0-3	1-7	15.1	- 1.29
R H Alner	7-30	0-10	0-3	1-4	6-13	23.3	- 7.09
K S Bridgwater	7-51	0-14	5-25	2-8	0-4	13.7	- 5.63
R J Hodges	7-56	0-11	4-20	0-8	3-17	12.5	+ 0.88
J M Bradley	7-69	1-23	2-26	2-8	2-12	10.1	- 25.23
R Lee	7-69	0-21	1-16	2-8	4-24	10.1	- 46.80
S Christian	6-19	5-12	1-5	0-0	0-2	31.6	+ 14.00
O Sherwood	6-20	3-9	1-3	1-4	1-4	30.0	+ 5.75
J White	6-37	2-16	3-11	0-5	1-5	16.2	- 7.50
R Dickin	6-50	0-15	1-9	2-11	3-15	12.0	- 15.00
Andrew Turnell	5-15	1-4	0-3	3-6	1-2	33.3	+ 6.70
Mrs H Parrott	5-18	1-5	1-3	0-3	3-7	27.8	+ 1.46

Leading Jockeys

	Total W-R	Per cent	£1 Level Stake	Best Trainer	W-R	Per cent	£1 Level Stake
D Bridgwater	25-118	21.2	+ 30.82	N Twiston-Davies	12-22	54.5	+ 44.88
R Dunwoody	22-78	28.2	+ 5.74	M C Pipe	5-14	35.7	+ 4.19
C Llewellyn	22-81	27.2	+ 8.00	N Twiston-Davies	10-31	32.3	+ 6.38
A P McCoy	14-60	23.3	+ 24.08	G B Balding	3-9	33.3	+ 0.60
J R Kavanagh	12-60	20.0	- 7.04	N J Henderson	6-15	40.0	+ 9.71
S McNeill	12-61	19.7	+ 0.48	Andrew Turnell	4-7	57.1	+ 12.61
M A FitzGerald	11-70	15.7	+ 4.04	N J Henderson	3-5	60.0	+ 1.91
J Osborne	10-40	25.0	- 2.32	O Sherwood	4-6	66.7	+ 14.75
N Mann	9-46	19.6	- 8.69	S Mellor	2-9	22.2	+ 4.38
A Maguire	9-56	16.1	- 28.17	D Nicholson	4-8	50.0	+ 3.46
Richard Davis	9-78	11.5	+ 12.25	N A Gaselee	1-1	100.0	+ 7.00
R Farrant	8-49	16.3	- 7.44	J M Bradley	3-15	20.0	+ 9.00

How the Favourites Fared

	W-R	Per cent	£1 Level Stake		W-R	Per cent	£1 Level Stake
Novice Hurdles	62-140	44.3	- 5.00	Novice Chases	30-65	46.2	- 4.33
H'cap Hurdles	39-120	32.5	- 13.59	H'cap Chases	36-94	38.3	- 4.56
N H Flat	5-23	21.7	- 12.42	Hunter Chases	15-34	44.1	+ 4.65
Totals	106-283	37.5	- 31.01	Totals	81-193	42.0	- 4.24
All favourites	187-476	39.3	- 35.25				

LEADING TRAINERS BY MONTH AT HEREFORD 1991-96

June

	Total W-R	Nov Hdles	H'cap Hdles	Nov Chses	H'cap Chses	Per cent	£1 Level Stake
Capt T A Forster	1-1	1-1	0-0	0-0	0-0	100.0	+ 12.00
R Lee	1-1	0-0	0-0	0-0	1-1	100.0	+ 2.50
Miss Laura Shally	1-1	0-0	1-1	0-0	0-0	100.0	+ 20.00

August

	Total W-R	Nov Hdles	H'cap Hdles	Nov Chses	H'cap Chses	Per cent	£1 Level Stake
M C Pipe	6-11	3-7	2-3	0-0	1-1	54.5	+ 8.74
R Lee	4-9	0-0	0-1	1-1	3-7	44.4	+ 3.00
K S Bridgwater	4-13	0-2	2-6	2-3	0-2	30.8	+ 3.13

September

	Total W-R	Nov Hdles	H'cap Hdles	Nov Chses	H'cap Chses	Per cent	£1 Level Stake
C D Broad	1-1	0-0	0-0	0-0	1-1	100.0	+ 5.50
R H Buckler	1-1	0-0	1-1	0-0	0-0	100.0	+100.00
D Burchell	1-1	1-1	0-0	0-0	0-0	100.0	+ 2.50

October

	Total W-R	Nov Hdles	H'cap Hdles	Nov Chses	H'cap Chses	Per cent	£1 Level Stake
M D McMillan	2-2	1-1	0-0	1-1	0-0	100.0	+ 8.25
K C Bailey	2-3	1-1	0-0	0-1	1-1	66.7	+ 3.70
M C Pipe	2-3	0-0	2-3	0-0	0-0	66.7	+ 19.00

November

	Total W-R	Nov Hdles	H'cap Hdles	Nov Chses	H'cap Chses	Per cent	£1 Level Stake
N J Henderson	4-4	0-0	0-0	2-2	2-2	100.0	+ 9.63
M C Pipe	4-18	3-11	1-4	0-3	0-0	22.2	+ 3.71
D Nicholson	3-10	3-6	0-0	0-0	0-4	30.0	- 2.78

December

	Total W-R	Nov Hdles	H'cap Hdles	Nov Chses	H'cap Chses	Per cent	£1 Level Stake
N Twiston-Davies	5-13	2-3	0-4	0-0	3-6	38.5	+ 5.32
R J Hodges	4-14	0-4	2-2	0-0	2-8	28.6	+ 17.50
M C Pipe	3-13	1-5	1-4	0-1	1-3	23.1	- 5.01

February

	Total W-R	Nov Hdles	H'cap Hdles	Nov Chses	H'cap Chses	Per cent	£1 Level Stake
D Nicholson	3-6	2-4	0-0	1-1	0-1	50.0	+ 4.38
M C Pipe	3-12	2-7	1-2	0-2	0-1	25.0	- 0.50
W R Muir	2-2	1-1	1-1	0-0	0-0	100.0	+ 4.25

March

	Total W-R	Nov Hdles	H'cap Hdles	Nov Chses	H'cap Chses	Per cent	£1 Level Stake
P J Hobbs	4-13	3-4	0-2	1-3	0-4	30.8	+ 0.30
N Twiston-Davies	3-9	1-4	2-5	0-0	0-0	33.3	+ 1.30
R H Alner	2-3	0-1	0-0	0-0	2-2	66.7	+ 6.75

April

	Total W-R	Nov Hdles	H'cap Hdles	Nov Chses	H'cap Chses	Per cent	£1 Level Stake
M C Pipe	4-7	4-7	0-0	0-0	0-0	57.1	+ 3.40
N Twiston-Davies	4-16	1-5	1-5	1-2	1-4	25.0	+ 14.63
C R Egerton	3-4	2-2	0-1	1-1	0-0	75.0	+ 5.73

May

	Total W-R	Nov Hdles	H'cap Hdles	Nov Chses	H'cap Chses	Per cent	£1 Level Stake
M C Pipe	11-41	4-20	3-10	2-4	2-7	26.8	- 7.46
N Twiston-Davies	8-26	4-9	1-6	1-4	2-7	30.8	- 0.42
K C Bailey	6-25	1-8	2-8	2-4	1-5	24.0	+ 1.43

HEXHAM (Group 4)

Leading Trainers 1991-96

	Total W-R	Nov Hdles	H'cap Hdles	Nov Chses	H'cap Chses	Per cent	£1 Level Stake
G Richards	20-88	12-33	1-9	4-24	3-22	22.7	+ 15.32
L Lungo	19-72	6-31	7-22	2-8	4-11	26.4	+ 24.86
Mrs M Reveley	17-66	4-21	3-18	3-13	7-14	25.8	+ 2.68
M D Hammond	15-106	8-50	2-20	3-13	2-23	14.2	- 58.97
P Monteith	14-54	3-21	2-10	2-9	7-14	25.9	- 2.81
J H Johnson	13-75	7-32	3-13	1-19	2-11	17.3	+ 5.00
W Bentley	9-32	5-13	3-13	1-3	0-3	28.1	+ 10.65
M A Barnes	9-55	1-17	2-11	2-8	4-19	16.4	- 6.62
G M Moore	9-66	7-33	1-14	1-10	0-9	13.6	- 32.17
W G Reed	9-67	1-24	0-4	4-21	4-18	13.4	- 21.22
J G M O'Shea	8-14	4-7	2-4	1-2	1-1	57.1	+ 13.23
Denys Smith	7-37	1-11	4-13	0-0	2-13	18.9	- 13.40
Mrs S J Smith	7-81	2-32	3-13	0-15	2-21	8.6	- 14.00
P Beaumont	6-54	0-22	2-8	3-11	1-13	11.1	- 14.00
M W Easterby	5-35	2-13	0-6	1-6	2-10	14.3	- 20.05
C Parker	5-49	0-16	0-6	2-9	3-18	10.2	- 29.57
S E Kettlewell	4-11	2-4	0-5	0-0	2-2	36.4	+ 4.60
J A C Edwards	4-13	3-12	0-0	1-1	0-0	30.8	- 3.92
A C Whillans	4-14	1-5	3-8	0-0	0-1	28.6	+ 7.00
T J Carr	4-17	1-9	0-3	2-2	1-3	23.5	+ 3.25

Leading Jockeys

	Total W-R	Per cent	£1 Level Stake	Best Trainer	W-R	Per cent	£1 Level Stake
T Reed	26-114	22.8	+ 32.35	L Lungo	13-31	41.9	+ 13.87
P Niven	22-93	23.7	- 12.65	Mrs M Reveley	12-35	34.3	+ 16.20
A Dobbin	19-94	20.2	- 16.37	P Monteith	6-25	24.0	- 3.65
N Bentley	15-53	28.3	+ 6.83	G M Moore	7-24	29.2	+ 4.33
A Thornton	10-67	14.9	- 10.68	Miss L V Russell	2-3	66.7	+ 2.75
M Dwyer	9-62	14.5	- 36.47	Mrs M Reveley	2-3	66.7	+ 4.50
J Callaghan	9-74	12.2	- 40.67	G M Moore	2-28	7.1	- 22.50
L O'Hara	8-54	14.8	- 12.87	Miss L A Perratt	3-12	25.0	+ 6.00
Richard Guest	8-61	13.1	+ 19.75	Mrs S J Smith	5-37	13.5	+ 4.00
K Johnson	8-75	10.7	- 20.02	F T Walton	3-8	37.5	+ 3.75
B Storey	8-160	5.0	-116.65	R Allan	3-16	18.8	+ 3.00
M A FitzGerald	7-20	35.0	+ 17.65	J G M O'Shea	5-9	55.6	+ 11.05

How the Favourites Fared

	W-R	Per cent	£1 Level Stake		W-R	Per cent	£1 Level Stake
Novice Hurdles	49-109	45.0	- 0.01	Novice Chases	30-65	46.2	+ 0.54
H'cap Hurdles	25-89	28.1	- 19.97	H'cap Chases	23-76	30.3	- 13.61
N H Flat	7-15	46.7	+ 3.64	Hunter Chases	5-15	33.3	- 0.37
Totals	81-213	38.0	- 16.34	Totals	58-156	37.2	- 13.44
All favourites	139-369	37.7	- 29.78				

LEADING TRAINERS BY MONTH AT HEXHAM 1991-96

August

	Total W-R	Nov Hdles	H'cap Hdles	Nov Chses	H'cap Chses	Per cent	£1 Level Stake
J G M O'Shea	5-6	3-3	1-2	1-1	0-0	83.3	+ 9.98
M D Hammond	3-11	1-4	1-4	0-0	1-3	27.3	- 2.25
M A Barnes	2-3	0-0	2-2	0-0	0-1	66.7	+ 16.00
T H Caldwell	1-1	1-1	0-0	0-0	0-0	100.0	+ 6.50

September

	Total W-R	Nov Hdles	H'cap Hdles	Nov Chses	H'cap Chses	Per cent	£1 Level Stake
J G M O'Shea	3-4	1-2	1-1	0-0	1-1	75.0	+ 7.25
P Monteith	2-2	1-1	0-0	0-0	1-1	100.0	+ 2.42
J J O'Neill	2-4	0-1	1-2	1-1	0-0	50.0	+ 0.28
Mrs M Reveley	2-5	0-2	0-1	0-0	2-2	40.0	+ 7.00

October

	Total W-R	Nov Hdles	H'cap Hdles	Nov Chses	H'cap Chses	Per cent	£1 Level Stake
Mrs M Reveley	5-13	1-4	1-3	1-2	2-4	38.5	+ 5.75
P Monteith	4-9	1-4	2-3	1-2	0-0	44.4	+ 1.93
G M Moore	3-8	2-5	1-2	0-1	0-0	37.5	+ 1.25
Mrs S J Smith	3-11	1-4	1-3	0-1	1-3	27.3	+ 36.00

November

	Total W-R	Nov Hdles	H'cap Hdles	Nov Chses	H'cap Chses	Per cent	£1 Level Stake
G Richards	7-23	3-6	0-2	3-10	1-5	30.4	+ 18.58
L Lungo	4-11	0-1	2-5	1-3	1-2	36.4	+ 5.54
P Monteith	4-17	0-6	0-2	0-3	4-6	23.5	+ 5.10
T P Tate	3-6	1-3	0-0	2-3	0-0	50.0	+ 5.25

December

	Total W-R	Nov Hdles	H'cap Hdles	Nov Chses	H'cap Chses	Per cent	£1 Level Stake
S E Kettlewell	2-2	1-1	0-0	0-0	1-1	100.0	+ 3.60
M A Barnes	2-4	1-2	0-0	0-1	1-1	50.0	+ 6.00
Miss L A Perratt	1-1	0-0	0-0	1-1	0-0	100.0	+ 3.00
Mrs S A Bramall	1-2	0-0	0-0	1-1	0-1	50.0	+ 7.00

March

	Total W-R	Nov Hdles	H'cap Hdles	Nov Chses	H'cap Chses	Per cent	£1 Level Stake
Mrs S A Bramall	3-6	0-1	0-1	1-1	2-3	50.0	+ 14.00
C Parker	3-12	0-5	0-1	1-3	2-3	25.0	+ 0.35
R Brewis	2-2	0-0	1-1	0-0	1-1	100.0	+ 15.00
A C Whillans	2-5	1-1	1-3	0-0	0-1	40.0	+ 5.50

April

	Total W-R	Nov Hdles	H'cap Hdles	Nov Chses	H'cap Chses	Per cent	£1 Level Stake
L Lungo	6-20	2-9	1-5	1-2	2-4	30.0	+ 2.57
G Richards	5-16	4-6	0-1	1-5	0-4	31.3	+ 0.28
Mrs M Reveley	3-9	1-5	0-1	1-2	1-1	33.3	+ 0.50
W G Reed	3-14	0-4	0-1	2-6	1-3	21.4	+ 8.50

May

	Total W-R	Nov Hdles	H'cap Hdles	Nov Chses	H'cap Chses	Per cent	£1 Level Stake
L Lungo	7-16	3-9	4-6	0-0	0-1	43.8	+ 16.25
J H Johnson	6-21	3-7	1-4	1-6	1-4	28.6	+ 14.92
W Bentley	5-10	3-4	1-4	1-1	0-1	50.0	+ 18.50
M D Hammond	5-18	4-10	0-3	1-1	0-4	27.8	+ 0.20

HUNTINGDON (Group 3)

Leading Trainers 1991-96

	Total W-R	Nov Hdles	H'cap Hdles	Nov Chses	H'cap Chses	Per cent	£1 Level Stake
F Murphy	20-123	4-37	3-14	2-23	11-49	16.3	+ 6.04
K C Bailey	16-50	4-17	2-6	5-15	5-12	32.0	+ 23.21
J T Gifford	16-74	6-27	2-6	3-20	5-21	21.6	+ 14.13
D Nicholson	15-54	8-29	0-1	3-10	4-14	27.8	+ 23.72
Mrs M Reveley	10-35	4-16	4-12	0-0	2-7	28.6	+ 0.50
Capt T A Forster	10-57	4-20	0-4	4-14	2-19	17.5	- 26.46
D R Gandolfo	9-31	2-12	1-4	4-6	2-9	29.0	+ 27.44
Mrs J Pitman	9-39	2-11	2-9	1-7	4-12	23.1	+ 0.24
J White	9-55	3-24	5-17	1-6	0-8	16.4	- 15.43
J R Jenkins	9-138	4-52	2-56	1-19	2-11	6.5	- 71.73
N J Henderson	8-37	2-13	2-11	4-6	0-7	21.6	+ 5.23
G A Hubbard	8-45	4-17	1-8	1-9	2-11	17.8	+ 6.46
O Brennan	8-61	3-28	4-17	1-7	0-9	13.1	- 21.59
J L Spearing	7-28	0-5	4-13	0-2	3-8	25.0	+ 52.25
K A Morgan	7-51	1-11	4-23	1-5	1-12	13.7	+ 17.38
J Pearce	6-26	2-15	1-8	2-2	1-1	23.1	+ 37.73
G B Balding	6-33	2-8	1-9	0-5	3-11	18.2	+ 1.25
J R Upson	6-49	2-17	1-5	0-8	3-19	12.2	- 11.25
Mrs S A Bramall	5-11	1-1	0-1	2-3	2-6	45.5	+ 7.96
M C Pipe	5-17	1-4	2-8	1-3	1-2	29.4	- 2.64

Leading Jockeys

	Total W-R	Per cent	£1 Level Stake	Best Trainer	W-R	Per cent	£1 Level Stake
A Maguire	23-123	18.7	- 2.62	F Murphy	8-39	20.5	+ 19.50
R Dunwoody	17-113	15.0	- 42.93	N J Henderson	4-11	36.4	+ 2.45
P Hide	14-51	27.5	+ 36.74	J T Gifford	9-31	29.0	+ 31.00
N Williamson	13-57	22.8	- 2.29	K C Bailey	6-15	40.0	+ 10.00
D Bridgwater	12-72	16.7	+ 7.04	M C Pipe	3-6	50.0	- 0.21
W Marston	9-48	18.8	+ 17.63	Mrs J Pitman	3-8	37.5	+ 0.63
D Gallagher	8-43	18.6	- 5.89	C T Nash	1-1	100.0	+ 4.00
J Ryan	8-50	16.0	+ 12.00	A S Reid	2-4	50.0	+ 10.00
J Railton	7-49	14.3	+ 12.75	K C Bailey	3-4	75.0	+ 16.75
A S Smith	7-51	13.7	+ 17.38	K A Morgan	7-43	16.3	+ 25.38
Martin Brennan	7-52	13.5	- 17.09	O Brennan	7-41	17.1	- 6.09
P Niven	6-30	20.0	- 8.05	Mrs M Reveley	6-22	27.3	- 0.05

How the Favourites Fared

	W-R	Per cent	£1 Level Stake		W-R	Per cent	£1 Level Stake
Novice Hurdles	42-116	36.2	- 26.20	Novice Chases	36-66	54.5	+ 5.87
H'cap Hurdles	37-98	37.8	- 1.99	H'cap Chases	45-108	41.7	- 2.66
N H Flat	3-15	20.0	- 7.95	Hunter Chases	7-17	41.2	- 2.06
Totals	82-229	35.8	- 36.14	Totals	88-191	46.1	+ 1.15
All favourites	170-420	40.5	- 34.99				

LEADING TRAINERS BY MONTH AT HUNTINGDON 1991-96

August

	Total W-R	Nov Hdles	H'cap Hdles	Nov Chses	H'cap Chses	Per cent	£1 Level Stake
F Murphy	3-5	1-2	0-1	0-0	2-2	60.0	+ 0.69
J White	2-2	0-0	2-2	0-0	0-0	100.0	+ 5.25
R Akehurst	1-1	1-1	0-0	0-0	0-0	100.0	+ 8.00

September

	Total W-R	Nov Hdles	H'cap Hdles	Nov Chses	H'cap Chses	Per cent	£1 Level Stake
Mrs S A Bramall	2-2	0-0	0-0	1-1	1-1	100.0	+ 8.80
M Meade	2-2	2-2	0-0	0-0	0-0	100.0	+ 5.00
N Tinkler	2-6	1-4	0-1	1-1	0-0	33.3	+ 3.17

October

	Total W-R	Nov Hdles	H'cap Hdles	Nov Chses	H'cap Chses	Per cent	£1 Level Stake
F Murphy	4-13	2-6	1-1	0-2	1-4	30.8	+ 31.00
J Fanshawe	2-2	1-1	1-1	0-0	0-0	100.0	+ 5.00
K C Bailey	2-6	1-3	0-0	1-1	0-2	33.3	- 1.63

November

	Total W-R	Nov Hdles	H'cap Hdles	Nov Chses	H'cap Chses	Per cent	£1 Level Stake
N J Henderson	6-13	0-1	2-6	4-4	0-2	46.2	+ 3.90
J T Gifford	6-23	1-6	0-0	1-9	4-8	26.1	+ 3.50
S Dow	3-7	2-4	0-2	0-0	1-1	42.9	+ 26.00

December

	Total W-R	Nov Hdles	H'cap Hdles	Nov Chses	H'cap Chses	Per cent	£1 Level Stake
D Nicholson	6-10	2-5	0-0	1-1	3-4	60.0	+ 14.95
J M Jefferson	3-4	0-1	0-0	0-0	3-3	75.0	+ 8.73
K C Bailey	3-8	1-4	1-1	0-1	1-2	37.5	+ 6.50

January

	Total W-R	Nov Hdles	H'cap Hdles	Nov Chses	H'cap Chses	Per cent	£1 Level Stake
J A C Edwards	2-2	0-0	0-0	2-2	0-0	100.0	+ 3.17
D R Gandolfo	2-5	1-2	1-3	0-0	0-0	40.0	+ 3.50
J L Spearing	1-1	0-0	0-0	0-0	1-1	100.0	+ 33.00

February

	Total W-R	Nov Hdles	H'cap Hdles	Nov Chses	H'cap Chses	Per cent	£1 Level Stake
F Murphy	4-21	0-4	1-1	2-7	1-9	19.0	+ 9.25
J T Gifford	3-12	1-4	1-2	1-4	0-2	25.0	+ 14.00
Mrs J Pitman	3-12	1-2	0-3	0-3	2-4	25.0	- 2.38

March

	Total W-R	Nov Hdles	H'cap Hdles	Nov Chses	H'cap Chses	Per cent	£1 Level Stake
G B Balding	3-6	1-4	0-0	0-0	2-2	50.0	+ 7.50
J Fanshawe	2-2	2-2	0-0	0-0	0-0	100.0	+ 3.00
B Preece	2-2	2-2	0-0	0-0	0-0	100.0	+ 3.44

April

	Total W-R	Nov Hdles	H'cap Hdles	Nov Chses	H'cap Chses	Per cent	£1 Level Stake
R Lee	3-5	0-0	0-0	0-1	3-4	60.0	+ 3.48
D Nicholson	3-7	2-4	0-0	1-3	0-0	42.9	+ 7.92
G A Hubbard	3-8	1-2	1-1	0-3	1-2	37.5	+ 6.66

May

	Total W-R	Nov Hdles	H'cap Hdles	Nov Chses	H'cap Chses	Per cent	£1 Level Stake
K C Bailey	7-10	2-2	1-3	2-3	2-2	70.0	+ 32.58
J F Bottomley	3-7	0-1	2-4	0-1	1-1	42.9	+ 7.48
R Rowe	3-8	0-3	1-2	1-1	1-2	37.5	+ 4.50

KELSO (Group 4)

Leading Trainers 1991-96

	Total W-R	Nov Hdles	H'cap Hdles	Nov Chses	H'cap Chses	Per cent	£1 Level Stake
Mrs M Reveley	45-142	22-63	9-40	3-11	11-28	31.7	+ 11.68
G Richards	30-126	6-40	6-30	6-24	12-32	23.8	+ 8.59
P Monteith	22-135	5-56	6-36	3-14	8-29	16.3	+ 11.29
M D Hammond	17-97	9-37	0-17	2-15	6-28	17.5	- 34.48
Mrs J Goodfellow	14-51	7-20	2-8	1-10	4-13	27.5	+ 22.87
G M Moore	12-63	2-30	6-17	4-11	0-5	19.0	- 13.75
J H Johnson	12-68	5-27	2-15	2-10	3-16	17.6	+ 6.50
R Allan	11-69	0-30	4-17	6-15	1-7	15.9	- 20.06
Mrs S C Bradburne	8-89	0-27	0-12	3-19	5-31	9.0	- 60.17
Mrs Jane Storey	6-13	0-0	0-0	6-13	0-0	46.2	+ 6.73
P Cheesbrough	6-64	3-27	0-5	3-20	0-12	9.4	- 13.28
L Lungo	6-71	3-47	1-13	2-8	0-3	8.5	- 52.13
N Tinkler	5-24	1-11	4-10	0-0	0-3	20.8	- 7.31
Mrs S J Smith	5-27	2-10	1-7	1-5	1-5	18.5	+ 40.25
A C Whillans	5-31	1-16	3-11	1-4	0-0	16.1	- 1.25
Mrs S A Bramall	5-42	0-11	0-4	3-15	2-12	11.9	+ 46.98
C Parker	5-56	0-21	1-13	1-7	3-15	8.9	- 7.30
Mrs M K Stirk	4-7	2-2	0-1	0-0	2-4	57.1	+ 15.00
T N Dalgetty	4-9	0-0	0-0	4-8	0-1	44.4	- 1.66
T P Tate	4-15	1-7	1-3	1-1	1-4	26.7	+ 7.63

Leading Jockeys

	Total W-R	Per cent	£1 Level Stake	Best Trainer	W-R	Per cent	£1 Level Stake
P Niven	54-145	37.2	+ 34.58	Mrs M Reveley	38-97	39.2	+ 17.94
B Storey	27-172	15.7	- 58.64	Mrs J Goodfellow	9-27	33.3	+ 16.65
A Dobbin	26-124	21.0	+ 27.26	P Monteith	11-57	19.3	+ 7.45
M Moloney	15-75	20.0	- 12.30	G Richards	10-24	41.7	+ 19.25
L Wyer	11-81	13.6	- 14.44	P Calver	2-2	100.0	+ 16.50
J Callaghan	10-66	15.2	- 28.92	G M Moore	7-25	28.0	+ 0.25
A Thornton	9-52	17.3	- 2.14	D McCune	1-1	100.0	+ 20.00
T Reed	9-97	9.3	- 46.55	L Lungo	5-33	15.2	- 16.38
Mr J M Dun	6-21	28.6	- 8.27	T N Dalgetty	4-8	50.0	- 0.65
M Dwyer	6-47	12.8	- 21.91	J J O'Neill	2-11	18.2	- 2.88
D J Moffatt	6-47	12.8	+ 28.00	J H Johnson	3-8	37.5	+ 15.50
B Harding	6-54	11.1	- 36.14	G Richards	4-17	23.5	- 5.39

How the Favourites Fared

	W-R	Per cent	£1 Level Stake		W-R	Per cent	£1 Level Stake
Novice Hurdles	53-106	50.0	+ 0.39	Novice Chases	25-53	47.2	- 4.92
H'cap Hurdles	32-85	37.6	- 9.59	H'cap Chases	24-74	32.4	- 20.91
N H Flat	1-4	25.0	- 2.67	Hunter Chases	13-27	48.1	- 2.61
Totals	86-195	44.1	- 11.87	Totals	62-154	40.3	- 28.44
All favourites	148-349	42.4	- 40.31				

LEADING TRAINERS BY MONTH AT KELSO 1991-96

September	Total W-R	Nov Hdles	H'cap Hdles	Nov Chses	H'cap Chses	Per cent	£1 Level Stake
W L Barker	1-1	0-0	1-1	0-0	0-0	100.0	+ 3.00
M J Camacho	1-1	1-1	0-0	0-0	0-0	100.0	+ 16.00
B Mactaggart	1-1	0-0	0-0	0-0	1-1	100.0	+ 14.00

October	Total W-R	Nov Hdles	H'cap Hdles	Nov Chses	H'cap Chses	Per cent	£1 Level Stake
Mrs M Reveley	10-24	6-12	3-10	0-0	1-2	41.7	+ 4.17
Mrs J Goodfellow	6-13	4-7	0-2	0-1	2-3	46.2	+ 16.67
G Richards	6-14	1-4	1-3	0-2	4-5	42.9	+ 4.73

November	Total W-R	Nov Hdles	H'cap Hdles	Nov Chses	H'cap Chses	Per cent	£1 Level Stake
G Richards	11-35	0-8	3-13	1-3	7-11	31.4	+ 5.43
Mrs M Reveley	11-42	3-13	0-13	2-4	6-12	26.2	- 10.96
G M Moore	4-18	1-5	2-7	1-3	0-3	22.2	- 0.50

December	Total W-R	Nov Hdles	H'cap Hdles	Nov Chses	H'cap Chses	Per cent	£1 Level Stake
Mrs M Reveley	4-13	2-7	0-3	0-0	2-3	30.8	+ 16.62
P Monteith	3-11	0-4	1-3	0-0	2-4	27.3	+ 27.95
G Richards	2-8	0-1	1-2	0-1	1-4	25.0	+ 9.00

January	Total W-R	Nov Hdles	H'cap Hdles	Nov Chses	H'cap Chses	Per cent	£1 Level Stake
P Monteith	4-13	1-5	1-3	0-0	2-5	30.8	+ 8.63
Mrs S C Bradburne	2-7	0-2	0-0	0-1	2-4	28.6	- 0.67
Mrs M Reveley	2-10	1-3	0-1	0-2	1-4	20.0	- 1.90

February	Total W-R	Nov Hdles	H'cap Hdles	Nov Chses	H'cap Chses	Per cent	£1 Level Stake
J H Johnson	5-13	1-6	1-1	1-2	2-4	38.5	+ 16.00
G Richards	5-13	3-8	0-0	2-2	0-3	38.5	- 1.94
Mrs M Reveley	4-19	3-10	0-3	1-2	0-4	21.1	- 10.43

March	Total W-R	Nov Hdles	H'cap Hdles	Nov Chses	H'cap Chses	Per cent	£1 Level Stake
M D Hammond	7-18	4-9	0-2	1-4	2-3	38.9	+ 11.24
Mrs M Reveley	6-11	5-7	1-2	0-1	0-1	54.5	+ 13.03
P Monteith	4-22	0-9	2-5	0-4	2-4	18.2	- 4.13

April	Total W-R	Nov Hdles	H'cap Hdles	Nov Chses	H'cap Chses	Per cent	£1 Level Stake
Mrs M Reveley	5-15	1-6	3-5	0-2	1-2	33.3	+ 1.75
Mrs Jane Storey	3-6	0-0	0-0	3-6	0-0	50.0	+ 7.75
P Cheesbrough	3-14	1-4	0-3	2-5	0-2	21.4	- 5.53

May	Total W-R	Nov Hdles	H'cap Hdles	Nov Chses	H'cap Chses	Per cent	£1 Level Stake
Mrs M Reveley	2-4	1-2	1-2	0-0	0-0	50.0	+ 1.50
J Barclay	1-1	0-0	0-0	1-1	0-0	100.0	+ 5.00
R H Goldie	1-1	0-0	0-0	0-0	1-1	100.0	+ 16.00

KEMPTON (Group 1)

Leading Trainers 1991-96

	Total W-R	Nov Hdles	H'cap Hdles	Nov Chses	H'cap Chses	Per cent	£1 Level Stake
N J Henderson	18-77	6-29	1-14	7-16	4-18	23.4	+ 7.35
D Nicholson	17-72	9-32	0-5	5-21	3-14	23.6	- 11.41
M C Pipe	15-71	8-34	2-14	3-15	2-8	21.1	+ 13.55
J T Gifford	14-104	3-34	2-13	5-29	4-28	13.5	- 20.11
K C Bailey	11-52	2-15	0-5	4-15	5-17	21.2	- 0.17
O Sherwood	9-48	2-14	1-8	6-14	0-12	18.8	- 19.14
D R C Elsworth	9-62	8-33	0-12	1-6	0-11	14.5	+ 11.23
Miss H C Knight	8-38	4-18	0-2	3-11	1-7	21.1	+ 5.47
R H Alner	7-21	1-5	0-1	4-11	2-4	33.3	+ 28.91
T Thomson Jones	7-22	1-10	2-6	3-5	1-1	31.8	+ 20.16
N Twiston-Davies	7-53	5-25	1-7	1-15	0-6	13.2	- 28.54
D R Gandolfo	5-15	1-5	2-3	2-5	0-2	33.3	+ 6.72
Mrs J Pitman	5-40	1-15	1-9	1-5	2-11	12.5	- 19.00
P J Hobbs	5-49	3-21	1-7	0-7	1-14	10.2	- 15.25
F Doumen (Fra)	4-12	0-2	0-1	3-5	1-4	33.3	+ 24.50
Lady Herries	4-13	3-10	1-3	0-0	0-0	30.8	- 1.00
P F Nicholls	4-13	1-3	0-1	2-5	1-4	30.8	- 1.20
J A C Edwards	4-14	1-3	0-1	3-8	0-2	28.6	+ 11.50
Capt T A Forster	4-14	0-0	0-2	1-2	3-10	28.6	+ 5.66
T Casey	4-17	1-6	0-1	2-5	1-5	23.5	- 4.26

Leading Jockeys

	Total W-R	Per cent	£1 Level Stake	Best Trainer	W-R	Per cent	£1 Level Stake
R Dunwoody	26-124	21.0	- 24.41	N J Henderson	6-19	31.6	- 0.62
J Osborne	25-130	19.2	- 12.77	O Sherwood	8-35	22.9	- 9.65
M A FitzGerald	16-82	19.5	+ 2.41	N J Henderson	8-35	22.9	+ 15.25
A Maguire	16-89	18.0	- 17.44	D Nicholson	9-27	33.3	+ 7.81
N Williamson	11-51	21.6	+ 3.37	K C Bailey	7-17	41.2	+ 10.41
P Hide	7-40	17.5	+ 2.81	J T Gifford	7-36	19.4	+ 6.81
E Murphy	6-24	25.0	- 5.33	Lady Herries	3-7	42.9	+ 3.01
A P McCoy	6-30	20.0	+ 9.30	P F Nicholls	3-5	60.0	+ 2.30
P Holley	6-53	11.3	+ 2.23	D R C Elsworth	6-40	15.0	+ 15.23
G Bradley	6-55	10.9	- 30.28	C P E Brooks	3-23	13.0	- 17.78
W Marston	5-20	25.0	+ 12.00	Mrs J Pitman	2-10	20.0	- 3.50
M Richards	5-47	10.6	- 29.25	S Sherwood	2-4	50.0	+ 3.25

How the Favourites Fared

	W-R	Per cent	£1 Level Stake		W-R	Per cent	£1 Level Stake
Novice Hurdles	33-82	40.2	- 5.69	Novice Chases	33-67	49.3	+ 0.12
H'cap Hurdles	15-50	30.0	- 11.08	H'cap Chases	17-54	31.5	- 12.76
N H Flat	3-9	33.3	- 1.50	Hunter Chases	2-5	40.0	- 1.83
Totals	51-141	36.2	- 18.27	Totals	52-126	41.3	- 14.47
All favourites	103-267	38.6	- 32.74				

LEADING TRAINERS BY MONTH AT KEMPTON 1991-96

October

	Total W-R	Nov Hdles	H'cap Hdles	Nov Chses	H'cap Chses	Per cent	£1 Level Stake
N J Henderson	3-6	0-0	0-1	1-2	2-3	50.0	+ 8.75
Miss H C Knight	3-8	1-1	0-0	2-4	0-3	37.5	+ 4.47
J T Gifford	3-17	0-4	0-1	2-4	1-8	17.6	- 4.10
Lady Herries	2-2	1-1	1-1	0-0	0-0	100.0	+ 5.38
S Christian	2-3	0-0	2-3	0-0	0-0	66.7	+ 3.00

November

	Total W-R	Nov Hdles	H'cap Hdles	Nov Chses	H'cap Chses	Per cent	£1 Level Stake
J T Gifford	8-27	3-10	2-2	1-7	2-8	29.6	+ 28.66
Capt T A Forster	3-4	0-0	0-0	1-2	2-2	75.0	+ 7.66
M C Pipe	3-5	2-2	0-0	0-1	1-2	60.0	+ 6.98
K C Bailey	3-14	1-5	0-1	2-5	0-3	21.4	- 1.67
N J Henderson	2-5	1-4	1-1	0-0	0-0	40.0	+ 0.75

December

	Total W-R	Nov Hdles	H'cap Hdles	Nov Chses	H'cap Chses	Per cent	£1 Level Stake
D Nicholson	5-15	1-3	0-1	3-8	1-3	33.3	+ 7.03
N J Henderson	4-19	2-4	0-5	1-6	1-4	21.1	+ 10.13
F Doumen (Fra)	3-8	0-2	0-0	3-5	0-1	37.5	+ 22.00
O Sherwood	3-9	0-0	1-3	2-3	0-3	33.3	+ 1.75
K C Bailey	3-12	0-2	0-0	1-7	2-3	25.0	- 0.67

January

	Total W-R	Nov Hdles	H'cap Hdles	Nov Chses	H'cap Chses	Per cent	£1 Level Stake
Miss H C Knight	3-5	2-3	0-1	0-0	1-1	60.0	+ 12.00
D R C Elsworth	3-11	2-5	0-1	1-3	0-2	27.3	+ 15.00
N Twiston-Davies	3-12	3-8	0-2	0-1	0-1	25.0	- 2.54
D Nicholson	3-13	2-6	0-0	0-4	1-3	23.1	+ 4.25
Mrs J Pitman	3-14	1-5	1-5	1-2	0-2	21.4	+ 0.50

February

	Total W-R	Nov Hdles	H'cap Hdles	Nov Chses	H'cap Chses	Per cent	£1 Level Stake
N J Henderson	7-26	3-15	0-1	3-3	1-7	26.9	+ 3.13
M C Pipe	7-28	4-17	1-2	2-7	0-2	25.0	+ 1.53
D Nicholson	5-30	4-19	0-2	1-5	0-4	16.7	- 17.14
R H Alner	3-5	1-1	0-0	1-3	1-1	60.0	+ 9.50
O Sherwood	3-12	2-6	0-3	1-3	0-0	25.0	- 4.14

LEICESTER (Group 3)

Leading Trainers 1991-96

	Total W-R	Nov Hdles	H'cap Hdles	Nov Chses	H'cap Chses	Per cent	£1 Level Stake
M C Pipe	22-78	13-39	2-11	7-18	0-10	28.2	- 18.57
Mrs J Pitman	16-64	4-19	1-6	8-24	3-15	25.0	- 6.11
D Nicholson	12-52	5-19	0-5	4-15	3-13	23.1	+137.94
N Twiston-Davies	7-25	4-15	0-0	3-7	0-3	28.0	+ 0.43
N J Henderson	6-19	0-6	2-4	3-6	1-3	31.6	+ 9.16
O Sherwood	5-17	2-7	1-1	1-4	1-5	29.4	+ 14.94
J White	5-17	4-12	0-0	1-3	0-2	29.4	+ 15.50
Mrs S A Bramall	5-21	0-4	0-0	2-6	3-11	23.8	+ 7.50
J Mackie	5-28	1-8	1-5	1-10	2-5	17.9	+ 8.30
H J Manners	4-7	1-2	1-2	2-3	0-0	57.1	+139.50
Miss C Saunders	4-11	0-0	0-0	4-11	0-0	36.4	+ 18.40
N Tinkler	4-12	1-6	1-1	2-4	0-1	33.3	+ 4.30
N A Gaselee	4-14	0-6	0-0	1-2	3-6	28.6	+ 16.25
Miss H C Knight	4-20	3-8	0-3	0-3	1-6	20.0	+ 1.25
Capt T A Forster	4-29	0-5	1-3	0-15	3-6	13.8	+ 8.25
J Fanshawe	3-4	2-3	1-1	0-0	0-0	75.0	+ 10.50
S Dow	3-6	0-0	2-5	1-1	0-0	50.0	+ 21.00
J S King	3-11	0-3	0-2	0-1	3-5	27.3	- 3.00
B Palling	3-11	2-8	1-3	0-0	0-0	27.3	+ 46.25
J G FitzGerald	3-12	2-5	0-2	0-1	1-4	25.0	- 4.43

Leading Jockeys

	Total W-R	Per cent	£1 Level Stake	Best Trainer	W-R	Per cent	£1 Level Stake
R Dunwoody	11-61	18.0	- 29.16	N J Henderson	2-7	28.6	+ 0.75
C Llewellyn	9-36	25.0	+ 17.54	N Twiston-Davies	4-14	28.6	+ 3.29
W Marston	9-61	14.8	+ 7.21	Mrs J Pitman	4-17	23.5	+ 4.50
A Maguire	9-61	14.8	- 28.96	D Nicholson	7-19	36.8	+ 6.29
J Osborne	8-42	19.0	- 4.55	C R Egerton	2-2	100.0	+ 7.88
D Bridgwater	7-39	17.9	- 15.93	N Twiston-Davies	3-6	50.0	+ 2.15
N Williamson	6-36	16.7	- 4.75	J A C Edwards	3-16	18.8	- 0.75
M A FitzGerald	6-38	15.8	- 7.59	N J Henderson	3-8	37.5	+ 5.41
M Dwyer	5-26	19.2	- 10.71	J G FitzGerald	3-9	33.3	- 1.43
G Bradley	5-32	15.6	- 5.77	N Tinkler	1-1	100.0	+ 4.00
D Parker	3-8	37.5	+ 13.00	Mrs S A Bramall	3-6	50.0	+ 15.00
J R Kavanagh	3-19	15.8	+ 10.00	N A Gaselee	1-1	100.0	+ 10.00

How the Favourites Fared

	W-R	Per cent	£1 Level Stake		W-R	Per cent	£1 Level Stake
Novice Hurdles	25-80	31.3	- 30.52	Novice Chases	24-49	49.0	- 1.55
H'cap Hurdles	7-37	18.9	- 14.50	H'cap Chases	19-50	38.0	+ 4.90
N H Flat	0-0	-	0.00	Hunter Chases	10-24	41.7	- 4.20
Totals	32-117	27.4	- 45.02	Totals	53-123	43.1	- 0.85
All favourites	85-240	35.4	- 45.87				

LEADING TRAINERS BY MONTH AT LEICESTER 1991-96

November

	Total W-R	Nov Hdles	H'cap Hdles	Nov Chses	H'cap Chses	Per cent	£1 Level Stake
D Nicholson	5-19	1-8	0-2	2-5	2-4	26.3	- 1.50
M C Pipe	5-21	3-12	2-5	0-2	0-2	23.8	- 5.80
N Tinkler	3-5	1-3	0-0	2-2	0-0	60.0	+ 5.80
J Mackie	3-12	1-6	1-2	0-2	1-2	25.0	+ 10.05
N A Gaselee	2-3	0-1	0-0	1-1	1-1	66.7	+ 13.00

December

	Total W-R	Nov Hdles	H'cap Hdles	Nov Chses	H'cap Chses	Per cent	£1 Level Stake
Mrs J Pitman	3-10	0-1	1-2	1-4	1-3	30.0	+ 1.75
A L Forbes	2-2	1-1	0-0	1-1	0-0	100.0	+ 7.50
J White	2-2	1-1	0-0	1-1	0-0	100.0	+ 19.00
M C Pipe	2-7	0-3	0-0	2-4	0-0	28.6	- 3.97
J Fanshawe	1-1	0-0	1-1	0-0	0-0	100.0	+ 3.00

January

	Total W-R	Nov Hdles	H'cap Hdles	Nov Chses	H'cap Chses	Per cent	£1 Level Stake
Mrs J Pitman	7-29	3-12	0-4	4-9	0-4	24.1	- 0.38
M C Pipe	4-19	3-9	0-6	1-3	0-1	21.1	- 4.96
N Twiston-Davies	3-11	2-7	0-0	1-3	0-1	27.3	- 3.19
J Fanshawe	2-2	2-2	0-0	0-0	0-0	100.0	+ 8.50
N J Henderson	2-5	0-1	0-1	2-3	0-0	40.0	+ 0.66

February

	Total W-R	Nov Hdles	H'cap Hdles	Nov Chses	H'cap Chses	Per cent	£1 Level Stake
M C Pipe	11-29	7-15	0-0	4-7	0-7	37.9	- 1.85
D Nicholson	4-8	2-2	0-0	2-5	0-1	50.0	+153.65
Mrs J Pitman	4-12	0-2	0-0	3-6	1-4	33.3	- 2.98
O Sherwood	2-2	1-1	0-0	0-0	1-1	100.0	+ 14.50
J G FitzGerald	2-6	1-2	0-0	0-1	1-3	33.3	0.00

March

	Total W-R	Nov Hdles	H'cap Hdles	Nov Chses	H'cap Chses	Per cent	£1 Level Stake
Miss C Saunders	4-11	0-0	0-0	4-11	0-0	36.4	+ 18.40
J S King	2-2	0-0	0-0	0-0	2-2	100.0	+ 3.25
H J Manners	2-2	0-0	0-0	2-2	0-0	100.0	+133.00
Mrs I McKie	2-3	0-0	0-0	1-2	1-1	66.7	+ 10.00
Andrew Turnell	2-3	0-0	0-0	1-1	1-2	66.7	+ 5.50

LINGFIELD (Group 2)

Leading Trainers 1991-96

	Total W-R	Nov Hdles	H'cap Hdles	Nov Chses	H'cap Chses	Per cent	£1 Level Stake
Miss B Sanders	21-66	9-30	11-34	1-2	0-0	31.8	- 2.14
R Akehurst	17-45	11-26	5-10	0-4	1-5	37.8	+ 16.24
S Dow	16-57	5-30	11-26	0-1	0-0	28.1	- 10.92
M C Pipe	13-53	7-28	1-11	4-10	1-4	24.5	- 12.95
R J O'Sullivan	13-65	5-32	4-18	2-5	2-10	20.0	- 16.53
T Thomson Jones	12-46	5-17	7-25	0-1	0-3	26.1	+ 1.34
Andrew Turnell	10-32	3-12	1-3	4-12	2-5	31.3	+ 5.00
P A Kelleway	9-15	7-9	2-6	0-0	0-0	60.0	+ 17.60
C Weedon	8-20	2-5	6-11	0-2	0-2	40.0	+ 1.04
J A B Old	8-21	3-7	5-11	0-0	0-3	38.1	+ 2.01
J L Spearing	8-22	4-8	4-14	0-0	0-0	36.4	+ 43.29
R Lee	8-27	1-7	6-13	0-2	1-5	29.6	+ 14.15
J White	8-46	4-26	4-15	0-4	0-1	17.4	- 17.20
R J Hodges	7-44	1-13	3-20	0-2	3-9	15.9	- 13.67
P F Nicholls	6-19	3-11	0-2	1-1	2-5	31.6	+ 1.95
N J Henderson	6-23	4-13	0-3	0-3	2-4	26.1	+ 8.16
R P C Hoad	6-50	1-17	4-25	0-4	1-4	12.0	- 18.63
D M Grissell	6-59	0-23	2-17	2-8	2-11	10.2	- 37.88
P W Hiatt	5-12	1-4	4-8	0-0	0-0	41.7	+ 20.08
D Nicholson	5-15	2-8	0-2	3-4	0-1	33.3	- 2.99

Leading Jockeys

	Total W-R	Per cent	£1 Level Stake	Best Trainer	W-R	Per cent	£1 Level Stake
A Maguire	23-104	22.1	- 30.83	Miss B Sanders	4-13	30.8	+ 1.41
A Dicken	21-60	35.0	+ 7.42	S Dow	15-39	38.5	+ 5.42
D O'Sullivan	13-93	14.0	- 35.03	R J O'Sullivan	12-56	21.4	- 11.03
D Bridgwater	12-43	27.9	+ 26.46	M C Pipe	5-15	33.3	+ 7.63
R Dunwoody	12-49	24.5	- 7.94	M C Pipe	3-5	60.0	- 1.55
J Osborne	11-46	23.9	- 10.61	C Weedon	4-5	80.0	+ 1.29
A Bates	9-18	50.0	+ 26.12	P A Kelleway	7-11	63.6	+ 16.45
D Gallagher	9-79	11.4	- 28.61	Mrs M E Long	1-1	100.0	+ 6.00
M A FitzGerald	8-31	25.8	+ 15.01	S E Kettlewell	1-1	100.0	+ 1.38
T Grantham	7-28	25.0	+ 5.77	J A B Old	6-16	37.5	+ 0.77
J R Kavanagh	7-39	17.9	- 4.34	N J Henderson	4-11	36.4	+ 11.16
M Richards	7-94	7.4	- 70.22	Miss B Sanders	2-5	40.0	- 1.97

How the Favourites Fared

	W-R	Per cent	£1 Level Stake		W-R	Per cent	£1 Level Stake
Novice Hurdles	73-133	54.9	+ 9.80	Novice Chases	16-38	42.1	- 5.73
H'cap Hurdles	76-158	48.1	+ 13.80	H'cap Chases	19-48	39.6	- 2.19
N H Flat	14-28	50.0	+ 0.21	Hunter Chases	2-7	28.6	- 4.06
Totals	163-319	51.1	+ 23.81	Totals	37-93	39.8	- 11.98
All favourites	200-412	48.5	+ 11.83				

LEADING TRAINERS BY MONTH AT LINGFIELD 1991-96

August

	Total W-R	Nov Hdles	H'cap Hdles	Nov Chses	H'cap Chses	Per cent	£1 Level Stake
R Akehurst	1-1	1-1	0-0	0-0	0-0	100.0	0.00

December

	Total W-R	Nov Hdles	H'cap Hdles	Nov Chses	H'cap Chses	Per cent	£1 Level Stake
R Akehurst	6-12	4-6	2-3	0-1	0-2	50.0	+ 13.13
N Twiston-Davies	3-8	1-4	1-1	1-3	0-0	37.5	+ 8.50
D Nicholson	3-11	2-6	0-2	1-2	0-1	27.3	- 3.74
M J Haynes	2-2	0-0	2-2	0-0	0-0	100.0	+ 5.50
Miss B Sanders	2-5	0-2	1-2	1-1	0-0	40.0	+ 1.38

January

	Total W-R	Nov Hdles	H'cap Hdles	Nov Chses	H'cap Chses	Per cent	£1 Level Stake
Miss B Sanders	11-33	7-19	4-13	0-1	0-0	33.3	+ 4.88
S Dow	10-31	2-14	8-16	0-1	0-0	32.3	- 2.27
T Thomson Jones	6-22	2-7	4-12	0-1	0-2	27.3	+ 6.52
R J O'Sullivan	6-26	5-17	1-4	0-2	0-3	23.1	- 8.37
Andrew Turnell	5-14	3-7	0-1	2-5	0-1	35.7	+ 0.66

February

	Total W-R	Nov Hdles	H'cap Hdles	Nov Chses	H'cap Chses	Per cent	£1 Level Stake
M C Pipe	7-17	5-10	0-2	2-5	0-0	41.2	- 5.07
Miss B Sanders	6-17	2-5	4-12	0-0	0-0	35.3	- 3.54
J White	6-18	3-12	3-6	0-0	0-0	33.3	- 2.20
P A Kelleway	5-6	3-4	2-2	0-0	0-0	83.3	+ 10.05
R Lee	5-13	1-5	4-6	0-1	0-1	38.5	+ 2.05

March

	Total W-R	Nov Hdles	H'cap Hdles	Nov Chses	H'cap Chses	Per cent	£1 Level Stake
D M Grissell	5-15	0-4	1-3	2-3	2-5	33.3	+ 3.62
J L Spearing	3-4	1-1	2-3	0-0	0-0	75.0	+ 4.75
G L Moore	3-5	1-2	2-2	0-0	0-1	60.0	+ 3.50
M J Wilkinson	3-5	0-0	0-0	2-3	1-2	60.0	+ 9.50
Andrew Turnell	3-7	0-1	0-1	2-3	1-2	42.9	+ 2.33

LUDLOW (Group 4)

Leading Trainers 1991-96

	Total W-R	Nov Hdles	H'cap Hdles	Nov Chses	H'cap Chses	Per cent	£1 Level Stake
D Nicholson	25-91	12-43	2-9	1-7	10-32	27.5	+ 2.83
K C Bailey	17-63	9-31	2-9	4-10	2-13	27.0	+ 11.79
M C Pipe	17-85	9-55	4-16	3-7	1-7	20.0	- 10.09
Capt T A Forster	13-80	3-31	0-6	2-14	8-29	16.3	- 32.27
P J Hobbs	12-60	4-23	2-12	0-1	6-24	20.0	+ 6.93
Miss H C Knight	11-73	5-34	2-13	4-14	0-12	15.1	- 23.08
S Sherwood	10-36	2-12	2-10	5-8	1-6	27.8	+ 6.02
N Twiston-Davies	10-100	2-40	4-20	1-11	3-29	10.0	- 45.23
J A C Edwards	9-54	1-26	0-2	1-7	7-19	16.7	+ 21.25
N J Henderson	8-26	4-12	0-2	1-4	3-8	30.8	+ 13.16
Mrs J Pitman	6-42	2-10	4-11	0-9	0-12	14.3	- 4.38
R J Hodges	6-44	2-13	1-14	0-3	3-14	13.6	- 14.27
Miss J Pidgeon	5-9	0-0	0-0	5-9	0-0	55.6	+ 1.26
S Christian	5-27	3-13	1-6	1-5	0-3	18.5	- 7.74
D Burchell	5-35	2-16	0-8	1-6	2-5	14.3	- 11.81
J L Spearing	5-36	3-12	0-11	1-7	1-6	13.9	- 9.50
B Preece	5-68	3-47	1-10	0-7	1-4	7.4	- 28.63
F Jordan	5-96	0-37	4-35	1-12	0-12	5.2	- 55.70
Mrs J Renfree-Barons	4-9	2-3	0-1	1-2	1-3	44.4	+ 17.38
R Curtis	4-12	0-3	3-4	0-0	1-5	33.3	+ 36.00

Leading Jockeys

	Total W-R	Per cent	£1 Level Stake	Best Trainer	W-R	Per cent	£1 Level Stake
R Dunwoody	20-68	29.4	+ 17.28	D Nicholson	4-10	40.0	+ 8.50
A Maguire	18-91	19.8	- 28.02	D Nicholson	11-40	27.5	- 5.42
N Williamson	12-79	15.2	- 19.97	J A C Edwards	8-31	25.8	+ 18.26
J Osborne	11-52	21.2	- 10.45	K C Bailey	3-5	60.0	+ 8.75
W Marston	10-68	14.7	+ 8.91	D Nicholson	3-9	33.3	+ 12.83
M A FitzGerald	9-60	15.0	- 16.37	N J Henderson	3-5	60.0	+ 9.63
C Llewellyn	9-68	13.2	- 32.85	Capt T A Forster	3-14	21.4	- 0.25
A P McCoy	8-39	20.5	- 2.54	Capt T A Forster	2-5	40.0	+ 3.23
B Powell	8-43	18.6	+ 3.08	R H Buckler	2-7	28.6	+ 8.33
J Railton	8-46	17.4	- 13.62	M Meade	2-3	66.7	+ 4.13
S McNeill	8-58	13.8	- 16.70	J C Tuck	2-5	40.0	+ 6.00
J R Kavanagh	8-63	12.7	- 12.74	N J Henderson	3-6	50.0	+ 5.66

How the Favourites Fared

	W-R	Per cent	£1 Level Stake		W-R	Per cent	£1 Level Stake
Novice Hurdles	52-123	42.3	- 1.00	Novice Chases	23-48	47.9	- 1.21
H'cap Hurdles	24-78	30.8	- 7.87	H'cap Chases	34-91	37.4	- 1.78
N H Flat	8-23	34.8	- 1.65	Hunter Chases	10-26	38.5	- 2.82
Totals	84-224	37.5	- 10.52	Totals	67-165	40.6	- 5.81
All favourites	151-389	38.8	- 16.33				

LEADING TRAINERS BY MONTH AT LUDLOW 1991-96

September

	Total W-R	Nov Hdles	H'cap Hdles	Nov Chses	H'cap Chses	Per cent	£1 Level Stake
Miss K S Allison	1-1	1-1	0-0	0-0	0-0	100.0	+ 1.25
T Casey	1-1	0-0	0-0	1-1	0-0	100.0	+ 0.91
G A Ham	1-1	1-1	0-0	0-0	0-0	100.0	+ 9.00

October

	Total W-R	Nov Hdles	H'cap Hdles	Nov Chses	H'cap Chses	Per cent	£1 Level Stake
J J O'Neill	3-3	2-2	0-0	0-0	1-1	100.0	+ 19.25
Dr J D Scargill	2-2	0-0	2-2	0-0	0-0	100.0	+ 4.38
N J Henderson	2-3	0-0	0-1	1-1	1-1	66.7	+ 3.13

November

	Total W-R	Nov Hdles	H'cap Hdles	Nov Chses	H'cap Chses	Per cent	£1 Level Stake
Capt T A Forster	3-3	1-1	0-0	1-1	1-1	100.0	+ 3.20
P J Hobbs	3-7	2-3	1-1	0-0	0-3	42.9	+ 4.70
D Nicholson	2-6	1-3	0-0	0-0	1-3	33.3	- 0.13

December

	Total W-R	Nov Hdles	H'cap Hdles	Nov Chses	H'cap Chses	Per cent	£1 Level Stake
D Nicholson	4-17	2-9	0-0	0-2	2-6	23.5	- 4.50
Mrs Renfree-Barons	3-5	2-2	0-0	0-1	1-2	60.0	+ 19.00
K C Bailey	3-10	1-3	0-1	1-2	1-4	30.0	+ 3.25

January

	Total W-R	Nov Hdles	H'cap Hdles	Nov Chses	H'cap Chses	Per cent	£1 Level Stake
D Nicholson	6-23	2-10	1-4	1-2	2-7	26.1	+ 8.76
Capt T A Forster	3-18	0-5	0-2	1-5	2-6	16.7	- 3.50
S Sherwood	2-4	1-1	0-0	1-2	0-1	50.0	+ 0.87

February

	Total W-R	Nov Hdles	H'cap Hdles	Nov Chses	H'cap Chses	Per cent	£1 Level Stake
D Nicholson	4-15	3-7	0-1	0-2	1-5	26.7	- 2.38
J A C Edwards	3-11	1-4	0-1	1-2	1-4	27.3	- 1.63
N J Henderson	2-4	0-2	0-0	0-0	2-2	50.0	+ 14.00

March

	Total W-R	Nov Hdles	H'cap Hdles	Nov Chses	H'cap Chses	Per cent	£1 Level Stake
D Nicholson	5-14	3-9	0-0	0-1	2-4	35.7	+ 4.25
M C Pipe	5-14	1-8	2-4	2-2	0-0	35.7	+ 6.06
R Curtis	2-2	0-0	1-1	0-0	1-1	100.0	+ 20.00

April

	Total W-R	Nov Hdles	H'cap Hdles	Nov Chses	H'cap Chses	Per cent	£1 Level Stake
K C Bailey	5-17	3-7	1-4	1-2	0-4	29.4	+ 14.00
N Twiston-Davies	4-19	0-5	2-8	0-1	2-5	21.1	- 1.88
Miss H C Knight	3-9	2-3	0-1	1-1	0-4	33.3	+ 6.00

May

	Total W-R	Nov Hdles	H'cap Hdles	Nov Chses	H'cap Chses	Per cent	£1 Level Stake
K C Bailey	5-11	2-6	1-2	1-1	1-2	45.5	+ 5.03
P J Hobbs	2-2	1-1	0-0	0-0	1-1	100.0	+ 14.73
H S Howe	1-1	1-1	0-0	0-0	0-0	100.0	+ 2.50

MARKET RASEN (Group 3)

Leading Trainers 1991-96

	Total W-R	Nov Hdles	H'cap Hdles	Nov Chses	H'cap Chses	Per cent	£1 Level Stake
Mrs M Reveley	20-83	6-30	1-14	8-12	5-27	24.1	- 17.53
N Tinkler	18-79	9-37	6-27	2-7	1-8	22.8	- 27.03
J G FitzGerald	17-101	4-56	4-13	3-8	6-24	16.8	- 9.51
M C Pipe	16-53	7-25	3-13	5-8	1-7	30.2	- 9.71
K A Morgan	15-103	7-40	6-38	1-10	1-15	14.6	- 8.50
O Brennan	15-143	3-56	3-42	4-15	5-30	10.5	- 48.34
J White	11-42	6-14	1-8	3-10	1-10	26.2	+ 2.14
Miss H C Knight	9-24	2-11	4-7	1-3	2-3	37.5	+ 17.31
K C Bailey	9-32	1-10	0-2	5-8	3-12	28.1	+ 1.23
J M Jefferson	8-32	2-14	0-6	3-4	3-8	25.0	+ 27.42
P Beaumont	8-50	3-14	1-8	2-13	2-15	16.0	+ 17.75
J J O'Neill	7-52	4-18	1-9	1-6	1-19	13.5	+ 11.50
M C Chapman	7-181	1-51	2-58	1-20	3-52	3.9	-118.63
F Murphy	6-26	1-6	2-5	2-3	1-12	23.1	- 2.25
M J Ryan	6-31	1-11	4-15	1-3	0-2	19.4	- 9.74
M D Hammond	6-50	4-28	0-17	0-1	2-4	12.0	- 22.77
Mrs J R Ramsden	5-17	3-11	2-4	0-1	0-1	29.4	+ 2.08
N Twiston-Davies	5-19	2-10	0-4	2-3	1-2	26.3	- 0.88
Miss L Siddall	5-35	1-17	2-10	0-0	2-8	14.3	- 4.50
P Cheesbrough	5-37	0-7	0-3	1-10	4-17	13.5	- 2.25

Leading Jockeys

	Total W-R	Per cent	£1 Level Stake	Best Trainer	W-R	Per cent	£1 Level Stake
P Niven	23-109	21.1	- 8.71	Mrs M Reveley	14-53	26.4	- 10.91
L Wyer	20-109	18.3	- 3.71	J M Jefferson	3-7	42.9	+ 28.50
M Dwyer	18-102	17.6	- 31.57	N Tinkler	4-13	30.8	- 2.25
A S Smith	17-118	14.4	- 19.75	K A Morgan	13-83	15.7	- 4.00
N Williamson	14-50	28.0	+ 8.47	K C Bailey	5-12	41.7	+ 2.73
A Maguire	12-76	15.8	- 29.51	J White	3-6	50.0	+ 1.36
Martin Brennan	12-130	9.2	- 46.59	O Brennan	11-98	11.2	- 24.59
R Dunwoody	10-63	15.9	- 17.33	Miss L Siddall	2-3	66.7	+ 7.00
D Byrne	9-62	14.5	- 19.68	J G FitzGerald	4-10	40.0	+ 9.83
J Ryan	9-63	14.3	+ 11.63	M J Ryan	5-28	17.9	- 9.87
R Garrity	9-85	10.6	- 17.67	Mrs J R Ramsden	3-10	30.0	- 1.67
D Bridgwater	8-47	17.0	- 12.34	M C Pipe	5-14	35.7	+ 4.66

How the Favourites Fared

	W-R	Per cent	£1 Level Stake		W-R	Per cent	£1 Level Stake
Novice Hurdles	60-145	41.4	- 12.34	Novice Chases	41-86	47.7	- 4.01
H'cap Hurdles	22-116	19.0	- 53.83	H'cap Chases	35-117	29.9	- 34.63
N H Flat	5-29	17.2	- 16.71	Hunter Chases	5-11	45.5	- 2.24
Totals	87-290	30.0	- 82.88	Totals	81-214	37.9	- 40.88
All favourites	168-504	33.3	-123.76				

LEADING TRAINERS BY MONTH AT MARKET RASEN 1991-96

	Total W-R	Nov Hdles	H'cap Hdles	Nov Chses	H'cap Chses	Per cent	£1 Level Stake
June							
J White	3-13	1-3	1-2	0-2	1-6	23.1	+ 9.50
W J Smith	2-2	0-0	2-2	0-0	0-0	100.0	+ 9.00
July							
Miss L Siddall	3-5	0-1	2-2	0-0	1-2	60.0	+ 10.50
J White	3-9	2-4	0-2	1-2	0-1	33.3	− 3.46
August							
N Tinkler	4-12	2-7	1-3	0-0	1-2	33.3	− 4.54
M C Chapman	4-17	0-5	1-7	0-0	3-5	23.5	+ 26.00
September							
M C Pipe	3-4	1-2	0-0	2-2	0-0	75.0	+ 4.03
J Wade	3-7	0-1	0-1	0-1	3-4	42.9	+ 8.75
October							
K C Bailey	4-8	0-2	0-0	3-3	1-3	50.0	+ 4.82
N Twiston-Davies	3-6	2-4	0-1	0-0	1-1	50.0	+ 6.75
November							
Mrs M Reveley	10-28	2-11	1-2	5-9	2-6	35.7	− 0.29
N Tinkler	5-13	3-7	1-3	1-2	0-1	38.5	+ 0.15
December							
J G FitzGerald	6-17	1-4	2-5	1-3	2-5	35.3	+ 18.63
S Christian	2-2	1-1	0-0	1-1	0-0	100.0	+ 2.29
January							
J A Glover	2-4	2-2	0-1	0-0	0-1	50.0	+ 14.00
M D Hammond	2-8	2-6	0-2	0-0	0-0	25.0	+ 2.25
February							
O Brennan	3-5	0-0	1-2	1-1	1-2	60.0	+ 19.50
M C Pipe	2-3	1-2	0-0	0-0	1-1	66.7	+ 2.83
March							
J G FitzGerald	2-4	0-1	1-2	0-0	1-1	50.0	+ 2.75
M C Pipe	2-4	2-4	0-0	0-0	0-0	50.0	− 0.37
April							
M C Pipe	5-8	3-4	0-1	2-2	0-1	62.5	+ 1.30
Miss H C Knight	5-14	2-7	2-3	0-2	1-2	35.7	+ 7.60
May							
Mrs M Reveley	5-11	1-2	0-2	2-2	2-5	45.5	+ 5.55
C Smith	3-10	0-4	3-4	0-2	0-0	30.0	+ 11.00

MUSSELBURGH (Group 4)

Leading Trainers 1991-96

	Total W-R	Nov Hdles	H'cap Hdles	Nov Chses	H'cap Chses	Per cent	£1 Level Stake
M D Hammond	28-116	10-47	7-25	2-18	9-26	24.1	+ 20.96
Mrs M Reveley	16-56	12-26	3-18	1-3	0-9	28.6	- 2.11
J H Johnson	13-86	2-35	2-14	5-16	4-21	15.1	- 21.75
N Tinkler	10-35	5-13	1-9	2-4	2-9	28.6	+ 0.27
P Monteith	10-68	5-33	1-18	1-8	3-9	14.7	+116.89
Mrs S C Bradburne	10-90	0-23	3-12	2-25	5-30	11.1	- 6.00
C Parker	9-41	0-8	6-11	0-10	3-12	22.0	+ 19.00
G M Moore	8-36	4-21	2-10	2-3	0-2	22.2	- 12.65
Denys Smith	7-53	1-23	1-12	1-6	4-12	13.2	- 28.67
J L Eyre	5-24	4-15	1-9	0-0	0-0	20.8	+ 1.87
L Lungo	5-35	2-17	1-13	0-2	2-3	14.3	+ 42.50
J M Jefferson	4-16	1-8	3-8	0-0	0-0	25.0	+ 22.62
C W Thornton	4-17	1-8	1-5	1-2	1-2	23.5	+ 4.50
J J O'Neill	4-19	1-9	2-7	0-0	1-3	21.1	+ 2.75
B S Rothwell	4-24	1-9	0-5	2-4	1-6	16.7	+ 35.88
W G Reed	4-40	0-9	1-5	2-11	1-15	10.0	+ 52.00
K C Bailey	3-6	1-2	0-1	2-2	0-1	50.0	+ 3.66
J Mackie	3-7	0-2	3-4	0-1	0-0	42.9	+ 3.75
J Pearce	3-9	2-6	1-2	0-1	0-0	33.3	+ 8.38
Mrs S A Bramall	3-18	1-5	1-4	1-8	0-1	16.7	- 2.92

Leading Jockeys

	Total W-R	Per cent	£1 Level Stake	Best Trainer	W-R	Per cent	£1 Level Stake
B Storey	18-125	14.4	+ 64.31	C Parker	5-17	29.4	+ 27.00
P Niven	14-65	21.5	+ 21.85	Mrs M Reveley	7-22	31.8	+ 5.35
T Reed	14-100	14.0	+ 89.50	Mrs S C Bradburne	4-10	40.0	+ 7.50
A Dobbin	9-81	11.1	+ 36.06	V Thompson	2-4	50.0	+ 41.00
J Callaghan	8-47	17.0	- 22.43	G M Moore	4-16	25.0	- 0.80
M Dwyer	7-37	18.9	- 14.93	G M Moore	2-4	50.0	- 1.80
P Williams	6-47	12.8	- 7.00	Mrs S C Bradburne	3-30	10.0	- 12.00
D Gallagher	5-13	38.5	+ 6.13	C P E Brooks	2-3	66.7	+ 7.50
A Maguire	5-20	25.0	+ 5.88	J H Johnson	4-11	36.4	+ 7.88
D Parker	5-31	16.1	- 9.50	C Parker	4-17	23.5	- 1.00
D Bentley	5-43	11.6	- 21.63	M D Hammond	5-26	19.2	- 4.63
A Thornton	5-68	7.4	- 48.75	J Barclay	2-7	28.6	+ 0.50

How the Favourites Fared

	W-R	Per cent	£1 Level Stake		W-R	Per cent	£1 Level Stake
Novice Hurdles	35-68	51.5	+ 5.27	Novice Chases	21-42	50.0	+ 6.63
H'cap Hurdles	22-61	36.1	- 1.83	H'cap Chases	17-51	33.3	- 3.31
N H Flat	5-10	50.0	+ 3.91	Hunter Chases	2-4	50.0	+ 0.42
Totals	62-139	44.6	+ 7.35	Totals	40-97	41.2	+ 3.74
All favourites	102-236	43.2	+ 11.09				

LEADING TRAINERS BY MONTH AT MUSSELBURGH 1991-96

December

	Total W-R	Nov Hdles	H'cap Hdles	Nov Chses	H'cap Chses	Per cent	£1 Level Stake
M D Hammond	11-34	4-11	1-6	0-6	6-11	32.4	+ 24.04
J H Johnson	5-24	0-6	2-6	3-8	0-4	20.8	+ 6.88
Mrs S C Bradburne	5-35	0-8	1-4	1-11	3-12	14.3	- 7.50
G M Moore	4-14	2-8	2-5	0-0	0-1	28.6	+ 2.83
N Tinkler	3-11	2-5	0-2	1-2	0-2	27.3	- 2.66

January

	Total W-R	Nov Hdles	H'cap Hdles	Nov Chses	H'cap Chses	Per cent	£1 Level Stake
Mrs M Reveley	9-30	6-12	2-13	1-1	0-4	30.0	- 0.09
M D Hammond	6-44	3-20	1-7	2-10	0-7	13.6	- 18.45
C Parker	5-12	0-2	2-5	0-2	3-3	41.7	+ 31.00
J H Johnson	5-26	2-10	0-5	2-5	1-6	19.2	- 2.50
N Tinkler	4-12	1-4	1-4	1-2	1-2	33.3	+ 7.17

February

	Total W-R	Nov Hdles	H'cap Hdles	Nov Chses	H'cap Chses	Per cent	£1 Level Stake
M D Hammond	10-35	3-14	4-11	0-2	3-8	28.6	+ 16.76
Mrs M Reveley	4-12	4-8	0-3	0-0	0-1	33.3	+ 4.50
Denys Smith	4-16	0-5	1-3	1-4	2-4	25.0	+ 0.75
K C Bailey	3-3	1-1	0-0	2-2	0-0	100.0	+ 6.66
N Tinkler	3-11	2-4	0-3	0-0	1-4	27.3	- 3.24

March

	Total W-R	Nov Hdles	H'cap Hdles	Nov Chses	H'cap Chses	Per cent	£1 Level Stake
J S Goldie	1-1	1-1	0-0	0-0	0-0	100.0	+ 6.00
Mrs J Goodfellow	1-1	0-0	0-0	1-1	0-0	100.0	+ 1.75
D McCain	1-2	0-1	0-0	0-0	1-1	50.0	+ 9.00
P Monteith	1-2	0-0	0-0	0-1	1-1	50.0	+ 1.25
M D Hammond	1-3	0-2	1-1	0-0	0-0	33.3	- 1.38

NEWBURY (Group 1)

Leading Trainers 1991-96

	Total W-R	Nov Hdles	H'cap Hdles	Nov Chses	H'cap Chses	Per cent	£1 Level Stake
D Nicholson	29-124	16-52	2-17	8-26	3-29	23.4	- 22.75
N J Henderson	25-119	9-51	4-26	8-17	4-25	21.0	- 6.08
O Sherwood	21-81	10-40	2-13	5-11	4-17	25.9	- 7.13
M C Pipe	18-96	8-33	4-27	1-9	5-27	18.8	- 5.54
D R C Elsworth	14-72	6-28	1-20	3-8	4-16	19.4	+ 5.05
Mrs J Pitman	12-74	7-30	1-14	2-7	2-23	16.2	- 25.99
Andrew Turnell	10-53	1-18	2-8	3-12	4-15	18.9	+ 3.58
P J Hobbs	10-80	5-35	1-19	0-7	4-19	12.5	- 20.88
J T Gifford	10-123	2-52	0-22	3-27	5-22	8.1	- 75.53
N Twiston-Davies	9-96	1-50	1-17	4-13	3-16	9.4	- 53.17
S Sherwood	7-43	0-17	1-8	2-5	4-13	16.3	- 14.53
C P E Brooks	7-52	1-18	0-7	0-7	6-20	13.5	- 22.58
G B Balding	7-97	5-43	1-26	0-12	1-16	7.2	- 49.00
M H Tompkins	6-21	4-15	2-6	0-0	0-0	28.6	+ 7.06
K C Bailey	6-64	4-35	0-5	0-8	2-16	9.4	- 30.63
G Harwood	5-20	2-9	3-10	0-1	0-0	25.0	+ 3.42
Mrs M Reveley	5-23	3-6	2-15	0-0	0-2	21.7	- 8.17
Capt T A Forster	5-36	1-11	1-8	0-5	3-12	13.9	- 11.88
N A Gaselee	5-61	1-19	0-8	1-9	3-25	8.2	- 42.25
Lady Herries	4-12	2-6	1-1	0-1	1-4	33.3	+ 7.18

Leading Jockeys

	Total W-R	Per cent	£1 Level Stake	Best Trainer	W-R	Per cent	£1 Level Stake
J Osborne	44-173	25.4	- 5.20	O Sherwood	20-57	35.1	+ 14.86
R Dunwoody	41-163	25.2	- 27.55	D Nicholson	16-48	33.3	- 6.04
A Maguire	20-129	15.5	+ 1.30	D Nicholson	9-44	20.5	- 8.31
P Holley	15-79	19.0	+ 0.05	D R C Elsworth	13-51	25.5	+ 15.05
C Llewellyn	11-108	10.2	- 48.92	N Twiston-Davies	4-47	8.5	- 25.17
S McNeill	10-68	14.7	- 15.49	Andrew Turnell	4-24	16.7	- 5.25
W Marston	9-47	19.1	+ 22.01	Mrs J Pitman	4-13	30.8	+ 11.00
M A FitzGerald	9-100	9.0	- 58.37	N J Henderson	6-35	17.1	- 9.70
N Williamson	7-49	14.3	+ 9.50	K C Bailey	4-21	19.0	+ 5.50
P Carberry	6-15	40.0	+ 44.00	Andrew Turnell	3-6	50.0	+ 11.50
P Niven	5-25	20.0	- 10.17	Mrs M Reveley	5-17	29.4	- 2.17
J R Kavanagh	5-44	11.4	- 18.95	N J Henderson	3-21	14.3	- 4.70

How the Favourites Fared

	W-R	Per cent	£1 Level Stake		W-R	Per cent	£1 Level Stake
Novice Hurdles	56-107	52.3	+ 22.03	Novice Chases	29-59	49.2	+ 4.11
H'cap Hurdles	23-75	30.7	- 2.31	H'cap Chases	33-89	37.1	- 8.78
N H Flat	4-15	26.7	- 5.87	Hunter Chases	4-10	40.0	- 2.10
Totals	83-197	42.1	+ 13.85	Totals	66-158	41.8	- 6.77
All favourites	149-355	42.0	+ 7.08				

LEADING TRAINERS BY MONTH AT NEWBURY 1991-96

October	Total W-R	Nov Hdles	H'cap Hdles	Nov Chses	H'cap Chses	Per cent	£1 Level Stake
P J Hobbs	4-12	2-6	1-2	0-0	1-4	33.3	+ 10.50
N J Henderson	3-13	1-4	0-4	2-2	0-3	23.1	+ 6.75
G Richards	2-3	0-0	0-1	1-1	1-1	66.7	+ 4.50
K C Bailey	2-4	1-2	0-1	0-0	1-1	50.0	+ 11.00
G Harwood	2-5	1-1	1-3	0-1	0-0	40.0	- 0.25

November	Total W-R	Nov Hdles	H'cap Hdles	Nov Chses	H'cap Chses	Per cent	£1 Level Stake
D Nicholson	9-38	8-20	0-1	1-6	0-11	23.7	- 10.96
O Sherwood	8-24	5-13	1-2	0-3	2-6	33.3	+ 7.23
N J Henderson	7-29	3-12	0-2	2-6	2-9	24.1	- 6.37
M C Pipe	6-21	4-12	1-1	0-0	1-8	28.6	+ 15.13
Andrew Turnell	6-21	1-8	0-1	2-5	3-7	28.6	+ 14.83

December	Total W-R	Nov Hdles	H'cap Hdles	Nov Chses	H'cap Chses	Per cent	£1 Level Stake
Mrs J Pitman	3-5	3-3	0-1	0-1	0-0	60.0	+ 10.08
O Sherwood	3-6	1-3	0-0	1-1	1-2	50.0	+ 2.26
M J Haynes	1-1	0-0	1-1	0-0	0-0	100.0	+ 1.38
T P Tate	1-1	0-0	0-0	0-0	1-1	100.0	+ 4.00
M H Tompkins	1-1	1-1	0-0	0-0	0-0	100.0	+ 1.25

January	Total W-R	Nov Hdles	H'cap Hdles	Nov Chses	H'cap Chses	Per cent	£1 Level Stake
M C Pipe	3-9	2-4	1-3	0-0	0-2	33.3	- 0.75
D Nicholson	3-10	2-5	0-0	0-1	1-4	30.0	- 1.25
Capt T A Forster	2-5	1-1	1-2	0-1	0-1	40.0	+ 5.75
N J Henderson	2-9	1-5	0-0	1-1	0-3	22.2	- 0.05
P Beaumont	1-1	0-0	0-0	0-0	1-1	100.0	+ 2.25

February	Total W-R	Nov Hdles	H'cap Hdles	Nov Chses	H'cap Chses	Per cent	£1 Level Stake
D Nicholson	10-32	3-11	0-2	5-13	2-6	31.3	- 4.52
O Sherwood	4-18	0-3	1-7	3-5	0-3	22.2	- 4.18
D R C Elsworth	4-22	3-7	0-7	1-4	0-4	18.2	+ 0.85
Miss C Saunders	3-4	0-0	0-0	3-4	0-0	75.0	+ 7.79
G Harwood	3-8	1-3	2-5	0-0	0-0	37.5	+ 10.67

March	Total W-R	Nov Hdles	H'cap Hdles	Nov Chses	H'cap Chses	Per cent	£1 Level Stake
N J Henderson	9-42	4-23	3-11	1-3	1-5	21.4	+ 5.45
D R C Elsworth	6-17	1-4	0-4	2-3	3-6	35.3	+ 15.28
O Sherwood	5-28	3-17	0-3	1-2	1-6	17.9	- 9.25
D Nicholson	5-32	3-13	1-11	1-2	0-6	15.6	- 0.14
Mrs J Pitman	4-19	2-11	0-1	1-1	1-6	21.1	- 4.70

NEWCASTLE (Group 1)

Leading Trainers 1991-96

	Total W-R	Nov Hdles	H'cap Hdles	Nov Chses	H'cap Chses	Per cent	£1 Level Stake
Mrs M Reveley	32-144	10-57	17-56	1-13	4-18	22.2	- 10.27
J H Johnson	17-126	5-49	3-25	1-16	8-36	13.5	- 62.70
M D Hammond	15-117	4-44	3-43	2-11	6-19	12.8	- 30.21
G Richards	13-69	2-30	3-14	5-11	3-14	18.8	- 14.70
G M Moore	13-81	9-41	2-25	2-12	0-3	16.0	- 6.91
P Cheesbrough	12-66	2-17	0-11	5-18	5-20	18.2	+ 6.06
M W Easterby	11-44	4-16	1-10	3-10	3-8	25.0	+ 28.25
J G FitzGerald	11-60	1-25	4-19	2-7	4-9	18.3	+ 43.53
J M Jefferson	8-29	5-14	2-11	0-2	1-2	27.6	+ 41.38
P Monteith	7-47	6-29	0-6	1-4	0-8	14.9	- 11.00
W G Reed	7-50	0-14	2-10	5-15	0-11	14.0	+ 4.13
M J Camacho	5-9	1-5	3-3	1-1	0-0	55.6	+ 5.62
R Allan	5-29	2-17	1-9	1-1	1-2	17.2	- 13.36
L Lungo	5-45	3-24	2-16	0-4	0-1	11.1	- 24.27
C Parker	4-28	1-11	0-6	2-2	1-9	14.3	+ 1.00
N Tinkler	4-29	1-9	0-16	1-1	2-3	13.8	- 17.76
Mrs S C Bradburne	4-41	1-10	2-7	0-9	1-15	9.8	- 12.00
W Storey	4-53	1-19	2-30	1-1	0-3	7.5	- 30.02
J I A Charlton	4-56	1-17	1-7	2-20	0-12	7.1	- 4.00
W A Bethell	3-6	0-0	2-4	1-2	0-0	50.0	+ 12.50

Leading Jockeys

	Total W-R	Per cent	£1 Level Stake	Best Trainer	W-R	Per cent	£1 Level Stake
P Niven	34-140	24.3	+ 0.61	Mrs M Reveley	23-86	26.7	- 14.41
L Wyer	17-103	16.5	- 14.79	J M Jefferson	3-7	42.9	+ 20.00
T Reed	15-100	15.0	- 2.31	W G Reed	6-33	18.2	+ 0.13
B Storey	14-139	10.1	- 77.88	R Allan	4-14	28.6	- 2.86
A Dobbin	13-91	14.3	- 4.22	P Monteith	6-25	24.0	+ 7.00
M Dwyer	12-72	16.7	- 21.04	J M Jefferson	4-8	50.0	+ 9.38
N Bentley	9-46	19.6	+ 62.38	G M Moore	5-27	18.5	+ 10.25
R Garrity	9-51	17.6	- 4.69	M W Easterby	4-11	36.4	+ 9.80
D Byrne	6-31	19.4	+ 6.33	M J Camacho	4-6	66.7	+ 3.13
A Thornton	6-37	16.2	- 4.54	P Cheesbrough	2-8	25.0	+ 5.83
B Harding	6-42	14.3	- 14.15	G Richards	4-16	25.0	- 0.90
Richard Guest	5-39	12.8	- 14.25	C P E Brooks	1-1	100.0	+ 5.00

How the Favourites Fared

	W-R	Per cent	£1 Level Stake		W-R	Per cent	£1 Level Stake
Novice Hurdles	39-87	44.8	- 2.68	Novice Chases	23-51	45.1	- 3.81
H'cap Hurdles	31-84	36.9	- 3.91	H'cap Chases	31-75	41.3	- 8.73
N H Flat	1-5	20.0	- 2.25	Hunter Chases	11-16	68.8	+ 5.66
Totals	71-176	40.3	- 8.84	Totals	65-142	45.8	- 6.88
All favourites	136-318	42.8	- 15.72				

LEADING TRAINERS BY MONTH AT NEWCASTLE 1991-96

October

	Total W-R	Nov Hdles	H'cap Hdles	Nov Chses	H'cap Chses	Per cent	£1 Level Stake
Mrs M Reveley	4-8	1-3	2-2	0-1	1-2	50.0	- 0.21
J H Johnson	4-12	0-3	0-1	0-2	4-6	33.3	+ 6.69
Mrs J Goodfellow	2-5	1-3	0-0	0-1	1-1	40.0	- 0.76
Mrs J Cecil	1-1	1-1	0-0	0-0	0-0	100.0	+ 0.62
J K M Oliver	1-1	0-0	0-0	1-1	0-0	100.0	+ 25.00

November

	Total W-R	Nov Hdles	H'cap Hdles	Nov Chses	H'cap Chses	Per cent	£1 Level Stake
Mrs M Reveley	10-40	2-17	6-13	1-4	1-6	25.0	- 7.43
G M Moore	5-20	4-12	0-5	1-2	0-1	25.0	+ 19.55
J H Johnson	5-27	2-11	2-6	0-3	1-7	18.5	- 13.44
P Cheesbrough	3-10	1-3	0-0	2-4	0-3	30.0	+ 12.25
J G FitzGerald	3-12	1-4	1-6	0-1	1-1	25.0	+ 28.00

December

	Total W-R	Nov Hdles	H'cap Hdles	Nov Chses	H'cap Chses	Per cent	£1 Level Stake
M D Hammond	4-16	0-7	1-6	1-1	2-2	25.0	+ 21.63
M W Easterby	3-5	1-2	0-0	0-1	2-2	60.0	+ 35.00
P Beaumont	2-4	2-3	0-0	0-0	0-1	50.0	+ 24.00
Miss S E Hall	2-4	0-2	2-2	0-0	0-0	50.0	+ 4.00
P Cheesbrough	2-5	0-1	0-1	0-0	2-3	40.0	+ 0.37

January

	Total W-R	Nov Hdles	H'cap Hdles	Nov Chses	H'cap Chses	Per cent	£1 Level Stake
Mrs M Reveley	4-23	1-10	3-10	0-2	0-1	17.4	- 10.44
J G FitzGerald	3-8	0-2	2-4	0-1	1-1	37.5	+ 40.00
J H Johnson	3-15	1-4	0-4	1-4	1-3	20.0	- 1.25
J White	2-2	0-0	1-1	0-0	1-1	100.0	+ 8.00
M W Easterby	2-9	0-3	1-4	0-0	1-2	22.2	+ 6.50

February

	Total W-R	Nov Hdles	H'cap Hdles	Nov Chses	H'cap Chses	Per cent	£1 Level Stake
Mrs M Reveley	6-23	3-7	1-10	0-1	2-5	26.1	+ 1.79
G Richards	3-25	0-10	1-7	1-3	1-5	12.0	- 11.30
W A Bethell	2-2	0-0	2-2	0-0	0-0	100.0	+ 13.00
J M Jefferson	2-6	2-2	0-3	0-0	0-1	33.3	+ 7.38
W Storey	2-12	0-5	1-5	1-1	0-1	16.7	+ 2.73

March

	Total W-R	Nov Hdles	H'cap Hdles	Nov Chses	H'cap Chses	Per cent	£1 Level Stake
Mrs M Reveley	6-37	3-15	3-14	0-5	0-3	16.2	+ 9.02
M D Hammond	5-23	2-7	2-12	0-2	1-2	21.7	+ 0.02
G Richards	4-14	0-7	1-3	2-2	1-2	28.6	+ 4.88
M W Easterby	4-18	2-6	0-5	2-5	0-2	22.2	- 5.95
P Cheesbrough	4-23	0-6	0-4	2-7	2-6	17.4	+ 0.11

May

	Total W-R	Nov Hdles	H'cap Hdles	Nov Chses	H'cap Chses	Per cent	£1 Level Stake
P Cheesbrough	3-7	1-2	0-2	1-1	1-2	42.9	+ 14.33
G M Moore	3-7	2-3	1-4	0-0	0-0	42.9	+ 5.50
W Bentley	2-2	0-0	2-2	0-0	0-0	100.0	+ 7.38
W G Reed	2-8	0-0	1-1	1-3	0-4	25.0	+ 4.75
T W Cunningham	1-1	0-0	0-0	0-0	1-1	100.0	+ 14.00

NEWTON ABBOT (Group 2)

Leading Trainers 1991-96

	Total W-R	Nov Hdles	H'cap Hdles	Nov Chses	H'cap Chses	Per cent	£1 Level Stake
M C Pipe	101-380	41-141	19-128	18-41	23-70	26.6	- 55.04
P J Hobbs	47-151	15-54	12-34	5-20	15-43	31.1	+ 42.21
P F Nicholls	26-118	2-25	2-22	7-28	15-43	22.0	+ 26.83
R G Frost	17-204	5-94	6-33	3-28	3-49	8.3	- 96.17
J White	15-69	5-23	5-21	4-10	1-15	21.7	- 18.13
R J Hodges	14-144	4-39	2-42	2-18	6-45	9.7	- 78.25
R J O'Sullivan	11-33	3-11	2-10	4-5	2-7	33.3	+ 24.73
G B Balding	11-67	0-16	4-15	3-10	4-26	16.4	- 2.16
N Twiston-Davies	10-63	6-29	2-15	0-6	2-13	15.9	- 19.32
Mrs J G Retter	10-85	2-30	6-38	1-12	1-5	11.8	+ 42.13
A G Newcombe	9-30	0-7	3-11	0-0	6-12	30.0	+ 8.51
K C Bailey	9-55	7-23	1-7	0-10	1-15	16.4	- 14.88
D H Barons	9-93	2-28	5-31	1-18	1-16	9.7	- 44.09
J A B Old	8-32	4-15	0-8	0-2	4-7	25.0	+ 9.10
S Sherwood	7-19	2-3	1-6	1-2	3-8	36.8	- 0.43
D Nicholson	7-22	4-14	1-5	2-2	0-1	31.8	+ 2.99
C P E Brooks	7-23	1-6	0-3	3-7	3-7	30.4	- 2.21
C R Egerton	7-30	1-7	3-12	1-3	2-8	23.3	- 3.49
K R Burke	7-31	2-10	3-10	2-5	0-6	22.6	+ 3.08
O Sherwood	6-34	4-12	2-6	0-5	0-11	17.6	- 18.99

Leading Jockeys

	Total W-R	Per cent	£1 Level Stake	Best Trainer	W-R	Per cent	£1 Level Stake
R Dunwoody	57-186	30.6	+ 52.62	M C Pipe	34-88	38.6	+ 34.61
D Bridgwater	24-102	23.5	- 13.83	M C Pipe	16-56	28.6	- 10.08
M A FitzGerald	20-148	13.5	- 17.40	Mrs J G Retter	5-42	11.9	+ 26.63
N Williamson	16-68	23.5	- 4.29	J A C Edwards	6-20	30.0	- 3.05
G Bradley	15-53	28.3	+ 5.61	C P E Brooks	6-20	30.0	- 0.49
J Frost	15-212	7.1	-110.56	R G Frost	12-164	7.3	- 75.67
C Maude	14-136	10.3	- 61.69	P J Hobbs	6-17	35.3	+ 11.87
A Thornton	13-54	24.1	+ 20.39	A G Newcombe	8-17	47.1	+ 16.51
J Osborne	13-62	21.0	- 14.61	S Sherwood	5-7	71.4	+ 7.28
A P McCoy	12-70	17.1	- 2.29	P F Nicholls	6-22	27.3	+ 2.83
A Maguire	12-75	16.0	- 35.76	J White	8-22	36.4	+ 0.66
C Llewellyn	12-84	14.3	+ 3.76	N Twiston-Davies	7-35	20.0	- 2.07

How the Favourites Fared

	W-R	Per cent	£1 Level Stake		W-R	Per cent	£1 Level Stake
Novice Hurdles	77-169	45.6	- 14.26	Novice Chases	40-86	46.5	- 14.54
H'cap Hurdles	66-187	35.3	- 9.08	H'cap Chases	59-146	40.4	- 21.96
N H Flat	7-16	43.8	+ 4.13	Hunter Chases	4-14	28.6	- 3.84
Totals	150-372	40.3	- 19.21	Totals	103-246	41.9	- 40.34
All favourites	253-618	40.9	- 59.55				

LEADING TRAINERS BY MONTH AT NEWTON ABBOT 1991-96

July

	Total W-R	Nov Hdles	H'cap Hdles	Nov Chses	H'cap Chses	Per cent	£1 Level Stake
M C Pipe	8-15	2-5	3-5	1-3	2-2	53.3	+ 7.90
J White	6-16	3-6	1-6	2-4	0-0	37.5	- 1.17

August

	Total W-R	Nov Hdles	H'cap Hdles	Nov Chses	H'cap Chses	Per cent	£1 Level Stake
M C Pipe	29-65	14-25	5-22	5-9	5-9	44.6	- 10.96
P J Hobbs	9-23	4-10	3-6	1-4	1-3	39.1	- 1.89

September

	Total W-R	Nov Hdles	H'cap Hdles	Nov Chses	H'cap Chses	Per cent	£1 Level Stake
M C Pipe	7-22	1-6	3-7	2-6	1-3	31.8	- 5.49
P J Hobbs	4-9	1-1	1-3	1-3	1-2	44.4	+ 9.10

October

	Total W-R	Nov Hdles	H'cap Hdles	Nov Chses	H'cap Chses	Per cent	£1 Level Stake
G B Balding	4-13	0-3	1-4	2-3	1-3	30.8	+ 9.00
P F Nicholls	4-13	0-1	0-4	2-4	2-4	30.8	+ 14.25

November

	Total W-R	Nov Hdles	H'cap Hdles	Nov Chses	H'cap Chses	Per cent	£1 Level Stake
M C Pipe	4-22	3-12	0-5	0-0	1-5	18.2	+ 2.83
K C Bailey	3-5	3-3	0-0	0-0	0-2	60.0	+ 16.88

December

	Total W-R	Nov Hdles	H'cap Hdles	Nov Chses	H'cap Chses	Per cent	£1 Level Stake
M C Pipe	10-37	5-11	2-15	0-2	3-9	27.0	- 0.18
P F Nicholls	9-25	0-6	1-3	2-9	6-7	36.0	+ 14.72

January

	Total W-R	Nov Hdles	H'cap Hdles	Nov Chses	H'cap Chses	Per cent	£1 Level Stake
M C Pipe	4-28	1-12	0-4	1-3	2-9	14.3	- 10.55
D Nicholson	3-3	2-2	0-0	1-1	0-0	100.0	+ 10.85

February

	Total W-R	Nov Hdles	H'cap Hdles	Nov Chses	H'cap Chses	Per cent	£1 Level Stake
M C Pipe	4-8	3-4	0-2	1-1	0-1	50.0	+ 3.50
G B Balding	1-1	0-0	0-0	1-1	0-0	100.0	+ 1.00

March

	Total W-R	Nov Hdles	H'cap Hdles	Nov Chses	H'cap Chses	Per cent	£1 Level Stake
M C Pipe	7-30	2-15	1-9	3-3	1-3	23.3	+ 0.96
P J Hobbs	6-13	4-8	1-2	0-1	1-2	46.2	+ 29.40

April

	Total W-R	Nov Hdles	H'cap Hdles	Nov Chses	H'cap Chses	Per cent	£1 Level Stake
P J Hobbs	11-27	4-10	2-6	1-2	4-9	40.7	+ 22.40
M C Pipe	9-72	2-22	3-30	2-5	2-15	12.5	- 39.02

May

	Total W-R	Nov Hdles	H'cap Hdles	Nov Chses	H'cap Chses	Per cent	£1 Level Stake
M C Pipe	17-60	7-19	2-24	2-6	6-11	28.3	+ 3.87
S Mellor	3-3	0-0	1-1	2-2	0-0	100.0	+ 7.13

PERTH (Group 4)

Leading Trainers 1991-96

	Total W-R	Nov Hdles	H'cap Hdles	Nov Chses	H'cap Chses	Per cent	£1 Level Stake
Mrs M Reveley	25-58	14-26	4-21	5-5	2-6	43.1	+ 10.20
M D Hammond	23-88	13-37	5-22	4-11	1-18	26.1	+ 3.63
G Richards	19-124	4-45	3-27	6-22	6-30	15.3	- 29.43
N Twiston-Davies	16-33	6-14	5-8	2-6	3-5	48.5	+ 35.50
P Monteith	16-87	2-36	3-23	4-14	7-14	18.4	- 2.15
K C Bailey	12-32	2-11	2-5	6-12	2-4	37.5	- 3.38
P J Hobbs	11-29	2-8	5-8	3-9	1-4	37.9	+ 8.43
Miss L A Perratt	10-49	2-15	3-20	2-5	3-9	20.4	- 15.01
L Lungo	8-25	3-16	2-5	2-3	1-1	32.0	+ 11.10
Mrs S C Bradburne	7-116	1-38	0-11	3-32	3-35	6.0	- 51.00
P Beaumont	6-23	1-9	2-9	2-2	1-3	26.1	+ 43.50
T Dyer	6-71	2-41	4-23	0-7	0-0	8.5	- 48.04
M C Pipe	5-6	2-3	2-2	1-1	0-0	83.3	+ 11.13
C Weedon	5-8	5-6	0-1	0-0	0-1	62.5	+ 17.38
N Tinkler	5-18	2-12	2-4	1-1	0-1	27.8	- 1.13
J G FitzGerald	5-19	1-9	1-4	0-1	3-5	26.3	+ 5.16
J S Goldie	5-25	1-8	4-17	0-0	0-0	20.0	+ 2.75
J J O'Neill	5-56	2-22	2-19	1-6	0-9	8.9	- 7.00
J H Johnson	5-58	2-23	0-13	2-11	1-11	8.6	- 22.17
S Mellor	4-7	2-3	1-2	1-1	0-1	57.1	+ 4.30

Leading Jockeys

	Total W-R	Per cent	£1 Level Stake	Best Trainer	W-R	Per cent	£1 Level Stake
P Niven	33-89	37.1	- 0.85	Mrs M Reveley	19-39	48.7	+ 7.07
M Dwyer	17-73	23.3	+ 4.47	J J O'Neill	4-18	22.2	+ 24.50
A Dobbin	15-81	18.5	+ 2.55	P Monteith	6-30	20.0	- 2.90
B Storey	15-140	10.7	- 41.59	R Allan	3-17	17.6	- 7.25
N Williamson	11-38	28.9	- 15.16	K C Bailey	10-19	52.6	+ 2.40
C Llewellyn	10-19	52.6	+ 28.73	N Twiston-Davies	10-19	52.6	+ 28.73
L O'Hara	9-68	13.2	- 8.62	Miss L A Perratt	4-18	22.2	- 0.15
D Bridgwater	8-17	47.1	+ 9.76	M C Pipe	4-5	80.0	+ 4.13
T Reed	8-55	14.5	- 18.25	L Lungo	6-12	50.0	+ 18.50
Richard Guest	6-29	20.7	+ 4.00	Mrs S J Smith	3-9	33.3	+ 1.75
R Dunwoody	6-34	17.6	- 16.35	P J Hobbs	2-2	100.0	+ 4.25
P G Cahill	5-24	20.8	+ 10.50	B Ellison	2-3	66.7	+ 12.50

How the Favourites Fared

	W-R	Per cent	£1 Level Stake		W-R	Per cent	£1 Level Stake
Novice Hurdles	38-96	39.6	- 18.38	Novice Chases	29-55	52.7	+ 2.24
H'cap Hurdles	28-81	34.6	- 15.63	H'cap Chases	28-58	48.3	+ 3.02
N H Flat	5-10	50.0	+ 1.44	Hunter Chases	5-10	50.0	- 0.44
Totals	71-187	38.0	- 32.57	Totals	62-123	50.4	+ 4.82
All favourites	133-310	42.9	- 27.75				

LEADING TRAINERS BY MONTH AT PERTH 1991-96

June	Total W-R	Nov Hdles	H'cap Hdles	Nov Chses	H'cap Chses	Per cent	£1 Level Stake
S Mellor	3-3	1-1	1-1	1-1	0-0	100.0	+ 4.30
J J Quinn	1-1	1-1	0-0	0-0	0-0	100.0	+ 3.50
Mrs M Reveley	1-1	0-0	0-0	0-0	1-1	100.0	+ 0.91
P Beaumont	1-2	1-1	0-1	0-0	0-0	50.0	+ 19.00
W T Kemp	1-2	0-1	1-1	0-0	0-0	50.0	+ 4.50

August	Total W-R	Nov Hdles	H'cap Hdles	Nov Chses	H'cap Chses	Per cent	£1 Level Stake
P J Hobbs	8-15	0-3	5-7	2-3	1-2	53.3	+ 7.43
M D Hammond	8-19	4-9	2-5	2-3	0-2	42.1	+ 8.33
Mrs M Reveley	7-10	5-8	2-2	0-0	0-0	70.0	+ 6.54
P Monteith	4-10	0-4	1-2	1-2	2-2	40.0	- 0.55
Mrs S C Bradburne	4-19	0-6	0-2	1-5	3-6	21.1	+ 30.00

September	Total W-R	Nov Hdles	H'cap Hdles	Nov Chses	H'cap Chses	Per cent	£1 Level Stake
N Twiston-Davies	16-33	6-14	5-8	2-6	3-5	48.5	+ 35.50
M D Hammond	6-16	4-10	1-4	1-2	0-0	37.5	+ 4.15
M C Pipe	5-6	2-3	2-2	1-1	0-0	83.3	+ 11.13
Miss L A Perratt	5-21	1-5	2-9	1-2	1-5	23.8	- 7.36
G Richards	5-34	1-16	0-6	2-4	2-8	14.7	- 7.71

April	Total W-R	Nov Hdles	H'cap Hdles	Nov Chses	H'cap Chses	Per cent	£1 Level Stake
K C Bailey	9-26	2-10	2-5	3-8	2-3	34.6	- 4.46
Mrs M Reveley	7-20	3-7	1-8	3-3	0-2	35.0	+ 0.26
M D Hammond	7-26	4-10	1-5	1-4	1-7	26.9	+ 7.82
P Monteith	7-29	2-10	1-8	3-7	1-4	24.1	+ 22.25
L Lungo	5-14	2-9	1-3	2-2	0-0	35.7	+ 10.50

May	Total W-R	Nov Hdles	H'cap Hdles	Nov Chses	H'cap Chses	Per cent	£1 Level Stake
Mrs M Reveley	8-16	4-6	1-6	2-2	1-2	50.0	+ 5.69
G Richards	6-25	1-8	1-7	2-6	2-4	24.0	- 3.75
P Beaumont	3-4	0-1	2-2	1-1	0-0	75.0	+ 25.50
J S Goldie	3-10	0-3	3-7	0-0	0-0	30.0	+ 5.75
L Lungo	2-3	0-0	1-2	0-0	1-1	66.7	+ 7.10

PLUMPTON (Group 3)

Leading Trainers 1991–96

	Total W–R	Nov Hdles	H'cap Hdles	Nov Chses	H'cap Chses	Per cent	£1 Level Stake
J White	42-144	10-45	11-38	11-35	10-26	29.2	+ 14.29
D M Grissell	13-72	6-29	1-13	2-6	4-24	18.1	- 23.54
J R Jenkins	13-87	4-34	3-30	4-17	2-6	14.9	- 48.40
C R Egerton	12-28	5-12	2-5	3-7	2-4	42.9	+ 1.76
R J Hodges	11-68	2-9	4-20	2-13	3-26	16.2	+ 33.63
R Rowe	11-79	3-20	2-23	1-9	5-27	13.9	- 6.50
J Ffitch-Heyes	11-129	2-45	9-58	0-14	0-12	8.5	- 43.05
M C Pipe	10-30	6-13	1-9	2-2	1-6	33.3	- 3.97
R J O'Sullivan	10-56	2-19	4-16	0-2	4-19	17.9	- 9.42
A Moore	10-133	3-43	4-56	2-17	1-17	7.5	- 54.50
Lady Herries	8-19	3-10	5-7	0-1	0-1	42.1	+ 16.25
T P McGovern	8-40	4-18	2-15	2-5	0-2	20.0	- 2.13
Mrs J Pitman	7-22	0-4	3-4	1-6	3-8	31.8	+ 18.28
R Akehurst	7-25	5-17	1-6	1-1	0-1	28.0	- 2.04
N J Henderson	7-25	2-10	0-2	4-7	1-6	28.0	+ 7.00
Mrs D Haine	6-18	5-14	0-2	1-1	0-1	33.3	+ 0.88
G Harwood	6-28	2-14	2-9	0-0	2-5	21.4	+ 1.29
R H Alner	6-33	0-7	0-0	2-10	4-16	18.2	- 11.88
J T Gifford	6-40	3-12	2-6	0-7	1-15	15.0	- 10.97
P J Jones	5-15	0-2	2-8	1-2	2-3	33.3	+ 10.00

Leading Jockeys

	Total W–R	Per cent	£1 Level Stake	Best Trainer	W–R	Per cent	£1 Level Stake
A Maguire	46-167	27.5	+ 7.06	J White	21-49	42.9	+ 18.37
R Dunwoody	21-112	18.8	- 37.47	J R Jenkins	5-25	20.0	- 7.92
D Bridgwater	16-32	50.0	+ 55.35	Mrs D Haine	3-3	100.0	+ 7.38
D O'Sullivan	13-80	16.3	- 14.91	R J O'Sullivan	8-39	20.5	- 2.16
J Osborne	12-55	21.8	- 13.52	C R Egerton	10-18	55.6	+ 7.98
A P McCoy	10-34	29.4	+ 5.25	J White	5-12	41.7	- 0.17
J R Kavanagh	10-62	16.1	- 21.87	N J Henderson	3-6	50.0	+ 8.00
M A FitzGerald	10-63	15.9	+ 1.25	N J Henderson	3-9	33.3	+ 1.50
M Richards	9-48	18.8	- 2.87	P R Hedger	5-9	55.6	+ 6.63
E Murphy	7-34	20.6	- 6.87	Lady Herries	5-11	45.5	+ 12.38
W McFarland	7-40	17.5	- 6.87	T P McGovern	3-13	23.1	+ 0.88
A Tory	6-47	12.8	- 10.62	R J Hodges	2-16	12.5	- 7.00

How the Favourites Fared

	W–R	Per cent	£1 Level Stake		W–R	Per cent	£1 Level Stake
Novice Hurdles	58-115	50.4	+ 8.31	Novice Chases	26-67	38.8	- 20.52
H'cap Hurdles	48-118	40.7	+ 1.46	H'cap Chases	37-94	39.4	- 12.17
N H Flat	0-0	-	0.00	Hunter Chases	3-7	42.9	- 1.45
Totals	106-233	45.5	+ 9.77	Totals	66-168	39.3	- 34.14
All favourites	172-401	42.9	- 24.37				

LEADING TRAINERS BY MONTH AT PLUMPTON 1991-96

August	Total W-R	Nov Hdles	H'cap Hdles	Nov Chses	H'cap Chses	Per cent	£1 Level Stake
J White	16-38	4-12	5-9	2-7	5-10	42.1	- 4.16
J R Jenkins	6-19	1-9	2-5	2-4	1-1	31.6	- 4.71
J Ffitch-Heyes	5-22	1-8	4-10	0-2	0-2	22.7	- 2.05

September	Total W-R	Nov Hdles	H'cap Hdles	Nov Chses	H'cap Chses	Per cent	£1 Level Stake
J White	3-13	1-5	0-3	2-5	0-0	23.1	+ 4.80
R J O'Sullivan	2-3	1-1	1-2	0-0	0-0	66.7	+ 2.75
J R Jenkins	2-8	1-1	0-4	1-3	0-0	25.0	0.00

October	Total W-R	Nov Hdles	H'cap Hdles	Nov Chses	H'cap Chses	Per cent	£1 Level Stake
J White	7-13	0-3	3-5	3-3	1-2	53.8	+ 13.73
C R Egerton	2-3	0-1	1-1	1-1	0-0	66.7	+ 4.30
M P Muggeridge	2-3	0-0	0-0	0-1	2-2	66.7	+ 5.25

November	Total W-R	Nov Hdles	H'cap Hdles	Nov Chses	H'cap Chses	Per cent	£1 Level Stake
C R Egerton	4-6	1-2	0-1	2-2	1-1	66.7	+ 1.47
A Moore	3-22	1-9	1-7	1-3	0-3	13.6	+ 12.00
Miss H C Knight	2-2	1-1	0-0	1-1	0-0	100.0	+ 3.13

December	Total W-R	Nov Hdles	H'cap Hdles	Nov Chses	H'cap Chses	Per cent	£1 Level Stake
G Harwood	3-5	2-2	1-2	0-0	0-1	60.0	+ 18.13
C R Egerton	3-6	1-2	1-2	0-1	1-1	50.0	+ 2.33
Mrs D Haine	2-2	1-1	0-0	1-1	0-0	100.0	+ 5.50

January	Total W-R	Nov Hdles	H'cap Hdles	Nov Chses	H'cap Chses	Per cent	£1 Level Stake
M C Pipe	2-2	1-1	1-1	0-0	0-0	100.0	+ 1.87
J White	2-8	2-4	0-1	0-2	0-1	25.0	- 2.25
P Butler	1-1	0-0	0-0	0-0	1-1	100.0	+ 9.00

February	Total W-R	Nov Hdles	H'cap Hdles	Nov Chses	H'cap Chses	Per cent	£1 Level Stake
M C Pipe	4-10	4-5	0-4	0-0	0-1	40.0	+ 3.57
C R Egerton	2-3	2-2	0-0	0-1	0-0	66.7	+ 0.91
Mrs J Pitman	2-3	0-0	1-1	0-1	1-1	66.7	+ 19.00

March	Total W-R	Nov Hdles	H'cap Hdles	Nov Chses	H'cap Chses	Per cent	£1 Level Stake
J White	6-17	2-5	1-6	2-3	1-3	35.3	+ 22.91
Lady Herries	3-5	1-2	2-3	0-0	0-0	60.0	+ 10.13
D M Grissell	3-12	1-5	0-2	1-2	1-3	25.0	- 1.88

April	Total W-R	Nov Hdles	H'cap Hdles	Nov Chses	H'cap Chses	Per cent	£1 Level Stake
D M Grissell	4-12	2-4	0-1	1-1	1-6	33.3	- 1.72
R Rowe	4-18	1-3	1-5	1-2	1-8	22.2	+ 16.25
J White	3-24	0-8	0-5	1-6	2-5	12.5	- 15.15

May	Total W-R	Nov Hdles	H'cap Hdles	Nov Chses	H'cap Chses	Per cent	£1 Level Stake
M C Pipe	2-3	1-2	0-0	1-1	0-0	66.7	+ 0.90
Miss K M George	1-1	0-0	1-1	0-0	0-0	100.0	+ 2.00
N J Henderson	1-1	1-1	0-0	0-0	0-0	100.0	+ 0.67

SANDOWN (Group 1)

Leading Trainers 1991-96

	Total W-R	Nov Hdles	H'cap Hdles	Nov Chses	H'cap Chses	Per cent	£1 Level Stake
D Nicholson	32-94	7-31	3-9	8-19	14-35	34.0	+ 59.05
J T Gifford	27-147	5-51	4-21	11-35	7-40	18.4	+ 4.41
M C Pipe	12-72	5-17	4-26	1-5	2-24	16.7	- 16.97
N J Henderson	12-96	7-41	0-18	1-13	4-24	12.5	- 8.19
O Sherwood	10-55	5-28	0-7	3-5	2-15	18.2	- 14.48
Andrew Turnell	8-24	1-8	1-2	2-5	4-9	33.3	+ 12.71
Capt T A Forster	8-34	1-6	1-5	2-6	4-17	23.5	+ 30.12
G B Balding	8-79	0-31	2-18	3-16	3-14	10.1	- 15.75
J A B Old	7-34	4-24	3-8	0-1	0-1	20.6	+ 57.50
C P E Brooks	7-49	0-18	1-5	3-7	3-19	14.3	- 18.88
D R C Elsworth	7-66	3-30	3-21	1-4	0-11	10.6	- 34.67
J G FitzGerald	6-16	1-2	2-6	0-2	3-6	37.5	+ 11.85
P F Nicholls	6-18	2-3	0-2	1-4	3-9	33.3	+ 10.88
G Harwood	6-20	4-10	2-8	0-1	0-1	30.0	+ 8.00
Mrs M Reveley	6-24	2-5	2-9	0-3	2-7	25.0	- 2.03
Miss H C Knight	6-30	3-13	1-5	1-7	1-5	20.0	- 2.34
R J Hodges	6-31	2-7	1-5	0-4	3-15	19.4	+ 6.75
S Dow	5-26	0-8	4-14	1-4	0-0	19.2	+ 5.50
P J Hobbs	5-36	2-9	0-7	1-6	2-14	13.9	- 13.58
N Twiston-Davies	5-78	2-30	1-14	2-15	0-19	6.4	- 42.00

Leading Jockeys

	Total W-R	Per cent	£1 Level Stake	Best Trainer	W-R	Per cent	£1 Level Stake
R Dunwoody	39-131	29.8	+ 31.48	D Nicholson	16-33	48.5	+ 27.21
A Maguire	20-102	19.6	- 13.66	D Nicholson	8-28	28.6	- 3.16
J Osborne	17-115	14.8	- 60.70	O Sherwood	7-41	17.1	- 19.73
A P McCoy	9-50	18.0	- 8.12	P F Nicholls	2-8	25.0	- 1.87
P Hide	9-67	13.4	- 11.80	J T Gifford	9-62	14.5	- 6.80
G Bradley	9-72	12.5	- 1.62	C P E Brooks	4-26	15.4	- 5.62
Mr C Ward Thomas	7-23	30.4	+ 25.50	Capt T A Forster	3-7	42.9	+ 23.25
B Powell	6-45	13.3	+ 25.07	Simon Earle	1-1	100.0	+ 0.91
M A FitzGerald	6-87	6.9	- 51.50	N J Henderson	3-34	8.8	- 16.50
J Frost	5-24	20.8	+ 41.50	R G Frost	2-6	33.3	+ 1.00
W Marston	5-29	17.2	+ 1.25	Mrs J Pitman	2-12	16.7	- 4.90
C Llewellyn	5-44	11.4	+ 25.50	Capt T A Forster	2-4	50.0	+ 25.00

How the Favourites Fared

	W-R	Per cent	£1 Level Stake		W-R	Per cent	£1 Level Stake
Novice Hurdles	22-65	33.8	- 14.97	Novice Chases	30-60	50.0	+ 2.02
H'cap Hurdles	21-68	30.9	- 9.24	H'cap Chases	37-89	41.6	- 5.97
N H Flat	4-15	26.7	- 0.40	Hunter Chases	7-15	46.7	- 0.30
Totals	47-148	31.8	- 24.61	Totals	74-164	45.1	- 4.25
All favourites	121-312	38.8	- 28.86				

LEADING TRAINERS BY MONTH AT SANDOWN 1991-96

October	Total W-R	Nov Hdles	H'cap Hdles	Nov Chses	H'cap Chses	Per cent	£1 Level Stake
J H Johnson	1-1	0-0	0-0	0-0	1-1	100.0	+ 1.38
G Thorner	1-1	0-0	1-1	0-0	0-0	100.0	+ 4.00
P R Hedger	1-2	0-1	1-1	0-0	0-0	50.0	+ 2.00
Miss H C Knight	1-2	1-2	0-0	0-0	0-0	50.0	+ 4.00
D Nicholson	1-2	1-1	0-1	0-0	0-0	50.0	+ 5.00

November	Total W-R	Nov Hdles	H'cap Hdles	Nov Chses	H'cap Chses	Per cent	£1 Level Stake
D Nicholson	4-8	0-3	1-1	0-1	3-3	50.0	+ 1.28
M C Pipe	3-6	2-4	1-2	0-0	0-0	50.0	+ 6.28
K C Bailey	3-10	1-3	0-1	0-0	2-6	30.0	+ 13.13
D R C Elsworth	3-12	1-5	2-6	0-0	0-1	25.0	+ 7.10
J A C Edwards	2-2	1-1	0-0	0-0	1-1	100.0	+ 10.91

December	Total W-R	Nov Hdles	H'cap Hdles	Nov Chses	H'cap Chses	Per cent	£1 Level Stake
D Nicholson	9-21	0-3	1-3	6-9	2-6	42.9	+ 11.74
J T Gifford	5-20	1-7	2-5	2-4	0-4	25.0	+ 11.25
S Dow	3-7	0-2	2-4	1-1	0-0	42.9	+ 9.50
P J Hobbs	3-10	1-3	0-1	0-1	2-5	30.0	- 2.08
Mrs M Reveley	3-12	1-2	1-6	0-2	1-2	25.0	- 0.40

January	Total W-R	Nov Hdles	H'cap Hdles	Nov Chses	H'cap Chses	Per cent	£1 Level Stake
G B Balding	2-8	0-1	1-2	1-3	0-2	25.0	+ 4.25
N Twiston-Davies	2-11	0-2	1-3	1-3	0-3	18.2	- 1.50
J T Gifford	2-14	0-5	0-3	1-4	1-2	14.3	- 8.88
D Nicholson	2-14	2-7	0-0	0-2	0-5	14.3	0.00
C C Elsey	1-1	1-1	0-0	0-0	0-0	100.0	+ 20.00

February	Total W-R	Nov Hdles	H'cap Hdles	Nov Chses	H'cap Chses	Per cent	£1 Level Stake
D Nicholson	8-26	3-12	0-1	2-3	3-10	30.8	+ 37.25
J T Gifford	8-47	2-19	1-6	3-10	2-12	17.0	- 12.86
N J Henderson	7-26	3-11	0-5	1-2	3-8	26.9	+ 11.72
J G FitzGerald	5-6	1-1	2-2	0-1	2-2	83.3	+ 14.85
J A B Old	5-17	4-12	1-4	0-0	0-1	29.4	+ 41.50

March	Total W-R	Nov Hdles	H'cap Hdles	Nov Chses	H'cap Chses	Per cent	£1 Level Stake
J T Gifford	10-42	2-14	0-2	4-13	4-13	23.8	+ 30.64
D Nicholson	8-22	1-5	1-3	0-4	6-10	36.4	+ 4.78
Capt T A Forster	5-21	0-5	0-3	1-4	4-9	23.8	+ 12.78
R J Hodges	4-12	1-1	1-2	0-3	2-6	33.3	+ 15.75
O Sherwood	4-12	2-6	0-2	2-2	0-2	33.3	+ 5.79

April	Total W-R	Nov Hdles	H'cap Hdles	Nov Chses	H'cap Chses	Per cent	£1 Level Stake
D H Barons	2-4	0-1	0-0	0-0	2-3	50.0	+ 12.50
O Sherwood	2-5	1-2	0-0	1-1	0-2	40.0	+ 8.10
N A Gaselee	1-1	0-0	0-0	0-0	1-1	100.0	+ 4.00
A P O'Brien (Ire)	1-1	0-0	0-0	0-0	1-1	100.0	+ 12.00
Mrs M Reveley	1-2	1-1	0-0	0-0	0-1	50.0	+ 1.50

SEDGEFIELD (Group 4)

Leading Trainers 1991–96

	Total W-R	Nov Hdles	H'cap Hdles	Nov Chses	H'cap Chses	Per cent	£1 Level Stake
Mrs M Reveley	75–262	25–80	16–82	14–34	20–66	28.6	+ 13.45
G M Moore	26–151	17–56	5–57	2–16	2–22	17.2	- 39.47
J H Johnson	24–175	3–52	4–36	7–40	10–47	13.7	- 81.78
J A Hellens	18–91	3–22	5–31	3–18	7–20	19.8	+ 9.00
J G FitzGerald	17–62	5–25	3–15	5–8	4–14	27.4	+ 40.91
P Beaumont	17–94	4–32	7–32	1–10	5–20	18.1	- 8.68
J Wade	15–144	1–49	6–39	4–32	4–24	10.4	- 36.97
Denys Smith	14–111	3–43	7–39	1–8	3–21	12.6	- 27.50
J J O'Neill	12–60	6–17	0–17	3–7	3–19	20.0	- 24.28
L Lungo	9–43	8–18	1–17	0–4	0–4	20.9	- 15.81
M W Easterby	8–63	0–25	2–9	1–13	5–16	12.7	- 34.68
Ian Park	7–27	4–14	2–10	0–0	1–3	25.9	+ 69.25
W Storey	7–51	2–15	4–28	1–6	0–2	13.7	+ 6.50
C W Thornton	6–24	5–15	1–6	0–1	0–2	25.0	+ 13.42
N B Mason	6–32	2–15	1–6	2–9	1–2	18.8	+ 0.67
B Ellison	6–60	0–18	2–26	1–7	3–9	10.0	- 15.50
V Thompson	6–108	0–22	3–35	2–35	1–16	5.6	- 55.00
P Bowen	5–8	0–0	1–2	0–0	4–6	62.5	+ 32.62
T P Tate	5–21	1–9	0–4	2–4	2–4	23.8	- 0.73
P Monteith	5–46	0–11	2–13	0–3	3–19	10.9	- 13.17

Leading Jockeys

	Total W-R	Per cent	£1 Level Stake	Best Trainer	W-R	Per cent	£1 Level Stake
P Niven	64–202	31.7	+ 26.05	Mrs M Reveley	50–136	36.8	+ 43.33
M Dwyer	28–140	20.0	+ 5.50	J G FitzGerald	9–32	28.1	+ 29.55
L Wyer	26–126	20.6	+ 46.05	Mrs M Reveley	2–2	100.0	+ 4.94
J Callaghan	20–125	16.0	- 41.01	G M Moore	13–67	19.4	- 10.39
A Maguire	17–83	20.5	- 19.76	J H Johnson	7–22	31.8	+ 2.29
T Reed	12–98	12.2	- 16.01	L Lungo	3–12	25.0	- 6.06
N Smith	12–105	11.4	+ 20.30	Ian Park	7–23	30.4	+ 73.26
B Storey	12–200	6.0	- 72.17	F S Storey	3–17	17.6	+ 17.83
A Dobbin	11–123	8.9	- 64.37	P Monteith	4–25	16.0	+ 2.83
A Larnach	10–79	12.7	- 27.21	J A Hellens	8–32	25.0	+ 12.38
J Supple	10–79	12.7	- 22.33	N B Mason	5–20	25.0	+ 7.17
G Lee	9–33	27.3	+ 6.62	Mrs M Reveley	7–24	29.2	+ 3.12

How the Favourites Fared

	W-R	Per cent	£1 Level Stake		W-R	Per cent	£1 Level Stake
Novice Hurdles	60–135	44.4	+ 4.03	Novice Chases	39–86	45.3	- 8.59
H'cap Hurdles	48–156	30.8	- 16.13	H'cap Chases	49–125	39.2	- 6.19
N H Flat	4–11	36.4	- 2.92	Hunter Chases	9–14	64.3	+ 14.31
Totals	112–302	37.1	- 15.02	Totals	97–225	43.1	- 0.47
All favourites	209–527	39.7	- 15.49				

LEADING TRAINERS BY MONTH AT SEDGEFIELD 1991-96

September

	Total W-R	Nov Hdles	H'cap Hdles	Nov Chses	H'cap Chses	Per cent	£1 Level Stake
Mrs M Reveley	7-21	3-10	2-6	1-2	1-3	33.3	+ 2.30
G M Moore	7-24	7-13	0-7	0-2	0-2	29.2	+ 1.58
J H Johnson	6-21	0-6	0-3	3-8	3-4	28.6	+ 2.13

October

	Total W-R	Nov Hdles	H'cap Hdles	Nov Chses	H'cap Chses	Per cent	£1 Level Stake
Mrs M Reveley	12-37	6-15	2-9	2-3	2-10	32.4	+ 16.41
J A Hellens	3-15	1-4	1-6	0-2	1-3	20.0	+ 2.25
G M Moore	3-17	2-5	0-8	1-3	0-1	17.6	+ 0.50

November

	Total W-R	Nov Hdles	H'cap Hdles	Nov Chses	H'cap Chses	Per cent	£1 Level Stake
Mrs M Reveley	11-34	3-10	3-11	3-8	2-5	32.4	+ 1.79
J J O'Neill	5-11	2-2	0-3	2-3	1-3	45.5	+ 7.93
J G FitzGerald	5-12	2-5	0-3	1-1	2-3	41.7	+ 35.25

December

	Total W-R	Nov Hdles	H'cap Hdles	Nov Chses	H'cap Chses	Per cent	£1 Level Stake
Mrs M Reveley	8-21	1-3	2-9	3-4	2-5	38.1	+ 5.81
P Monteith	2-10	0-1	1-3	0-0	1-6	20.0	- 0.67
J A Hellens	2-11	0-0	1-6	0-1	1-4	18.2	+ 1.00

January

	Total W-R	Nov Hdles	H'cap Hdles	Nov Chses	H'cap Chses	Per cent	£1 Level Stake
Mrs M Reveley	7-23	2-9	1-7	1-1	3-6	30.4	+ 8.53
J J Quinn	2-4	1-1	1-3	0-0	0-0	50.0	+ 15.00
P Beaumont	2-6	0-3	1-1	1-1	0-1	33.3	+ 2.57

February

	Total W-R	Nov Hdles	H'cap Hdles	Nov Chses	H'cap Chses	Per cent	£1 Level Stake
Mrs M Reveley	9-32	3-8	1-9	2-5	3-10	28.1	+ 3.00
P Beaumont	4-15	2-7	0-1	0-3	2-4	26.7	+ 0.75
G M Moore	4-24	3-8	1-8	0-3	0-5	16.7	- 3.25

March

	Total W-R	Nov Hdles	H'cap Hdles	Nov Chses	H'cap Chses	Per cent	£1 Level Stake
Mrs M Reveley	8-34	1-7	2-9	2-6	3-12	23.5	- 8.36
J G FitzGerald	5-11	0-3	2-3	1-1	2-4	45.5	+ 7.48
J H Johnson	4-25	2-6	0-4	1-5	1-10	16.0	- 9.34

April

	Total W-R	Nov Hdles	H'cap Hdles	Nov Chses	H'cap Chses	Per cent	£1 Level Stake
Mrs M Reveley	7-38	3-12	1-14	0-4	3-8	18.4	- 12.88
G M Moore	4-22	1-12	1-6	1-2	1-2	18.2	- 10.05
J G FitzGerald	3-11	2-6	0-3	1-2	0-0	27.3	+ 3.62

May

	Total W-R	Nov Hdles	H'cap Hdles	Nov Chses	H'cap Chses	Per cent	£1 Level Stake
Mrs M Reveley	6-23	3-7	2-8	0-1	1-7	26.1	- 4.15
Ian Park	3-6	1-4	1-1	0-0	1-1	50.0	+ 18.38
P Beaumont	3-8	0-3	0-2	0-0	3-3	37.5	+ 5.00

SOUTHWELL (Group 4)

Leading Trainers 1991-96

	Total W-R	Nov Hdles	H'cap Hdles	Nov Chses	H'cap Chses	Per cent	£1 Level Stake
W Clay	27-150	15-84	11-51	0-9	1-6	18.0	+ 42.28
R Hollinshead	23-103	15-60	6-37	0-0	2-6	22.3	- 36.22
J L Harris	22-141	9-65	13-72	0-0	0-4	15.6	- 20.57
M C Pipe	19-80	16-47	1-21	2-9	0-3	23.8	- 29.15
Mrs M Reveley	14-35	2-14	4-7	3-4	5-10	40.0	+ 11.09
K C Bailey	13-56	3-12	0-7	4-17	6-20	23.2	+ 21.47
D Burchell	9-59	4-27	4-27	1-3	0-2	15.3	- 5.73
J R Jenkins	9-71	5-30	1-24	2-9	1-8	12.7	- 29.63
J E Banks	8-23	5-15	1-6	2-2	0-0	34.8	+ 4.25
O Brennan	8-70	2-29	2-23	3-9	1-9	11.4	- 39.88
Mrs S J Smith	8-70	1-24	2-9	1-13	4-24	11.4	+ 0.38
S Sherwood	7-22	1-7	0-3	4-5	2-7	31.8	- 0.55
P F Nicholls	6-15	2-7	0-2	0-1	4-5	40.0	+ 7.38
O Sherwood	6-29	1-9	1-4	2-8	2-8	20.7	- 12.40
J G FitzGerald	6-34	4-25	1-3	1-3	0-3	17.6	- 0.17
J White	6-42	2-22	2-10	2-6	0-4	14.3	- 25.80
K S Bridgwater	6-51	1-20	5-30	0-0	0-1	11.8	- 17.00
Capt T A Forster	5-14	2-3	0-0	2-4	1-7	35.7	+ 26.00
J A C Edwards	5-18	0-3	2-4	1-6	2-5	27.8	- 0.13
N Tinkler	5-19	3-9	2-7	0-1	0-2	26.3	- 2.13

Leading Jockeys

	Total W-R	Per cent	£1 Level Stake	Best Trainer	W-R	Per cent	£1 Level Stake
S Wynne	20-111	18.0	- 54.06	R Hollinshead	18-81	22.2	- 29.19
A Maguire	19-71	26.8	+ 0.86	D Nicholson	5-9	55.6	+ 5.08
Diane Clay	18-77	23.4	+ 35.85	W Clay	18-77	23.4	+ 35.85
R Dunwoody	15-50	30.0	- 4.16	M C Pipe	10-23	43.5	- 0.76
P Niven	15-59	25.4	- 3.20	Mrs M Reveley	10-22	45.5	+ 9.64
N Williamson	14-59	23.7	+ 1.05	K C Bailey	5-13	38.5	+ 1.97
J Osborne	11-36	30.6	+ 15.74	O Sherwood	4-9	44.4	+ 2.11
R Garrity	11-44	25.0	+ 18.47	W Clay	1-1	100.0	+ 7.00
R Supple	11-81	13.6	- 8.37	J R Upson	3-15	20.0	- 6.37
A P McCoy	9-25	36.0	+ 6.13	P F Nicholls	3-5	60.0	+ 4.13
M A FitzGerald	9-68	13.2	- 11.87	N J Henderson	2-5	40.0	+ 2.25
Martin Brennan	9-74	12.2	- 34.87	O Brennan	7-53	13.2	- 25.87

How the Favourites Fared

	W-R	Per cent	£1 Level Stake		W-R	Per cent	£1 Level Stake
Novice Hurdles	84-199	42.2	- 14.32	Novice Chases	22-62	35.5	- 12.22
H'cap Hurdles	51-179	28.5	- 42.82	H'cap Chases	40-99	40.4	- 0.12
N H Flat	8-23	34.8	- 6.30	Hunter Chases	3-7	42.9	+ 0.55
Totals	143-401	35.7	- 63.44	Totals	65-168	38.7	- 11.79
All favourites	208-569	36.6	- 75.23				

LEADING TRAINERS BY MONTH AT SOUTHWELL 1991-96

	Total W-R	Nov Hdles	H'cap Hdles	Nov Chses	H'cap Chses	Per cent	£1 Level Stake
June							
G C Bravery	1-1	1-1	0-0	0-0	0-0	100.0	+ 6.00
N J Henderson	1-1	0-0	0-0	0-0	1-1	100.0	+ 3.50
July							
A Harrison	2-2	1-1	1-1	0-0	0-0	100.0	+ 21.50
M C Pipe	2-6	2-2	0-2	0-1	0-1	33.3	- 3.50
August							
Mrs S C Bradburne	2-2	0-0	0-0	1-1	1-1	100.0	+ 2.19
J A Glover	2-3	2-3	0-0	0-0	0-0	66.7	+ 3.00
September							
J P Leigh	2-2	0-0	1-1	0-0	1-1	100.0	+ 6.73
C L Popham	2-2	0-0	0-0	0-0	2-2	100.0	+ 8.00
October							
J L Harris	5-11	2-6	3-5	0-0	0-0	45.5	+ 18.13
Mrs M Reveley	4-5	0-0	1-1	1-1	2-3	80.0	+ 4.06
November							
J L Harris	4-16	4-7	0-9	0-0	0-0	25.0	+ 11.10
Capt T A Forster	3-3	2-2	0-0	0-0	1-1	100.0	+ 14.00
December							
W Clay	3-10	2-5	1-4	0-1	0-0	30.0	+ 16.00
T P McGovern	2-3	1-2	1-1	0-0	0-0	66.7	+ 9.00
January							
W Clay	9-34	3-21	6-12	0-1	0-0	26.5	+ 48.85
M C Pipe	8-27	6-19	1-7	1-1	0-0	29.6	- 5.76
February							
R Hollinshead	7-24	4-14	3-10	0-0	0-0	29.2	- 7.95
J L Harris	5-23	1-10	4-13	0-0	0-0	21.7	+ 1.13
March							
W Clay	7-20	5-14	2-5	0-1	0-0	35.0	+ 9.58
R Hollinshead	5-12	4-8	0-2	0-0	1-2	41.7	+ 7.51
April							
K C Bailey	4-8	1-1	0-1	2-2	1-4	50.0	+ 28.50
O Brennan	2-8	0-2	0-1	1-2	1-3	25.0	- 1.25
May							
K C Bailey	6-16	0-2	0-1	2-5	4-8	37.5	+ 4.47
Mrs V C Ward	3-9	1-1	1-4	1-2	0-2	33.3	+ 16.50

STRATFORD (Group 3)

Leading Trainers 1991-96

	Total W-R	Nov Hdles	H'cap Hdles	Nov Chses	H'cap Chses	Per cent	£1 Level Stake
M C Pipe	29-111	12-51	6-31	5-14	6-15	26.1	+ 18.48
K C Bailey	15-78	2-20	2-12	3-20	8-26	19.2	+ 6.98
D Nicholson	14-63	5-25	2-7	3-14	4-17	22.2	- 19.30
P J Hobbs	13-65	0-13	2-16	3-12	8-24	20.0	- 24.45
G B Balding	12-67	2-15	4-19	1-8	5-25	17.9	+ 57.52
J White	12-82	7-33	1-29	4-9	0-11	14.6	- 33.71
Capt T A Forster	11-60	4-18	1-10	2-14	4-18	18.3	+ 18.58
N Twiston-Davies	10-64	4-20	3-17	2-16	1-11	15.6	+ 2.25
O Sherwood	8-28	3-10	1-2	1-7	3-9	28.6	- 1.23
Mrs J Pitman	7-50	2-12	2-16	2-11	1-11	14.0	+ 16.83
P F Nicholls	6-15	3-4	0-2	1-4	2-5	40.0	+ 16.05
S Sherwood	6-35	2-8	1-9	1-8	2-10	17.1	+ 6.50
C R Barwell	5-23	0-4	4-12	1-5	0-2	21.7	+ 13.75
J R Upson	5-23	1-7	1-4	0-3	3-9	21.7	+ 8.50
G Richards	5-24	0-4	0-2	1-4	4-14	20.8	- 8.50
R J O'Sullivan	4-17	2-4	1-4	1-3	0-6	23.5	- 4.13
C D Broad	4-20	2-7	1-12	0-0	1-1	20.0	+ 6.63
Andrew Turnell	4-21	2-8	0-5	0-4	2-4	19.0	+ 14.00
J G FitzGerald	4-22	2-6	0-5	1-3	1-8	18.2	- 0.43
N J Henderson	4-22	2-10	0-1	1-2	1-9	18.2	- 4.25

Leading Jockeys

	Total W-R	Per cent	£1 Level Stake	Best Trainer	W-R	Per cent	£1 Level Stake
A Maguire	24-98	24.5	+ 32.51	D Nicholson	5-16	31.3	- 0.75
R Dunwoody	21-103	20.4	- 25.33	M C Pipe	8-21	38.1	+ 12.96
N Williamson	17-111	15.3	- 0.24	K C Bailey	6-36	16.7	- 9.62
C Llewellyn	16-78	20.5	+ 31.00	N Twiston-Davies	6-26	23.1	+ 23.25
A P McCoy	13-66	19.7	+ 5.04	G B Balding	6-24	25.0	+ 9.33
J Osborne	10-61	16.4	- 4.90	O Sherwood	4-17	23.5	- 3.15
S McNeill	10-78	12.8	+ 19.75	Miss A J Whitfield	2-5	40.0	+ 8.50
D Bridgwater	10-97	10.3	- 32.22	M C Pipe	4-19	21.1	+ 0.03
S Wynne	8-26	30.8	+ 28.10	R Hollinshead	3-9	33.3	+ 2.00
J A McCarthy	8-30	26.7	+ 10.25	O Sherwood	4-8	50.0	+ 4.92
T Eley	6-33	18.2	+ 17.75	A Streeter	3-4	75.0	+ 15.25
J Lower	5-21	23.8	- 2.11	M C Pipe	5-20	25.0	- 1.11

How the Favourites Fared

	W-R	Per cent	£1 Level Stake		W-R	Per cent	£1 Level Stake
Novice Hurdles	40-108	37.0	- 14.50	Novice Chases	23-58	39.7	- 6.80
H'cap Hurdles	34-115	29.6	- 21.27	H'cap Chases	36-96	37.5	- 1.34
N H Flat	0-0	-	0.00	Hunter Chases	10-29	34.5	- 3.81
Totals	74-223	33.2	- 35.77	Totals	69-183	37.7	- 11.95
All favourites	143-406	35.2	- 47.72				

LEADING TRAINERS BY MONTH AT STRATFORD 1991-96

June

	Total W-R	Nov Hdles	H'cap Hdles	Nov Chses	H'cap Chses	Per cent	£1 Level Stake
M C Pipe	8-25	3-7	2-10	1-2	2-6	32.0	+ 4.85
K C Bailey	3-7	0-1	1-4	0-0	2-2	42.9	+ 2.58

July

	Total W-R	Nov Hdles	H'cap Hdles	Nov Chses	H'cap Chses	Per cent	£1 Level Stake
J White	4-9	1-2	1-2	2-3	0-2	44.4	+ 13.17
J R Upson	2-4	1-2	1-1	0-0	0-1	50.0	+ 7.50

August

	Total W-R	Nov Hdles	H'cap Hdles	Nov Chses	H'cap Chses	Per cent	£1 Level Stake
M D Hammond	1-1	0-0	0-0	1-1	0-0	100.0	+ 2.75
P W Hiatt	1-1	1-1	0-0	0-0	0-0	100.0	+ 3.00

September

	Total W-R	Nov Hdles	H'cap Hdles	Nov Chses	H'cap Chses	Per cent	£1 Level Stake
M C Pipe	5-14	3-9	0-2	2-3	0-0	35.7	+ 10.18
P J Hobbs	4-6	0-0	0-1	1-2	3-3	66.7	+ 4.25

October

	Total W-R	Nov Hdles	H'cap Hdles	Nov Chses	H'cap Chses	Per cent	£1 Level Stake
K C Bailey	4-18	0-6	1-2	0-4	3-6	22.2	- 0.88
P F Nicholls	3-5	3-3	0-0	0-1	0-1	60.0	+ 20.50

November

	Total W-R	Nov Hdles	H'cap Hdles	Nov Chses	H'cap Chses	Per cent	£1 Level Stake
D Nicholson	3-5	1-2	0-0	1-1	1-2	60.0	+ 4.75
Capt T A Forster	2-6	1-4	0-0	0-1	1-1	33.3	- 0.25

December

	Total W-R	Nov Hdles	H'cap Hdles	Nov Chses	H'cap Chses	Per cent	£1 Level Stake
D Nicholson	2-4	1-1	0-0	0-0	1-3	50.0	+ 0.57
Mrs R Brackenbury	1-1	0-0	0-0	0-0	1-1	100.0	+ 4.50

February

	Total W-R	Nov Hdles	H'cap Hdles	Nov Chses	H'cap Chses	Per cent	£1 Level Stake
G B Balding	3-6	0-2	1-2	0-0	2-2	50.0	+ 44.50
M C Pipe	2-6	2-3	0-1	0-1	0-1	33.3	- 1.96

March

	Total W-R	Nov Hdles	H'cap Hdles	Nov Chses	H'cap Chses	Per cent	£1 Level Stake
Miss J S Doyle	2-2	1-1	1-1	0-0	0-0	100.0	+ 5.38
N Twiston-Davies	2-3	0-0	2-2	0-1	0-0	66.7	+ 15.50

April

	Total W-R	Nov Hdles	H'cap Hdles	Nov Chses	H'cap Chses	Per cent	£1 Level Stake
D Nicholson	3-11	1-6	0-1	1-3	1-1	27.3	- 2.38
N A Gaselee	2-5	1-2	1-1	0-1	0-1	40.0	+ 5.85

May

	Total W-R	Nov Hdles	H'cap Hdles	Nov Chses	H'cap Chses	Per cent	£1 Level Stake
M C Pipe	9-34	3-13	3-12	1-6	2-3	26.5	+ 20.31
K C Bailey	5-18	0-3	0-3	2-4	3-8	27.8	- 5.73

TAUNTON (Group 4)

Leading Trainers 1991-96

	Total W-R	Nov Hdles	H'cap Hdles	Nov Chses	H'cap Chses	Per cent	£1 Level Stake
M C Pipe	46-194	24-72	16-86	5-13	1-23	23.7	- 32.58
P J Hobbs	22-94	10-33	5-29	2-9	5-23	23.4	+ 61.46
R J Hodges	19-201	0-45	6-84	6-27	7-45	9.5	- 87.67
P F Nicholls	9-81	4-25	1-14	1-14	3-28	11.1	- 46.00
J A B Old	8-21	5-12	3-8	0-0	0-1	38.1	+ 24.56
Mrs J G Retter	7-58	0-15	3-22	1-10	3-11	12.1	- 12.00
Miss H C Knight	6-29	1-11	2-4	3-6	0-8	20.7	+ 9.00
N J Henderson	6-36	3-19	0-6	1-5	2-6	16.7	- 11.65
R H Buckler	6-55	1-14	5-18	0-10	0-13	10.9	- 18.77
G B Balding	6-58	0-16	3-15	1-7	2-20	10.3	- 21.00
J S King	5-23	0-4	1-5	1-4	3-10	21.7	- 0.25
K Bishop	5-40	0-8	2-16	1-6	2-10	12.5	- 7.50
C L Popham	5-95	2-37	2-19	1-14	0-25	5.3	- 55.17
F Murphy	4-14	1-6	2-5	1-3	0-0	28.6	+ 10.50
P R Hedger	4-20	2-9	1-8	1-2	0-1	20.0	- 3.15
O Sherwood	4-22	1-7	0-5	1-3	2-7	18.2	- 2.75
S Sherwood	4-24	0-5	1-9	3-3	0-7	16.7	- 13.48
Mrs S D Williams	4-30	1-11	2-11	0-4	1-4	13.3	+ 10.00
G F Edwards	4-31	0-4	3-20	1-3	0-4	12.9	+ 9.50
G A Ham	4-45	0-11	3-22	0-5	1-7	8.9	- 25.75

Leading Jockeys

	Total W-R	Per cent	£1 Level Stake	Best Trainer	W-R	Per cent	£1 Level Stake
M A FitzGerald	18-125	14.4	- 12.82	Mrs J G Retter	4-27	14.8	- 6.50
D Bridgwater	14-88	15.9	- 42.12	M C Pipe	7-27	25.9	- 7.38
J Osborne	11-44	25.0	+ 5.93	C Weedon	2-2	100.0	+ 7.33
C Maude	11-86	12.8	+ 4.05	P J Hobbs	7-17	41.2	+ 55.55
R Dunwoody	11-104	10.6	- 57.71	M C Pipe	5-38	13.2	- 24.97
M Richards	10-43	23.3	+ 9.76	W R Muir	3-6	50.0	+ 8.08
A P McCoy	9-57	15.8	- 7.34	G B Balding	2-6	33.3	+ 4.00
S Burrough	9-87	10.3	- 32.52	H T Cole	2-6	33.3	+ 3.73
J Lower	7-29	24.1	- 2.58	M C Pipe	7-28	25.0	- 1.58
J R Kavanagh	7-38	18.4	- 0.75	N J Henderson	4-12	33.3	+ 7.75
A Tory	7-72	9.7	- 32.75	R J Hodges	5-50	10.0	- 31.25
B Powell	7-121	5.8	- 77.60	R H Buckler	2-26	7.7	- 14.60

How the Favourites Fared

	W-R	Per cent	£1 Level Stake		W-R	Per cent	£1 Level Stake
Novice Hurdles	59-119	49.6	+ 16.65	Novice Chases	20-42	47.6	+ 4.61
H'cap Hurdles	29-112	25.9	- 16.86	H'cap Chases	20-69	29.0	- 14.95
N H Flat	0-0	-	0.00	Hunter Chases	6-14	42.9	+ 0.38
Totals	88-231	38.1	- 0.21	Totals	46-125	36.8	- 9.96
All favourites	134-356	37.6	- 10.17				

LEADING TRAINERS BY MONTH AT TAUNTON 1991-96

September

	Total W-R	Nov Hdles	H'cap Hdles	Nov Chses	H'cap Chses	Per cent	£1 Level Stake
P J Hobbs	4-11	3-7	0-0	0-1	1-3	36.4	+ 3.05
M R Channon	3-4	2-2	1-2	0-0	0-0	75.0	+ 33.50
M C Pipe	3-15	2-9	1-4	0-0	0-2	20.0	- 9.58
Miss H C Knight	2-2	1-1	0-0	1-1	0-0	100.0	+ 7.50

October

	Total W-R	Nov Hdles	H'cap Hdles	Nov Chses	H'cap Chses	Per cent	£1 Level Stake
M C Pipe	3-15	2-7	0-5	1-2	0-1	20.0	- 8.64
P F Nicholls	2-3	1-1	1-1	0-1	0-0	66.7	+ 3.00
G F Edwards	2-5	0-1	1-3	1-1	0-0	40.0	+ 19.50
P J Hobbs	2-6	2-4	0-1	0-1	0-0	33.3	+ 29.50

November

	Total W-R	Nov Hdles	H'cap Hdles	Nov Chses	H'cap Chses	Per cent	£1 Level Stake
M C Pipe	8-29	3-10	4-13	1-2	0-4	27.6	+ 12.85
M W Davies	2-2	2-2	0-0	0-0	0-0	100.0	+ 2.53
C R Egerton	2-3	1-2	0-0	0-0	1-1	66.7	+ 13.25
J W Mullins	2-3	0-1	0-0	0-0	2-2	66.7	+ 5.75

December

	Total W-R	Nov Hdles	H'cap Hdles	Nov Chses	H'cap Chses	Per cent	£1 Level Stake
P J Hobbs	7-13	4-6	0-3	0-0	3-4	53.8	+ 29.75
M C Pipe	5-27	3-12	2-11	0-0	0-4	18.5	- 10.64
R J Hodges	4-38	0-12	1-14	0-0	3-12	10.5	- 6.75
N J Henderson	3-7	2-5	0-1	0-0	1-1	42.9	+ 6.10

January

	Total W-R	Nov Hdles	H'cap Hdles	Nov Chses	H'cap Chses	Per cent	£1 Level Stake
M C Pipe	6-19	3-7	2-8	0-0	1-4	31.6	- 0.55
T T Bill	1-1	0-0	0-0	0-0	1-1	100.0	+ 20.00
R H Buckler	1-1	0-0	1-1	0-0	0-0	100.0	+ 3.33
R Callow	1-1	1-1	0-0	0-0	0-0	100.0	+ 12.00

February

	Total W-R	Nov Hdles	H'cap Hdles	Nov Chses	H'cap Chses	Per cent	£1 Level Stake
M C Pipe	4-24	3-5	0-15	1-2	0-2	16.7	- 13.43
P J Hobbs	3-13	0-2	1-6	2-3	0-2	23.1	- 2.84
O Sherwood	2-4	0-1	0-0	0-0	2-3	50.0	+ 8.00
J A B Old	2-6	2-4	0-2	0-0	0-0	33.3	+ 6.25

March

	Total W-R	Nov Hdles	H'cap Hdles	Nov Chses	H'cap Chses	Per cent	£1 Level Stake
M C Pipe	12-35	6-16	4-12	2-4	0-3	34.3	+ 13.38
R J Hodges	5-35	0-8	2-15	3-7	0-5	14.3	+ 9.50
J A B Old	3-5	2-3	1-2	0-0	0-0	60.0	+ 7.31
P J Hobbs	3-17	1-5	2-7	0-3	0-2	17.6	+ 11.00

April

	Total W-R	Nov Hdles	H'cap Hdles	Nov Chses	H'cap Chses	Per cent	£1 Level Stake
M C Pipe	5-30	2-6	3-18	0-3	0-3	16.7	- 15.98
R J Hodges	5-36	0-1	1-22	2-4	2-9	13.9	- 21.92
W R Muir	2-2	1-1	0-0	1-1	0-0	100.0	+ 6.08
N G Ayliffe	2-3	0-0	2-3	0-0	0-0	66.7	+ 19.00

TOWCESTER (Group 4)

Leading Trainers 1991-96

	Total W-R	Nov Hdles	H'cap Hdles	Nov Chses	H'cap Chses	Per cent	£1 Level Stake
O Brennan	26-121	8-49	9-38	0-8	9-26	21.5	+ 10.42
D Nicholson	21-61	11-37	0-1	3-9	7-14	34.4	+ 69.04
Mrs I McKie	15-60	0-19	2-9	3-9	10-23	25.0	+ 14.08
Miss C Saunders	14-23	0-0	0-0	14-23	0-0	60.9	+ 11.58
Mrs J Pitman	13-55	8-25	1-9	3-8	1-13	23.6	- 3.23
Capt T A Forster	13-97	3-22	0-5	3-24	7-46	13.4	- 31.90
N Twiston-Davies	12-88	3-34	3-19	6-22	0-13	13.6	- 23.83
J R Upson	11-73	1-29	3-14	2-12	5-18	15.1	- 16.50
J T Gifford	10-74	5-23	0-10	3-15	2-26	13.5	- 29.77
D R Gandolfo	9-48	5-26	1-7	2-3	1-12	18.8	- 4.34
K C Bailey	9-63	1-18	1-13	2-14	5-18	14.3	- 25.59
C P E Brooks	8-32	0-9	1-3	6-11	1-9	25.0	- 7.97
J A B Old	7-39	3-12	3-15	1-3	0-9	17.9	+ 6.75
M C Pipe	7-49	5-30	1-6	1-6	0-7	14.3	- 21.15
R J Hodges	6-25	1-3	1-7	0-1	4-14	24.0	+ 12.00
P T Dalton	6-27	0-6	1-5	1-3	4-13	22.2	+ 9.75
T Thomson Jones	6-31	0-6	0-8	0-2	6-15	19.4	- 8.25
J S Moore	5-17	2-8	3-8	0-0	0-1	29.4	+ 46.40
J A C Edwards	5-27	1-10	0-2	0-2	4-13	18.5	- 8.25
J White	5-45	4-24	0-13	0-5	1-3	11.1	- 15.71

Leading Jockeys

	Total W-R	Per cent	£1 Level Stake	Best Trainer	W-R	Per cent	£1 Level Stake
Martin Brennan	25-103	24.3	+ 24.44	O Brennan	25-95	26.3	+ 32.44
R Dunwoody	19-92	20.7	- 12.52	R J Hodges	4-9	44.4	+ 8.00
A Maguire	17-78	21.8	- 10.61	D Nicholson	12-20	60.0	+ 25.74
L Harvey	15-109	13.8	- 27.28	Mrs I McKie	11-45	24.4	+ 11.09
W Marston	12-69	17.4	- 6.26	Mrs J Pitman	4-14	28.6	- 1.87
N Williamson	11-63	17.5	- 18.74	J A C Edwards	4-11	36.4	+ 2.26
D Gallagher	10-52	19.2	+ 19.00	C P E Brooks	2-6	33.3	+ 1.00
D Bridgwater	9-89	10.1	- 44.82	N Twiston-Davies	4-16	25.0	+ 6.18
R Supple	8-90	8.9	- 16.50	J R Upson	5-39	12.8	- 15.50
C Llewellyn	8-94	8.5	- 53.52	J A B Old	2-4	50.0	+ 7.50
G Bradley	6-39	15.4	- 15.46	C P E Brooks	4-18	22.2	- 6.71
T Grantham	6-42	14.3	- 3.75	J A B Old	5-30	16.7	+ 4.25

How the Favourites Fared

	W-R	Per cent	£1 Level Stake		W-R	Per cent	£1 Level Stake
Novice Hurdles	43-118	36.4	- 19.65	Novice Chases	26-55	47.3	+ 2.75
H'cap Hurdles	28-87	32.2	- 2.55	H'cap Chases	36-109	33.0	- 16.10
N H Flat	4-11	36.4	- 0.28	Hunter Chases	20-33	60.6	+ 20.49
Totals	75-216	34.7	- 22.48	Totals	82-197	41.6	+ 7.14
All favourites	157-413	38.0	- 15.34				

LEADING TRAINERS BY MONTH AT TOWCESTER 1991-96

October

	Total W-R	Nov Hdles	H'cap Hdles	Nov Chses	H'cap Chses	Per cent	£1 Level Stake
Mrs J Pitman	3-3	2-2	0-0	1-1	0-0	100.0	+ 5.58
P T Dalton	2-2	0-0	0-0	0-0	2-2	100.0	+ 22.00
Mrs I McKie	2-8	0-2	1-1	1-2	0-3	25.0	- 1.00
A P Jones	2-10	0-1	0-1	0-2	2-6	20.0	+ 26.75

November

	Total W-R	Nov Hdles	H'cap Hdles	Nov Chses	H'cap Chses	Per cent	£1 Level Stake
J R Upson	4-14	0-4	1-4	2-3	1-3	28.6	+ 8.75
Mrs I McKie	3-11	0-4	0-1	0-0	3-6	27.3	+ 1.00
D Nicholson	3-11	2-6	0-0	0-2	1-3	27.3	+ 37.60
J T Gifford	3-19	3-8	0-2	0-3	0-6	15.8	- 4.25

December

	Total W-R	Nov Hdles	H'cap Hdles	Nov Chses	H'cap Chses	Per cent	£1 Level Stake
N Twiston-Davies	5-18	2-8	0-1	3-6	0-3	27.8	+ 6.68
D Nicholson	4-17	2-9	0-0	1-4	1-4	23.5	+ 7.75
N J Henderson	3-11	1-7	0-0	1-2	1-2	27.3	- 2.03
Mrs J Pitman	3-15	2-8	0-0	0-1	1-6	20.0	- 0.50

January

	Total W-R	Nov Hdles	H'cap Hdles	Nov Chses	H'cap Chses	Per cent	£1 Level Stake
D Nicholson	6-13	3-9	0-0	0-1	3-3	46.2	+ 2.12
C R Egerton	2-4	0-0	1-1	0-1	1-2	50.0	+ 14.50
J T Gifford	2-9	1-5	0-0	1-2	0-2	22.2	+ 2.73
Mrs J Pitman	2-9	1-6	0-0	1-1	0-2	22.2	- 3.75

February

	Total W-R	Nov Hdles	H'cap Hdles	Nov Chses	H'cap Chses	Per cent	£1 Level Stake
D Nicholson	4-10	1-7	0-0	2-2	1-1	40.0	+ 1.07
D R Gandolfo	3-6	2-4	0-1	1-1	0-0	50.0	+ 12.29
Mrs I McKie	2-2	0-0	0-0	0-0	2-2	100.0	+ 6.75
Miss C Saunders	2-3	0-0	0-0	2-3	0-0	66.7	+ 1.29

March

	Total W-R	Nov Hdles	H'cap Hdles	Nov Chses	H'cap Chses	Per cent	£1 Level Stake
Mrs I McKie	4-7	0-2	1-1	2-2	1-2	57.1	+ 22.83
Miss C Saunders	3-6	0-0	0-0	3-6	0-0	50.0	- 1.03
H J Collingridge	2-5	0-1	2-4	0-0	0-0	40.0	+ 6.50
P T Dalton	2-5	0-0	0-1	1-1	1-3	40.0	+ 1.13

April

	Total W-R	Nov Hdles	H'cap Hdles	Nov Chses	H'cap Chses	Per cent	£1 Level Stake
O Brennan	6-18	1-6	3-6	0-0	2-6	33.3	+ 4.29
T Thomson Jones	4-11	0-1	0-4	0-0	4-6	36.4	+ 1.38
Capt T A Forster	4-15	1-2	0-1	2-5	1-7	26.7	+ 7.50
Miss C Saunders	3-4	0-0	0-0	3-4	0-0	75.0	+ 0.98

May

	Total W-R	Nov Hdles	H'cap Hdles	Nov Chses	H'cap Chses	Per cent	£1 Level Stake
O Brennan	13-36	5-15	4-13	0-1	4-7	36.1	+ 20.88
Miss C Saunders	6-10	0-0	0-0	6-10	0-0	60.0	+ 10.35
R J Hodges	5-13	1-1	1-5	0-1	3-6	38.5	+ 20.00
K C Bailey	4-19	0-4	1-7	1-4	2-4	21.1	- 2.97

UTTOXETER (Group 3)

Leading Trainers 1991-96

	Total W-R	Nov Hdles	H'cap Hdles	Nov Chses	H'cap Chses	Per cent	£1 Level Stake
M C Pipe	45-159	22-64	7-44	9-20	7-31	28.3	+ 2.50
K C Bailey	25-108	11-40	3-18	7-20	4-30	23.1	+ 0.36
N Twiston-Davies	23-106	12-48	5-12	4-20	2-26	21.7	+ 2.56
O Sherwood	18-61	8-28	1-2	5-9	4-22	29.5	+ 23.04
D Nicholson	18-83	10-45	2-15	3-6	3-17	21.7	+ 0.98
P J Hobbs	12-76	2-22	2-15	2-8	6-31	15.8	- 18.06
Capt T A Forster	11-49	0-12	1-4	5-7	5-26	22.4	- 4.28
J G FitzGerald	9-38	3-14	1-14	3-6	2-4	23.7	+ 1.83
P T Dalton	9-56	2-17	2-15	1-13	4-11	16.1	- 0.50
Miss H C Knight	9-61	4-28	2-9	2-10	1-14	14.8	- 14.46
Mrs J Pitman	9-72	0-23	1-21	1-9	7-19	12.5	- 28.10
N J Henderson	8-29	2-7	3-8	0-3	3-11	27.6	- 2.40
J J O'Neill	8-29	2-10	5-11	0-4	1-4	27.6	+ 17.28
G Richards	8-55	2-17	0-5	0-6	6-27	14.5	- 24.29
J Mackie	8-103	1-32	3-35	1-9	3-27	7.8	- 57.94
W Clay	8-165	5-65	3-72	0-19	0-9	4.8	- 88.25
M H Tompkins	7-24	3-15	2-6	1-2	1-1	29.2	+ 12.80
J A B Old	7-25	5-12	0-7	0-0	2-6	28.0	+ 10.82
R Lee	7-59	2-25	2-16	0-6	3-12	11.9	- 16.90
C J Mann	6-20	1-9	0-3	2-2	3-6	30.0	+ 1.73

Leading Jockeys

	Total W-R	Per cent	£1 Level Stake	Best Trainer	W-R	Per cent	£1 Level Stake
R Dunwoody	40-173	23.1	- 52.95	M C Pipe	17-46	37.0	+ 2.42
J Osborne	28-96	29.2	+ 43.16	O Sherwood	12-30	40.0	+ 17.25
N Williamson	24-149	16.1	- 25.32	K C Bailey	12-47	25.5	+ 9.38
A Maguire	21-125	16.8	- 6.66	D Nicholson	6-25	24.0	- 2.64
C Llewellyn	15-92	16.3	- 12.23	N Twiston-Davies	9-37	24.3	- 0.34
D Bridgwater	15-106	14.2	- 45.57	M C Pipe	4-15	26.7	- 5.99
T Eley	15-142	10.6	- 17.04	Miss S J Wilton	4-21	19.0	+ 24.00
S McNeill	12-59	20.3	+ 8.30	K C Bailey	3-7	42.9	+ 0.63
A P McCoy	10-41	24.4	- 1.13	M C Pipe	3-3	100.0	+ 5.10
M A FitzGerald	10-81	12.3	+ 16.58	Mrs J G Retter	3-13	23.1	+ 2.25
W Marston	10-108	9.3	- 52.34	Mrs J Pitman	3-17	17.6	+ 1.10
G Bradley	9-41	22.0	+ 32.00	C P E Brooks	3-11	27.3	+ 2.50

How the Favourites Fared

	W-R	Per cent	£1 Level Stake		W-R	Per cent	£1 Level Stake
Novice Hurdles	63-158	39.9	- 10.69	Novice Chases	35-75	46.7	- 11.35
H'cap Hurdles	43-154	27.9	- 23.62	H'cap Chases	53-138	38.4	- 9.99
N H Flat	4-23	17.4	- 15.12	Hunter Chases	21-39	53.8	+ 9.05
Totals	110-335	32.8	- 49.43	Totals	109-252	43.3	- 12.29
All favourites	219-587	37.3	- 61.72				

LEADING TRAINERS BY MONTH AT UTTOXETER 1991-96

June	Total W-R	Nov Hdles	H'cap Hdles	Nov Chses	H'cap Chses	Per cent	£1 Level Stake
N Twiston-Davies	3-9	1-3	0-1	2-3	0-2	33.3	- 2.61
M C Pipe	3-11	1-3	0-4	0-1	2-3	27.3	- 2.90

August	Total W-R	Nov Hdles	H'cap Hdles	Nov Chses	H'cap Chses	Per cent	£1 Level Stake
M C Pipe	6-9	4-6	0-1	2-2	0-0	66.7	+ 7.43
P J Hobbs	2-3	0-0	1-1	0-0	1-2	66.7	+ 1.08

September	Total W-R	Nov Hdles	H'cap Hdles	Nov Chses	H'cap Chses	Per cent	£1 Level Stake
K C Bailey	3-6	0-1	2-2	0-1	1-2	50.0	+ 4.75
G Richards	3-9	2-2	0-1	0-2	1-4	33.3	+ 4.75

October	Total W-R	Nov Hdles	H'cap Hdles	Nov Chses	H'cap Chses	Per cent	£1 Level Stake
N Twiston-Davies	5-15	1-5	1-2	2-4	1-4	33.3	+ 2.78
O Sherwood	4-6	3-3	0-0	0-1	1-2	66.7	+ 19.00

November	Total W-R	Nov Hdles	H'cap Hdles	Nov Chses	H'cap Chses	Per cent	£1 Level Stake
K C Bailey	6-16	4-7	0-0	1-5	1-4	37.5	+ 15.45
O Sherwood	4-11	1-5	0-1	2-2	1-3	36.4	- 2.66

December	Total W-R	Nov Hdles	H'cap Hdles	Nov Chses	H'cap Chses	Per cent	£1 Level Stake
M C Pipe	7-23	5-12	0-2	2-3	0-6	30.4	+ 3.07
D Nicholson	5-12	3-5	0-2	1-1	1-4	41.7	+ 16.46

January	Total W-R	Nov Hdles	H'cap Hdles	Nov Chses	H'cap Chses	Per cent	£1 Level Stake
M C Pipe	3-8	0-3	1-2	1-1	1-2	37.5	- 0.50
R H Alner	1-1	1-1	0-0	0-0	0-0	100.0	+ 0.67

February	Total W-R	Nov Hdles	H'cap Hdles	Nov Chses	H'cap Chses	Per cent	£1 Level Stake
J G FitzGerald	3-9	2-4	0-2	1-2	0-1	33.3	+ 6.00
C J Mann	2-3	0-1	0-0	1-1	1-1	66.7	+ 1.75

March	Total W-R	Nov Hdles	H'cap Hdles	Nov Chses	H'cap Chses	Per cent	£1 Level Stake
J A B Old	3-9	2-5	0-2	0-0	1-2	33.3	+ 3.25
D Nicholson	3-14	3-7	0-2	0-1	0-4	21.4	- 5.18

April	Total W-R	Nov Hdles	H'cap Hdles	Nov Chses	H'cap Chses	Per cent	£1 Level Stake
O Sherwood	5-12	2-5	1-1	0-2	2-4	41.7	+ 16.00
P J Hobbs	5-17	2-7	0-3	1-2	2-5	29.4	+ 9.25

May	Total W-R	Nov Hdles	H'cap Hdles	Nov Chses	H'cap Chses	Per cent	£1 Level Stake
M C Pipe	14-35	5-10	4-15	3-4	2-6	40.0	+ 8.69
N Twiston-Davies	7-16	3-7	3-4	0-3	1-2	43.8	+ 26.67

WARWICK (Group 3)

Leading Trainers 1991-96

	Total W-R	Nov Hdles	H'cap Hdles	Nov Chses	H'cap Chses	Per cent	£1 Level Stake
M C Pipe	32-128	14-65	5-27	7-10	6-26	25.0	- 23.31
D Nicholson	25-116	13-50	3-17	6-20	3-29	21.6	+ 9.96
Mrs J Pitman	17-91	3-28	4-25	4-16	6-22	18.7	+ 63.05
N Twiston-Davies	12-74	7-47	2-7	2-9	1-11	16.2	+ 3.52
O Sherwood	10-49	6-21	0-7	3-10	1-11	20.4	+ 2.27
N J Henderson	10-51	6-23	1-8	1-8	2-12	19.6	- 2.26
Miss H C Knight	9-39	3-15	3-12	0-5	3-7	23.1	+ 22.50
N A Gaselee	9-40	2-9	2-9	2-9	3-13	22.5	+ 3.75
G B Balding	7-77	1-27	3-24	1-12	2-14	9.1	- 45.17
P J Hobbs	6-42	3-14	1-8	1-9	1-11	14.3	+ 3.25
J T Gifford	6-46	0-10	3-14	1-10	2-12	13.0	- 22.30
R J Price	5-19	2-9	2-9	0-0	1-1	26.3	+ 16.08
J L Spearing	5-29	2-20	3-7	0-2	0-0	17.2	0.00
R Dickin	5-38	2-12	2-13	0-6	1-7	13.2	+ 0.50
K C Bailey	5-39	1-16	0-1	2-11	2-11	12.8	- 23.13
A J Wilson	5-47	1-13	3-21	0-5	1-8	10.6	+ 5.50
Capt T A Forster	5-77	1-38	1-14	1-9	2-16	6.5	- 50.13
R C Wilkins	4-5	0-0	0-0	4-5	0-0	80.0	+ 1.55
W G M Turner	4-9	1-3	1-2	1-2	1-2	44.4	+ 36.91
G Harwood	4-11	0-1	1-3	2-4	1-3	36.4	+ 0.03

Leading Jockeys

	Total W-R	Per cent	£1 Level Stake		Best Trainer	W-R	Per cent	£1 Level Stake
R Dunwoody	40-107	37.4	+ 24.49		M C Pipe	11-19	57.9	+ 10.78
A Maguire	17-88	19.3	+ 35.14		D Nicholson	8-31	25.8	+ 7.81
J Osborne	15-86	17.4	- 29.07		O Sherwood	8-28	28.6	+ 8.27
N Williamson	11-57	19.3	- 0.33		K C Bailey	3-14	21.4	- 4.46
W Marston	10-86	11.6	- 23.93		Mrs J Pitman	5-21	23.8	+ 2.37
T Jenks	8-37	21.6	+ 2.29		N Twiston-Davies	3-16	18.8	0.00
C Llewellyn	8-48	16.7	- 7.77		N A Gaselee	3-8	37.5	+ 10.25
D Bridgwater	8-62	12.9	- 18.30		M C Pipe	5-11	45.5	+ 13.29
A P McCoy	7-25	28.0	+ 7.71		J L Spearing	2-2	100.0	+ 12.00
B Powell	6-68	8.8	- 45.75		P J Hobbs	1-1	100.0	+ 2.75
R Johnson	5-30	16.7	- 7.00		W Jenks	1-1	100.0	+ 3.50
J R Kavanagh	5-34	14.7	+ 11.00		N J Henderson	2-8	25.0	+ 15.00

How the Favourites Fared

	W-R	Per cent	£1 Level Stake		W-R	Per cent	£1 Level Stake
Novice Hurdles	46-89	51.7	+ 18.80	Novice Chases	28-58	48.3	- 2.27
H'cap Hurdles	29-86	33.7	+ 5.37	H'cap Chases	29-75	38.7	- 0.45
N H Flat	5-26	19.2	- 8.08	Hunter Chases	9-27	33.3	- 8.11
Totals	80-201	39.8	+ 16.09	Totals	66-160	41.3	- 10.83
All favourites	146-361	40.4	+ 5.26				

LEADING TRAINERS BY MONTH AT WARWICK 1991-96

October

	Total W-R	Nov Hdles	H'cap Hdles	Nov Chses	H'cap Chses	Per cent	£1 Level Stake
D Nicholson	3-6	3-6	0-0	0-0	0-0	50.0	+ 4.78
K C Bailey	2-7	1-2	0-0	0-3	1-2	28.6	+ 0.25
Mrs J Pitman	2-10	0-5	1-2	0-2	1-1	20.0	+ 6.25
M C Pipe	2-11	2-5	0-3	0-0	0-3	18.2	− 3.50
J L Harris	1-1	0-0	1-1	0-0	0-0	100.0	+ 10.00

November

	Total W-R	Nov Hdles	H'cap Hdles	Nov Chses	H'cap Chses	Per cent	£1 Level Stake
Mrs J Pitman	6-26	2-12	1-5	0-0	3-9	23.1	+ 23.10
J T Gifford	4-10	0-1	2-3	1-3	1-3	40.0	+ 2.95
O Sherwood	4-11	3-5	0-1	1-2	0-3	36.4	+ 2.24
M C Pipe	4-15	2-8	0-2	0-0	2-5	26.7	− 5.02
R Dickin	3-5	1-1	1-2	0-1	1-1	60.0	+ 19.00

December

	Total W-R	Nov Hdles	H'cap Hdles	Nov Chses	H'cap Chses	Per cent	£1 Level Stake
M C Pipe	5-15	1-7	1-3	1-2	2-3	33.3	+ 6.88
N Twiston-Davies	4-18	3-13	0-1	1-2	0-2	22.2	+ 10.75
D Nicholson	3-19	1-9	0-1	2-3	0-6	15.8	− 13.05
C T Nash	2-2	0-0	0-0	1-1	1-1	100.0	+ 9.38
N A Gaselee	2-6	1-3	0-0	0-1	1-2	33.3	+ 1.00

January

	Total W-R	Nov Hdles	H'cap Hdles	Nov Chses	H'cap Chses	Per cent	£1 Level Stake
D Nicholson	10-36	4-12	3-9	0-5	3-10	27.8	+ 9.68
M C Pipe	8-38	2-12	1-12	4-6	1-8	21.1	− 12.69
Mrs J Pitman	5-21	0-2	1-7	3-8	1-4	23.8	+ 18.62
J R Jenkins	2-3	1-2	1-1	0-0	0-0	66.7	+ 7.50
J A B Old	2-4	0-0	2-3	0-0	0-1	50.0	+ 17.00

February

	Total W-R	Nov Hdles	H'cap Hdles	Nov Chses	H'cap Chses	Per cent	£1 Level Stake
D Nicholson	5-25	3-12	0-3	2-6	0-4	20.0	+ 0.30
O Sherwood	4-12	3-6	0-1	1-3	0-2	33.3	+ 13.50
Mrs J Pitman	3-12	1-5	1-3	0-2	1-2	25.0	+ 35.25
N J Henderson	3-15	1-7	1-1	1-4	0-3	20.0	+ 10.19
N Twiston-Davies	3-16	2-11	0-1	1-3	0-1	18.8	+ 6.60

March

	Total W-R	Nov Hdles	H'cap Hdles	Nov Chses	H'cap Chses	Per cent	£1 Level Stake
M C Pipe	3-13	2-9	1-3	0-0	0-1	23.1	− 5.63
P R Webber	2-2	1-1	0-0	1-1	0-0	100.0	+ 3.94
R C Wilkins	2-3	0-0	0-0	2-3	0-0	66.7	+ 1.20
K O C-Brown	1-1	0-0	1-1	0-0	0-0	100.0	+ 4.00
G P Enright	1-1	0-0	1-1	0-0	0-0	100.0	+ 6.00

May

	Total W-R	Nov Hdles	H'cap Hdles	Nov Chses	H'cap Chses	Per cent	£1 Level Stake
M C Pipe	9-18	4-11	2-3	2-2	1-2	50.0	+ 12.03
P Bowen	3-4	0-0	0-1	3-3	0-0	75.0	+ 4.54
N A Gaselee	3-5	1-1	2-2	0-0	0-2	60.0	+ 8.25
G Harwood	3-6	0-0	1-3	1-2	1-1	50.0	+ 3.50
N Twiston-Davies	3-9	1-6	1-1	0-0	1-2	33.3	+ 0.67

WETHERBY (Group 2)

Leading Trainers 1991-96

	Total W-R	Nov Hdles	H'cap Hdles	Nov Chses	H'cap Chses	Per cent	£1 Level Stake
Mrs M Reveley	48-172	18-68	18-60	3-13	9-31	27.9	- 19.03
G Richards	28-131	6-28	2-29	8-27	12-47	21.4	- 21.69
M W Easterby	18-112	7-59	2-20	4-13	5-20	16.1	- 36.69
J G FitzGerald	18-112	4-52	6-23	3-12	5-25	16.1	+ 6.94
D Nicholson	17-53	4-23	0-4	7-14	6-12	32.1	+ 7.61
M D Hammond	17-141	6-58	6-31	1-16	4-36	12.1	- 59.05
J H Johnson	16-83	3-27	6-18	2-9	5-29	19.3	+ 91.17
P Cheesbrough	10-89	2-23	1-12	1-24	6-30	11.2	- 41.95
Mrs S J Smith	9-112	1-44	2-20	2-24	4-24	8.0	- 53.25
N Tinkler	8-70	5-33	2-33	0-1	1-3	11.4	- 32.42
G M Moore	7-69	4-34	2-20	1-5	0-10	10.1	- 43.59
P Beaumont	6-48	4-23	0-16	2-6	0-3	12.5	- 11.60
N Twiston-Davies	5-20	2-8	0-2	2-8	1-2	25.0	+ 1.99
J I A Charlton	5-23	0-5	1-2	0-2	4-14	21.7	- 3.08
J J O'Neill	5-43	1-12	2-17	1-7	1-7	11.6	- 18.92
T P Tate	5-45	0-20	1-10	1-6	3-9	11.1	- 13.00
T D Easterby	4-13	0-5	2-6	0-0	2-2	30.8	+ 6.75
J T Gifford	4-18	0-0	1-3	3-5	0-10	22.2	- 2.75
J A Hellens	4-30	2-12	1-6	0-4	1-8	13.3	- 13.25
J Mackie	4-30	1-10	3-13	0-0	0-7	13.3	+ 21.00

Leading Jockeys

	Total W-R	Per cent	£1 Level Stake	Best Trainer	W-R	Per cent	£1 Level Stake
P Niven	46-180	25.6	- 8.24	Mrs M Reveley	35-109	32.1	+ 10.15
L Wyer	41-170	24.1	+ 16.58	T D Easterby	3-6	50.0	+ 8.75
A Maguire	20-77	26.0	+ 55.03	D Nicholson	10-31	32.3	+ 11.03
M Dwyer	19-173	11.0	- 106.08	J G FitzGerald	9-69	13.0	- 32.33
A Dobbin	14-84	16.7	- 14.39	G Richards	7-28	25.0	- 2.97
R Garrity	11-124	8.9	- 55.00	M W Easterby	5-30	16.7	- 4.25
B Storey	9-89	10.1	- 54.08	J I A Charlton	3-14	21.4	- 6.08
R Dunwoody	8-32	25.0	+ 0.27	D Nicholson	3-8	37.5	+ 0.27
J Callaghan	8-85	9.4	- 36.37	G M Moore	4-30	13.3	- 14.87
D Byrne	7-50	14.0	+ 11.63	B E Wilkinson	2-5	40.0	+ 27.50
K Johnson	6-59	10.2	- 34.25	P Cheesbrough	4-30	13.3	- 15.25
Richard Guest	6-61	9.8	- 32.12	Mrs S J Smith	3-41	7.3	- 19.00

How the Favourites Fared

	W-R	Per cent	£1 Level Stake		W-R	Per cent	£1 Level Stake
Novice Hurdles	59-120	49.2	+ 21.74	Novice Chases	31-64	48.4	- 5.03
H'cap Hurdles	40-101	39.6	+ 3.13	H'cap Chases	38-107	35.5	- 9.91
N H Flat	2-5	40.0	+ 3.25	Hunter Chases	12-18	66.7	+ 5.59
Totals	101-226	44.7	+ 28.12	Totals	81-189	42.9	- 9.35
All favourites	182-415	43.9	+ 18.77				

LEADING TRAINERS BY MONTH AT WETHERBY 1991-96

October	Total W-R	Nov Hdles	H'cap Hdles	Nov Chses	H'cap Chses	Per cent	£1 Level Stake
Mrs M Reveley	15-40	5-16	6-10	1-6	3-8	37.5	+ 1.22
D Nicholson	6-20	1-8	0-1	3-6	2-5	30.0	+ 13.91
J H Johnson	5-26	1-12	1-2	0-3	3-9	19.2	+ 39.00
N Twiston-Davies	4-13	2-6	0-0	2-6	0-1	30.8	+ 6.11

November	Total W-R	Nov Hdles	H'cap Hdles	Nov Chses	H'cap Chses	Per cent	£1 Level Stake
Mrs M Reveley	8-24	5-13	2-5	0-1	1-5	33.3	+ 6.25
J G FitzGerald	7-19	1-7	2-3	2-3	2-6	36.8	+ 16.75
J H Johnson	3-13	2-3	1-2	0-2	0-6	23.1	+ 48.50
D Nicholson	2-7	0-3	0-0	0-1	2-3	28.6	- 2.38

December	Total W-R	Nov Hdles	H'cap Hdles	Nov Chses	H'cap Chses	Per cent	£1 Level Stake
G Richards	8-33	3-5	0-9	3-7	2-12	24.2	- 5.72
Mrs M Reveley	5-20	2-7	2-7	0-0	1-6	25.0	- 2.33
D Nicholson	3-8	0-1	0-2	2-3	1-2	37.5	- 1.74
M D Hammond	3-30	0-11	2-7	0-4	1-8	10.0	- 9.00

January	Total W-R	Nov Hdles	H'cap Hdles	Nov Chses	H'cap Chses	Per cent	£1 Level Stake
Mrs M Reveley	5-17	1-7	1-4	1-2	2-4	29.4	- 3.17
M W Easterby	2-9	1-5	0-2	1-1	0-1	22.2	- 3.00
N Tinkler	2-9	1-5	1-4	0-0	0-0	22.2	+ 3.63
T J Etherington	1-1	0-0	1-1	0-0	0-0	100.0	+ 8.00

February	Total W-R	Nov Hdles	H'cap Hdles	Nov Chses	H'cap Chses	Per cent	£1 Level Stake
G Richards	4-15	1-3	0-5	2-5	1-2	26.7	+ 2.32
Miss C Saunders	3-3	0-0	0-0	3-3	0-0	100.0	+ 3.90
J G FitzGerald	3-13	1-8	1-1	0-1	1-3	23.1	+ 45.17
D Nicholson	2-5	1-3	0-1	1-1	0-0	40.0	- 1.18

March	Total W-R	Nov Hdles	H'cap Hdles	Nov Chses	H'cap Chses	Per cent	£1 Level Stake
Mrs S J Smith	2-10	1-6	0-2	0-1	1-1	20.0	- 2.75
J W P Curtis	1-1	0-0	0-0	0-0	1-1	100.0	+ 33.00
N J Henderson	1-1	1-1	0-0	0-0	0-0	100.0	+ 1.63
Mrs M Morris	1-1	0-0	0-0	1-1	0-0	100.0	+ 1.88

April	Total W-R	Nov Hdles	H'cap Hdles	Nov Chses	H'cap Chses	Per cent	£1 Level Stake
G Richards	6-18	1-2	1-4	2-4	2-8	33.3	+ 6.03
M W Easterby	6-23	2-12	0-0	1-3	3-8	26.1	+ 6.50
Mrs M Reveley	6-28	1-6	3-16	1-1	1-5	21.4	- 11.20
P Cheesbrough	4-21	1-8	1-5	0-2	2-6	19.0	- 4.25

May	Total W-R	Nov Hdles	H'cap Hdles	Nov Chses	H'cap Chses	Per cent	£1 Level Stake
Mrs M Reveley	8-18	4-10	3-6	0-0	1-2	44.4	+ 8.70
M D Hammond	6-11	4-4	1-3	0-1	1-3	54.5	+ 14.45
M W Easterby	6-19	2-9	2-6	0-0	2-4	31.6	- 1.26
J H Johnson	5-15	0-4	2-5	2-2	1-4	33.3	+ 3.67

WINCANTON (Group 3)

Leading Trainers 1991-96

	Total W-R	Nov Hdles	H'cap Hdles	Nov Chses	H'cap Chses	Per cent	£1 Level Stake
M C Pipe	38-142	24-76	5-31	8-20	1-15	26.8	+ 18.04
Mrs J Pitman	22-77	5-22	4-13	7-27	6-15	28.6	+ 65.65
P F Nicholls	19-113	1-37	2-16	5-18	11-42	16.8	- 30.03
P J Hobbs	18-121	4-43	9-38	1-8	4-32	14.9	- 9.92
J T Gifford	16-91	6-36	1-9	7-21	2-25	17.6	- 40.05
R J Hodges	14-155	1-52	6-48	0-18	7-37	9.0	- 44.46
N Twiston-Davies	12-53	5-24	1-5	2-10	4-14	22.6	+ 8.87
O Sherwood	11-35	9-22	0-2	1-3	1-8	31.4	+ 3.12
R H Alner	11-76	4-38	2-5	3-15	2-18	14.5	- 29.04
K C Bailey	10-59	5-26	0-8	2-12	3-13	16.9	- 17.58
Capt T A Forster	10-69	1-22	1-11	3-12	5-24	14.5	- 15.65
G B Balding	10-105	2-30	3-20	0-17	5-38	9.5	- 44.05
Mrs J G Retter	9-56	1-20	4-16	2-7	2-13	16.1	- 7.50
N J Henderson	9-61	4-29	1-10	2-6	2-16	14.8	- 16.43
Andrew Turnell	8-50	2-17	2-11	3-11	1-11	16.0	+ 23.25
J S King	8-61	3-20	3-19	0-7	2-15	13.1	+ 3.54
Miss H C Knight	7-33	4-15	0-6	2-6	1-6	21.2	- 11.99
D R Gandolfo	7-36	3-23	2-6	2-6	0-1	19.4	+ 6.56
D R C Elsworth	7-61	2-23	0-12	1-12	4-14	11.5	- 9.10
S Sherwood	6-37	1-15	2-6	3-7	0-9	16.2	+ 4.25

Leading Jockeys

	Total W-R	Per cent	£1 Level Stake	Best Trainer	W-R	Per cent	£1 Level Stake
R Dunwoody	33-155	21.3	- 57.48	M C Pipe	12-29	41.4	+ 16.65
J Osborne	14-68	20.6	+ 2.58	O Sherwood	5-18	27.8	- 0.75
C Llewellyn	11-73	15.1	- 0.45	N Twiston-Davies	4-16	25.0	+ 8.05
M A FitzGerald	11-120	9.2	- 65.00	Mrs J G Retter	7-35	20.0	+ 5.00
A P McCoy	10-58	17.2	- 20.58	P F Nicholls	4-13	30.8	+ 0.41
P Holley	10-94	10.6	- 16.10	D R C Elsworth	5-40	12.5	+ 0.90
S McNeill	9-73	12.3	+ 2.38	Andrew Turnell	3-16	18.8	+ 27.25
M Hourigan	8-36	22.2	+ 34.66	P J Hobbs	4-15	26.7	+ 33.25
G Bradley	8-46	17.4	+ 0.23	Mrs J Pitman	5-6	83.3	+ 31.23
J Lower	7-23	30.4	+ 11.42	M C Pipe	7-23	30.4	+ 11.42
A Maguire	7-78	9.0	- 44.87	J White	2-3	66.7	+ 1.63
B Powell	7-120	5.8	- 74.50	Capt T A Forster	2-14	14.3	- 7.00

How the Favourites Fared

	W-R	Per cent	£1 Level Stake		W-R	Per cent	£1 Level Stake
Novice Hurdles	53-122	43.4	+ 3.82	Novice Chases	37-69	53.6	- 0.55
H'cap Hurdles	26-77	33.8	- 9.94	H'cap Chases	31-88	35.2	- 3.11
N H Flat	1-9	11.1	- 7.00	Hunter Chases	10-16	62.5	+ 5.13
Totals	80-208	38.5	- 13.12	Totals	78-173	45.1	+ 1.47
All favourites	158-381	41.5	- 11.65				

LEADING TRAINERS BY MONTH AT WINCANTON 1991-96

October	Total W-R	Nov Hdles	H'cap Hdles	Nov Chses	H'cap Chses	Per cent	£1 Level Stake
M C Pipe	6-15	3-9	1-2	2-2	0-2	40.0	- 2.36
O Sherwood	4-7	3-4	0-0	0-0	1-3	57.1	+ 3.92
Andrew Turnell	4-10	1-2	1-2	1-4	1-2	40.0	+ 15.00
P J Hobbs	4-18	0-4	0-6	0-0	4-8	22.2	+ 25.25

November	Total W-R	Nov Hdles	H'cap Hdles	Nov Chses	H'cap Chses	Per cent	£1 Level Stake
Mrs J Pitman	6-11	0-2	0-2	1-1	5-6	54.5	+ 24.75
O Sherwood	4-9	3-5	0-0	1-1	0-3	44.4	+ 2.20
M C Pipe	4-15	2-4	2-7	0-1	0-3	26.7	+ 3.00
N Twiston-Davies	4-15	2-5	0-2	1-2	1-6	26.7	+ 1.87

December	Total W-R	Nov Hdles	H'cap Hdles	Nov Chses	H'cap Chses	Per cent	£1 Level Stake
Mrs J G Retter	2-3	0-0	1-1	0-1	1-1	66.7	+ 7.00
Mrs J Pitman	2-8	0-0	2-4	0-2	0-2	25.0	+ 3.54
R J Hodges	2-13	1-2	1-4	0-0	0-7	15.4	+ 26.00
I A Balding	1-1	1-1	0-0	0-0	0-0	100.0	+ 1.25

January	Total W-R	Nov Hdles	H'cap Hdles	Nov Chses	H'cap Chses	Per cent	£1 Level Stake
N Twiston-Davies	4-8	1-2	1-2	0-1	2-3	50.0	+ 14.93
P F Nicholls	4-19	0-2	2-5	0-2	2-10	21.1	+ 8.25
Mrs J Pitman	4-23	1-8	0-2	2-8	1-5	17.4	- 2.94
M C Pipe	4-25	2-9	1-8	1-4	0-4	16.0	- 10.63

February	Total W-R	Nov Hdles	H'cap Hdles	Nov Chses	H'cap Chses	Per cent	£1 Level Stake
M C Pipe	9-35	6-25	0-3	3-7	0-0	25.7	+ 19.50
Mrs J Pitman	4-17	1-5	0-0	3-12	0-0	23.5	+ 18.50
S Sherwood	3-4	1-1	0-0	2-2	0-1	75.0	+ 14.25
P J Hobbs	3-12	1-8	2-3	0-0	0-1	25.0	- 0.50

March	Total W-R	Nov Hdles	H'cap Hdles	Nov Chses	H'cap Chses	Per cent	£1 Level Stake
M C Pipe	6-24	4-16	0-3	2-4	0-1	25.0	+ 5.92
J T Gifford	4-12	2-5	0-0	2-5	0-2	33.3	+ 4.30
R J Hodges	4-19	0-9	2-5	0-2	2-3	21.1	+ 13.08
P J Hobbs	4-24	1-11	3-8	0-3	0-2	16.7	- 2.50

April	Total W-R	Nov Hdles	H'cap Hdles	Nov Chses	H'cap Chses	Per cent	£1 Level Stake
M C Pipe	4-10	4-8	0-2	0-0	0-0	40.0	+ 5.10
R H Alner	3-9	3-7	0-0	0-1	0-1	33.3	+ 11.75
P F Nicholls	3-17	0-8	0-2	1-4	2-3	17.6	- 6.10
G B Balding	2-6	0-2	1-1	0-0	1-3	33.3	+ 7.00

May	Total W-R	Nov Hdles	H'cap Hdles	Nov Chses	H'cap Chses	Per cent	£1 Level Stake
M C Pipe	4-8	3-4	1-1	0-0	0-3	50.0	+ 3.50
P J Hobbs	3-8	1-2	2-4	0-0	0-2	37.5	+ 0.83
P F Nicholls	3-10	0-1	0-3	0-0	3-6	30.0	- 3.47
R J Hodges	2-11	0-2	1-5	0-0	1-4	18.2	- 5.38

WINDSOR (Group 3)

Leading Trainers 1991–96

	Total W–R	Nov Hdles	H'cap Hdles	Nov Chses	H'cap Chses	Per cent	£1 Level Stake
K C Bailey	11-59	3-17	1-7	2-15	5-20	18.6	+ 1.76
N J Henderson	10-45	6-21	1-5	0-6	3-13	22.2	- 11.19
P J Hobbs	9-48	3-16	0-7	1-3	5-22	18.8	- 5.13
Miss H C Knight	9-51	3-19	3-11	3-14	0-7	17.6	- 3.43
J White	7-64	3-27	0-9	1-11	3-17	10.9	+ 10.50
C P E Brooks	6-20	1-11	0-0	2-4	3-5	30.0	+ 2.00
D R C Elsworth	6-22	0-10	3-6	2-3	1-3	27.3	+ 3.80
Andrew Turnell	6-29	3-10	2-5	1-10	0-4	20.7	- 7.59
R Akehurst	6-34	4-19	1-8	1-4	0-3	17.6	- 11.81
P R Hedger	5-28	1-14	1-7	0-1	3-6	17.9	- 5.70
N A Gaselee	5-31	1-12	0-4	3-10	1-5	16.1	- 3.25
D R Gandolfo	4-21	4-10	0-3	0-2	0-6	19.0	- 2.88
G B Balding	4-25	0-8	1-3	1-5	2-9	16.0	+ 10.38
M C Pipe	4-27	3-14	0-7	0-3	1-3	14.8	- 13.05
D M Grissell	4-28	2-12	2-9	0-2	0-5	14.3	+ 13.50
J T Gifford	4-33	2-12	0-1	2-11	0-9	12.1	- 15.63
Mrs J Pitman	4-38	1-17	1-9	2-10	0-2	10.5	- 27.88
S Mellor	4-43	1-26	3-8	0-3	0-6	9.3	- 3.00
R J Hodges	4-58	1-14	1-14	0-11	2-19	6.9	- 34.88
J R Upson	3-9	0-3	0-0	2-3	1-3	33.3	+ 1.50

Leading Jockeys

	Total W–R	Per cent	£1 Level Stake	Best Trainer	W–R	Per cent	£1 Level Stake
J Osborne	10-72	13.9	- 2.55	Miss H C Knight	5-24	20.8	+ 2.20
R Dunwoody	9-52	17.3	- 27.00	N J Henderson	4-12	33.3	- 0.20
N Williamson	9-65	13.8	+ 10.96	K C Bailey	4-23	17.4	+ 1.33
M Richards	9-89	10.1	- 5.20	P R Hedger	5-23	21.7	- 0.70
D Gallagher	6-33	18.2	+ 10.66	C P E Brooks	2-4	50.0	+ 6.25
J R Kavanagh	6-38	15.8	- 14.45	N J Henderson	3-12	25.0	- 2.20
M A FitzGerald	6-42	14.3	- 11.79	N J Henderson	3-14	21.4	- 1.79
J Railton	6-58	10.3	- 12.37	C J Drewe	2-5	40.0	+ 14.00
A Maguire	5-21	23.8	+ 4.88	M Madgwick	1-1	100.0	+ 2.50
P Holley	5-31	16.1	- 12.70	D R C Elsworth	5-12	41.7	+ 6.30
S McNeill	5-45	11.1	- 16.75	Andrew Turnell	3-14	21.4	- 0.75
T J Murphy	4-9	44.4	+ 8.80	K C Bailey	3-5	60.0	+ 8.30

How the Favourites Fared

	W–R	Per cent	£1 Level Stake		W–R	Per cent	£1 Level Stake
Novice Hurdles	30-77	39.0	- 7.66	Novice Chases	16-38	42.1	- 4.02
H'cap Hurdles	15-50	30.0	- 10.00	H'cap Chases	13-53	24.5	- 20.37
N H Flat	2-2	100.0	+ 4.38	Hunter Chases	2-5	40.0	- 1.13
Totals	47-129	36.4	- 13.28	Totals	31-96	32.3	- 25.52
All favourites	78-225	34.7	- 38.80				

LEADING TRAINERS BY MONTH AT WINDSOR 1991-96

November

	Total W-R	Nov Hdles	H'cap Hdles	Nov Chses	H'cap Chses	Per cent	£1 Level Stake
Miss H C Knight	5-20	1-8	1-3	3-6	0-3	25.0	+ 7.13
P J Hobbs	4-15	2-4	0-4	1-1	1-6	26.7	+ 3.00
C P E Brooks	3-7	1-4	0-0	0-0	2-3	42.9	+ 2.00
Andrew Turnell	3-8	2-4	0-0	1-4	0-0	37.5	+ 0.41
N J Henderson	3-12	1-3	0-2	0-2	2-5	25.0	- 2.37

December

	Total W-R	Nov Hdles	H'cap Hdles	Nov Chses	H'cap Chses	Per cent	£1 Level Stake
R Akehurst	3-6	2-5	1-1	0-0	0-0	50.0	+ 4.23
K C Bailey	3-6	1-1	0-0	0-0	2-5	50.0	+ 13.83
N J Henderson	2-8	1-3	0-1	0-0	1-4	25.0	+ 1.50
R J Hodges	2-11	0-5	0-0	0-0	2-6	18.2	+ 5.62
Mrs Althea Barclay	1-1	0-0	0-0	0-0	1-1	100.0	+ 3.50

January

	Total W-R	Nov Hdles	H'cap Hdles	Nov Chses	H'cap Chses	Per cent	£1 Level Stake
D R C Elsworth	4-8	0-4	3-3	1-1	0-0	50.0	+ 8.30
K C Bailey	3-16	0-4	1-3	1-2	1-7	18.8	+ 4.50
D R Gandolfo	2-8	2-2	0-2	0-0	0-4	25.0	+ 4.62
N A Gaselee	2-8	1-3	0-2	0-0	1-3	25.0	+ 7.50
P R Hedger	2-8	0-3	0-2	0-0	2-3	25.0	0.00

February

	Total W-R	Nov Hdles	H'cap Hdles	Nov Chses	H'cap Chses	Per cent	£1 Level Stake
J R Upson	2-3	0-0	0-0	2-3	0-0	66.7	+ 4.25
O Sherwood	2-5	1-3	1-1	0-1	0-0	40.0	+ 17.00
N J Henderson	2-6	1-3	1-2	0-1	0-0	33.3	+ 3.00
M C Pipe	2-7	1-6	0-0	0-0	1-1	28.6	- 0.75
J White	2-8	1-3	0-1	1-2	0-2	25.0	+ 0.25

March

	Total W-R	Nov Hdles	H'cap Hdles	Nov Chses	H'cap Chses	Per cent	£1 Level Stake
K C Bailey	4-7	2-2	0-0	1-2	1-3	57.1	+ 8.93
R Barber	2-2	0-0	0-0	2-2	0-0	100.0	+ 1.87
Miss H C Knight	2-4	1-1	1-2	0-1	0-0	50.0	+ 0.45
P J Hobbs	2-5	0-2	0-0	0-0	2-3	40.0	+ 4.63
S Mellor	2-7	0-4	2-2	0-0	0-1	28.6	+ 21.00

WORCESTER (Group 3)

Leading Trainers 1991-96

	Total W-R	Nov Hdles	H'cap Hdles	Nov Chses	H'cap Chses	Per cent	£1 Level Stake
M C Pipe	36-140	18-57	7-36	5-20	6-27	25.7	- 5.04
P J Hobbs	30-127	9-41	9-33	4-17	8-36	23.6	+ 18.31
D Nicholson	22-92	10-49	5-10	4-13	3-20	23.9	+ 34.99
K C Bailey	20-100	2-40	1-11	8-19	9-30	20.0	+ 10.84
G B Balding	19-103	6-32	5-29	1-11	7-31	18.4	+ 30.71
O Sherwood	18-61	3-20	1-9	4-14	10-18	29.5	+ 24.84
N Twiston-Davies	16-118	8-57	2-21	2-19	4-21	13.6	- 58.26
Miss H C Knight	12-48	5-19	1-8	3-7	3-14	25.0	+ 16.13
P F Nicholls	12-48	1-14	1-6	5-11	5-17	25.0	+ 23.00
C P E Brooks	8-31	3-12	3-7	1-2	1-10	25.8	+ 4.82
Capt T A Forster	8-91	1-32	0-7	1-18	6-34	8.8	- 61.58
K R Burke	7-42	2-18	4-18	1-5	0-1	16.7	+ 12.88
Mrs J Pitman	7-57	2-18	0-8	2-14	3-17	12.3	- 13.00
R Rowe	7-57	3-18	2-14	2-12	0-13	12.3	- 9.13
R Dickin	7-90	0-24	0-17	2-12	5-37	7.8	- 65.88
C R Barwell	6-30	2-12	3-14	1-2	0-2	20.0	+ 55.08
S Sherwood	6-34	0-12	1-7	3-4	2-11	17.6	+ 3.75
R J Hodges	6-35	0-9	0-5	0-3	6-18	17.1	+ 13.00
F Murphy	6-37	2-13	0-6	1-6	3-12	16.2	- 13.13
N J Henderson	6-43	4-20	0-3	2-9	0-11	14.0	- 24.90

Leading Jockeys

	Total W-R	Per cent	£1 Level Stake		Best Trainer	W-R	Per cent	£1 Level Stake
R Dunwoody	38-229	16.6	- 54.43		D Nicholson	8-20	40.0	+ 30.80
J Osborne	29-117	24.8	+ 74.75		O Sherwood	14-38	36.8	+ 21.70
A Maguire	27-162	16.7	- 46.00		F Murphy	5-11	45.5	+ 9.38
N Williamson	21-116	18.1	+ 13.98		K C Bailey	14-44	31.8	+ 40.85
A P McCoy	18-76	23.7	+ 19.96		G B Balding	12-30	40.0	+ 38.71
C Llewellyn	18-146	12.3	- 0.44		N Twiston-Davies	8-52	15.4	- 18.57
W Marston	15-133	11.3	- 10.33		D Nicholson	5-19	26.3	+ 18.98
B Powell	13-129	10.1	- 40.24		B Smart	3-3	100.0	+ 12.38
D Bridgwater	12-130	9.2	- 68.78		N Twiston-Davies	4-27	14.8	- 13.42
G Bradley	11-50	22.0	+ 19.57		C P E Brooks	6-20	30.0	+ 9.44
M A FitzGerald	9-119	7.6	- 78.39		J G M O'Shea	2-8	25.0	+ 1.23
J Frost	8-78	10.3	+ 11.63		R G Frost	4-52	7.7	- 1.37

How the Favourites Fared

	W-R	Per cent	£1 Level Stake		W-R	Per cent	£1 Level Stake
Novice Hurdles	55-146	37.7	- 16.04	Novice Chases	36-83	43.4	- 3.97
H'cap Hurdles	49-145	33.8	- 6.54	H'cap Chases	46-149	30.9	- 35.23
N H Flat	7-27	25.9	- 6.27	Hunter Chases	4-7	57.1	+ 8.00
Totals	111-318	34.9	- 28.85	Totals	86-239	36.0	- 31.20
All favourites	197-557	35.4	- 60.05				

LEADING TRAINERS BY MONTH AT WORCESTER 1991-96

June	Total W-R	Nov Hdles	H'cap Hdles	Nov Chses	H'cap Chses	Per cent	£1 Level Stake
G B Balding	3-5	2-2	0-2	0-0	1-1	60.0	+ 27.00
R Rowe	2-4	1-2	0-1	1-1	0-0	50.0	+ 24.00

July	Total W-R	Nov Hdles	H'cap Hdles	Nov Chses	H'cap Chses	Per cent	£1 Level Stake
G B Balding	5-7	3-4	1-1	0-0	1-2	71.4	+ 20.88
K R Burke	1-1	0-0	1-1	0-0	0-0	100.0	+ 10.00

August	Total W-R	Nov Hdles	H'cap Hdles	Nov Chses	H'cap Chses	Per cent	£1 Level Stake
M C Pipe	7-20	4-9	1-4	1-4	1-3	35.0	− 2.49
P J Hobbs	7-21	0-5	5-7	0-2	2-7	33.3	+ 16.00

September	Total W-R	Nov Hdles	H'cap Hdles	Nov Chses	H'cap Chses	Per cent	£1 Level Stake
P J Hobbs	7-30	2-9	2-7	1-5	2-9	23.3	− 1.10
K C Bailey	6-18	1-7	0-2	2-3	3-6	33.3	+ 22.63

October	Total W-R	Nov Hdles	H'cap Hdles	Nov Chses	H'cap Chses	Per cent	£1 Level Stake
K C Bailey	4-17	1-5	0-1	2-6	1-5	23.5	+ 3.13
G B Balding	4-19	0-4	2-4	0-5	2-6	21.1	0.00

November	Total W-R	Nov Hdles	H'cap Hdles	Nov Chses	H'cap Chses	Per cent	£1 Level Stake
D Nicholson	4-17	1-9	1-1	2-3	0-4	23.5	+ 6.24
M C Pipe	3-11	1-4	1-4	0-1	1-2	27.3	+ 0.06

December	Total W-R	Nov Hdles	H'cap Hdles	Nov Chses	H'cap Chses	Per cent	£1 Level Stake
P J Hobbs	2-2	0-0	0-0	0-0	2-2	100.0	+ 13.25
D Nicholson	2-4	1-1	0-0	0-0	1-3	50.0	+ 5.73

January	Total W-R	Nov Hdles	H'cap Hdles	Nov Chses	H'cap Chses	Per cent	£1 Level Stake
M C Pipe	2-2	0-0	0-0	2-2	0-0	100.0	+ 2.35
P F Nicholls	1-1	0-0	1-1	0-0	0-0	100.0	+ 4.00

February	Total W-R	Nov Hdles	H'cap Hdles	Nov Chses	H'cap Chses	Per cent	£1 Level Stake
J Parkes	2-2	0-0	1-1	0-0	1-1	100.0	+ 46.00
R Dickin	2-3	0-0	0-1	1-1	1-1	66.7	+ 3.13

March	Total W-R	Nov Hdles	H'cap Hdles	Nov Chses	H'cap Chses	Per cent	£1 Level Stake
M C Pipe	9-28	7-14	0-6	0-1	2-7	32.1	+ 11 14
O Sherwood	5-14	0-5	0-2	2-3	3-4	35.7	+ 3.13

April	Total W-R	Nov Hdles	H'cap Hdles	Nov Chses	H'cap Chses	Per cent	£1 Level Stake
F Murphy	4-11	2-4	0-2	0-0	2-5	36.4	+ 5.63
M C Pipe	4-13	2-7	1-2	0-1	1-3	30.8	+ 8.41

May	Total W-R	Nov Hdles	H'cap Hdles	Nov Chses	H'cap Chses	Per cent	£1 Level Stake
Miss H C Knight	7-11	5-7	0-1	2-2	0-1	63.6	+ 39.75
M C Pipe	6-26	2-12	3-8	1-3	0-3	23.1	− 3.76

447

TRAINERS' FAVOURITES AT AINTREE 1991-96

	Total W-R	Nov Hdles	H'cap Hdles	Nov Chses	H'cap Chses	Per cent	£1 Level Stake
M C Pipe	4-9	2-4	0-1	1-2	1-2	44.4	+ 1.00
K C Bailey	3-6	0-1	0-0	2-2	1-3	50.0	+ 1.47
G Richards	3-8	1-3	1-1	1-3	0-1	37.5	- 0.38
N Twiston-Davies	3-8	0-2	0-0	1-3	2-3	37.5	+ 3.38
J T Gifford	2-2	0-0	0-0	2-2	0-0	100.0	+ 3.25
G B Balding	2-3	1-1	0-0	0-0	1-2	66.7	+ 1.80
D Nicholson	2-13	0-3	2-3	0-4	0-3	15.4	- 9.00
J I A Charlton	1-1	0-0	0-0	0-0	1-1	100.0	+ 3.50
P J Bevan	1-1	1-1	0-0	0-0	0-0	100.0	+ 5.00
Andrew Turnell	1-1	0-0	0-0	0-0	1-1	100.0	+ 1.20
S Christian	1-1	0-0	0-0	1-1	0-0	100.0	+ 1.20
J A C Edwards	1-1	0-0	0-0	1-1	0-0	100.0	+ 1.75
D W P Arbuthnot	1-1	1-1	0-0	0-0	0-0	100.0	+ 1.10
I A Balding	1-1	0-0	1-1	0-0	0-0	100.0	+ 1.63

TRAINERS' FAVOURITES AT ASCOT 1991-96

	Total W-R	Nov Hdles	H'cap Hdles	Nov Chses	H'cap Chses	Per cent	£1 Level Stake
D Nicholson	11-25	4-9	2-3	3-8	2-5	44.0	+ 5.07
O Sherwood	10-22	5-10	1-5	4-6	0-1	45.5	+ 1.54
N J Henderson	6-18	3-6	1-5	1-3	1-4	33.3	- 1.38
M C Pipe	5-17	3-8	2-4	0-1	0-4	29.4	- 4.78
K C Bailey	5-17	0-2	1-1	1-4	3-10	29.4	- 3.93
J T Gifford	5-17	2-5	0-1	1-5	2-6	29.4	- 4.77
Mrs J Pitman	4-6	1-2	0-0	0-0	3-4	66.7	+ 6.91
D R C Elsworth	4-10	2-4	1-1	1-3	0-2	40.0	- 2.41
N Tinkler	3-4	2-2	1-1	0-0	0-1	75.0	+ 1.63
I A Balding	3-4	2-2	0-0	0-1	1-1	75.0	+ 2.70
R Akehurst	3-8	2-4	1-4	0-0	0-0	37.5	- 0.47
G B Balding	3-10	1-3	0-1	0-0	2-6	30.0	- 3.98
N Twiston-Davies	3-16	0-5	1-4	1-2	1-5	18.8	- 5.79
J R Jenkins	2-2	2-2	0-0	0-0	0-0	100.0	+ 3.25

TRAINERS' FAVOURITES AT AYR 1991-96

	Total W-R	Nov Hdles	H'cap Hdles	Nov Chses	H'cap Chses	Per cent	£1 Level Stake
Mrs M Reveley	35-67	12-26	13-21	7-9	3-11	52.2	+ 5.05
G Richards	28-52	4-5	6-9	7-14	11-24	53.8	+ 9.42
J J O'Neill	9-15	4-7	3-4	1-3	1-1	60.0	+ 8.67
M D Hammond	6-18	2-5	1-7	2-2	1-4	33.3	- 2.99
P Monteith	6-22	3-6	0-5	2-3	1-8	27.3	- 8.46
C W Thornton	5-9	5-7	0-1	0-0	0-1	55.6	+ 0.18
G M Moore	5-10	4-6	0-1	1-1	0-2	50.0	- 3.07
L Lungo	5-15	3-6	1-5	0-0	1-4	33.3	- 2.80
J T Gifford	4-8	1-2	0-1	1-2	2-3	50.0	+ 2.32
C Parker	4-9	0-0	0-2	2-3	2-4	44.4	- 1.03
A C Whillans	3-3	0-0	1-1	0-0	2-2	100.0	+ 9.25
P Cheesbrough	3-4	1-1	0-0	1-1	1-2	75.0	+ 2.50
F S Storey	2-2	1-1	1-1	0-0	0-0	100.0	+ 6.25
W Hamilton	2-2	0-0	0-0	2-2	0-0	100.0	+ 3.13

TRAINERS' FAVOURITES AT BANGOR 1991-96

	Total W-R	Nov Hdles	H'cap Hdles	Nov Chses	H'cap Chses	Per cent	£1 Level Stake
G Richards	21-37	4-8	1-2	8-10	8-17	56.8	+ 1.83
M C Pipe	14-34	8-19	2-5	3-5	1-5	41.2	- 1.66
R Dickin	6-7	0-0	3-4	2-2	1-1	85.7	+ 9.71
J White	6-11	4-7	1-1	0-2	1-1	54.5	+ 0.72
D Nicholson	6-13	3-7	1-1	0-1	2-4	46.2	- 0.41
N Twiston-Davies	6-15	3-7	2-5	1-2	0-1	40.0	+ 0.75
M D Hammond	4-6	1-1	1-3	1-1	1-1	66.7	+ 7.38
Miss C Saunders	4-7	0-0	0-0	4-7	0-0	57.1	- 0.21
J J O'Neill	4-12	0-5	0-2	3-4	1-1	33.3	- 3.91
Capt T A Forster	3-6	0-0	0-0	2-3	1-3	50.0	+ 3.03
O Sherwood	3-6	2-2	1-1	0-0	0-3	50.0	+ 2.47
R J Hodges	2-2	0-0	0-0	1-1	1-1	100.0	+ 2.88
R Hollinshead	2-3	1-2	1-1	0-0	0-0	66.7	+ 1.37
Mrs A R Hewitt	2-3	0-1	0-0	0-0	2-2	66.7	+ 2.41

TRAINERS' FAVOURITES AT CARLISLE 1991-96

	Total W-R	Nov Hdles	H'cap Hdles	Nov Chses	H'cap Chses	Per cent	£1 Level Stake
G Richards	19-46	6-13	1-7	7-16	5-10	41.3	- 2.61
Mrs M Reveley	17-38	7-16	6-15	0-0	4-7	44.7	+ 2.06
C Parker	7-17	2-5	1-2	1-3	3-7	41.2	+ 0.10
L Lungo	6-13	4-7	1-3	0-2	1-1	46.2	+ 1.74
J I A Charlton	5-7	2-2	0-0	0-0	3-5	71.4	+ 8.53
J G FitzGerald	5-8	2-4	1-1	2-3	0-0	62.5	+ 10.13
G M Moore	5-14	2-5	1-4	2-3	0-2	35.7	- 1.77
M D Hammond	5-15	3-5	0-2	0-2	2-6	33.3	- 1.38
J J O'Neill	5-16	2-5	1-4	2-5	0-2	31.3	- 6.69
W Storey	4-5	1-1	3-3	0-1	0-0	80.0	+ 5.79
J H Johnson	4-8	3-3	0-0	1-2	0-3	50.0	- 1.02
Mrs A Swinbank	3-3	3-3	0-0	0-0	0-0	100.0	+ 5.00
J M Jefferson	3-11	2-5	0-2	0-1	1-3	27.3	- 4.10
J A C Edwards	2-5	1-3	0-0	1-1	0-1	40.0	- 0.20

TRAINERS' FAVOURITES AT CARTMEL 1991-96

	Total W-R	Nov Hdles	H'cap Hdles	Nov Chses	H'cap Chses	Per cent	£1 Level Stake
G Richards	9-20	1-5	0-2	3-5	5-8	45.0	- 3.84
J White	8-20	2-5	2-3	4-9	0-3	40.0	- 1.92
Mrs M Reveley	6-11	3-5	1-4	1-1	1-1	54.5	- 0.60
D Moffatt	5-6	1-1	4-5	0-0	0-0	83.3	+ 6.30
G M Moore	4-9	2-6	1-2	0-0	1-1	44.4	+ 0.04
J J O'Neill	2-3	0-0	1-2	1-1	0-0	66.7	+ 0.13
M C Pipe	2-4	1-1	0-2	1-1	0-0	50.0	- 0.29
J A C Edwards	2-4	1-2	0-0	1-1	0-1	50.0	- 0.36
M A Barnes	2-4	0-0	1-1	1-2	0-1	50.0	- 0.10
N Tinkler	2-5	1-2	1-2	0-0	0-1	40.0	+ 1.00
L Lungo	2-5	1-1	1-3	0-1	0-0	40.0	+ 1.75
M D Hammond	2-6	1-2	0-1	0-1	1-2	33.3	- 0.75
K A Morgan	1-1	1-1	0-0	0-0	0-0	100.0	+ 1.75
G B Balding	1-1	0-0	1-1	0-0	0-0	100.0	+ 2.00

TRAINERS' FAVOURITES AT CATTERICK 1991-96

	Total W–R	Nov Hdles	H'cap Hdles	Nov Chses	H'cap Chses	Per cent	£1 Level Stake
Mrs M Reveley	13–34	3–11	4–8	2–3	4–12	38.2	– 1.70
L Lungo	6–7	0–0	4–5	1–1	1–1	85.7	+ 8.50
N Tinkler	6–13	2–4	1–1	2–5	1–3	46.2	+ 0.78
J G FitzGerald	6–13	4–8	0–2	2–2	0–1	46.2	+ 2.40
Mrs V A Aconley	4–4	2–2	0–0	1–1	1–1	100.0	+ 8.57
J I A Charlton	4–9	0–1	0–0	3–5	1–3	44.4	+ 2.45
G M Moore	4–14	2–11	2–3	0–0	0–0	28.6	+ 1.23
M D Hammond	4–22	2–10	0–5	0–1	2–6	18.2	– 12.19
J J Quinn	3–3	1–1	0–0	1–1	1–1	100.0	+ 3.33
G Richards	3–11	0–3	0–1	1–5	2–2	27.3	– 6.47
Mrs J Goodfellow	2–2	0–0	1–1	1–1	0–0	100.0	+ 5.58
Mrs P Sly	2–2	0–0	2–2	0–0	0–0	100.0	+ 4.50
W Bentley	2–3	1–1	0–0	1–2	0–0	66.7	+ 7.00
Mrs P A Barker	2–3	1–1	1–2	0–0	0–0	66.7	+ 0.39

TRAINERS' FAVOURITES AT CHELTENHAM 1991-96

	Total W–R	Nov Hdles	H'cap Hdles	Nov Chses	H'cap Chses	Per cent	£1 Level Stake
D Nicholson	19–43	7–17	1–5	6–10	5–11	44.2	+ 3.85
N Twiston-Davies	18–41	5–9	6–14	4–7	3–11	43.9	+ 20.89
M C Pipe	18–54	8–18	5–15	2–11	3–10	33.3	+ 0.95
K C Bailey	14–25	4–6	0–2	7–7	3–10	56.0	+ 11.82
J T Gifford	7–14	1–2	0–1	2–5	4–6	50.0	+ 5.52
O Sherwood	7–16	4–8	2–3	0–1	1–4	43.8	+ 5.97
Mrs J Pitman	6–16	0–2	1–2	1–2	4–10	37.5	+ 0.50
G B Balding	5–9	1–3	0–0	1–2	3–4	55.6	+ 4.65
G Richards	5–10	0–0	1–1	1–4	3–5	50.0	+ 4.53
N J Henderson	5–19	0–6	2–4	2–6	1–3	26.3	– 4.92
R C Wilkins	4–4	0–0	0–0	4–4	0–0	100.0	+ 2.37
N Tinkler	3–4	2–2	1–1	0–1	0–0	75.0	+ 4.17
I A Balding	3–5	1–1	0–1	1–2	1–1	60.0	+ 2.46
P Monteith	2–2	0–0	0–0	0–0	2–2	100.0	+ 2.57

TRAINERS' FAVOURITES AT CHEPSTOW 1991-96

	Total W–R	Nov Hdles	H'cap Hdles	Nov Chses	H'cap Chses	Per cent	£1 Level Stake
M C Pipe	43–90	20–36	10–26	7–10	6–18	47.8	– 0.42
N Twiston-Davies	10–22	4–9	2–4	3–5	1–4	45.5	+ 5.17
D Nicholson	8–14	5–8	1–3	2–2	0–1	57.1	+ 5.83
P J Hobbs	7–14	2–3	1–3	1–1	3–7	50.0	+ 4.14
J A B Old	5–11	1–2	0–4	1–1	3–4	45.5	+ 3.49
N J Henderson	4–11	2–4	0–1	1–2	1–4	36.4	– 1.83
D Burchell	3–4	3–4	0–0	0–0	0–0	75.0	+ 3.63
Mrs J G Retter	3–4	0–0	1–1	0–1	2–2	75.0	+ 1.89
G B Balding	3–11	0–1	0–2	2–4	1–4	27.3	– 2.25
Andrew Turnell	2–5	0–0	1–2	0–1	1–2	40.0	0.00
J A C Edwards	2–5	0–0	1–2	1–2	0–1	40.0	– 0.75
J White	2–5	0–1	1–2	1–1	0–1	40.0	+ 0.75
R H Alner	2–5	0–0	2–3	0–2	0–0	40.0	+ 1.50
C P E Brooks	2–6	1–1	1–2	0–1	0–2	33.3	– 1.50

TRAINERS' FAVOURITES AT DONCASTER 1991-96

	Total W-R	Nov Hdles	H'cap Hdles	Nov Chses	H'cap Chses	Per cent	£1 Level Stake
Mrs M Reveley	10-23	5-13	2-5	2-3	1-2	43.5	− 1.77
D Nicholson	7-11	2-3	0-0	2-2	3-6	63.6	+ 6.43
J G FitzGerald	5-14	3-7	0-2	1-2	1-3	35.7	− 4.28
O Sherwood	4-9	2-3	0-0	2-3	0-3	44.4	+ 0.19
M C Pipe	3-3	2-2	1-1	0-0	0-0	100.0	+ 4.60
N Tinkler	3-5	0-2	1-1	0-0	2-2	60.0	+ 2.73
M D Hammond	3-7	0-2	1-1	1-1	1-3	42.9	+ 1.13
G Richards	3-9	1-1	0-1	2-4	0-3	33.3	− 2.53
N J Henderson	2-2	0-0	2-2	0-0	0-0	100.0	+ 6.33
Miss L A Perratt	2-2	1-1	1-1	0-0	0-0	100.0	+ 3.33
Mrs J R Ramsden	2-3	0-0	2-3	0-0	0-0	66.7	+ 3.63
J White	2-3	2-3	0-0	0-0	0-0	66.7	+ 1.38
K C Bailey	2-8	0-1	0-1	1-1	1-5	25.0	− 2.50
J A B Old	1-1	0-0	1-1	0-0	0-0	100.0	+ 1.75

TRAINERS' FAVOURITES AT EXETER 1991-96

	Total W-R	Nov Hdles	H'cap Hdles	Nov Chses	H'cap Chses	Per cent	£1 Level Stake
M C Pipe	59-126	35-64	11-35	7-15	6-12	46.8	− 11.68
Miss H C Knight	15-28	6-9	5-11	2-4	2-4	53.6	+ 13.48
P J Hobbs	11-25	1-5	2-7	2-5	6-8	44.0	+ 2.88
I A Balding	8-13	7-10	1-1	0-1	0-1	61.5	+ 4.16
G B Balding	6-15	1-3	2-5	2-3	1-4	40.0	+ 0.81
D R C Elsworth	5-6	1-1	2-3	2-2	0-0	83.3	+ 6.57
N J Henderson	4-7	1-2	0-1	3-3	0-1	57.1	− 0.07
A J K Dunn	4-7	1-2	1-1	1-1	1-3	57.1	+ 1.52
R G Frost	4-8	0-1	1-2	2-4	1-1	50.0	+ 6.16
O Sherwood	3-5	3-4	0-1	0-0	0-0	60.0	+ 0.55
Mrs A Knight	3-6	0-1	3-5	0-0	0-0	50.0	+ 0.55
R H Alner	3-6	0-1	0-0	2-3	1-2	50.0	+ 0.35
R J Hodges	3-7	0-0	1-2	1-1	1-4	42.9	+ 0.80
Mrs J G Retter	3-10	0-0	1-5	0-2	2-3	30.0	− 2.38

TRAINERS' FAVOURITES AT FAKENHAM 1991-96

	Total W-R	Nov Hdles	H'cap Hdles	Nov Chses	H'cap Chses	Per cent	£1 Level Stake
O Brennan	5-7	0-0	4-6	1-1	0-0	71.4	+ 5.40
K C Bailey	5-10	1-3	0-0	2-2	2-5	50.0	+ 0.11
Miss C Saunders	4-4	0-0	0-0	4-4	0-0	100.0	+ 4.76
Mrs D Haine	3-4	0-0	0-0	2-2	1-2	75.0	+ 1.91
D R Gandolfo	2-2	0-0	0-0	2-2	0-0	100.0	+ 1.60
D Nicholson	2-2	1-1	0-0	1-1	0-0	100.0	+ 2.95
J T Gifford	2-2	0-0	0-0	1-1	1-1	100.0	+ 2.49
O Sherwood	2-3	0-0	0-0	2-3	0-0	66.7	+ 1.24
J M Turner	2-3	0-0	0-0	2-3	0-0	66.7	+ 1.43
G C Bravery	2-3	0-0	2-3	0-0	0-0	66.7	+ 2.00
W J Warner	2-3	0-0	0-0	2-3	0-0	66.7	+ 0.39
M C Pipe	2-4	0-1	1-1	1-2	0-0	50.0	− 0.72
M H Tompkins	2-4	0-0	2-4	0-0	0-0	50.0	+ 3.70
T J Naughton	2-4	0-0	2-4	0-0	0-0	50.0	+ 4.00

TRAINERS' FAVOURITES AT FOLKESTONE 1991-96

	Total W-R	Nov Hdles	H'cap Hdles	Nov Chses	H'cap Chses	Per cent	£1 Level Stake
J T Gifford	9-18	2-8	0-0	4-5	3-5	50.0	+ 0.36
M C Pipe	7-14	3-7	3-6	1-1	0-0	50.0	+ 2.39
Mrs D Haine	5-6	2-2	0-1	0-0	3-3	83.3	+ 5.81
N J Henderson	5-9	1-1	1-3	3-5	0-0	55.6	+ 1.00
Miss H C Knight	3-4	0-1	0-0	1-1	2-2	75.0	+ 2.53
S Dow	3-5	2-3	1-1	0-0	0-1	60.0	+ 3.21
D M Grissell	3-9	0-0	1-3	1-1	1-5	33.3	+ 0.08
F Murphy	2-2	0-0	0-0	0-0	2-2	100.0	+ 2.75
T Thomson Jones	2-3	0-0	0-0	0-0	2-3	66.7	+ 1.98
H Wellstead	2-3	0-0	0-0	2-3	0-0	66.7	+ 3.00
Capt T A Forster	2-4	0-0	0-0	0-1	2-3	50.0	+ 2.13
O Sherwood	2-5	0-1	0-2	2-2	0-0	40.0	- 0.25
R Akehurst	2-6	1-3	0-2	1-1	0-0	33.3	- 1.50
R Rowe	2-11	0-0	1-6	1-4	0-1	18.2	- 6.93

TRAINERS' FAVOURITES AT FONTWELL 1991-96

	Total W-R	Nov Hdles	H'cap Hdles	Nov Chses	H'cap Chses	Per cent	£1 Level Stake
M C Pipe	22-41	10-21	4-8	7-10	1-2	53.7	+ 9.36
R Curtis	11-14	0-0	0-0	1-2	10-12	78.6	+ 11.19
P J Hobbs	11-24	2-4	2-5	2-5	5-10	45.8	+ 2.38
G Harwood	10-18	2-4	7-11	1-3	0-0	55.6	+ 4.36
J T Gifford	10-22	3-11	4-4	1-3	2-4	45.5	+ 0.76
R H Alner	9-12	0-0	0-0	5-5	4-7	75.0	+ 5.96
G B Balding	9-22	3-5	0-4	4-7	2-6	40.9	- 5.83
J White	8-14	3-6	3-3	1-3	1-2	57.1	+ 5.86
R J O'Sullivan	7-15	5-6	0-5	1-1	1-3	46.7	+ 0.54
K C Bailey	5-10	2-4	0-2	0-0	3-4	50.0	+ 4.38
R Rowe	5-16	0-2	2-8	0-0	3-6	31.3	- 0.09
Mrs J Pitman	4-8	0-0	1-1	1-3	2-4	50.0	+ 4.63
D M Grissell	4-10	0-2	0-0	3-3	1-5	40.0	- 1.29
J Ffitch-Heyes	3-4	1-1	0-0	1-1	1-2	75.0	+ 2.11

TRAINERS' FAVOURITES AT HAYDOCK 1991-96

	Total W-R	Nov Hdles	H'cap Hdles	Nov Chses	H'cap Chses	Per cent	£1 Level Stake
M C Pipe	20-47	13-28	2-10	3-5	2-4	42.6	- 9.54
G Richards	17-30	1-2	1-4	10-12	5-12	56.7	+ 4.09
D Nicholson	7-20	5-11	0-1	2-5	0-3	35.0	- 6.47
N Twiston-Davies	6-13	1-5	0-1	3-3	2-4	46.2	- 0.11
J G FitzGerald	6-16	3-4	1-4	0-3	2-5	37.5	- 1.34
Mrs M Reveley	5-12	1-3	4-8	0-0	0-1	41.7	+ 2.93
T P Tate	4-5	3-4	0-0	1-1	0-0	80.0	+ 1.80
Capt T A Forster	3-4	1-1	0-0	0-1	2-2	75.0	+ 1.93
C P E Brooks	3-6	0-0	0-0	2-3	1-3	50.0	+ 1.58
Miss H C Knight	3-7	0-0	1-4	0-1	2-2	42.9	- 1.62
R Akehurst	2-2	0-0	2-2	0-0	0-0	100.0	+ 6.75
J J O'Neill	2-2	0-0	0-0	1-1	1-1	100.0	+ 1.60
C R Egerton	2-2	2-2	0-0	0-0	0-0	100.0	+ 1.58
D McCain	2-3	0-0	0-0	0-0	2-3	66.7	+ 1.35

TRAINERS' FAVOURITES AT HEREFORD 1991-96

	Total W-R	Nov Hdles	H'cap Hdles	Nov Chses	H'cap Chses	Per cent	£1 Level Stake
M C Pipe	19-45	9-24	4-11	2-5	4-5	42.2	- 2.43
N Twiston-Davies	12-27	6-11	2-8	1-2	3-6	44.4	+ 3.31
K C Bailey	10-24	5-10	0-1	4-8	1-5	41.7	- 2.18
N J Henderson	8-10	2-3	1-1	2-2	3-4	80.0	+ 9.49
D Nicholson	8-12	7-9	0-0	1-1	0-2	66.7	+ 6.04
R H Alner	5-10	0-0	0-1	1-4	4-5	50.0	+ 1.41
P J Hobbs	5-12	3-6	1-3	1-1	0-2	41.7	+ 0.96
P F Nicholls	4-14	1-2	0-0	2-7	1-5	28.6	- 4.07
M R Channon	3-3	0-0	3-3	0-0	0-0	100.0	+ 6.75
N Tinkler	3-4	2-2	0-0	0-0	1-2	75.0	+ 2.78
R H Buckler	3-4	0-0	3-3	0-0	0-1	75.0	+ 6.38
C P E Brooks	3-4	0-0	1-1	1-2	1-1	75.0	+ 3.28
R Lee	3-8	0-0	0-1	1-1	2-6	37.5	+ 1.20
O Sherwood	3-11	1-4	1-3	1-3	0-1	27.3	- 2.50

TRAINERS' FAVOURITES AT HEXHAM 1991-96

	Total W-R	Nov Hdles	H'cap Hdles	Nov Chses	H'cap Chses	Per cent	£1 Level Stake
M D Hammond	10-24	5-11	2-6	3-4	0-3	41.7	+ 0.63
G Richards	10-27	6-8	0-2	2-10	2-7	37.0	- 4.05
Mrs M Reveley	9-23	3-6	1-5	2-6	3-6	39.1	- 1.07
P Monteith	8-15	3-3	1-3	1-2	3-7	53.3	+ 5.82
L Lungo	8-18	2-5	2-4	2-3	2-6	44.4	+ 5.61
G M Moore	6-11	5-8	0-1	1-1	0-1	54.5	+ 3.58
W Bentley	5-9	2-2	2-5	1-2	0-0	55.6	+ 3.15
J H Johnson	5-14	3-6	0-1	1-3	1-4	35.7	- 0.75
W G Reed	4-6	1-3	0-0	1-1	2-2	66.7	+ 7.45
Denys Smith	4-7	0-0	3-5	0-0	1-2	57.1	+ 5.60
J A C Edwards	4-7	3-6	0-0	1-1	0-0	57.1	+ 2.08
M W Easterby	4-11	2-4	0-2	1-2	1-3	36.4	- 0.05
J G M O'Shea	3-6	1-2	1-3	1-1	0-0	50.0	+ 0.10
J J O'Neill	3-8	0-0	2-5	1-3	0-0	37.5	- 0.23

TRAINERS' FAVOURITES AT HUNTINGDON 1991-96

	Total W-R	Nov Hdles	H'cap Hdles	Nov Chses	H'cap Chses	Per cent	£1 Level Stake
D Nicholson	10-16	3-4	0-1	3-4	4-7	62.5	+ 10.72
K C Bailey	9-17	1-4	1-2	3-6	4-5	52.9	+ 8.71
F Murphy	7-11	1-2	1-1	1-2	4-6	63.6	+ 7.04
Mrs M Reveley	6-11	2-5	2-2	0-0	2-4	54.5	+ 6.00
Capt T A Forster	6-13	2-6	0-0	3-5	1-2	46.2	+ 1.04
J T Gifford	6-13	1-2	2-2	1-3	2-6	46.2	+ 8.88
Mrs J Pitman	5-12	1-3	0-1	1-2	3-6	41.7	+ 0.49
D R Gandolfo	4-5	2-2	0-1	2-2	0-0	80.0	+ 4.44
J Fanshawe	4-6	3-4	1-2	0-0	0-0	66.7	+ 6.00
M C Pipe	4-10	1-4	1-3	1-2	1-1	40.0	- 2.64
N J Henderson	4-13	0-3	1-5	3-3	0-2	30.8	- 6.10
F Jordan	3-3	0-0	2-2	1-1	0-0	100.0	+ 3.82
G A P-Gordon	3-3	1-1	2-2	0-0	0-0	100.0	+ 5.08
Mrs S A Bramall	3-5	1-1	0-0	1-1	1-3	60.0	- 0.04

TRAINERS' FAVOURITES AT KELSO 1991-96

	Total W-R	Nov Hdles	H'cap Hdles	Nov Chses	H'cap Chses	Per cent	£1 Level Stake
Mrs M Reveley	28-64	16-31	6-19	1-2	5-12	43.8	- 2.95
G Richards	13-26	3-7	2-3	4-8	4-8	50.0	- 1.62
M D Hammond	8-19	5-9	0-2	2-4	1-4	42.1	+ 0.69
P Monteith	8-21	3-3	3-8	1-3	1-7	38.1	- 2.96
Mrs J Goodfellow	7-13	2-4	0-1	1-4	4-4	53.8	+ 3.37
L Lungo	5-11	3-6	1-4	1-1	0-0	45.5	+ 1.87
G M Moore	5-13	1-3	1-5	3-5	0-0	38.5	- 1.25
T N Dalgetty	4-7	0-0	0-0	4-7	0-0	57.1	+ 0.34
Mrs S J Smith	3-4	2-2	1-2	0-0	0-0	75.0	+ 3.25
N Tinkler	3-6	1-2	2-3	0-0	0-1	50.0	+ 0.19
P Beaumont	3-6	0-1	0-1	2-3	1-1	50.0	- 0.98
Mrs S C Bradburne	3-6	0-0	0-2	2-2	1-2	50.0	- 0.50
R Allan	3-9	0-2	0-1	2-3	1-3	33.3	- 4.39
W Storey	2-3	0-0	1-2	1-1	0-0	66.7	+ 1.94

TRAINERS' FAVOURITES AT KEMPTON 1991-96

	Total W-R	Nov Hdles	H'cap Hdles	Nov Chses	H'cap Chses	Per cent	£1 Level Stake
D Nicholson	10-27	6-11	0-1	3-10	1-5	37.0	- 8.16
M C Pipe	9-25	6-14	1-4	2-5	0-2	36.0	- 6.45
N J Henderson	7-19	2-4	0-1	4-9	1-5	36.8	+ 0.35
N Twiston-Davies	5-8	4-6	1-2	0-0	0-0	62.5	+ 5.96
O Sherwood	5-12	1-3	1-2	3-5	0-2	41.7	- 1.48
J T Gifford	5-13	1-2	1-5	2-3	1-3	38.5	- 1.53
D R Gandolfo	4-4	1-1	1-1	2-2	0-0	100.0	+ 6.72
K C Bailey	4-8	1-3	0-1	1-2	2-2	50.0	+ 3.66
Lady Herries	3-4	2-3	1-1	0-0	0-0	75.0	+ 3.50
T Casey	3-4	0-1	0-0	2-2	1-1	75.0	+ 3.24
T Thomson Jones	3-4	0-0	1-2	2-2	0-0	75.0	+ 5.66
C P E Brooks	3-5	0-0	0-1	1-2	2-2	60.0	+ 0.22
R H Alner	3-5	1-1	0-1	2-2	0-1	60.0	+ 1.41
Miss H C Knight	3-6	2-4	0-0	1-2	0-0	50.0	+ 2.97

TRAINERS' FAVOURITES AT LEICESTER 1991-96

	Total W-R	Nov Hdles	H'cap Hdles	Nov Chses	H'cap Chses	Per cent	£1 Level Stake
M C Pipe	16-39	9-23	0-2	7-10	0-4	41.0	- 9.57
Mrs J Pitman	8-17	1-2	1-1	5-10	1-4	47.1	+ 1.39
D Nicholson	5-14	1-5	0-1	3-5	1-3	35.7	- 2.81
N J Henderson	4-6	0-2	1-1	2-2	1-1	66.7	+ 6.16
J S King	3-3	0-0	0-0	0-0	3-3	100.0	+ 5.00
J G FitzGerald	3-4	2-2	0-0	0-0	1-2	75.0	+ 3.57
N Twiston-Davies	3-5	3-4	0-0	0-0	0-1	60.0	+ 0.68
Capt T A Forster	2-4	0-1	1-1	0-1	1-1	50.0	+ 5.25
J Mackie	2-4	0-1	1-1	0-0	1-2	50.0	+ 1.05
Miss C Saunders	2-4	0-0	0-0	2-4	0-0	50.0	+ 1.15
E J Alston	1-1	0-0	0-0	1-1	0-0	100.0	+ 2.00
N Tinkler	1-1	1-1	0-0	0-0	0-0	100.0	+ 0.80
C James	1-1	0-0	1-1	0-0	0-0	100.0	+ 2.75
K C Bailey	1-1	0-0	0-0	1-1	0-0	100.0	+ 1.00

TRAINERS' FAVOURITES AT LINGFIELD 1991-96

	Total W-R	Nov Hdles	H'cap Hdles	Nov Chses	H'cap Chses	Per cent	£1 Level Stake
Miss B Sanders	14-22	5-6	8-14	1-2	0-0	63.6	+ 4.77
R J O'Sullivan	10-16	5-8	3-5	0-0	2-3	62.5	+ 13.97
S Dow	10-17	3-9	7-7	0-1	0-0	58.8	+ 4.33
R Akehurst	9-15	6-9	3-6	0-0	0-0	60.0	+ 8.66
M C Pipe	8-18	5-8	0-2	3-6	0-2	44.4	- 4.57
C Weedon	7-7	1-1	6-6	0-0	0-0	100.0	+ 9.04
T Thomson Jones	6-11	4-6	2-5	0-0	0-0	54.5	+ 1.59
P A Kelleway	5-5	5-5	0-0	0-0	0-0	100.0	+ 4.60
J L Spearing	5-8	3-3	2-5	0-0	0-0	62.5	+ 5.79
J A B Old	5-9	2-3	3-5	0-0	0-1	55.6	+ 2.63
R J Hodges	5-12	0-0	3-8	0-1	2-3	41.7	+ 0.33
Andrew Turnell	4-6	2-2	0-0	2-3	0-1	66.7	+ 1.00
R Lee	4-7	1-1	3-4	0-0	0-2	57.1	+ 1.40
K C Bailey	4-8	2-2	0-1	1-3	1-2	50.0	- 0.06

TRAINERS' FAVOURITES AT LUDLOW 1991-96

	Total W-R	Nov Hdles	H'cap Hdles	Nov Chses	H'cap Chses	Per cent	£1 Level Stake
D Nicholson	17-37	9-19	1-2	1-5	6-11	45.9	+ 6.50
M C Pipe	12-31	7-23	3-5	2-3	0-0	38.7	+ 2.53
Capt T A Forster	8-13	2-3	0-0	1-2	5-8	61.5	+ 4.23
S Sherwood	7-7	2-2	1-1	3-3	1-1	100.0	+ 10.77
P J Hobbs	6-18	3-6	0-4	0-0	3-8	33.3	- 5.07
Miss J Pidgeon	5-8	0-0	0-0	5-8	0-0	62.5	+ 2.26
Miss H C Knight	5-10	2-3	1-4	2-3	0-0	50.0	+ 3.92
N Twiston-Davies	5-20	1-8	2-6	1-2	1-4	25.0	- 5.48
J A C Edwards	4-9	1-4	0-0	1-2	2-3	44.4	+ 2.75
K C Bailey	4-13	2-3	0-3	2-5	0-2	30.8	- 4.09
I A Balding	3-3	2-2	1-1	0-0	0-0	100.0	+ 3.20
R J Hodges	3-4	1-2	1-1	0-0	1-1	75.0	+ 6.73
D Burchell	3-4	1-1	0-1	1-1	1-1	75.0	+ 3.69
Mrs J Pitman	3-10	1-1	2-4	0-4	0-1	30.0	- 0.38

TRAINERS' FAVOURITES AT MARKET RASEN 1991-96

	Total W-R	Nov Hdles	H'cap Hdles	Nov Chses	H'cap Chses	Per cent	£1 Level Stake
N Tinkler	14-32	8-17	4-10	1-3	1-2	43.8	- 1.53
Mrs M Reveley	12-32	2-13	1-3	6-6	3-10	37.5	- 8.73
M C Pipe	11-28	7-15	1-4	3-5	0-4	39.3	- 8.21
J White	7-13	5-7	0-1	2-4	0-1	53.8	+ 1.89
J G FitzGerald	7-22	2-9	1-3	1-3	3-7	31.8	- 4.51
Miss H C Knight	4-8	1-3	1-2	1-2	1-1	50.0	+ 1.31
F Murphy	4-8	1-2	1-1	2-2	0-3	50.0	+ 3.25
J A C Edwards	3-5	1-1	0-0	2-2	0-2	60.0	+ 2.36
N J Henderson	3-6	1-2	0-0	0-0	2-4	50.0	+ 0.82
J R Upson	3-7	0-1	0-0	1-2	2-4	42.9	- 0.67
K C Bailey	3-9	0-1	0-0	2-3	1-5	33.3	- 4.02
K A Morgan	3-11	2-3	1-6	0-2	0-0	27.3	0.00
O Brennan	3-16	0-2	0-6	2-4	1-4	18.8	- 9.84
Andrew Turnell	2-2	1-1	0-0	1-1	0-0	100.0	+ 3.00

TRAINERS' FAVOURITES AT MUSSELBURGH 1991–96

	Total W-R	Nov Hdles	H'cap Hdles	Nov Chses	H'cap Chses	Per cent	£1 Level Stake
M D Hammond	11–26	3–9	4–6	1–4	3–7	42.3	+ 3.21
Mrs M Reveley	9–17	7–10	1–4	1–1	0–2	52.9	+ 1.39
N Tinkler	7–12	4–5	0–3	2–3	1–1	58.3	+ 5.52
G M Moore	7–14	4–8	1–4	2–2	0–0	50.0	+ 1.35
Denys Smith	5–6	1–1	0–0	1–1	3–4	83.3	+ 9.33
P Monteith	5–9	2–2	1–4	1–1	1–2	55.6	+ 2.39
J H Johnson	5–15	1–3	0–2	3–4	1–6	33.3	− 1.50
C Parker	4–6	0–0	2–2	0–1	2–3	66.7	+ 5.50
K A Morgan	2–2	1–1	0–0	0–0	1–1	100.0	+ 4.00
K C Bailey	2–2	1–1	0–0	1–1	0–0	100.0	+ 2.66
J M Jefferson	2–2	1–1	1–1	0–0	0–0	100.0	+ 5.62
I A Balding	2–2	1–1	0–0	0–0	1–1	100.0	+ 1.75
J L Eyre	2–2	2–2	0–0	0–0	0–0	100.0	+ 3.62
J Barclay	2–2	0–0	1–1	1–1	0–0	100.0	+ 5.50

TRAINERS' FAVOURITES AT NEWBURY 1991–96

	Total W-R	Nov Hdles	H'cap Hdles	Nov Chses	H'cap Chses	Per cent	£1 Level Stake
D Nicholson	16–38	8–13	1–4	5–10	2–11	42.1	− 2.00
N J Henderson	14–26	2–5	1–4	8–11	3–6	53.8	+ 7.08
O Sherwood	11–25	8–14	0–3	2–3	1–5	44.0	+ 2.53
M C Pipe	9–26	5–11	1–5	1–4	2–6	34.6	− 0.79
Mrs J Pitman	8–13	5–5	1–2	1–2	1–4	61.5	+ 9.51
Mrs M Reveley	4–10	3–4	1–5	0–0	0–1	40.0	+ 0.50
S Sherwood	4–12	0–2	0–1	2–3	2–6	33.3	− 2.03
P J Hobbs	4–13	2–6	0–3	0–0	2–4	30.8	− 3.13
J T Gifford	4–14	2–5	0–3	0–2	2–4	28.6	− 0.40
G Harwood	3–3	2–2	1–1	0–0	0–0	100.0	+ 3.42
I A Balding	3–4	1–1	0–1	2–2	0–0	75.0	+ 2.40
R H Alner	3–5	1–1	1–1	1–1	0–2	60.0	+ 2.47
M H Tompkins	3–6	3–6	0–0	0–0	0–0	50.0	+ 1.23
C P E Brooks	3–8	1–2	0–1	0–1	2–4	37.5	+ 0.18

TRAINERS' FAVOURITES AT NEWCASTLE 1991–96

	Total W-R	Nov Hdles	H'cap Hdles	Nov Chses	H'cap Chses	Per cent	£1 Level Stake
Mrs M Reveley	18–49	8–19	8–15	0–4	2–11	36.7	− 10.43
J H Johnson	9–14	4–5	1–2	1–2	3–5	64.3	+ 6.22
M D Hammond	9–24	3–5	0–7	1–4	5–8	37.5	− 0.21
G Richards	7–13	0–2	3–3	3–5	1–3	53.8	+ 5.80
M W Easterby	5–10	2–3	0–2	2–2	1–3	50.0	+ 2.00
M J Camacho	4–5	1–2	3–3	0–0	0–0	80.0	+ 4.12
L Lungo	4–8	2–2	2–5	0–1	0–0	50.0	+ 3.73
P Cheesbrough	4–10	0–1	0–2	3–5	1–2	40.0	− 2.44
G M Moore	4–11	3–5	0–3	1–3	0–0	36.4	− 2.66
J G FitzGerald	3–10	0–5	1–3	1–1	1–1	30.0	− 1.84
J M Jefferson	2–2	2–2	0–0	0–0	0–0	100.0	+ 3.13
J White	2–2	0–0	1–1	0–0	1–1	100.0	+ 4.00
K C Bailey	2–3	1–1	0–0	0–0	1–2	66.7	+ 1.98
B E Wilkinson	2–3	0–0	0–0	0–0	2–3	66.7	+ 2.20

TRAINERS' FAVOURITES AT NEWTON ABBOT 1991-96

	Total W-R	Nov Hdles	H'cap Hdles	Nov Chses	H'cap Chses	Per cent	£1 Level Stake
M C Pipe	66-166	26-66	12-44	13-25	15-31	39.8	- 40.42
P J Hobbs	28-59	8-14	7-15	5-11	8-19	47.5	+ 2.39
J White	9-25	2-8	3-8	3-3	1-6	36.0	- 4.08
P F Nicholls	8-24	0-2	2-6	1-4	5-12	33.3	- 0.75
R G Frost	7-12	2-3	3-4	0-0	2-5	58.3	+ 10.33
O Sherwood	6-13	4-7	2-2	0-2	0-2	46.2	+ 2.01
J A B Old	5-9	3-5	0-1	0-0	2-3	55.6	+ 1.10
D Nicholson	5-9	3-6	1-2	1-1	0-0	55.6	+ 3.66
D H Barons	5-11	1-1	2-5	1-3	1-2	45.5	+ 5.41
K C Bailey	5-15	5-8	0-0	0-2	0-5	33.3	- 1.75
R J Hodges	5-18	2-4	2-7	0-1	1-6	27.8	- 3.00
J G M O'Shea	4-4	1-1	1-1	1-1	1-1	100.0	+ 5.67
A G Newcombe	4-4	0-0	0-0	0-0	4-4	100.0	+ 5.51
S Sherwood	4-7	0-0	1-2	0-0	3-5	57.1	+ 0.82

TRAINERS' FAVOURITES AT PERTH 1991-96

	Total W-R	Nov Hdles	H'cap Hdles	Nov Chses	H'cap Chses	Per cent	£1 Level Stake
Mrs M Reveley	19-31	11-15	1-8	5-5	2-3	61.3	+ 5.45
K C Bailey	10-12	2-2	1-2	5-5	2-3	83.3	+ 7.62
P Monteith	8-15	0-3	1-4	1-1	6-7	53.3	+ 5.35
N Twiston-Davies	8-16	2-5	3-3	1-4	2-4	50.0	+ 2.50
M D Hammond	7-21	4-7	1-8	1-3	1-3	33.3	- 5.33
G Richards	7-28	1-8	0-6	4-7	2-7	25.0	- 12.18
Miss L A Perratt	6-13	1-5	2-4	0-0	3-4	46.2	+ 0.99
P J Hobbs	5-10	0-1	3-4	1-2	1-3	50.0	- 1.57
M C Pipe	4-4	1-1	2-2	1-1	0-0	100.0	+ 5.13
L Lungo	4-8	2-5	2-3	0-0	0-0	50.0	+ 2.10
S Mellor	3-3	1-1	1-1	1-1	0-0	100.0	+ 4.30
N Tinkler	3-7	2-6	1-1	0-0	0-0	42.9	+ 1.63
J White	3-9	1-4	0-1	2-4	0-0	33.3	- 3.72
B Mactaggart	2-2	0-0	1-1	0-0	1-1	100.0	+ 4.33

TRAINERS' FAVOURITES AT PLUMPTON 1991-96

	Total W-R	Nov Hdles	H'cap Hdles	Nov Chses	H'cap Chses	Per cent	£1 Level Stake
J White	29-60	8-16	8-13	5-16	8-15	48.3	+ 3.29
C R Egerton	10 15	4-6	1-2	3-5	2-2	66.7	+ 4.76
D M Grissell	8-11	4-4	1-1	1-1	2-5	72.7	+ 7.62
M C Pipe	6-10	3-3	1-3	1-1	1-3	60.0	+ 0.28
J R Jenkins	6-13	1-5	3-5	1-1	1-2	46.2	- 1.98
R Akehurst	5-11	4-7	0-2	1-1	0-1	45.5	- 0.54
R J O'Sullivan	5-11	2-4	2-4	0-2	1-1	45.5	+ 2.33
G Harwood	5-11	1-3	2-6	0-0	2-2	45.5	+ 1.29
Mrs D Haine	4-5	4-5	0-0	0-0	0-0	80.0	+ 6.38
R Rowe	4-9	1-2	1-3	1-1	1-3	44.4	+ 2.50
J Ffitch-Heyes	4-10	0-3	4-6	0-1	0-0	40.0	- 0.55
R Curtis	4-10	1-1	0-1	1-3	2-5	40.0	+ 0.60
N J Henderson	4-15	2-7	0-1	1-2	1-5	26.7	- 6.00
T G Mills	3-3	2-2	1-1	0-0	0-0	100.0	+ 4.58

TRAINERS' FAVOURITES AT SANDOWN 1991-96

	Total W-R	Nov Hdles	H'cap Hdles	Nov Chses	H'cap Chses	Per cent	£1 Level Stake
D Nicholson	20-41	3-7	2-5	5-8	10-21	48.8	+ 9.40
J T Gifford	13-24	1-5	1-4	7-8	4-7	54.2	+ 7.79
M C Pipe	6-13	3-5	2-6	0-0	1-2	46.2	- 0.47
O Sherwood	6-13	3-7	0-2	2-2	1-2	46.2	+ 0.52
Capt T A Forster	4-7	0-0	0-1	2-2	2-4	57.1	- 0.13
P F Nicholls	3-4	2-2	0-0	0-0	1-2	75.0	+ 4.38
C P E Brooks	3-6	0-0	1-1	1-1	1-4	50.0	+ 1.04
Mrs M Reveley	3-7	0-1	2-2	0-1	1-3	42.9	+ 1.98
N Twiston-Davies	3-8	0-3	1-2	2-3	0-0	37.5	+ 5.00
D R C Elsworth	3-10	3-8	0-1	0-1	0-0	30.0	- 3.55
N J Henderson	3-19	3-12	0-1	0-3	0-3	15.8	- 12.78
J H Johnson	2-2	0-0	0-0	0-0	2-2	100.0	+ 3.63
D J Caro	2-2	0-0	0-0	2-2	0-0	100.0	+ 1.63
J A B Old	2-3	2-3	0-0	0-0	0-0	66.7	+ 3.50

TRAINERS' FAVOURITES AT SEDGEFIELD 1991-96

	Total W-R	Nov Hdles	H'cap Hdles	Nov Chses	H'cap Chses	Per cent	£1 Level Stake
Mrs M Reveley	46-103	15-27	10-31	10-18	11-27	44.7	+ 16.45
J H Johnson	12-37	2-7	2-10	4-9	4-11	32.4	- 5.78
G M Moore	11-26	7-11	3-10	1-3	0-2	42.3	+ 6.03
J J O'Neill	9-13	5-7	0-0	3-3	1-3	69.2	+ 1.22
L Lungo	8-13	7-8	1-3	0-0	0-2	61.5	+ 8.19
J A Hellens	6-12	0-1	2-4	0-1	4-6	50.0	+ 6.88
M W Easterby	6-14	0-3	2-2	1-2	3-7	42.9	+ 2.82
J G FitzGerald	5-9	1-2	0-1	2-3	2-3	55.6	+ 2.16
Denys Smith	5-12	1-4	2-4	1-1	1-3	41.7	+ 2.50
P Beaumont	5-13	2-5	0-3	1-1	2-4	38.5	+ 1.57
P Cheesbrough	4-6	0-1	1-1	1-1	2-3	66.7	+ 4.56
J Wade	4-13	0-0	0-7	2-2	2-4	30.8	- 2.09
C W Thornton	3-4	3-3	0-1	0-0	0-0	75.0	+ 5.42
F Murphy	3-4	1-1	1-1	0-1	1-1	75.0	+ 3.68

TRAINERS' FAVOURITES AT SOUTHWELL 1991-96

	Total W-R	Nov Hdles	H'cap Hdles	Nov Chses	H'cap Chses	Per cent	£1 Level Stake
R Hollinshead	17-23	13-16	4-6	0-0	0-1	73.9	+ 15.28
M C Pipe	13-32	11-19	0-9	2-4	0-0	40.6	- 8.02
Mrs M Reveley	9-16	2-5	2-3	2-3	3-5	56.3	+ 4.84
W Clay	9-24	4-7	4-15	0-1	1-1	37.5	+ 4.65
J L Harris	6-22	4-8	2-14	0-0	0-0	27.3	- 6.32
J E Banks	5-6	3-3	1-2	1-1	0-0	83.3	+ 4.50
S Sherwood	5-9	1-2	0-1	2-2	2-4	55.6	+ 3.70
O Brennan	5-13	2-4	0-6	3-3	0-0	38.5	+ 0.63
O Sherwood	5-13	1-5	0-0	2-5	2-3	38.5	+ 0.10
D Nicholson	4-7	0-1	0-0	1-3	3-3	57.1	+ 2.75
S P C Woods	4-7	0-0	4-7	0-0	0-0	57.1	+ 2.84
D Burchell	4-9	2-3	1-4	1-2	0-0	44.4	- 0.73
J A C Edwards	4-9	0-0	2-3	0-1	2-5	44.4	+ 3.38
J White	4-16	2-9	1-3	1-3	0-1	25.0	- 6.05

TRAINERS' FAVOURITES AT STRATFORD 1991-96

	Total W-R	Nov Hdles	H'cap Hdles	Nov Chses	H'cap Chses	Per cent	£1 Level Stake
M C Pipe	18-47	9-22	3-14	3-6	3-5	38.3	– 8.44
D Nicholson	9-22	4-8	1-2	1-6	3-6	40.9	+ 2.45
J White	8-16	5-8	1-3	2-2	0-3	50.0	+ 8.29
P J Hobbs	7-18	0-4	1-4	1-3	5-7	38.9	+ 0.80
K C Bailey	7-23	0-3	0-1	2-7	5-12	30.4	– 5.48
O Sherwood	6-13	3-6	1-1	0-3	2-3	46.2	+ 4.27
G B Balding	4-13	0-1	1-5	0-0	3-7	30.8	+ 3.69
R J O'Sullivan	3-5	1-2	1-1	1-1	0-1	60.0	+ 1.87
Capt T A Forster	3-7	1-3	0-0	1-1	1-3	42.9	– 0.18
P F Nicholls	3-8	0-0	0-1	1-3	2-4	37.5	– 2.45
N Twiston-Davies	3-12	1-2	1-4	0-3	1-3	25.0	– 3.00
Mrs M Reveley	3-13	0-0	1-5	1-4	1-4	23.1	– 6.08
P D Evans	2-2	0-0	2-2	0-0	0-0	100.0	+ 4.25
F Murphy	2-2	0-0	0-0	0-0	2-2	100.0	+ 2.63

TRAINERS' FAVOURITES AT TAUNTON 1991-96

	Total W-R	Nov Hdles	H'cap Hdles	Nov Chses	H'cap Chses	Per cent	£1 Level Stake
M C Pipe	30-71	21-36	7-27	1-3	1-5	42.3	– 4.83
R J Hodges	9-27	0-2	3-12	4-5	2-8	33.3	+ 3.08
P J Hobbs	8-16	3-5	1-5	2-2	2-4	50.0	+ 3.71
P F Nicholls	5-20	2-3	1-6	1-5	1-6	25.0	– 6.25
S Sherwood	4-6	0-0	1-2	3-3	0-1	66.7	+ 4.52
R H Buckler	3-6	1-1	2-3	0-0	0-2	50.0	+ 4.23
J A B Old	3-8	3-5	0-3	0-0	0-0	37.5	– 1.44
N J Henderson	3-9	2-4	0-0	1-3	0-2	33.3	– 1.65
Mrs J G Retter	3-12	0-0	1-7	0-2	2-3	25.0	– 1.00
P R Hedger	2-2	2-2	0-0	0-0	0-0	100.0	+ 3.35
M W Davies	2-2	2-2	0-0	0-0	0-0	100.0	+ 2.53
Sidney J Smith	2-3	0-0	0-0	2-3	0-0	66.7	+ 2.00
G A Ham	2-5	0-1	1-1	0-0	1-3	40.0	+ 3.75
I A Balding	2-5	1-2	0-1	1-1	0-1	40.0	– 0.25

TRAINERS' FAVOURITES AT TOWCESTER 1991-96

	Total W-R	Nov Hdles	H'cap Hdles	Nov Chses	H'cap Chses	Per cent	£1 Level Stake
O Brennan	12-20	3-6	6-9	0-1	3-4	60.0	+ 13.54
Miss C Saunders	11-13	0-0	0-0	11-13	0-0	84.6	+ 9.33
D Nicholson	10-15	5-9	0-0	2-2	3-4	66.7	+ 7.79
Mrs J Pitman	10-17	6-7	0-2	3-6	1-2	58.8	+ 9.77
N Twiston-Davies	6-14	1-3	1-5	4-5	0-1	42.9	+ 0.18
Mrs I McKie	5-13	0-1	1-3	0-1	4-8	38.5	+ 1.13
M C Pipe	5-18	3-10	1-2	1-4	0-2	27.8	– 5.65
J L Spearing	4-4	1-1	3-3	0-0	0-0	100.0	+ 8.00
J A C Edwards	4-7	1-2	0-0	0-1	3-4	57.1	+ 6.25
T Thomson Jones	4-8	0-1	0-0	0-0	4-7	50.0	+ 4.00
C P E Brooks	4-9	0-2	0-0	3-4	1-3	44.4	+ 1.28
J T Gifford	4-15	3-8	0-1	1-3	0-3	26.7	– 6.77
Capt T A Forster	4-16	0-0	0-1	2-4	2-11	25.0	– 5.65
P J Hobbs	3-4	2-3	1-1	0-0	0-0	75.0	+ 4.25

TRAINERS' FAVOURITES AT UTTOXETER 1991-96

	Total W-R	Nov Hdles	H'cap Hdles	Nov Chses	H'cap Chses	Per cent	£1 Level Stake
M C Pipe	30-62	12-23	7-16	7-12	4-11	48.4	+ 7.42
K C Bailey	15-34	6-11	3-8	4-8	2-7	44.1	+ 11.36
N Twiston-Davies	11-15	6-8	1-1	3-5	1-1	73.3	+ 9.31
D Nicholson	10-30	6-15	1-7	2-4	1-4	33.3	− 1.64
N J Henderson	7-14	1-3	3-5	0-1	3-5	50.0	+ 4.10
J A C Edwards	6-12	0-2	1-2	3-3	2-5	50.0	+ 6.43
P J Hobbs	6-14	0-2	1-1	2-3	3-8	42.9	+ 0.74
O Sherwood	6-18	3-9	0-1	3-5	0-3	33.3	− 6.96
Capt T A Forster	5-8	0-1	0-0	2-2	3-5	62.5	+ 5.72
Mrs J Pitman	5-14	0-4	0-1	1-3	4-6	35.7	+ 0.40
G Richards	5-15	1-4	0-1	0-1	4-9	33.3	− 3.63
O Brennan	4-6	0-0	3-5	0-0	1-1	66.7	+ 7.71
S A Brookshaw	4-7	0-0	0-0	4-7	0-0	57.1	+ 0.12
C J Mann	4-7	0-2	0-0	2-2	2-3	57.1	+ 2.73

TRAINERS' FAVOURITES AT WARWICK 1991-96

	Total W-R	Nov Hdles	H'cap Hdles	Nov Chses	H'cap Chses	Per cent	£1 Level Stake
M C Pipe	22-47	10-19	4-14	5-5	3-9	46.8	+ 7.99
D Nicholson	16-32	10-17	1-2	3-6	2-7	50.0	+ 5.46
Mrs J Pitman	7-19	1-3	0-2	3-6	3-8	36.8	− 2.45
N J Henderson	6-13	4-7	0-1	1-3	1-2	46.2	+ 0.74
R C Wilkins	4-5	0-0	0-0	4-5	0-0	80.0	+ 1.55
J T Gifford	4-6	0-1	2-2	1-2	1-1	66.7	+ 8.70
G B Balding	4-11	0-5	3-3	1-2	0-1	36.4	+ 4.83
O Sherwood	4-12	2-7	0-1	2-4	0-0	33.3	− 3.23
R J Hodges	3-4	0-0	1-2	0-0	2-2	75.0	+ 2.17
N A Gaselee	3-6	1-2	0-0	1-2	1-2	50.0	+ 1.50
N Twiston-Davies	3-6	2-5	0-0	1-1	0-0	50.0	+ 3.27
J G FitzGerald	3-9	2-4	1-3	0-1	0-1	33.3	− 2.30
Miss H C Knight	3-10	1-3	1-3	0-2	1-2	30.0	0.00
P R Webber	2-2	1-1	0-0	1-1	0-0	100.0	+ 3.94

TRAINERS' FAVOURITES AT WETHERBY 1991-96

	Total W-R	Nov Hdles	H'cap Hdles	Nov Chses	H'cap Chses	Per cent	£1 Level Stake
Mrs M Reveley	33-62	14-24	10-20	3-6	6-12	53.2	+ 12.97
G Richards	12-28	4-4	0-4	2-5	6-15	42.9	+ 1.97
D Nicholson	11-21	3-7	0-1	5-9	3-4	52.4	+ 0.11
J G FitzGerald	10-27	3-9	5-8	2-5	0-5	37.0	− 1.31
M W Easterby	9-16	5-5	1-2	2-5	1-4	56.3	+ 4.06
M D Hammond	7-22	3-5	2-5	1-4	1-8	31.8	− 0.30
P Cheesbrough	5-10	1-2	0-1	1-3	3-4	50.0	+ 4.30
N Tinkler	4-13	4-10	0-1	0-1	0-1	30.8	− 2.17
T D Walford	3-4	0-0	0-0	3-4	0-0	75.0	+ 1.37
P Beaumont	3-5	1-3	0-0	2-2	0-0	60.0	+ 0.65
J T Gifford	3-6	0-0	1-1	2-2	0-3	50.0	+ 2.25
Mrs S J Smith	3-7	0-2	1-1	0-1	2-3	42.9	+ 3.25
J H Johnson	3-8	0-0	1-3	2-2	0-3	37.5	+ 0.17
G M Moore	3-9	1-4	1-3	1-1	0-1	33.3	− 1.59

TRAINERS' FAVOURITES AT WINCANTON 1991-96

	Total W-R	Nov Hdles	H'cap Hdles	Nov Chses	H'cap Chses	Per cent	£1 Level Stake
M C Pipe	20-47	12-32	2-5	6-10	0-0	42.6	- 5.59
J T Gifford	11-18	5-6	0-0	5-8	1-4	61.1	+ 8.25
P F Nicholls	8-21	1-5	0-2	2-5	5-9	38.1	- 2.16
N Twiston-Davies	7-12	1-3	1-1	2-4	3-4	58.3	+ 6.87
O Sherwood	6-10	4-6	0-0	1-1	1-3	60.0	+ 5.12
P J Hobbs	6-12	3-5	2-5	0-0	1-2	50.0	+ 4.58
Mrs J Pitman	6-18	0-3	1-3	2-5	3-7	33.3	- 4.85
Capt T A Forster	5-11	0-1	0-2	3-3	2-5	45.5	+ 2.85
R H Alner	5-12	1-1	2-2	1-3	1-6	41.7	+ 1.71
R J Hodges	5-13	0-0	3-5	0-1	2-7	38.5	+ 2.71
K C Bailey	5-13	2-5	0-2	2-3	1-3	38.5	- 3.83
N J Henderson	5-14	3-8	0-2	2-2	0-2	35.7	- 3.80
J White	4-4	3-3	0-0	1-1	0-0	100.0	+ 6.87
D R Gandolfo	4-7	1-3	1-1	2-3	0-0	57.1	+ 2.56

TRAINERS' FAVOURITES AT WINDSOR 1991-96

	Total W-R	Nov Hdles	H'cap Hdles	Nov Chses	H'cap Chses	Per cent	£1 Level Stake
Miss H C Knight	5-10	2-3	2-4	1-2	0-1	50.0	+ 4.07
N J Henderson	5-12	5-9	0-0	0-0	0-3	41.7	- 0.53
Andrew Turnell	4-6	2-2	1-2	1-1	0-1	66.7	+ 6.16
Mrs J Pitman	4-11	1-1	1-4	2-6	0-0	36.4	- 0.88
R Akehurst	3-4	2-3	0-0	1-1	0-0	75.0	+ 4.36
P R Hedger	3-4	1-2	0-0	0-0	2-2	75.0	+ 5.80
C P E Brooks	3-4	1-1	0-0	0-0	2-3	75.0	+ 5.00
D R C Elsworth	3-6	0-1	2-4	1-1	0-0	50.0	+ 2.80
J T Gifford	3-7	1-2	0-0	2-3	0-2	42.9	+ 0.37
P J Hobbs	3-8	1-1	0-1	1-1	1-5	37.5	+ 0.88
R Barber	2-2	0-0	0-0	2-2	0-0	100.0	+ 1.87
D R Gandolfo	2-3	2-3	0-0	0-0	0-0	66.7	+ 0.12
M C Pipe	2-5	2-2	0-1	0-1	0-1	40.0	- 0.30
G B Balding	2-5	0-1	1-1	0-0	1-3	40.0	+ 2.00

TRAINERS' FAVOURITES AT WORCESTER 1991-96

	Total W-R	Nov Hdles	H'cap Hdles	Nov Chses	H'cap Chses	Per cent	£1 Level Stake
M C Pipe	19-59	11-26	3-13	4-11	1-9	32.2	- 18.13
P J Hobbs	16-39	3-10	6-11	3-6	4-12	41.0	+ 2.68
D Nicholson	12-25	7-11	2-2	2-5	1-7	48.0	+ 7.74
N Twiston-Davies	12-31	6-10	2-4	2-6	2-11	38.7	+ 2.74
O Sherwood	10-18	2-6	0-1	4-5	4-6	55.6	+ 7.97
Miss H C Knight	8-12	2-4	1-1	2-3	3-4	66.7	+ 11.13
K C Bailey	7-20	1-6	0-0	4-7	2-7	35.0	- 3.16
Capt T A Forster	6-14	1-1	0-2	1-3	4-8	42.9	+ 5.43
C J Mann	4-4	1-1	0-0	2-2	1-1	100.0	+ 5.83
N J Henderson	4-10	3-5	0-0	1-4	0-1	40.0	- 0.90
K R Burke	3-3	1-1	2-2	0-0	0-0	100.0	+ 8.88
R Rowe	3-5	2-2	1-3	0-0	0-0	60.0	+ 6.25
C P E Brooks	3-8	0-1	2-4	0-1	1-2	37.5	+ 6.44
R Dickin	3-11	0-0	0-2	1-3	2-6	27.3	- 2.75

TOP PERCENTAGE COURSES FOR FAVOURITES 1991-96

	W-R	Per cent	£1 Level Stake		W-R	Per cent	£1 Level Stake
Lingfield	200-412	48.5	+ 11.83	Hereford	187-476	39.3	- 35.25
Fontwell	215-460	46.7	+ 34.59	Nottingham	110-280	39.3	- 14.25
Ayr	156-353	44.2	- 23.90	Ludlow	151-389	38.8	- 16.33
Wetherby	182-415	43.9	+ 18.77	Sandown	121-312	38.8	- 28.86
Musselburgh	102-236	43.2	+ 11.09	Kempton	103-267	38.6	- 32.74
Plumpton	172-401	42.9	- 24.37	Fakenham	69-180	38.3	- 13.04
Perth	133-310	42.9	- 27.75	Towcester	157-413	38.0	- 15.34
Newcastle	136-318	42.8	- 15.72	Bangor	148-392	37.8	- 45.69
Folkestone	93-218	42.7	- 5.35	Hexham	139-369	37.7	- 29.78
Kelso	148-349	42.4	- 40.31	Ascot	115-305	37.7	- 24.57
Newbury	149-355	42.0	+ 7.08	Taunton	134-356	37.6	- 10.17
Carlisle	135-323	41.8	- 0.84	Cheltenham	176-468	37.6	- 19.76
Doncaster	82-196	41.8	- 2.00	Uttoxeter	219-587	37.3	- 61.72
Cartmel	63-151	41.7	- 13.09	Southwell	208-569	36.6	- 75.23
Haydock	121-290	41.7	- 32.15	Worcester	197-557	35.4	- 60.05
Wincanton	158-381	41.5	- 11.65	Leicester	85-240	35.4	- 45.87
Exeter	189-456	41.4	- 32.16	Stratford	143-406	35.2	- 47.72
Chepstow	143-349	41.0	- 31.25	Windsor	78-225	34.7	- 38.80
Newton Abbot	253-618	40.9	- 59.55	Aintree	52-152	34.2	- 3.04
Huntingdon	170-420	40.5	- 34.99	Market Rasen	168-504	33.3	-123.76
Warwick	146-361	40.4	+ 5.26	Catterick	101-305	33.1	- 74.42
Sedgefield	209-527	39.7	- 15.49				

FAVOURITES BY TYPE OF RACE AND DISTANCE 1991-96

	2 Miles - 2M 3F			2M 4F - 2M 7F		
	W-R	Per cent	£1 Level Stake	W-R	Per cent	£1 Level Stake
Novice Hurdles	1327-3078	43.1	- 139.57	533-1173	45.4	- 36.09
Handicap Hurdles	684-2173	31.5	- 309.68	435-1252	34.7	- 66.33
Novice Chases	412-871	47.3	- 61.11	423-876	48.3	- 14.05
Handicap Chases	427-1129	37.8	- 137.40	407-1062	38.3	- 68.99
Hunter Chases	20-43	46.5	+ 4.46	102-206	49.5	+ 37.81
N H Flat	160-547	29.3	- 135.96	0-0	-	0.00
Totals	3030-7841	38.6	- 779.26	1900-4569	41.6	-147.65

	3 Miles +			All Favourites		
Novice Hurdles	117-282	41.5	- 19.93	1977-4533	43.6	-195.59
Handicap Hurdles	198-556	35.6	- 21.31	1317-3981	33.1	-397.32
Novice Chases	333-718	46.4	- 21.95	1168-2465	47.4	- 97.11
Handicap Chases	486-1375	35.3	- 139.63	1320-3566	37.0	-346.02
Hunter Chases	197-426	46.2	+ 15.31	319-675	47.3	+ 57.58
N H Flat	0-0	-	0.00	160-547	29.3	-135.96
Totals	1331-3357	39.6	- 187.51	6261-15767	39.7	-1114.42

When there is more than one favourite in a race then the £1 stake has been equally divided on each one. Only one favourite is counted for each race.

TRAINER SUMMARIES

LEADING JUMPS TRAINERS 1995-96

	Total W-R	Hurdles	Chases	Per cent	£1 Level Stake
M C Pipe	176-770	124-555	52-215	22.9	- 61.01
D Nicholson	86-377	54-261	32-116	22.8	- 10.69
Mrs M Reveley	86-397	72-313	14-84	21.7	- 71.91
P J Hobbs	77-375	42-225	35-150	20.5	- 33.73
N Twiston-Davies	74-494	51-318	23-176	15.0	-104.31
G Richards	69-225	19-89	50-136	30.7	+ 18.65
K C Bailey	68-430	25-199	43-231	15.8	-131.17
Miss H C Knight	59-312	36-212	23-100	18.9	- 25.47
P F Nicholls	53-265	14-82	39-183	20.0	- 48.55
Mrs J Pitman	48-256	21-125	27-131	18.8	+ 47.60
N J Henderson	47-278	24-163	23-115	16.9	- 52.27
O Sherwood	46-242	30-148	16-94	19.0	- 25.07
G B Balding	45-307	21-186	24-121	14.7	- 40.33
J T Gifford	40-267	19-138	21-129	15.0	- 41.29
J H Johnson	35-216	13-112	22-104	16.2	- 23.51
J White	35-255	21-165	14-90	13.7	- 95.86
Capt T A Forster	34-178	16-95	18-83	19.1	+ 1.36
M D Hammond	34-299	22-196	12-103	11.4	-133.43
C P E Brooks	29-185	10-97	19-88	15.7	- 16.84
M H Easterby	28-95	19-74	9-21	29.5	+ 0.81
J R Jenkins	28-278	25-236	3-42	10.1	-123.99
R H Alner	25-198	4-76	21-122	12.6	- 66.71
R J Hodges	25-217	11-122	14-95	11.5	- 58.29
Mrs S J Smith	25-247	9-137	16-110	10.1	- 29.36
P Monteith	24-141	11-78	13-63	17.0	- 56.15
D R Gandolfo	24-169	15-129	9-40	14.2	- 55.11
J G FitzGerald	22-141	13-87	9-54	15.6	+ 47.01
P Beaumont	21-108	12-74	9-34	19.4	+ 16.53
S Mellor	21-185	12-140	9-45	11.4	- 41.32
F Murphy	19-117	12-73	7-44	16.2	- 10.38
J J O'Neill	18-166	17-122	1-44	10.8	- 89.94
C J Mann	17-128	13-101	4-27	13.3	- 31.84
J A B Old	17-146	13-118	4-28	11.6	- 50.06
G M Moore	17-148	12-127	5-21	11.5	- 65.33
R Rowe	17-155	11-105	6-50	11.0	- 41.96
R Curtis	16-87	5-40	11-47	18.4	+ 0.02
K A Morgan	16-114	16-106	0-8	14.0	- 18.14
R H Buckler	16-172	12-89	4-83	9.3	+ 66.40
Andrew Turnell	15-128	9-73	6-55	11.7	- 41.25
J M Bradley	15-190	8-131	7-59	7.9	- 89.30
A Streeter	14-56	10-50	4-6	25.0	+ 27.68
T Thomson Jones	14-66	8-41	6-25	21.2	+ 27.51
T D Easterby	14-84	11-74	3-10	16.7	- 15.77
J M Jefferson	14-90	10-78	4-12	15.6	+ 68.53
N Tinkler	14-99	6-61	8-38	14.1	- 41.61
D R C Elsworth	14-103	10-73	4-30	13.6	- 50.54
C Parker	14-118	3-61	11-57	11.9	- 46.12
N A Gaselee	14-126	5-51	9-75	11.1	- 26.37
L Lungo	14-138	10-122	4-16	10.1	- 50.32
I A Balding	13-46	9-38	4-8	28.3	- 1.42
Noel T Chance	13-53	10-45	3-8	24.5	+ 9.09
J Mackie	13-90	12-80	1-10	14.4	+ 5.73
M W Easterby	13-100	7-66	6-34	13.0	- 31.93
P R Webber	13-108	10-77	3-31	12.0	+ 36.77

C R Egerton	13-109	11-74	2-35	11.9	- 55.69
J S King	13-141	4-76	9-65	9.2	- 66.73
W Storey	12-77	11-67	1-10	15.6	- 13.95
Miss L V Russell	12-80	0-18	12-62	15.0	- 18.12
J G M O'Shea	12-108	9-76	3-32	11.1	- 31.64
O Brennan	12-131	6-97	6-34	9.2	- 74.65
A G Newcombe	11-45	6-34	5-11	24.4	+ 15.14
R Akehurst	11-48	11-48	0-0	22.9	- 18.68
Denys Smith	11-61	7-50	4-11	18.0	- 9.00
W G M Turner	11-80	7-74	4-6	13.8	- 18.12
Mrs S C Bradburne	11-86	3-26	8-60	12.8	+ 45.08
J L Eyre	10-49	10-48	0-1	20.4	- 16.52
K G Wingrove	10-66	10-56	0-10	15.2	+ 22.13
B Ellison	10-79	3-52	7-27	12.7	+ 0.63
S Sherwood	10-82	3-50	7-32	12.2	- 47.90
R J O'Sullivan	10-93	10-76	0-17	10.8	- 7.75
R Dickin	10-129	1-55	9-74	7.8	- 76.91
J A C Edwards	10-130	3-95	7-35	7.7	- 89.59
G M McCourt	9-35	0-13	9-22	25.7	+ 8.69
Mrs M A Jones	9-54	7-41	2-13	16.7	+ 30.75
J I A Charlton	9-61	1-30	8-31	14.8	- 26.59
G A Hubbard	9-72	8-47	1-25	12.5	- 20.00
R D E Woodhouse	9-73	4-53	5-20	12.3	- 17.79
Mrs S A Bramall	9-96	4-46	5-50	9.4	- 31.92
M J Wilkinson	9-99	4-66	5-33	9.1	- 48.25
H J Manners	9-103	5-59	4-44	8.7	+ 30.50
J Wade	9-115	2-46	7-69	7.8	- 69.71
D Burchell	9-117	7-96	2-21	7.7	- 60.25
A C Whillans	8-37	4-30	4-7	21.6	+ 4.00
T P McGovern	8-43	8-38	0-5	18.6	+ 1.50
T P Tate	8-45	2-23	6-22	17.8	+ 12.20
G L Moore	8-45	8-45	0-0	17.8	+ 6.92
R Allan	8-48	6-38	2-10	16.7	+ 1.33
R T Phillips	8-48	4-18	4-30	16.7	- 14.27
J Pearce	8-56	7-46	1-10	14.3	- 2.52
S E Kettlewell	8-56	1-38	7-18	14.3	- 21.85
J L Harris	8-57	8-52	0-5	14.0	+ 11.50
P R Hedger	8-66	6-43	2-23	12.1	- 30.36
D M Grissell	8-70	6-44	2-26	11.4	- 6.37
R J Price	8-88	7-66	1-22	9.1	- 27.50
K R Burke	8-93	7-73	1-20	8.6	- 36.00
C L Popham	8-118	6-78	2-40	6.8	- 44.00
R G Frost	8-131	7-88	1-43	6.1	- 82.00
Miss C Saunders	7-19	0-0	7-19	36.8	- 2.15
Lady Herries	7-39	7-38	0-1	17.9	- 1.62
B Mactaggart	7-43	6-39	1-4	16.3	+ 2.47
C W Thornton	7-48	4-35	3-13	14.6	- 1.42
Miss V Williams	7-52	4-25	3-27	13.5	+ 13.75
P Bowen	7-56	1-26	6-30	12.5	+ 3.12
Mrs D Haine	7-59	5-35	2-24	11.9	- 12.89
T Casey	7-61	2-30	5-31	11.5	- 38.26
J J Quinn	7-63	5-53	2-10	11.1	- 24.76
W Jenks	7-66	7-54	0-12	10.6	- 9.75
J R Upson	7-84	6-70	1-14	8.3	- 38.42
D L Williams	7-86	2-45	5-41	8.1	- 27.67
M C Chapman	7-110	2-62	5-48	6.4	- 38.25
F Jordan	7-121	4-98	3-23	5.8	- 82.93
T Dyer	7-139	7-123	0-16	5.0	-103.04

LEADING JOCKEYS 1995-96

	1st	2nd	3rd	Unpl	Total Mts	Per cent	£1 Level Stake
A P McCoy	175	131	89	364	759	23.1	+ 90.71
D Bridgwater	131	94	70	305	600	21.8	- 70.94
R Dunwoody	101	78	76	238	493	20.5	-100.87
P Niven	84	62	37	222	405	20.7	- 79.96
A Dobbin	68	42	40	179	329	20.7	- 55.24
M A Fitzgerald	68	75	62	288	493	13.8	-151.45
L Wyer	66	46	43	195	350	18.9	+ 11.81
A Maguire	61	54	55	140	310	19.7	- 64.68
C Llewellyn	58	50	42	274	424	13.7	- 65.26
J Osborne	53	46	36	177	312	17.0	- 82.43
J Titley	50	33	37	164	284	17.6	- 40.70
A Thornton	50	65	51	321	487	10.3	-192.34
P Carberry	46	40	36	143	265	17.4	+ 59.54
M Dwyer	45	47	45	210	347	13.0	- 56.94
G Bradley	44	22	35	203	304	14.5	+ 25.95
W Marston	44	42	32	274	392	11.2	-163.55
P Hide	39	27	19	160	245	15.9	- 42.07
C Maude	38	19	18	177	252	15.1	- 25.67
J R Kavanagh	37	29	29	250	345	10.7	-125.81
B Storey	36	47	43	242	368	9.8	-162.07
R Garrity	35	32	23	98	188	18.6	- 11.27
Richard Guest	33	32	32	204	301	11.0	- 88.29
J A McCarthy	32	28	28	111	199	16.1	- 12.63
A S Smith	29	18	18	147	212	13.7	- 57.02
D Gallagher	27	22	24	210	283	9.5	-118.19
B Powell	27	33	49	345	454	5.9	-237.23
N Williamson	24	17	19	48	108	22.2	+ 21.01
R Farrant	24	23	17	145	209	11.5	- 35.69
R Supple	24	50	46	234	354	6.8	-200.37
G McCourt	23	10	9	86	128	18.0	+ 40.55
Peter Hobbs	23	19	23	77	142	16.2	- 36.91
D O'Sullivan	23	13	17	147	200	11.5	- 33.86
T Eley	22	16	21	129	188	11.7	- 43.57
G Upton	22	32	25	192	271	8.1	-155.17
S McNeill	22	25	23	236	306	7.2	-140.95
J Railton	21	43	22	160	246	8.5	-125.84
J Lower	19	12	15	73	119	16.0	- 7.03
M Richards	18	23	22	128	191	9.4	- 28.16
J Ryan	16	19	15	108	158	10.1	+ 18.88
T Reed	16	18	20	144	198	8.1	-123.40
D Byrne	15	18	11	68	112	13.4	+ 26.38
J Callaghan	15	9	20	135	179	8.4	- 94.96
S Wynne	14	17	21	114	166	8.4	- 58.87
B M Clifford	13	11	13	109	146	8.9	- 33.52
N Bentley	12	7	9	65	93	12.9	- 15.78
L Harvey	12	15	18	180	225	5.3	-138.67
D Skyrme	11	6	7	49	73	15.1	+ 19.83
M Foster	11	12	11	88	122	9.0	- 71.37
T Jenks	11	14	16	138	179	6.1	-124.25
Martin Brennan	10	12	10	86	118	8.5	- 57.90
L O'Hara	10	12	13	100	135	7.4	- 35.90

LEADING CONDITIONAL JOCKEYS 1995-96

	1st	2nd	3rd	Unpl	Total Mts	Per cent	£1 Level Stake
R Johnson	53	61	62	299	475	11.2	-151.50
P G Cahill	33	24	21	120	198	16.7	+ 44.21
B Harding	30	42	21	206	299	10.0	-164.52
B Fenton	29	18	37	221	305	9.5	- 2.93
T J Murphy	26	18	21	117	182	14.3	- 18.50
T Dascombe	26	34	33	172	265	9.8	- 72.92
G E Tormey	24	22	21	140	207	11.6	- 69.97
D Walsh	21	19	21	118	179	11.7	+ 13.89
S Curran	17	23	28	174	242	7.0	- 65.75
L Aspell	16	11	8	74	109	14.7	- 8.62
G Hogan	16	20	21	214	271	5.9	-163.25
A J Roche	14	7	11	70	102	13.7	- 42.08
E Husband	14	17	14	84	129	10.9	- 40.68
K P Gaule	13	15	10	85	123	10.6	- 3.67
Christopher Webb	13	20	10	94	137	9.5	- 66.20
Guy Lewis	13	16	22	175	226	5.8	-113.62
P McLoughlin	12	14	20	121	167	7.2	- 78.50
E Callaghan	11	13	8	69	101	10.9	- 41.82
G Lee	11	11	11	75	108	10.2	- 39.90
R McGrath	10	10	7	46	73	13.7	- 12.04
F Leahy	10	8	12	84	114	8.8	+ 30.13
R Massey	10	14	11	101	136	7.4	- 80.37
D Parker	10	13	17	148	188	5.3	-115.75
O Burrows	9	9	6	43	67	13.4	- 16.40
C Rae	9	12	11	51	83	10.8	- 37.45
S Ryan	8	6	2	32	48	16.7	- 27.09
D Fortt	8	3	7	43	61	13.1	- 9.75
A Larnach	8	10	10	67	95	8.4	- 38.92
Sophie Mitchell	8	7	9	89	113	7.1	- 35.67
S Melrose	6	2	3	32	43	14.0	+ 7.25
B D Grattan	6	6	4	43	59	10.2	- 26.50
S Fox	6	15	8	61	90	6.7	- 54.42
W Fry	6	5	7	78	96	6.3	- 65.84
F Perratt	6	10	7	111	134	4.5	- 87.09
A Bates	5	3	2	11	21	23.8	+ 20.63
D Finnegan	5	3	4	39	51	9.8	- 11.60
G Ryan	5	5	11	48	69	7.2	- 24.75
J Supple	5	6	12	85	108	4.6	- 89.67
D Leahy	5	13	16	124	158	3.2	-111.60

LEADING AMATEUR RIDERS 1995-96

	1st	2nd	3rd	Unpl	Total Mts	Per cent	£1 Level Stake
Mr J Culloty	39	32	32	141	244	16.0	- 33.66
Mr P Henley	15	23	24	90	152	9.9	- 72.79
Mr C Bonner	14	31	18	104	167	8.4	-104.43
Mr K Whelan	9	10	9	51	79	11.4	+ 45.75
Mr Richard White	8	1	3	10	22	36.4	+ 13.25
Mr M Rimell	8	7	8	60	83	9.6	- 48.62
Mr J Jukes	7	3	3	38	51	13.7	+ 2.50
Mr C Storey	6	4	2	7	19	31.6	- 4.25
Mr E James	6	7	6	29	48	12.5	- 20.34
Mr S Swiers	6	6	7	36	55	10.9	+ 38.50

LEADING TRAINERS FIRST TIME OUT 1991-96

	Total W-R	Hurdles	Chases	Per cent	£1 Level Stake
M C Pipe	168-754	121-551	47-203	22.3	- 20.00
Mrs M Reveley	118-437	82-332	36-105	27.0	+ 14.03
N Twiston-Davies	83-409	54-286	29-123	20.3	+ 39.66
D Nicholson	80-393	46-246	34-147	20.4	+256.22
K C Bailey	65-374	27-209	38-165	17.4	- 35.19
N J Henderson	64-347	31-231	33-116	18.4	- 66.67
P J Hobbs	64-398	42-289	22-109	16.1	+ 14.99
O Sherwood	61-276	40-172	21-104	22.1	- 5.21
J White	54-348	37-258	17-90	15.5	-135.33
G Richards	54-352	18-202	36-150	15.3	-107.32
J T Gifford	51-365	29-220	22-145	14.0	- 45.52
J G FitzGerald	42-267	25-203	17-64	15.7	+ 61.39
Mrs J Pitman	42-285	26-200	16-85	14.7	+ 94.55
M D Hammond	39-312	24-232	15-80	12.5	-114.29
Capt T A Forster	36-296	17-176	19-120	12.2	- 88.74
Miss H C Knight	35-263	23-176	12-87	13.3	- 36.58
C P E Brooks	32-202	10-124	22-78	15.8	- 27.95
P F Nicholls	31-183	14-100	17-83	16.9	- 24.66
G B Balding	31-304	16-216	15-88	10.2	- 93.94
J H Johnson	30-228	13-159	17-69	13.2	+ 45.47
Andrew Turnell	29-161	12-91	17-70	18.0	+ 23.98
G M Moore	25-197	22-163	3-34	12.7	- 57.66
C R Egerton	22-112	15-85	7-27	19.6	+ 51.72
R Akehurst	22-123	21-108	1-15	17.9	- 19.04
D R C Elsworth	21-138	17-121	4-17	15.2	- 16.61
S Sherwood	21-158	6-92	15-66	13.3	- 34.73
J J O'Neill	21-206	15-157	6-49	10.2	- 81.53
T Thomson Jones	20-117	13-85	7-32	17.1	+ 36.13
J A B Old	20-144	19-131	1-13	13.9	+ 39.99
D R Gandolfo	20-187	13-151	7-36	10.7	- 25.43
Miss C Saunders	19-47	0-0	19-47	40.4	+ 29.20
R H Alner	18-121	4-71	14-50	14.9	- 1.89
N Tinkler	17-140	13-125	4-15	12.1	- 79.08
M H Tompkins	16-113	16-108	0-5	14.2	- 58.78
R Lee	16-154	6-84	10-70	10.4	- 35.90
J A C Edwards	16-189	9-123	7-66	8.5	- 63.25
J R Jenkins	16-216	12-181	4-35	7.4	-149.82
S Christian	15-110	11-76	4-34	13.6	- 25.62
F Murphy	15-146	12-93	3-53	10.3	- 46.19
G Harwood	14-66	11-56	3-10	21.2	- 15.87
C W Thornton	14-77	14-70	0-7	18.2	+ 8.80
R J O'Sullivan	14-91	6-66	8-25	15.4	- 5.96
R Rowe	14-161	8-103	6-58	8.7	- 61.74
R J Hodges	14-273	6-191	8-82	5.1	-174.28
D Murray Smith	13-50	8-32	5-18	26.0	+ 38.90
K R Burke	13-122	9-93	4-29	10.7	- 11.50
J M Bradley	13-165	7-133	6-32	7.9	- 66.05
O Brennan	13-169	6-135	7-34	7.7	- 46.27
I A Balding	12-53	9-47	3-6	22.6	- 16.05
R Allan	12-77	7-62	5-15	15.6	- 26.01
J M Jefferson	12-85	8-70	4-15	14.1	+ 80.82
Mrs D Haine	12-93	8-69	4-24	12.9	- 31.21
J S King	12-146	6-99	6-47	8.2	- 40.75
Mrs J G Retter	11-131	7-106	4-25	8.4	+ 23.58

	Total W-R	Hurdles	Chases	Per cent	£1 Level Stake
M W Easterby	11-140	5-99	6-41	7.9	- 66.67
D H Barons	11-142	7-93	4-49	7.7	- 39.50
N A Gaselee	11-147	4-81	7-66	7.5	- 67.25
M R Channon	10-42	8-39	2-3	23.8	+ 46.76
C J Mann	10-58	8-43	2-15	17.2	+ 21.21
D M Grissell	10-105	6-79	4-26	9.5	+ 34.38
J Mackie	10-126	7-93	3-33	7.9	- 54.25
D Burchell	10-139	10-122	0-17	7.2	- 73.62
S Mellor	10-139	8-122	2-17	7.2	- 37.62
J R Upson	10-145	1-77	9-68	6.9	- 93.91
S Dow	9-87	6-79	3-8	10.3	+ 4.33
Mrs S A Bramall	9-106	4-59	5-47	8.5	- 14.67
R Curtis	9-106	1-65	8-41	8.5	- 75.16
C D Broad	9-119	5-101	4-18	7.6	- 57.54
P Monteith	9-130	3-103	6-27	6.9	-102.96
L Lungo	9-156	7-139	2-17	5.8	- 69.19
Mrs S J Smith	9-193	7-130	2-63	4.7	- 27.50
J Fanshawe	8-22	8-22	0-0	36.4	+ 10.25
Mrs J R Ramsden	8-44	8-40	0-4	18.2	- 14.76
W R Muir	8-45	8-45	0-0	17.8	+ 33.33
N B Mason	8-68	5-46	3-22	11.8	+ 4.00
T P Tate	8-78	1-53	7-25	10.3	- 24.25
Denys Smith	8-109	5-88	3-21	7.3	- 77.39
K A Morgan	8-128	6-105	2-23	6.3	- 75.40
P Beaumont	8-132	6-89	2-43	6.1	- 58.45
W G M Turner	8-146	6-130	2-16	5.5	- 33.50
R Barber	7-23	0-0	7-23	30.4	+ 17.12
Lady Herries	7-37	6-31	1-6	18.9	+ 7.26
P C Haslam	7-39	7-37	0-2	17.9	- 7.62
C James	7-40	6-35	1-5	17.5	+ 82.83
J Pearce	7-41	5-38	2-3	17.1	+ 28.11
T P McGovern	7-48	5-39	2-9	14.6	- 8.42
J Akehurst	7-56	7-56	0-0	12.5	+ 26.25
Miss L A Perratt	7-59	6-51	1-8	11.9	- 31.81
D Moffatt	7-75	7-73	0-2	9.3	- 18.89
J G M O'Shea	7-76	6-68	1-8	9.2	- 25.12
B Preece	7-95	7-88	0-7	7.4	- 15.47
R Hollinshead	7-96	7-89	0-7	7.3	- 57.88
K S Bridgwater	7-107	5-102	2-5	6.5	- 44.62
W Clay	7-163	6-146	1-17	4.3	- 69.75
M J Camacho	6-21	6-20	0-1	28.6	+ 35.67
H Wellstead	6-21	0-0	6-21	28.6	- 7.83
Miss J S Doyle	6-37	6-36	0-1	16.2	+ 17.00
J A Glover	6-54	6-48	0-6	11.1	- 8.02
P T Dalton	6-56	2-41	4-15	10.7	+ 22.00
Miss B Sanders	6-59	6-56	0-3	10.2	- 28.12
S E Kettlewell	6-60	4-53	2-7	10.0	+ 4.50
P D Evans	6-69	6-66	0-3	8.7	- 29.75
W Storey	6-76	6-72	0-4	7.9	- 7.67
M A Barnes	6-85	5-69	1-16	7.1	- 14.37
C Weedon	6-87	5-75	1-12	6.9	- 48.30
B S Rothwell	6-90	5-67	1-23	6.7	- 4.33
F Jordan	6-120	6-106	0-14	5.0	- 65.50
C Parker	6-127	3-90	3-37	4.7	- 53.00
A Moore	6-137	4-104	2-33	4.4	- 8.00
R Dickin	6-144	3-98	3-46	4.2	-114.62

LEADING TRAINERS BY MONTH 1991-96
June/July

	Total W-R	Hurdles	Chases	Per cent	£1 Level Stake
M C Pipe	22-55	14-36	8-19	40.0	+ 8.97
J White	22-87	12-54	10-33	25.3	+ 2.48
G B Balding	11-24	8-16	3-8	45.8	+ 53.18
P J Hobbs	8-29	5-20	3-9	27.6	- 8.45
K R Burke	5-13	4-8	1-5	38.5	+ 19.00
N Twiston-Davies	4-18	1-12	3-6	22.2	+ 4.00
A Harrison	3-5	3-4	0-1	60.0	+ 22.83
G Richards	3-6	1-2	2-4	50.0	+ 9.13
C J Mann	3-9	3-6	0-3	33.3	+ 27.50
N Tinkler	3-10	2-8	1-2	30.0	- 0.75
Miss L Siddall	3-12	2-7	1-5	25.0	+ 3.50
B S Rothwell	3-12	1-4	2-8	25.0	+ 10.63
M D Hammond	3-13	0-8	3-5	23.1	+ 2.75
S Mellor	3-14	2-7	1-7	21.4	- 6.70
W Clay	3-28	2-24	1-4	10.7	+ 4.00

August

	Total W-R	Hurdles	Chases	Per cent	£1 Level Stake
M C Pipe	66-152	44-109	22-43	43.4	- 0.54
J White	51-165	32-99	19-66	30.9	- 25.07
P J Hobbs	34-88	24-61	10-27	38.6	+ 15.19
M D Hammond	17-57	11-41	6-16	29.8	- 4.00
J R Jenkins	16-81	12-65	4-16	19.8	- 33.00
R J O'Sullivan	14-29	8-17	6-12	48.3	+ 36.23
G Richards	13-61	4-33	9-28	21.3	- 21.43
J G M O'Shea	12-41	10-33	2-8	29.3	+ 2.04
K C Bailey	10-31	4-18	6-13	32.3	- 7.82
Mrs M Reveley	9-21	9-19	0-2	42.9	- 0.13
N Tinkler	9-37	8-35	1-2	24.3	- 17.48
K R Burke	8-26	7-23	1-3	30.8	+ 7.38
R Curtis	8-37	1-11	7-26	21.6	- 16.20
J R Upson	8-46	3-20	5-26	17.4	- 3.96
R J Hodges	8-50	5-28	3-22	16.0	- 21.57
M C Chapman	8-52	4-39	4-13	15.4	+ 14.75
J M Bradley	8-58	4-38	4-20	13.8	- 20.98
D Moffatt	7-15	7-15	0-0	46.7	+ 7.47
C J Mann	7-16	7-15	0-1	43.8	+ 6.68
R Lee	7-20	0-6	7-14	35.0	+ 9.50
N Twiston-Davies	7-25	5-19	2-6	28.0	+ 13.68
M A Barnes	6-13	5-11	1-2	46.2	+ 25.73
Mrs S C Bradburne	6-24	0-8	6-16	25.0	+ 29.19
Mrs A Knight	6-45	6-44	0-1	13.3	+ 29.00
W G M Turner	6-53	6-53	0-0	11.3	- 9.25
R T Juckes	6-68	3-53	3-15	8.8	- 19.50

September

	Total W-R	Hurdles	Chases	Per cent	£1 Level Stake
M C Pipe	48-157	35-115	13-42	30.6	- 16.73
N Twiston-Davies	32-107	25-77	7-30	29.9	+ 14.66
P J Hobbs	31-109	17-59	14-50	28.4	+ 19.93
K C Bailey	25-78	11-31	14-47	32.1	+ 35.26
G Richards	21-82	9-42	12-40	25.6	- 4.14
Mrs M Reveley	18-59	12-46	6-13	30.5	+ 5.21
M D Hammond	14-68	10-55	4-13	20.6	- 22.83
J White	14-85	8-54	6-31	16.5	- 22.61
O Sherwood	13-32	3-12	10-20	40.6	+ 11.47
G M Moore	13-59	11-46	2-13	22.0	- 11.66
N Tinkler	12-40	11-38	1-2	30.0	+ 0.28
J G M O'Shea	11-41	5-26	6-15	26.8	- 4.79
J R Jenkins	11-99	10-73	1-26	11.1	- 23.64
J H Johnson	9-37	2-18	7-19	24.3	+ 12.63
J Wade	9-43	6-31	3-12	20.9	+ 32.63
Miss L A Perratt	8-31	5-20	3-11	25.8	- 2.12
W G M Turner	8-32	7-30	1-2	25.0	+ 35.12
J J O'Neill	8-41	7-29	1-12	19.5	+ 28.58
Miss H C Knight	7-30	3-15	4-15	23.3	- 2.37
D R Gandolfo	7-35	4-20	3-15	20.0	+ 10.75
Denys Smith	7-56	3-40	4-16	12.5	- 26.00
G B Balding	7-70	4-36	3-34	10.0	- 22.29
C P E Brooks	6-12	3-3	3-9	50.0	+ 23.00
P F Nicholls	6-24	2-13	4-11	25.0	- 2.62

October

	Total W-R	Hurdles	Chases	Per cent	£1 Level Stake
Mrs M Reveley	73-206	49-141	24-65	35.4	+ 30.13
M C Pipe	50-212	40-168	10-44	23.6	- 39.21
K C Bailey	43-177	15-71	28-106	24.3	- 15.05
G Richards	40-156	12-68	28-88	25.6	- 6.66
N Twiston-Davies	38-201	25-121	13-80	18.9	- 34.29
P J Hobbs	33-165	13-87	20-78	20.0	+ 45.60
D Nicholson	31-122	15-64	16-58	25.4	+ 10.00
O Sherwood	25-93	18-48	7-45	26.9	+ 3.83
G B Balding	25-158	10-82	15-76	15.8	- 58.37
Andrew Turnell	23-81	7-31	16-50	28.4	+ 53.06
P F Nicholls	21-80	7-32	14-48	26.3	+ 18.99
J H Johnson	21-97	10-57	11-40	21.6	+ 53.32
Miss H C Knight	20-109	10-71	10-38	18.3	- 20.35
J White	20-114	16-78	4-36	17.5	- 30.88
Mrs J Pitman	19-86	6-34	13-52	22.1	+ 0.21
G M Moore	19-88	13-70	6-18	21.6	- 26.45
N J Henderson	18-76	3-26	15-50	23.7	+ 6.17
J T Gifford	18-120	7-50	11-70	15.0	- 35.09
P Monteith	17-66	11-44	6-22	25.8	+ 12.18
J J O'Neill	16-78	12-50	4-28	20.5	- 7.86
M D Hammond	15-112	7-73	8-39	13.4	- 52.87
S Sherwood	14-68	3-35	11-33	20.6	+ 10.25
N Tinkler	14-79	12-71	2-8	17.7	- 35.96
D R Gandolfo	14-85	6-52	8-33	16.5	+ 36.96

November

	Total W-R	Hurdles	Chases	Per cent	£1 Level Stake
Mrs M Reveley	93-350	60-240	33-110	26.6	- 50.57
M C Pipe	82-343	64-241	18-102	23.9	- 12.14
D Nicholson	78-292	41-158	37-134	26.7	+ 22.37
G Richards	70-289	27-142	43-147	24.2	- 8.36
J T Gifford	59-297	26-131	33-166	19.9	- 3.16
N Twiston-Davies	52-283	29-158	23-125	18.4	- 33.89
K C Bailey	48-232	20-87	28-145	20.7	- 18.76
N J Henderson	42-171	20-89	22-82	24.6	- 33.49
O Sherwood	42-173	23-95	19-78	24.3	- 23.86
J G FitzGerald	40-157	22-106	18-51	25.5	+ 54.21
Capt T A Forster	36-187	13-84	23-103	19.3	- 41.54
Mrs J Pitman	35-173	12-97	23-76	20.2	+ 76.52
P J Hobbs	35-218	19-118	16-100	16.1	- 1.15
G B Balding	33-233	15-121	18-112	14.2	- 10.43
J H Johnson	25-127	15-69	10-58	19.7	+ 23.30
Miss H C Knight	25-132	13-75	12-57	18.9	- 13.74
C P E Brooks	23-122	5-55	18-67	18.9	- 29.72
N Tinkler	22-128	14-105	8-23	17.2	- 47.73
G M Moore	21-141	18-112	3-29	14.9	- 16.32
J J O'Neill	21-146	10-98	11-48	14.4	- 77.78
M D Hammond	20-180	9-116	11-64	11.1	-111.33
P F Nicholls	18-128	5-39	13-89	14.1	- 40.79
R J Hodges	17-174	8-93	9-81	9.8	- 52.50
J A C Edwards	16-87	5-42	11-45	18.4	+ 35.29

December

	Total W-R	Hurdles	Chases	Per cent	£1 Level Stake
M C Pipe	90-372	60-253	30-119	24.2	+ 11.07
D Nicholson	81-272	36-128	45-144	29.8	+ 26.17
Mrs M Reveley	48-183	31-129	17-54	26.2	- 0.00
N Twiston-Davies	38-230	18-126	20-104	16.5	- 28.86
N J Henderson	36-170	16-93	20-77	21.2	+ 12.96
P J Hobbs	32-164	15-79	17-85	19.5	+ 4.96
G Richards	31-194	9-83	22-111	16.0	- 82.06
M D Hammond	31-194	16-126	15-68	16.0	- 3.91
J T Gifford	31-199	11-83	20-116	15.6	- 40.45
J G FitzGerald	28-161	12-99	16-62	17.4	- 42.06
K C Bailey	28-178	8-72	20-106	15.7	- 52.24
O Sherwood	25-130	15-76	10-54	19.2	- 35.65
Mrs J Pitman	24-156	12-80	12-76	15.4	- 55.18
Miss H C Knight	23-123	14-71	9-52	18.7	+ 6.51
R J Hodges	21-173	11-106	10-67	12.1	- 7.85
P F Nicholls	20-97	5-33	15-64	20.6	- 21.58
D R C Elsworth	19-102	13-75	6-27	18.6	+ 1.24
Capt T A Forster	18-122	4-50	14-72	14.8	- 18.64
G B Balding	18-186	8-99	10-87	9.7	- 88.47
R Akehurst	16-73	15-62	1-11	21.9	- 8.61
N Tinkler	16-87	13-70	3-17	18.4	- 20.40
C P E Brooks	16-95	2-40	14-55	16.8	- 40.75
J H Johnson	16-98	9-51	7-47	16.3	- 1.36
G M Moore	16-106	14-86	2-20	15.1	- 16.42

January

	Total W-R	Hurdles	Chases	Per cent	£1 Level Stake
M C Pipe	94-419	62-289	32-130	22.4	- 91.37
D Nicholson	63-254	32-138	31-116	24.8	+ 38.65
Mrs M Reveley	54-221	35-158	19-63	24.4	- 37.66
Mrs J Pitman	36-201	16-108	20-93	17.9	- 17.55
N Twiston-Davies	32-215	19-136	13-79	14.9	- 47.09
G Richards	30-151	12-80	18-71	19.9	- 20.55
Capt T A Forster	26-135	9-66	17-69	19.3	+ 24.90
J T Gifford	22-228	6-109	16-119	9.6	- 64.31
M D Hammond	19-181	11-116	8-65	10.5	- 95.98
J White	18-108	14-80	4-28	16.7	+ 3.54
Miss H C Knight	18-116	11-76	7-40	15.5	- 26.64
J G FitzGerald	18-124	13-82	5-42	14.5	+ 9.33
N J Henderson	18-149	8-87	10-62	12.1	- 71.26
K C Bailey	18-152	5-80	13-72	11.8	- 43.06
T Thomson Jones	16-85	11-57	5-28	18.8	+ 18.43
J A C Edwards	16-106	10-54	6-52	15.1	- 33.19
G B Balding	15-166	10-83	5-83	9.0	- 73.70
S Dow	14-53	14-47	0-6	26.4	+ 5.07
O Sherwood	14-129	8-74	6-55	10.9	- 83.16
P J Hobbs	14-173	7-94	7-79	8.1	-102.12
N Tinkler	13-76	8-56	5-20	17.1	- 18.84
Andrew Turnell	13-82	8-41	5-41	15.9	- 30.70
J H Johnson	13-105	4-57	9-48	12.4	- 20.75
Miss B Sanders	12-49	11-42	1-7	24.5	- 9.45

February

	Total W-R	Hurdles	Chases	Per cent	£1 Level Stake
M C Pipe	96-444	68-306	28-138	21.6	- 72.42
D Nicholson	63-287	30-162	33-125	22.0	+120.59
Mrs M Reveley	42-202	27-141	15-61	20.8	- 49.11
N J Henderson	41-178	21-114	20-64	23.0	+ 44.16
O Sherwood	32-145	17-81	15-64	22.1	+ 14.45
Mrs J Pitman	31-198	13-98	18-100	15.7	+ 1.52
J G FitzGerald	30-157	18-100	12-57	19.1	+ 8.42
J T Gifford	30-228	9-121	21-107	13.2	- 83.50
M D Hammond	25-156	15-107	10-49	16.0	+ 2.89
P J Hobbs	24-154	11-98	13-56	15.6	- 25.76
G Richards	24-178	7-85	17-93	13.5	- 98.49
N Twiston-Davies	23-254	13-162	10-92	9.1	- 95.96
C P E Brooks	19-107	6-56	13-51	17.8	+ 6.38
Miss H C Knight	19-126	15-72	4-54	15.1	- 13.20
Capt T A Forster	19-150	4-56	15-94	12.7	- 26.86
G B Balding	18-151	6-84	12-67	11.9	+ 18.15
Miss C Saunders	17-48	0-0	17-48	35.4	+ 4.29
Andrew Turnell	17-82	7-42	10-40	20.7	+ 56.58
J A B Old	17-86	14-77	3-9	19.8	+ 19.98
J White	17-112	13-79	4-33	15.2	- 47.16
K C Bailey	17-142	8-79	9-63	12.0	- 61.56
C R Egerton	15-61	9-31	6-30	24.6	+ 25.01
T Thomson Jones	15-80	10-51	5-29	18.8	- 22.67
P F Nicholls	15-97	7-51	8-46	15.5	- 14.22

March

	Total W-R	Hurdles	Chases	Per cent	£1 Level Stake
M C Pipe	104-565	73-415	31-150	18.4	- 57.45
D Nicholson	52-274	29-170	23-104	19.0	- 58.42
Mrs M Reveley	45-227	36-164	9-63	19.8	- 20.42
P J Hobbs	40-225	25-136	15-89	17.8	+ 21.33
N J Henderson	37-242	25-155	12-87	15.3	- 49.54
J T Gifford	37-246	14-127	23-119	15.0	- 49.83
G Richards	34-202	11-86	23-116	16.8	- 33.90
O Sherwood	33-173	16-98	17-75	19.1	- 32.17
N Twiston-Davies	30-260	18-165	12-95	11.5	- 34.42
R J Hodges	27-166	13-89	14-77	16.3	+ 22.65
Capt T A Forster	26-187	5-78	21-109	13.9	- 38.33
M D Hammond	25-173	16-114	9-59	14.5	- 54.90
J G FitzGerald	24-146	15-108	9-38	16.4	- 43.54
K C Bailey	24-196	14-101	10-95	12.2	- 89.03
Miss H C Knight	22-156	10-97	12-59	14.1	- 76.55
Miss C Saunders	20-51	0-0	20-51	39.2	+ 21.04
P F Nicholls	20-143	6-62	14-81	14.0	- 48.05
J A B Old	19-102	16-85	3-17	18.6	- 8.86
C P E Brooks	19-113	7-50	12-63	16.8	- 29.23
J White	19-116	11-82	8-34	16.4	- 30.92
L Lungo	18-105	14-84	4-21	17.1	- 13.13
O Brennan	18-112	14-86	4-26	16.1	- 1.01
Mrs J Pitman	18-199	10-115	8-84	9.0	- 72.62
G M Moore	17-106	13-85	4-21	16.0	- 47.35

April

	Total W-R	Hurdles	Chases	Per cent	£1 Level Stake
M C Pipe	69-369	49-265	20-104	18.7	- 87.24
K C Bailey	49-256	21-146	28-110	19.1	+ 22.28
Mrs M Reveley	48-200	32-143	16-57	24.0	- 43.26
N Twiston-Davies	40-236	23-141	17-95	16.9	+ 40.15
P J Hobbs	36-185	20-113	16-72	19.5	- 15.30
G Richards	34-233	12-108	22-125	14.6	- 27.02
J T Gifford	31-188	16-86	15-102	16.5	- 24.47
D Nicholson	30-195	21-123	9-72	15.4	- 15.86
G B Balding	23-168	8-96	15-72	13.7	- 8.61
J G FitzGerald	22-115	13-76	9-39	19.1	+ 0.31
O Sherwood	22-133	13-78	9-55	16.5	- 21.13
N J Henderson	22-180	12-117	10-63	12.2	-101.80
Miss H C Knight	21-124	15-84	6-40	16.9	+ 1.60
O Brennan	19-99	11-72	8-27	19.2	- 4.10
Mrs J Pitman	19-161	10-81	9-80	11.8	- 4.19
L Lungo	18-96	12-81	6-15	18.8	- 23.42
M D Hammond	18-165	12-103	6-62	10.9	- 61.80
Capt T A Forster	17-131	6-62	11-69	13.0	- 32.62
J A B Old	15-82	8-65	7-17	18.3	+ 9.75
P F Nicholls	15-105	3-44	12-61	14.3	- 39.32
R J Hodges	15-137	3-68	12-69	10.9	- 74.80
C R Egerton	14-49	9-32	5-17	28.6	+ 20.83
J R Upson	14-69	5-37	9-32	20.3	+ 13.75
P Cheesbrough	14-102	5-45	9-57	13.7	- 47.44

May

	Total W-R	Hurdles	Chases	Per cent	£1 Level Stake
M C Pipe	137-464	96-348	41-116	29.5	+ 14.01
K C Bailey	59-222	19-112	40-110	26.6	+ 2.28
Mrs M Reveley	46-153	30-112	16-41	30.1	- 16.52
N Twiston-Davies	38-162	24-96	14-66	23.5	+ 3.40
G Richards	31-122	10-61	21-61	25.4	- 3.65
O Brennan	29-143	21-115	8-28	20.3	+ 6.10
P J Hobbs	28-141	12-80	16-61	19.9	- 16.64
N J Henderson	26-111	16-61	10-50	23.4	- 22.83
J White	25-166	16-109	9-57	15.1	- 53.77
D Nicholson	24-80	19-55	5-25	30.0	+ 30.09
Miss H C Knight	22-87	16-65	6-22	25.3	+ 35.67
G B Balding	22-128	9-72	13-56	17.2	+ 10.69
J H Johnson	20-118	10-68	10-50	16.9	- 18.70
M D Hammond	19-98	13-60	6-38	19.4	- 21.99
R J Hodges	19-105	7-57	12-48	18.1	+ 4.80
J A C Edwards	16-98	5-57	11-41	16.3	- 44.62
P Beaumont	15-93	7-59	8-34	16.1	- 5.26
P Cheesbrough	14-65	5-31	9-34	21.5	- 5.18
G M Moore	14-77	13-62	1-15	18.2	- 15.29
P F Nicholls	13-54	2-25	11-29	24.1	- 14.60
Mrs J G Retter	13-68	7-49	6-19	19.1	+ 63.88
L Lungo	12-39	11-35	1-4	30.8	+ 11.83
D Burchell	12-61	10-45	2-16	19.7	+ 16.31
Mrs J Pitman	11-74	5-37	6-37	14.9	- 21.13

LEADING TRAINERS BY TYPE OF RACE 1991-96

Novice Hurdles

	W-R	Per cent	£1 Level Stake		W-R	Per cent	£1 Level Stake
M C Pipe	331-1116	29.7	- 16.35	N Tinkler	35-246	14.2	-137.58
D Nicholson	155-625	24.8	+136.98	L Lungo	34-241	14.1	- 56.73
Mrs M Reveley	153-516	29.7	- 33.10	I A Balding	31-112	27.7	- 15.55
N Twiston-Davies	108-614	17.6	- 33.70	J A B Old	31-182	17.0	+ 5.62
K C Bailey	86-479	18.0	- 68.04	J H Johnson	31-283	11.0	- 40.58
O Sherwood	80-364	22.0	- 43.26	Capt T A Forster	30-280	10.7	- 74.69
N J Henderson	80-428	18.7	- 67.95	C R Egerton	27-133	20.3	- 31.97
P J Hobbs	78-431	18.1	- 11.90	D R Gandolfo	27-224	12.1	- 91.01
G M Moore	70-351	19.9	- 19.95	J R Jenkins	27-382	7.1	-258.73
J White	65-416	15.6	- 139.07	Andrew Turnell	26-201	12.9	- 71.28
G Richards	63-419	15.0	- 103.02	J J O'Neill	25-232	10.8	- 88.93
M D Hammond	61-436	14.0	- 205.04	P F Nicholls	23-149	15.4	- 35.12
J T Gifford	57-455	12.5	- 127.15	T Thomson Jones	23-150	15.3	- 24.06
Miss H C Knight	49-303	16.2	- 43.40	K A Morgan	22-135	16.3	+ 22.48
R Akehurst	46-222	20.7	- 11.77	P Monteith	22-231	9.5	- 36.65
Mrs J Pitman	42-304	13.8	- 37.16	O Brennan	21-185	11.4	- 65.31
M H Tompkins	39-197	19.8	- 61.26	J A C Edwards	21-220	9.5	-127.26
J G FitzGerald	38-300	12.7	- 91.66	W Clay	21-248	8.5	- 59.45
G B Balding	37-360	10.3	- 150.67	R J O'Sullivan	20-136	14.7	- 25.65
D R C Elsworth	36-225	16.0	- 10.58				

Handicap Hurdles

	W-R	Per cent	£1 Level Stake		W-R	Per cent	£1 Level Stake
M C Pipe	136-779	17.5	- 117.68	R Rowe	26-182	14.3	- 16.31
Mrs M Reveley	125-533	23.5	- 48.98	J White	26-205	12.7	- 94.17
N Twiston-Davies	59-343	17.2	- 10.54	N Tinkler	26-208	12.5	- 84.40
P J Hobbs	59-345	17.1	- 30.79	J T Gifford	26-234	11.1	-104.35
G Richards	44-271	16.2	- 31.60	J L Spearing	25-152	16.4	+ 20.75
Miss H C Knight	41-192	21.4	+ 35.37	J A B Old	25-152	16.4	+ 66.06
G B Balding	41-357	11.5	- 84.33	O Sherwood	25-155	16.1	- 22.96
D Nicholson	37-211	17.5	+ 3.93	K C Bailey	25-217	11.5	- 82.81
M D Hammond	37-318	11.6	- 104.89	G Harwood	23-104	22.1	- 7.30
J J O'Neill	35-244	14.3	- 26.38	R H Buckler	23-143	16.1	+190.46
N J Henderson	33-230	14.3	- 42.69	J Mackie	23-148	15.5	+ 19.92
Mrs J Pitman	33-262	12.6	+ 10.12	K A Morgan	22-207	10.6	- 50.37
R J Hodges	33-290	11.4	- 61.62	J L Harris	20-142	14.1	+ 7.88
S Dow	31-158	19.6	- 17.76	P Monteith	19-124	15.3	+ 14.97
J G FitzGerald	31-192	16.1	+ 26.43	Capt T A Forster	19-140	13.6	- 10.29
J R Jenkins	30-327	9.2	- 117.95	W Clay	19-219	8.7	- 79.87
Mrs J G Retter	28-210	13.3	- 7.29	Miss B Sanders	18-89	20.2	- 29.41
O Brennan	28-238	11.8	- 57.31	J H Johnson	18-165	10.9	- 53.34
G M Moore	28-238	11.8	- 103.87	R Dickin	18-172	10.5	- 53.04
L Lungo	26-141	18.4	- 20.38				

Novice Chases

	W-R	Per cent	£1 Level Stake		W-R	Per cent	£1 Level Stake
M C Pipe	131-390	33.6	- 42.06	Andrew Turnell	28-155	18.1	- 3.86
D Nicholson	100-320	31.3	+ 36.90	J H Johnson	27-166	16.3	- 60.08
G Richards	93-329	28.3	- 40.49	D R Gandolfo	24-97	24.7	+ 6.11
K C Bailey	90-353	25.5	- 12.58	R H Alner	24-113	21.2	- 21.07
J T Gifford	71-362	19.6	- 40.46	M D Hammond	24-144	16.7	- 35.17
Mrs M Reveley	63-174	36.2	- 11.98	J J O'Neill	19-95	20.0	- 39.39
N Twiston-Davies	62-321	19.3	- 65.33	N A Gaselee	19-117	16.2	- 14.42
N J Henderson	56-198	28.3	- 23.02	Mrs S A Bramall	18-130	13.8	+ 63.80
O Sherwood	55-194	28.4	- 33.17	G M Moore	17-94	18.1	- 41.61
Mrs J Pitman	49-252	19.4	- 58.90	O Brennan	16-72	22.2	- 14.89
J White	46-213	21.6	- 26.47	C Parker	15-84	17.9	- 19.92
C P E Brooks	40-143	28.0	- 3.50	J R Upson	15-96	15.6	+ 20.34
Capt T A Forster	40-204	19.6	- 26.15	W G Reed	15-104	14.4	+ 53.13
P F Nicholls	36-177	20.3	- 31.90	P Beaumont	15-104	14.4	- 38.51
Miss H C Knight	36-181	19.9	- 25.23	P Monteith	14-73	19.2	+ 5.92
G B Balding	36-222	16.2	+ 7.32	N Tinkler	13-46	28.3	- 10.81
P J Hobbs	33-188	17.6	- 76.06	D R C Elsworth	13-68	19.1	- 19.51
J G FitzGerald	31-113	27.4	+ 17.67	M W Easterby	13-81	16.0	- 47.13
S Sherwood	29-110	26.4	+ 20.30	Mrs S C Bradburne	13-139	9.4	- 15.52
J A C Edwards	29-139	20.9	- 44.39	R J Hodges	13-156	8.3	-109.86

Handicap Chases

	W-R	Per cent	£1 Level Stake		W-R	Per cent	£1 Level Stake
G Richards	115-510	22.5	- 62.64	Andrew Turnell	36-176	20.5	+ 8.60
P J Hobbs	108-476	22.7	+ 50.42	R H Alner	35-180	19.4	- 3.73
M C Pipe	106-535	19.8	- 74.91	R Lee	35-242	14.5	- 44.13
K C Bailey	98-478	20.5	- 53.04	Mrs S J Smith	35-245	14.3	+111.02
D Nicholson	91-427	21.3	- 53.50	J R Upson	33-208	15.9	- 36.70
Mrs M Reveley	89-350	25.4	- 20.49	F Murphy	31-208	14.9	- 16.40
Capt T A Forster	72-380	18.9	- 34.22	P Monteith	30-138	21.7	+ 42.79
J T Gifford	68-425	16.0	- 94.92	Miss H C Knight	29-187	15.5	- 64.71
G B Balding	66-435	15.2	+ 13.65	J S King	28-178	15.7	- 33.15
N J Henderson	65-331	19.6	- 37.19	Mrs S C Bradburne	28-227	12.3	- 56.98
N Twiston-Davies	63-402	15.7	- 26.76	R Dickin	28-247	11.3	- 53.03
Mrs J Pitman	62-346	17.9	+ 9.33	M W Easterby	27-127	21.3	- 9.33
M D Hammond	60-310	19.4	- 13.52	R Curtis	27-141	19.1	- 28.15
R J Hodges	58-354	16.4	- 35.44	J White	27-177	15.3	- 51.63
P F Nicholls	57-288	19.8	- 41.53	P Cheesbrough	26-166	15.7	- 20.85
C P E Brooks	48-220	21.8	+ 14.86	O Brennan	24-133	18.0	- 18.85
J H Johnson	47-258	18.2	+ 52.49	N A Gaselee	24-175	13.7	- 29.50
J G FitzGerald	45-221	20.4	- 26.70	S Sherwood	22-143	15.4	- 54.70
O Sherwood	43-273	15.8	- 67.37	C Parker	22-153	14.4	- 55.78
J A C Edwards	39-245	15.9	- 24.34				

Selling

	W-R	Per cent	£1 Level Stake		W-R	Per cent	£1 Level Stake
M C Pipe	101-426	23.7	- 65.74	A Moore	10-131	7.6	- 63.75
J White	49-223	22.0	- 38.56	P Beaumont	9-35	25.7	+ 37.50
N Tinkler	25-101	24.8	- 3.60	R P C Hoad	9-76	11.8	+ 16.13
W Clay	23-220	10.5	+ 52.88	H J Manners	9-93	9.7	- 11.25
D Burchell	22-124	17.7	+ 11.50	B J Llewellyn	9-99	9.1	+ 37.96
R J Hodges	18-194	9.3	- 44.04	K A Morgan	8-66	12.1	- 14.75
O Brennan	15-93	16.1	+ 11.03	D J Wintle	8-98	8.2	- 39.50
J R Jenkins	14-153	9.2	- 70.54	R G Frost	8-123	6.5	- 52.00
P J Hobbs	13-57	22.8	+ 23.08	R J O'Sullivan	7-24	29.2	+ 2.28
W G M Turner	13-103	12.6	- 0.12	M D I Usher	7-26	26.9	+ 5.38
K R Burke	13-119	10.9	- 17.17	Mrs S J Smith	7-60	11.7	- 9.50
J S Moore	12-62	19.4	+ 54.00	R Hollinshead	7-65	10.8	- 33.59
J Parkes	12-117	10.3	- 19.52	P D Evans	7-73	9.6	- 31.52
J M Bradley	12-141	8.5	- 20.75	Miss S J Wilton	7-89	7.9	- 41.00
N Twiston-Davies	11-50	22.0	- 2.25	Miss B Sanders	6-14	42.9	+ 17.55
P Monteith	11-65	16.9	+ 5.42	G B Balding	6-28	21.4	+ 15.83
Mrs M Reveley	11-69	15.9	- 18.99	J G FitzGerald	6-39	15.4	+ 1.75
J Ffitch-Heyes	11-78	14.1	- 5.55	F J Yardley	6-41	14.6	+ 10.70
M D Hammond	10-57	17.5	- 12.60	C C Trietline	6-57	10.5	- 23.64
C L Popham	10-89	11.2	+ 2.58	F Jordan	6-98	6.1	- 47.00

Amateur

	W-R	Per cent	£1 Level Stake		W-R	Per cent	£1 Level Stake
M C Pipe	24-82	29.3	+ 4.28	A Harrison	3-9	33.3	+ 0.25
Mrs M Reveley	13-44	29.5	- 12.01	M J Coombe	3-13	23.1	+ 1.50
K C Bailey	12-38	31.6	+ 3.66	F Murphy	3-14	21.4	+ 8.50
P J Hobbs	9-55	16.4	- 2.21	P Cheesbrough	3-15	20.0	+ 26.00
N Twiston-Davies	7-46	15.2	+ 2.00	J White	3-16	18.8	- 3.25
Capt T A Forster	6-29	20.7	+ 17.63	C P E Brooks	3-19	15.8	- 7.59
P Beaumont	6-29	20.7	+ 28.16	J H Johnson	3-22	13.6	- 2.75
M D Hammond	6-36	16.7	- 15.75	J S King	3-23	13.0	- 5.75
G Richards	6-37	16.2	+ 8.00	K S Bridgwater	2-4	50.0	+ 7.50
Andrew Turnell	5-9	55.6	+ 12.88	Mrs J Goodfellow	2-4	50.0	+ 3.10
Mrs S A Bramall	5-15	33.3	+ 27.10	D J Wintle	2-6	33.3	+ 6.25
D Nicholson	5-19	26.3	+ 9.13	N Tinkler	2-8	25.0	- 1.50
T Thomson Jones	5-25	20.0	- 4.40	A Moore	2-9	22.2	+ 65.00
J T Gifford	5-40	12.5	+ 10.20	N A Gaselee	2-11	18.2	+ 8.50
A P Jones	4-17	23.5	+ 35.75	C James	2-12	16.7	- 4.25
C Parker	4-18	22.2	- 2.50	J R Jenkins	2-13	15.4	+ 41.00
R H Alner	4-21	19.0	+ 2.11	O Sherwood	2-16	12.5	- 9.62
R J Hodges	4-24	16.7	- 3.67	J M Bradley	2-19	10.5	- 13.80
P F Nicholls	4-31	12.9	- 10.92	J A C Edwards	2-30	6.7	- 16.00
J A B Old	3-5	60.0	+ 17.00	G B Balding	2-42	4.8	- 22.00

Hunter Chases

	W-R	Per cent	£1 Level Stake
Miss C Saunders	56-166	33.7	+ 10.99
P Cheesbrough	19-48	39.6	- 11.74
R C Wilkins	15-21	71.4	+ 18.63
S A Brookshaw	14-56	25.0	- 19.93
W J Warner	13-38	34.2	- 2.59
H Wellstead	12-44	27.3	- 15.77
Miss J Pidgeon	11-25	44.0	- 4.08
S L Pike	11-45	24.4	- 4.16
Mrs Jane Storey	10-29	34.5	+ 0.18
R Barber	10-41	24.4	+ 2.02
P R Chamings	9-29	31.0	+ 17.00
P Bowen	8-28	28.6	+ 10.72
Sidney J Smith	8-37	21.6	- 8.41
T D Walford	7-20	35.0	- 5.97
D J Caro	7-28	25.0	- 4.07
J W Dufosse	7-81	8.6	- 46.79
Miss H C Knight	6-10	60.0	+ 6.53
G Richards	6-26	23.1	- 6.20
D L Williams	6-29	20.7	+ 10.92
Mrs D M Grissell	6-29	20.7	- 9.74
C C Trietline	6-46	13.0	- 16.91
J M Turner	6-52	11.5	- 28.82
Lee Bowles	6-80	7.5	- 33.00
Mrs S Cobden	5-12	41.7	+ 9.75
D E Nicholls	5-15	33.3	+ 20.25
Mrs J G Griffith	5-16	31.3	+ 11.71
M J Trickey	5-16	31.3	+ 7.24
Mrs C Hardinge	5-19	26.3	- 1.92
Mrs Jean Brown	5-28	17.9	- 14.35
T N Dalgetty	4-12	33.3	- 4.65
J Wall	4-12	33.3	+ 5.87
H J Manners	4-13	30.8	+133.75
H W Lavis	4-14	28.6	+ 4.83
M J Felton	4-17	23.5	- 2.34
S J Leadbetter	4-18	22.2	- 8.67
M C Pipe	4-19	21.1	+ 3.75
D Nicholson	4-20	20.0	- 7.20
N Twiston-Davies	4-25	16.0	- 9.99
D R Bloor	4-32	12.5	+ 7.50
Mrs C Hicks	4-32	12.5	- 1.50

N H Flat Races

	W-R	Per cent	£1 Level Stake
D Nicholson	33-178	18.5	+ 31.83
J G FitzGerald	26-120	21.7	+ 13.58
M C Pipe	25-205	12.2	- 34.34
Mrs M Reveley	22-148	14.9	- 46.97
N Twiston-Davies	20-190	10.5	- 52.05
P J Hobbs	15-97	15.5	- 12.95
Miss H C Knight	14-119	11.8	- 20.50
J J O'Neill	13-52	25.0	+ 8.68
O Sherwood	12-76	15.8	- 7.25
J A C Edwards	12-110	10.9	- 14.93
C W Thornton	10-54	18.5	+ 5.43
J A B Old	9-59	15.3	- 8.25
K C Bailey	9-75	12.0	- 18.26
N J Henderson	9-81	11.1	- 22.42
Mrs J Pitman	9-93	9.7	- 10.25
J T Gifford	8-45	17.8	+ 31.50
G M Moore	8-58	13.8	- 16.33
J M Jefferson	8-59	13.6	- 11.12
J H Johnson	8-60	13.3	- 26.82
M D Hammond	8-86	9.3	- 27.00
D R Gandolfo	7-67	10.4	+ 6.25
S Christian	6-37	16.2	+ 3.62
T Thomson Jones	6-43	14.0	- 25.63
L Lungo	6-66	9.1	+ 10.00
Miss S E Hall	5-25	20.0	+ 6.75
J Norton	5-37	13.5	+ 10.50
C P E Brooks	5-51	9.8	- 2.25
P F Nicholls	5-53	9.4	- 36.05
B Preece	5-54	9.3	+ 4.38
D H Barons	5-66	7.6	- 18.50
J F Bottomley	4-17	23.5	+ 14.88
D R C Elsworth	4-23	17.4	- 2.07
P R Webber	4-23	17.4	+ 14.50
P Beaumont	4-27	14.8	- 12.50
D Eddy	4-34	11.8	- 14.25
Mrs J G Retter	4-35	11.4	+ 34.00
R Rowe	4-45	8.9	- 10.00
Capt T A Forster	4-49	8.2	- 18.00
G B Balding	4-69	5.8	- 42.00
O Brennan	4-72	5.6	- 14.50

LEADING TRAINERS' FAVOURITES 1991-96

	W-R	Per cent	£1 Level Stake	% of Runners that Started Favourite	% of Winners that Started Favourite
M C Pipe	416-997	41.7	-105.82	28.1	48.5
Mrs M Reveley	253-580	43.6	+ 8.94	31.6	52.9
D Nicholson	212-496	42.7	+ 12.58	27.5	49.8
G Richards	145-342	42.4	- 23.80	20.4	43.8
K C Bailey	133-367	36.2	- 42.51	21.9	41.3
P J Hobbs	127-308	41.2	+ 1.93	18.7	40.3
N Twiston-Davies	126-327	38.5	+ 19.20	16.4	37.7
N J Henderson	100-263	38.0	- 14.69	20.2	40.8
J White	99-271	36.5	- 36.99	20.9	45.6
O Sherwood	98-265	37.0	- 20.44	24.2	44.5
J T Gifford	86-206	41.7	+ 17.16	13.2	36.4
M D Hammond	75-231	32.5	- 36.82	16.5	36.4
Miss H C Knight	71-176	40.3	+ 10.01	17.4	39.7
Capt T A Forster	67-169	39.6	+ 10.73	15.4	39.0
Mrs J Pitman	67-187	35.8	+ 0.48	14.7	34.2
N Tinkler	60-157	38.2	- 13.78	22.2	51.7
J G FitzGerald	59-176	33.5	- 20.75	17.9	33.3
G M Moore	51-135	37.8	- 2.13	14.7	37.0
P F Nicholls	49-154	31.8	- 33.37	18.6	35.0
J J O'Neill	43-116	37.1	- 24.12	13.8	39.1
G B Balding	43-172	25.0	- 59.29	11.3	22.2
J A C Edwards	42-96	43.8	+ 16.34	11.6	37.5
J H Johnson	42-121	34.7	- 14.02	12.2	30.2
R H Alner	38-103	36.9	- 16.84	18.7	44.7
C R Egerton	36-88	40.9	+ 5.49	22.4	49.3
P Monteith	35-97	36.1	- 15.64	14.4	35.4
C P E Brooks	35-114	30.7	- 27.74	15.3	27.1
O Brennan	34-84	40.5	+ 11.52	10.6	31.5
R J Hodges	34-109	31.2	+ 3.05	8.6	24.8
D R Gandolfo	33-90	36.7	- 14.49	12.8	34.7
Andrew Turnell	32-89	36.0	- 4.16	13.9	28.8
L Lungo	32-92	34.8	- 10.24	15.0	32.3
I A Balding	29-57	50.9	+ 5.05	28.1	54.7
S Sherwood	29-91	31.9	- 15.49	14.7	32.6
F Murphy	28-58	48.3	+ 12.79	9.5	34.6
M H Tompkins	27-69	39.1	- 2.36	17.6	43.5
R Akehurst	27-71	38.0	- 4.85	17.1	40.3
D R C Elsworth	27-72	37.5	- 3.73	12.7	32.1
J A B Old	25-74	33.8	- 7.07	15.1	42.9
Miss C Saunders	24-47	51.1	+ 3.29	28.3	42.9
R J O'Sullivan	24-61	39.3	+ 4.68	15.7	38.1
G Harwood	23-53	43.4	+ 3.78	18.7	40.4
T Thomson Jones	23-69	33.3	- 8.27	12.9	28.0
J R Jenkins	23-87	26.4	- 26.65	7.6	24.2
R Rowe	22-64	34.4	- 1.21	8.4	28.9
P Cheesbrough	21-48	43.8	- 1.14	9.0	30.4
C J Mann	21-59	35.6	- 9.59	19.7	43.8
N A Gaselee	20-60	33.3	- 7.47	9.3	25.6
M W Easterby	20-68	29.4	- 23.19	12.7	29.9

TRAINER TIPS FOR 1996-97

R Akehurst   –   Runners at Lingfield

N J Henderson   –   Runners at Hereford

P J Hobbs   –   Runners at Newton Abbot

Miss H C Knight   –   Runners at Exeter & Market Rasen

D Nicholson   –   Runners at Huntingdon, Sandown & Towcester
                         –   Chasers first time out

R J O'Sullivan   –   Runners in August

Miss C Saunders –   Runners in March

N Twiston-Davies –   Runners at Perth

R C Wilkins   –   Runners in Hunter Chases

INDEX TO TRAINERS

INDEX TO COURSES

NOTES

NOTES

NOTES

NOTES

NOTES

NOTES

NOTES

NOTES

NOTES

NOTES